Modes of Organization in the New Institutional Economics

The International Library of the New Institutional Economics

Editor: Claude Ménard
Professor of Economics
and Director of ATOM (Center for Analytical Theory of Organizations and Markets)
University of Paris Panthéon-Sorbonne, France

1 The Foundations of the New Institutional Economics
2 Transaction Costs and Property Rights
3 Contracts in the New Institutional Economics
4 Modes of Organization in the New Institutional Economics
5 Institutional Dimensions of the Modern Corporation
6 The Political Economy of Institutions
7 Controversies and Challenges in the New Institutional Economics

Wherever possible, the articles in these volumes have been reproduced as originally published using facsimile reproduction, inclusive of footnotes and pagination to facilitate ease of reference.

Modes of Organization in the New Institutional Economics

Edited by

Claude Ménard

Professor of Economics
and Director of ATOM (Center for Analytical Theory of Organizations and Markets)
University of Paris Panthéon-Sorbonne, France

THE INTERNATIONAL LIBRARY OF THE NEW INSTITUTIONAL ECONOMICS

An Elgar Reference Collection
Cheltenham, UK • Northampton, MA, USA

Published by
Edward Elgar Publishing Limited
Glensanda House
Montpellier Parade
Cheltenham
Glos GL50 1UA
UK

Edward Elgar Publishing, Inc.
136 West Street
Suite 202
Northampton
Massachusetts 01060
USA

A catalogue record for this book is available from the British Library.

ISBN 1 84376 663 9
1 84064 382 X (7 volume set)

Printed and bound in Great Britain by MPG Books Ltd, Bodmin, Cornwall

Contents

Acknowledgements

The editor and publishers wish to thank the authors and the following publishers who have kindly given permission for the use of copyright material.

Administrative Science Quarterly for articles: William G. Ouchi (1980), 'Markets, Bureaucracies, and Clans', *Administrative Science Quarterly*, **25** (1), March, 129–41; Oliver E. Williamson (1991), 'Comparative Economic Organization: The Analysis of Discrete Structural Alternatives', *Administrative Science Quarterly*, **36** (2), June, 269–96.

American Economic Association for articles: Oliver E. Williamson (1971), 'The Vertical Integration of Production: Market Failure Considerations', *American Economic Review, Papers and Proceedings*, **LXI** (2), May, 112–23; Bengt Holmström and John Roberts (1998), 'The Boundaries of the Firm Revisited', *Journal of Economic Perspectives*, **12** (4), Fall, 73–94.

Blackwell Publishing Ltd for article: James G. March (1962), 'The Business Firm as a Political Coalition', *Journal of Politics*, **24**, 662–78.

Elsevier for articles and excerpt: Robert G. Eccles (1981), 'The Quasifirm in the Construction Industry', *Journal of Economic Behavior and Organization*, **2** (4), 335–57; Walter W. Powell (1990), 'Neither Market nor Hierarchy: Network Forms of Organization', in Barry M. Staw and L.L. Cummings (eds), *Research in Organizational Behavior*, Volume 12, 295–336, re-set; Bruce R. Lyons (1995), 'Specific Investment, Economies of Scale, and the Make-or-Buy Decision: A Test of Transaction Cost Theory', *Journal of Economic Behavior and Organization*, **26** (3), May, 431–43.

Journal of Law and Economics and the University of Chicago Law School for articles: Benjamin Klein, Robert G. Crawford and Armen A. Alchian (1978), 'Vertical Integration, Appropriable Rents, and the Competitive Contracting Process', *Journal of Law and Economics*, **XXI** (2), October, 297–326; Steven N.S. Cheung (1983), 'The Contractual Nature of the Firm', *Journal of Law and Economics*, **XXVI** (1), April, 1–21; Scott E. Masten (1984), 'The Organization of Production: Evidence from the Aerospace Industry', *Journal of Law and Economics*, **XXVII** (2), October, 403–17.

MIT Press Journals and the President and Fellows of Harvard College and the Massachusetts Institute of Technology for article: George Baker, Robert Gibbons and Kevin J. Murphy (2002), 'Relational Contracts and the Theory of the Firm', *Quarterly Journal of Economics*, **CXVII** (1), February, 39–84.

Mohr Siebeck Tübingen for article: Claude Menard (1996), 'On Clusters, Hybrids, and Other Strange Forms: The Case of the French Poultry Industry', *Journal of Institutional and Theoretical Economics*, **152** (1), March, 154–83.

Nobel Foundation for article: R.H. Coase (1992), 'The Institutional Structure of Production', *American Economic Review*, **82** (4), September, 713–19.

Oxford University Press for articles: Paul L. Joskow (1985), 'Vertical Integration and Long-term Contracts: The Case of Coal-burning Electric Generating Plants', *Journal of Law, Economics, and Organization*, **1** (1), Spring, 33–80; Paul L. Joskow (1988), 'Asset Specificity and the Structure of Vertical Relationships: Empirical Evidence', *Journal of Law, Economics, and Organization*, **4** (1), Spring, 95–117; George John and Barton A. Weitz (1988), 'Forward Integration into Distribution: An Empirical Test of Transaction Cost Analysis', *Journal of Law, Economics, and Organization*, **4** (2), Fall, 337–55; Joanne E. Oxley (1997), 'Appropriability Hazards and Governance in Strategic Alliances: A Transaction Cost Approach', *Journal of Law, Economics, and Organization*, **13** (2), October, 387–409; Bengt Holmstrom (1999), 'The Firm as a Subeconomy', *Journal of Law, Economics, and Organization*, **15** (1), April, 74–102.

Presses de Sciences PO for article: Claude Ménard (1997), 'The Governance of Hybrid Organizational Forms', *Revue Économique*, **48** (3), May, 741–50 [originally published as 'Le Pilotage des Formes Organisationnelles Hybrides'].

RAND for articles: Kirk Monteverde and David J. Teece (1982), 'Supplier Switching Costs and Vertical Integration in the Automobile Industry', *Bell Journal of Economics*, **13** (1), Spring, 206–13; Erin Anderson and David C. Schmittlein (1984), 'Integration of the Sales Force: An Empirical Examination', *RAND Journal of Economics*, **15** (3), Autumn, 385–95.

University of Chicago Press for article: Francine Lafontaine and Kathryn L. Shaw (1999), 'The Dynamics of Franchise Contracting: Evidence from Panel Data', *Journal of Political Economy*, **107** (5), October, 1041–80.

Every effort has been made to trace all the copyright holders but if any have been inadvertently overlooked the publishers will be pleased to make the necessary arrangement at the first opportunity.

In addition the publishers wish to thank the Marshall Library of Economics, Cambridge University, the Library of the University of Warwick and the Library of Indiana University at Bloomington, USA for their assistance in obtaining these articles.

General Introduction

Claude Ménard

A Remarkable Development

From a historical standpoint, the New Institutional Economics (NIE) is a very young theory. With the exception of the now famous article from Ronald Coase, 'The Nature of the Firm' (1937), this new approach slowly took shape in the 1960s, but really took off in the 1970s, with major contributions from Alchian, Coase, Demsetz, North, Williamson, and many others. It was only in the 1980s and 1990s that it established itself as a fully developed and acknowledged research program.[1] Looking retrospectively at this short period of time, the accomplishments are quite remarkable. The contributions collected in these seven volumes illustrate the variety and richness of the analyses elaborated during that period. The difficulties in selecting the articles reprinted in the series provide an indication of the quality of these contributions.

The developments occurred mostly along two complementary and interdependent axes; one oriented towards the analysis of the modes of organization, while the other focused on the institutional environment in which these arrangements are embedded.

The transaction costs analysis of the tradeoff among modes of organization, the explanation provided to vertical integration, the centrality of contractual arrangements, and the insights on some fundamental characteristics of the different modes of organization have all become standard references in economics (and beyond), even among those who do not share the NIE interpretation. Similarly, the recognition of the central role played by the institutional environment in making possible the development of market economies, the importance of laws and political rules in order to have lower transaction costs and a larger volume of transactions, and the comparative analysis of the impact of different political regimes on development and growth, have now permeated all social sciences as well as mainstream economics. The present series is intended to show how NIE has contributed to these developments.

Main Axes of Analysis

In a recent synthesis reproduced in the last volume of this series,[2] Williamson proposed a distinction between four levels of analysis, corresponding to different time perspectives. Although the chronology suggested may be debatable, the general scheme provides a helpful framework for encapsulating the varied set of contributions that developed under the NIE umbrella.

In the *very long run*, spanning over centuries, customs, traditions, and beliefs tend to predominate. Although they change very slowly, they contribute to shaping the institutional environment, as illustrated in many articles of this series. Their importance comes from their role in defining rules and support in the organization of transactions and in contributing to the determination of the level of transaction costs, particularly in environments with no public enforcers or very weak ones. However, they can also create obstacles to the development of transactions, as with customs that isolate a social group from its environment. Douglass North has repeatedly brought attention to the importance of these factors for understanding the evolution of transactions over time and, ultimately, on development and growth. Several recent researches, particularly by historians and anthropologists, have substantiated this view and some of them are presented in the following volumes.

Over a more restricted time span, but still in a *long run* perspective, political and legal institutions define rules within which transactions can develop, thus creating possibilities or inhibitions for trading activities. Coase has opened the way here in showing the significance of laws and the legal regime in a world with positive transaction costs. Three aspects have particularly captured the attention of new institutionalists in that respect. First, a comparative approach to political systems, using transaction costs and contractual lenses, has allowed substantial progress in our understanding of how the polity interacts with the organization of exchanges. At the same time, Douglass North has also played an important role here, by showing the way political systems operate can be analysed as a 'market' of a specific type, on which political transactions occur that explain the adoption of certain forms and the reasons why some have been more successful than others in supporting development and growth. The many articles on federalism collected in this series illustrate this.

Second, parallel to and interacting with political institutions, the legal system also plays a major role in determining how transactions can be organized and at what costs. Legal issues have been part of the research program in NIE from very early on, particularly under the influence of Ronald Coase. One important lesson of these studies is that they tend to show that no legal system is superior to another one per se, contrary to what has been suggested by competing theories. What really matters is the fitness of a legal system, that is: (1) its adaptation to what we can call the institutional endowments of a society at some point in its history, particularly its endowments in public servants and personnel with legal competences; (2) its relevance to the nature of transactions at stake, since institutions adapted to some activities, for example the financial system, do no necessarily correspond to those needed for regulating other activities, for example markets for perishable goods; (3) its reliability in defining, implementing, and enforcing property rights.

Last, a flow of recent studies has substantiated this concern for the long-run impact of political and legal regimes through the analysis of the successes and failures of regulations, with a special attention to the reform of public utilities. All these faces of the durable influence of institutions on the way transactions are organized are represented in this series. They constitute the hard core of that part of the NIE research program that North and Davis have synthesized as the 'institutional environment'.

In the *medium* and short run, the analysis concentrates on the variety of modes of organization that shape an economy and that North and Davis encapsulated as 'institutional arrangements'. These arrangements are embedded in existing legal and political institutions as well as in ideologies and traditions that shape the behavior of transactors. However, their time horizon is shorter and they are more malleable, and more prone to voluntary changes. Coase opened the way to the analysis of these modes of organization that provide differentiated supports to transactions, and Williamson has become the leading figure here.

By using a transaction costs lens, this approach has exhibited the diversity of ways in which to organize trading activities in order to take advantage of specialization. The booming literature on modes of organization has switched us from a bipolar perspective, focusing on the tradeoff between markets and 'hierarchies' (or integrated organizations), to a multi-polar vision with the increasing acknowledgement of the importance of intermediate or 'hybrid' forms. However, and even more importantly, NIE has provided a theoretical framework that has become a point of reference for explaining the tradeoff among these modes of organization, that is, why one form is preferred to another one under the specific attributes that characterize a transaction. The initial attention went to the explanation of vertical integration, as an alternative to market solutions, and it is now widely acknowledged that this represented both an important theoretical breakthrough and an empirical 'success story'. More recently, the attention has turned to ways of organizing transactions that correspond neither to integration nor to the usual features characterizing market relations. The analysis of these non-standard contractual relationships has become an important component of the NIE research program.

Also related to a medium-run perspective, there is an increasing interest for identifying and examining the internal structures and characteristics of alternative modes of organizations. The idea here, reflected in many articles in this series, is that using the concepts developed in NIE could help to understand better why one mode fits better than another with the attributes of transactions at stake. One important issue concerns the theoretical status of these factors in the effort to explain the tradeoff among modes of organizations. Are these factors orthogonal to an explanation of the tradeoff, for example are costs of bureaucracy orthogonal to transaction costs? If they must be mobilized for substantiating the transaction costs explanation, how can we model them so as to avoid getting trapped into a tautology, that is, a mode of organization prevails because it has a superior mode of organization!

Lastly, *short run* elements and variations also influence the way transactions are organized, and the way relative costs are incurred. According to Williamson, and most new institutionalists would likely agree on this, the short-run perspective focuses on marginal adaptation, as in the price theory or with incentives issues, and it prevails in mainstream economics. NIE has surely contributed less to this aspect than other theories, for example agency theory. However, it has paid attention to the role of these variations in comparing modes of organization. It has also contributed to refocusing on the short perspective in pointing out the need to examine how these variables of adjustments are embedded in specific modes of organizations. One illustration, developed in this series, concerns the role of organizational motivations and values, beyond monetary incentives and their variations.

All these developments result in a complex and highly diversified research program, as illustrated by this series. At the same time it is a unified research program.

A Unifying Set of Concepts Paired to a Methodological Vision

Indeed, a striking aspect of the NIE research program is the presence under this diversity of object and levels of analysis of a coherent set of concepts that provides unity to the whole. Transaction costs, contracts, and property rights form the core of this analytical apparatus.

Within this triad, *transaction costs* occupy a very central position, for historical as well as theoretical reasons. The historical priority goes back to the pioneering role of Coase's article on 'The Nature of the Firm'. The theoretical centrality of the concept refers to more subtle reasons, as so many misinterpretations testify (for example the idea that transaction costs would at best neglect, at worst ignore production costs). Several chapters in this series explicitly point out why transaction costs matter so much in the NIE perspective. It all boils down to an argument rooted in Adam Smith: there is no possibility of taking advantage of the division of labor and of specialization without organizing transactions, and all arrangements that can be implemented for doing so have a cost. This approach gives its full sense to the definition of transaction costs as 'the cost of running the economic system' (Arrow, 1970).

How exactly to pin down these costs and how to approximate them is a more complex question, and is one that is discussed in several chapters of the series. At least two different views have developed. One considers that transaction costs make sense only for analysing market exchanges, thus transaction costs are what it costs to trade on markets. A more extensive definition considers transaction costs as the costs of transferring rights of usage, which makes the concept a relevant tool for analysing modes of organization alternative to markets as well. However, whether the restrictive or the wider interpretation prevails, the concept remains a powerful tool for examining micro arrangements as well as global institutions and for exploring the interaction between these levels. At the same time, the issue of measuring transaction costs remains an open one, that is, whether it is relevant or not to try measuring them remains debatable; and if it is relevant to measure them, then the question arises of how this can be done. Again, several chapters in the series discuss these issues.

Whatever are the answers to these important and difficult questions, there is a general agreement among new institutionalists that transaction costs particularly matter when in comes to the establishment and transfer of *property rights*. Identifying the different types of property rights and the consequences of their allocation has been on the agenda of NIE since very early in its development. Indeed, in a world of positive transaction costs, the distribution of rights and the devices for transferring them are of the utmost importance and have a significant impact on the performance of the alternative modes of organization as well as on growth. Therefore, the two concepts of transaction costs and of property rights have been linked from the very beginning of the research program, as is already visible in 'The Problem of Social Costs' (Coase, 1960). NIE has continuously contributed to a better understanding of the nature and role of property rights. It has also continuously emphasized the centrality of their enforcement, that is, the need for institutions to implement and secure property rights, thus reducing contractual hazards and risk of opportunism. In doing so it establishes a link with the microfoundations of transaction costs, as well illustrated with the credibility issue, discussed in several papers of this series.[3]

In a developed market economy, *contracts* represent one of the major supports for transferring property rights and, more generally, for organizing transactions. Coase had the intuition of the importance of contracts in his pioneering discussion (1937) of the integration issue and of what differentiates the allocation of resources and tasks in a firm by contrast with markets. However, Williamson deserves the main credit here because he has led the crowd in establishing the centrality of contracts for organizing and coordinating transactions. In an apparent paradox he has done so while exhibiting the incompleteness of contracts. In a world in which uncertainties combine with positive transaction costs, contracts remain inevitably incomplete, thus generating hazards that require safeguards. These safeguards may be entrenched in the contracts themselves; they may also rely on complementary governing devices or on external enforcers, among which courts and governments are major actors. An entire branch of NIE has developed this research program and is well represented in this series.

One element that contributes to explain the incompleteness of contracts, besides the importance of unanticipated events, may lie in the *behavior* of parties to contractual arrangements. NIE paid early attention to the strategizing behavior of agents and, more generally, to exploring a more complex representation of agents than the one dominating the standard approach in economics. References to bounded rationality and to opportunistic behavior may be considered as relatively primitive efforts in this direction. They have been seriously substantiated by more recent researches, mainly coming from two different perspectives: experimental economics on the one hand, and cognitive sciences on the other hand. Several chapters of the series illustrate this movement. Among others, Ostrom provides particularly important insights based on experiments and field studies; and North indicates how cognitive sciences may help in developing sound microfoundations to the analysis of organizations and institutions through the analytical explanation of how agents combine rational calculation and beliefs in their behavior and their choices.

Hence, the NIE research program reposes on a solid and dense web of concepts tightly interwoven. These fundamental concepts and assumptions, and their refinements developed in numerous chapters in the series, are complemented by a *methodological approach* quite universally shared among new institutionalists. Indeed, the NIE approach is deliberately and systematically comparative. Institutions and modes of organizations cannot be assessed in isolation; they can only be evaluated through comparison. New institutionalists go even further in considering that all institutions and all modes of organizations have their own flaws. This happens quite naturally from the concepts introduced above. As soon as the existence of positive transaction costs is acknowledged, and that the efficiency in the allocation and reallocation of rights depends on the characteristics of the devices required by these transfers, no one optimal solution that could serve as a benchmark exists. The only way to assess successes and failures, and to estimate costs and benefits, is through comparisons.

An Open Approach

In implementing this comparative approach on these kinds of issues, NIE has necessarily developed major intersections with other disciplines. Among the different and often competing paradigms that characterize modern economics, NIE figures as exceptionally interactive with legal scholars, social scientists, management scientists, and so on. Because NIE regards agents and organizations as socially embedded in institutions, the intersection with non-economic disciplines has become increasingly significant. Since it acknowledges the fact that agents are calculators and that costs matter in their choice, bridges have also remained open with mainstream economists. NIE is all but an isolated and closed paradigm.

Open to other disciplines as well as to other approaches in economics, new institutionalists naturally acknowledge weaknesses and problems in their paradigm. Numerous articles selected for this series identify problems and flaws; some even challenge corner stones of the edifice. This is precisely what in my view makes NIE a 'progressive' research program, that is, a research program turned in the direction of problems to be explored further and of domains to develop. Understanding institutional and organization changes, establishing more rigorously the channels through which modes of organization and institutions interact, and integrating the analysis of technology and technological dynamics are some of the challenges facing NIE. Several contributions show that these issues, and others, are high on the agenda of NIE researchers. If one main goal should be assigned to this series, it is to help the readers identify these terrains that are open to future research.

Organization of the Series: Some Caveats

The series is organized in seven books structured by themes so that each one forms an autonomous entity. Volume 1 collects articles that provided foundations to the field and opened the domain of NIE, and more recent articles that identify the major axes that have since developed and review some important issues, many of which remain under-explored. Volume 2 summarizes the behavioral assumptions that distinguish NIE from other approaches. Then, it proceeds to examine two building blocks of the theory: the nature and role of transaction costs, and the status of property rights. Volume 3 completes the golden triangle of NIE by thoroughly reviewing what contracts are, their characteristics, and how they are enforced. Volume 4 assembles articles on a leading theme in NIE, that is, the existence of alternative modes of organization and the tradeoff among them. The emblematic case of vertical integration definitively occupies a central place here. However, I have also included some exploratory articles on hybrid arrangements. Volume 5 develops the specific case of large modern corporations, since this case provides the support of most of what has been published in a NIE perspective on the internal characteristics of firms, an underdeveloped topic in NIE (and more generally in economic theory). Part of this volume also explores the impact of institutions on structural choices made within or among modes of organization. In Volume 6, I have assembled a set of articles focusing on the analysis of institutions, with a particular attention to what relates institutions to development and growth. Therefore, the emphasis here is less on the general impact of institutions at the organizational level, as in the previous volume, and more on the impact of political institutions and legal systems on the dynamics of transactions over time. Volume 7 concludes the series with articles examining critical issues in NIE and, for some of them, challenging the relevance of the approach. The confrontation of these different and often controversial perspectives should not only help to determine some of the main problems and flaws in NIE, but also identify where the action is or should be expected.

Through all seven volumes, I have selected articles that emphasize the testability of the theory. Indeed, one major characteristic of NIE from the very beginning has been its reluctance towards 'blackboard economics' and its emphasis on the urgent need to build a theory that continually confronts facts and adjusts to observed realities.

One last thing deserves clarification here. The introductions to the different volumes are intended to explain the logic underlying my choices. Ordering the chapters and suggesting specific links among them obviously involves interpretation. I have done my best to not distort or bias the main messages the authors wanted to get across. However, I have put the articles in a perspective that authors may not always share. Moreover, there is clearly a selection bias. Although the series is quite extensive, I was forced to discard some articles that would have deserved being here.

Acknowledgements

A project like this one develops over a long period of time. It requires support and encouragement. In preparing the series, I have benefited from a particularly generous environment.

First, I owe a lot to numerous friends and colleagues who made suggestions regarding the selection of articles for the series. I am particularly indebted to Ronald Coase, Philip Keefer, Gary Libecap, Douglass C. North, Emmanuel Raynaud, Stephane Saussier, Mary Shirley, and Oliver E. Williamson. Of course none of them is responsible for errors or omissions in the final selection. I have also received technical support from research assistants (Caroline Berteau, Stephanie Polin, and Anne Yvrande-Billon) and from the staff at Edward Elgar (particularly Nicola Mills and Ben Booth, whom I thank for their patience). Several institutions have supported and/or hosted me at different times in this project. The University of Paris (Panthéon-Sorbonne), the French Ministry of Education and Research, the Centre National de la Recherche Scientifique, the University of California at Berkeley, and the Massachusetts Institute of Technology have all provided facilities and support without which this project could not have been achieved.

However, my most significant debt is towards the contributors who all enthusiastically supported the project and helped to attain the copyrights. I want to express them my deepest gratitude.

Notes

1. The creation of the International Society for New Institutional Economics at a Conference held in St. Louis in 1997, with almost all major contributors to the field attending, can be considered as the institutional consolidation of the developments of the previous period.
2. Williamson (2000); Chapter 30, Volume 7.
3. All these aspects clearly distinguish NIE from the so-called 'new' property rights theory in which the existence and definition of these rights as well as the institutions required are assumed as given and costless.

References

Arrow, Kenneth (1970), 'The Organization of Economic Activity: Issues Pertinent to the Choice of Market versus Non-market Allocation', in Robert Haveman and Julius Margolis (eds), *Public Expenditures and Policy Analysis*. Chicago: Markham Pub. Co., pp. 39–73.

Coase, R.H. (1937), 'The Nature of the Firm', *Economica*, New Series, **4** (16), November, 386–405.

Coase, R.H. (1960), 'The Problem of Social Costs', *Journal of Law and Economics*, **3**, October, 1–44.

Williamson, O.E. (2000), 'The New Institutional Economics: Taking Stock, Looking Ahead', *Journal of Economic Literature*, **XXXVIII** (3), September, 596–613.

Introduction

Claude Ménard

The analysis of alternative modes of organization has had a special status from the very beginning of the development of New Institutional Economics.[1] First, the paper that can be considered as the initial step in that direction raised the central issue of the nature of the firm, particularly in relation to markets (Coase, 1937; see Volume 1, Chapter 3). Second, the pioneering empirical studies derived from NIE were about organizational issues, from the analysis by Coase of the telecommunications industry to Williamson's *Markets and Hierarchies*.[2]

In the 1980s discussions and developments in NIE regarding modes of organization focused essentially on the paradigmatic case of vertical integration. Hundreds of case studies and econometric tests have been published on these issues that continue to inspire researchers. In the 1990s the heuristic model was extended to incorporate institutional arrangements that did not correspond to integrated firms, but that could not be described as usual market relationships either. The concept of 'hybrid' was developed and an abundant literature is now available on these non-standard agreements.

This volume assembles a small subset of the vast literature now available on these issues. It does so with a view to illustrating the major problems that continue to feed research. Part I focuses on the theoretical characterization of the modes of organization identified in the literature. Part II contains some of the most significant papers in the initial wave of studies on vertical integration. Part III sheds some light on the under-researched domain of non-standard agreements.

Part I: Markets, Hierarchies, Hybrid Forms

Part I collects contributions that identify and characterize different 'institutional structures of production'. It includes papers from authors who are not new institutionalists, but whose views have been deeply influenced by the ideas of Coase and Williamson on organizations.

The Nobel lecture delivered by Coase (1992, Chapter 1) is a perfect opening to this part. The paper adequately summarizes the facts and arguments that convinced Coase to look at firms as an alternative to the organization of transactions through markets. The paper also identifies some questions that remain high on the agenda of new institutionalists. Let me emphasize two of them. First, the paper correctly points out how little we still know about the institutional arrangements needed for markets to work. Second, it sharply criticizes the lack of interest by economists in the internal arrangement of firms, although it is crucial for understanding how economies work. Things may have evolved somewhat on these issues, but resistance persists. The good news is that transaction costs provide a powerful tool to go further. Coase also reminds us why they matter so much: they result from assigning rights to those who can use them productively, and from transferring these rights.

Williamson's paper (1991, Chapter 2) is complementary to Coase's – it expands the analysis of institutional structures of production to cases that are neither markets nor hierarchies – cases that he calls 'hybrids'. Therefore, we end up with three generic modes of organization that can support transactions. The presumption that needs empirical confirmation (see Part III of this volume, and also Parts I and II of Volume 5) is that each mode has characteristics of its own, particularly with respect to contract laws and governance attributes (with specific attention to adaptation). Williamson provides insights on these characteristics and reassesses the 'discrete alignment principle', according to which the choice of a specific arrangement can find its explanation in the search for the mode that fits relatively better with the attributes of the transaction at stake. The model he proposes also helps understanding of how shifts in parameters – for example, institutional changes – have an impact on transaction costs, and therefore on the tradeoff among modes of organization. Therefore, this framework introduces the major themes developed in the rest of this volume.

The next five papers focus on specific modes of organization, three on firms and two on inter-firm relationships (hybrids). The first one, by Cheung (1983, Chapter 3), somehow challenges the vision of the firm as a discrete structure proposed by Coase and Williamson. Indeed, it develops the idea of the firm as a nexus of contracts. This conception extends the analysis initially proposed by Alchian and Demsetz (see Volume 1, Chapter 8), making the examination of the internal characteristics of firms a relatively minor issue. What really matters for understanding market economies is the diversity and complexity of contractual arrangements. This approach represents an important trend among new institutionalists.

Holmstrom (1999, Chapter 4) would likely not identify himself as a new institutionalist, but his paper shows, beside its own interest, how much his vision of the firm is influenced by transaction cost economics. His paper is an attempt at integrating this theory with the so-called 'new' property rights approach developed by Hart *et al.* (see Volume II, Chapter 21). In Holmstrom's view, what matters is not the allocation of property rights *per se*, as in Hart *et al.*, but the power that unified ownership confers over deciding who should do what and how. Ownership gives control on (physical) assets, providing the firm leverage over human assets, which is what essentially characterizes a firm and determines its boundaries. In that perspective, contracts are incomplete and they offer only limited means for guiding the action of employees. The paper also explores how the combination of high ownership incentives with low-powered employee incentives for encouraging cooperation might allow a better overall design of activities.

In that context, firms can be interpreted as complex coalitions of interest in which parties play complex games. In a pioneering paper, March (1962, Chapter 5) anticipated several related themes that are making their way on the agenda of economists. By adopting a decision-making approach, he emphasizes the nature of business firms as conflict systems, with dispute solving a main activity since it determines the capacity to coordinate. Firms can thus be interpreted as political coalitions, and entrepreneurs or executives as political brokers. Two consequences are of particular significance in a new institutional perspective. First, this characterization gives a positive role to managers as conflict solvers. Second, it explicitly introduces the role of institutional constraints in the formation and stability of the coalition that gives a firm its identity.

The next two papers turn to what Williamson called 'hybrids'. Using the model developed in Chapter 2 and in several empirical studies, Ménard (1997, Chapter 6) explores some characteristics of these arrangements by differentiating them from firms and making them viable substitutes to pure market agreements. The paper suggests that three elements are of particular importance for understanding hybrids: the combination of autonomous property rights, the pooling of substantial subsets of decisions, and the implementation of coordinating mechanisms that do not rely on prices. It also assesses some properties of these mechanisms, particularly the delineation of a domain of 'tolerance' allowing adjustments, provisions for anticipated renegotiations, contractual safeguards against risks of free riding, and the design of endogenous coordinating bodies.

Baker, Gibbons, and Murphy (2002, Chapter 7) go in the same direction, although from a different perspective. By acknowledging the diversity of arrangements for coordinating activities across firms, they focus on devices developed for monitoring externalities (spill-over effects) and *ex post* behaviors of partners. They concur with the idea that contracts do not do the entire job, which in their view explains the key role of relational adaptation among firms mutually committed; thus, strategic alliances provide a good illustration. This relational dimension would summarize the fundamental difference between inter-firm agreements and an integrated firm.

Part II: Vertical Integration

Integration is precisely the object of the set of papers in Part II. This theme is a landmark, or a 'success story', in the development of NIE.

Indeed, in identifying vertical integration as a way to model and to test the intuition of Coase regarding the tradeoff between make or buy, Williamson (1971, Chapter 8) gave a major impact to the development of the new research program. By taking exception from the dominating view of the time that vertical integration was an anomaly when not justified by technological considerations, this paper posited integration as an efficient response to 'transactional failures' – that is, to market transaction costs high enough to make the internalization of the transactions advantageous. In the process of explaining how this could happen, the paper also introduced some themes that later became central pieces of the NIE program: the advantages and limits of internal organization, the role of contracts and their incompleteness, and the need for a comparative approach in assessing the costs and benefits of alternative modes of governance.

Klein, Crawford, and Alchian (1978, Chapter 9) complemented this view, but also introduced considerations that reoriented part of the research program thus defined. Their paper caught on the idea that the 'action' in a contractual arrangement is mostly *ex post*, when opportunistic behavior can emerge. By focusing on the role of relationship-specific investments, they emphasized the risk of 'hold up', which is one party trying to take advantage of that dependence to absorb the quasi-rent. By circumventing this risk, agents have different possibilities. One is the implementation of long-term enforceable contracts. However, this can be too costly due to the importance of unanticipated contingencies, of the social loss that the threat of termination could represent, and/or of the high costs of arbitration. Vertical integration is another response. The authors then illustrate the tradeoff between these solutions with the now famous case of the integration of Fisher Body by General Motors in 1926. This potential role of misbehavior ('hold up') when specific assets are made or needed has generated a heated debate (see Volume 7, Chapters 10 and 11).

In the next papers tests of the model underlying the previous two papers are presented. Five papers focus on upstream integration, while two look at downstream integration. Like most of the tests based on transaction cost theory so far, the papers use sector data.[3]

Monteverde and Teece (1982, Chapter 10) delivered one of the very first econometric tests of the transaction cost explanation to vertical integration. By using qualitative data based on the evaluation of engineer-specific components in the automobile industry, they measure the importance of know-how in the development of all components in order to show its high correlation with the decision to 'make' or to 'buy'. The test was very corroborative.

Not long after, Masten (1984, Chapter 11) examined a similar question through the case of procurement practices in the aerospace industry. One characteristic of some defense-related production is the importance of specialized design and the limited alternative value of investments. According to the theory (Williamson, 1971, Chapter 8; Klein *et al.*, 1978, Chapter 9), the degree of specialization of assets involved should be closely related to the decision to make internally rather than dealing with an external organization. It should also reflect in the contract provisions if externalization is chosen. Using data provided by questionnaires about the specificity of the design, the site specificity, and the complexity of 1887 components, the study showed that notwithstanding some reluctance to internalize, the choice to make rather than buy prevails when exposure to hazards of market exchanges become too high, which happens with complex and specialized assets.

Joskow (1985, Chapter 12) also tested the impact of specificity, but in a different context. Working on a highly regulated industry, electric power supply, which is the main consumer of coal produced in the USA (over 80 per cent at the time of the paper), he could not test directly the 'make or buy' tradeoff because of the regulatory constraints on integration. On the other hand, coal suppliers and electric-generating plants are interdependent, but with wide variations according to the type of coal used, the quantity needed, and the respective location of mines and power plants. Joskow then hypothesized that parties should be expected to implement contracts that minimize the reliance on the legal system and that minimize their transaction costs. In this paper, which is part of a set of contributions on this issue, he used the extensive set of contracts available (almost 300) to show the strong relation between the specificity of assets at stake and the choice of a governance structure approximated through the duration of contracts.[4]

Lyons (1995, Chapter 13) complements the previous studies; as in Chapters 10 and 11, he proceeded through a questionnaire (102 firms responded) in order to measure the specificity of assets approximated with the specificity of the technologies chosen. The test innovated in two aspects: it is one of the very first econometric studies based on European data, and it intended to evaluate the respective importance of specific investments and of economies of scale in the decision made. As such, it is an early effort to compare alternative explanations, including transaction-cost economics and the technological approach. The study confirmed the importance of specific investments, but also showed the significance of economies of scale in the decisions made. The paper also contains interesting remarks on the limits of tests based on questionnaires.

The next two papers turn to downstream integration. Anderson and Schmittlein (1984, Chapter 14) pioneered the transaction cost approach to integration in distribution. More specifically, they analyzed the tradeoff between employees and independent representatives as sales people. Starting from the attributes of transactions identified by Williamson, they found proxies for measuring the respective role of specific assets, uncertainty, and frequency. Data came from questionnaires circulated in the electronic components industry. The results show the importance of uncertainty, particularly in measuring individual performance, in the decision to 'integrate' – that is, to have house-based salesmen. Specificity of assets came second in the estimation, but may overlap partially with uncertainty, as discussed in the paper.

John and Weitz (1988, Chapter 15) similarly examine the role of transaction costs in choices made in distribution. Their paper focuses on the tradeoff between direct channels, with resellers employed by the firm, and indirect channels, in which independent resellers can sell to other resellers, to individual customers, etc. One puzzling result that re-emerged later in several papers on franchising is the coexistence of both forms in many firms. The study was based on data provided by 87 firms answering an extensive questionnaire. It also confirmed the significant effect of uncertainty and of the specificity of assets, although the latter is less significant when explaining mixed channels.

A synthesis provided by Joskow (1988, Chapter 16) concludes this section. Although the review dates back from the 1980s, it gives an interesting perspective on the early evolution of transaction cost economics. But more important, it identifies through the examination of the first generation of econometric tests some major problems that are still relevant. Measurement difficulties are particularly emphasized: difficulties of comparing alternative solutions, difficulties of evaluating the specificity of assets or measuring the other attributes, and difficulties related to the questionnaire method. These problems do not belong solely to NIE. They are of particular importance there, though, because the emphasis is put on empirical verification and interaction with the theory.

Part III: Non-Standard Agreements

The problems mentioned above become even more significant with the analysis of non-standard agreements, of 'hybrids'. Actually the analyses of the tradeoff between 'make' or 'buy' in the previous sections already identified arrangements that corresponded neither to full integration nor to standard market relationships. They signaled the presence of intermediate forms, the importance of which was not yet fully acknowledged though. It is in the 1990s that the analysis of these forms took off.

Two papers from the early 1980s particularly anticipated this movement. In a discussion of the Coase–Williamson explanation to markets and firms, Ouchi (1980, Chapter 17) vigorously supported the idea that a third form should be incorporated, that he called 'clans' (the literature later referred to these forms as networks[5]). Notwithstanding the positive role of 'bureaucracies' (integrated organizations) when markets fail to provide efficient tools for coordinating through prices, as established by transaction cost economics, there are situations in which ambiguity of performance evaluation may be significantly greater than what already caused market failures, so that hierarchies may fail as well. 'Clans' offer an alternative, based on reputation, on regular relationships, and on shared social norms.

Almost simultaneously, Eccles (1981, Chapter 18) published an empirical study illustrating the importance *and* stability of intermediate forms. Also referring to Williamson, he wondered what happens when investments are only moderately specific and when specialization is incomplete, while consequential uncertainty requires great flexibility. Through a detailed examination of subcontracting in the construction industry, he showed the role of networks of partners based on durable relations combined with constant renegotiations. Organization as a pool provides the flexibility that vertical integration could not offer for adapting to continuously changing projects and circumstances. It also allows recurrent testing of the market, while the stability of the set of partners reduces coordination costs. Therefore, intermediate forms have logic of their own.

This was progressively acknowledged by Williamson (1991, Chapter 2) and confirmed by numerous studies in the 1990s. Powell (1990, Chapter 19) contributed to this evolution, particularly with his analysis of networks. Their importance in craft industries (construction, publishing, films, and recording) and in high-technology sectors (biotechnologies) points to the crucial role of inter-firm cooperation when sharing know-how and/or dealing with rapid changes that make consequences of choices unpredictable. The paper also identifies characteristics necessary to make networks stable – for example, the homogeneity of participants or the frequency of transactions. Powell joins Eccles in challenging the preeminence of asset specificity and in emphasizing the role of uncertainty to explain these forms.

The analysis of the high-quality segment in the French poultry industry by Ménard (1996, Chapter 20) exhibits arrangements that combine subcontracting and networks, along with confirming the significance of uncertainty, but only when it is paired with idiosyncratic investments. More precisely, the examination of an extended set of contracts in the successful 'label system' shows that the tight coordination required for guaranteeing quality and meeting the standards that differentiate products generated well-structured forms of governance. Three types of private order were identified that correspond neither to an integrated firm nor to market arrangements.

Focusing on modes of organization in the case of technology transfer, Oxley (1997, Chapter 21) confirms the differentiation among hybrids. She also identifies three forms of alliances; and they also correspond to different property rights. In her typology, unilateral contracts (licensing) are close to market arrangements, bilateral contracts (technology sharing agreements) involve tighter coordination, and equity joint-ventures are close to quasi-integration. As in Ménard, the study also emphasizes the role of specific devices, designed to better coordinate without the burden (and lower incentives) of integration. Her database of 9000 agreements, mostly in the 1980s, shows that more hierarchical forms prevail when appropriability hazards become severe.

Lafontaine and Shaw (1999, Chapter 22) do not strictly endorse a transaction approach, but they do look at a problem that arose by several new institutionalists studying hybrids (see John and Weitz, 1988, Chapter 15; Powell, 1990, Chapter 19; Ménard, 1996, Chapter 20) – that is, the coexistence of mixed forms within the same arrangement. By examining why franchisors quite systematically combine company-owned outlets and independent franchisees, they also take note of a quite general evolution of the pattern over time, and its stabilization in similar terms across sectors. Alternative explanations are tested, mainly in relation to specificity of assets and to agency problems, but no satisfactory answer seems to be available yet.

Holmström and Roberts (1998, Chapter 23) conclude this volume by a comparison of transaction cost economics and property rights theory, which are the two approaches that dominate the recent literature on the nature of firms and their boundaries. The paper summarizes well several issues at stake, although it may underestimate the consequences of the different assumptions made.[6] It points out the necessity to dig deeper in the internal characteristics of firms in order to understand their role in comparison to markets, and the authors urge that more research on hybrids is needed. Most new institutionalists should concur.

Notes

1. Hereafter NIE.
2. Coase, Ronald (1959), 'The Federal Communications Commission', *Journal of Law and Economics*, **2** (October), 1–40; Williamson, Oliver E. (1975), *Markets and Hierarchies: Analysis and Antitrust Implications*. New York: Free Press.
3. For a methodological discussion of some problems involved see Masten and Snyder, Volume 5, Chapter 5.
4. He also looked at the importance of non-price provisions.
5. Thorelli identified and nicely characterized networks in a paper that we were unfortunately not able to include here: Thorelli, Hans B. (1986), 'Networks: Between Markets and Hierarchies', *Strategic Management Journal*, **7** (1), 37–51.
6. These differences are discussed in Williamson, Oliver (2002), 'The Theory of the Firm as Governance Structure: From Choice to Contract', *Journal of Economic Perspectives*, **16** (3), 171–94.

References

Coase, Ronald H. (1937), 'The Nature of the Firm', *Economica*, New Series, November, **4** (16), 386–405.

Masten, Scott E., James W. Meehan Jr. and Edward A. Snyder (1991), 'The Costs of Organization', *Journal of Law, Economics, and Organization*, **7** (1), Spring, 1–25.

Williamson, O.E. (2002), 'The Theory of the Firm as Governance Structure: From Choice to Contract', *Journal of Economic Perspectives*, **16** (3), 171–94.

Part I
Markets, Hierarchies, Hybrid Forms

[1]

The Institutional Structure of Production

By R. H. COASE*

In my long life I have known some great economists, but I have never counted myself among their number nor walked in their company. I have made no innovations in high theory. My contribution to economics has been to urge the inclusion in our analysis of features of the economic system so obvious that, like the postman in G. K. Chesterton's Father Brown tale, "The Invisible Man," they have tended to be overlooked. Nonetheless, once included in the analysis, they will, as I believe, bring about a complete change in the structure of economic theory, at least in what is called price theory or microeconomics. What I have done is to show the importance for the working of the economic system of what may be termed the institutional structure of production. In this lecture I shall explain why, in my view, these features of the economic system were ignored and why their recognition will lead to a change in the way we analyze the working of the economic system and in the way we think about economic policy, changes which are already beginning to occur. I will also speak about the empirical work that needs to be done if this transformation in our approach is to increase our understanding. In speaking about this transformation, I do not wish to suggest that it is the result of my work alone. Oliver Williamson, Harold Demsetz, and Steven Cheung, among others, have made outstanding contributions to the subject, and without their work and that of many others, I doubt whether the significance of my writings would have been recognized. While it has been a great advantage of the creation of the Prize in Economic Sciences in Memory of Alfred Nobel that, by drawing attention to the significance of particular fields of economics, it encourages further research in them, the highlighting of the work of a few scholars, or, in my case, one scholar, tends to obscure the importance of the contributions of other able scholars whose researches have been crucial to the development of the field.

I will be speaking of that part of economics which has come to be called industrial organization, but to understand its present state, it is necessary to say something about the development of economics in general. During the two centuries since the publication of *The Wealth of Nations*, the main activity of economists, it seems to me, has been to fill the gaps in Adam Smith's system, to correct his errors, and to make his analysis vastly more exact. A principal theme of *The Wealth of Nations* was that government regulation or centralized planning were not necessary to make an economic system function in an orderly way. The economy could be coordinated by a system of prices (the "invisible hand") and, furthermore, with beneficial results. A major task of economists since the publication of *The Wealth of Nations*, as Harold Demsetz (1988 p. 145) has explained, has been to formalize this proposition of Adam Smith. The given factors are technology and the tastes of consumers, and individuals, who follow their own interest, are governed in their choices by a system of prices. Economists have uncovered the conditions necessary if Adam Smith's results are to be achieved and where, in the real world, such conditions do not appear to be found, they have proposed changes which are designed to bring them about. It is what one finds in the textbooks. Harold Demsetz has said rightly that what this theory analyzes is a system of extreme decentralization. It has

*University of Chicago Law School, 1111 East 60th Street, Chicago, IL 60637.

This article is the lecture R. H. Coase delivered in Stockholm, Sweden, December 9, 1991, when he received the Alfred Nobel Memorial Prize in Economic Sciences.

been a great intellectual achievement, and it throws light on many aspects of the economic system. But it has not been by any means all gain. The concentration on the determination of prices has led to a narrowing of focus which has had as a result the neglect of other aspects of the economic system. Sometimes, indeed, it seems as though economists conceive of their subject as being concerned only with the pricing system and anything outside this is considered as no part of their business. Thus, my old chief and wonderful human being, Lionel Robbins, wrote, in *The Nature and Significance of Economic Science*, about the "glaring deficiencies" of the old treatment of the theory of production with its discussion of peasant proprietorships and industrial forms: "It suggests that from the point of view of the economist 'organisation' is a matter of internal industrial (or agricultural) arrangement—if not internal to the firm, at any rate internal to 'the' industry. At the same time it tends to leave out completely the governing factor of all productive organisation—the relationship of prices and cost... (Robbins, 1932 p. 70). What this comes down to is that, in Robbins's view, an economist does not interest himself in the internal arrangements within organizations but only in what happens on the market, the purchase of factors of production, and the sale of the goods that these factors produce. What happens in between the purchase of the factors of production and the sale of the goods that are produced by these factors is largely ignored. I do not know how far economists today share Robbins's attitude but it is undeniable that microeconomics is largely a study of the determination of prices and output; indeed, this part of economics is often called price theory.

This neglect of other aspects of the system has been made easier by another feature of modern economic theory—the growing abstraction of the analysis, which does not seem to call for a detailed knowledge of the actual economic system or, at any rate, has managed to proceed without it. Bengt Holmstrom and Jean Tirole (1989) writing on "The Theory of the Firm" in the recently published *Handbook of Industrial Organization*, conclude at the end of their article of 63 pages that "the evidence/theory ratio...is currently very low in this field." Sam Peltzman (1991) has written a scathing review of the *Handbook* in which he points out how much of the discussion in it is theory without any empirical basis. What is studied is a system which lives in the minds of economists but not on earth. I have called the result "blackboard economics." The firm and the market appear by name but they lack any substance. The firm in mainstream economic theory has often been described as a "black box." And so it is. This is very extraordinary given that most resources in a modern economic system are employed within firms, with how these resources are used dependent on administrative decisions and not directly on the operation of a market. Consequently, the efficiency of the economic system depends to a very considerable extent on how these organizations conduct their affairs, particularly, of course, the modern corporation. Even more surprising, given their interest in the pricing system, is the neglect of the market or more specifically the institutional arrangements which govern the process of exchange. As these institutional arrangements determine to a large extent what is produced, what we have is a very incomplete theory. All this is beginning to change, and in this process I am glad to have played my part. The value of including such institutional factors in the corpus of mainstream economics is made clear by recent events in Eastern Europe. These ex-communist countries are advised to move to a market economy, and their leaders wish to do so, but without the appropriate institutions no market economy of any significance is possible. If we knew more about our own economy, we would be in a better position to advise them.

What I endeavored to do in the two articles cited by the Royal Swedish Academy of Sciences was to attempt to fill these gaps or more exactly to indicate the direction in which we should move if they are ultimately to be filled. Let me start with "The Nature of the Firm." I went as a student to the London School of Economics in 1929 to study for a Bachelor of Commerce degree, specializing in the Industry group, supposedly designed for people who wished to become works managers, a choice of occupation for which I was singularly ill-suited. However, in 1931 I had a great stroke of luck. Arnold Plant was appointed Professor of Commerce in 1930. He was a wonderful teacher. I began to attend his seminar in 1931, some five months before I took the final examinations. It was a revelation. He quoted Sir Arthur Salter: "The normal economic system works itself." And he explained how a competitive economic system coordinated by prices would lead to the production of goods and services which consumers valued most highly. Before being exposed to Plant's teaching, my notions on how the economy worked were extremely woolly. After Plant's seminar I had a coherent view of the economic system. He introduced me to Adam Smith's "invisible hand." As I had taken the first year of university work while still at high school, I managed to complete the requirements for a degree in two years. However, University regulations required three years of residence before a degree could be granted. I had therefore a year to spare. I then had another stroke of luck. I was awarded a Cassel travelling scholarship by the University of London. I decided to spend the year in the United States, this being treated as a year's residence at the London School of Economics, the regulations being somewhat loosely interpreted.

I decided to study vertical and lateral integration of industry in the United States. Plant had described in his lectures the different ways in which various industries were organized, but we seemed to lack any theory which would explain these differences. I set out to find it. There was also another puzzle which, in my mind, needed to be solved and which seemed to be related to my main project. The view of the pricing system as a coordinating mechanism was clearly right, but there were aspects of the argument which troubled me. Plant was opposed to all schemes, then very fashionable during the Great Depression, for the coordination of industrial production by some form of planning. Competition, according to Plant, acting through a system of prices, would do all the coordination necessary. And yet we had a factor of production, management, whose function was to coordinate. Why was it needed if the pricing system provided all the coordination necessary? The same problem presented itself to me at that time in another guise. The Russian Revolution had taken place only 14 years earlier. We knew then very little about how planning would actually be carried out in a communist system. Lenin had said that the economic system in Russia would be run as one big factory. However, many economists in the West maintained that this was an impossibility. And yet there were factories in the West, and some of them were extremely large. How did one reconcile the views expressed by economists on the role of the pricing system and the impossibility of successful central economic planning with the existence of management and of these apparently planned societies, firms, operating within our own economy?[1]

I found the answer by the summer of 1932. It was to realize that there were costs of using the pricing mechanism. What the prices are have to be discovered. There are negotiations to be undertaken, contracts have to be drawn up, inspections have to be made, arrangements have to be made to settle disputes, and so on. These costs have come to be known as transaction costs. Their existence implies that methods of coordination alternative to the market, which are themselves costly and in various ways imperfect, may nonetheless be preferable to relying on the pricing mechanism, the only method of coordination normally analyzed by economists. It was the avoidance of the costs of carrying out transactions through the market that could explain the existence of the firm in which the allocation of factors came about as a result of administrative decisions (and I thought it did). In my 1937 article I argued that in a competitive system

[1]A fuller account of these events will be found in Oliver E. Williamson and Sidney G. Winter (1991 pp. 34–47).

there would be an optimum of planning since a firm, that little planned society, could only continue to exist if it performed its coordination function at a lower cost than would be incurred if it were achieved by means of market transactions and also at a lower cost than this same function could be performed by another firm. To have an efficient economic system it is necessary not only to have markets but also areas of planning within organizations of the appropriate size. What this mix should be we find as a result of competition. This is what I said in my article of 1937. However, as we know from a letter I wrote in 1932 which has been preserved, all the essentials of this argument had been presented in a lecture I gave in Dundee at the beginning of October, 1932 (see Williamson and Winter, 1991 pp. 34–5). I was then 21 years of age, and the sun never ceased to shine. I could never have imagined that these ideas would become some 60 years later a major justification for the award of a Nobel Prize. And it is a strange experience to be praised in my eighties for work I did in my twenties.

There is no doubt that the recognition by economists of the importance of the role of the firm in the functioning of the economy will prompt them to investigate its activities more closely. The work of Oliver Williamson and others has led to a greater understanding of the factors which govern what a firm does and how it does it. And we can also hope to learn much more in future from the studies of the activities of firms which have recently been initiated by the Center for Economic Studies of the Bureau of the Census of the United States. But it would be wrong to think that the most important consequence for economics of the publication of "The Nature of the Firm" has been to direct attention to the importance of the firm in our modern economy, a result which, in my view, would have come about in any case. What I think will be considered in the future to have been the important contribution of this article is the explicit introduction of transaction costs into economic analysis. I argued in "The Nature of the Firm" that the existence of transaction costs leads to the emergence of the firm. But the effects are pervasive in the economy. Businessmen in deciding on their ways of doing business and on what to produce have to take into account transaction costs. If the costs of making an exchange are greater than the gains which that exchange would bring, that exchange would not take place and the greater production that would flow from specialization would not be realized. In this way transaction costs affect not only contractual arrangements, but also what goods and services are produced. Not to include transaction costs in the theory leaves many aspects of the working of the economic system unexplained, including the emergence of the firm, but much else besides. In fact, a large part of what we think of as economic activity is designed to accomplish what high transaction costs would otherwise prevent or to reduce transaction costs so that individuals can freely negotiate and we can take advantage of that diffused knowledge of which Hayek has told us.

I know of only one part of economics in which transaction costs have been used to explain a major feature of the economic system, and that relates to the evolution and use of money. Adam Smith pointed out the hindrances to commerce that would arise in an economic system in which there was a division of labor but in which all exchange had to take the form of barter. No one would be able to buy anything unless he possessed something that the producer wanted. This difficulty, he explained, could be overcome by the use of money. A person wishing to buy something in a barter system has to find someone who has this product for sale but who also wants some of the goods possessed by the potential buyer. Similarly, a person wishing to sell something has to find someone who both wants what he has to offer and also possesses something that the potential seller wants. Exchange in a barter system requires what W. S. Jevons called "this double coincidence." Clearly the search for partners in exchange with suitable qualifications is likely to be very costly and will prevent many potentially beneficial exchanges from taking place. The benefit brought about by the use of money consists of a reduction in transaction costs.

The use of money also reduces transaction costs by facilitating the drawing up of contracts as well as by reducing the quantity of goods that need to be held for purposes of exchange. However, the nature of the benefits secured by the use of money seems to have faded into the background so far as economists are concerned, and it does not seem to have been noticed that there are other features of the economic system which exist because of the need to mitigate transaction costs.

I now turn to that other article cited by the Swedish Academy, "The Problem of Social Cost," published some 30 years ago. I will not say much here about its influence on legal scholarship, which has been immense, but will mainly consider its influence on economics, which has not been immense, although I believe that in time it will be. It is my view that the approach used in that article will ultimately transform the structure of microeconomics—and I will explain why. I should add that in writing this article I had no such general aim in mind. I thought that I was exposing the weaknesses of Pigou's analysis of the divergence between private and social products, an analysis generally accepted by economists, and that was all. It was only later, and in part as a result of conversations with Steven Cheung in the 1960's that I came to see the general significance for economic theory of what I had written in that article and also to see more clearly what questions needed to be further investigated.

Pigou's conclusion and that of most economists using standard economic theory was (and perhaps still is) that some kind of government action (usually the imposition of taxes) was required to restrain those whose actions had harmful effects on others (often termed negative externalities). What I showed in that article, as I thought, was that in a regime of zero transaction costs, an assumption of standard economic theory, negotiations between the parties would lead to those arrangements being made which would maximize wealth and this irrespective of the initial assignment of rights. This is the infamous Coase theorem, named and formulated by George Stigler, although it is based on work of mine. Stigler argues that the Coase theorem follows from the standard assumptions of economic theory. Its logic cannot be questioned, only its domain (Stigler, 1989 pp. 631–3). I do not disagree with Stigler. However, I tend to regard the Coase theorem as a stepping stone on the way to an analysis of an economy with positive transaction costs. The significance to me of the Coase theorem is that it undermines the Pigovian system. Since standard economic theory assumes transaction costs to be zero, the Coase theorem demonstrates that the Pigovian solutions are unnecessary in these circumstances. Of course, it does not imply, when transaction costs are positive, that government actions (such as government operation, regulation, or taxation, including subsidies) could not produce a better result than relying on negotiations between individuals in the market. Whether this would be so could be discovered not by studying imaginary governments but what real governments actually do. My conclusion: let us study the world of positive transaction costs.

If we move from a regime of zero transaction costs to one of positive transaction costs, what becomes immediately clear is the crucial importance of the legal system in this new world. I explained in "The Problem of Social Cost" that what are traded on the market are not, as is often supposed by economists, physical entities, but the rights to perform certain actions, and the rights which individuals possess are established by the legal system. While we can imagine in the hypothetical world of zero transaction costs that the parties to an exchange would negotiate to change any provision of the law which prevents them from taking whatever steps are required to increase the value of production, in the real world of positive transaction costs, such a procedure would be extremely costly and would make unprofitable, even where it was allowed, a great deal of such contracting around the law. Because of this, the rights which individuals possess, with their duties and privileges, will be, to a large extent, what the law determines. As a result, the legal system will have a profound effect on the working of the economic system and may in certain respects be said to control it. It is obviously desirable that these rights should be assigned to those who can use them most productively and with incentives that lead them to do so and that, to discover (and maintain) such a distribution of rights, the costs of their transference should be low, through clarity in the law and by making the legal requirements for such transfers less onerous. Since this can come about only if there is an appropriate system of property rights (and they are enforced), it is easy to understand why so many academic lawyers (at least in the United States) have found so attractive the task of uncovering the character of such a property-rights system and why the subject of "law and economics" has flourished in American law schools. Indeed, work is going forward at such a pace that I do not consider it overoptimistic to believe that the main outlines of the subject will be drawn within five or ten years.

Until quite recently, most economists seem to have been unaware of this relationship between the economic and legal systems except in the most general way. Stock and produce exchanges are often used by economists as examples of perfect or near-perfect competition. But these exchanges regulate in great detail the activities of traders (and this quite apart from any public regulation there may be). What can be traded, when it can be traded, the terms of settlement, and so on are all laid down by the authorities of the exchange. There is, in effect, a private law. Without such rules and regulations, the speedy conclusion of trades would not be possible. Of course, when trading takes place outside exchanges (and this is almost all trading) and where the dealers are scattered in space and have very divergent interests, as in retailing and wholesaling, such a private law would be difficult to establish, and their activities will be regulated by the laws of the State. It makes little sense for economists to discuss the process of exchange without specifying the institutional setting within which the trading takes place, since this affects the incentives to produce and the costs of transacting. I think this is now beginning to be recognized and has been made crystal-clear by what is going on in Eastern Europe today. The time has surely gone in which economists could analyze in great detail two individuals exchanging nuts for berries on the edge of the forest and then feel that their analysis of the process of exchange was complete, illuminating though this analysis may be in certain respects. The process of contracting needs to be studied in a real-world setting. We would then learn of the problems that are encountered and of how they are overcome, and we would certainly become aware of the richness of the institutional alternatives between which we have to choose.

Oliver Williamson has ascribed the nonuse or limited use of my thesis in "The Nature of the Firm" to the fact that it has not been made "operational," by which he means that the concept of transaction costs has not been incorporated into a general theory. I think this is correct. There have been two reasons for this. First, incorporating transaction costs into standard economic theory, which has been based on the assumption that they are zero, would be very difficult, and economists who, like most scientists, as Thomas Kuhn has told us, are extremely conservative in their methods, have not been inclined to attempt it. Second, Williamson has also pointed out that although I was correct in making the choice between organization within the firm or through the market the centerpiece of my analysis, I did not indicate what the factors were that determined the outcome of this choice and thus made it difficult for others to build on what is often described as a "fundamental insight." This also is true. But the interrelationships which govern the mix of market and hierarchy, to use Williamson's terms, are extremely complex, and in our present state of ignorance it will not be easy to discover what these factors are. What we need is more empirical work. In a paper written for a conference of the National Bureau of Economic Research, I explained why I thought this was so. This is what I said: "An inspired theoretician might do as well without such empirical work, but my own feeling is that the inspiration is most likely to come through the stimulus provided by the patterns, puzzles, and anomalies revealed by the systematic gathering of data, particularly when the prime need is to break our existing habits of thought (Coase, 1988 p. 71). This statement was made in 1970. I still think that in essentials it is true today. Although much interesting and important research was done in the 1970's and 1980's and we certainly know much more than we did in 1970, there is little doubt that a great deal more empirical work is needed. However, I have come to the conclusion that the main obstacle faced by researchers in industrial organization is the lack of available data on contracts and the activities of firms. I have therefore decided to do something about it.

Believing that there is a great deal of data on contracts and the activities of firms in the United States available in government departments and agencies in Washington, DC, and that this information is largely unknown to economists, I organized a conference at the University of Chicago Law School in the summer of 1990 at which government officials presented papers in which they described what data was available and how to get access to it and also reported on some of the research being carried out within their departments. The audience consisted of academic economists. It was, as a colleague remarked, a case of supply meeting demand. The proceedings of this conference will be published in a special issue of the *Journal of Law and Economics*. Another development with which I am associated is the establishment of the Center for the Study of Contracts and the Structure of Enterprise at the Business School of the University of Pittsburgh. This Center will make large-scale collections of business contracts and will prepare data bases which will be made available to all researchers, whatever their institution. Nor should we forget the work now getting started at the Center for Economic Studies of the Bureau of the Census. This greater availability of data and the encouragement given to all researchers working on the institutional structure of production by the award to me of the Nobel Prize should result in a reduction in that elegant but sterile theorizing so commonly found in the economics literature on industrial organization and should lead to studies which increase our understanding of how the real economic system works.

My remarks have sometimes been interpreted as implying that I am hostile to the mathematization of economic theory. This is untrue. Indeed, once we begin to uncover the real factors affecting the performance of the economic system, the complicated interrelations between them will clearly necessitate a mathematical treatment, as in the natural sciences, and economists like myself, who write in prose, will take their bow. May this period soon come.

I am very much aware that many economists whom I respect and admire will not agree with the opinions I have expressed, and some may even be offended by them. But a scholar must be content with the knowledge that what is false in what he says will soon be exposed and, as for what is true, he can count on ultimately seeing it accepted, if only he lives long enough.

REFERENCES

Coase, R. H., *The Firm, The Market, and the Law*, Chicago: University of Chicago Press, 1988.

Demsetz, Harold, *Ownership, Control, and the Firm*, Vol. I, Oxford: Blackwell, 1988.

Holmstrom, Bengt and Tirole, Jean, "The Theory of the Firm," in Richard Schmalensee and Robert D. Willig, eds., *Handbook of Industrial Organization*, Amsterdam: North-Holland, 1989, pp. 61–128.

Peltzman, Sam, "The Handbook of Industrial Organization: A Review Article," *Journal of Political Economy*, February 1991, *99*, 201–17.

Robbins, Lionel, *The Nature and Significance of Economic Science*, London: Macmillan, 1932.

Stigler, George J., "Two Notes on the Coase Theorem," *Yale Law Journal*, December 1989, *99*, 631–3.

Williamson, Oliver E. and Winter, Sidney G., eds., *The Nature of the Firm, Origins, Evolution, and Development*, Oxford: Oxford University Press, 1991.

[2]

Comparative Economic Organization: The Analysis of Discrete Structural Alternatives

Oliver E. Williamson
University of California, Berkeley

This paper combines institutional economics with aspects of contract law and organization theory to identify and explicate the key differences that distinguish three generic forms of economic organization—market, hybrid, and hierarchy. The analysis shows that the three generic forms are distinguished by different coordinating and control mechanisms and by different abilities to adapt to disturbances. Also, each generic form is supported and defined by a distinctive type of contract law. The cost-effective choice of organization form is shown to vary systematically with the attributes of transactions. The paper unifies two hitherto disjunct areas of institutional economics—the institutional environment and the institutions of governance—by treating the institutional environment as a locus of parameters, changes in which parameters bring about shifts in the comparative costs of governance. Changes in property rights, contract law, reputation effects, and uncertainty are investigated.•

Although microeconomic organization is formidably complex and has long resisted systematic analysis, that has been changing as new modes of analysis have become available, as recognition of the importance of institutions to economic performance has grown, and as the limits of earlier modes of analysis have become evident. Information economics, game theory, agency theory, and population ecology have all made significant advances.

This paper approaches the study of economic organization from a comparative institutional point of view in which transaction-cost economizing is featured. Comparative economic organization never examines organization forms separately but always in relation to alternatives. Transaction-cost economics places the principal burden of analysis on comparisons of transaction costs—which, broadly, are the "costs of running the economic system" (Arrow, 1969: 48).

My purpose in this paper is to extend and refine the apparatus out of which transaction-cost economics works, thereby to respond to some of the leading criticisms. Four objections to prior work in this area are especially pertinent. One objection is that the two stages of the new institutional economics research agenda—the institutional environment and the institutions of governance—have developed in disjunct ways. The first of these paints on a very large historical canvas and emphasizes the institutional rules of the game: customs, laws, politics (North, 1986). The latter is much more microanalytic and focuses on the comparative efficacy with which alternative generic forms of governance—markets, hybrids, hierarchies—economize on transaction costs. Can this disjunction problem be overcome? Second, transaction-cost economics has been criticized because it deals with polar forms—markets and hierarchies—to the neglect of intermediate or hybrid forms. Although that objection has begun to be addressed by recent treatments of long-term contracting in which bilateral dependency conditions are supported by a variety of specialized governance features (hostages, arbitration, take-or-pay procurement clauses, tied sales, reciprocity, regulation, etc.), the abstract attributes

0001-8392/91/3602-0269/$1.00.

•

The author is Transamerica Professor of Business, Economics, and Law at the University of California, Berkeley and Senior Research Scientist of the Institute for Policy Reform. The paper benefitted from presentations at workshops at the University of California, Berkeley, the University of California, Los Angeles/University of Southern California, the University of California, Irvine, the University of Michigan, and the Netherlands Institute for Advanced Studies. Helpful comments from workshop participants and from Glenn Carroll, Melvin Eisenberg, Bengt Holmstrom, David Kreps, Gillian Hadfield, Scott Masten, Vai-Lam Mui, Richard Nelson, Dan Ostas, Michael Riordan, Roberta Romano, Richard Stewart, Jean Tirole, and Birger Wernerfelt as well as the referees, editor, and managing editor of this journal are gratefully acknowledged. A much shorter version was prepared for and presented as the opening address to the annual meeting of German Academic Business Economists at Frankfurt, Germany in June 1990. A German translation of that address has since been published in the papers and proceedings. The final version of this paper was produced while I was at Saarbrücken University as Distinguished U.S. Senior Scientist, Alexander von Humboldt-Stiftung, for which support I express appreciation.

that characterize alternative modes of governance have remained obscure. What are the key attributes and how do they vary among forms? This is responsive to the third objection, namely, that efforts to operationalize transaction-cost economics have given disproportionate attention to the abstract description of transactions as compared with the abstract description of governance. The dimensionalization of both is needed. Finally, there is the embeddedness problem: Transaction-cost economics purports to have general application but has been developed almost entirely with reference to Western capitalist economies (Hamilton and Biggart, 1988). Is a unified treatment of Western and non-Western, capitalist and noncapitalist economies really feasible? This paper attempts to address these objections by posing the problem of organization as one of discrete structural analysis.

DISCRETE STRUCTURAL ANALYSIS

The term discrete structural analysis was introduced into the study of comparative economic organization by Simon (1978: 6–7), who observed that

> As economics expands beyond its central core of price theory, and its central concern with quantities of commodities and money, we observe in it . . . [a] shift from a highly quantitative analysis, in which equilibration at the margin plays a central role, to a much more qualitative institutional analysis, in which discrete structural alternatives are compared. . . .
>
> [S]uch analyses can often be carried out without elaborate mathematical apparatus or marginal calculation. In general, much cruder and simpler arguments will suffice to demonstrate an inequality between two quantities than are required to show the conditions under which these quantities are equated at the margin.

But what exactly is discrete structural analysis? Is it employed only because "there is at present no [satisfactory] way of characterizing organizations in terms of continuous variation over a spectrum" (Ward, 1967: 38)? Or is there a deeper rationale?

Of the variety of factors that support discrete structural analysis, I focus here on the following: (1) firms are not merely extensions of markets but employ different means, (2) discrete contract law differences provide crucial support for and serve to define each generic form of governance, and (3) marginal analysis is typically concerned with second-order refinements to the neglect of first-order economizing.

Different Means

Although the study of economic organization deals principally with markets and market mechanisms, it is haunted by a troublesome fact: a great deal of economic activity takes place within firms (Barnard, 1938; Chandler, 1962, 1977). Conceivably, however, no novel economizing issues are posed within firms, because technology is largely determinative—the firm is mainly defined by economies of scale and scope and is merely an instrument for transforming inputs into outputs according to the laws of technology—and because market mechanisms carry over into firms. I have taken exception with the technology view elsewhere (Williamson, 1975). Consider, therefore, the latter.

(Williamson, 1983). Franchising is another way of preserving semi-autonomy, but added supports are needed (Klein, 1980; Hadfield, 1990). More generally, long-term, incomplete contracts require special adaptive mechanisms to effect realignment and restore efficiency when beset by unanticipated disturbances.

Disturbances are of three kinds: inconsequential, consequential, and highly consequential. Inconsequential disturbances are ones for which the deviation from efficiency is too small to recover the costs of adjustment. The net gains from realignment are negative for minor disturbances because (as discussed below) requests for adjustments need to be justified and are subject to review, the costs of which exceed the prospective gains.

Middle-range or consequential disturbances are ones to which neoclassical contract law applies. These are transactions for which Karl Llewellyn's concept of "contract as framework" is pertinent. Thus Llewellyn (1931: 737) refers to contract as "a framework highly adjustable, a framework which almost never accurately indicates real working relations, but which affords a rough indication around which such relations vary, an occasional guide in cases of doubt, and a norm of ultimate appeal when the relations cease in fact to work." The thirty-two-year coal supply agreement between the Nevada Power Company and the Northwest Trading Company illustrates the elastic mechanisms employed by a neoclassical contract. That contract reads in part as follows:

> . . . In the event an inequitable condition occurs which adversely affects one Party, it shall then be the joint and equal responsibility of both Parties to act promptly and in good faith to determine the action required to cure or adjust for the inequity and effectively to implement such action. Upon written claim of inequity served by one Party upon the other, the Parties shall act jointly to reach an agreement concerning the claimed inequity within sixty (60) days of the date of such written claim. An adjusted base coal price that differs from market price by more than ten percent (10%) shall constitute a hardship. The Party claiming inequity shall include in its claim such information and data as may be reasonably necessary to substantiate the claim and shall freely and without delay furnish such other information and data as the other Party reasonably may deem relevant and necessary. If the Parties cannot reach agreement within sixty (60) days the matter shall be submitted to arbitration.

By contrast with a classical contract, this contract (1) contemplates unanticipated disturbances for which adaptation is needed, (2) provides a tolerance zone (of ±10%) within which misalignments will be absorbed, (3) requires information disclosure and substantiation if adaptation is proposed, and (4) provides for arbitration in the event voluntary agreement fails.

The forum to which this neoclassical contract refers disputes is (initially, at least) that of arbitration rather than the courts. Fuller (1963: 11–12) described the procedural differences between arbitration and litigation:

> [T]here are open to the arbitrator . . . quick methods of education not open to the courts. An arbitrator will frequently interrupt the examination of witnesses with a request that the parties educate

Comparative Economic Organization

In parallel with von Clausewitz's (1980) views on war, I maintain that hierarchy is not merely a contractual act but is also a contractual instrument, a continuation of market relations by other means. The challenge to comparative contractual analysis is to discern and explicate the different means. As developed below, each viable form of governance—market, hybrid, and hierarchy—is defined by a syndrome of attributes that bear a supporting relation to one another. Many hypothetical forms of organization never arise, or quickly die out, because they combine inconsistent features.

Contract Law

The mapping of contract law onto economic organization has been examined elsewhere (Williamson, 1979, 1985). Although some of that is repeated here, there are two significant differences. First, I advance the hypothesis that each generic form of governance—market, hybrid, and hierarchy—needs to be supported by a different form of contract law. Second, the form of contract law that supports hierarchy is that of forbearance.

Classical contract law. Classical contract law applies to the ideal transaction in law and economics—"sharp in by clear agreement; sharp out by clear performance" (Macneil, 1974: 738)—in which the identity of the parties is irrelevant. "Thick" markets are ones in which individual buyers and sellers bear no dependency relation to each other. Instead, each party can go its own way at negligible cost to another. If contracts are renewed period by period, that is only because current suppliers are continuously meeting bids in the spot market. Such transactions are monetized in extreme degree; contract law is interpreted in a very legalistic way: more formal terms supercede less formal should disputes arise between formal and less formal features (e.g., written agreements versus oral amendments), and hard bargaining, to which the rules of contract law are strictly applied, characterizes these transactions. Classical contract law is congruent with and supports the autonomous market form of organization (Macneil, 1974, 1978).

Neoclassical contract law and excuse doctrine. Neoclassical contract law and excuse doctrine, which relieves parties from strict enforcement, apply to contracts in which the parties to the transaction maintain autonomy but are bilaterally dependent to a nontrivial degree. Identity plainly matters if premature termination or persistent maladaptation would place burdens on one or both parties. Perceptive parties reject classical contract law and move into a neoclassical contracting regime because this better facilitates continuity and promotes efficient adaptation.

As developed below, hybrid modes of contracting are supported by neoclassical contract law. The parties to such contracts maintain autonomy, but the contract is mediated by an elastic contracting mechanism. Public utility regulation, in which the relations between public utility firms and their customers are mediated by a regulatory agency, is one example (Goldberg, 1976; Williamson, 1976). Exchange agreements or reciprocal trading in which the parties experience (and respond similarly to) similar disturbances is another illustration

him to the point where he can understand the testimony being received. This education can proceed informally, with frequent interruptions by the arbitrator, and by informed persons on either side, when a point needs clarification. Sometimes there will be arguments across the table, occasionally even within each of the separate camps. The end result will usually be a clarification that will enable everyone to proceed more intelligently with the case.

Such adaptability notwithstanding, neoclassical contracts are not indefinitely elastic. As disturbances become highly consequential, neoclassical contracts experience real strain, because the autonomous ownership status of the parties continuously poses an incentive to defect. The general proposition here is that when the "lawful" gains to be had by insistence upon literal enforcement exceed the discounted value of continuing the exchange relationship, defection from the spirit of the contract can be anticipated.

When, in effect, arbitration gives way to litigation, accommodation can no longer be presumed. Instead, the contract reverts to a much more legalistic regime—although, even here, neoclassical contract law averts truly punitive consequences by permitting appeal to exceptions that qualify under some form of excuse doctrine. The legal system's commitment to the keeping of promises under neoclassical contract law is modest, as Macneil (1974: 731) explained:

> . . . contract remedies are generally among the weakest of those the legal system can deliver. But a host of doctrines and techniques lies in the way even of those remedies: impossibility, frustration, mistake, manipulative interpretation, jury discretion, consideration, illegality, duress, undue influence, unconscionability, capacity, forfeiture and penalty rules, doctrines of substantial performance, severability, bankruptcy laws, statutes of frauds, to name some; almost any contract doctrine can and does serve to make the commitment of the legal system to promise keeping less than complete.

From an economic point of view, the tradeoff that needs to be faced in excusing contract performance is between stronger incentives and reduced opportunism. If the state realization in question was unforeseen and unforeseeable (different in degree and/or especially in kind from the range of normal business experience), if strict enforcement would have truly punitive consequences, and especially if the resulting "injustice" is supported by (lawful) opportunism, then excuse can be seen mainly as a way of mitigating opportunism, ideally without adverse impact on incentives. If, however, excuse is granted routinely whenever adversity occurs, then incentives to think through contracts, choose technologies judiciously, share risks efficiently, and avert adversity will be impaired. Excuse doctrine should therefore be used sparingly—which it evidently is (Farnsworth, 1968: 885; Buxbaum, 1985).

The relief afforded by excuse doctrine notwithstanding, neoclassical contracts deal with consequential disturbances only at great cost: arbitration is costly to administer and its adaptive range is limited. As consequential disturbances and, especially, as highly consequential disturbances become more frequent, the hybrid mode supported by arbitration and excuse doctrine incurs added costs and comes under added strain. Even more elastic and adaptive arrangements warrant consideration.

Forbearance. Internal organization, hierarchy, qualifies as a still more elastic and adaptive mode of organization. What type of contract law applies to internal organization? How does this have a bearing on contract performance?

Describing the firm as a "nexus of contracts" (Alchian and Demsetz, 1972; Jensen and Meckling, 1976; Fama, 1980) suggests that the firm is no different from the market in contractual respects. Alchian and Demsetz (1972: 777) originally took the position that the relation between a shopper and his grocer and that between an employer and employee was identical in contractual respects:

> The single consumer can assign his grocer to the task of obtaining whatever the customer can induce the grocer to provide at a price acceptable to both parties. That is precisely all that an employer can do to an employee. To speak of managing, directing, or assigning workers to various tasks is a deceptive way of noting that the employer continually is involved in renegotiation of contracts on terms that must be acceptable to both parties. . . . Long-term contracts between employer and employee are not the essence of the organization we call a firm.

That it has been instructive to view the firm as a nexus of contracts is evident from the numerous insights that this literature has generated. But to regard the corporation only as a nexus of contracts misses much of what is truly distinctive about this mode of governance. As developed below, bilateral adaptation effected through fiat is a distinguishing feature of internal organization. But wherein do the fiat differences between market and hierarchy arise? If, moreover, hierarchy enjoys an "advantage" with respect to fiat, why can't the market replicate this?

One explanation is that fiat has its origins in the employment contract (Barnard, 1938; Simon, 1951; Coase, 1952; Masten, 1988). Although there is a good deal to be said for that explanation, I propose a separate and complementary explanation: The implicit contract law of internal organization is that of forbearance. Thus, whereas courts routinely grant standing to firms should there be disputes over prices, the damages to be ascribed to delays, failures of quality, and the like, courts will refuse to hear disputes between one internal division and another over identical technical issues. Access to the courts being denied, the parties must resolve their differences internally. Accordingly, hierarchy is its own court of ultimate appeal.

What is known as the "business judgment rule" holds that "Absent bad faith or some other corrupt motive, directors are normally not liable to the corporation for mistakes of judgment, whether those mistakes are classified as mistakes of fact or mistakes of law" (Gilson, 1986: 741). Not only does that rule serve as "a quasi-jurisdictional barrier to prevent courts from exercising regulatory powers over the activities of corporate managers" (Manne, 1967: 271), but "The courts' abdication of regulatory authority through the business judgment rule may well be the most significant common law contribution to corporate governance" (Gilson, 1986: 741). The business judgment rule, which applies to the relation between shareholders and directors, can be interpreted as a particular manifestation of forbearance doctrine, which applies to the management of the firm more generally. To review alleged mistakes of judgment or to adjudicate internal disputes would sorely test the competence of courts and would undermine the efficacy of hierarchy.

Accordingly, the reason why the market is unable to replicate the firm with respect to fiat is that market transactions are defined by contract law of an altogether different kind. There is a logic to classical market contracting and there is a logic for forbearance law, and the choice of one regime precludes the other. Whether a transaction is organized as make or buy—internal procurement or market procurement, respectively—thus matters greatly in dispute-resolution respects: the courts will hear disputes of the one kind and will refuse to be drawn into the resolution of disputes of the other. Internal disputes between one division and another regarding the appropriate transfer prices, the damages to be ascribed to delays, failures of quality, and the like, are thus denied a court hearing.

To be sure, not all disputes within firms are technical. Personnel disputes are more complicated. Issues of worker safety, dignity, the limits of the "zone of acceptance," and the like sometimes pose societal spillover costs that are undervalued in the firm's private net benefit calculus. Underprovision of human and worker rights could ensue if the courts refused to consider issues of these kinds. Also, executive compensation agreements can sometimes be written in ways that make it difficult to draw a sharp line between personnel and technical issues. Even with personnel disputes, however, there is a presumption that such differences will be resolved internally. For example, unions may refuse to bring individual grievances to arbitration (Cox, 1958: 24):

> [G]iving the union control over all claims arising under the collective agreement comports so much better with the functional nature of a collective bargaining agreement. . . . Allowing an individual to carry a claim to arbitration whenever he is dissatisfied with the adjustment worked out by the company and the union . . . discourages the kind of day-to-day cooperation between company and union which is normally the mark of sound industrial relations—a relationship in which grievances are treated as problems to be solved and contracts are only guideposts in a dynamic human relationship. When . . . the individual's claim endangers group interests, the union's function is to resolve the competition by reaching an accommodation or striking a balance.

As compared with markets, internal incentives in hierarchies are flat or low-powered, which is to say that changes in effort expended have little or no immediate effect on compensation. That is mainly because the high-powered incentives of markets are unavoidably compromised by internal organization (Williamson, 1985, chap. 6; 1988). Also, however, hierarchy uses flat incentives because these elicit greater cooperation and because unwanted side effects are checked by added internal controls (see Williamson, 1988; Holmstrom, 1989). Not only, therefore, will workers and managers be more willing to accommodate, because their compensation is the same whether they "do this" or "do that," but an unwillingness to accommodate is interpreted not as an excess of zeal but as a predilection to behave in a noncooperative way. Long-term promotion prospects are damaged as a consequence. Defection from the spirit of the agreement in favor of litigiousness is quite perverse if neither immediate nor long-term gains are thereby realized. The combination of fiat with low-powered incentives is a manifestation of the syndrome condition of economic organization to which I referred earlier (and develop more fully below).

The underlying rationale for forbearance law is twofold: (1) parties to an internal dispute have deep knowledge—both about the circumstances surrounding a dispute as well as the efficiency properties of alternative solutions—that can be communicated to the court only at great cost, and (2) permitting internal disputes to be appealed to the court would undermine the efficacy and integrity of hierarchy. If fiat were merely advisory, in that internal disputes over net receipts could be pursued in the courts, the firm would be little more than an "inside contracting" system (Williamson, 1985: 218–222). The application of forbearance doctrine to internal organization means that parties to an internal exchange can work out their differences themselves or appeal unresolved disputes to the hierarchy for a decision. But this exhausts their alternatives. When push comes to shove, "legalistic" arguments fail. Greater reliance on instrumental reasoning and mutual accommodation result. This argument contradicts Alchian and Demsetz's (1972: 777) claim that the firm "has no power of fiat, no authority, no disciplinary action any different in the slightest degree from ordinary market contracting." That is exactly wrong: firms can and do exercise fiat that markets cannot. Prior neglect of contract law differences and their ramifications explain the error.

First-Order Economizing

Although the need to get priorities straight is unarguable, first-order economizing—effective adaptation and the elimination of waste—has been neglected. Adaptation is especially crucial. As developed below, it is the central economic problem. But as Frank Knight (1941: 252) insisted, the elimination of waste is also important:

> . . . men in general, and within limits, wish to behave economically, to make their activities and their organization "efficient" rather than wasteful. This fact does deserve the utmost emphasis; and an adequate definition of the science of economics . . . might well make it explicit that the main relevance of the discussion is found in its relation to social policy, assumed to be directed toward the end indicated, of increasing economic efficiency, of reducing waste.

Relatedly, but independently, Oskar Lange (1938: 109) held that "the real danger of socialism is that of the bureaucratization of economic life, and not the impossibility of coping with the problem of allocation of resources." Inasmuch, however, as Lange (1938: 109) believed that this argument belonged "in the field of sociology" he concluded that it "must be dispensed with here." Subsequent informed observers of socialism followed this lead, whereupon the problems of bureaucracy were, until recently, given scant attention. Instead, the study of socialism was preoccupied with technical features—marginal cost pricing, activity analysis, and the like—with respect to which a broadly sanguine consensus took shape (Bergson, 1948; Montias, 1976; Koopmans, 1977).

Comparative Economic Organization

The natural interpretation of the organizational concerns expressed by Knight and Lange—or, at least, the interpretation that I propose here—is that economics was too preoccupied with issues of allocative efficiency, in which marginal analysis was featured, to the neglect of organizational efficiency, in which discrete structural alternatives were brought under scrutiny. Partly that is because the mathematics for dealing with clusters of attributes is only now beginning to be developed (Topkis, 1978; Milgrom and Roberts, 1990; Holmstrom and Milgrom, 1991). Even more basic, however, is the propensity to focus exclusively on market mechanisms to the neglect of discrete structural alternatives. The argument, for example, that all systems of honest trade are variants on the reputation-effect mechanisms of markets (Milgrom, North, and Weingast, 1990: 16) ignores the possibility that some ways of infusing contractual integrity (e.g., hierarchy) employ altogether different means. Market-favoring predispositions need to be disputed, lest the study of economic organization in all of its forms be needlessly and harmfully truncated.

DIMENSIONALIZING GOVERNANCE

What are the key attributes with respect to which governance structures differ? The discriminating alignment hypothesis to which transaction-cost economics owes much of its predictive content holds that transactions, which differ in their attributes, are aligned with governance structures, which differ in their costs and competencies, in a discriminating (mainly, transaction-cost-economizing) way. But whereas the dimensionalization of transactions received early and explicit attention, the dimensionalization of governance structures has been relatively slighted. What are the factors that are responsible for the aforementioned differential costs and competencies?

One of those key differences has been already indicated: market, hybrid, and hierarchy differ in contract law respects. Indeed, were it the case that the very same type of contract law were to be uniformly applied to all forms of governance, important distinctions between these three generic forms would be vitiated. But there is more to governance than contract law. Crucial differences in adaptability and in the use of incentive and control instruments are also germane.

Adaptation As the Central Economic Problem

Hayek (1945: 523) insistently argued that "economic problems arise always and only in consequence of change" and that this truth was obscured by those who held that "technological knowledge" is of foremost importance. He disputed the latter and urged that "the economic problem of society is mainly one of rapid adaptation in the particular circumstances of time and place" (Hayek, 1945: 524). Of special importance to Hayek was the proposition that the price system, as compared with central planning, is an extraordinarily efficient mechanism for communicating information and inducing change (Hayek, 1945: 524–527).

Interestingly, Barnard (1938) also held that the main concern of organization was that of adaptation to changing circumstances, but his concern was with adaptation within internal organization. Confronted with a continously fluctuating environment, the "survival of an organization depends upon the maintenance of an equilibrium of complex character. . . . [This] calls for readjustment of processes internal to the organization. . . , [whence] the center of our interest is the processes by which [adaptation] is accomplished" (Barnard, 1938: 6).

That is very curious. Both Hayek and Barnard hold that the central problem of economic organization is adaptation. But whereas Hayek locates this adaptive capacity in the market, it was the adaptive capacity of internal organization on which Barnard focused attention. If the "marvel of the market" (Hayek) is matched by the "marvel of internal organization" (Barnard), then wherein does one outperform the other?

The marvel to which Hayek (1945: 528) referred had spontaneous origins: "The price system is . . . one of those formations which man has learned to use . . . after he stumbled on it without understanding it." The importance of such spontaneous cooperation notwithstanding, it was Barnard's experience that intended cooperation was important and undervalued. The latter was defined as "that kind of cooperation among men that is conscious, deliberate, purposeful" (Barnard, 1938: 4) and was realized through formal organization, especially hierarchy.

I submit that adaptability is the central problem of economic organization and that both Hayek and Barnard are correct, because they are referring to adaptations of different kinds, both of which are needed in a high-performance system. The adaptations to which Hayek refers are those for which prices serve as sufficient statistics. Changes in the demand or supply of a commodity are reflected in price changes, in response to which "individual participants . . . [are] able to take the right action" (Hayek, 1945: 527). I will refer to adaptations of this kind as adaptation (A), where (A) denotes autonomy. This is the neoclassical ideal in which consumers and producers respond independently to parametric price changes so as to maximize their utility and profits, respectively.

That would entirely suffice if all disturbances were of this kind. Some disturbances, however, require coordinated responses, lest the individual parts operate at cross-purposes or otherwise suboptimize. Failures of coordination may arise because autonomous parties read and react to signals differently, even though their purpose is to achieve a timely and compatible combined response. The "nonconvergent expectations" to which Malmgren (1961) referred is an illustration. Although, in principle, convergent expectations could be realized by asking one party to read and interpret the signals for all, the lead party may behave strategically—by distorting information or disclosing it in an incomplete and selective fashion.

More generally, parties that bear a long-term bilateral dependency relation to one another must recognize that incomplete contracts require gapfilling and sometimes get out of alignment. Although it is always in the collective interest of autonomous parties to fill gaps, correct errors, and effect efficient realignments, it is also the case that the distribution of the resulting gains is indeterminate. Self-interested bargaining predictably obtains. Such bargaining is itself costly.

The main costs, however, are that transactions are maladapted to the environment during the bargaining interval. Also, the prospect of ex post bargaining invites ex ante prepositioning of an inefficient kind (Grossman and Hart, 1986).

Recourse to a different mechanism is suggested as the needs for coordinated investments and for uncontested (or less contested) coordinated realignments increase in frequency and consequentiality. Adaptations of these coordinated kinds will be referred to as adaptation (C), where (C) denotes cooperation. The conscious, deliberate, and purposeful efforts to craft adaptive internal coordinating mechanisms were those on which Barnard focused. Independent adaptations here would at best realize imperfect realignments and could operate at cross-purposes. Lest the aforementioned costs and delays associated with strategic bargaining be incurred, the relation is reconfigured by supplanting autonomy by hierarchy. The authority relation (fiat) has adaptive advantages over autonomy for transactions of a bilaterally (or multilaterally) dependent kind.

Instruments

Vertical and lateral integration are usefully thought of as organization forms of last resort, to be employed when all else fails. That is because markets are a "marvel" in adaptation (A) respects. Given a disturbance for which prices serve as sufficient statistics, individual buyers and suppliers can reposition autonomously. Appropriating, as they do, individual streams of net receipts, each party has a strong incentive to reduce costs and adapt efficiently. What I have referred to as high-powered incentives result when consequences are tightly linked to actions in this way (Williamson, 1988). Other autonomous traders have neither legitimate claims against the gains nor can they be held accountable for the losses. Accounting systems cannot be manipulated to share gains or subsidize losses.

Matters get more complicated when bilateral dependency intrudes. As discussed above, bilateral dependency introduces an opportunity to realize gains through hierarchy. As compared with the market, the use of formal organization to orchestrate coordinated adaptation to unanticipated disturbances enjoys adaptive advantages as the condition of bilateral dependency progressively builds up. But these adaptation (C) gains come at a cost. Not only can related divisions within the firm make plausible claims that they are causally responsible for the gains (in indeterminate degree), but divisions that report losses can make plausible claims that others are culpable. There are many ways, moreover, in which the headquarters can use the accounting system to effect strategic redistributions (through transfer pricing changes, overhead assignments, inventory conventions, etc.), whatever the preferences of the parties. The upshot is that internal organization degrades incentive intensity, and added bureaucratic costs result (Williamson, 1985: chap. 6; 1988).

These three features—adaptability of type A, adaptability of type C, and differential incentive intensity—do not exhaust the important differences between market and hierarchy. Also important are the differential reliance on administrative controls and, as developed above, the different contract law regimes to which each is subject. Suffice it to observe here that (1) hierarchy is buttressed by the differential efficacy of administrative controls within firms, as compared with between firms, and (2) incentive intensity within firms is sometimes deliberately suppressed. Incentive intensity is not an objective but is merely an instrument. If added incentive intensity gets in the way of bilateral adaptability, then weaker incentive intensity supported by added administrative controls (monitoring and career rewards and penalties) can be optimal.

Markets and hierarchies are polar modes. As indicated at the outset, however, a major purpose of this paper is to locate hybrid modes—various forms of long-term contracting, reciprocal trading, regulation, franchising, and the like—in relation to these polar modes. Plainly, the neoclassical contract law of hybrid governance differs from both the classical contract law of markets and the forbearance contract law of hierarchies, being more elastic than the former but more legalistic than the latter. The added question is How do hybrids compare with respect to adaptability (types A and C), incentive intensity, and administrative control?

The hybrid mode displays intermediate values in all four features. It preserves ownership autonomy, which elicits strong incentives and encourages adaptation to type A disturbances (those to which one party can respond efficiently without consulting the other). Because there is bilateral dependency, however, long-term contracts are supported by added contractual safeguards and administrative apparatus (information disclosure, dispute-settlement machinery). These facilitate adaptations of type C but come at the cost of incentive attenuation. Concerns for "equity" intrude. Thus the Nevada Power Company–Northwest Trading Company coal contract, whose adaptation mechanics were set out above, begins with the following: "It is the intent of the Parties hereto that this agreement, as a whole and in all of its parts, shall be equitable to both Parties throughout its term." Such efforts unavoidably dampen incentive-intensity features.

One advantage of hierarchy over the hybrid with respect to bilateral adaptation is that internal contracts can be more incomplete. More importantly, adaptations to consequential disturbances are less costly within firms because (1) proposals to adapt require less documentation, (2) resolving internal disputes by fiat rather than arbitration saves resources and facilitates timely adaptation, (3) information that is deeply impacted can more easily be accessed and more accurately assessed, (4) internal dispute resolution enjoys the support of informal organization (Barnard, 1938; Scott, 1987), and (5) internal organization has access to additional incentive instruments—including especially career reward and joint profit sharing—that promote a team orientation. Furthermore, highly consequential disturbances that would occasion breakdown or costly litigation under the hybrid mode can be accommodated more easily. The advantages of hierarchy over hybrid in adaptation C respects are not, however, realized without cost. Weaker incentive intensity (greater bureaucratic costs) attend the move from hybrid to hierarchy, ceteris paribus.

Comparative Economic Organization

Summarizing, the hybrid mode is characterized by semi-strong incentives, an intermediate degree of administrative apparatus, displays semi-strong adaptations of both kinds, and works out of a semi-legalistic contract law regime. As compared with market and hierarchy, which are polar opposites, the hybrid mode is located between the two of these in all five attribute respects. Based on the foregoing, and denoting strong, semi-strong, and weak by + +, +, and 0, respectively, the instruments, adaptive attributes, and contract law features that distinguish markets, hybrids, and hierarchies are shown in Table 1.

Table 1

Distinguishing Attributes of Market, Hybrid, and Hierarchy Governance Structures*

	Governance structure		
Attributes	Market	Hybrid	Hierarchy
Instruments			
Incentive intensity	+ +	+	0
Administrative controls	0	+	+ +
Performance attributes			
Adaptation (A)	+ +	+	0
Adaptation (C)	0	+	+ +
Contract law	+ +	+	0

* + + = strong; + = semi-strong; 0 = weak.

DISCRIMINATING ALIGNMENT

Transaction-cost economics subscribes to Commons' view (1924, 1934) that the transaction is the basic unit of analysis. That important insight takes on operational significance upon identifying the critical dimensions with respect to which transactions differ. Without purporting to be exhaustive, these include the frequency with which transactions recur, the uncertainty to which transactions are subject, and the type and degree of asset specificity involved in supplying the good or service in question (Williamson, 1979). Although all are important, transaction-cost economics attaches special significance to this last (Williamson, 1975, 1979; Klein, Crawford, and Alchian, 1978; Grossman and Hart, 1986).

Asset specificity has reference to the degree to which an asset can be redeployed to alternative uses and by alternative users without sacrifice of productive value. Asset-specificity distinctions of six kinds have been made: (1) site specificity, as where successive stations are located in a cheek-by-jowl relation to each other so as to economize on inventory and transportation expenses; (2) physical asset specificity, such as specialized dies that are required to produce a component; (3) human-asset specificity that arises in learning by doing; (4) brand name capital; (5) dedicated assets, which are discrete investments in general purpose plant that are made at the behest of a particular customer; and (6) temporal specificity, which is akin to technological nonseparability and can be thought of as a type of site specificity in which timely responsiveness by on-site human assets is vital (Masten, Meehan, and Snyder, 1991). Asset specificity, especially in its first five forms, creates bilateral dependency and poses added contracting hazards. It has played a central role in the conceptual and empirical work in transaction-cost economics.

The analysis here focuses entirely on transaction costs: neither the revenue consequences nor the production-cost savings that result from asset specialization are included. Although that simplifies the analysis, note that asset specificity increases the transaction costs of all forms of governance. Such added specificity is warranted only if these added governance costs are more than offset by production-cost savings and/or increased revenues. A full analysis will necessarily make allowance for effects of all three kinds (Riordan and Williamson, 1985). Only a truncated analysis appears here.

Reduced-Form Analysis

The governance-cost expressions set out herein are akin to reduced forms, in that governance costs are expressed as a function of asset specificity and a set of exogenous variables. The structural equations from which these reduced forms are derived are not set out. The key features that are responsible for cost differences among governance structures are nonetheless evident in the matrix version of the model set out below.[1]

Although asset specificity can take a variety of forms, the common consequence is this: a condition of bilateral dependency builds up as asset specificity deepens. The ideal transaction in law and economics—whereby the identities of buyers and sellers is irrelevant—obtains when asset specificity is zero. Identity matters as investments in transaction-specific assets increase, since such specialized assets lose productive value when redeployed to best alternative uses and by best alternative users.

Assume, for simplicity, that asset specificity differences are entirely due to physical or site specificity features. I begin with the situation in which classical market contracting works well: autonomous actors adapt effectively to exogenous disturbances. Internal organization is at a disadvantage for transactions of this kind, since hierarchy incurs added bureaucratic costs to which no added benefits can be ascribed. That, however, changes as bilateral dependency sets in. Disturbances for which coordinated responses are required become more numerous and consequential as investments in asset specificity deepen. The high-powered incentives of markets here impede adaptability, since each party to an autonomous exchange that has gotten out of alignment and for which mutual consent is needed to effect an adjustment will want to appropriate as much as possible (ideally, all but epsilon) of the adaptive gains to be realized. When bilaterally dependent parties are unable to respond quickly and easily, because of disagreements and self-interested bargaining, maladaptation costs are incurred. Although the transfer of such transactions from market to hierarchy creates added bureaucratic costs, those costs may be more than offset by the bilateral adaptive gains that result.

1
Developing the deeper structure that supports the reduced forms—by explicating contractual incompleteness and its consequences in a more microanalytic way and by developing the bureaucratic cost consequences of internal organization more explicitly—is an ambitious but important undertaking.

Comparative Economic Organization

Let M = M(k;θ) and H = H(k;θ) be reduced-form expressions that denote market and hierarchy governance costs as a function of asset specificity (k) and a vector of shift parameters (θ). Assuming that each mode is constrained to choose the same level of asset specificity, the following comparative-cost relations obtain: $M(0) < H(0)$ and $M' > H' > 0$.[2] The first of these two inequalities reflects the fact that the bureaucratic costs of internal organization exceed those of the market because the latter is superior in adaptation (A) respects—which is the only kind that matters if asset specificity is negligible. The intercept for market governance is thus lower than is the intercept for hierarchy. The second inequality reflects the marginal disability of markets as compared with hierarchies in adaptation (C) respects as asset specificity, hence bilateral dependency, becomes more consequential.

As described above, the hybrid mode is located between market and hierarchy with respect to incentives, adaptability, and bureaucratic costs. As compared with the market, the hybrid sacrifices incentives in favor of superior coordination among the parts. As compared with the hierarchy, the hybrid sacrifices cooperativeness in favor of greater incentive intensity. The distribution of branded product from retail outlets by market, hierarchy, and hybrid, where franchising is an example of this last, illustrates the argument.

Forward integration out of manufacturing into distribution would be implied by hierarchy. That would sacrifice incentive intensity but would (better) assure that the parts do not operate at cross-purposes with one another. The market solution would be to sell the good or service outright. Incentive intensity is thereby harnessed, but suboptimization (free riding on promotional efforts, dissipation of the brand name, etc.) may also result. Franchising awards greater autonomy than hierarchy but places franchisees under added rules and surveillance as compared with markets. Cost control and local adaptations are stronger under franchising than hierarchy, and suboptimization is reduced under franchising as compared with the market. The added autonomy (as compared with hierarchy) and the added restraints (as compared with the market) under which franchisees operate nevertheless come at a cost. If, for example, quality assurance is realized by constraining the franchisee to use materials supplied by the franchisor, and if exceptions to that practice are not permitted because of the potential for abuse that would result, then local opportunities to make "apparently" cost-effective procurements will be prohibited. Similarly, the added local autonomy enjoyed by franchisees may get in the way of some global adjustments.

Transactions for which the requisite adaptations to disturbances are neither predominantly autonomous nor bilateral, but require a mixture of each, are candidates to be organized under the hybrid mode. Over some intermediate range of k, the mixed adaptation (A/C) that hybrids afford could well be superior to the A-favoring or C-favoring adaptations supported by markets and hierarchies, respectively.

Letting X = X(k;θ) denote the governance costs of the hybrid mode as a function of asset specificity, the argument is

2
A more general optimizing treatment in which the level of asset specificity varies with organization form is set out in Riordan and Williamson (1985). Also see Masten (1982).

that M(0) < X(0) < H(0) and that M′ > X′ > H′ > 0.[3] The relations shown in Figure 1 then obtain. Efficient supply implies operating on the envelope, whence, if k^* is the optimal value of k, the rule for efficient supply is as follows: I, use markets for $k^* < \bar{k}_1$; II, use hybrids for $\bar{k}_1 < k^* < k_2$; and III, use hierarchy for $k^* > \bar{k}_2$.

Figure 1. Governance costs as a function of asset specificity.

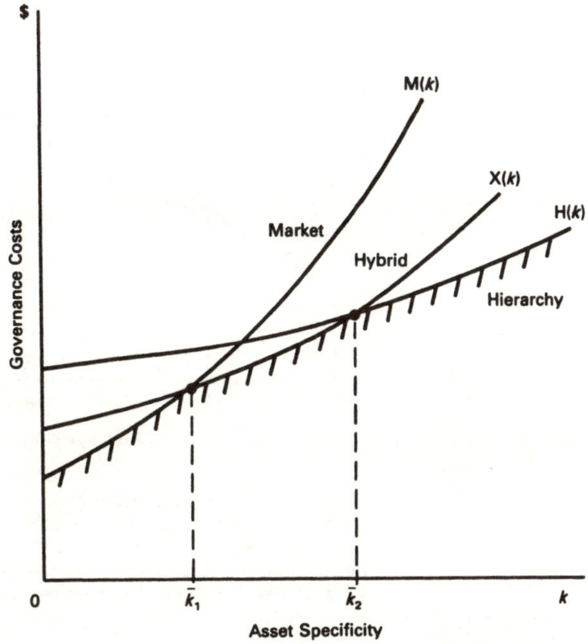

In a very heuristic way, moreover, one can think of moving along one of these generic curves as moving toward more intrusive controls. Thus, consider two forms of franchising, one of which involves less control than the other. If $X^1(k)$ and $X^2(k)$ refer to franchising with little and much control, respectively, then $X^2(k)$ will be located to the right of $X^1(k)$ in Figure 2. Or consider the M-form (multidivisional) and U-form (unitary or functionally organized) corporation. Because the former provides more market-like divisionalization than does the latter, the M-form is given by $H^1(k)$ and is located closer to $\bar{k}_2$ in Figure 2.

A Matrix Representation

Suppose that disturbances are distinguished in terms of the type of response—autonomous or bilateral—that is needed to effect an adaptation. Suppose further that the type of adaptation depends on the degree of asset specificity. Let asset specificity be denoted by k_i and suppose that it can take on any of three values: $k_1 = 0$ (generic investment), $k_2 > 0$ (semi-specific investment), or $k_3 \gg 0$ (highly specific investment). Assume that adjustments to disturbances can be any

3
This assumes that X(0) is less than H(0) to a nontrivial degree, since otherwise the hybrid mode could be dominated throughout by the least-cost choice of either market or hierarchy, which may occur for certain classes of transactions, as discussed below.

Comparative Economic Organization

Figure 2. Governance differences within discrete structural forms.

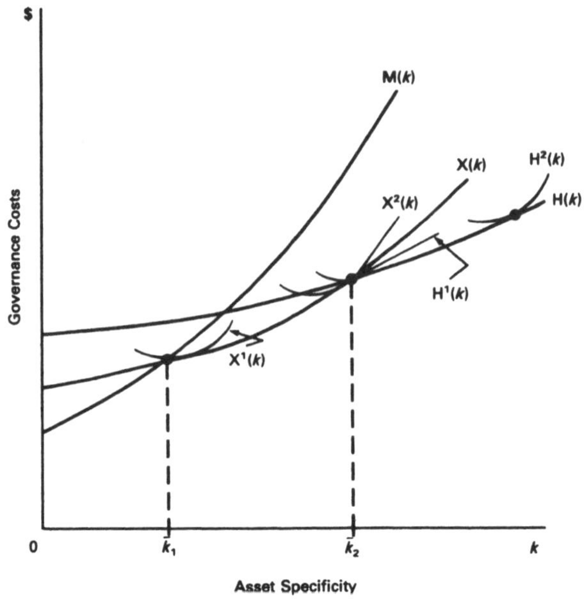

of four kinds: I, strictly autonomous; II, mainly autonomous; III, mainly coordinated; or IV, strictly coordinated. Let p_{ij} be the probability that an adaptation of type i = I, II, . . . , IV will be required if asset-specificity condition k_j (j = 1, 2, 3) obtains and let the matrix $[p_{ij}]$ be given by

		k_1	k_2	k_3
$[p_{ij}]$:	I	1.00	.25	.10
	II	.00	.25	.10
	III	.00	.25	.40
	IV	.00	.25	.40

Note that, the k_1 column excepted, positive probability is associated with every element in the matrix. What added asset specificity does is shift the distribution of required responses in favor of greater cooperativeness.

Assume that each adaptation, if costlessly and successfully implemented, would yield identical expected cost savings. For the reasons given above, however, the efficacy with which different modes adapt to disturbances of different kinds varies. Let e_{im} be the efficacy with which mode m (m = M, X, H) is able to implement adaptations of type i (i = I, II, . . . , IV) and assume that the matrix e_{im} is given by

		M	X	H
$[e_{im}]$:	I	1.0	0.9	0.7
	II	0.7	0.9	0.4
	III	0.2	0.5	0.5
	IV	−0.2	0.0	0.5

where 1.0 is the ideal degree of adaptiveness and 0.0 is equivalent (in terms of efficacy) to no adaptation.

The efficacy assumptions embedded in this last matrix warrant remark: (1) Only the entry e_{IM} has a value of 1.0. This condition—market adaptations to a disturbance for which strictly autonomous adaptation is appropriate—corresponds to the ideal transaction in law and economics (classical market contracting); (2) The efficacy of the market falls off as bilateral dependency builds up, becoming negative (worse than no adaptation at all) for the strictly cooperative case (IV). This last reflects the conflictual nature of market exchange for transactions of the bilaterally dependent kind; (3) The hybrid mode is almost as good as the market for strictly autonomous adaptations, is better than the market in all other adaptation categories, and is as good or better than hierarchy in all categories save that for which strict coordination is indicated; (4) Hierarchy is burdened by bureaucracy and never scores high in efficacy for any category of adaptation.[4] What matters, however, is comparative efficacy. The hierarchy comes into its own (comparatively) where adaptations of a strictly cooperative kind are needed; and (5) The efficacy of hierarchy is lowest for disturbances requiring a mainly autonomous adaptation. As compared with strictly autonomous disturbances, where bureaucratic costs are held in check by an objective market standard, ready recourse to the market is compromised by the need for some coordination. Because, however, the gains from coordination are not great, efforts to coordinate are problematic. If efforts to adapt autonomously are protested (my costs are greater because you moved without consulting me) while failures to adapt quickly are costly, the hierarchy is caught between the proverbial rock and a hard place.

Let C_{jm} be the expected maladaptation costs of using mode m to effect adaptations if asset specificity is of type k_j. Since inefficacy is given by $1 - e_{im}$, the expected maladaptation costs are $C_{jm} = \Sigma_i p_{ij} (1 - e_{im})$. That matrix is given by

		M	X	H
	k_1	**.000**	.100	.300
$[C_{jm}]$:	k_2	.575	**.425**	.475
	k_3	.830	.620	**.490**

The lowest values in each row are realized by matching market, hybrid, and hierarchy with asset specificity conditions k_1, k_2, and k_3, respectively. These costs are consonant with the reduced-form relations shown in Figure 1. Thus if $\beta \geq 0$ is the irreducible setup costs of economic participation, then the bureaucratic cost intercepts associated with zero asset specificity (k_1) for market, hybrid, and hierarchy will be given by β plus .000, .100, and .300, respectively. Also, the relation between the implied slopes associated with each mode in the matrix (expressed as a function of asset specificity) is that $M' > X' > H'$, which corresponds exactly to the relations shown in Figure 1.

COMPARATIVE STATICS

Transaction-cost economics maintains that (1) transaction-cost economizing is the "main case," which is not to be confused with the only case (Williamson, 1985: 22–23; 1989: 137–138), and (2) transaction costs vary with governance structures in the manner described above. Assuming

4
Hierarchy is able to deal with type I (strictly autonomous) disturbances reasonably well by instructing the operating parts to respond to local disturbances on their own motion and by using the market as an alternate source of supply and/or standard.

that the institutional environment is unchanging, transactions should be clustered under governance structures as indicated. Variance will be observed, but the main case should be as described.

The purpose of this section is to consider how equilibrium distributions of transactions will change in response to disturbances in the institutional environment. That is a comparative static exercise. Both parts of the new institutional economics—the institutional environment and the institutions of governance—are implicated. The crucial distinctions are these (Davis and North, 1971: 6–7):

The *institutional environment* is the set of fundamental political, social and legal ground rules that establishes the basis for production, exchange and distribution. Rules governing elections, property rights, and the right of contract are examples. . . .

An *institutional arrangement* is an arrangement between economic units that governs the ways in which these units can cooperate and/or compete. It . . . [can] provide a structure within which its members can cooperate . . . or [it can] provide a mechanism that can effect a change in laws or property rights.

The way that I propose to join these two is to treat the institutional environment as a set of parameters, changes in which elicit shifts in the comparative costs of governance. An advantage of a three-way setup—market, hybrid, and hierarchy (as compared with just market and hierarchy)—is that much larger parameter changes are required to induce a shift from market to hierarchy (or the reverse) than are required to induce a shift from market to hybrid or from hybrid to hierarchy. Indeed, as developed below, much of the comparative static action turns on differential shifts in the intercept and/or slope of the hybrid mode. The critical predictive action is that which is located in the neighborhood of $\bar{k}_1$ (M to X) and $\bar{k}_2$ (X to H) in Figure 1. Parameter changes of four kinds are examined: property rights, contract law, reputation effects, and uncertainty.

Among the limitations of the discrete structural approach is that parameter changes need to be introduced in a special way. Rather than investigate the effects of increases (or decreases) in a parameter (a wage rate, a tax, a shift in demand), as is customary with the usual maximizing setup, the comparative governance cost setup needs to characterize parameter changes as improvements (or not). It is furthermore limited by the need for these improvements to be concentrated disproportionately on one generic mode of governance. Those limitations notwithstanding, it is informative to examine comparative static effects.

Property Rights

What has come to be known as the economics of property rights holds that economic performance is largely determined by the way in which property rights are defined. Ownership of assets is especially pertinent to the definition of property rights, where this "consists of three elements: (a) the right to use the asset [and delimitations that apply thereto] . . . , (b) the right to appropriate returns from the asset . . . , and (c) the right to change the asset's form and/or substance" (Furubotn and Pejovich, 1974: 4).

Most discussions of property rights focus on definitional issues. As is generally conceded, property rights can be costly to define and enforce and hence arise only when the expected benefits exceed the expected costs (Demsetz, 1967). That is not my concern here. Rather, I focus on the degree to which property rights, once assigned, have good security features. Security hazards of two types are pertinent: expropriation by the government and expropriation by commerce (rivals, suppliers, customers).

Governmental expropriation. Issues of "credible commitments" (Williamson, 1983) and "security of expectations" (Michelman, 1967) are pertinent to expropriation by the government. If property rights could be efficiently assigned once and for all, so that assignments, once made, would not subsequently be undone—especially strategically undone—governmental expropriation concerns would not arise. Firms and individuals would confidently invest in productive assets without concern that they would thereafter be deprived of their just desserts.

If, however, property rights are subject to occasional reassignment, and if compensation is not paid on each occasion (possibly because it is prohibitively costly), then strategic considerations enter the investment calculus. Wealth will be reallocated (disguised, deflected, consumed) rather than invested in potentially expropriable assets if expropriation is perceived to be a serious hazard. More generally, individuals or groups who either experience or observe expropriation and can reasonably anticipate that they will be similarly disadvantaged in the future have incentives to adapt.

Michelman (1967) focused on cost-effective compensation. He argued that if compensation is costly and if the "demoralization costs" experienced by disadvantaged individuals and interested observers are slight, then compensation is not needed. If, however, demoralization costs can be expected to be great and losses can be easily ascertained, compensation is warranted. Michelman proposed a series of criteria by which to judge how this calculus works out. Suppose that the government is advised of these concerns and "promises" to respect the proposed criteria. Will such promises be believed? This brings us to the problem of credible commitments.

Promises are easy to make, but credible promises are another thing. Kornai's (1986: 1705–1706) observation that craftsmen and small shopkeepers fear expropriation in Hungary despite "repeated official declarations that their activity is regarded as a permanent feature of Hungarian socialism" is pertinent. That "many of them are myopic profit maximizers, not much interested in building up lasting goodwill . . . or by investing in long-lived fixed assets" (1986: 1706) is partly explained by the fact that "These individuals or their parents lived through the era of confiscations in the forties" (Kornai, 1986: 1705).

But there is more to it than that. Not only is there a history of expropriation, but, as of 1986, the structure of the government had not changed in such a way as to assuredly forestall subsequent expropriations. Official declarations will be more credible only with long experience or if accompanied by a credible (not easily reversible) reorganization of politics. As one Polish entrepreneur recently remarked, "I don't want expensive machines. If the situation changes, I'll get stuck with them" (Newman, 1989: A10). Note, in this connection, that the objectivity of law is placed in jeopardy if the law and its enforcement are under the control of a one-party state (Berman, 1983: 37). Credibility will be enhanced if a monarch who has made the law "may not make it arbitrarily, and until he has remade it—lawfully—he is bound by it" (Berman, 1983: 9). Self-denying ordinances and, even more, inertia that has been crafted into the political process have commitment benefits (North and Weingast, 1989).

That this has not fully registered on Eastern Europe and the Soviet Union is suggested by the following remarks of Mikhail Gorbachev (advising U.S. firms to invest quickly in the Soviet Union rather than wait): "Those [companies] who are with us now have good prospects of participating in our great country . . . [whereas those who wait] will remain observers for years to come—*we will see to it*" (*International Herald Tribune,* 1990: 5). That the leadership of the Soviet Union "will see to it" that early and late movers will be rewarded and punished, respectively, reflects conventional carrot-and-stick incentive reasoning. What it misses is that ready access to administrative discretion is the source of contractual hazard. The paradox is that fewer degrees of freedom (rules) can have advantages over more (discretion) because added credible commitments can obtain in this way. Effective economic reform thus requires that reneging options be foreclosed if investor confidence is to be realized.

Lack of credible commitment on the part of the government poses hazards for durable, immobile investments of all kinds—specialized and unspecialized alike—in the private sector. If durability and immobility are uncorrelated with asset specificity, then the transaction costs of all forms of private-sector governance increase together as expropriation hazards increase. In that event, the values of $\bar{k}_1$ and $\bar{k}_2$ might then change little or not at all. What can be said with assurance is that the government sector will have to bear a larger durable investment burden in a regime in which expropriation risks are perceived to be great. Also, private-sector durable investments will favor assets that can be smuggled or are otherwise mobile—such as general-purpose human assets (skilled machinists, physicians) that can be used productively if emigration is permitted to other countries.

Leakage. Not only may property rights be devalued by governments, but the value of specialized knowledge and information may be appropriated and/or dissipated by suppliers, buyers, and rivals. The issues here have recently been addressed by Teece (1986) in conjunction with "weak regimes of appropriability" and are related to earlier discussions by Arrow (1962) regarding property rights in information. If investments in knowledge cannot lawfully be protected or if nominal protection (e.g., a patent) is ineffective, then (1) the ex ante incentives to make such investments are impaired and (2) the ex post incentives to embed such investments in protective governance structures are increased. As Teece (1986) discussed, vertical or lateral integration into related stages of production where the hazards of leakage are greatest is sometimes undertaken for precisely these protective purposes. Trade secret protection is an example.

Interpreted in terms of the comparative governance cost apparatus employed here, weaker appropriability (increased risk of leakage) increases the cost of hybrid contracting as compared with hierarchy. The market and hybrid curves in Figure 1 are both shifted up by increased leakage, so that $\bar{k}_1$ remains approximately unchanged and the main effects are concentrated at $\bar{k}_2$. The value of $\bar{k}_2$ thus shifts to the left as leakage hazards increase, so that the distribution of transactions favors greater reliance on hierarchy.

Contract Law

Improvements or not in a contract law regime can be judged by how the relevant governance-cost curve shifts. An improvement in excuse doctrine, for example, would shift the cost of hybrid governance down. The idea here is that excuse doctrine can be either too lax or too strict. If too strict, then parties will be reluctant to make specialized investments in support of one another because of the added risk of truly punitive outcomes should unanticipated events materialize and the opposite party insist that the letter of the contract be observed. If too lax, then incentives to think through contracts, choose technologies judiciously, share risks efficiently, and avert adversity will be impaired.

Whether a change in excuse doctrine is an improvement or not depends on the initial conditions and on how these trade-offs play out. Assuming that an improvement is introduced, the effect will be to lower the cost of hybrid contracting—especially at higher values of asset specificity, where a defection from the spirit of the contract is more consequential. The effect of such improvements would be to increase the use of hybrid contracting, especially as compared with hierarchy.

Hadfield (1990: 981–982) has recently examined franchise law and has interpreted the prevailing tendency by the courts to fill in the gaps of an incomplete contract "by according the franchisor unfettered discretion, much as it would enjoy if it [the franchisor] were a vertically integrated corporation" as a mistaken application of forbearance reasoning from hierarchy (where the logic holds) to neoclassical contracting (where the logic fails). Such a failure of franchise law would increase the cost of franchising in relation to forward integration into distribution (Hadfield, 1990: 954). This would imply a shift in the value of $\bar{k}_2$ in Figure 1 to the left.

A change in forbearance doctrine would be reflected in the governance cost of hierarchy. Thus, mistaken forbearance doctrine—for example, a willingness by the courts to litigate intrafirm technical disputes—would have the effect of shifting the costs of hierarchical governance up. This would disadvantage hierarchy in relation to hybrid modes of contracting ($\bar{k}_2$ would shift to the right).

Reputation Effects

One way of interpreting a network is as a nonhierarchical contracting relation in which reputation effects are quickly and accurately communicated. Parties to a transaction to which reputation effects apply can consult not only their own experience but can benefit from the experience of others. To be sure, the efficacy of reputation effects is easily overstated (Williamson, 1991b), but comparative efficacy is all that concerns us here and changes in comparative efficacy can often be established.

Thus, assume that it is possible to identify a community of traders in which reputation effects work better (or worse). Improved reputation effects attenuate incentives to behave opportunistically in interfirm trade—since the immediate gains from opportunism in a regime where reputation counts must be traded off against future costs. The hazards of opportunism in interfirm trading are greatest for hybrid transactions—especially those in the neighborhood of $\bar{k}_2$. Since an improvement in interfirm reputation effects will reduce the cost of hybrid contracting, the value of $\bar{k}_2$ will shift to the right. Hybrid contracting will therefore increase, in relation to hierarchy, in regimes where interfirm reputation effects are more highly perfected, ceteris paribus. Reputation effects are pertinent within firms as well. If internal reputation effects improve, then managerial opportunism will be reduced and the costs of hierarchical governance will fall.

Ethnic communities that display solidarity often enjoy advantages of a hybrid contracting kind. Reputations spread quickly within such communities and added sanctions are available to the membership (Light, 1972). Such ethnic communities will predictably displace nonethnic communities for activities for which interfirm reputation effects are important. Nonethnic communities, to be viable, will resort to market or hierarchy (in a lower or higher k niche, respectively).

Uncertainty

Greater uncertainty could take either of two forms. One is that the probability distribution of disturbances remains unchanged but that more numerous disturbances occur. A second is that disturbances become more consequential (due, for example, to an increase in the variance).

One way of interpreting changes of either kind is through the efficacy matrix, above. I conjecture that the effects of more frequent disturbances are especially pertinent for those disturbances for which mainly coordinated or strictly coordinated responses are required. Although the efficacy of all forms of governance may deteriorate in the face of more frequent disturbances, the hybrid mode is arguably the most susceptible. That is because hybrid adaptations cannot be made unilaterally (as with market governance) or by fiat (as with hierarchy) but require mutual consent. Consent, however, takes time. If a hybrid mode is negotiating an adjustment to one disturbance only to be hit by another, failures of adaptation predictably obtain (Ashby, 1960). An increase in market and hierarchy and a decrease in hybrid will thus be associated with an (above threshold) increase in the frequency of disturbances. As shown in Figure 3, the hybrid mode could well become nonviable when the frequency of disturbances reaches high levels.[5]

5
The range of asset specificity is from zero (purely generic) to complete (purely firm-specific). The range of frequency is from "low" (a positive lower bound in a nearly unchanging environment) to "very high."

Figure 3. Organization form responses to changes in frequency.

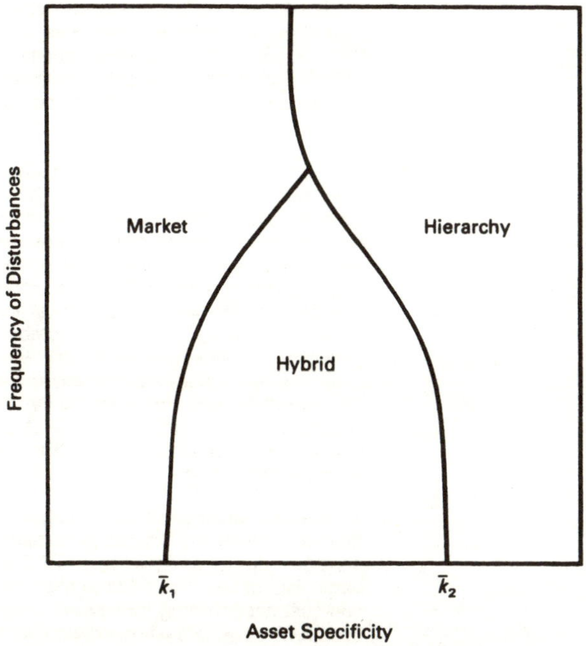

If an increase in the variance of the disturbances uniformly increases the benefits to be associated with each successful adaptation, then the effect of increasing the consequentiality of disturbances can again be assessed through the effects on efficacy. Since outliers induce greater defection on the spirit of the agreement for hybrid modes, the efficacy of the hybrid is adversely affected by added variance. Unless similar disabilities can be ascribed to market or hierarchy, the hybrid is disfavored by greater variance, ceteris paribus.

DISCUSSION

The foregoing is concerned with the organization of transactions for mature goods and services and introduces parameter shifts one at a time. Added complications arise when innovation is introduced and when a series of parameter shifts occur together.

Innovation

Some of the added problems posed by innovation take the form of weak property rights. These are discussed above in conjunction with leakage. A second class of problems that confront innovation is that of timeliness. Nonstandard forms of organization, such as parallel R&D (Nelson, 1961) and joint ventures, are sometimes employed because these facilitate timely entry.

Timing can be crucial if a party expects to be a "player" when events are fast-moving or if learning-by-doing is essential. Although transaction-cost economics can relate to some of the pertinent issues, such as those posed by tacit knowledge (Polanyi, 1962) and the limits of imitation (Williamson, 1975: 31–32, 203–207), added apparatus is needed to deal with the full set of issues that arise when responsiveness in real time, rather than equilibrium contracting, is the central concern. Awaiting such developments, the apparatus developed here should not be applied uncritically. For example, joint ventures are sometimes described as hybrids. If, however, joint ventures are temporary forms of organization that support quick responsiveness, and if that is their primary purpose, then both successful and unsuccessful joint ventures will commonly be terminated when contracts expire. Successful joint ventures will be terminated because success will often mean that each of the parties, who chose not to merge but, instead, decided to combine their respective strengths in a selective and timely way, will have learned enough to go it alone. Unsuccessful joint ventures will be terminated because the opportunity to participate will have passed them by. Joint ventures that are designed to give a respite should be distinguished from the types of hybrid modes analyzed here, which are of an equilibrium kind.

The need to distinguish continuing from temporary supply does not, however, mean that transaction-cost economizing principles do not apply to each. To the contrary, although the particulars differ, I would urge that the same general transaction-cost economizing framework has application (Williamson, 1985). The quasi-firms described by Eccles (1981), for example, can be interpreted as the efficient solution to a particular type of recurrent contracting problem. But the details do matter.

Simultaneous Parameter Shifts

The comparative static analysis set out above treats each generic form of organization as a syndrome of attributes and introduces parameter shifts one at a time. Suppose, instead, that a series of shifts were to occur together. Could these be processed as a sequence of independent changes? If such changes were in fact independent, that is precisely what I would propose. If, however, a related set of changes is made simultaneously, it will not do to treat these independently. If strong interaction effects exist, these must be treated as a cluster.

Relying extensively on the recent work of Aoki (1988, 1990), I have elsewhere interpreted the Japanese corporation as follows: (1) three key factors—employment, subcontracting, and banking—are fundamentally responsible for the success of the Japanese firm; (2) the efficacy of each of these rests on distinctive institutional supports; and (3) the three factors bear a complementary relation to each other (Williamson, 1991a).

The search for key factors and their institutional supports is wholly consistent with the spirit of this paper. Because employment, subcontracting, and banking changes are linked, however, the American corporation cannot expect to replicate the Japanese corporation by making changes in only one of these practices and not in the others. That is not to say that American firms cannot learn by observing subcontracting practices in Japanese firms. Exact replication of individual practices will be suboptimal, however, if linkages are important.

Similar considerations apply to economic reforms in China and Eastern Europe. If, for example, the efficacy of privatization turns crucially on the manner in which banking is organized and on the security of property rights, then piecemeal proposals that ignore the support institutions are fraught with hazard. The study of viable clusters of organization is a combined law, economics, and organizations undertaking. Although the apparatus in this paper is pertinent, applications to economic reform need to make express provision for contextual differences between alternative forms of capitalism (Hamilton and Biggart, 1988).

CONCLUSION

This paper advances the transaction-cost economics research agenda in the following five respects: (1) the economic problem of society is described as that of adaptation, of which autonomous and coordinated kinds are distinguished; (2) each generic form of governance is shown to rest on a distinctive form of contract law, of which the contract law of forbearance, which applies to internal organization and supports fiat, is especially noteworthy; (3) the hybrid form of organization is not a loose amalgam of market and hierarchy but possesses its own disciplined rationale; (4) more generally, the logic of each generic form of governance—market, hybrid, and hierarchy—is revealed by the dimensionalization and explication of governance herein developed; and (5) the obviously related but hitherto disjunct stages of institutional economics—the institutional environment and the institutions of governance—are joined by interpreting the institutional environment as a locus of shift parameters, changes in which parameters induce shifts in the comparative costs of governance. A large number of refutable implications are derived from the equilibrium and comparative static analyses of governance that result. The growing empirical literature, moreover, is broadly corroborative (for summaries, see Williamson, 1985: chap. 5; Joskow, 1988; Shelanski, 1990).

Further developments of conceptual, theoretical, and empirical kinds are needed. Taken together with related developments in information economics, agency theory, and population ecology, there is reason to be optimistic that a "new science of organization" will take shape during the decade of the 1990s (Williamson, 1990). Whether that materializes or not, organization theory is being renewed in law, economics, and organizational respects. These are exciting times for interdisciplinary social theory.

REFERENCES

Alchian, Armen, and Harold Demsetz
1972 "Production, information costs, and economic organization." American Economic Review, 62: 777–795.

Aoki, Masahiko
1988 Information, Incentives, and Bargaining in the Japanese Economy. New York: Cambridge University Press.

1990 "Toward an economic model of the Japanese firm." Journal of Economic Literature, 28: 1–27.

Comparative Economic Organization

Arrow, Kenneth J.
1962 "Economic welfare and the allocation of resources of invention." In National Bureau of Economic Research (ed.), The Rate and Direction of Inventive Activity: Economic and Social Factors: 609–625. Princeton, NJ: Princeton University Press.
1969 "The organization of economic activity: Issues pertinent to the choice of market versus nonmarket allocation." In The Analysis and Evaluation of Public Expenditure, Vol. 1: The PPB System: 59–73. U.S. Joint Economic Committee, 91st Congress, 1st Session. Washington, DC: U.S. Government Printing Office.

Ashby, W. Ross
1960 Design for a Brain. New York: Wiley.

Barnard, Chester
1938 The Functions of the Executive. Cambridge, MA: Harvard University Press.

Bergson, Abram
1948 "Socialist economics." In Howard Ellis (ed.), Survey of Contemporary Economics: 430–458. Philadelphia: Blakiston.

Berman, Harold
1983 Law and Revolution. Cambridge, MA: Harvard University Press.

Buxbaum, Richard M.
1985 "Modification and adaptation of contracts: American legal developments." Studies in Transnational Economic Law, 3: 31–54.

Chandler, Alfred D., Jr.
1962 Strategy and Structure. Cambridge, MA: MIT Press.
1977 The Visible Hand: The Managerial Revolution in American Business. Cambridge, MA: Harvard University Press.

Clausewitz, Karl von
1980 Vom Kriege, 19th ed. (Originally published in 1832.) Bonn: Dremmler.

Coase, R. H.
1952 "The nature of the firm." In George J. Stigler and Kenneth E. Boulding (eds.), Readings in Price Theory: 331–351. Homewood, IL: Irwin.

Commons, John R.
1924 "Law and economics." Yale Law Journal, 34: 371–382.
1934 Institutional Economics. Madison, WI: University of Wisconsin Press.

Cox, Archibald
1958 "The legal nature of collective bargaining agreements." Michigan Law Review, 57: 1–36.

Davis, Lance E., and Douglass C. North
1971 Institutional Change and American Economic Growth. Cambridge: Cambridge University Press.

Demsetz, Harold
1967 "Toward a theory of property rights." American Economic Review, 57: 347–359.

Eccles, Robert
1981 "The quasifirm in the construction industry." Journal of Economic Behavior and Organization, 2: 335–357.

Fama, Eugene F.
1980 "Agency problems and the theory of the firm." Journal of Political Economy, 88: 288–307.

Farnsworth, Edward Allan
1968 "Disputes over omissions in contracts." Columbia Law Review, 68: 860–891.

Fuller, Lon L.
1963 "Collective bargaining and the arbitrator." Wisconsin Law Review, January: 3–46.

Furubotn, Eirik, and Svetozar Pejovich
1974 The Economics of Property Rights. Cambridge, MA: Ballinger.

Gilson, Ronald
1986 The Law and Finance of Corporate Acquisitions. Mineola, NY: Foundation Press.

Goldberg, Victor
1976 "Regulation and administered contracts." Bell Journal of Economics, 7: 426–452.

Grossman, Sanford J., and Oliver D. Hart
1986 "The costs and benefits of ownership: A theory of vertical and lateral integration." Journal of Political Economy, 94: 691–719.

Hadfield, Gillian
1990 "Problematic relations: Franchising and the law of incomplete contracts." Stanford Law Review, 42: 927–992.

Hamilton, Gary, and Nicole Biggart
1988 "Market, culture, and authority." American Journal of Sociology (Supplement), 94: S52–S94.

Hayek, Friedrich
1945 "The use of knowledge in society." American Economic Review, 35: 519–530.

Holmstrom, Bengt
1989 "Agency costs and innovation." Journal of Economic Behavior and Organization, 12: 305–327.

Holmstrom, Bengt, and Paul Milgrom
1991 "Multi-task principal-agent analysis." Journal of Law, Economics, and Organization (in press).

International Herald Tribune
1990 "Soviet economic development." June 5: 5.

Jensen, Michael, and William Meckling
1976 "Theory of the firm: Managerial behavior, agency costs, and capital structure." Journal of Financial Economics, 3: 305–360.

Joskow, Paul
1988 "Asset specificity and the structure of vertical relationships." Journal of Law, Economics, and Organization, 4: 95–117.

Klein, Benjamin
1980 "Transaction cost determinants of 'unfair' contractual arrangements." American Economic Review, 70: 356–362.

Klein, Benjamin, R. A. Crawford, and A. A. Alchian
1978 "Vertical integration, appropriable rents, and the competitive contracting process." Journal of Law and Economics, 21: 297–326.

Knight, Frank H.
1941 Review of Melville J. Herskovits, *Economic Anthropology*. Journal of Political Economy, 49: 247–258.

Koopmans, Tjalling
1977 "Concepts of optimality and their uses." American Economic Review, 67: 261–274.

Kornai, Janos
1986 "The Hungarian reform process." Journal of Economic Literature, 24: 1687–1737.

Lange, Oskar
1938 "On the theory of economic socialism." In Benjamin Lippincott (ed.), On the Economic Theory of Socialism: 55–143. Minneapolis: University of Minnesota Press.

Light, Ivan
1972 Ethnic Enterprise in America: Business and Welfare among Chinese, Japanese, and Blacks. Berkeley, CA: University of Calfornia Press.

Llewellyn, Karl N.
1931 "What price contract? An essay in perspective." Yale Law Journal, 40: 704–751.

Macneil, Ian R.
1974 "The many futures of contracts." Southern California Law Review, 47: 691–816.
1978 "Contracts: Adjustments of long-term economic relations under classical, neoclassical, and relational contract law." Northwestern University Law Review, 72: 854–906.

Malmgren, Harold
1961 "Information, expectations and the theory of the firm." Quarterly Journal of Economics, 75: 399–421.

Manne, Henry
1967 "Our two corporation systems: Law and economics." University of Virginia Law Review, 53: 259–285.

Masten, Scott
1982 "Transaction costs, institutional choice, and the theory of the firm." Unpublished Ph.D. dissertation, University of Pennsylvania.
1988 "A legal basis for the firm." Journal of Law, Economics, and Organization, 4: 181–198.

Masten, Scott, James Meehan, and Edward Snyder
1991 "The costs of organization." Journal of Law, Economics, and Organization, Vol. 7 (in press).

Michelman, Frank
1967 "Property, utility and fairness: The ethical foundations of 'just compensation' law." Harvard Law Review, 80: 1165–1257.

Milgrom, Paul, Douglass North, and Barry Weingast
1990 "The role of institutions in the revival of trade." Economics and Politics, 2: 1–23.

Milgrom, Paul, and John Roberts
1990 "The economics of modern manufacturing: Technology, strategy, and organization." American Economic Review, 80: 511–528.

Montias, Michael
1976 The Structure of Economic Systems. New Haven, CT: Yale University Press.

Nelson, Richard R.
1961 "Uncertainty, learning, and the economics of parallel R&D." Review of Economics and Statistics, 43: 351–364.

Newman, Barry
1989 "Poland's farmers put the screws to leaders by holding back crops." Wall Street Journal, October 25: A1 and A10.

North, Douglass
1986 "The new institutional economics." Journal of Theoretical and Institutional Economics, 142: 230–237.

North, Douglass, and Barry Weingast
1989 "Constitutions and commitment: The evolution of institutions governing public choice in 17th century England." Journal of Economic History, 49: 803–832.

Polanyi, Michael
1962 Personal Knowledge: Towards a Post-Critical Philosophy. New York: Harper & Row.

Riordan, Michael, and Oliver Williamson
1985 "Asset specificity and economic organization." International Journal of Industrial Organization, 3: 365–378.

Scott, W. Richard
1987 Organizations, 2d ed. Englewood Cliffs, NJ: Prentice-Hall.

Shelanski, Howard
1990 "A survey of empirical research in transaction cost economics." Unpublished manuscript, University of California, Berkeley.

Simon, Herbert
1951 "A formal theory of the employment relation." Econometrica, 19: 293–305.
1978 "Rationality as process and as product of thought." American Economic Review, 68: 1–16.

Teece, David J.
1986 "Profiting from technological innovation." Research Policy, 15 (December): 285–305.

Topkis, Donald
1978 "Maximizing a submodular function on a lattice." Operations Research, 26: 305–321.

Ward, B. N.
1967 The Socialist Economy: A Study of Organizational Alternatives. New York: Random House.

Williamson, Oliver E.
1975 Markets and Hierarchies. New York: Free Press.
1976 "Franchise bidding for natural monopoly—In general and with respect to CATV." Bell Journal of Economics, 7: 73–104.
1979 "Transaction-cost economics: The governance of contractual relations." Journal of Law and Economics, 22: 233–261.
1983 "Credible commitments: Using hostages to support exchange." American Economic Review, 73: 519–540.
1985 The Economic Institutions of Capitalism. New York: Free Press.
1988 "The logic of economic organization." Journal of Law, Economics, and Organization, 4: 65–93.
1989 "Transaction cost economics." In Richard Schmalensee and Robert Willig (eds.), Handbook of Industrial Organization, 1: 136–182. New York: North-Holland.
1990 "Chester Barnard and the incipient science of organization." In Oliver E. Williamson (ed.), Organization Theory: 172–207. New York: Oxford University Press.
1991a "Strategizing, economizing, and economic organization." Strategic Management Journal (in press).
1991b "Economic institutions: Spontaneous and intentional governance." Journal of Law, Economics, and Organization (in press).

[3]

THE CONTRACTUAL NATURE OF THE FIRM*

STEVEN N. S. CHEUNG
University of Hong Kong

ALMOST half a century has elapsed since R. H. Coase wrote "The Nature of the Firm."[1] The impact of this paper is now increasing.[2] At about twenty years of age and before receiving a bachelor's degree from the London School of Economics, Coase conceived the thesis of that work during a traveling scholarship to the United States in 1931–32.[3] Consider-

* For their helpful comments I am grateful to Armen A. Alchian, Yoram Barzel, Keith Leffler, John S. McGee, and Dean Worcester.

[1] Ronald H. Coase, The Nature of the Firm, 4 Economica 386 (1937). The paper, however, was written several years earlier (see note 3 *infra*).

[2] The *Social Sciences Citation Index* provides the following information. Breaking down the period of 1966–80 into three five-year periods, the total citations of Coase's "firm" paper for each subperiod are: 1966–70, 17 citations; 1971–75, 47 citations; and 1976–80, 105 citations.

[3] In personal correspondence Coase wrote me his recollections as follows:

> About the firm. I spent the year 1931–1932 in the United States where I studied the problem of vertical and lateral integration in American industry. From pondering on these problems came my views on the nature of the firm. The basic idea in the article on the Nature of the Firm was certainly worked out by October, 1932 as a letter which I then wrote (and which has been preserved) shows. Also I completed a draft of the article by the Spring of 1934 while still in Dundee. As to why I waited until 1937 to publish, the reasons are various. I did not feel under any great pressure to publish it. I did in fact publish some other pieces before the firm article but the ideas in these papers were in fact developed after those on the firm. Remember that I was a young lecturer having to learn a lot in order to teach courses on subjects on which I knew very little and this took up a good deal of time. And I was interested in many other aspects of economics. I have never been one to rush into print—indeed I find it difficult to express exactly what I have in mind and have never thought that the world would suffer much if it didn't have the opportunity to read my views. I did in fact make some changes in the period between 1934 and 1937 but there was no change in my main position. But I did not feel any need to publish before I had expressed my thoughts as well as I could. Some of the projects on which I worked in the 1930s have still not been completed although I hope one day to do so.
>
> About dates. As I completed the first year of University work while still at high school (not unusual at that time), I completed my University work and passed the degree examinations in 1931 (after 2 years at LSE). I was awarded a travelling scholarship by the University of London in 1931 and spent the next year in the United States. At that time, 3 years residence was required for the award of a degree but the regulations were loosely interpreted so as to allow my year in the United States to be counted as a year of residence

[*Journal of Law & Economics*, vol. XXVI (April 1983)]
 0022-2186/83/2601-0007$01.50

ing the work started out as the equivalent of an undergraduate term paper one stands in awe of the insights that prompted it.

The issues surrounding what has been called "the firm" and the scope of economic behavior encompassed by Coase's thesis are far from resolved. At present, different versions abound of what Coase meant, along with varied criticisms.[4] I do not propose to evaluate this growing body of literature or to argue that my interpretation is necessarily an accurate presentation of Coase's position. Rather, once inspired by Coase's early work to do research on contracts, I wish to return and expound on that work in light of my own findings.

Anyone who investigates the economics of contractual arrangements will recognize that Coase's "firm" paper relates to the choice of contracts.[5] Yet Coase, aware of the significance and relevance of the measurement problem, suggested in 1969 that I look into the various measurements adopted in the timber industry. However, the difficulty of obtaining data blocked that attempt. By 1974 I had reached the view that piece-rate contracts offer a useful gateway to an understanding of the firm as an organization, because payment by the piece falls squarely in between the

---

at LSE. This explains why I was awarded my degree in 1932 although I had passed the examination in 1931. When I worked out my views on the nature of the firm, I was 20 or 21. A letter written in October 1932 (and the independent recollections of Duncan Black) indicate I had them by October 1932 and presumably I developed them earlier—between October 1931 and the summer of 1932. My date of birth is December 29th, 1910.

[4] For some examples which seem most directly related to Coase's work, see H. B. Malmgren, Information, Expectations and the Theory of the Firm, 75 Q. J. Econ. 399 (1961); G. B. Richardson, The Organization of Industry, 82 Econ. J. 883 (1972); Armen A. Alchian & Harold Demsetz, Production, Information Costs, and Economic Organization, 62 Am. Econ. Rev. 777 (1972); Paul H. Rubin, The Expansion of Firms, 81 J. Pol. Econ. 936 (1973); A. Michael Spence, The Economics of Internal Organization: An Introduction, 6 Bell. J. Econ. 163 (1975); John C. McManus, The Costs of Alternative Economic Organizations, 8 Can. J. Econ. 334 (1975); Oliver E. Williamson, Markets and Hierarchies (1975); Lloyd R. Cohen, The Firm: A Revised Definition, 46 S. Econ. J. 580 (1979); and Yoram Barzel, Measurement Costs and the Organization of Markets, 25 J. Law & Econ. 27 (1982). Each of these works has a different interpretation of Coase, and they all disagree with Coase in different ways. This lack of consensus leaves room for further interpretation, although in the area of transaction costs the lack of a standardized terminology makes it difficult to tell where the disagreements lie.

[5] See Steven N. S. Cheung, Transaction Costs, Risk Aversion, and the Choice of Contractual Arrangements, 12 J. Law & Econ. 23 (1969). With great reluctance I brought in risk sharing to explain the choice of share contracts in agriculture: several attempts made in 1968 to discard "risk" had not succeeded. Certain types of risk, such as the uncertainty of whether a promise will be honored or whether a product will live up to its advertisement, can be viewed as transaction costs. In such a case my preference is always for treating the problem in that light because testable implications are easier to derive. In agriculture, however, risk resulting from nature poses a different problem.

market and what Coase called the firm. My investigation of the piece-rate contract began in 1975 and continues.[6]

What I propose to do here, therefore, is to try to interpret Coase's arguments in light of my findings about contracts in general and about the piece-rate contract in particular. I shall then argue that we do not exactly know what the firm is—nor is it vital to know. The word "firm" is simply a shorthand description of a way to organize activities under contractual arrangements that differ from those of ordinary product markets.

I. The Firm as a Form of Contractual Arrangement

Coase's central thesis is that differences in the costs of operating institutions (transaction costs) lead to the emergence of a firm to supersede a market. On the one hand, market transactions involve products or commodities; on the other, "firm transactions" involve factors of production. The growth of a firm may then be viewed as the replacement of a product market by a factor market, resulting in a saving in transaction costs. This thesis is not easy to understand because Coase does not define "the firm"; nor, as we shall see, is there a clear distinction between a product market and a factor market.

Private ownership of productive inputs is assumed. Each input owner therefore has the option of (1) producing and marketing goods himself, (2) selling his input outright, or (3) entering into a contractual arrangement surrendering the use of his input to an agent in exchange for an income. The firm emerges with the third option: the entrepreneur or the agent who holds a limited set of use rights by contract directs production activities without immediate reference to the price of each activity, and the commodities so produced are then sold in the market. Herein lies the puzzle. If private property rights are absent and hence the above options are not available, it is relatively easy to understand why the activities of a worker or an input are directed by an agent instead of by market prices. But why should a private property owner *voluntarily* surrender his rights and be told what to do by a visible hand?

This choice, according to Coase, is made to reduce transaction costs.

[6] Joseph E. Stiglitz analyzes the piece-rate versus the wage contract in terms of risk and information, while explicitly stating that he ignores the costs of supervision. It appears to me that his "incentive and risk" problems can be treated as problems of transaction costs. In any event, the Stiglitz approach is quite different from that in the present paper. See Joseph E. Stiglitz, Incentives, Risk, and Information: Notes towards a Theory of Hierarchy, 6 Bell J. Econ. 552 (1975). Another interesting paper on the piece-rate contract, again based on a different orientation from mine, is found in Edward P. Lazear & Sherwin Rosen, Rank-Order Tournaments as Optimum Labor Contracts, 89 J. Pol. Econ. 841 (1981).

Some have suggested that such an argument is tautological. But it is not, because other reasons are also advanced for the emergence of the firm, including division of labor, risk, and the coordination of production activities. Coase considered these factors and rejected them all. To him, transaction costs constitute the prime consideration. His argument is subject to refutation because the list of other plausible factors makes it possible to conceive that total transaction costs might rise as the firm emerges.

Even if transaction costs constitute the only relevant factor, or if all other factors are forcibly interpreted as belonging in the domain of transaction costs, Coase's argument is still not tautological if one can identify different types of transaction costs and how they will vary under different circumstances. Generality in the extreme renders an argument tautological, whereas a total lack of general applicability renders an argument ad hoc. Testable implications are to be found somewhere in between, and how the costs are to be specified is a matter of choice, depending on the problem at hand.

An emphasis on transaction costs does not negate the potential gain from specialization through the division of labor or from more efficient coordination of productive efforts. Consider, for example, the classic "pin factory" in which each of the multiple input owners specializes by working on only one part. If all costs of transaction were zero, a customer buying a pin would make a separate payment to each of the many contributing to its production. Comparative advantage guides each to specialize in his own skill, and if it appears desirable to hire a coordinator of activities, the buyer of the pin will simply make an additional payment to him. In such a case, a large number of product prices would direct the production of the single pin.

In such a world it would be redundant to speak of a product market and a factor market. The two would be inseparable: the buyer would be paying simultaneously for the product and for the contribution of the input owner. To separate a product from a factor market requires that an agent pay input owners while receiving from customers payment for the products he hands out. Whereas the standard approach assumes the number of products as given, Coase's view is that this number is determinate only if transaction costs are explicitly incorporated into the analysis.

The problem can be stated more fundamentally. Any productive input is a *private* property if, within well-defined limits, its owner has (1) the right to exclude others so that he alone may decide on its use, (2) the right to extract exclusive income from its use, and (3) the right to transfer the property (including labor) to or to exchange with anyone he sees fit. The right to exchange implies the right to contract, and property rights may be transacted through a wide variety of contractual arrangements. When these rights are exchanged it is, of course, for the purpose of yielding higher income to the owner, and the choice of contracts will be constrained by the costs of transaction.

Our main concern here is not the transaction itself but the contractual arrangements through which the right to use the input is delegated to another party and commodities produced by this use are sold to consumers. No outright transfer is made, and when the input owner retains some other rights the contract becomes a structured document.[7] A delimited set of use rights is surrendered in exchange for an income, under a form of contract that binds the input owner to follow directions instead of determining his own course by continual reference to the market prices of a variety of activities he may perform.

The surrender of use rights is a matter of degree, and the delimitation of the rights delegated is the subject of contracting, often supplemented by an implicit understanding, by custom, and by common law. It goes without saying that a clerk will not be asked to do work normally reserved for a janitor. The payment tendered is often based on a measured property (for example, hours per day) that bears no resemblance to the measured properties of the final commodities priced for sale. For this reason, observed market prices cannot directly guide the owner of the input to perform in the same manner as if every activity he performs were measured and priced. Hence the surrender of use rights often implies the delegation of the right to decide what to do.

With private property rights, economic analysis asserts as an axiom that when an input owner enters into a contract of the type described (joining the firm) he expects a gain relative to his other options, for he has had the option of not joining. What must be explained is why that increase occurs. Could it be that letting someone else make the decision is often more productive? The answer is no. We have noted that delegating the right to make a decision is the result of the difference in pricing and measuring properties. It cannot in general be the case that management decisions are superior to consumer decisions reached through the price mechanism. Errors are bound to be less frequent when price information guides every activity performed.

Could it be that specialization, coordination, and economy of scale achieved by pooling input resources from many owners will yield higher incomes for all, so that each chooses to join the firm? Again the answer is no. As noted earlier, if every activity is measured and priced, then benefits arising from specialization and coordination can be realized with-

[7] See Steven N. S. Cheung, The Structure of a Contract and the Theory of a Non-Exclusive Resource, 13 J. Law & Econ. 49 (1970).

out the "factor market"—the right to decide and use one's input need not be delegated to some agent or entrepreneur, because in a product market the input owner will receive a payment for every contribution.

Could the firm emerge because people shirk, cheat, or are opportunistic—as some recent theses imply?[8] Maybe. But the problem is that this sort of behavior is ubiquitous and will vary only in degree and in kind depending on the form of contract chosen or on how the property transacted is measured and priced. The behavior of a factory worker whose shirking requires the service of a monitor results from the worker's delegation of the right to use his labor. He would not shirk, or at least he would shirk differently, if for every small contribution he were paid a price.

Coase's answer is bold: "The main reason why it is profitable to establish a firm would seem to be that there is a cost of using the price mechanism. The most obvious cost of 'organising' production through the price mechanism is that of *discovering what the relevant prices are*" (emphasis added).[9] He offers several reasons why the discovery and negotiation of prices are costly, although his explanation seems incomplete. I propose to offer here four general reasons, at least two of them derivatives of Coase's reasoning.

Perhaps the most obvious reason why the cost of discovering prices is higher in the absence of a firm is that significantly more transactions are required, each calling for a separate price. If the consumer were to pay for each contribution to or each component of the commodity, instead of for a single finished product, the cost would often be prohibitive. As an alternative, all cooperating input owners might contract with one another, each agreeing on a price for his services, and all the prices then might be aggregated for the final product. As a substitute for these contracts a central agent might contract with each input owner, paying him a price for the use rights rendered and selling the final product at another price. On this form of contract reduction Coase wrote: "A factor of production (or the owner thereof) does not have to make a series of contracts with the factors with whom he is co-operating within the firm, as would be necessary, of course, if this co-operation were as a direct result of the working of the price mechanism. For this series of contracts is substituted one."[10]

A second factor apparently not considered by Coase is the information

[8] See, in particular, Williamson, *supra* note 4; and Benjamin Klein, Robert G. Crawford, & Armen A. Alchian, Vertical Integration, Appropriable Rents, and the Competitive Contracting Process, 21 J. Law & Econ. 297 (1978).

[9] Coase, *supra* note 1, at 390.

[10] Coase, *supra* note 1, at 391.

cost of knowing a product. When parts or components of a product considered separately have no easily recognizable usage, agreement on price between producer and consumer of each and every part tends to be more costly than the whole product. Reaching agreement on the price of a spring inside a camera incurs a proportionately higher cost than does the camera. Although the consumer has the final say in assessing the worth of the whole product, he cannot be expected to recognize the value of each component part—he may not even know what some of them are or even that they exist. It simply costs too much to learn about everything in every commodity we buy. As we shall see, in piece-rate contracts the parts or components of a commodity are often directly measured and priced, but these negotiations are between specialist agents and input owners. That is, for a component which by itself has no readily identifiable value, agreement on price is less costly between specialists and input owners than it would be between input owners and consumers or between specialists and consumers. The one who produces component parts tends to know more about them than the one who consumes.

A third cost of discovering price is that of measurement. In every transaction, some characteristics or attributes must be measured, whether the deal is between an agent and a customer, an agent and an input owner, or an input owner and a customer. If the activities performed by an input owner change frequently, if these activities vary greatly, or if some of the activities to be performed cannot be conveniently stipulated in advance, it tends to be more economical to forgo any direct measurement of these activities and substitute another measurement to serve as a proxy. Thus an agent may hire a worker by the hour or lease a building by the square foot without going through the process of metering every contribution the input performs. The varied input activities which, in fact, are the source of product value are not priced at all because measurement would be too costly. The input owner receives payment for his varied contributions by measuring an attribute totally different from those of his actual contributions or of the final product sold to customers. The agent deals with two different sets of measurements, absorbing any gain or loss by directing and monitoring the performance of input owners and providing to consumers total commodities with specified characteristics.

Coase seemed to have in mind the use of a "proxy" measurement to avoid the cost of measuring greatly varied activities when he wrote the following:

It may well be a matter of indifference to the person supplying the service or commodity which of several courses of action is taken, but not to the purchaser of that service or commodity. But the purchaser will not know which of these several courses he will want the supplier to take. Therefore, the service which is being provided is expressed in general terms, the exact details being left until a later date. All that is stated in the contract is the limits to what the person supplying the commodity or service is expected to do. The details of what the supplier is expected to do is not stated in the contract but is decided later by the purchaser. When the direction of resources (within the limits of the contract) becomes dependent on the buyer in this way, that relationship which I term a "firm" may be obtained. . . . It is obviously of more importance in the case of services—labour—than it is in the case of . . . commodities. In the case of commodities, the main items can be stated in advance and the details which will be decided later will be of minor significance.[11]

Finally, the problem of separating contributions generates cost in reaching price agreement. When input owners work in collaboration, in some situations the contribution of each may not be easily delineated and each may claim more than he deserves. It is true that competition among input owners will reduce excessive claims, but the problem will not be eliminated. An agent hiring the collaborating participants may therefore exercise a right similar to that of eminent domain, offering a price for each on a take-it-or-leave-it basis by again measuring a proxy instead of the contribution itself.[12]

As examples of the gain from collaboration and the difficulty of delineating contributions, Alchian and Demsetz[13] cite the examples of loading and of fishing. My own favorite example is riverboat pulling in China before the communist regime, when a large group of workers marched along the shore towing a good-sized wooden boat. The unique interest of this example is that the collaborators actually agreed to the hiring of a monitor to whip them. The point here is that even if every puller were perfectly "honest," it would still be too costly to measure the effort each has contributed to the movement of the boat, but to choose a different measurement agreeable to all would be so difficult that the arbitration of an agent is essential.

With regard to this example, Alchian and Demsetz argue that the moni-

[11] Coase, *supra* note 1, at 391–92. Coase argues that the diverse activities described in this quotation lead to the use of a long-term contract—which I do not consider important to his thesis. The training of workers or the remodeling of a rented building, like improvements made on agricultural land by a tenant, appears to be a more incisive reason for the choice of a long-term contract because of the difficulty of recapturing the investments committed. See Cheung, *supra* note 5; and Klein, Crawford, & Alchian, *supra* note 8. The latter paper employs the concept of quasi rent to interpret the choice of a long-term contract.

[12] In a 1968 discussion, Coase expressed doubt that the power of eminent domain would be necessary to reduce transaction costs. Yet in my later study of the problem of evicting tenants for housing reconstruction under rent control the evidence is incontrovertible that in certain circumstances the power of eminent domain reduces transaction costs. See Steven N. S. Cheung, Rent Control and Housing Reconstruction: The Postwar Experience of Prewar Premises in Hong Kong, 22 J. Law & Econ. 27 (1979), particularly at 50–52.

[13] Alchian & Demsetz, *supra* note 4.

tor (that is, the "firm") enters the picture because of the shirking.[14] My argument goes further back, asserting that the behavior has itself originated because a proxy instead of effort was chosen for measurement; the concept of shirking is, therefore, an indirect way of expressing that there is a cost in discovering prices for relative contributions. Within what Coase calls a firm, then, shirking takes place in a way that differs from dishonesty in the market.

Let me summarize the arguments of this lengthy section. In principle, all contributions of input owners as well as the services of the coordinator can be separately priced and sold to customers by measuring directly various attributes related to each contribution.[15] In this case product and factor markets coincide. But the determination of prices is costly because of the number of transactions, because consumers lack detailed information on the use of each component or contribution to a commodity, because of the difficulty of measuring varied and changing activities, and because of the need to separate contributions.

One effective way to reduce the costs of discovering prices is to substitute some device other than the direct and separate pricing of activities. This substitution may be as simple as the use of the piece-rate contract or as complex as the establishment of a communist regime.[16] Coase's main concern is substitution that entails the delegation of use rights from *private* input owners, to the extent that the contribution or activity of each is not directly priced. This implies measurement by a proxy. An "entrepreneur" therefore emerges.

Specialization and coordination are relevant here to the extent that they typically involve multiple input owners and tend to compound the costs of discovering prices. Had there been no cost of measuring and pricing performance there would be no firm, and the value of the social outputs would be maximal. But these costs do exist, and product market transactions decline as they are being partly superseded by factor-market contracts. The agency costs of a monitor, a director, or a manager—which

[14] Following Knight, Alchian & Demsetz (*supra* note 4) also define a firm to have a residual claimant. Coase notes, however, that under share contracts no residual claimant exists (*supra* note 1, at 392).

[15] While in the total absence of transaction costs the services of a monitor or an agent would not be necessary, those of a coordinator might still be wanted. That is, the services of a conductor in a symphony orchestra or of a coach in a team sport have little to do with transaction costs. In practice, of course, one who coordinates may also perform some functions of an agent.

[16] The communist regime is a "superfirm" within which citizens lack the option of not joining. I have argued elsewhere that this lack necessarily implies higher transaction costs in the operation of the economy. See Steven N. S. Cheung, Will China Go "Capitalist"? (1982).

are also transaction costs—rise as the costs of discovering prices fall.[17] And the supersession will go no further when at the margin the saving in one type of cost equals the rise in the other.

Textbooks typically depict the product market as consisting of outright sales of goods and services at prices determined by supply and demand. No reference is made to any contractual arrangement under which the producer (supplier) may be paid by measuring a proxy rather than the product. The factor market then crops up in another chapter, typically under the theory of marginal productivity. Each input owner receives remuneration equaling the value of his marginal product, and no mention is made of any delegation of rights to an agent. Indeed, how an input owner gets paid and by whom seem irrelevant.

It is *not* quite correct to say that a "firm" supersedes "the market." Rather, one type of contract supersedes another type. Coase's main concern is a type of contract under which an input owner surrenders a delimited set of rights to use his input in exchange for income. He is therefore directed by a visible hand, not by the invisible hand of a price mechanism. It takes remarkable insight to see that as this type of contract increases there will be fewer product markets.

II. The Piece-Rate Contract as an Illustration

One appealing aspect of the piece-rate arrangement is that no other labor contract so clearly reveals productivity differentials among workers. This provides useful observations for testing a number of implications of the marginal productivity theory. Our present interest is in another important aspect: piece-rate workers in a factory (a "firm") are paid on the basis of direct count of their production contributions (a "market"). Hence, to identify a "firm," which we shall later argue is a futile task, one would have difficulty coping with the piece-rate arrangement. But precisely because this arrangement does have a dual nature, tracing the transition from the simplest form of a piece-rate contract to a wage contract will usefully illustrate our earlier interpretation of the organization of production. What is or is not a firm is immaterial: what counts are the various ways of organizing economic activities under different transaction costs.

Since my investigation on the piece-rate contract was conducted in Hong Kong, all factual examples provided here will be taken from that

[17] The term "agency costs" is taken from Michael C. Jensen & William H. Meckling, Theory of the Firm: Managerial Behavior, Agency Costs and Ownership Structure, 3 J. Financial Econ. 305 (1976). In Coase's early work, an agent is regarded as the same as an entrepreneur.

city. This choice was made to avoid complications attendant on labor unions and minimum wage laws.[18]

Let us begin with the case of a middleman in Hong Kong who buys shirts from manufacturers by piece count and sells them to an importer in the United States. He shops around, gathers samples, makes offers, and quotes prices to his clients. Seldom will he tell a manufacturer what to produce, and never will he tell the factory workers what to do. He makes his living by specialization: he makes contacts, learns the preferences of a particular market, and has a good knowledge of prices. In short, he does not direct resource use; he merely transmits price signals. Few would claim that the middleman uses a piece-rate contract even though, in fact, he pays for the shirts by the piece.

The transmission of price signals through specialization in contacts and price information may involve several steps. Consider the laying of hardwood floors. A landlord who wants to build a high-rise finds a building contractor. This contractor subcontracts with a hardwood floor contractor on an agreed price per square foot—a piece count. The subcontractor, who imports the wood materials and adds finishing work to the wood on a piece-rate basis, in turn finds a sub-subcontractor, provides him wood, and offers him a price per square foot laid. Finally, the sub-subcontractor hires workers and again pays them per square foot laid.

At each stage of contracting a price signal is transmitted, at a cost, and each successive contractor holds different contacts and information. Of course, a middleman or a contractor may conceal price information to his own advantage, but a price signal is nonetheless transmitted because his decision to buy or to subcontract is based on his own price information. Furthermore, competition in contracting will curb the success of his effort to conceal price.

Other than the number of steps involved, it is difficult to see any difference between the hardwood floor example and the earlier example of the shirt exporter. But while few would say the middleman buys shirts on a piece-rate contract, everyone somehow agrees that the hardwood floor is produced under piece rate. The key distinction seems to be that the middleman does not make payments directly to the workers who make shirts,

[18] For example, whereas under piece rate an unusually slow worker may receive an income below minimum wage, the establishment of a minimum piece rate would be nearly impossible because of the great variety of such work. It is said that when the United Auto Workers was formed some forty-five years ago, the abolition of the piece-rate arrangement was regarded as one of the union's major accomplishments. One popular argument against the piece rate is that the rate for a hard worker will be revised downward by the management. This is flatly contradicted by my Hong Kong findings which, as will be elaborated elsewhere, show that a hard worker often receives bonuses when some specified level of output is attained.

whereas the sub-subcontractor pays his workers directly. Yet a resident homeowner who wants his floor replaced may also pay per square foot to a worker directly, as some do, although most choose to order through a contractor. It is not all that easy to separate a factor market from the product market.

The hardwood floor example clearly illustrates the advantage of the piece-rate contract. Square footage is a straightforward measure which leaves little room for argument. In fact, the hardwood floor in Hong Kong is typically set in squares of one square foot each, and both the workers and the contractors are so expert at estimating partial squares that they often agree on the dimensions without using a tape. The quality of a finished floor is also easily judged by the specialist subcontractor in a few minutes of inspection.

Another piecework advantage in this case is that, because of Hong Kong's humid climate, hardwood floor of a particular type is routinely used in all the highrises. The market price of the flooring per square foot is well known, and the price between contractor and worker is easily negotiated because the workmen know their alternatives. Since the worker is seldom given job direction other than time and place, he is delegating little of his use rights. A price is paid for his service per square foot laid.

For this industry, payment by the hour—a wage contract—would not be practical to negotiate and enforce. Different workers have such varied speeds that a uniform wage will guarantee quarrels. On the other hand, the cost of assessing different abilities is sufficient to assure that varying wage rates would have to be determined somewhat arbitrarily and would require considerably more background information about the workers. Moreover, only a long-term relationship between contractor and workman can assure, under a wage contract, that the work will be done diligently. When many among the labor force work on call from job to job such a contract invites lethargy. To monitor the work is costly; yet a general slowdown can add up to a great deal of unproductive time.

The stringing of beads for belts and headbands is another task routinely done on a piece-rate basis. Little equipment is required, and the workers do the task at home. Each piece is usually a complete commodity, and payments are based on piece count and quality inspection. Outstanding pieces are awarded small premiums; they are used as samples or are placed on top of others in packaging. Typically, about the only direction given to the worker over what would be provided by the consumer in the market is a color pattern for the beads. In transmitting the price, the contractor also transmits an estimated consumer preference as to color and pattern. The worker is told what to do about color because the piece rate he receives contains one less signal than would the price if paid directly by the consumer.

It is always the case that the less explicitly the transmitted price indicates consumer preferences or product specifications, the more direction will the worker receive from a "visible hand." Directions may be given by an agent or by a consumer; in either case, the giving of directions means that the input owner has to some extent relinquished his use rights. Direction under the piece-rate contract tends to be far less than under the wage contract because measurement by the piece is a more direct measure of the actual contribution than is measurement by hours of work.

In the garment and toy industries, as well as in a variety of industries involving light metallic and plastic products, piece-rate contracts are popular. In the vast majority of cases the piece-rate worker specializes at any one time in producing only one component of a product. Examples include the painting of a doll's eyes, the assembling of a toy, the polishing of one part of a flashlight, or the cutting of materials for a coat. Indeed, an entire shirt may be the product of a whole combination of piece-rate works. Among the requisite conditions are that each piece can be easily counted and that a standardized set of measures governs inspection (by random sampling, for low-rate works).

The pricing and measurements adopted for piece components differ from those of an assembled product. Nonetheless, under piece rate it is the contribution of the worker which is directly measured and priced. Pieceworkers may work either in a factory where space and tools are provided or at home using their own equipment—understandably in this case at a higher rate to compensate for the rental value of the equipment and space. In either event, the component worker is given specifications because (as the component is seldom sold separately in a final-product market) the piece rate offers little information about consumer preference. Those working at home are also assigned a deadline for delivery to integrate with the schedule for other components. Coordination of activities is improved when all workers perform under one roof, supplementing with work sent out to home craftsmen only at times of peak loads.

Pieceworkers in factories are often assigned specific machines to avoid careless use under random rotation, and fast workers are often assigned the better equipment. We may put this in the context of Coase's thesis: the home worker is paid a piece rate for the contribution of his labor plus his equipment, whereas the factory worker is paid only for his labor. The contribution of the factory equipment is priced in terms of implicit rental values. Thus the assignment of machines to specific workers and the occasional monitoring of the workers themselves may be viewed as "directions" given to the machines in lieu of a direct pricing of their contributions. Predictably, piece-rate works which require the use of heavy machinery tend to be produced in a factory. Such machinery is awkward in a home, dangerous to children, and requires prompt repair; it may also be so costly that few home workers would willingly invest without assurance of long-term use.

To equalize the marginal productivities of similar machines requires that their rental values be equal. Yet given the same piece rate the rental yield to a machine will be higher with a faster worker. Thus in addition to assigning a better machine to a faster worker, when costly machines are used a bonus over a standard piece rate is paid for quick work (that is, a lump-sum bonus if a worker exceeds a certain number of pieces a day). Thus one with double the output of another often receives more than double total pay. The home worker receives no bonus even though he is using a costly machine, because his piece rate reflects the total contribution of all inputs except the materials provided him.

The determination of the piece rate—a price—illustrates the cost of "discovering" prices. For a part or a component of a market product, there is often no market price to serve as a frame of reference. For many components, however, there are standard piece rates, long used in the industry, established by reference to the daily wage paid or to piece rates offered by competing factories for similar work. Minor modifications in the piecework may promptly lead, through rough estimation, to minor changes in the piece rate. But a greater problem concerns major changes, particularly in the plastic and light metallic industries, where models often change significantly between orders and where each factory tends to originate unique models. The management must decide, in such cases, whether the new component promises sufficient volume to justify the costs of negotiating a new piece rate.

Test runs are an unsuitable basis for determining such a rate, because workers beginning an unfamiliar task will take several days to pick up speed, and they tend to overstate the difficulty of the new job. The standard procedure therefore is to employ a motion specialist, sometimes recruited from outside, to negotiate with a representative of the workers. The basic reference is that an average worker moves his hands or feet approximately 8,500 times on a normal working day, the number varying with the extent of the required motion and with its duration. The number and types of motion required to complete the new component are first assessed, then a daily wage, or the average daily earning of a piece-rate worker in a comparable trade, is used as a frame of reference in setting the new rate of pay.

This negotiation process may be cumbersome because the worker representative must gain consent from the workers. Moreover, a rate so negotiated is seldom binding, and either side has the right to demand renegotiation after a few days of work. These negotiation costs—that is, the cost of discovering price—will of course be lower if the component to be produced, like a string of beads or a square foot of hardwood floor, commands a well-established price in the final product market which may be used as a reference. But, as noted in the preceding section, few customers would even recognize the function of some components.

That is why piece rates are not applicable when components or contributions either change often or entail a variety of activities by the same worker. The point is illustrated by the polishing of flashlights or gas lamps. Workers doing routine finishing with a motor and wax are paid a piece rate; but when defects are found, such as some minor scratches or burns from electroplating, workers correcting the flaws are paid a wage. Similarly, other employees receive wages: the janitor, the office clerk, the accountant, the model designer, and the chemist in the electroplating shop.

When components are assembled in a way that makes separation of workers' contributions costly, the piece-rate contract is also difficult to establish. In one sort of collaboration, a group of workers polishes flashlights and places them in separate baskets which, after counting and inspection, are moved to another group which inserts switches. Both activities are paid by the piece. But in another type of collaboration, when the flashlights are being electroplated or anodized, one worker monitors the tank of chemicals, another rotates the articles in the solution, and a third rinses them as they are handed to him on a hanger. The relative contribution of each worker is thus difficult to separate. Similar difficulty attends the planning of a new product: one member searches the market for ideas, a committee evaluates alternatives, and the export manager solicits feedback from potential buyers. Where each of these workers has incentive to claim more credit because his share is difficult to delineate, it becomes less costly to price by measuring a proxy under the arbitration of an agent.

A proxy such as an hour or a day is easily measured; it does not change as components or contributions do; it can be separately measured for each worker; and it can embrace a host of activities to be performed by each worker, some of them too trivial to be subject to contracting. These advantages result in lower costs of determining wage rates than would be possible if contributions were measured in the complicated situations just described. But a unit of time in itself contributes no productive value; it merely represents what a worker presumably can perform. More stringent monitoring and direction are thus required under a wage contract because the activity itself is not directly priced. From this we infer that in some cases the piece rate may be chosen even if the costs of determining that rate are higher than those for a wage rate.

A piece rate transmits a price signal, although we have shown that the information it provides may vary greatly and, as a result, specifications and directions vary in degree. While the inspection of output is more demanding for piece-rate work because the worker has an incentive to rush, the total costs of monitoring are necessarily lower than under a wage contract. This is because the piece-rate worker's pay is proportional to his contribution, which reduces the need to contract for the use of his input. On the other hand, pricing by measurement of a proxy necessitates greater control of the use rights before profitable contributions can be expected. This delegation of rights by the input owners is a delimited package within which the entrepreneur can pick and direct production activities without pricing contributions. Management is a cost; decision error is also a cost. These costs are higher in pricing a proxy; the benefit is a reduction in the costs of discovering prices.

In this section I have traced the transitions from the simple service of a middleman, through various piece-rate arrangements, to wage contracts. The measurements adopted range respectively from a whole product to a component to a proxy measure. The information of the price signal moves from a full valuation of the contribution to no direct signal at all.[19] Direction and monitoring by the agent correspondingly rise in complexity. Delegation of the right to use the input also increases until full control is granted in terms of some contractual limits. The supersession of market transactions ranges from a possible doubling of transactions under the middleman arrangement to the making of piece-rate payments on a collective scale to the clear emergence of factor-market transactions superseding product-market transactions.

Throughout these transitions I have, following Coase, emphasized the costs of discovering prices, including the costs of information, of measurement, and of negotiation. When these costs change, different contracts appear. I do *not* claim that price determination is the only transaction cost which matters in all choices of the forms of contracts or organizations. But with regard to the central point made by Coase, my own investigation supports his view: under private property rights, any movement toward the contractual delegation of use rights results mainly from the constraints of pricing costs.

III. The Ambiguity of Firm Size

Some ten years ago I posed to Coase the following question: If an apple orchard owner contracts with a beekeeper to pollinate his fruits, is the

[19] Strictly speaking, not all valuable characteristics in a product are directly measured and priced. Properties such as vitamin C in an orange or the use of salt in a restaurant are not measured in transaction, although their presence is known and implicit in the product prices. This and related implications should not detain us here.

result one firm or two firms? This question has no clear answer. The contract involved may be a hive-rental contract, a wage contract, a contract sharing the apple yield, or, in principle, some combination of these and still other arrangements. In each case the beekeeper receives a remuneration for his service, and the orders he expects from the orchard owner vary with the form of contract.

The taxing agent of a government may treat the beekeeper and the orchard owner as one or two firms, depending on tax laws and business registrations adopted in the relevant area. But what is the viewpoint of economics? Most economists would probably opt for only one firm if the beekeeper is hired on a wage contract but for two if the hives are rented. Does it make sense to say that the number of firms, hence firm size, depends on the chosen form of contract? If so, in what sense? Is it not true that different directions will be given by the orchard owner under different contracts? What about the case of the sharing arrangement? And what if, instead of renting beehives, the orchard operator rents out the orchard itself? The basic problem here is that examples can easily be found to counter almost any definition of a firm that one can offer.

Consider our earlier example of the hardwood floor. There are three stages of subcontracting between the building contractor and the workers. How many firms are there? One? Or four? Hong Kong laws hold that all parties are separately responsible for tax, and all but the worker hold business licenses. Yet economists may well argue that because they are all vertically integrated by contracts, with transfer pricing, only one firm exists.

Consider, further, the case of a big department store bearing only one name but consisting in fact of separate sellers, each leasing a space under one roof, paying a rent to one central agent, and governed by a set of rules on the line of products each can sell and his hours of operation. That would seem to represent a single firm. However, *exactly* the same arrangements are found in most shopping centers, except that the shops bear various names. Why should that matter in determining firm size? Of course, some names are worth more than others, as is evident in the case of franchises, but it is also true that a single corporation may establish a number of subsidiaries, each bearing a different name for a different business.

The truth is that according to one's view a "firm" may be as small as a contractual relationship between two input owners or, if the chain of contracts is allowed to spread, as big as the whole economy. We have noted that the delegation of use rights and the transmission of price information are matters of degree. Given, then, that every individual is an input owner, it is highly likely that each has some contractual relationship with others in addition to the goods he sells or buys in the product market. Seldom in a modern society would an individual operate single-handedly in production and in exchange of his output in the marketplace.

Thus it is futile to press the issue of what is or is not a firm. If each individual is a private input owner—of his own labor, if nothing else—then almost all individuals in society are bound by contracts when they compete and interact.[20] The important questions are why contracts take the forms observed and what are the economic implications of different contractual and pricing arrangements.

In the domain of price theory, the traditional concerns of economists have been income distribution and resource allocation. Contractual arrangements, and their effects on income distribution and resource allocation, have been slighted. This oversight would be irrelevant if all transactions were costless: in that case, various contractual arrangements would never have been devised. But transaction costs *are* positive and significant. Hence, real-world observations are often not satisfactorily explained by the traditional approach. In an indirect way, Coase's early paper on the firm made this same complaint.

In spite of his attempt to seek a definition of the firm, Coase was well aware of the difficulty of drawing a boundary. He stated in a footnote that "it is not possible to draw a hard fast line which determines whether there is a firm or not."[21] His concern was not so much with the firm as with production and exchange activities observed to have been organized in different ways. In particular, he concentrated on the observations of direction by price signal versus direction by an entrepreneur. We need not reiterate here the different types of contracts and their implications.

We have noted that equilibrium is reached when the saving of transaction (pricing) costs incurred in the product market is equaled at the margin by the rising agency costs (also transaction costs) within an emerging "factor market." This is identical to Coase's condition that "a firm will tend to expand until the costs of organising an extra transaction within the firm become equal to the costs of carrying out the same transaction by means of an exchange on the open market."[22] But the condition does not really determine firm size. Rather, it determines the extent of contract substitution.

We have stated that the costs of discovering and agreeing on prices in

[20] In the Chinese communist regime, not even labor is privately owned: workers have no rights either to choose their profession or to contract and negotiate their wages. See Cheung, *supra* note 16, at 33.

[21] Coase, *supra* note 1, at 392.

[22] Coase, *supra* note 1, at 395.

the product markets include those of information, measurement, and negotiation. In different dimensions and magnitudes these costs also exist in the factor markets. For factor markets Coase cites various agency costs, including those of organizing activities and of making errors. He also adds changes in the supply price of factors, the relevance of which I do not see. Coase equates "rising supply price" with "diminishing returns to management,"[23] which appear to have been popular subjects among British economists of that period. But this point seems redundant once we recognize that (1) pricing by measurement of a proxy incurs extra costs of management and increased chance of decision errors and (2) these costs rise as the price signals transmitted contain less information, thus requiring greater control of use rights delegated by input owners.

Perhaps the most interesting confirmation of the fruitfulness of the approach presented here is that we cannot say much about firm size because we do not know precisely what a firm is. Stated differently, under the Coase approach we *can* identify clearly what a firm is and hence its size if the following conditions are met. First, producers or agents sell directly to consumers in outright transactions. Second, agents or entrepreneurs hold only wage or rental contracts with input owners. And third, there is no contractual relationship between agents. Ignoring the producer who owns all his input resources outright, these conditions yield the polar cases of (1) consumers buying commodities from agents (the product market) and (2) each separate agent holding wage and rental contracts with input owners (the firm). With any contractual relationship between agents assumed away, firms become separately identifiable and are literally "islands of conscious power."[24] To say that one type of contract supersedes another will then be the same as saying that the firm supersedes the product market. Firm size becomes determinate at the moment contractual supersession is determinate.

But the world is more complex. The polar cases are complicated by middlemen and subcontractors; agents contract among themselves; and any type of input may support a variety of contractual arrangements. We surmise that these very complications, which render the "firm" ambiguous, have arisen from attempts to save transaction costs that were not avoidable in the polar cases.[25] As one example, we have shown that the

[23] Coase, *supra* note 1, at 396–97.

[24] Coase cites D. H. Robertson at 333: "[Firms are like] islands of conscious power in [the] ocean of unconscious co-operation like lumps of butter coagulating in a pail of buttermilk."

[25] Governmental regulations may complicate the choice of contracts, but this we ignore here.

piece-rate contract lies somewhere in between, with a lower pricing cost than if the components were sold directly in the market and a lower agency cost than wage or rental contracts. The total of transaction costs is reduced by the piece-rate contract. The Coase thesis is therefore strengthened at the trivial sacrifice of acknowledging that we now know less about the definition and size of the firm.

IV. Concluding Remarks

In Hong Kong in 1969, I sat on an empty wooden box by the roadside and let a boy shine my shoes at an agreed price of twenty cents. As soon as his work began another boy approached and, without saying a word, started to polish my other shoe. "How do I pay?" I asked. "Ten cents for each of us," one boy replied. Not knowing the pricing practice, I was surprised to find out that the two boys did not know each other at all. But it dawned on me that this must illustrate what Coase meant by the market: the splitting of one transaction into two could not have gone so smoothly had I worn a shoe on one foot and an uncommon boot on the other. This little episode led me to reread "The Nature of the Firm" with a different orientation, and the subsequent research on contracts, which forms the basis of my present interpretation, followed to satisfy my own curiosity.

Few would deny that Coase's work on social cost is his most important and his most famous.[26] But I hold the "firm" paper in special regard because its insights are the spring at the headwaters of his most important subsequent writings. The surging interest in the "firm" paper during the past decade is one measure of the change in view among economists about the importance of the real-world applicability of theory which Coase and others have helped to promote.

It is not long since external economies or diseconomies constituted a prime subject in the field of economic development, presented along with such dubious terms as "bottleneck," "take off," "vicious circle," and "balanced versus unbalanced growth." These seem archaic concepts now. Only twenty years ago the word "contract" was confined to the "contract curve" in the Edgeworth-Bowley box; now it has become a household word in the discipline. Property rights were an untouchable area for doctoral theses; now centers have emerged and the subject is taught even at the undergraduate level. The transaction-cost paradigm is here to stay.

[26] Coase, The Problem of Social Cost, 3 J. Law & Econ. 1 (1960). This may well be the most cited economic paper of our time: 1966–70, 88 citations; 1971–75, 286 citations; and 1976–80, 331 citations.

Coase was not alone in promoting this paradigm. Knight and Hayek, among others, shared an early interest in Coase's subject matter. But came the Keynesian revolution, and whatever observations economists did not understand found refuge in various "imperfections." It was a different era when, in 1960, Coase published his paper on social cost. In the same period Stigler wrote on information and Arrow on the appropriability of returns.[27] Students once frustrated by the inept explanatory power of price theory were now told of something other than imperfections. At roughly the same time, Aaron Director's interest in tie-in sales was spreading, and Armen Alchian was persistently interpreting price and competition in terms of property rights. Students at UCLA were buying duplicate copies of Friedman's price theory lectures in the gray market, sweating over the questions provided at the end in fear that some of them might be used in an upcoming preliminary examination. That Friedman's lectures had little to do with his questions on mergers and various forms of pricing behavior foretold what was to come.

Coase was fortunate in that his important work on social cost (and transaction costs) took shape just as a tide was turning. The call for policy recommendation, which had dominated economic thinking, was subsiding as a desire for economic explanation began to swell. The turning tide surged far more strongly because of what Coase had to say. My view is that transaction costs and contracting will someday be regarded as a basis for analysis rivaling marginalism in neoclassical economics.

[27] George J. Stigler, The Economics of Information, 69 J. Pol. Econ. 213 (June 1961); and Kenneth J. Arrow, Economic Welfare and the Allocation of Resources for Invention, in The Rate and Direction of Inventive Activity 609–25 (1962).

[4]

The Firm as a Subeconomy

Bengt Holmstrom
Massachusetts Institute of Technology

This article explores the economic role of the firm in a market economy. The analysis begins with a discussion and critique of the property rights approach to the theory of the firm as exposited in the recent work by Hart and Moore ("Property Rights and the Nature of the Firm"). It is argued that the Hart–Moore model, taken literally, can only explain why individuals own assets, but not why firms own assets. In particular, the logic of the model suggests that each asset should be free standing in order to provide maximal flexibility for the design of individual incentives. These implications run counter to fact. One of the key features of the modern firm is that it owns essentially all the productive assets that it employs. Employees rarely own any assets; they only contribute human capital. Why is the ownership of assets clustered in firms? This article outlines an answer based on the notion that control over physical assets gives control over contracting rights to those assets. Metaphorically, the firm is viewed as a miniature economy, an "island" economy, in which asset ownership conveys the CEO the power to define the "rules of the game," that is, the ability to restructure the incentives of those that accept to do business on (or with) the island. The desire to regulate trade in this fashion stems from contractual externalities characteristic of imperfect information environments. The inability to regulate all trade through a single firm stems from the value of exit rights as an incentive instrument and a tool to discipline the abuse of power.

First version presented at the conference, "The Theory of the Firm and Economic Transition," Beijing, China, September 1–2, 1996. This version presented at the conference, "Bureaucracy: Issues and Apparatus," Marconi Center, Marshal, California, April 4–5, 1998. Portions of this article stem from my third Yrjö Jahnsson Lecture, delivered in November 1992. The research was partially funded by the National Science Foundation. I want to thank Oliver Hart, David Kreps, Paul Milgrom, John Roberts, Jean Tirole, and Oliver Williamson for many fruitful conversations on this topic and Abhijit Banerjee, Tore Ellington, Guido Friebel, Robert Gibbons, Benjamin Hermalin, Peter Högfeldt, Jon Levin, Lars Stole, Michael Waldman, and Robin Wells for comments on earlier drafts.

1. Introduction

Coase's (1937) key insight was to observe that in organizing transactions, there is a choice between placing a transaction in a market and locating it inside a firm, and that therefore this choice must have a bearing on understanding both forms of trade. It took a long time for Coase's insight to sink in, but today, thanks to the efforts of Arrow, Alchian, Demsetz, Williamson, and many others, institutional theory has again found a major place in economic theorizing. Initially theorists focused on problems of contracting under asymmetric information, developing new methods to deal with the strategic use of information and the attendant incentive problems. Equipped with insights from basic contract theory, theorists have again returned to the classic question raised by Coase: What determines the boundaries of the firm? The economic significance of this question is easy to appreciate today as mergers and acquisition activity has reached unprecedented levels in this past decade.[1]

The new theories remain scattered and it would take a long article to survey all approaches and strands. That is not my intent. Rather my objective is to suggest a partial synthesis of the theory of the firm, integrating aspects of internal organization with the leading modeling approach to boundaries, the modern property rights theory. In the envisioned synthesis, measurement costs of the kind originally stressed by Alchian and Demsetz will return to center stage. For this reason, I will start out reviewing Alchian and Demsetz's (1972) vision of the firm as a monitor of inputs. Their model will also serve as an important backdrop for interpreting the influential work of Grossman, Hart, and Moore on incomplete contracting and asset ownership. Incomplete contract models stress the importance of asset ownership as an instrument for influencing individual incentives. Ownership both creates and resolves holdup problems, altering the returns to investment in human capital. The most advanced exposition of this line of analysis is found in Hart and Moore (1990). I provide a sketch of the Hart–Moore model in Section 3, followed by a critique. I argue that this model, despite its express objective to explain the boundaries of firms, fails to do so, at least if the model is interpreted literally. The model offers a theory of individual ownership of assets, that is, how control over assets should be distributed among individuals, but it does not explain why firms own assets, let alone why firms tend to own or have control over all the alienable, nonhuman assets that they use to produce goods or in other ways serve customers. I take the ownership of assets by firms, and the attendant feature that economic contracts are made with firms, not with their employees or owners, as one of the most significant and robust empirical regularities to be explained by any theory of the firm.[2]

Having said this let me confess at the start that I am unable myself to offer a well-developed explanation of asset ownership by firms. But I have a conjecture that is inspired by the Hart–Moore article. The conjecture is that the firm gains

1. Transactions worth over $900 billion occurred in 1997 in the United States.

2. The "nexus of contracts" view, discussed in Alchian and Demsetz (1972), suggests as an explanation the costs of writing bilateral contracts between parties in a network of relationships, but I have not found a coherent explanation of why these costs are any less within firms.

power over human capital through ownership and control of assets. Ownership confers contracting rights that allow the firm to decide who should be offered the opportunity to work with particular assets and on what terms.[3] The firm uses its rights to set "internal rules of the game" and to design incentives in a manner that internalizes some of the contractual externalities that are present in markets due to asymmetric information. The hold-up problem is just one example of a contractual externality. There are several others, as I will illustrate.

In effect, I see the firm as a subeconomy in which the executive office has the power to regulate trade by assigning tasks, delegating authority, and delineating principles for how explicit and implicit incentives are to be structured. There is an obvious analogy between my vision of the firm as a regulator of trade and the role that a government plays in determining tax and other rules for an economy. It is interesting to ask which tasks should be left for the government given that firms can internalize a lot of externalities within their local trading environments. I will not pursue that question here, except to note that the principles of second-best, which commonly have been used in the context of public finance, seem to have much greater applicability and relevance in the context of the theory of the firm. Of importance, the second-best logic can explain why firms make extensive use of low-powered incentives and narrow job designs: to encourage employee cooperation in situations where incentives for cooperation would be compromised by excessively strong market incentives. In this view the much-lamented lack of individual initiative in bureaucratic firms should be seen as an essential element in providing incentives for cooperative activities. Section 4 illustrates this idea with a few simple examples, which are variations on my earlier work with Milgrom on multitask agency (Holmstrom and Milgrom, 1991, 1994; see also Laffont and Tirole, 1991).

Section 5 turns to the question of boundaries, applying the examples from Section 4 to the multifirm case. Section 6 compares the subeconomy view with the property rights view. The predictions are empirically distinguishable, because in the subeconomy view measurement costs play a central role in explaining contractual externalities and the need to internalize them. More importantly, though, the subeconomy view suggests that the boundary question is of interest, not so much in isolation as in the context of how firm boundaries condition what kinds of incentives can be structured on markets as well as within firms. The strength of the property rights view is that it articulates so clearly the role of market incentives and how they can be altered by shifts in asset ownership. But it says nothing about the incentives that can be created within firms. The real challenge is to understand how the two forms of organization complement each other as well as compete with each other as mechanisms for

3. Models of incomplete contracting have almost exclusively focused on the ex post bargainning rights and implied residual returns that come with ownership. My emphasis is on ex ante contracting rights. Tirole (1994) also stresses that ownership entails broader contracting rights than typically considered in the property rights theory. Rajan and Zingales (1998) emphasize the fact that the owner controls employee access to assets, human as well as physical. This is very similar to my approach, which is based on Holmstrom and Milgrom (1991, 1994).

influencing individual incentives. The main objective of this article is to point research in that direction.

2. Alchian and Demsetz Revisited

2.1 The Free-Rider Problem

The earliest theories by Coase (1937) and Simon (1951) suggested that the distinguishing characteristic of a firm is its use of authority. In firms, resources are allocated by fiat rather than by prices. Alchian and Demsetz (1972) objected to this interpretation by noting that market participants seem to have similar authority by virtue of their right to withdraw from trade. An individual who stops buying from her grocer is just as much "firing" her grocer as an employer who terminates an employee. The context and consequences are different, but the economic mechanism is the same. Instead of authority, they suggested that the key characteristic of a firm is the monitoring of inputs rather than outputs. The need for monitoring arises, because much output is jointly produced so that individual contributions get disguised by the contributions of other parties. This results in free riding and a suboptimal level of performance. It is useful to sketch a formal model of their argument, since it will facilitate the interpretation of Hart and Moore's model.[4]

Suppose there are n workers supplying inputs into a production process that yields a joint output $y = y(e_1, \ldots, e_n)$, where e_i is the input of worker i. Assume each e_i, referred to generically as effort, is unobservable and represents the private cost to worker i of choosing effort level e_i. Only output y is observable. As such, y can be used as a basis for a contract between the workers. Let $s_i(y)$ represent worker i's share of output in the contract and assume for the moment that shares are chosen so that $\Sigma_i s_i(y) = y$, that is, total output is exactly distributed among the workers, because workers form a partnership. The question then arises: Can the sharing rules s_i be chosen so that they induce workers to choose inputs efficiently? If we take workers to be risk neutral and assume that they have sufficient wealth, an efficient vector of inputs e^* is found by maximizing total surplus. Assuming a differentiable, strictly concave production function, the following first-order conditions fully characterize e^*:

$$\frac{\partial y(e^*)}{\partial e_i} = 1, \quad \text{for all } i = 1, \ldots, n. \tag{1}$$

Since inputs are privately chosen, it is natural to assume that they are chosen noncooperatively with a Nash equilibrium characterizing the equilibrium outcome. Assuming that sharing rules are differentiable, an assumption that simplifies the exposition, but is inconsequential for the conclusion, we have the following first-order conditions for a Nash equilibrium e^{NE}:

$$\frac{ds_i(y(e^{NE}))}{dy}\frac{\partial y(e^{NE})}{\partial e_i} = 1, \text{ for all } i = 1, \ldots, n. \tag{2}$$

4. The model is from Holmstrom (1982).

If we are to have $e^{NE} = e^*$, we must have

$$\frac{ds_i(y(e^*))}{dy} = 1, \text{ for all } i = 1, \ldots, n. \tag{3}$$

This is just the standard result that efficiency requires each worker to obtain the marginal social surplus from his actions. On the other hand, since sharing rules have to add up to the output level y no matter what y is, we see, by differentiating the budget constraint, that

$$\sum_i \frac{ds_i(y(e^*))}{dy} = 1. \tag{4}$$

Evidently, Equations (3) and (4) are inconsistent, implying that a Nash equilibrium e^{NE} can never equal the efficient choice e^*. The problem is that there are not enough margins to go around. By Equation (3), each worker should receive 100% of his marginal product, but the budget offers only a total margin of 100% to be divided among the workers. The split of the total margin leads to a suboptimal choice of inputs.

It is worth emphasizing that the free-rider problem has nothing to do with externalities in the production function (as argued by Alchian and Demsetz). As shown above, the problem arises just as easily with an additive production function in which there are no interactions between the workers' inputs. The free-rider problem is exclusively driven by informational externalities caused by the inability to identify individual contributions.[5]

2.2 Two Solutions to the Free-Rider Problem

There are two solutions to the free-rider problem. The first one is to allow for budget-breaking sharing rules that do not add up to the total output at all levels of y (Holmstrom, 1982). The second is to expand on measures through additional monitoring. Let me start with the budget-breaking solution. If we allow sharing rules satisfying the weaker constraint $\Sigma_i s_i(y) \leq y$ for all y, then efficiency can be restored. All one has to do is to let every worker suffer sufficiently if output falls below the efficient level $y(e^*)$. For instance, let $s_i(y) = \frac{y}{n}$, if $y \geq y(e^*)$ and $s_i(y) = \frac{y(e^*)}{n} + y - y(e^*)$, if $y < y(e^*)$. This rule burdens each agent with the full social cost of shirking. It breaks the budget by requiring the partnership to throw away some of the output if the efficient output level is not reached. But since the rule will induce workers to choose the efficient level of effort, no output needs to be thrown away in equilibrium. There is a question, of course, whether such a self-imposed threat is credible. To deal with potential credibility problems, one can bring in a passive outsider that breaks the budget. This has its own problems with collusion, but I will not go further into that issue here.

Alchian and Demsetz (1972) suggested that the free-rider problem be solved by introducing a monitor to assess worker inputs. A monitor, who is able to

5. That technological externalities as such don't determine firm boundaries is evident. Just think of a car or any other complex product, in which almost all components are tightly engineered to fit, yet hundreds of firms are involved in the production process.

perfectly discern individual inputs, can use a simple forcing contract to induce the right choice of effort. In such a contract, the worker is paid only if he performs to the standard. This suggestion leaves two questions unanswered: What assures that the monitor doesn't cheat on payments when performance meets the standard? And what gives the monitor the incentive to monitor? The latter question, according to Alchian and Demsetz, is resolved by giving the monitor the claim on the residual, that is, the output net of payments to the workers. In their interpretation, this arrangement makes the monitor also the owner. The first question they never address, but one can imagine that in a repeated game, the owner's concern for her reputation will prevent cheating [see Bull (1987) and Baker, Gibbons, and Murphy (1997)]. I will not pursue this point either. Instead, let me look at the question of monitoring from a more abstract perspective, namely as a method to create a richer system of performance measures.

2.3 Additional Performance Measures

When will an additional performance measure, say $z = z(e_1, \ldots, e_n)$, add value by enabling a better Nash equilibrium? To make the analysis more transparent, assume that there are just two workers whose joint output y is additively separable. With an appropriate transformation of variables, we can write $y = e_1 + e_2$, leaving the workers with strictly convex cost functions $c_1(e_1)$ and $c_2(e_2)$. Let $z = e_1 + \gamma e_2$ be the additional performance measure with γ a constant. Note that we can restrict attention to linear sharing rules, $s_1(y, z) = \alpha y + \beta z + \delta$ and $s_2(y, z) = (1 - \alpha)y - \beta z - \delta$. Any set of sharing rules that implements a particular vector of efforts (e_1, e_2) can be replaced by a set of linear sharing rules with weights equal to the derivatives of the general rules evaluated at the implemented vector of efforts. Because of budget balancing, the weights of y have to add to one and the weights of z have to add to zero. Noting this, the workers' choice of efforts will be described by the first-order conditions

$$\begin{aligned} \alpha + \beta &= c_1'(e_1) \\ (1 - \alpha) - \beta\gamma &= c_2'(e_2). \end{aligned} \tag{5}$$

According to Equation (5), the workers will respond to changes in β as follows:

$$\begin{aligned} \frac{de_1}{d\beta} &= \frac{1}{c_1''} \\ \frac{de_2}{d\beta} &= \frac{-\gamma}{c_2''}. \end{aligned}$$

The effect of a change in β on net output, $y - c_1 - c_2$, can after a bit of algebra be expressed as

$$\left[(1 - \alpha)\frac{1}{c_1''} - \alpha\frac{\gamma}{c_2''}\right] d\beta. \tag{6}$$

Evidently the additional measure z will be valuable if and only if the bracketed term is nonzero, since then we can choose a nonzero β that makes Equation (6) positive.

If $\gamma = 1$, then $z = y$. In this case, of course, the additional measure adds no value. Formally, this is true because changes in β are equivalent to changes in α. It follows that for the second-best value of α (the value that maximizes net output when y is the only available measure), the bracket in Equation (6) must be zero (I am assuming an interior solution, which is guaranteed if the cost functions have zero derivatives at zero). Consequently, as long as γ is different from 1, the expression in Equation (6) must be nonzero at the second-best value of α and hence net output can be raised either by increasing or decreasing β. Specifically, if $\gamma > 1$, then net profit is raised by some $\beta < 0$ and conversely if $\gamma < 1$. This is perfectly intuitive. When $\gamma > 1$, the z measure is more sensitive to changes in e_2 than to e_1 and hence worker 2 should be given a positive share of z, that is, β should be negative.

The economic point of this exercise is simple. As long as the additional measure z is not collinear with output y, it provides additional information about the inputs and such information can always be used to strengthen worker incentives somewhat. This can best be seen by adding up the incentive coefficients of the two workers, the terms on the left-hand side of the expressions in Equation (5). The sum is $1 + (1 - \gamma)\beta$, which is greater than 1, because we will set $\beta > 0$ (< 0) when $\gamma < 1$ (> 1). In contrast, when output y is the only measure, and budget balancing is imposed, the incentive coefficients necessarily sum up to one. The important effect of an additional measure is to "break the margin budget" so that more incentive margins can be distributed to the workers. This observation will have an interesting parallel in the Hart–Moore model.

The analysis above extends readily to n workers with separable output. In order for z to admit a marginal improvement in the equilibrium outcome, the vectors $[dy/de_1, \ldots, dy/de_n]$ and $[dz/de_1, \ldots, dz/de_n]$, evaluated at the second-best Nash equilibrium e^{EN}, must not be collinear.

3. Ownership and Incomplete Contracts

3.1 The Role of Incomplete Contracts

Alchian and Demsetz' idea of monitoring has been criticized because it fails to explain where the boundaries between firms are drawn. The argument is that the proposed solution is insensitive to the institutional context. Any contract between the owner-monitor and the workers could just as well be carried out in a market as within a firm. The organizational location of the parties is inconsequential, since the contract specifies all the relevant contingencies.[6]

When contracts are incomplete in the sense that they cannot incorporate all future contracting opportunities, governance becomes consequential. Contractual incompleteness is of course endemic, both because contingencies are too numerous to deal with and because many relevant contingencies cannot

6. This critique is most compelling if we think of the contract as explicitly written. Similar enforcement rules apply inside and outside the firm when it comes to human capital. The argument is weaker if we think of the contract as implicitly enforced, say through repeated interactions.

be foreseen. When unspecified contingencies occur, the continuation of the relationship must rest on negotiating how the old contract should be completed or negotiating an entirely new contract. The outcome of these negotiations will generally depend on the organizational affiliation of the involved parties. Two individuals will negotiate under very different incentives as employees of a single firm than as owners of separate firms, for instance.

The role of governance was first discussed in the context of vertical integration (Williamson, 1979; Klein, Crawford, and Alchian 1978). When there are two separate firms, each owning assets that are critical for production, either side can cause economic damage to the other by withholding use of its assets. The possibility of holdups can be troublesome if the relationship requires initial investments that cannot be fully recouped by the investing party when the relationship is severed. The mere threat of terminating the relationship may allow the noninvesting side to appropriate enough of the rents so that, even when the relationship is continued under a new agreement, the investing side will not be able to recover its initial investment outlays. Under such a threat, the investing party will rationally underinvest in the relationship.

Businessmen are acutely aware of the holdup problem. For instance, joint venture agreements pay careful attention to the potential for holdups (showing that holdup problems often are dealt with contractually rather than by integration; see Holmstrom and Roberts, 1998). Various contractual levers are given to each side to protect relationship-specific investments, such as exclusive selling rights, long-term delivery agreements, rights to veto expansions, and so on. Also, these agreements are quite explicit about exit rights: what to do in case of an impasse in negotiations over how to handle unstipulated events. Some variant of "Russian roulette" (also known as the "Texas Shoot Out") is commonly employed as a termination rule. The rule requires one side to propose a price, which the other side can accept either as a selling price or as a buying price of the joint venture. In both cases, the outcome is 100% ownership by one of the parties.

Applied to vertical integration, the logic of holdup suggests that when investments entail a high degree of asset specificity—that is, assets are much more valuable within a relationship than outside it—integration is preferred to having two separate firms. Williamson (1985) provides a detailed discussion of the role of asset specificity. He stresses that asset specificity, particularly in conjunction with environmental uncertainty and transaction frequency are conducive to integration. A key premise of his transaction cost economics is that one can predict integration based on the characteristics of individual transactions rather than bundles of transactions.

Hart (1995) has argued that Williamson's transaction cost approach does not explain exactly what changes when two firms integrate. Specifically, why is the holdup problem mitigated by integration and what costs are associated with the decision? Hart's own answer, first presented in his work with Grossman (Grossman and Hart, 1986), identifies changes in residual rights as the critical variable. Ownership, by legal definition, determines who has the residual right to decide how to use the asset. An owner can contract out some of the rights, say by leasing the asset for a specified time, but apart from such contractually assigned specific decision rights, an owner is free to use the asset as he sees fit (subject to legal and social constraints, of course). Ownership gives formal control over the asset for uses that have not been preassigned—it gives "residual rights of control."

While ownership may save a firm from being held up by another firm, it also provides a lever to hold up other parties that make valuable investments. There is both a benefit and a cost to a switch in ownership. "Entrepreneurship" or "initiative" are terms we hear when the positive incentive effects of ownership dominate. "Holdup" is reserved for the negative effects. Which term is used varies with the context, but the basic mechanism is the same. The fact that the property rights theory applies one and the same logic to characterize both benefits and costs is a significant conceptual advantage. Another big advantage is that the idea can be readily translated into formal models, as evidenced by the many articles on incomplete contracting written in recent years. The most elegant exposition of the theory is offered by Hart and Moore (1990). Let me turn to a simplified version of their model.

3.2 The Hart–Moore Model

The model can handle many parties, but I will assume that there are only two, a buyer B and a seller S. There are two dates, 1 and 2. There is a set of alienable assets A, the ownership of which can be assigned in various configurations to B and S (or possibly some unrelated outsider O). At date 1 both the seller and the buyer make unobserved investments, denoted b and s, respectively. A critical assumption of the model is that these investments enhance the value of each party's human capital rather than the value of the assets directly. The value of the assets may go up indirectly, however, as there are interaction effects between assets and human capital.

It is assumed that no contract can be written at date 1 regarding the use of the assets at date 2, nor can a meaningful contract be written regarding trades at date 2. This, of course, is quite unrealistic, but it serves to highlight the role of asset ownership in the starkest way possible. Because there is no contract ex ante, the parties have to negotiate about what if any trade should take place at date 2. Rather than specify a particular production technology and the associated revenues and costs from trading, it is sometimes more illuminating to define the outcome of the process abstractly in terms of values that accrue to the parties at date 2 as a function of their investments and the assets that they control in the final agreement. There are two possible outcomes at date 2. Either the parties agree to trade, or they go their own ways. If they trade, they split the total surplus, denoted $v(b, s)$, in a fashion to be determined momentarily. Note that the notation $v(b, s)$ assumes that if an agreement is reached, all the assets will be under the control of B and S; it will become clear shortly that it is never desirable to introduce a third party, who might have ownership of some of the assets, so this notation is justified. If the parties fail to reach an agreement, the buyer receives his best alternative payoff $v_b(b|A_b)$ and the seller her outside option $v_s(s|A_s)$. Here $A_b(A_s)$ is the set of assets that the buyer (seller) has control over at date 2. Note that v_b does not depend on the seller's investment s, because without the seller's participation her human capital cannot benefit B. Similarily for v_s. This is the import of assuming that investments are in human rather than nonhuman capital.

Assume that $v \geq v_b + v_s$. In that case it is always desirable to reach agreement and divide the value of v between B and S in a fashion that gives b at least v_b and the seller at least v_s. The predictions of the model are (unfortunately) sensitive to the particular bargaining assumptions used to determine how the surplus $v - v_b - v_s$ is split (see DeMeza and Lockwood, 1997). The standard bargaining assumption is a 50:50 split, in which case the payoffs to the parties at date 2 will be

$$\begin{aligned} s_b(b, s|A_b, A_s) &= v_b(b|A_b) + 1/2[v(b, s) - v_b(b|A_b) - v_s(s|A_s)] \\ &= 1/2v(b, s) + 1/2v_b(b|A_b) - 1/2v_s(s|A_s), \qquad (7) \\ s_s(b, s|A_b, A_s) &= 1/2v(b, s) - 1/2v_b(b|A_b) + 1/2v_s(s|A_s). \end{aligned}$$

The sum of the payoffs add up to v, of course. Foreseeing these date 2 payoffs, B and S make their investment decisions b and s at date 1. It is assumed that the choices will be made noncooperatively (since they cannot be observed) and that a Nash equilibrium will result.

The value functions v, v_b, and v_s are exogenous to the model. The only endogenous variable influencing the parties choice of investment is the allocation of assets A_b and A_s. Note from Equation (7) that it is only through a change in the outside options that the asset allocation matters.

In order to study the effects of ownership on investment decisions, one needs to make further assumptions about how the endogenous variables interact. Hart and Moore make the plausible assumption that with more assets under one's control, the marginal incentive to invest increases. That is, $\partial v_b/\partial b(\partial v_s/\partial s)$ increases as B (S) controls more assets. Also, they assume that b and s are complementary inputs in the joint production function $v(b, s)$; the cross-partial is positive. Finally, the marginal contributions of b and s are assumed to be highest when the parties work together: $\partial v/\partial b \geq \partial v_b/\partial b$ and correspondingly for s.[7]

The first implication is that the equilibrium level of investment is at or below the efficient level. Consider the decision of B, for instance. Starting from the efficient level, B's investment incentives will be driven by $1/2\partial v/\partial b + 1/2\partial v_b/\partial b \leq \partial v/\partial b$. If the inequality is strict, B will underinvest. But the more B underinvests, the lower are S's marginal returns from investing, because investments are complementary. Once S reduces her investment, B again lowers his and so it goes until a suboptimal equilibrium is reached. This is all a straightforward consequence of supermodularity, of course.

A second implication of supermodularity is that it never pays to have joint ownership. In joint ownership either side can veto the use of an asset.[8] That

7. In more technical jargon, these assumptions state that the value functions are supermodular, that is, the marginal return from increasing a variable increases with the other variables.

8. The assumption that both sides can veto the use of an asset may not represent reality. As I

means that in the event of disagreement, some assets will be made unavailable for use by either side. Looking at Equation (7), it is clear that it would always be better to reassign a jointly owned asset to sole ownership by one party, say B for concreteness, since that increases B's incentives to invest without directly affecting S's incentives. The fact that joint ownership is suboptimal also means that it is never desirable to give control over an asset to an outsider who makes no investments. Doing so would just reduce the incentives for B and S to invest for the same reasons as discussed above. In addition, the shares in the value functions allocated to B and S would go down (using Shapley value as the extended bargaining outcome), reducing investments still further.

Supermodularity further implies that assets that are complementary, in the strict sense that one asset is worthless without access to the other asset, should be owned by the same party. If the two assets were owned separately, this would be equivalent to joint ownership in which both sides can veto the use of the assets, an arrangement we have just seen to be suboptimal. Conversely, if the assets are unrelated (in the sense that no person's investment affects both assets), they should be owned separately.[9]

Finally, note that multidimensional investment decisions, for instance, B allocating his investment between enhancing the outside value v_b and enhancing the joint value v, will always bias investments excessively toward the outside option. This is a form of rent seeking, where total value is sacrificed in order to achieve a larger share of the common pie (Holmstrom and Tirole, 1991; Rajan and Zingales, 1998). I will return to the organizational implications of this case shortly.

3.3 A Comparison with Alchian and Demsetz

It is illuminating to compare the Hart–Moore model to the free-rider model discussed in the previous section. To this end, first observe that the two models deal with exactly the same type of problem. In the Hart–Moore model the joint output is $y = v(b, s)$ and the issue is how to provide the parties with incentives to supply unobserved inputs $e_1 = b$ and $e_2 = s$. The only difference between the models is in the instruments they use to motivate the agents. In the free-rider model it is assumed that the joint product can be split between the workers according to arbitrary sharing rules. In the Hart–Moore model, instead of general sharing rules, the parties are constrained to use sharing rules that arise out of varying asset allocations as described in Equation (7). At first, this may appear to offer much more limited choices. For instance, when there is a single asset that has to be fully allocated to one party or the other, only two sharing

mentioned earlier, irreconcilable differences will often lead to termination *and* a transfer of assets to one party.

9. One might think that supermodularity also implies that when the marginal value of B's investment, say, goes up in the total surplus function v, then B should be given no fewer assets than before. In other words, the more important B becomes as an investor, the more assets (weakly) B should control. This is not true in general and requires additional assumptions that I will not get into.

rules are available. However, if one allows ex post randomization so that asset ownership can be determined not just ex ante, but also ex post through an ex ante agreed upon lottery, the set of possible payoffs in the Hart–Moore model expands to include all linear combinations of Equation (7). In another respect, the incentives in Equation (7) may be richer than in the free-rider model. The payoffs in Equation (7) cannot in general be written as a function of the joint output v, because b and s enter not just through v but also through the outside options v_b and v_s.[10]

Let me elaborate on this important distinction. Alchian and Demsetz (1972) suggested that organizations can deal with the free-rider problem by *internal* monitoring, which as we saw, serves to break the "margin budget," that is, the constraint that margins cannot add up to more than 1. The Hart–Moore model highlights the fact that the market can also break the margin budget in a different way, through external monitoring. When the parties bargain over the split of the surplus v, it is implicitly assumed that they can observe each other's outside options v_b and v_s; else it would not be possible to write the payoffs in the form of Equation (7). Unless v_b and v_s are collinear with v, they then qualify as additional, valuable measures of performance as discussed earlier. This is well illustrated by considering the special case where, for some asset allocation (A_b, A_s) the outside options add up exactly to total surplus:

$$v(b, s) = v_b(b|A_b) + v_s(s|A_s), \quad \text{for all } b, s. \tag{8}$$

Since the outside options are as valuable as the inside options, it is natural to think of this case as representing a perfectly competitive market. Computing the bargaining payoffs according to Equation (7) one finds that $\partial s_b/\partial b = \partial v/\partial b$ and $\partial s_s/\partial s = \partial v/\partial s$, that is, both B's and S's marginal returns from investment coincide with the social return. This results in an efficient level of investment. While both sides get only 50% of the marginal social return through the first term in Equation (7), they pick up another 50% of the margin through the additional performance measures v_b and v_s. Market monitoring breaks the margin budget, allowing both sides to receive 100% of the social return.

I am trying to make two points here. The first is that bargaining generates information, and this feature is a central part of the Hart–Moore model. Indeed, the model captures very nicely the essence of market competition: the right to exit a relationship and the information and incentives that the ensuing bargaining process generates. The role of the market had always been somewhat of an enigma in organizational analyses prior to the property rights models. It was common to take the market as a first-best default with internal organization

10. One option that is unavailable in the Hart–Moore model is budget breaking of the kind that can prove effective in the free-rider model. While third-party ownership can reduce the stakes of the buyer and the seller, this will merely weaken incentives rather than strengthen them. The problem is that the third party cannot punish the workers by taking part ownership. Nor can the third party add more rewards, because ownership shares have to add up to 100%. However, with richer contract options, budget breaking may be achieved also in incomplete contract models; see Maskin and Tirole (1999).

emerging where the market failed (e.g., Williamson, 1975). That view did not explain exactly what makes markets so useful and how asset ownership could influence the outcome.

My second point is almost a converse of the first. While markets generate information through bargaining, this process is certainly not costless. Someone has to invest effort into finding the information required to reach an agreement of the kind described in Equation (7). Also, the bargaining process may itself generate undesirable rent seeking as the parties try to influence the outside options in order to get a bigger share of the total (Milgrom and Roberts, 1992). Such information and bargaining costs need to be compared with alternative ways of generating performance information. It is likely that in many situations, particularly ones with few participants, information can be produced in less costly ways outside the market. To go back to Alchian and Demsetz' original idea, perhaps the owner-monitor has expertise in evaluating the contributions of the input suppliers, making internal monitoring more efficient than allowing the parties to bargain privately. In this respect the assumption that the parties can observe ex post either the investment levels made or the actual value of the outside options deserves more scrutiny.

3.4 Empirical Issues[11]

The prediction of the Hart–Moore model that joint production never is optimal is counterfactual. Joint ventures (and shared ownership, more generally) have always been an important part of the corporate landscape, and if anything they seem to have become more prevalent in recent years [for instance, Stuckey (1983) reports that more than 50% of the world's primary aluminum was produced through joint ventures in the 1980s]. In fact, the theoretical predictions concerning joint ventures, sole ownership of complementary assets and outside ownership are all quite fragile. Multidimensional investments, as discussed later, can overturn these results. Different bargaining rules and dynamic considerations can alter the conclusions (Halonen, 1994; Baker, Gibbons, and Murphy; 1997, DeMeza and Lockwood, 1998). Also, if one assumes that investments add value to alienable assets rather than just human assets, things can change. Consider two parties that invest in a single alienable asset. If only one of them owns the asset, the other party will have no incentive to invest. If the investments are sufficiently complementary, a better arrangement is to let both sides veto the use of the asset. This will give each side a marginal return of one-half of v and both will invest. Of interest, joint ventures with a 50:50 ownership are quite common.

Sensitivity to details about bargaining rules and about the nature of the unobserved investments is likely to be empirically problematic. Another potential problem for property rights models is the interpretation of asset specificity. Consider again the competitive case where $v = v_b + v_s$ for all investment deci-

11. Whinston (1997) offers a much more detailed discussion of the empirical implications and problems with the property rights approach. Holmstrom and Roberts (1998) describes recent trends in organizational forms in reference to property rights and transaction cost theories.

sions. There is no asset specificity and, as we saw earlier, investment levels will be efficient. However, the same is true if one adds an arbitrary constant to the joint surplus, while leaving the outside options the same. In other words, there can be arbitrary amounts of asset specificity (measured by the constant) without any effect on the optimal distribution of assets. Again, this is an implication that is sensitive to the particular bargaining game being used. Even so, it is clear that the meaning of asset specificity in the Hart–Moore model, if there is one, is very different from the standard definition underlying all the empirical work on transaction cost economics. It cannot be measured by ex post dependency as in Williamson (1975, 1985). Rather, the degree to which asset specificity is a problem has to do with how investments influence the marginal values v, v_b, and v_s. It is challenging to think of ways to measure these effects, since they involve investments and associated margins that according to the theory cannot be observed or priced.

3.5 Why Do Firms Own Assets?

Let me turn to the most serious question concerning the model. To what extent is it about the firm?

The problem is that the theory, as presented, really is a theory about asset ownership by individuals rather than by firms, at least if one interprets it literally. Assets are like bargaining chips in an entirely autocratic market. There are neither firms nor workers. The same critique that was directed at Alchian and Demsetz' vision of the firm, that organizational affiliations did not matter for transactions, could be directed at the Hart–Moore model just as well. Individual ownership of assets does not offer a theory of organizational identities unless one associates individuals with firms. So why not think of the model as an entrepreneurial theory of the firm? Suppose unobserved human capital investments are investments in some sort of organizational capital or capabilities. The main problem with this interpretation is that it takes firms and their activities as exogenously given. If one tries to explain how assets get distributed across firms, given a set of investment activities, this is all right. But if one tries to explain how activities get distributed across firms, it obviously is not. And yet the boundary question is in my view fundamentally about the distribution of activities: What do firms do rather than what do they own?[12] Understanding asset configurations should not become an end in itself, but rather a means toward understanding activity configurations.

Going back to the literal (individualistic) interpretation of the model, its logic would seem to suggest that assets should be distributed widely across individuals, just as shares in the joint output would typically be widely distributed in the free-rider model. If we look inside firms, we should see workers own assets either outright or perhaps intermittently in some way in order to create optimal incentives. Clearly we don't see anything like that. Instead, the overwhelming

12. This agrees with Coase's (1988) view of what needs explaining. Levin (1998) offers a model in which activities get clustered because of externalities in reputation building.

evidence is that firms own essentially all the productive alienable assets and employees rarely any.

One can present this critique a bit more pointedly as follows. When firms own assets, these assets are tied together in a fashion that makes it impossible for a person to own 30% of one of the firm's assets and 50% of another of the firm's assets. If I own 10% of firm A, I own 10% of all its assets. But in a model where assets provide the only incentives, it is clear that this is generally inefficient. It would always be weakly better to have each asset be separately sold and available for individual purchase. Such an arrangement would permit maximum flexibility in distributing ownership shares in assets. It cannot be worse, since if indeed I want to own 10% of all the assets of firm A, I could purchase 10% of each asset in the free market.[13]

So why do firms own essentially all the nonhuman assets it uses in production? Why do workers—or for that matter any other stakeholder—rarely own any such assets? This strikes me as one of the most basic regularities that a theory of the firm needs to explain.

One possible explanation is that ownership strengthens the firm's bargaining power vis-à-vis outsiders. Suppliers and other outsiders will have to deal with the firm as a unit rather than as individual members. It is readily seen that in the Shapley value formula (which Hart and Moore use in the multiperson case), a coalition that supplies substitute inputs will get more as a collective bargaining unit than individually. United the firm's members stand stronger than divided, just as a union can extract better terms for its members. On the other hand, if the inputs are complements, then workers can extract more of the surplus (according to Shapley value) by bargaining individually, so this line of reasoning is not so clear-cut. The general point though is that institutional affiliation, and not just asset allocation, can significantly influence the nature of bargaining. Note that this type of argument does not require any ex ante investments. Ownership coalitions could reflect the equilibrium of a power game.

Another plausible and related reason for bundling assets is that it influences the terms of financing asset purchases. Integration can assure the financier that there are fewer holdups if the financing terms ever have to be renegotiated. Also, with assets that can collectively be pledged as collateral, the firm may increase its financial leverage and this way obtain more as well as cheaper financing (Conning, 1997). In effect, the firm can be a valuable financial intermediary. The recent literature on corporate finance is relevant here, but there have been very few models that try to characterize the division of labor between direct market finance and firm-mediated finance.

A third reason is that by having the assets under a single authority (at least formally) the firm can assign workers to assets in a manner that is richer and more varied than what would be possible with separate ownership. The firm

13. This statement may need qualification, if as seems likely, there are externalities in the market for assets. See Bolton and Whinston (1993).

can shift workers around over time and across contingencies because ownership of assets gives it the right to design jobs associated with those assets. The firm can promote workers it deems deserving and it can demote or fire workers it thinks have underperformed, but only to jobs that are associated with assets that it owns. A firm cannot promote a worker to a job in another firm, nor can it typically assign a worker to a job that requires assets controlled by another firm. The fact that contingencies are hard to specify ex ante makes the firm a potentially important operator of an internal human capital market.

This last point is part of a broader explanation. By focusing on holdups alone, the property rights approach overlooks the great variety of instruments that can be used to influence employee incentives. If all a firm can do is pay its employees based on their holdup power, its ability to provide incentives will be quite limited. Actually the firm has a great variety of instruments with which to influence worker incentives. The firm can pay bonuses, based on either an explicit formula or subjective performance evaluations. It can design jobs, set work rules, assign tasks, decide on strategic plans, delegate authority, control information channels, espouse a particular corporate culture, and so on.[14] What gives the firm the power to dictate all these things? The reason is apparent: by owning and hence holding contracting rights to all the alienable assets, the firm gains considerable leverage over its human assets. Hart and Moore suggest likewise, but in their case the power is merely used to alter the constellation of holdups and the resulting bargaining payoffs rather than to give the firm access to a wider range of instruments. Indeed, their logic fits better the first explanation given above, that concentrated ownership gives leverage over outsiders.

Why should the firm have any such power? My argument is that it allows the firm to internalize many of the externalities that are associated with incentive design in a world characterized by informational imperfections. As the theory of second best suggests, an uncoordinated application of the available incentive instruments will lead to significant externalities. By having access to more instruments, the firm can set up a more coherent system of incentives. Often this involves suppressing excessively strong incentives on individually measured performance for the benefit of enhancing the effectiveness of more delicate and subtle instruments aimed at encouraging cooperation and other less easily measured activities. In other words, high-powered ownership incentives are replaced by lower-powered employee incentives, because that enables a better overall design. This view stands in sharp contrast with the commonly heard complaints about lack of individual initiative in large hierarchical firms. That type of critique does not appreciate the inevitable trade-off between individual initiative and cooperation when performance is imperfectly measured.

Let me stress that viewing the firm as a subeconomy, which regulates trade according to second-best principles, does not imply that one firm should own

14. Of course, a firm could and does pay bonuses to independent contractors as well (and implicitly "promote" such contractors by awarding them increasingly valuable jobs), but the evidence suggests that the nature of external contracting is quite different from internal contracting.

all the assets. As the property rights approach shows, separate ownership does allow market-based bargaining, which cannot be emulated within a firm that owns all the assets. Indeed, the very fact that workers can exit a firm at will and go to other firms, and that consumers and input suppliers and other trading partners can do likewise, limits the firm's ability to exploit these constituents. This in turn makes it feasible for the firm to go about its business of setting "internal rules of the game" in a relatively unfettered fashion.[15] By comparison, a government, which faces a similar regulation problem, does not have the luxury to use nonanonymous rules. Its regulations must apply equally to all firms and citizens that face verifiably similar circumstances. Also, voice has to replace exit as the instrument that limits government abuse (Hirschman, 1970). Democracy is a costly governance procedure, but it appears to be the best one available when exit is precluded.[16]

4. Regulating Trade Within the Firm

4.1 Various Measurement Costs

In this section I will illustrate some of the principles and implications of coherent incentive design based on Holmstrom and Milgrom (1991, 1994). I will use a moral hazard model in which explicit incentive payments are possible, but it will become evident that the basic insights I am after do not depend on this feature. In particular, other incentive drivers, such as asset ownership, can often replace explicit contracts without altering the main point.

Moral hazard stems from imperfect performance measurement. There are (at least) three types of measurement imperfections one can envision. The standard one is that performance is a joint product of what the agent does and what nature does:

$$x = f(e, \theta),$$

where e is the agent's choice of input, θ is the realized state of nature, and x is the observed performance (which may not equal output y). Now the problem is akin to joint production in the free-rider model: one doesn't know exactly how to apportion blame (or praise). This is not a problem if the agent is risk neutral and has sufficient wealth to buy out the productive assets and become a residual claimant. But if the agent is risk averse or has too little wealth, there is a trade-off between stronger incentives and sharing of risk.

The second type of measurement problem arises when performance measures are biased. Suppose

$$x = \theta e$$

15. Thus markets and firms are not mere substitutes, as Coase argued, but also complements insofar as strong market discipline permits the successful operation of large and powerful firms. This is an aspect that the organizational literature has completely overlooked, because the focus has been on individual transactions rather than on the system as a whole.

16. Large firms feel similar pressures to be democratic and nonpartial when exit is costly for its members.

and output $y = e$. Assume that the agent can observe θ before he chooses e, that the unobserved cost function $c(e)$ is strictly convex, and that in expectation x is an unbiased measure of output: $E(\theta) = 1$. The problem then is that the agent's choice will vary with θ even though the marginal product of his choice in the production function is constant. Even if the agent were risk neutral, paying him according to the sharing rule, $s(x) = x+$ constant, would be inefficient because this rule induces excessive variation in effort choice, which is costly due to the convexity of the cost function c (Baker, 1992). The situation is very similar to the one analyzed many years back by Weitzman (1974) in his seminal article on prices and quantities [for more on the comparison, see Courtey (1997)]. There is a misalignment between what is measured and what is produced.

The third type of measurement cost stems from the agent's ability to manipulate the performance measure (Holmstrom and Milgrom, 1991; Allen and Gale, 1992). Let

$$x = e + m, \tag{9}$$

where m is the (unobserved) degree to which the agent manipulates x. If manipulation is privately costly, then this case will also lead to contracting costs even though the agent is risk neutral. I will use this framework, because it is convenient and not unrealistic. One interpretation of "manipulation" a la Equation (9) is that the agent can shade on quality: real quality is e, while observed quality is x, with m measuring the degree of shading.

4.2 A Simple Model

To be concrete, assume that the costs of effort and manipulation are separable and take the form

$$\text{private cost} = c(e) + d(m) = 1/2(e^2 + \lambda m^2), \tag{10}$$

where λ is a parameter measuring the relative cost of manipulation. Let the value of output be $y = pe$, where p is the value of the agent's input. I restrict attention to linear sharing rules of the form $s(x) = \alpha x + \beta$. In this setting of certainty there is no loss of generality in doing so. (Quantity constraints would do just as well; the incentive on x would be represented by a shadow price.) The agent's response is to choose $e(\alpha) = \alpha$ and $m(\alpha) = \alpha/\lambda$. Note that the ratio $e/m = \lambda$ will be the same no matter what incentive scheme is used (even if it is nonlinear).

The optimal choice of α is found by maximizing total surplus

$$S(\alpha) = p(e(\alpha)) - c(e(\alpha)) - d(m(\alpha)) = p\alpha - 1/2(\alpha^2 + \alpha^2/\lambda). \tag{11}$$

The best choice is to set $\alpha = \lambda p/(1 + \lambda)$. This contrasts with the first-best choice, which is $\alpha = p$. In the second-best choice, the incentive provision is always weaker than in first-best.[17]

17. By using total surplus as my welfare measure, it would seem that I have made the principal carry part of the agent's direct cost of cheating. Can't the principal just give the agent an incentive scheme with the surplus splitting parameter β set so that the agent meets his participation constraint

This model isn't very interesting as such. But it provides the seed for discussing richer variations, namely variations in which the agent's input e is multidimensional, as when the agent can engage in many different tasks. In reality, the problem of providing sufficient effort may often be of second-order importance to the problem of having the agent allocate effort efficiently among several tasks. For simplicity I will introduce multitasking with just two measured tasks and assume that they represent time spent on each task. Denote the two inputs e_1 and e_2 and let the new cost function be

$$\text{private cost} = 1/2(e_1 + e_2)^2 + 1/2\lambda m^2. \tag{12}$$

Let the principal's return function be $y = p_1 R(e_1) + p_2 e_2$, where R is an increasing, strictly concave function (in order to avoid corner solutions). The inputs can be observed via two performance measures:

$$x_1 = R(e_1)$$
$$x_2 = e_2 + m.$$

I have simplified things by not letting the payoff from e_1 be manipulable; the effects of adding manipulation to x_1 will be evident. The return from e_2 can be manipulated at the marginal cost λm.

Payments to the agent take the form $s(x_1, x_2) = \alpha_1 x_1 + \alpha_2 x_2 + \beta$. The choice of the optimal incentive coefficients proceeds as before. The first step is to determine how the agent responds to an arbitrary pair of incentive coefficients (α_1, α_2). The agent chooses e_1, e_2, and m to

$$\max \alpha_1 R(e_1) + \alpha_2(e_2 + m) - 1/2(e_1 + e_2)^2 - 1/2\lambda m^2.$$

The first-order conditions for e_1 and e_2 are:

$$\alpha_1 R'(e_1) = \alpha_2,$$
$$e_2 = \alpha_2 - e_1. \tag{13}$$

The first-order condition for m is

$$m = \alpha_2/\lambda. \tag{14}$$

Of course, the principal can figure out exactly the amount of manipulation that takes place, so he is not fooled. Yet there is a deadweight loss from the manipulation activity, just as in any signaling model. The loss is

$$1/2\lambda m^2 = \frac{\alpha_2^2}{2\lambda}, \tag{15}$$

which increases as λ is reduced. The easier it is to manipulate the performance measure, the more wasteful this activity becomes.

The second step in the analysis is to choose the incentive coefficients α_1 and α_2, given the agent's response functions [Equations (13) and (14)]. There is little point in showing the details, so let me just report the main features. In the

only if he does not manipulate? Not so. If such a scheme is chosen, the agent will actually do strictly better than his reservation utility.

first-best solution (corresponding to infinitely costly manipulation; $\lambda = \infty$), the principal sets $\alpha_1 = p_1$ and $\alpha_2 = p_2$. In the second-best solution, incentives on e_2 are muted (low-powered) in order to reduce wasteful manipulation. This makes it optimal to set weaker incentives for e_1, as well, because e_1 and e_2 compete for the agent's attention. It is easy to check that both activities will in fact be performed at lower levels of intensity than in the first-best solution. Also, as manipulation becomes less costly to the agent (λ decreases), the distortion in inputs will increase, making it desirable to reduce the incentives further; this follows from Equation (15), using a revealed preference argument. The economic point is that when performance measures have less integrity, there will be more wasteful manipulation. To reduce the waste without creating a significant imbalance in the allocation of effort, it is optimal to lower incentives on both activities.

An instructive way to think of this second-best result is that there are two ways to increase incentives for the problematic task e_2. Either the principal can increase the reward on e_2 or he can reduce the reward on e_1. The benefit of the latter alternative is that, by reducing the opportunity cost of e_2, incentives improve without any increase in manipulation. The general idea that an optimal incentive design should consider not only rewards but also instruments for influencing the agent's opportunity cost is evident in the many constraints firms impose on their employees.

4.3 Freedom and Constraints

A more direct way of seeing the role of the opportunity cost is by considering the following variant. Go back to the one-task case, but add a parameter τ in the agent's cost function so that now

$$\text{private cost} = c(e; \tau) + d(m; \lambda).$$

The agent will choose e and m so that

$$c'(e; \tau) = \alpha = d'(m; \lambda).$$

Thus as α goes up, both e and m go up. For simplicity, let d be of the same functional form as in Equation (12). For c, assume that the second derivative with respect to e is constant and denote it $C''(\tau)$. Since $de/d\alpha = 1/C''$, C'' measures how responsive the agent is to the incentive coefficient α. Assume further that $dC''/d\tau < 0$, so that a higher τ corresponds to a more responsive agent, and that the marginal cost c' increases with τ. These assumptions will be satisfied, for instance, if the agent can engage in (unobserved) private activities as well as in the principal's activity e, and only the total time spent on all activities determines the agent's cost of effort (that is, total time is limited by a set number of hours). In that case, if τ represents the number of private tasks that are permissible, the conditions stated above will be met. In this case, we can think of τ as measuring the agent's freedom from rules and restrictions. Other interpretations are possible. For instance, τ could represent the choice of a less or more flexible technology.

Total surplus, expressed as a function of the endogenous design variables α

and τ and the exogenous parameters, p and λ, is

$$TS(\alpha, \tau; p, \lambda) = pe(\alpha, \tau) - c(e(\alpha, \tau); \tau) - d(m(\alpha, \lambda); \lambda). \tag{16}$$

In order to see how the optimal design changes with changes in the parameters, one must consider the interaction effects of the variables in TS. To illustrate, consider the interaction terms with α. We have

$$dTS/d\alpha = (p - \alpha)\partial e/\partial\alpha - \alpha\partial m/\partial\alpha, \tag{17}$$

which is set to zero at the optimal value of α. Taking the derivative of Equation (17) with respect to τ, we see that $\partial^2 TS/\partial\alpha\partial\tau > 0$, because $\partial^2 e/\partial\alpha\partial\tau$ is positive (by assumption), the elasticity of effort is constant, and $p > \alpha$ (in any meaningful design). For the other cross-partials we find that $\partial^2 TS/\partial\alpha\partial p > 0$ and $\partial^2 TS/\partial\alpha\partial\lambda = 0$. Also, $\partial^2 TS/\partial\tau\partial p < 0$ and $\partial^2 TS/\partial\tau\partial\lambda = 0$.

As we can see, the total surplus function is not supermodular in all variables. This is not a problem in predicting the effects of changes in λ, the cost of manipulating performance. It will unambiguously increase α as well as τ. The less there is of a measurement problem, the stronger the incentives and the more freedom the agent will be given. Now consider changes in p, the value of the agent's effort. Here we encounter a problem. The problem is that an increase in p calls for a strengthening of incentives through a higher α, and a reduction in the opportunity cost through a lower τ, yet when α increases τ should also increase, other things equal. The two effects go in opposite directions and the prediction becomes ambiguous. If the interaction between α and τ is strong enough, an increase in p will raise both α and τ. If the effect is sufficiently weak, an increase in p will raise α and lower τ.

These comparative exercises are meant to illustrate two points. The first is that with more than one instrument, one needs to think about coherence in the overall design. Contracting separately on the different instruments will create externalities. The second, more subtle point is that predictions regarding coherence can be quite sensitive to the external factors that drive the change. Thus if the principal's activity becomes more important, it will imply stronger emphasis on performance, but whether that is followed by more or less freedom depends on how strong the interaction between α and τ is.

Firms extensively use the option to constrain their employees. Many of these constraints are so obvious as to elude our recognition. For instance, it is standard praxis that ordinary employees cannot work for two firms at the same time. Also, while working at home may be becoming more common, the majority of employees are still required to come into the office during work hours. Another example is the restriction on the use of money as a means to curry favors and compete for services within the firm.[18] Allowing employees to do so would diminish or destroy some of the more delicate incentives employed by firms, such as social norms.

18. Excessively generous gifts to a shared secretary are well known to cause tensions, for instance. In a related vein, Prendergast and Stole (1997) discuss why money can be harmful in maintaining effective social and reputational networks.

5. Back to Boundaries

The previous section dealt with designing incentives within a single firm. It made the point that incentive design can benefit greatly from controlling a wider range of instruments. Because many of the instruments are accessed through ownership of assets, this perspective has implications for the boundary of the firm. If the instruments are under the control of separate firms, it is more difficult to have them designed in a coordinated fashion than when the instruments are controlled by one firm. Separate design will create contractual externalities, which integration can help to resolve. Let me illustrate this idea with two variations on the first of the examples from the previous section.

5.1 Variation 1—Asset Ownership[19]

In this variation incentives stem exclusively from asset ownership, as in the Hart–Moore model. There are two agents, 1 and 2. There is one asset A. The asset can only be operated by agent 1, who can produce outputs $y_1 = R(e_1)$ and $y_2 = e_2$ with it, choosing unobserved inputs (e_1, e_2). The agent's private cost function is given by Equation (12) with $m = 0$, so manipulation is not possible. By bargaining with an outsider, agent 1 can get p_1 for each unit of output y_1. Agent 2 is an expert on marketing output y_2, but has no investment decisions. His human capital is essential for selling output y_2 at a positive price p_2 per unit.

In keeping with incomplete contract models, assume that revenues cannot be verified and hence contracts based on y_1 and y_2 cannot be written. Instead, revenues from y_1 and y_2 get divided between the agents through a bargaining process. The division depends on who owns the only alienable asset A. If agent 1 owns asset A, he can appropriate $1/2 p_2 y_2$ from agent 2's revenue by threatening to withhold output y_2. In addition, he will get $p_1 R(e_1)$ from his bargain with outsiders, since production of y_1 does not involve agent 2. Agent 2's payoff is $1/2 p_2 y_2$. If agent 2 owns asset A, the payoffs to agent 1 are determined by his right to withhold his human capital in the production of y_1 and y_2. With a 50-50 split of the surplus, he will appropriate $1/2[p_1 R(e_1) + p_2 e_2]$. The same amount will go to agent 2.

With these reduced form payoffs, the analysis maps into the general framework laid out in Section 4.3. If agent 1 owns asset A he faces incentive coefficients $\alpha_1 = p_1$ and $\alpha_2 = 1/2 p_2$. If he doesn't own the asset, the implied incentives are $\alpha_1 = 1/2 p_1$ and $\alpha_2 = 1/2 p_2$. Agent 2 makes no investments so the optimal ownership structure is determined entirely by the effect it has on agent 1's incentives. Agent 1's allocation of effort when he owns A is given by

$$\begin{aligned} e_1 &= p_1 R'(e_1) - e_2, \\ e_2 &= \tfrac{1}{2} p_2 - e_1. \end{aligned} \tag{18}$$

It follows that e_1 is above the efficient level of effort, while e_2 is below it. When

19. This variation was inspired by Rajan and Zingales (1998).

agent 1 does not own A, the allocation of effort is

$$e_1 = \tfrac{1}{2}p_1 R'(e_1) - e_2$$
$$e_2 = \tfrac{1}{2}p_2 - e_1. \qquad (19)$$

Now e_1 is at the first-best level, while e_2 is below it. However, e_2 is closer to first-best in Equation (19) than in Equation (18). Consequently, the case where agent 1 *does not* own asset A provides strictly better incentives than the case where he does own A, irrespectively of parameter values. The logic is the following. When agent 1 does not own the asset, incentives have the right balance. Since the choice of e_1 only depends on the right balance, it will be chosen efficiently. While e_2 will be below the first-best level, it will be higher than when agent 1 owns the asset and α_1 equals p_1, because in the latter case e_1 is too high, driving down e_2.

The purpose of this example is to illustrate—with asset ownership rather than explicit payments as the incentive driver—that balanced incentives, even when low powered, can be better than imbalanced incentives. Ownership by agent 1 can be costly, not only because the asset cannot then be used to motivate agent 2; indeed, agent 2 needs no motivation here. Rather, ownership can be directly detrimental for agent 1's incentives because it deflects attention from activity e_2 . For this reason, it may be desirable to have assets owned by a third party with no inputs at all (agent 2 can act as a third party here). It is easy to envision an extension of the example in which assets get clustered in the hands of a third party in order to remove excessively strong incentives that deflect attention to outside opportunities (Rajan and Zingales, 1998). The third party could be a firm, but there is no particular reason for that. Any individual would do as well.[20] In either case, the logic of integration is not one of asset complementarities as defined in Hart and Moore (1990), but rather of incentive complementarities caused by contractual externalities as in Holmstrom and Milgrom (1994).

A final note on this case: The result that agent 1 should never own asset A depends on the assumption that surplus is split 50-50 in the bargain between agents. Suppose agent 1's human capital is not indispensable, so that agent 2, if he owns the asset, could find a substitute for agent 1. As long as agent 1 is better than the substitute, he will be retained and get a share of the y_2 revenue, though less than 1/2 of it. The better the substitute is, the smaller agent 1's share of the surplus will be. Eventually there will come a point when it is better to have agent 1 focus solely on maximizing y_1. At that point, agent 1 should own asset A.

5.2 Variation 2—Contracts and Job Design

Let me return to the example in Section 4.2, reinterpreting it in an institutional context. A worker works for firm A. He can allocate his time between two

20. This is a form of beneficial budget-breaking in the context of ownership.

activities e_1 and e_2. Both tasks require an asset that firm A owns and therefore only firm A can contract with the worker for the supply of e_1 and e_2. Outputs are, as before, $y_1 = R(e_1)$ and $y_2 = e_2$. Firm A can sell output y_1 to an outside market at price p_1 per unit. Output y_2 is used exclusively by firm B, which values it at p_2 per unit. Contracting between firm A and the worker can be based on the performance measures $x_1 = y_1$ and $x_2 = y_2 + m$, where m is a variable that the worker can choose to manipulate actual output. Assume that by virtue of its contracting rights, only firm A can observe the contract it makes with the worker and that firm B cannot offer the worker any secret side payments. This is in accordance with employment laws. I will shortly suggest why such side payments may indeed be undesirable. The only way firm B can induce the worker to pay attention to e_2 is by signing a contract with firm A based on the observed measure x_2. I do not allow firm B to pay based on x_1. In practice, firm B is unlikely to observe firm A's internal performance measures. More importantly, firm B cannot control the worker's assignment, so if it tried to discourage the worker from working on e_1 through a contract on x_1 (in order to increase attention on e_2) firm A could reassign the worker to an alternative, third task, with the same effect as if firm B could not use x_1; (or firm A could side contract with the worker to mitigate firm B's influence).

The analysis now proceeds as in Section 4.2 with the difference that firm B only has access to one incentive variable: the piece rate contract $rx_2 + b$ that it uses to reimburse firm A for the services of the worker. Taking this piece rate contract as given, firm A designs an incentive scheme (as in Section 4.2) to induce the worker to choose effort and manipulation in a way that maximizes the joint surplus $p_1 R(e_1) + r(e_2 + m) - 1/2\lambda m^2 - 1/2(e_1 + e_2)^2$. This surplus is the sum of the worker's and firm A's payoffs. The worker's incentives are determined by Equations (13) and (14) as before. What coefficients α_1 and α_2 will maximize the joint surplus? Evidently, the optimal choice is $\alpha_1 = p_1$ and $\alpha_2 = r$, since then Equations (13) and (14) will coincide with the first-order conditions for maximizing the joint surplus by direct choice of e_1, e_2, and m.

Return now to firm B's choice of a piece rate contract. Suppose manipulation is infinitely costly. Then the first-best outcome will obtain by setting $r = p_2$. But as manipulation becomes more attractive (λ decreases), there will be more waste and firm B will decrease r in response. (Note that firm B cannot decrease r at the same rate as if it controlled both incentive coefficients, because e_2 has to compete with e_1, and firm A keeps the incentive for e_1 at p_1.) Eventually, as the misallocation of effort gets sufficiently large due to a mispricing of the returns to effort, firm B will stop buying y_2 from firm A and choose one of two alternatives. It will either buy the asset from firm A in order to get access to both incentive instruments α_1 and α_2 and that way get a better handle on the effort distortion problem. Or it can simply give up on y_2 altogether. Which of the two alternatives firm B chooses depends on the relative values of y_1 and y_2. Actually, if firm B chooses to buy the asset, it also has the option to start producing y_1 for firm A in a reversal of the originally envisioned trade. Indeed, if firm B could appropriate all of $p_1 y_1$ in such a trade, it would be optimal (first-best, in fact) to have firm B own the productive asset and employ the worker, since y_1 can be measured without error and hence there are no contractual externalities. However, assume that firm A is run by an entrepreneur whose services are essential for getting the return from y_1. In that case firm B will appropriate less than the social surplus by bargaining with the entrepreneur and this again creates distortions, possibly of such magnitude that it will not be worthwhile for firm B to produce y_1 at all.

In sum, depending on the degree of measurement costs and the returns to the various activities, we can have three different configurations: (a) the worker could be working for firm A, which owns the asset and produces both y_1 and y_2; (b) the worker could be working for firm B, which owns the asset and produces both y_1 and y_2; or (c) either y_1 or y_2 are not produced at all.

The point of this example is to show that measurement costs can play an important role in determining boundaries. A way to express the measurement problem illustrated by the example is to say that market instruments, such as output prices, do not always allow agents to communicate their needs and desires sufficiently well. With measurement costs of the kind described here, a price contract does not permit firm B to express and get exactly what it wants from firm A. Ownership of the asset expands on firm B's ability to communicate its preferences to and extend its leverage over the worker. This contrasts with Bernheim and Whinston's (1986) work on common agency. [My example is also one of common agency in that both firms (principals) have an interest in influencing the worker (agent).] In Bernheim and Whinston's model, the problem is resolved by having all principals transfer their preferences to a single principal along with the decision rights. This internalizes the common agency externality because the contracts between the principals incorporate all means of influence.

Of course, markets use more instruments than prices to influence incentives and mediate transactions. It is easy to come up with examples where market transactions specify exclusion of activities, choice of technology, special work assignments, and so on. For instance, firms may insist on being served by a particular consultant in a larger agency; car manufactures, including General Motors, typically insist on expensive quality measures, such as the installation of an ISO 9000 standard, before certifying a supplier; and recently, in a break with tradition, Sears has started to demand that incentives paid to their suppliers be passed onto those individually responsible for the work. These kinds of measures are evidently taken to assure quality through inputs rather than outputs. Does that nullify the ideas expressed above? Not really. First, these examples show that information problems of the sort I have emphasized do exist. Second, the theory does not assume that only prices can be used in markets, even though the examples were designed that way. It merely instructs us to look at the relative costs of controlling incentives within firms versus on markets, suggesting that control of assets provides control over a number of indirect incentive measures that typically, but not always, can be inaccessible or very costly to use in the market.

Finally, note that in this illustrative example, the boundary is most naturally defined by the set of activities undertaken by each firm. In a simple extension, one can see that if, for instance, firm B only ends up undertaking activity y_2, firm A may want to buy a duplicate asset and hire its own worker to produce y_1, underlining the sense in which asset ownership follows the choice of activities rather than the reverse. In most cases, if one were only told what assets a firm owns, but not what it is doing, it would be difficult to guess its lines of business. But if one were told what line of business the firm is engaged in, it would in many cases be easier to suggest the types of assets it owns.

5.3 Measurement Cost versus Holdup—Empirical Distinctions

The theory advocated here argues that boundaries will be drawn with intent to internalize significant contractual externalities stemming from measurement costs. How does this differ empirically from the predictions of the holdup logic? Before answering that question, note first that the holdup problem is also one that involves externalities. The investments cannot be observed and the future contingencies cannot be contractually specified. Integration solves the problem by allowing the firm to structure the incentives for its managers so that they come to terms with each other more easily than they would if they were in separate firms. This requires that the firm puts the managers inside the firm on weaker individual incentives in order to improve cooperation or, alternatively, that it does not allow the managers any power to negotiate internal trades (see Holmstrom and Tirole, 1991). Both solutions are associated with costs, as individual incentives are muted.

Now, back to the comparison with holdups. Consider the following two scenarios. In one case, ex post trade is perfectly enforceable, but it cannot be specified ex ante. There are no measurement costs ex post, but there is a potential for holdup as there is just one supplying firm. In the other case, there are a large number of suppliers and potential buyers and hence no asset specificity. But each supplier-buyer relationship faces the sort of measurement problem described earlier. The holdup theory would predict integration in the first scenario, but not the second. Measurement cost theory would predict just the reverse. This thought experiment illustrates how the two ideas are empirically distinct, though they are by no means mutually exclusive.

One case in which the measurement story has been shown to be empirically relevant is the study by Anderson and Schmittlein (1984). They found that firms, when deciding between an in-house sales office versus use of an external sales firm, the key factor explaining this choice was the difficulties with measuring a salesperson's performance. The biggest problems occurred when the salesperson worked in teams assigned to sell many different brands. This is very much in the spirit of the examples above.[21]

21. Additional evidence can be found in Brickley (1995), Slade and Lafontaine (1995), and Slade (1996), among others. Evidence against measurement costs is reported in Wernerfelt (1997).

6. Concluding Remarks

The modern property rights theory, developed by Hart and his coauthors, has had a major influence on the evolution of the theory of the firm. By emphasizing incomplete contracting and residual decision rights, in place of imperfect contracts and agency costs, it has brought much needed clarity to the meaning of ownership and the significance of exit as a defining characteristic of the market. Thanks to this theory, we have an improved understanding of how market incentives operate and, importantly, a modeling technology with which to investigate them.

Despite these significant contributions, I have argued that the property rights theory, as articulated in Hart and Moore (1990) and other representative pieces, says very little about the firm.[22] The problem is that there really are no firms in these models, just representative entrepreneurs. This focuses all the attention on the question of boundaries, which admittedly has been the outstanding puzzle to solve ever since Coase raised it more than 50 years ago. However, we also have to ask why Coase thought (or we think) that the question of boundaries is such an interesting and essential one to address. In my view, the boundary question is interesting primarily because we cannot claim to fully understand either the internal organization of firms or the operation of markets by studying the two in isolation. We need to analyze how they interact as organizations; how they compete as well as complement each other in matching individuals with tasks and in providing proper individual incentives for carrying out those tasks. It is in this spirit that I have suggested that we take a broader view of ownership than is common in the current property rights models.

References

Alchian, Armen, and Harold Demsetz. 1972. "Production, Information Costs, and Economic Organization," 62 *American Economic Review* 777–795.

Allen, Franklin, and Douglas Gale. 1992. "Measurement Distortion and Missing Contingencies in Optimal Contracts," 2 *Economic Theory* 1–26.

Andersen, Erin, and David Schmittlein. 1984. "Integration of the Sales Force: An Empirical Examination," 15 *Rand Journal of Economics* 385–395.

Arrow, Kenneth. 1974. *The Limits of Organization*. New York: W. W. Norton.

Baker, George. 1992. "Incentive Measures and Performance Measurement," 100 *Journal of Political Economy* 598–614.

Baker, George, Robert Gibbons, and Kevin J. Murphy. "Relational Contracts and the Theory of the Firm," draft, MIT.

Bernheim, Douglas, and Michael Whinston. 1986. "Common Agency," 54 *Econometrica* 911–930.

Bolton, Patrick, and Michael Whinston. 1993. "Incomplete Contracts, Vertical Integration and Supply Assurance," 60 *Review of Economic Studies* 121–148.

Brickley, James. 1995. "Incentive Conflicts and Contracting: Evidence from Franchising," FR 95-26, Rochester University.

Bull, Clive. 1987. "The Existence of Self-Enforcing Contracts," 102 *Quarterly Journal of Economics* 147–159.

Coase, Ronald. 1937. "The Nature of the Firm," 4 *Economica* 386–405.

22. The paper by Rajan and Zingales (1998) is an exception.

———. 1988. "Industrial Organization: A Proposal for Research," in *The Firm, the Market and the Law*. Chicago: University of Chicago Press.

Conning, Jonathan. 1997. "Joint Liability, Peer Monitoring, and the Creation of Social Collateral," mimeo, Yale University.

Courty, Pascal. 1997. "Strategy Communication and Measurement Systems," mimeo, Universitat Pompeu Fabra.

DeMeza, David, and Ben Lockwood. 1998. "Does Asset Ownership Always Motivate Managers? Outside Options and the Property Rights Theory of the Firm," 113 *Quarterly Journal of Economics* 361–386.

Grossman, Sanford, and Oliver Hart. 1986. "The Costs and Benefits of Ownership: A Theory of Lateral and Vertical Integration," 94 *Journal of Political Economy* 691–719.

Halonen, Maija. 1994. "Reputation and Allocation of Ownership," STICERD Theoretical Economics Discussion Paper, London School of Economics.

Hart, Oliver. 1995. *Firms, Contracts, and Financial Structure*. Oxford: Clarendon Press.

Hart, Oliver, and John Moore. 1990. "Property Rights and the Nature of the Firm," 98 *Journal of Political Economy* 1119–1158.

Hirschman, Albert O. 1970. *Exit, Voice and Loyalty*. Cambridge: Harvard University Press.

Holmström, Bengt. 1982. "Moral Hazard in Teams," 13 *Bell Journal of Economics* 324–340.

———, and Paul Milgrom. 1991. "Multitask Principal-Agent Analyses: Incentive Contracts, Asset Ownership, and Job Design," 7 *Journal of Law, Economics, & Organization* 24–51.

———. 1994. "The Firm as an Incentive System," 84 *American Economic Review* 972–991.

———, and John Roberts. 1998. "Boundaries of the Firm Revisited," 12 *Journal of Economic Perspectives* 73–94.

———, and Jean Tirole. 1991. "Transfer Pricing and Organizational Form," 7 *Journal of Law, Economics, & Organization* 201–228.

Klein, Benjamin, Robert Crawford, and Armen Alchian. 1978. "Vertical Integration, Appropriable Rents, and the Competitive Contracting Process," 21 *Journal of Law and Economics* 297–326.

Laffont, Jean-Jacques, and Jean Tirole. 1991. "Provision of Quality and Power of Incentive Schemes in Regulated Industries," in J. Gabszewicz and A. Mas-Colell, eds., *Equilibrium Theory and Applications*. Cambridge: Cambridge University Press.

Levin, Jon. 1998. "Multilateral Contracting and Organizational Design," draft, MIT.

Maskin, Eric, and Jean Tirole. 1999. "Two Remarks on the Property Rights Literature," *Review of Economic Studies*, forthcoming.

Milgrom, Paul, and John Roberts. 1992. "Bargaining Costs, Influence Costs, and the Organization of Economic Activity," in J. Alt and K. Shepsle, eds., *Perspectives on Positive Political Economy*. Cambridge: Cambridge University Press.

Prendergast, Canice, and Lars Stole. 1997. "Monetizing Social Exchange," draft, University of Chicago.

Rajan, Raghuram, and Luigi Zingales. 1998. "Power in a Theory of the Firm," 113 *Quarterly Journal of Economics* 387–432.

Simon, Herbert. 1951. "A Formal Theory of the Employment Relationship," 19 *Econometrica* 293–305.

Slade, Margaret. 1996. "Multitask Agency and Contract Choice: An Empirical Exploration," 37 *International Economic Review* 465–486.

———, and Francine Lafontaine. 1995. "Retail Contracting: Theory and Practice," draft, The University of British Columbia.

Stuckey, John. 1983. *Vertical Integration and Joint Ventures in the Aluminum Industry*. Cambridge: Harvard University Press.

Tirole, Jean. 1994. "Incomplete Contracts: Where Do We Stand?" Walras-Bowley lecture delivered at the North American Summer Meetings of the Econometric Society, Quebec City.

Weitzman, Martin. 1974. "Prices vs Quantities," *Review of Economic Studies* 477–491.

Wernerfelt, Birger. 1997. "On the Nature and Scope of the Firm: An Adjustment Cost Theory," 70 *Journal of Business* 489–514.

Whinston, Michael. 1997. "On the Transaction Cost Determinants of Vertical Integration," draft, Northwestern University.

Williamson, Oliver. 1975. *Markets and Hierarchies: Analysis and Antitrust Implications*. New York: Free Press.
______. 1979. "Transaction-Cost Economics: The Governance of Contractual Relations," 22 *Journal of Law and Economics* 233–271.
______. 1985. *The Economic Institutions of Capitalism*. New York: Free Press.

[5]

THE BUSINESS FIRM AS A POLITICAL COALITION[1]

JAMES G. MARCH
Carnegie Institute of Technology

THE MODERN BUSINESS FIRM is an organization for making and implementing decisions within a market economy. In most major industries of well-developed economies, most firms are large, complex organizations. These organizations render a set of key decisions for the economy. They establish prices, determine outputs, make investments, and allocate resources. These decisions and the consequences ensuing from them are the focus for the economic study of the firm. The economic theory of the firm attempts (1) to specify the decisions that business firms will make (as a basis for more aggregate predictions of the economy) and (2) to prescribe appropriate decision rules for a rational firm operating in a market economy.

Except as it enters as a participant in the general political arena, the business firm has not been a focus of study for political scientists. Political scientists have generally defined their field in a relatively modest way, limiting their attention to phenomena that occur in, or in close conjunction with, explicitly governmental institutions. Except for a few attempts to define the field in terms of the study of power (or its variants), the major criterion for delimiting the field has been descriptive rather than analytic. By any reasonable descriptive definition of political science, the business firm is outside the domain. Similarly, economists have largely ignored political systems except as they impinge on the market. Although it is conventional for economists to identify their field in terms of an analytic definition (e.g., the study of the allocation of scarce resources), the vast bulk of economic research is linked to a descriptive definition of the field. For practical purposes, economics is the study of

[1]This paper is based on a paper presented at the annual meetings of the American Political Science Association in St. Louis, September 7, 1961. The research underlying it was conducted jointly with R. M. Cyert under a grant from the Ford Foundation for the study of organizational behavior. I wish to acknowledge the major contribution of Professor Cyert to the ideas expressed here.

markets. The main attention to politics comes as a side issue in the area of economic policy.

At the risk of offending both economists and political scientists, I will assert that this division of labor is dysfunctional. It contributes to our inability as students to understand and predict the firm; it contributes to our inability as public policy makers to control and direct the firm. More specifically, I will argue that the business organization is properly viewed as a political system and that viewing the firm as such a system both clarifies conventional economic theories of the firm and (in conjunction with recent developments in theoretical languages) suggests some ways of dealing with classical problems in the theory of political systems generally. The argument depends on a general statement of the theoretical problem involved in decision models of complex systems, an evaluation of two major alternative approaches to that problem, and an examination of the implications of some recent attempts to develop a revised theory of the firm on the basis of a few key political concepts.

CONFLICT SYSTEMS

Consider a general class of purposive systems characterized by two attributes:

1. *There are consistent basic units.* Each elementary unit in the system can be described as having a consistent preference ordering defined over the possible states of the system. By a consistent preference ordering is meant an ordering such that for any realizable subset of possible states of the system there exists at least one state as good as any other state in the subset. Thus we require that the elementary units be able to make a choice among alternatives states of the system (allowing for a chance decision rule for the special case in which there is more than one state at least as good as all other states).

2. *There is conflict.* The preference orderings of the elementary units are mutually inconsistent relative to the resources of the system. Conflict, in this sense, arises when the most preferred states of all elementary units cannot be simultaneously realized. In order for conflict (in this sense) to exist it must be true that there is no allocative decision such that

no one of the elementary units would prefer an alternative state of the system.

These two simple postulated attributes underlie a wide variety of theories about conflict resolution, choice, or the allocation of scarce resources. Whether we are talking about the behavior of individuals in a simple learning experiment, the internal dynamics of a small group solving a problem, the interaction of parties and pressure groups in a legislative setting, or the pricing of commodities in a market system, we frequently make these two postulates. For convenience, let us call them the postulates of conflict. Any system satisfying the postulates we can call a conflict system.

One feature of studies of conflict systems that is puzzling from the point of view of the postulates of conflict is the extent to which the elementary units in one study are the conflict systems of another. The individual is treated as the system in some cases (e.g., in learning) and as the elementary unit in other (e.g., studies of small groups). Similarly, small groups are treated both as systems and as elementary units (e.g., in studies of organizations). Since the first postulate of conflict is essentially that the basic units themselves not be conflict systems, it seems awkward to be able to view a single system as either an elementary unit or a conflict system depending on the level of aggregation involved. In fact, most systems studied in the social sciences are apparently conflict systems of conflict systems.

The assumption of consistent basic units is justified by asserting either of two other characteristics of the macro-system involved. We may assert that the preference ordering of the subsystem (which we wish to identify as the elementary unit) is causally antecedent, and independent of, the decisions of the larger system. In such a case, we treat the preference ordering of the subsystem as given without considering the way in which that ordering is derived. Alternatively, we may assert that variation in system behavior due to conflict within the subsystem is trivial because of scale differences between the conflict within the subsystem on the one hand and conflict among subsystems on the other. In such a case, we take the preference ordering of the subsystem as subject to some minor error without attempting to eliminate the error entirely.

Such assertions are not simple technicalities. Consider, for example, either labor-management bargaining or bargaining among nations. Most of the literature and models of these phenomena accept the postulates of conflict. Since it is clear that (at the least) labor unions and nation states are themselves conflict systems, the theories are required to make some assertions that will allow the postulates of conflict to be made. A casual reading of this literature would suggest that either the assumption of causal antecedence or the assumption of scale difference is typically made. A casual reading of the literature also suggests, however, that the assumptions are suspect. In fact, one of the major recent developments in the study of these particular conflict systems has been a consideration of the complexities of interaction between the resolution of conflict within the subsystems and the resolution of conflict within the larger system.

Despite such observations on the difficulties of satisfying the first postulate of conflict, most theories of conflict resolution essentially accept it as a reasonable approximation. If we restrict our attention to more or less well-defined theories susceptible to technical manipulation, virtually all theories use the postulate.

Political theory deals primarily with conflict systems as thus defined; and a rather large proportion of studies of the political process are concerned with discovering how conflict is resolved within a system revolving around some explicitly political institutions. Similarly, economic theory and economic studies focus to a large extent on conflict systems identified with explicitly economic institutions. In recent years a modest resurgence of political economy as a field of study has led to some important applications of economic concepts to the analysis of political conflict systems. This is particularly conspicuous in the work of Downs,[2] Davis and Whinston,[3] and Buchanan and Tullock.[4] In these attempts, allocation problems in politics have been studied from the point of view of concepts developed for economic systems. In some cases (e.g., Downs), this has meant the translation of a standard form of economic analysis into political terms. In other cases (e.g., Davis and Whinston), the general approach is clearly economic but the detailed form of analysis is relatively new for economics as well as politics. At the same time, some recent work in organization theory seems

[2] A. Downs, *An Economic Theory of Democracy* (New York, 1957).

[3] O. A. Davis and A. B. Whinston, "The Economics of Urban Renewal," *Law and Contemporary Problems*, 26 (1961), 105-117.

[4] J. M. Buchanan and G. Tullock, *The Calculus of Consent* (Ann Arbor, 1962).

to indicate the utility of applying political concepts to the study of economic systems, particularly to the study of economic organizations. In many resepcts, March and Simon,[5] Thompson,[6] and Cyert and March[7] view the business organization as a socio-political conflict system subject to economic constraints.

THEORIES OF CONFLICT RESOLUTION

Given that we wish to describe a system as satisfying the postulates of conflict, and given that we wish to describe this system as "acting," "behaving," "choosing," or "deciding," we are required to introduce some mode of conflict resolution. By saying that the system does in fact "act," we accept the proposition that the system *in some sense* prefers some state of the world to other possible states of the world. By describing the system as a conflict system, we assert that the system does not have a preference ordering in the usual sense of that term. The devices used to move from conflict to conflict resolution comprise the core of a theory of a conflict system. In general, extant theories take one of two directions for resolving conflict. Either they impute a superordinate goal in terms of which the conflict can be mediated, or they describe a process by which decisions are reached without explicit comparison of utilities. The latter approach is typical of theories of political coalitions; the former is typical of theories of business firms.

The imputation of a superordinate goal.

Any conflict system that can be observed and that can be described as "behaving" is susceptible to description in terms of a superordinate goal. Given a sequence of behaviors, we impute a superordinate goal by accepting two simple assumptions: First, we assume there exists a joint preference ordering for the system at any particular point in time. Second, we assume the system always chooses the alternative behavior that is most preferred. Consider, for example, the familiar example of a conspicuous conflict system —a tree.[8] Is it reasonable to say that a tree seeks to maximize its

[5] J. G. March and H. A. Simon, *Organizations* (New York, 1958).

[6] V. A. Thompson, *Modern Organization* (New York, 1961).

[7] R. M. Cyert and J. G. March, *A Behavioral Theory of the Firm* (New York, forthcoming).

[8] M. Friedman, *Essays in Positive Economics* (Chicago, 1953), pp. 3-43; E. Rotwein, "On the 'Methodolgy of Positive Economics'," *Quarterly Journal of Economics,* 73 (1959), 554-578.

total exposure to the sun subject to certain behavior limitations on the species, nutrients available, and environmental conditions? If, in fact, the behavior of the tree is such as to resolve conflict over a scarce resource (sunlight) so as to maximize total exposure, there is no reason why we cannot impute such a goal to a tree. Moreover, there may be many reasons why we would want to do so.

The usual objection to the imputation of a superordinate goal to conflict systems other than the human organism (or perhaps animals generally) is a curious one. Any such effort bears the onus of anthropomorphism. Yet insofar as a goal is simply an inferred rule for allocating resources, it is no more unique to anthropoids than is change of state. In the tree example, in fact, it can be argued that the concept of a goal is (under the assumed conditions) a more powerful tool for studying trees than it is for studying human beings. It permits us to make predictions about a variety of important phenomena (e.g., the location and movement of leaves and branches).

The tree example suggests two necessary conditions for effective use of an imputed superordinate goal in the construction of a theory. First, the goal must be stable (or at least change in a predictable way). Second, the goal must be meaningful. If the goal is not meaningful, it cannot be used for predictive purposes and simply becomes a restatement of the axiom that the system always chooses the most preferred alternative. A goal of maximizing subjective utility can, for example, be imputed to any system; but the imputation is largely useless unless operational meaning that is independent of the choices studied can be given to subjective utility. If the goal is not stable, the axioms underlying the importance of a superordinate goal are largely futile since the theory can only be applied a posteriori.

The description of a conflict resolution process.

Just as any system that "behaves" can be described as having a superordinate goal, it can also be described as having a conflict resolving process. If we adopt the process approach to a conflict system, we do not attempt to identify a joint preference ordering with respect to the ultimate decision. We replace the axioms of superordinate goals with two different assumptions. First, we assume that the ultimate decision results from a series of elementary decisions. Second, we assume that some sort of joint preference ordering exists for the elementary decisions.

If we consider the case of the tree again, it is clear that we can describe the tree in terms of a conflict resolution process. In fact, this is apparently the more common theoretical tool. We might, for example, stipulate a series of elementary decisions by individual leaves that, taken together, allocate sunshine to the various parts of the tree. Furthermore, we might be able to demonstrate the consistency of the process and a particular superordinate goal. This would be true, for example, if we could demonstrate that the elementary leaf decisions necessarily resulted in an ultimate allocation that maximized total exposure for the tree. The botanical invisible hand as it were.

The usual objection to a process description of a conflict system is its tendency to become analytically grotesque. A large elm tree has more than a million leaves on it. Even if we had a theory of leaf decision making and could (conceptually) link leaf decisions to an aggregate exposure allocation, it is not easy to see how we analyze such a system.

Thus, two necessary conditions for effective use of a process description in the development of a theory for conflict systems are (1) that the elementary decision processes be susceptible to treatment as consistent basic units, and (2) that analytic procedures be available with which to explore the properties of the model. The first is required to make the theory well-defined; the second is required to permit the theory to make meaningful predictions.

Studies of the firm as an economic conflict system.

Economic treatment of the firm as a conflict system is heavily influenced by the fact that the firm in economic theory is more commonly treated as the basic unit of a larger conflict system (industry, market, economic system) than as a conflict system itself. As a result, the economic theory of the firm is almost invariably constructed by explicitly imputing a superordinate goal to the conflict system represented by a business firm. In its classic form the theory asserts that the objective of the firm is to maximize long-run expected profits. The objective is accomplished by determining an output to be produced given a production function, a cost function, and a price. Given a set of factor prices, the firm determines the minimum cost factor mix and the optimum output. Theories of imperfect competition are primarily modifications of this basic structure and do not change the basic approach. In the main, they modify the market structure faced by the firm or introduce new decision variables (e.g., price).

Thus, the economic theory of the firm assumes a joint preference ordering for the firm. In the standard form, that joint preference ordering is defined by profit maximization. Such a characterization of business firm objectives has been subject to more or less continuous minority attack. Part of that attack we can ignore for present purposes. It stems from some misgivings about the social welfare implications of profit maximization as a goal. The other source of the attack is more critical, however. It suggests that a theory assuming a profit maximization goal is a poor predictive theory. Consequently, in some attempts at revision, profit maximization is replaced by a more general utility function[9] or by an alternative goal (e.g., revenue maximization).[10] In some revisions the preference ordering is a partial rather than complete ordering.[11] For the most part, the theory suppresses as outside its domain the process by which an organization composed of a rather complex mixture of people with considerable heterogeneity of individual goals generates a single preference ordering. It is assumed that conflict is resolved by the employment contract, or—more generally—by the factor prices and that the result is a joint preference ordering of some sort or other.

This implicit assumption that the firm represents a conflict system susceptible to useful description in terms of a superordinate goal (whether profit maximization or some other) is shared by most economists. It is apparently convenient for the construction of theories of macro-economic systems. Most economic theories build upon it (although not all necessarily depend upon it). It is relatively amenable to theoretical manipulation. It lends itself to the geometry and calculus familiar to economic thought.

Nevertheless, the assumption is almost certainly wrong as a micro-description of a business firm. It was proved extremely dif-

[9] A. Papandreau, "Some Basic Problems in the Theory of the Firm," in B. F. Haley, ed., *A Survey of Contemporary Economics*, Vol. 2 (Homewood, Ill., 1952).

[10] W. J. Baumol, *Business Behavior, Value and Growth* (New York, 1959).

[11] H. A. Simon, *The New Science of Management Decision* (New York, 1961).

ficult to define a superordinate goal for a business firm that meets the two technical requirements of stability and meaningfulness as well as the empirical requirement of validity. Generally speaking, profit maximization can be made perfectly meaningful (with some qualifications); but when made meaningful, it usually turns out to be invalid as a description of firm behavior. To achieve validity, we can substitute utility maximization; but this turns out to be either not stable or not meaningful. Thus, Machlup, who set out to save the profit maximization assumption be generalizing it to utility maximization, ended by reducing it largely to a definition[12] insofar as a micro theory is concerned. With few exceptions, modern observers of actual firm behavior report persistent and significant contradictions between firm behavior and the classical assumptions.[13]

Despite their inadequacies, the assumptions have persisted. They have persisted for a simple but compelling reason. The alternative mode of theory—the process description of a conflict system —also has generally failed to satisfy its technical requirements. Until quite recently, case descriptions of the decision process in a business firm had approximately the same impact on a theorist of economic behavior as experiments on ESP had on a theorist of human perception. They were horror stories. They tended to demonstrate that there existed some unexplained variance in received theories. They did not provide us devices for reducing the variance. No matter how much we might think we knew about the decision process within the firm, we had no analytical apparatus for dealing with a process model. Such a disability means that few of the implications of the process could be determined except by direct observation and that a revised theory of the firm could not satisfactorily be grafted to existing economic theory. For most economists, such difficulties have seemed of decisive importance.

Studies of political conflict systems.

Whatever the reason may be, analytical disabilities appear to have had less impact on the development of political science than

[12]F. Machlup, "Marginal Analysis and Empirical Research," *American Economic Review,* 36 (1946), 519-554; F. Machlup, "Rejoinder to an Antimarginalist," *American Economic Review,* 37 (1947), 148-154.

[13]For example, R. L. Hall and C. J. Hitch, "Price Theory and Business Behavior," in T. Wilson, ed., *Oxford Studies in Price Mechanisms* (Oxford, 1951); B. Fog, *Industrial Pricing Policies* (Amsterdam, 1960); Cyert and March, *op. cit.*

on economics. There is no political theory in the sense in which there is economic theory; and with only a few exceptions, little effort has been made to develop analytically tractable theories of political conflict systems. Generally speaking, there has been little pressure for simplification comparable to the pressure for simplification in the theory of the firm imposed by the needs of aggregation. The major exception (and only a partial one) is the study of international relations. In some treatments of bargaining among nation states, attempts have been made to characterize the behavior of the individual states in terms of simple models analogous in a loose way to the marginalist assumptions of economic theory.[14]

Most conspicuous by its absence in most of the modern literature on political conflict resolution is the imputation of a superordinate goal to political organizations. Except for some students of international relations, most modern observers have viewed concepts of the "general will," "national interest," or the "common interest" as unsatisfactory concepts in the development of a theory of how political systems behave. "Public interest" as a theoretical tool suffers from the standard problems of superordinate goals. It is almost impossible to make it simultaneously meaningful, stable, and valid. Because of such difficulties and because the existence of unresolved conflict is conspicuous in political systems, students of such systems have moved heavily toward process descriptive case studies of specific political organizations or decisions. By and large, these case studies have not yielded a set of theoretical propositions on which there is general agreement. The richness of specific case detail has tended to emphasize the uniqueness of the cases rather than contribute to theoretical model building.

Nevertheless, the basic outline of a process-oriented political theory of conflict resolution can be detected.[15] The theory assumes that there exist various interest groups in the system and that these groups make various demands. It further assumes that decisions within the system on the allocation of resources (i.e., in response to demands) are made by coalitions of interest groups and that each potential coalition has a certain potential control over the system. The process postulated is one in which a broker—the politician—

[14] A. Rapoport, "Lewis Richard's Mathematical Theory of War," *Journal of Conflict Resolution*, 1 (1957), 249-299.

[15] For example, see D. B. Truman, *The Governmental Process* (New York, 1951); R. A. Dahl and C. E. Lindblom, *Politics, Economics, and Welfare* (New York, 1953).

attempts to organize a coalition of interests that is viable (that is, one in which the demands are less than or equal to the resources available to the coalition). The theory ordinarily highlights phenomena such as bargaining, compromise, negotiation, inconsistency, and more or less continual conflict. In the descriptions of political systems there is an emphasis of power, internal struggle, and expediency; a de-emphasis of order, cooperation, and problem solving.

Insofar as the interest group theory of political decision making is a theory, it is a theory with modest analytic pretensions but rather impressive generality as a framework for observation. Most recent students of political organizations accept it in one form or another despite the obvious fact that the theory neither is particularly well-defined nor has a particularly powerful language. Thus, where the economic theory of the firm has moved to the imputation of a superordinate goal in order to gain analytic simplicity, the political theory of decision making has moved to process description in order to gain empirical validity.

THE FIRM AS A POLITICAL COALITION

The choice between an analytically elegant but empirically sterile theory on the one hand and an empirically fecund but analytically crude theory on the other is hardly a happy choice. Nor, I think, any longer a necessary one. To illustrate, let me outline a revised theory of the business firm and particularly a revised theory of the goals of a business firm. It is a theory that in some respects is more pristinely classic than many currently conventional economic conceptions of the firm, but it also bears a rather close relationship to current conceptions of political conflict systems. It is a theory that R. M. Cyert and I have used in developing some behavioral models of business firm decision making.[16]

Basically, we assume that a business firm is a political coalition and that the executive in the firm is a political broker. The composition of the firm is not given; it is negotiated. The goals of the firm are not given; they are bargained.

We assume that there is a set of potential participants in the firm. At least initially, we think of such classes of potential participants as investors (stockholders), suppliers, customers, governmental agents, and various types of employees. More realistically, we

[16] Cyert and March, *op. cit.*

might supplement such a list with such actual or potential participants as investment analysts, trade associations, political parties, and labor unions. Each potential participant makes demands on the system. These demands are essentially the price required for participation in the coalition. The demands are partly in the form of payments commonly assumed in economic theories (e.g., money) but they also are partly in the form of demands for policy commitments, personal treatment, etc. Thus, each set of demands can be characterized as having some degree of consistency with each combination of other demands. Some pairs of demands may be strictly inconsistent (under no circumstances can they both be satisfied). Some pairs of demands may be more or less consistent depending on external conditions (e.g., so long as the resources available to the coalition are substantial they may be consistent). Some pairs of demands may be completely complementary (e.g., if one demand is satisfied so also is the other one necessarily and without additional resource expenditure). As a result of this complementarity, we can describe the marginal "cost" of any participant to any given coalition.

At the same time, we assume that the demands of the potential participants are subject to two important dynamic properties. First, the level of demands shifts in response to experience (both actual and vicarious). Second, attention to demands—the extent to which they are seen as relevant to action—shifts in response to the perception of problems.

We also assume that each possible coalition of participants has a certain "value" with respect to the environment involved. It can gain a certain return from that environment. Thus, an over-simple model of a governmental coalition in a parliamentary democracy might assume that any coalition including more than 50% of the voters would be able to do anything permissible within the system (thus would have maximum power) and that any coalition including less than 50% of the voters would be able to do nothing (thus would have minimum power). In a similar way, alternative business coalitions can gain different returns from the economic system in which they operate; and we can (at least approximately) specify the marginal value of a particular given participant to a particular given coalition.

One way (not the only one) of describing the theory is from the point of view of the executive. Assume that the executive wishes to use the organization to maximize his own utility. His problem then is (insofar as he is able) to select a coalition so as to maximize the difference between the demands of his coalition members and the potential return from the environment of the coalition. The executive-political broker problem is twofold. On the one hand, he must select a coalition that has relatively low "costs" of maintenance and relatively high returns from the environment. On the other hand, he must so structure the payments made to coalition members as to make the shifts in demands conducive to increasing the difference between total demands and total resources. The theory to this point becomes well-defined when we can specify the dimensions of participant demands, some measure of their complementarity, the functions by which they change over time, and the short run internal constraints on the bargaining process by which goals are formed.

The terms "marginal cost" and "marginal value" suggest the sense in which this theory of business coalitions is close to classic economic views. Why do we describe the coalition involved as a political coalition? There are four critical ways in which the theory deviates from conventional economic views in the direction of a more "political" treatment.

First, the focus of attention shifts from the owners (and their objectives) to the actual, operating organizers of the coalition—whoever they may be. In general, we view stockholders much as a theory of political systems might view citizens. Their demands form loose constraints on the more active members of the coalition. Their initiative in policy formation and in determining the nature of the coalitions is small.

Second, the theory emphasizes the non-uniqueness of short run solutions to the coalition problem. At any point in time, there are a number of possible coalitions that are viable (that is, their total value exceeds their total cost of maintenance). As in the case of most political theories, some of the more interesting features of the theory depend on short run deviations from a long run position of equilibrium.

Third, the theory does not solve the problem of conflict by simple payments to participants and agreement on a superordinate goal. Rather it emphasizes the importance of policy demands and payments and of sequential rather than simultaneous mediation of demands.

Fourth, the theory emphasizes the importance of institutional constraints on the solution of the coalition problem. Most conspicuously there are constraints imposed (1) by the institutionalization of commitments through the organizational structure, precedents, and budgetary agreements, (2) by the reification of attachments through identification and indoctrination, and (3) by the limitations in coordination and control imposed on an executive.

A theory of the business firm as a political coalition has both face validity and a certain amount of empirical support. In particular, such a theory seems more consistent than other available theories with the following widely observed attributes of business decision making:

1. Organization goals seem to be a series of more or less independent constraints.
2. Business firms seem to tolerate a rather large amount of apparent inconsistency in goals and decisions, both over time and from one part of the organization to another.
3. Goals and decisions tend to be paired and decentralized with loose cross connections.
4. The extent to which decisions within the firm involve extensive conflict and "marginal" decisions varies with the munificence of the environment.
5. The goals and commitments of business firms shift slowly over time in response to shifts in the coalition represented in the firm.

The fact (if it is one) that a description of a business firm as a political coalition is a more valid description than the classic economic description of the firm as an entrepreneur does not, however, solve the theoretical dilemma posed by the classic problems of analysis. For many years, economists as well as others have belabored the point that firms are organizations rather than entrepreneurs; only in the last few years have such strictures had any impact on the theory of the firm. Those students who were prepared to accept the evidence had no choice but to abandon not only the theory but also the field, since few of them were sympathetic intellectually with the journalist role implicit in the proliferation of case studies.

In recent years, the introduction of the computer and the computer program model to the repertoire of the theorist has changed dramatically the theoretical potential of process description models of conflict systems. Complex process description models of organizational behavior permit the development of a micro-economic theory of the firm. To illustrate, let me mention briefly three specific models:

First, a model of discretionary pricing and ordering decisions in a large department store. Cyert, March, and Moore have been able to simulate quite well three kinds of pricing decisions: regular pricing, scheduled sale pricing, and markdown pricing. In addition, they have been able to predict the amount and timing of orders (both original orders and reorders) with (as nearly as can be determined) reasonable accuracy.[17]

Second, a model of output determination in a duopoly, the American Can industry. On the basis of a few theoretical assumptions about differences between American and Continental Can Companies, Cyert, Feigenbaum, and March have been able to develop a model of decision-making within the industry. This model predicts quite well both the profit ratio of the two firms and their share of market over the 1913-1956 period.[18]

Third, a general model of price and output determination. As a framework for other specific models and as a basis for investigation of the macro-economic implications of a behavioral theory of the firm (including the assumption that the firm is a political coalition), Cohen, Cyert, March, and Soelberg have developed a general model of price and output determination in a modern oligopoly. The model has not been fully analyzed, but preliminary results seem to indicate a general correspondence between the output of the model and empirical data.[19]

Each of these models is written in the language of a computer program. All of them are process description models. Other comparable models of organizational behavior built on assumptions that differ in detail but are generally process descriptive, are in various stages of development. Balderston and Hoggatt have developed a model of the wholesale lumber market.[20] Howard has developed a model of another wholesale market.[21] Clarkson has developed a

[17] *Ibid.*

[18] *Ibid.*

[19] *Ibid.*

[20] F. E. Balderston and A. C. Hoggatt, *The Simulation of Market Processes* (Berkeley, 1960).

[21] J. A. Howard, *Marketing: Executive and Buyer Behavior* (New York, forthcoming), Chap. 2.

model of the investment decisions of a trust bank.[22] Haines has developed a model of decision making by an experimental group playing a complex business game.[23]

Not all of these models assume that the best characterization of a business firm is as a political coalition; however, they all illustrate the point that we are now in a position to explore the implications of viewing the firm as such a coalition. Process-descriptive, computer models are a natural form of theory in this area. As a result, theoretically oriented students of the firm can afford to take seriously the detailed case studies of conflict systems both economic and political. For example, the recent work on a behavioral theory of the firm described briefly above has drawn rather heavily on political concepts. Within these models, it has been possible to introduce such "political" features as unmediated conflict, multi-dimensional goals, and sequential attention to sub-unit pressures.

IMPLICATIONS FOR THE STUDY OF POLITICAL CONFLICT SYSTEMS

With a few exceptions, studies of political conflict systems have been largely atheoretical or quasi-theoretical in the past. Lacking an adequate theoretical language, we have had to work within the confines of simple verbal formulations. Nevertheless, some of these formulations seem to contribute to an understanding of the operation of the business firm, particularly when they are introduced into computer models of organizational decision making. In the context of such models, I think it is quite likely that we will be able to expose both the theory of the firm as a coalition and the theory of political coalitions in general to new analytic attention.

Thus, we can identify three major implications for political science of recent research on the business firm as a decision making coalition: (1) Recent experience indicates that the business firm can plausibly be conceived as a political conflict system; indeed the firm provides a useful test of the extent to which political phenomena are modified by a non-governmental setting. (2) Successes with computer program models in the analysis of political systems within business firms support the view that computer programs provide

[22] G. P. E. Clarkson, *Portfolio Selection: A Simulation of Trust Investment* (New York, 1962).

[23] G. H. Haines, Jr., "The Rote Marketer," *Behavioral Science*, 6 (1961), 357-365.

a powerful language for treatment of political conflict systems generally. (3) The apparent theoretical similarity between the political coalition in business and the political coalition in governmental organizations suggests that the substantive features of recent behavioral models of the firm may be useful as a basis for comparable models of governmental decision making.

Finally, we should identify the major theoretical job that remains to be done. Although they are adaptive in many respects, the models of firm decision making discussed above have not gone beyond the static implications of the fact that firms are political coalitions. Essentially they assert that certain phenomena occur in the firm because of its character as a coalition. They do not attempt to reflect shifts in coalitions per se. The latter task—leading to a more general theory of coalition development—has hardly been touched except conceptually. The significance of such a theory to a theory of the business firm and its growth is obvious. Even more obvious, however, is the significance of such a theory to the development of a theory of politics.

[6]

The Governance of Hybrid Organizational Forms

Claude Ménard[1]

This paper analyzes 'hybrid' organizational forms. The main idea is that hybrid forms are a distinctive governance structure, implemented in order to supplement incomplete contractual relationships developed among partners involved in joint transactions. Based on recent and ongoing studies, the paper explores the key role of AUTHORITY in the capacity of hybrid forms, under certain conditions, to allocate resources more efficiently than other arrangements. The paper also examines the role of this device in the sharing of rents among partners.

Classification *JEL*: A1; D2; L1; L2

Introduction

The attention of economists has, for a long time, been almost exclusively centered on the markets and their characteristics. Nevertheless, transaction cost economics, derived from the pioneering work of Coase (1937), altered this state of mind by emphasizing the role of 'hierarchies', or formal organizations, as being an alternative method in supporting transactions (Williamson, 1975, 1985). But, it quickly became clear that the market/organization pair did not sufficiently reflect the diversity of these 'governance structures'.

The uncertain description of the interspersed forms within the two polar cases finally opened the door to a new concept, that of 'hybrid forms' (Williamson, 1991). This concept covers a wide variety of arrangements, such as franchise, long-term inter-firm contracts, cyber businesses, lending consistency by identifying the characteristics that they have in common, in particular, the partial transfer of the power to allocate resources without a simultaneous transfer of property rights. More precisely, the hybrid forms represent a category of 'governance structures' that assures control over transactions involving a significant dependence between the assets held by independent units, without having this specificity justify the integration into a unified business. We are therefore in a situation where the dependence requires a continuous relationship as well as control and coordination mechanisms more powerful than those of the market, however, without the necessity of establishing an entity that is economically and legally unified. The question therefore is to find out exactly what the properties are with regard to such structures.

The objective of this paper is to examine some of these properties with the help of recent studies carried out in very diversified fields, from the agro-food sector to biotechnology. I will concentrate on one area, the governance of these hybrid forms. I will maintain that there exists a specific method of 'government' of these forms, intended to stabilize the shortcomings of the contractual relationship, calling on a principle of *authority*, clearly different from the hierarchical relationship as well as the price relationship that are characteristic of organizations and markets respectively. To develop further this point of view, I will first examine certain distinctive features of contracts specific to hybrid forms. In a second part, I will analyze the nature and the role of authority as a method of governance, applying it to the case of sharing of rents that is particularly problematic when it is part of such an arrangement.

The Nature of Hybrid Forms

My analysis of hybrid forms comes within the scope of neo-institutional economics where the term originated. While the content of the concept is present in Coase (1937), we must call on Davis and North (1971) to explicitly recognize the diversity of 'institutional arrangements' serving as vectors for transactions. It is precisely these agreements that Williamson (1985, 1991) will later describe as 'governance structures'.

The Basic Model

The deciding step in the identification of the nature of hybrid forms results from the operationalization effort of the concept of transaction costs, as per Williamson. Beginning in the 1970s he developed a research program now well known where he describes the transactions in such a way that their costs may explain the relative advantages of a certain governance structure. There are three characteristics of transactions that must be taken into account: the *uncertainty* affecting a transaction (or a family of homogenous transactions), the *frequency* in which it takes place and most of all, the *degree of specificity* of the assets involved in the transaction.

Therefore, a strong hypothesis is put forth (Williamson, 1985, 1991), i.e., the alignment, in order to minimize transaction costs, from certain governance structures to certain types of transactions. Asset specificity, the variable that is most often tested (Shelanski and Klein, 1995), supports the proposition that the market constitutes the most efficient structure (the less expensive in terms of transaction costs) when the level of specificity of the assets is low, while the integrated organization has a comparative advantage in the governance of transactions involving assets with a high level of specificity. But what happens when the degree of specificity is intermediate, high enough to create a bilateral dependence requiring a more precise reciprocal coordination and control than the markets allow; but too low to justify the integration into a unique business, where the 'administrative' costs are likely to cancel out the gains on the transaction costs? This is where the hybrid organizational form comes into play. It is set precisely where competition and collaboration unite, it coincides with the structures identified by Gibbons et al. (1994, chapter 2) in the field of new technologies, where there exists: (**i**) a strong competition between independent businesses fighting for market shares; (**ii**) but, also, cooperation, which is necessary because of the need to share the high cost of research and development expenses, and because the selection by the market has more to do with groups than individual businesses (selection of a standard for quality, of technical standards, of configuration of an object).

Williamson (1991) has summarized his hypothesis regarding the tradeoffs among alternative modes of organization in the following representation, where M represents market, H hybrid form and O organization. If we admit that the economic entities try to minimize their transaction costs, then they should be situated on the inferior envelope of the curves, which explains (and may eventually guide) their choices regarding the structure best adapted to govern the corresponding family of transactions.

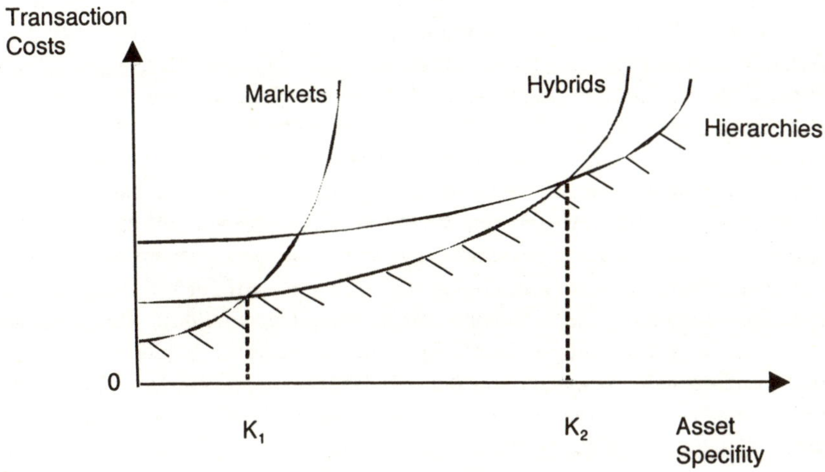

Figure 1: The tradeoffs among organizational forms

Then the question that arises is that of the property of hybrid forms likely to explain its comparative advantage when transactions have the expected characteristics, for example, a moderate level of specificity of the assets involved.

A Specific Contractual Arrangement

A topic that is particularly important to our discussion concerns the contractual relationship between entities involved in a hybrid organizational form. Inter-firm R & D agreements (for example in the field of biotechnology), franchise relationships as well as certain agro-food arrangements (for example, the poultry label) are examples that substantially clarify this point.

Transaction cost economics suggests the existence of a category of contracts specific to the hybrid form, often called 'neo-classical contracts' (Williamson, 1985, chapter 3). If C is the contract relating to a transaction; p is the price; k is the degree of specificity of the assets involved and s represents the safeguard clause, we would have the relationship (Williamson, 1991):

$$C = C\ (p, k, s)$$

Given the characteristics of the transactions for which the hybrid form has a relative advantage, the theory predicts that in its contractual arrangement, the 'neo-classical' contract, prices play a lesser role than in classical market contracts, while the presence of a strong complementarity of assets will put considerable emphasis on the clauses relating to the pooling of these assets, most particularly the safeguard clauses, that are difficult to precisely define and leave a great margin for interpretation, leading to the apparition of adaptation mechanisms, a subject that I will come back to later.

Numerous empirical studies, in the field of transportation, energy, poultry, distribution (franchise), strengthen and clarify this hypothesis. It seems, in fact, that the hybrid forms generally involve *multilateral contracts*, with the presence of a significant number of partners having specific and complementary assets at their disposal. This characteristic, coupled with the uncertainty affecting future transactions, leads to a weakening of the price variable as an adjustment variable. In almost all of the cases studied, procedures are set out for the intention of harmonizing prices and smoothing them out from one period to the next. Such procedures reveal that the management of specific assets tends to predominate in these contracts (elevated value of k), while the safeguard clauses are revealed to be complex and difficult to implement (we may refer to the control of the 'free rider' in agreements in which partners are pooling their resources for the development of a new technology or a truly innovative product). These contracts are, in most cases, *long-term contracts*, or *short-term contracts with an almost automatic renewal*. For example, in the poultry industry, the contracts theoretically relate to a lot, but are in fact almost systematically renewed (Knoeber, 1989; Ménard, 1996b). This characteristic is supported by the importance of continuity of the relationship between the partners as a condition for efficiency when complementarity of the assets exists.

Finally, the contracts of hybrid form carry *clauses of adaptation and control* directed at protecting the partners from opportunistic behaviors. Such behaviors are promoted by bilateral dependence inherent in the complementarity of the assets and will often magnify the significant disturbances of the environment. This results in high contractual risks ('*contractual hazards*'), in particular the risk of a 'hold up' of the rent generated by the hybrid arrangement (Klein et al., 1978). We may classify these clauses into four types. **[a]** First of all, we find clauses that provide *procedures for the resolution* of conflicts that may arise in cases of significant environmental disturbances. A recurring example is that of the procedures that provide for the management and distribution of costs resulting from exogenous shock (e.g., multiparty committee; designation of the procedures that would arbitrate the adjustments required between partners). **[b]** These contracts systematically define a *tolerance zone* with regard to certain key variables, for example, prices (fluctuation margins are forecasted with regard to prices fixed *ex ante*, or with regard to an adjustment index), or quality (hence, acceptable variation margins are defined, indicating a range for the rejection rate that is considered tolerable), **[c]** *Procedures for disclosure of information*, for example information that is to be supplied (to which partners and under which circumstances), or yet, the indicators agreed upon *ex ante* by the partners, are also included in the typical contracts for hybrid forms. They try to guarantee a certain transparency of the reasons that may lead to unforeseen adjustments. **[d]** Finally, we systematically find *arbitration procedures* intended to avoid recourse to procedures outside the arrangement (for example, the courts), a recourse that would be expensive and would put the continuity of the relationship between the partners at risk. Such clauses are all the more important, strictly speaking, since the hybrid form does not contain any hierarchical system that would tend to use its discretionary power for arbitration. These procedures may possess a rather mechanical character, a type of clause that is 'take-or-pay', or, on the contrary, be of a more 'organic' nature, for example, the approval *ex ante* of the design of a system for solving disagreements.

All these contractual characteristics point in the same direction: they try to establish coordination between the partners to the transaction in situations where the market indicators are not sufficient or are available too late, and where these partners remain legally autonomous. It remains to be seen how the implementation of the contractual relationship, full of holes, translates with regard to effective governance of the hybrid form.

Modes of Governance

How can we fill in the amount of 'blanks' that we have just identified, given that the hybrid form does not possess a hierarchical system that would act as a 'court of appeal of last resort' as is the case in an integrated organization? The answer lies in the establishment of methods, supplement to the contracts, methods that would take form under an *AUTHORITY*, distinct from the hierarchical relationship as well as the market relationship. These properties are particularly important in managing the sharing of the rent, given the imbrications of property rights in the hybrid form.

Authority

I have developed elsewhere a number of justifications concerning the introduction of the authority relationship as a specific method of governance, distinct from the hierarchical relationship (Ménard, 1994, 1996a, 1996b).

The hierarchical relationship constitutes the hard core of coordination in an integrated organization. It is characterized by the existence of *non-negotiable* asymmetries, where a 'superior' holds the control and supervision rights. Also the *ability to command* is crucial: the superior may assign tasks in a rather discretionary manner, determine the respective positions for the members, and constrain their actions (within the limits defined in the institutional environment: labor law, etc.). Formally, the hierarchy defines an order, described by an inversed tree. The ability to command is supported by the asymmetry of *property* rights, which allows the hierarchy to operate as its own court of appeal of last resort (Williamson, 1985, chapter 3).

Therefore, it is clear that this 'hierarchical' relationship does not take into account the methods of coordination at work in the hybrid forms. In the latter, we have, in fact, an arrangement where the property rights of the partners remain distinct and where there is no system with the ability a priori to impose the required arbitrations. This introduces the concept of *AUTHORITY* as a means of knowing what coordination is at work in the hybrid forms. I understand 'authority' as a *delegation by the legally distinct entities of the power of decision-making over a subclass of their operating range*. An entity, **i**, has the authority over entity **j** when **j** consents to the transfer *ex ante* to **i** of the ability for decision-making for a category of operations **A**, all the while maintaining his property rights regarding the effects of this action. Authority may play a part in an integrated organization; but remains in second place with regard to the hierarchical relationship. On the other hand, it is at the *heart of the adaptation mechanism of hybrid forms*. Its main characteristic is *intentionality*, which requires an explicit form of consent between partners and the possibility of reversibility. This requirement of mutual consent signifies that the choices made may always be re-examined: this contributes, for example, to explaining that in the hybrid forms, the contracts are either short term, with an almost tacit renewal; or long term, but with clauses defining the methods for exercising authority (for example, defining the status of certifying organizations in the high quality segment of the poultry industry). In a relationship of authority, the *symmetry* (at least formally) of the property rights leads to the problem of the efficiency of the system responsible for implementing the decisions of common interest, resulting in explicit mechanisms for determination of choices (as is the case for an assembly of co-owners), or mechanisms calling for reciprocal confidence.

This point brings about the question of possible methods of exercising this authority. I will identify four methods of governance, from the weakest to the most formal. The first method relates to the *influence* that certain entities may exercise over others, for historical reasons (for example, taking the initiative: LOUÉ is an illustration of this within the poultry label), for competency reasons (when certain decisions are turned over to the most experienced partner, for example, in a network of R & D), or for connivance reasons (e.g., one of the partners benefits from the concentrated listening of the public decision-makers who distribute research assistance). A second method relates to *confidence*. Powell (1996) displayed this with regard to biotechnology. In sectors that are evolving rapidly, with uncertainty affecting the transactions between partners, the contractual relationship is often replaced by other more efficient forms of cooperation, founded in mutual confidence developed in the continuity of the transactional relationship (reputation therefore plays the role of the safeguard clause). A third, even stronger method, relates to *leadership*. In the pharmaceutical industry, the R & D agreements between a large business and a group of small businesses carrying out the latest research often depends on the financial and decision-making abilities of the strongest partner, despite the formal equality of rights. However we must not confuse this arrangement with subcontracting: when the technological assets and the know-how are greatly specific, the ability to innovate of small entities is a determinant and bilateral dependence tends to develop further. Finally, in the last method, the authority may exercise its rights in a more formal and constraining manner with the creation of an '*ad hoc institution*' responsible for establishing order in the relationships among the participants. This is the case with the executive council in a co-ownership, in which this private 'government' subjects the represented parties to a set of rules that are themselves often stabilized by a public order (the assemblies are, for example, subjected to a regulation).

Therefore, authority corresponds to the *establishment of a private order* between autonomous entities. It constitutes a discretionary method of governance, distinct from the hierarchical relationship specific to integrated organizations, but also from a pure market relationship based on adjustment by prices. With regard to the methods of governance mentioned above, the transaction cost theory allows putting forth a testable proposition: *the more the assets involved in the transaction are specific the greater the authority will be. The presence of a high degree of uncertainty strengthens this tendency*. Therefore, in an environment that is relatively stable with a degree of specificity that is relatively weak, influence should prevail. When uncertainty increases and/or when the assets become more specific, the authority becomes stronger and culminates in the creation of an ad hoc institution. In this last form, we approach the boundaries of the integrated organization.

Sharing of the Rent

One of the major problems that the *authority* must manage is that of the sharing of the rent generated by the hybrid form. This problem results from the specificity of this arrangement regarding property rights and the difficulty in implementing the distribution mechanisms when taking into account the importance of the non-observable factors and the risk of opportunistic behavior.

The specificity of the allocation of property rights clearly appears in the businesses operating by network to ensure the production of new knowledge. The unpredictable character of the results, but also the difficulty, or the impossibility, of *ex ante* valuing of the respective contributions of the partners, resulting from the research, makes contractual specification of the rights and their distribution almost impossible. This problem is, however, not exclusive to the high technology businesses: we also find it in traditional sectors, as soon as strong coordination constraints arise (in the case of the poultry label), or as soon as cooperation generates significant externalities (in the case of franchise systems).

In a developed market economy, the polar structures have a system for allocation of rights that is relatively well defined. In markets or integrated organizations, the rights of 'residual claimants' are relatively well specified.[2] The case of hybrid forms proves to be much more delicate since, by definition, there is a pooling of resources that can generate the rent, but with the maintenance of total or partial separation of property rights. The situation becomes even more complicated when the arrangement results in the private management of the sharing of the rent, but relies on public regulation, as is the case with the certifying organizations in the agro-food sector, or when R & D projects involve the State.

Therefore, the very reason for hybrid forms to exist lies in the pooling of *some* resources between entities otherwise autonomous, so as to produce a rent.[3] But this combination in itself favours opportunistic behaviour, of which the risk increases and at the same rate as the uncertainty affecting the environment. Under these conditions, *the choice of incentive mechanisms* becomes particularly difficult.

A certain number of empirical studies (Knoeber, 1989; Ménard, 1996b; Arrunada et al., 1996) reveal some characteristics that we may divide into two subsets: incentives related to observable data and that result in a governance that is relatively 'automatic'; and incentives related to non-observable elements of the rent, resulting in a governance that is 'discretionary', and in which the *authority* plays the determining role.

The observable component leads to incentive measures that we also find in organizations, to which are added provisions explicitly destined to stabilize the hybrid form. Let me give two examples. One, practiced in poultry farming, leads to the distribution of the rent based on the ordinal classification of the relative performances of the partners (Knoeber, 1989; Ménard, 1996b). We have here a tournament type system, including a component that is in proportion with the relative output, destined to share the risk with the partners and reduce opportunistic behaviors; and a component, for example, in the form of a bonus, depending on the difference of the individual performances compared to the average performances. Another method, observed in the fishing sector (Arrunada et al., 1996), relies on fixed shares relating to costs, with control provisions regarding these costs in order to check on partners whose decisions remain mainly autonomous (which could encourage them to neglect the relative costs); and on flexible shares relating to gains, with weighting according to the specificity of the assets involved. In accordance with the provisions of the theory, these regulation systems are generally short term, but with an almost tacit renewal. As a result, there is some control over the risk of opportunistic behaviors by the threat of non-renewal of the agreement if deviance is observed and by the maintenance of the continuity of the relationship by tacit renewal in the majority of cases.

Evidently the problem becomes more complicated when a significant non-observable component exists. The cases mentioned above were relatively simple due to the observability of the results (poultry, fishing), the uncertainty originating mainly in the efforts of the partners in activities involving strong externalities. The management of the rent in the hybrid form is similar to the management of remunerations for team production. But, in numerous cases, the hybrid form is implemented to confront situations where uncertainty is much greater and is related to the processes themselves. This is the case in R & D agreements, where it is difficult or even impossible to anticipate the contributions of each party (and therefore the determination of the relatively precise contractual clauses *ex ante*) and measuring the weight of these contributions in the final result. The contractual risks ('contractual hazards') therefore are considerable and can only be managed in a discretionary manner. The distribution of the rent depends on the methods used for exercising the *authority*, identified above. Transaction costs economics suggests that *the more the assets involved are specific, the stronger the tendency to substitute an ad hoc form of government for mechanisms such as mutual confidence or leadership in the distribution of the rent.*

Conclusion

In this article, I have tackled the question of the nature of hybrid organizational forms as structures distinct from the polar cases that are markets and organizations. I have focused the attention on the mode of governance of these forms since this is where their adaptation abilities are played out and therefore the conditions of their relative efficiency.

First, I emphasized the characteristics that are specific to contractual relationships that develop in this type of arrangement and have the function of managing the multiplicity of the assets involved, their interdependence and the incompleteness factors that result. Using several recent researches, I have been able to identify the most favorable method of governance of hybrid forms, *authority*, intended to respond to the important shortcomings in contractual relationships. This method of governance is distinguished clearly from the allocation of resources by price, but most of all, from the allocation of resources by hierarchy, such as it is implemented in integrated organizations. I have also determined certain methods of operationalization of the relationship of authority, applying it to the sharing of the rent. Along the way, I have established a significant number of testable propositions, open to argument.

Notes

1. Centre ATOM, Université de Paris I (Panthéon-Sorbonne), 106 Bd de l'Hôpital, 75647-Paris Cedex 13. E-mail: menard@univ-paris l.fr! This paper was initially published as 'Le Pilotage des formes organisationnelles hybrides', *Revue Economique*, **48** (2), 741–51. English translation by Kathy Blair, revised by Claude Ménard.
2. In an integrated business, the 'residual claimants' are the capital holders, and the contracts must specify the share that is owed to the other participants, including the members of the hierarchy.
3. For example, a study of the INAO revealed that in 1992, the gross margin on a kilo of 'live' label poultry was 1,92 F, as compared to 0,67 for standard poultry.

References

Arrunada, B., M. Gonzalez and B. Lopez (1996), 'The Role of Competition in Controlling Team Production: The Case of Fishing Firms', working paper, Universitat Pompeu Fabra.

Coase, R. (1937), 'The Nature of the Firm', *Economica*, **2** (1), 386–405.

Davis, L. and D.C. North (1971), *Institutional Change and American Economic Growth*, Cambridge, UK: Cambridge University Press.

Gibbons, M. et al. (1994), *The New Production of Knowledge*, London: Sage Publications.

Klein, B., R.G. Crawford and A.A. Alchian (1978), 'Vertical Integration, Appropriable Rents and the Competitive Contracting Process', *Journal of Law and Economics*, **21** (2), 297–326.

Knoeber, C. (1989), 'A Real Game of Chicken: Contracts, Tournaments, and the Production of Broilers', *Journal of Law, Economics and Organization*, **5** (2), 271–92.

Ménard, C. (1994), 'Organization as Coordinating Devices', *Metroeconomica*, **45** (3), 224–47.

Ménard, C. (1996a), 'Inside the Black Box', in John Groenewegen (ed.), *Transaction Costs and Beyond*, Dordrecht and Boston: Kluwer Academic Press, pp. 149–70.

Ménard, C. (1996b), 'On Clusters, Hybrids and Other Strange Forms. The Case of the French Poultry Industry', *Journal of Institutional and Theoretical Economics*, **152** (1), 154–83.

Powell, W. (1996), 'Trust-Based Forms of Governance', in Roderick M. Kramer et al., *Trust in Organizations*, London: Sage Publications, pp. 51–67.

Shelanski, H.A. and P.G. Klein (1995), 'Empirical Research in Transaction Cost Economics: A Review and Assessment', *Journal of Law, Economics and Organization*, **7** (2), 335–61.

Williamson, O.E. (1975), *Markets and Hierarchies*, New York: The Free Press.

Williamson, O.E. (1985), *The Economic Institutions of Capitalism*, New York: The Free Press.

Williamson, O.E. (1991), 'Comparing Economic Organizations: The Analysis of Discrete Structural Analysis', *Administrative Science Quarterly*, **36** (2), 269–96.

[7]

RELATIONAL CONTRACTS AND THE THEORY OF THE FIRM*

George Baker
Robert Gibbons
Kevin J. Murphy

Relational contracts—informal agreements sustained by the value of future relationships—are prevalent within and between firms. We develop repeated-game models showing why and how relational contracts within firms (vertical integration) differ from those between (nonintegration). We show that integration affects the parties' temptations to renege on a given relational contract, and hence affects the best relational contract the parties can sustain. In this sense, the integration decision can be an instrument in the service of the parties' relationship. Our approach also has implications for joint ventures, alliances, and networks, and for the role of management within and between firms.

I. Introduction

Firms are riddled with relational contracts: informal agreements and unwritten codes of conduct that powerfully affect the behaviors of individuals within firms. There are often informal quid pro quos between coworkers, as well as unwritten understandings between bosses and subordinates about task-assignment, promotion, and termination decisions.[1] Even ostensibly formal processes such as compensation, transfer pricing, internal auditing, and capital budgeting often cannot be understood without consideration of their associated informal agreements.[2]

Business dealings are also riddled with relational contracts. Supply chains often involve long-run, hand-in-glove supplier relationships through which the parties reach accommodations when unforeseen or uncontracted-for events occur.[3] Similar rela-

* We are grateful for research support from the Division of Research at the Harvard Business School (Baker); the Massachusetts Institute of Technology's Sloan School and Center for Innovation in Product Development, and the National Science Foundation (through grant SBR-9809107) (Gibbons); and the University of Southern California Marshall School (Murphy). We thank Alexander Dyck, Oliver Hart, Rebecca Henderson, Bengt Holmstrom, Edward Lazear, Patrick Legros, Jonathan Levin, Bentley MacLeod, John Matsusaka, Kevin Murdoch, Canice Prendergast, Julio Rotemberg, Steven Tadelis, Michael Waldman, Michael Whinston, the referees, and especially Benjamin Klein for helpful comments.

1. Many observers have emphasized the importance of informal agreements in organizations, including Barnard [1938], Simon [1947], Selznick [1949], Gouldner [1954], and Blau [1955].

2. See Lawler [1971] on compensation, Eccles [1985] on transfer pricing, Dalton [1959] on internal auditing, and Bower [1970] on capital budgeting.

3. Macaulay [1963] emphasized the importance of such "non-contractual

The Quarterly Journal of Economics, February 2002

tionships also exist horizontally, as in the networks of firms in the fashion industry or the diamond trade, and in strategic alliances, joint ventures, and business groups.[4] Whether vertical or horizontal, these relational contracts influence the behaviors of firms in their dealings with other firms.

Relational contracts within and between firms help circumvent difficulties in formal contracting (i.e., contracting enforced by a third party, such as a court). For example, a formal contract must be specified ex ante in terms that can be verified ex post by the third party, whereas a relational contract can be based on outcomes that are observed by only the contracting parties ex post, and also on outcomes that are prohibitively costly to specify ex ante. A relational contract thus allows the parties to utilize their detailed knowledge of their specific situation and to adapt to new information as it becomes available. For the same reasons, however, relational contracts cannot be enforced by a third party and so must be self-enforcing: the value of the future relationship must be sufficiently large that neither party wishes to renege.[5]

In this paper we develop repeated-game models of relational contracts both within and between firms. We show why and how relational contracts within firms differ from those between. In particular, we find that integration affects the parties' temptations to renege on a given relational contract. Thus, in a given environment, a desirable relational contract might be feasible under integration but not under nonintegration (or the reverse). This result motivates a new perspective on vertical integration: a major factor in the vertical-integration decision is whether integration or nonintegration facilitates the superior relational con-

relations" between various businesses. Dore [1983] was the first of many to describe Japanese supply relationships in these terms; see Cusumano and Takeishi [1991], Nishiguchi [1994], and Sako and Helper [1998] for recent contributions.

4. In "Neither Market Nor Hierarchy: Network Forms of Organization," Powell [1990] describes a variety of networks and emphasizes their differences from markets and firms; see Podolny and Page [1998] for a summary and critique of subsequent work. On alliances, see Gerlach [1991] and Gulati and Singh [1998]; on joint ventures, Kogut [1989] and Pisano [1989]; on business groups, Granovetter [1995] and Dyer [1996]; and on "virtual" firms, Chesbrough and Teece [1996].

5. Accordingly, contracts we call "relational" are sometimes called "self-enforcing" [Telser 1981; Klein 1996], "implicit" [MacLeod and Malcomson 1989], or both [Bull 1987]. Our use of "relational" follows the legal literature, particularly Macneil [1978]. Those who call relational contracts "implicit" naturally call formal contracts "explicit," but this usage risks connoting that implicit contracts are vague, when in practice it is often important that relational contracts be clearly understood.

tract. In short, integration can be an instrument in the service of the parties' relationship.

Section II develops a model in which an upstream party uses an asset to produce a good that can be used in a downstream party's production process. We follow Grossman and Hart's [1986] terminology: when the upstream party owns the asset, we call the transaction nonintegrated—the upstream party is an independent contractor, working with an asset she owns; when the downstream party owns the asset, we call the transaction integrated—the upstream party is an employee, working with an asset owned by the firm. We assume that ownership of the asset conveys ownership of the good. (In fact, the asset could simply be the legal title to the good.) Thus, if the upstream party owns the asset, then the downstream party cannot use the good without buying it from the upstream party, whereas if the downstream party owns the asset, then he already owns the good. In addition, we assume that the good produced by the upstream party can be used either in the downstream party's production process or in an alternative use, and that the upstream party's actions affect the good's value in both these uses.

Under either ownership structure, the downstream party would like the upstream party to take actions that improve the value of the good in the downstream production process. We focus on actions that are unobservable (moral hazard) and outcomes that are observable but not verifiable (noncontractibility). In such a setting, relational contracts can encourage useful actions: the downstream party can promise to pay the upstream party a bonus if she produces a good of high value. Because this promise is based on noncontractible outcomes, it provides incentives to the upstream party only if it is self-enforcing (i.e., the short-run value of reneging must be less than the long-run value of the relationship).

The key question in our analysis is whether choosing appropriate asset ownership (integration or nonintegration) can make a given promise self-enforcing. Under integration, if the downstream party reneges on the bonus, he still owns the good. But under nonintegration, if the downstream party reneges on the bonus, he cannot use the good without buying it for at least its value in its alternative use. In this sense, nonintegration gives the upstream party more recourse if the downstream party should renege on the promised bonus. But nonintegration has a drawback: it creates an incentive for the upstream party to increase the value of the good in its alternative use, in order to improve her bargaining position with the downstream party. These two conflicting effects (recourse and bargaining position) produce our main proposition: integration affects the parties' temptations to renege on a relational contract, and hence affects the best relational contract the parties can sustain.

Our proposition leads to an interesting corollary: in our model, it is impossible for a firm to mimic the spot-market outcome after it brings a transaction inside the firm, because the reneging temptation is then too great. This corollary is a first step toward a formal underpinning for Williamson's [1985, p. 135] observation that "selective intervention" must be impossible: if firms could mimic markets, intervening only when the market outcome would be inefficient, then we would observe one enormous firm. This corollary is also a cautionary tale for those who would "bring the market inside the firm" via empowerment, transfer pricing, performance measurement (such as "Economic Value Added"), and the like; we expand on this in Baker, Gibbons, and Murphy [2001].

We establish our main proposition and its corollary in Section III. In Section IV we explore the implications of our main proposition by deriving five further results. Our first result is that vertical integration is an efficient response to widely varying supply prices, because integration reduces reneging temptations in such situations. Our second result is that high-powered incentives create bigger reneging temptations under integration than under nonintegration, with the consequence that performance payments in relational incentive contracts will be smaller in firms than in (otherwise equivalent) markets. Although our first two results are driven by differences in reneging temptations under relational contracts, qualitatively similar results arise in a static analysis of our model, and in other static models in the tradition of Grossman and Hart. Our third, fourth, and fifth results, however, emphasize unique aspects of our repeated-game approach. Our third result is that, holding all other parameters constant, the optimal integration decision can depend on the discount rate. Our fourth result is that, holding all marginal incentives constant (and hence holding constant the optimal integration decision in the static model), the optimal integration decision can depend on the payoff levels. Finally, our fifth result extends the corollary in Section III: to complement the corollary that a firm cannot mimic the spot-market outcome, we show that a firm may be unable to improve upon the spot-market outcome (even if that outcome is inefficient) because the availability of the spot-market as a fall-back after reneging may render infeasible any desirable relational-employment contract.

Section V concludes by discussing four additional ideas. First, we describe how our approach relates to the extensive sociological literature on the formal and informal aspects of organizational structure. Second, we suggest how our approach can be applied to understanding organizational forms other than firms, such as joint ventures, strategic alliances, and business groups. Third, we explore the implications of our analysis for internal organizational processes such as transfer pricing, capital allocation, compensation, and corporate governance. Finally, we argue that our focus on relational contracts suggests a natural role for managers in the economic theory of the firm: managers formulate, communicate, implement, and change relational contracts. Such management can be as important in relationships between firms as within.

II. Economic Environment

We consider an economic environment consisting of an upstream party, a downstream party, and an asset. Both parties and the asset live forever (or die together at a random date, as per the usual interpretation of "infinitely" repeated games). Both parties are risk-neutral and share the interest rate r per period. Initially, the downstream party owns the asset.

In each period, the upstream party may use the asset to produce a good. The downstream party values the good, but the good also has an alternative use. We assume that the good's value to the downstream party always exceeds its value in the alternative use. (For example, there might be other similar downstream parties but the asset might be tailored to this downstream party's needs. Alternatively, the upstream party might be able to set up shop as a downstream party, but lack the expertise to do so efficiently.) Regardless of how the good is used, its value falls to zero at the end of the period in which it was produced.

Ownership of the asset conveys ownership of the good produced using the asset. That is, if the downstream party owns the asset, then he could simply take the good, refusing to pay the upstream party anything, whereas if the upstream party owns the asset, then she could consign the good to its alternative use, paying no heed to objections from the downstream party.[6] Of course, the latter scenario will not occur: because the value of the good to the downstream party exceeds its value in its alternative use, the efficient outcome when the upstream party owns the asset is for the parties to trade, exchanging money for the good.

Each period, the upstream party chooses a vector of n actions $\mathbf{a} = (a_1, a_2, \ldots, a_n)$ at cost $c(\mathbf{a})$. The actions in a given period affect both the downstream value (Q) and alternative-use value (P) of the good in that period. In particular, the downstream value is either high or low (Q_H or Q_L), the alternative-use value is either high or low (P_H or P_L, where $P_L < P_H < Q_L < Q_H$), and the upstream party's actions affect the probabilities that high values will be realized:

$$Q = \begin{cases} Q_H \text{ with probability} & q(a) \\ Q_L \text{ with probability} & 1 - q(a) \end{cases}$$

$$P = \begin{cases} P_H \text{ with probability} & p(a) \\ P_L \text{ with probability} & 1 - p(a) \end{cases}.$$

Given the upstream party's actions, the downstream and alternative-use values are conditionally independent. We assume that $c(0) = 0$, $q(0) = 0$, and $p(0) = 0$, so that when the upstream party fails to take any actions, she bears no costs but also has no chance of realizing the high outcomes Q_H or P_H. We write $\Delta Q \equiv Q_H - Q_L$ and $\Delta P \equiv P_H - P_L$.

The first-best actions $\mathbf{a}^*$ maximize the expected value of the good in its efficient use minus the cost of actions, $Q_L + q(\mathbf{a})\,\Delta Q - c(\mathbf{a})$, and so produce total surplus

$$S^* \equiv Q_L + q(\mathbf{a}^*)\Delta Q - c(\mathbf{a}^*). \tag{1}$$

The actions are unobservable to anyone but the upstream party, so contracts contingent on actions cannot be enforced. Achieving the first-best would still be possible if contracts dependent on Q could be enforced, but we assume that a contract that depends on

6. As this discussion makes clear, the "asset" in our model could simply be legal title to the good. Similarly, one could interpret our asset-ownership model in terms of alternative contracts between nonintegrated parties, where "downstream asset ownership" corresponds to a specific-performance contract that requires the upstream party to deliver the good to the downstream party and "upstream asset ownership" corresponds to the absence of a contract. We thank a referee for noting this contracting reinterpretation and for suggesting Maskin and Tirole [1999] for further remarks about the analogies between asset-ownership models and contracting models.

the realized value of Q or P cannot be enforced by a third party.[7] On the other hand, both Q and P can be observed by the upstream and downstream parties, so there are two potential ways to influence the upstream party's choice of actions: asset ownership and relational contracts. That is, if the upstream party owns the asset, she can negotiate with the downstream party over the price of the good. Alternatively, independent of who owns the asset, the realized values of Q and P can form the basis of a relational contract sustained by the value of future relationships.

We follow Grossman and Hart in interpreting asset ownership as integration, but our multitask economic environment is closer in spirit to Holmstrom and Milgrom [1991], Holmstrom and Tirole [1991], and especially Holmstrom [1999], except that these multitask models are static and hence analyze formal rather than relational contracts. As an illustration of our environment, consider the following two-dimensional linear example: the vector of actions has two components, $\mathbf{a} = (a_1, a_2)$, and the production functions $q(\mathbf{a})$ and $p(\mathbf{a})$ are

$$q(\mathbf{a}) = q_1 a_1 + q_2 a_2,$$

and

$$p(\mathbf{a}) = p_1 a_1 + p_2 a_2,$$

where $q_1, q_2, p_1, p_2 \geq 0$. This example nests two standard cases: (1) one-dimensional effort ($q_2 = p_2 = 0$), where attempts to increase the probability of realizing the high alternative-use value (P_H) also increase the probability of the high downstream value (Q_H), and (2) unproductive multitasking ($q_2 = p_1 = 0$), where attempts to influence P are costly but have no effect on Q, and so strictly reduce social surplus. Other values of q_1, q_2, p_1, and p_2 capture cases such as academics, where research contributes to internal and external productivity ($q_1, p_1 > 0$), but ad-

7. As in most of the incomplete-contracts literature, we acknowledge but do not model the role for formal contracts. That is, we interpret Q and P as representing the noncontractible elements of the exchange between the upstream and downstream parties, and assume that the contractible (i.e., observable and verifiable) elements are covered through formal contracts. As an illustration of the potential importance of relational contracts even in the presence of formal contracts, see Blumenstein and Stern [1996] on how the 1700-page contract between General Motors and the United Auto Workers has important gaps that are covered by informal agreements. But note that our suppression of the formal contracts in our analysis ignores potential interactions between the noncontractible and contractible elements of exchange; see Baker, Gibbons, and Murphy [1994], Bernheim and Whinston [1998], and Che and Yoo [2001] for analyses of such interactions.

	Ownership Environment	
Governance Environment	Nonintegrated Asset Ownership	Integrated Asset Ownership
Spot	Spot Outsourcing	Spot Employment
Relational	Relational Outsourcing	Relational Employment

FIGURE I

Combinations of Ownership and Governance Regimes That Define Four Organizational Forms: Spot Outsourcing, Spot Employment, Relational Outsourcing, and Relational Employment

ministration contributes only to internal value ($q_2 > p_2 = 0$). Section III analyzes our general environment; Section IV focuses on this two-dimensional linear example.

Figure I summarizes the four combinations of asset ownership (upstream or downstream) and governance regimes (spot or relational) that are feasible in this environment. Consistent with common usage, we refer to the vertically integrated case as "employment," and the nonintegrated case as "outsourcing." We therefore call the four governance structures in Figure I "Spot Outsourcing" (where the upstream party owns the asset but there is no relational contract), "Spot Employment" (where the downstream party owns the asset but there is no relational contract), "Relational Employment" (where the downstream party owns the asset and there is a relational contract), and "Relational Outsourcing" (where the upstream party owns the asset and there is a relational contract).

Several of the classic contributions to organizational economics can be described using Figure I. For example, static analyses of integration in the absence of relational contracting (e.g., Grossman and Hart [1986]) are analogous to our comparison of spot outsourcing to spot employment (the top row in Figure I). Similarly, repeated-game analyses of relationships within firms (e.g., Bull [1987]) are analogous to our comparison of spot employment to relational employment (the right column) and repeated-game analyses of relationships between firms (e.g., Klein and Leffler [1981]) are analogous to our comparison of spot outsourcing to relational outsourcing (the left column). Finally, Williamson [1975, Chapters 4 and 5] emphasized that the advantage of firms over markets lies in the firm's ability to enforce relational contracts, which is analogous to our comparison of spot outsourcing to relational employment (the main diagonal).

The central focus of this paper is the comparison of relational outsourcing to relational employment (the bottom row of Figure I). Two important precursors to our analysis are Klein and Williamson. Both begin by arguing that court-enforceable explicit contracts between firms are typically incomplete, but each then focuses on half the story we wish to tell. Klein emphasizes that, under nonintegration, relational contracts between firms often supplement incomplete explicit contracts and a shock may cause one of the firms to renege on the relational contract by enforcing the terms of the explicit contract [Klein, Crawford, and Alchian 1978; Klein 1996, 2000; Klein and Murphy 1988, 1997]. But Klein is virtually silent about life under integration, except to argue that there will not be an explicit contract inside a firm so reneging by enforcing the terms of an explicit contract will not be possible. In contrast, Williamson [1975] built on Simon [1951] to emphasize the importance of relational contracts within firms, but was virtually silent about relational contracts between firms. Subsequently, Williamson [1985, Chapter 3] built on Macneil [1978] to incorporate relational contracts between firms into his framework; in our view, however, this extension allowed for the existence of relational forms of nonintegration but hardly explored their limits or advantages relative to relational contracts within firms.[8]

Our model attempts an even-handed and formal analysis of relational contracts both within and between firms. Compared with Klein's argument, our model emphasizes not only that integration eliminates one important reneging temptation present under nonintegration but also that integration creates its own reneging temptation. Compared with Williamson's [1975] argument, our analysis of the reneging temptation under integration adds an important dimension to Williamson's [1975, Chapter 7; 1985, Chapter 6] discussions of the limitations of integrated gov-

8. Williamson's [1985] main comment about relational contracts between firms was to construe the resulting "hybrid" organizational forms as lying on a continuum between markets and hierarchies [p. 83], and Williamson [1996, Chapter 4] offers a deeper analysis in this spirit. But our Figure I suggests that the set of alternative governance structures is two-dimensional, so it is not possible to locate all governance structures on a line between markets and hierarchies. In this sense, our Figure I is consistent with the large sociological literature beginning with Powell [1990] that argues that networks and other relational forms of nonintegration are not simply "hybrid" combinations of markets and hierarchies.

ernance. Finally, compared with both Klein and Williamson, our formal model derives several key concepts that they treat in reduced form, such as the size of the reneging temptations under nonintegration and integration and the level of "relational capital" that each party could lose if it reneged.

III. Outsourcing and Employment under Spot and Relational Governance

In this section we analyze the four governance structures defined in Figure I. These four separate analyses allow us to derive our main proposition that asset ownership affects reneging temptations in relational contracts.[9] We then conduct a comparative analysis in Section IV.

A. Spot Outsourcing

We first consider spot outsourcing. Once the actions are taken and the good is produced, the upstream party either sells the good to the downstream party or puts the good to its alternative use. Although upstream and downstream cannot contract directly on the realized values of Q and P, they can negotiate over the price of the good. We use the Nash bargaining solution (with equal bargaining powers) to arrive at this price: downstream will pay upstream the alternative-use value, P_j, plus half of the surplus from use by the downstream party, $Q_i - P_j$, so the price is $\frac{1}{2}(Q_i + P_j)$, where $i = H, L$ and $j = H, L$.

The upstream party's payoff under spot outsourcing is the price $\frac{1}{2}(Q_i + P_j)$ less the cost of actions $c(\mathbf{a})$. Upstream therefore chooses actions $\mathbf{a}^{SO}$ to solve

$$(2) \quad \max_{a} \tfrac{1}{2}[Q_L + q(\mathbf{a})\Delta Q] + \tfrac{1}{2}[P_L + p(\mathbf{a})\Delta P] - c(\mathbf{a}) \equiv U^{SO}.$$

The spot-outsourcing actions are thus likely to differ from the first-best actions. For example, consider the extreme case when

9. Garvey [1995] and Halonen [1994] also explore the effect of asset ownership on relational contracting, akin to our models of relational outsourcing and relational employment. Both Garvey and Halonen analyze repeated versions of the original Grossman-Hart model, whereas our static model captures a rich variety of multitask settings. Also, Halonen assumes that ownership is fixed forever, even after reneging on the relational contract, whereas Garvey and we assume that ownership after reneging reverts to the efficient ownership at that point (with an appropriate transfer payment between parties). Finally, Garvey and Halonen do not present the results or interpretations we offer in Sections III, IV, and V.

$\Delta Q = 0$: the downstream party cannot benefit from effort, so the first-best levels of effort are all zero, but the upstream party will expend effort because P_j influences the price of the good under Nash bargaining. More generally, even when ΔQ and ΔP are positive, the upstream party may choose the wrong actions—exerting effort on activities that increase P even if they have no effect on Q.[10]

After Q_i and P_j are realized and trade occurs, the downstream party's total payoff is $Q_i - \frac{1}{2}(Q_i + P_j) = \frac{1}{2}(Q_i - P_j)$. Define $D^{SO} \equiv \frac{1}{2}E[Q_i - P_j | \mathbf{a} = \mathbf{a}^{SO}]$ as downstream's expected payoff under spot outsourcing, conditional on upstream's optimal action choices. The total surplus under spot outsourcing is therefore

$$(3) \qquad S^{SO} \equiv D^{SO} + U^{SO} = Q_L + q(\mathbf{a}^{SO})\Delta Q - c(\mathbf{a}^{SO}).$$

B. Spot Employment

When the downstream party owns the asset but there is no relational contract, the downstream party can simply take the output without paying the upstream party. In anticipation of this outcome, the upstream party will refuse to take any costly actions, so the downstream value of the output will be Q_L with certainty. Thus, the total surplus from spot employment is $S^{SE} = Q_L$, which can again be divided into upstream and downstream components, $U^{SE} + D^{SE} \equiv S^{SE}$. Although we defer our main discussion of the comparative efficiency of spot outsourcing and spot employment until Section IV, we note here that spot employment dominates spot outsourcing only when the net benefit from upstream actions under spot governance is negative, $q(\mathbf{a}^{SO})\Delta Q - c(\mathbf{a}^{SO}) < 0$. This could occur, for example, when the actions that affect the alternative-use value, P, are unproductive or even counterproductive to the downstream value Q, yet under spot outsourcing these actions are undertaken by the upstream party to improve her bargaining position.

Our model of spot employment may seem trivial and unreal-

10. Our model illustrates an important distinction in the literature concerning underinvestment in specific assets. Asset specificity is usually measured in terms of the levels of asset values (for example, $Q_L - P_H > 0$ might be used as a measure of asset specificity in our model), whereas investment decisions are determined by margins (here ΔP and ΔQ). Hence, assets can be very specific ($Q_L \gg P_H$) and yet induce overinvestment (if $\Delta P \gg \Delta Q$). This point is obscured in models that tie asset levels to marginal returns in such a way that asset specificity necessarily produces underinvestment.

istic: the upstream party refuses to take any actions whatsoever with respect to the noncontractible elements of exchange. But recall that we have ignored the possibility of formal contracts. One could add formal contracts and generate situations in which spot employment induces positive (although generally not first-best) effort. We do so in Baker, Gibbons, and Murphy [2001], but in this paper we omit such formal contracts in order to focus on relational contracts.

C. Relational Employment

In relational employment, as in spot employment, the downstream party owns the asset. But in relational employment (like Simon's [1951] employment relationships) there is also a relational contract based on the observable but noncontractible realizations Q and P. We follow Bull [1987] in constructing a repeated-game model of such a relational contract between employer and employee. Unlike the spot-employment case, the relational-employment contract may provide upstream incentives, even though the downstream party owns the asset, provided that the parties value their reputations sufficiently. The core of the analysis is therefore checking whether reputation concerns in fact outweigh the temptation to renege on a given relational contract.

An important part of this calculation is the payoff after reneging. We analyze trigger-strategy equilibria, in which the party who did not renege refuses to enter into any new relational contract with the party who reneged. Because there are only two parties (one downstream and one upstream), this trigger-strategy assumption implies that the parties live under spot governance forever after one reneges. To determine whether such spot governance takes the form of a spot outsourcing or spot employment, we allow the parties to negotiate over asset ownership after reneging. Thus, the downstream party will retain ownership when $S^{SE} > S^{SO}$, but will sell the asset to the upstream party (at some price π) when $S^{SO} > S^{SE}$.

Consider the relational compensation contract $(s, b_{HH}, b_{HL}, b_{LH}, b_{LL}) \equiv (s, \{b_{ij}\})$, where salary s is paid by downstream to upstream at the beginning of each period and b_{ij} is supposed to be paid when $Q = Q_i$ and $P = P_j$, respectively (for $i, j = H, L$). For the moment, suppose that the upstream party is confident that the downstream party will indeed pay b_{ij} as promised (and that the upstream party will make any promised payments if $b_{ij} < 0$).

If the upstream party accepts the contract, she will choose a vector of actions $\mathbf{a}^{RE}$ to solve

$$(4)\quad \max_{a}\ s + b_{LL}(1-q)(1-p) + b_{HL}q(1-p) + b_{LH}(1-q)p + b_{HH}qp - c(\mathbf{a}) \equiv U^{RE},$$

where $q \equiv q(\mathbf{a})$ and $p \equiv p(\mathbf{a})$. The expected downstream payoff is then

$$E[Q_i - s - b_{ij}|\mathbf{a} = \mathbf{a}^{RE}] = Q_L + \Delta Q q(\mathbf{a}^{RE}) - [U^{RE} + c(\mathbf{a}^{RE})] \equiv D^{RE},$$

so the total surplus generated under relational employment is

$$(5)\qquad S^{RE} \equiv U^{RE} + D^{RE} = Q_L + q(\mathbf{a}^{RE})\Delta Q - c(\mathbf{a}^{RE}).$$

The relational-employment contract $(s, \{b_{ij}\})$ is self-enforcing if both parties choose to honor the contract for all possible realizations of Q_i and P_j. The downstream party reneges if he refuses to pay the promised bonus b_{ij} to the upstream party, instead simply taking the good and paying nothing. After reneging, the downstream party will either retain ownership and earn the spot-employment payoff $D^{SE} = Q_L$ in perpetuity (when $S^{SE} > S^{SO}$), or sell the asset upstream for π and earn spot-outsourcing payoff D^{SO} in perpetuity (when $S^{SO} > S^{SE}$).

Assume first that $S^{SE} > S^{SO}$, so that if reneging occurs then the downstream party will retain ownership and earn D^{SE} in perpetuity. The downstream party will honor the relational-employment contract as long as the present value of honoring the contract exceeds the present value of reneging. Since the present value of honoring the contract is $-b_{ij} + \frac{1}{r} D^{RE}$, the downstream owner will honor rather than renege on the relational contract when, for all i and j,

$$(6)\qquad -b_{ij} + \tfrac{1}{r}D^{RE} \geq \tfrac{1}{r}D^{SE}.$$

The upstream party reneges on the relational-employment contract by refusing to accept a promised payment b_{ij} when it was offered (or by refusing to make a promised payment if $b_{ij} < 0$), earning U^{SE} thereafter. Thus, the upstream party will honor rather than renege on the relational contract when, for all i and j,

(7) $$b_{ij} + \tfrac{1}{r}U^{RE} \geq \tfrac{1}{r}U^{SE}.$$

If (6) holds for all i and j, then it must hold for the largest b_{ij}, while if (7) holds for all i and j it must hold for the smallest b_{ij}. Combining these two extreme versions of (6) and (7) yields a necessary condition for the relational-employment contract $(s,\{b_{ij}\})$ to be self-enforcing when $S^{SE} > S^{SO}$:

(8) $$\max b_{ij} - \min b_{ij} \leq \tfrac{1}{r}(S^{RE} - S^{SE}).$$

Next assume that $S^{SO} > S^{SE}$, so that if reneging occurs, then the upstream party will purchase the ownership right from the downstream party for some price π, after which the upstream and downstream parties earn U^{SO} and D^{SO}, respectively. In this case, the right-hand side of (6) becomes $\tfrac{1}{r}D^{SO} + \pi$, and the right-hand side of (7) becomes $\tfrac{1}{r}U^{SO} - \pi$, so combining the extreme versions of the resulting incentive constraints yields a necessary condition for the relational-employment contract $(s,\{b_{ij}\})$ to be self-enforcing when $S^{SO} > S^{SE}$:

(9) $$\max b_{ij} - \min b_{ij} \leq \tfrac{1}{r}(S^{RE} - S^{SO}).$$

Combining (8) and (9) yields a single necessary condition for a self-enforcing relational-employment contract:

(10) $$\max b_{ij} - \min b_{ij} \leq \tfrac{1}{r}(S^{RE} - \max(S^{SE},S^{SO})).$$

In fact, (10) is sufficient as well as necessary, because for any max b_{ij} and min b_{ij} satisfying (10), a fixed payment, s, can always be chosen that satisfies (6) and (7) (when $S^{SE} > S^{SO}$) or their analogs (when $S^{SO} > S^{SE}$). The left-hand side of (10) is the maximum total temptation to renege on the relational-employment contract (i.e., the upstream party's temptation plus the downstream's). The right-hand side is the present value of the net total surplus (i.e., the total surplus from continuing the relationship, S^{RE}, less the best fallback if either party should renege, $\max[S^{SO},S^{SE}]$). The efficient relational-employment contract maximizes the total surplus S^{RE} in (5), subject to the feasibility constraint (10).[11]

11. Note that the same derivation would hold for arbitrary finite sets of possible realizations for Q and P: $Q \in \{Q_1, \ldots, Q_I\}$ and $P \in \{P_1, \ldots, P_J\}$, where $Q_1 > \ldots > Q_I > P_1 > \ldots > P_J$. In fact, the derivation persists even without all the possible realizations of Q being above all those of P, as long as the joint distribution of Q and P puts positive probability on (Q_i,P_j) only if $Q_i > P_j$. The fact that the many constraints in (6) and (7) reduce to the single constraint in

Given functional forms for $q(\mathbf{a})$ and $p(\mathbf{a})$ and values for the parameters ΔQ, ΔP, and r, we could now determine whether (i) relational employment can achieve first-best upstream actions, (ii) relational employment can exist (i.e., there exist payments and associated actions satisfying (4) and (10) that produce higher total surplus than spot employment) but cannot achieve the first-best, or (iii) relational employment cannot exist (i.e., the payments and actions from spot employment are the only solution to (4) and (10)). We do not pause here to explore these three possibilities because for many functional-form assumptions and parameter values some other organizational form (i.e., spot outsourcing, relational outsourcing, or spot employment) will be more efficient; see below.

D. Relational Outsourcing

We next consider relational outsourcing—relational contracts where the upstream party owns the asset. Such relational contracts in nonintegrated supply transactions have been analyzed at least since Klein and Leffler [1981] and Telser [1981], but there has been no formal comparison of these Klein-Leffler-Telser-style models of relationships between firms to the Bull-Simon-style models of relationships within firms. We show that relational contracts between nonintegrated parties (outsourcing) differ from those between integrated parties (employment) in the ways they tempt each party to renege.

If the promised payment b_{ij} is greater than the price that would be negotiated under spot outsourcing, $\frac{1}{2}(Q_i + P_j)$, the downstream purchaser would be better off this period if he reneged on the relational-outsourcing contract. Similarly, if the promised payment b_{ij} is less than $\frac{1}{2}(Q_i + P_j)$, then the upstream producer would be better off this period if she reneged. Thus, a key difference between relational contracts under outsourcing versus under employment is that the good's value in its alternative use, P_j, affects the reneging decision under relational outsourcing but not under relational employment. This difference drives our main Proposition and several of our subsequent results.

(8), and likewise in deriving (9), is well-known in the literature; see MacLeod and Malcomson [1989, 1998] and Levin [2000]. The appearance of the maximum total reneging temptation on the left-hand sides of (8) and (9) also is familiar, and leads to Levin's result on "bang-bang" contracts.

The analysis of relational outsourcing parallels that of relational employment. If the upstream party is confident that the downstream party will honor the contract $(s,\{b_{ij}\})$, then the upstream party will choose a vector of actions $\mathbf{a}^{RO}$ to solve

$$\max_a s + b_{LL}(1-q)(1-p) + b_{HL}q(1-p) + b_{LH}(1-q)p + b_{HH}qp - c(\mathbf{a}) \equiv U^{RO},$$

where $q \equiv q(\mathbf{a})$ and $p \equiv p(\mathbf{a})$. The expected downstream payoff is then $E[Q_i - s - b_{ij}|\mathbf{a} = \mathbf{a}^{RO}] \equiv D^{RO}$, so the total surplus under relational-outsourcing contract is

$$S^{RO} \equiv U^{RO} + D^{RO} = Q_L + q(\mathbf{a}^{RO})\Delta Q - c(\mathbf{a}^{RO}). \tag{11}$$

Note that a given relational contract $(s,\{b_{ij}\})$ produces the same actions and the same surplus under relational outsourcing as under relational employment (assuming that the relational contract satisfies the relevant reneging constraints in each case). But, as we show next, the temptation to renege on a relational employment contract differs from the temptation to renege under relational outsourcing.

Once Q_i and P_j have been realized, the downstream party is supposed to receive the net payoff $Q_i - b_{ij}$. If he reneges on the relational-outsourcing contract, he negotiates to buy the good for the spot-outsourcing price of $\frac{1}{2}(Q_i + P_j)$ instead of for b_{ij}, realizing a current payoff of $Q_i - \frac{1}{2}(Q_i + P_j)$. Likewise, once Q_i and P_j have been realized, the upstream party is supposed to sell the good for the price b_{ij}. If she reneges, she negotiates to sell the good for the spot price of $\frac{1}{2}(Q_i + P_j)$.

Assume first that $S^{SO} > S^{SE}$, so that it is efficient for the upstream party to retain ownership of the asset after either party reneges on the relational contact. In this case, the downstream party will honor rather than renege on the relational contract when, for all i and j,

$$Q_i - b_{ij} + \frac{1}{r}D^{RO} \geq \frac{1}{2}(Q_i - P_j) + \frac{1}{r}D^{SO},$$

or

$$b_{ij} - \frac{1}{2}(Q_i + P_j) \leq \frac{1}{r}(D^{RO} - D^{SO}). \tag{12}$$

Likewise, the upstream party will honor rather than renege on the relational-outsourcing contract when, for all i and j,

$$b_{ij} - \frac{1}{2}(Q_i + P_j) \geq \frac{1}{r}(U^{SO} - U^{RO}). \tag{13}$$

If (12) holds for all i and j, then it must hold for the largest value of $b_{ij} - \frac{1}{2}(Q_i + P_j)$, while if (13) holds for all i and j, it must hold for the smallest value of $b_{ij} - \frac{1}{2}(Q_i + P_j)$. Combining these two extreme versions of (12) and (13) yields a single necessary condition for the relational-outsourcing contract $(s,\{b_{ij}\})$ to be self-enforcing when $S^{SO} > S^{SE}$.

$$(14) \quad \max(b_{ij} - \tfrac{1}{2}(Q_i + P_j)) - \min(b_{ij} - \tfrac{1}{2}(Q_i + P_j)) \leq \tfrac{1}{r}(S^{RO} - S^{SO}).$$

As in the analysis of relational employment, this necessary condition is also sufficient.

Next assume that $S^{SE} > S^{SO}$, so that it is efficient for the upstream party to sell the asset downstream at some price π after either party reneges on the relational contact. In this case, the right-hand side of (12) becomes $\frac{1}{r}(D^{RO} - D^{SE}) - \pi$, and the right-hand side of (13) becomes $\frac{1}{r}(U^{SO} - U^{RE}) + \pi$, so combining the extreme versions of the resulting incentive constraints yields a single necessary condition for the relational-outsourcing contract $(s,\{b_{ij}\})$ to be self-enforcing when $S^{SE} > S^{SO}$:

$$(15) \quad \max(b_{ij} - \tfrac{1}{2}(Q_i + P_j)) - \min(b_{ij} - \tfrac{1}{2}(Q_i + P_j)) \leq \tfrac{1}{r}(S^{RO} - S^{SE}).$$

Combining (14) and (15) yields a single necessary condition for a self-enforcing relational-outsourcing contract:

$$(16) \quad \max(b_{ij} - \tfrac{1}{2}(Q_i + P_j)) - \min(b_{ij} - \tfrac{1}{2}(Q_i + P_j)) \leq \tfrac{1}{r}(S^{RO} - \max[S^{SO}, S^{SE}]).$$

As in the analysis of relational employment, this necessary condition is also sufficient (and, as noted in footnote 11, the argument can be generalized to arbitrary finite sets of realizations for Q and P). Parallel to (10), the left-hand side of (16) is the maximum total temptation to renege on the relational-outsourcing contract, and the right-hand side is the present value of the total surplus from continuing the relationship S^{RO}, less the best fall-back if either party should renege, $\max[S^{SO}, S^{SE}]$. The efficient relational-outsourcing contract maximizes the total surplus S^{RO} in (11), subject to the feasibility constraint (16).

Given functional forms for $q(\mathbf{a})$ and $p(\mathbf{a})$ and values for the parameters ΔQ, ΔP, and r, we could again determine whether (i) relational outsourcing can achieve first-best upstream actions, (ii) relational outsourcing can exist but cannot achieve the first-best, or (iii) relational outsourcing cannot exist. We again defer our exploration of these possibilities.

We conclude this section by stating our main proposition and its corollary.

PROPOSITION. Asset ownership affects the parties' temptations to renege on a relational contract, and hence affects whether a given relational contract is feasible. Formally, the relational contract $(s,\{b_{ij}\})$ produces the same actions and total surplus under either ownership structure, but the maximum total reneging temptation is $\max(b_{ij}) - \min(b_{ij})$ in (10) under relational employment versus $\max(b_{ij} - ½(Q_i + P_j)) - \min(b_{ij} - ½(Q_i + P_j))$ in (16) under relational outsourcing.

The proposition reveals that whether the parties are integrated or nonintegrated affects their temptations to renege on a given relational contract. In some situations, the reneging temptation is lower between integrated parties; in others, the reneging temptation is lower between nonintegrated parties. This result motivates an underexplored perspective on vertical integration: a major factor in the vertical-integration decision is whether integration or nonintegration facilitates the superior relational contract.

Before beginning to explore the implications of this proposition in Section IV, we pause to compare it with some of the work discussed in connection with Figure I above. For example, consider Bull's model of a subjective bonus (or any other model of relational contracts within firms): the words describe an informal agreement within a firm, but could the model be reinterpreted as concerning a hand-in-glove supply relationship between two firms? Similarly, consider Klein and Leffler's model of a supply relationship (or any other model of relational contracts between firms): the words describe an informal agreement between firms, but could the model be reinterpreted as concerning transfer payments between upstream and downstream divisions of a single firm? In short, in a typical repeated-game model, it is unclear whether the relational contract is within or between firms, and consequently also unclear whether this distinction matters. By including asset ownership in our model, we both clarify this distinction and show that it does matter: asset ownership affects the parties' temptations to renege, and so affects what relational contracts are feasible and what asset ownership pattern is efficient.[12]

Our proposition can also be compared with Grossman and Hart's [1986] perspective on integration. Although we adopt their assumptions that bringing a transaction inside a firm does not create any additional information, or render formerly noncontractible outcomes contractible, or change the preferences of any actor, we depart from their assertion that "the benefits of integration must surely be more than the ability to choose a new payment method" [p. 694]. In our model, one important benefit of integration is precisely the ability to choose a new payment method (i.e., a different relational contract).

Finally, our main proposition produces the following corollary.

COROLLARY. It is impossible for a firm to mimic the spot-market outcome after it brings a transaction inside the firm because the reneging temptation is too great. Formally, the relational contract that replicates the payoffs of spot outsourcing—namely, $(s = 0, \{b_{ij} = -\frac{1}{2}(Q_i + P_j)\})$—of course produces the same actions and surplus as spot outsourcing, but fails to satisfy (10) because the maximum total reneging temptation under relational employment—namely, $\max(b_{ij}) - \min(b_{ij}) = \frac{1}{2}(Q_H + P_H) - \frac{1}{2}(Q_L + P_L)$—is positive whereas the difference in surplus—namely, $\frac{1}{r}(S^{SO} - \max[S^{SO}, S^{SE}])$—cannot exceed zero.[13]

If firms could write contracts with employees that provide incentives identical to those created in markets, then firms could try to mimic the market in cases where the market outcome is efficient but intervene in cases where the market outcome is inefficient. Williamson [1985, p. 135] argued that such "selective intervention" must be impossible, or else we would observe one enormous firm. This corollary offers a first step toward formal

12. Kreps's [1990] classic paper on corporate culture provides another example in this vein. Some readers have interpreted Kreps's analysis as within a firm (e.g., culture as a promise to employees), while others have interpreted the analysis as between firms (e.g., culture as a promise to suppliers or customers). Kreps is clearly correct that corporate culture is important to both internal and external constituencies, but our proposition implies that a single repeated-game model (i.e., a model without an asset-ownership variable or its equivalent) cannot simultaneously describe both of these important relational contracts.

13. Note that the reverse is also true: it is impossible under nonintegration to mimic the spot-employment outcome after the transaction is brought outside the firm, because the reneging temptation is too great.

support for Williamson's argument: relational employment contracts cannot replicate incentives from spot markets. We extend this corollary in Section IV by showing that the availability of inefficient spot outsourcing may prevent the existence of more efficient relational employment. That is, not only will a firm be unable to mimic the spot-market outcome after it brings a transaction inside the firm, it may also be unable to improve upon the spot-market outcome, because the relational contract necessary for such improvements has too great a reneging temptation when spot-market governance is available after reneging.

IV. A Comparative Analysis of Organizational Forms

The preceding section characterized upstream actions and total surplus under four alternative governance structures. In a given environment, the efficient organizational form maximizes the total surplus. For some parameter values, relational employment will be the efficient organizational form; for others, relational outsourcing will dominate; for still other parameters, neither relational outsourcing nor employment will be feasible and spot outsourcing or spot employment will dominate.

In this section we begin to explore the implications of our main proposition by deriving five additional results. We emphasize that these additional results are exploratory and suggestive, in two senses. First, they are derived for specific functional forms rather than for the more general model in Section III. And second, they only begin to probe what we expect to be a broad set of applications of our main proposition, some of which we sketch in Section V.

In this section we also solve an example for which we compute and display the efficient organizational form as a function of parameters such as r, ΔQ, and ΔP. That is, for this example, we conduct a formal version of the comparative analysis proposed by Coase [1937] and elaborated by Williamson [1975, 1985, 1996]: when will a given transaction occur within a single firm rather than between two? Relative to static versions of this formal comparison in the tradition of Grossman and Hart (such as Hart and Moore [1990] and Hart [1995]), our analysis encourages a richer conception of life within and between firms, by emphasizing the importance of relational contracts in both cases. Relative to informal comparisons of relational contracts within and between firms, such as Williamson [1996, Chapter 4], our analysis derives rather than assumes the "relational capital" and reneging temptations that are critical to this comparison.

Our first result is that vertical integration is an efficient response to widely varying supply prices (even when all parties are risk-neutral), because integration reduces reneging temptations in such settings. We show that under nonintegrated ownership, an extreme realization of the supply price creates a large temptation to renege on a relational contract. This reneging temptation limits the incentive power of the best relational contract that can be implemented under nonintegrated ownership. Under integrated ownership, however, we show that the reneging temptation is independent of the supply price, making integration the more efficient governance structure when the supply price can vary widely. As we discuss below, this result may help explain a puzzle noted by Carlton [1979]: why would risk-neutral companies pursue vertical mergers to achieve certainty of supply?

Our second result is that high-powered incentives create bigger reneging temptations under integration than under nonintegration, with the consequence that performance payments in relational incentive contracts will be smaller under integration than under (otherwise equivalent) nonintegration. In our repeated-game model, the downstream party promises the upstream party a bonus for delivering high quality. In the integrated case, the upstream employee has no recourse if the downstream firm refuses to pay the promised bonus; in the nonintegrated case, however, if the upstream independent contractor is not paid a promised bonus, she can still extract some payment for the good through bargaining. Reneging on the bonus owed to an independent contractor thus saves only the amount of the bonus over and above the payment that would be determined by such bargaining. The downstream party's temptation not to pay the bonus is therefore smaller under nonintegration than under integration. This reduced temptation makes it credible to promise a larger bonus payment to an independent contractor than to an employee.

Because Q and P are not contractible, the promised bonus b_{ij} is not a court-enforceable contract, but the bonus payment might nonetheless be measurable by examining payroll records or the like. Our predicted difference in measurable bonus payments to independent contractors versus employees is thus potentially testable. In this sense, our second result can be seen as a testable version of Williamson's [1985, Ch. 6] observation that incentives are "higher-powered" in markets than in firms. That is, Williamson's observation seems to focus on total incentives (which may be difficult to measure), whereas our result matches Williamson's observation about total incentives but produces a prediction in terms of measurable bonus payments. In contrast, many static models in the Grossman-Hart tradition also match Williamson's observation about total incentives but generate this prediction from the effects of asset ownership on marginal incentives (which again seem hard to measure), without producing any prediction about the levels of measurable payments. Whinston [2000] develops a parallel critique of the testability of asset-ownership models by emphasizing the difference between measurable levels of asset specificity versus hard-to-measure marginal effects.

Our third result is that, holding all other parameters constant, the optimal integration decision can depend on the discount rate (which is of course irrelevant in a static model). At sufficiently low discount rates, ownership is irrelevant because the first-best can be achieved under either relational outsourcing or relational employment. But the relational contract that achieves the first-best has different maximum total reneging temptations under integration versus nonintegration, so there is a critical discount rate at which it becomes impossible to achieve the first-best under one ownership structure but is still possible under the other. Thus, moving from low to moderate discount rates can change the optimal ownership structure. Similarly, we show that a slight increase in the discount rate can change the efficient organizational form from second-best relational employment to (spot or relational) outsourcing.

Our fourth result is that, holding all marginal incentives constant, the optimal integration decision can depend on the payoff levels (which play no separate role our in static model, if marginal incentives are held constant). For example, imagine increasing ΔP but holding marginal incentives constant (by correspondingly decreasing another appropriate parameter), and suppose that these constant marginal incentives make spot outsourcing more efficient than spot employment. This increase in ΔP increases the maximum total reneging temptation in relational outsourcing but not in relational employment (and the decrease in the other parameter has no effect on reneging temptations). As a result, relational employment may be feasible when relational outsourcing is not, reversing the conclusion of the static model.

Our fifth result extends the corollary in Section III, which showed that a firm will be unable to mimic the spot-market outcome after it brings a transaction inside the firm. We now show that a mediocre spot market may prevent the existence of *any* firm, including a firm that would be more efficient than the spot market. More precisely, a firm may be unable to improve upon the spot-market outcome because the availability of the spot-market outcome as a fallback after reneging may ruin any relational-employment contract that could improve on the spot-market outcome. One interesting implication of this result is that a small change in parameters can force firms to abandon more efficient employment relationships in favor of less efficient outsourcing.

Our fifth result is in the spirit of the Coase-Williamson argument that a firm arises only if a spot market would perform sufficiently poorly, but our reasoning is new. In our model, the market may supplant a firm in governing a particular transaction not because the market wins the head-to-head competition between governance structures implicitly envisioned by Coase and Williamson, but rather because the existence of the market as a fallback after reneging may prevent the existence of the firm in the first place. This result again distinguishes our repeated-game approach from existing static models, because in static models either there are no contracts (as in Grossman and Hart) or the feasible set of contracts does not depend on asset ownership (as in Holmstrom), whereas this result shows that the feasible set of relational contracts under one ownership structure depends on the desirability of changing asset ownership after reneging.

A. Additional Assumptions

We prove these five results for a special case of the model developed in Section III. We assume henceforth that the vector of actions $\mathbf{a}$ has two components, the production functions $q(\mathbf{a})$ and $p(\mathbf{a})$ are linear, and the cost function $c(\mathbf{a})$ is quadratic:

$$\begin{aligned} \mathbf{a} &= (a_1, a_2), \\ q(\mathbf{a}) &= q_1 a_1 + q_2 a_2, \\ p(\mathbf{a}) &= p_1 a_1 + p_2 a_2, \text{ and} \\ c(\mathbf{a}) &= \tfrac{1}{2} a_1^2 + \tfrac{1}{2} a_2^2, \end{aligned}$$

where q_1, q_2, p_1, $p_2 \geq 0$ and $q_1 p_2 \neq q_2 p_1$. For this linear-quadratic case, the first-best actions are

$$a_1^{FB} = q_1 \Delta Q \quad \text{and} \quad a_2^{FB} = q_2 \Delta Q.$$

In contrast, under spot outsourcing the upstream party chooses a_1 and a_2 to maximize $\frac{1}{2}(Q_L + P_L) + \frac{1}{2}q(\mathbf{a})\Delta Q + \frac{1}{2}p(\mathbf{a})\Delta P - c(\mathbf{a})$, so

$$(17) \qquad \begin{aligned} a_1^{SO} &= \tfrac{1}{2}q_1\Delta Q + \tfrac{1}{2}p_1\Delta P \\ a_2^{SO} &= \tfrac{1}{2}q_2\Delta Q + \tfrac{1}{2}p_2\Delta P. \end{aligned}$$

And under spot employment the upstream party has no incentive to take costly actions and so chooses $a_1^{SE} = a_2^{SE} = 0$.

With some loss of generality but substantial gain in expositional efficiency, we also assume henceforth that the bonus payments b_{ij} in any relational contract satisfy

$$b_{HH} = b_H + \beta_H, \quad b_{HL} = b_H + \beta_L,$$
$$b_{LH} = b_L + \beta_H, \quad b_{LL} = b_L + \beta_L.$$

This restriction on bonus payments amounts to assuming that the downstream party pays a bonus $\Delta b \equiv b_H - b_L$ if $Q = Q_H$ and a bonus $\Delta\beta \equiv \beta_H - \beta_L$ if $P = P_H$, with no further bonus payable if both Q and P achieve their high values.[14] Under this assumption about bonus payments in relational contracts, the upstream party chooses a_1 and a_2 to maximize $(s + b_L + \beta_L) + q(\mathbf{a})\Delta b + p(\mathbf{a})\Delta\beta - c(\mathbf{a})$, so

$$(18) \qquad \begin{aligned} a_1^R &= q_1\Delta b + p_1\Delta\beta \\ a_2^R &= q_2\Delta b + p_2\Delta\beta, \end{aligned}$$

where R connotes relational contract (and will be replaced by either RO for relational outsourcing or RE for relational employment below). As we show in Appendix 1, the necessary and sufficient conditions for self-enforcing relational-employment contracts (10) and relational-outsourcing contracts (16) then take the simpler forms (10′) and (16′):

$$(10') \qquad |\Delta b| + |\Delta\beta| \leq \tfrac{1}{r}(S^{RE} - \max[S^{SO}, S^{SE}]),$$

14. In combination with our assumption that $q_1p_2 \neq q_2p_1$, these restricted bonus payments imply a one-to-one correspondence between action vectors and bonus payments, which greatly simplifies the computations underlying Figure II and some of the results below.

$$(16') \quad |\Delta b - \tfrac{1}{2}\Delta Q| + |\Delta\beta - \tfrac{1}{2}\Delta P| \leq \tfrac{1}{r}(S^{RO} - \max[S^{SO}, S^{SE}]).$$

Given (18), the first-best can be achieved under a relational contract if and only if $\Delta b = \Delta Q$ and $\Delta\beta = 0$, so (10′) implies that the first-best can be achieved under relational employment if and only if

$$(19) \qquad \Delta Q \leq \tfrac{1}{r}(S^{FB} - \max[S^{SO}, S^{SE}]),$$

where S^{FB} is the first-best total surplus, $Q_L + \tfrac{1}{2}q^2\Delta Q^2$. Similarly, (16′) implies that the first-best can be achieved under relational outsourcing if and only if

$$(20) \qquad \tfrac{1}{2}(\Delta Q + \Delta P) \leq \tfrac{1}{r}(S^{FB} - \max[S^{SO}, S^{SE}]).$$

From (19) and (20) we see that at sufficiently small discount rates the first-best is achievable under either relational employment or outsourcing. But if $\Delta P > \Delta Q$, then there exist intermediate discount rates where the first-best is achievable under relational employment but not under relational outsourcing; and if $\Delta P < \Delta Q$, then there are discount rates where the first-best is achievable under relational outsourcing but not under relational employment. As noted above, these observations generate a first illustration of Result 3: the optimal integration decision can depend on the discount rate.

B. Additional Results

In this subsection we state and interpret formal versions of our five additional results. (Proofs are in Appendix 2.)

Before proving these results, we build intuition via the following "unproductive multitasking" example: the agent can take one action that affects Q and another that affects P (i.e., $q_2 = p_1 = 0$, so the probabilities of realizing $Q = Q_H$ and $P = P_H$ can be written as $q(\mathbf{a}) = qa_1$ and $p(\mathbf{a}) = pa_2$, respectively). Figure II plots the efficient organizational form for this unproductive-multitasking example, as a function of r and ΔP. The figure contains five regions indicating the governance structure that produces the highest total surplus in each region of parameter space. When discount rates are high, relational contracts are not feasible, so either spot outsourcing or spot employment is efficient. Spot outsourcing yields total surplus $S^{SO} = Q_L + \tfrac{3}{8}q^2\Delta Q^2 - \tfrac{1}{8}p^2\Delta P^2$ while spot employment yields $S^{SE} = Q_L$, so spot outsourcing dominates spot employment if and only if $p\Delta P > \sqrt{3}q\Delta Q$, as can be seen at the top of the figure. At intermediate

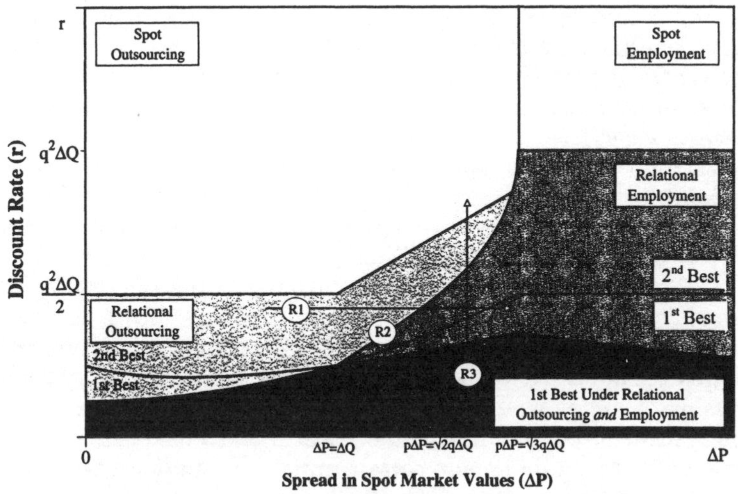

FIGURE II

Efficient Organization Form as a Function of r and ΔP
($q(a) = qa_1$, $p(a) = pa_2$, and $c(a) = \frac{1}{2}a_1^2 + \frac{1}{2}a_2^2$)

The figure shows how the efficient organizational form varies with the discount rate (r) and the difference between the high and low market valuations (ΔP), assuming that $p = q = 1$. Our first three results are illustrated in ($R1$) through ($R3$) (see the text for a complete discussion).

discount rates, total surplus is maximized by relational outsourcing or relational employment (at either second- or first-best surplus, depending on the discount rate). Finally, when discount rates are sufficiently low, the first-best can be achieved through both relational outsourcing and relational employment. Figure II is thus a formal version of the Coase-Williamson horse race between markets and firms, but we will also use it to illustrate several of the following results.

RESULT 1. Vertical integration is an efficient response to widely varying supply prices. Formally, given q_1, q_2, p_1, p_2, ΔQ, and r, there exists ΔP^* such that if $\Delta P > \Delta P^*$, then the downstream party owns the asset in the efficient governance structure.

Under relational outsourcing, the upstream party could consign the good to its alternative use, so current market conditions (that is, realizations of P_L or P_H) play an important role in determining whether the parties will honor the relational-outsourcing contract. In contrast, under relational employment, current market conditions do not affect the reneging decision because the downstream owner can simply take the good, without any restitution to the upstream party whatsoever. This distinction is clear from the reneging constraints: ΔP appears in the constraint for relational outsourcing, (16′), but not in the constraint for relational employment, (10′). As a result, increases in ΔP cause relational outsourcing to become infeasible (follow the arrow labeled $R1$ in Figure II).

This difference between relational outsourcing and relational employment offers an explanation for Carlton's [1979, p. 189] observation that companies vertically integrate to reduce uncertainty of supply. "It has always been somewhat of a mystery why businessmen, as well as researchers, so often conclude that the significant force explaining . . . vertical integration . . . has been the desire to obtain a more certain supply of inputs . . . Why are markets not doing their jobs of allocating resources, and why should uncertainty create incentives for vertical integration?" While Carlton proposes an answer to this question that depends on price rigidities that keep supply from equaling demand in some circumstances, our model suggests an alternative answer that does not depend on such nonmarket-clearing mechanisms. In our model, anticipated price fluctuations make vertical integration efficient not because of ex ante uncertainty associated with a volatile market price, but rather because of the ex post temptation to renege on a relational contract.[15] Specifically, the upstream producer faces a large temptation to renege when the price is high, and the downstream consumer faces a large temptation when the price is low. These temptations make it difficult to sustain a relational-outsourcing contract, but after vertical integration the market price P no longer serves as a temptation to either party.[16]

RESULT 2. High-powered incentives create bigger reneging temptations under integration than under nonintegration, with

15. In our model, a high ΔP represents a large variability in the value of the good in its next-best use. We interpret a high ΔP as meaning that the market price of the good is highly variable.

16. See Goldberg and Erickson [1987], Klein [1996], and Klein and Murphy [1997] for similar arguments applied to particular industries. Arrow [1975] also suggests that variation in supply prices may explain vertical integration, but his result is based on acquiring information to improve price forecasting rather than on the temptation to renege on relational contracts.

the consequence that performance payments in relational incentive contracts will be smaller in firms than in (otherwise equivalent) markets. Formally, given $q_1, q_2, p_1, p_2, \Delta Q, \Delta P$, and r, if the most efficient relational-employment contract yields $a_1^{RE} < a_1^{FB}$ and $a_2^{RE} < a_2^{FB}$, then either the most efficient relational-outsourcing contract yields $a_1^{RO} > a_1^{RE}$ and $a_2^{RO} > a_2^{RE}$, or no relational-outsourcing contract exists.

As explained earlier, under relational outsourcing the temptation for the downstream party to renege is not the full amount of a promised payment but only the difference between the promised payment and the payment that would be determined by bargaining. More formally, the upstream party's actions are determined by Δb and $\Delta\beta$ (these are the "bonuses" paid for achieving high realizations of Q and P, respectively), so holding Δb and $\Delta\beta$ fixed, the total surplus from relational contracting does not depend on who owns the asset. But the temptation to renege, shown on the left-hand sides of (10′) and (16′), does depend on asset ownership. In particular, if strong incentives are desirable (i.e., $\Delta b > \frac{1}{2}\Delta Q$ and $\Delta\beta > \frac{1}{2}\Delta P$), then the total reneging temptation is smaller under relational outsourcing than under relational employment (namely, $|\Delta b - \frac{1}{2}\Delta Q| + |\Delta\beta - \frac{1}{2}\Delta P|$ rather than $|\Delta b| + |\Delta\beta|$). Thus, when strong incentives are desirable, relational employment is an inefficient governance mechanism compared with relational outsourcing.

Result 2 corresponds to a thought experiment: fix the environment, measure the incentive payments in the optimal organizational form, and consider what incentive payments would emerge if the organizational form were changed. But an empirical test along these lines would require that nonoptimal organizational forms exist in the given environment. Fortunately, a related result also holds: choose a data set with a narrow range of environments in which both relational outsourcing and employment exist. In this range of environments, outsourcing contracts will have larger incentive payments than employment contracts will have.

As an example of the latter thought experiment, consider the boundary between relational outsourcing and relational employment denoted by $R2$ in Figure II. Along this boundary (which occurs when $\Delta Q < \Delta P < \sqrt{2}q\Delta Q/p$), the surpluses generated under the two relational contracts are identical, but the contracts themselves are different: the optimal contract under relational employment is $\Delta b^{RE} > 0$ and $\Delta \beta^{RE} = 0$, while the optimal contract under relational outsourcing is $\Delta b^{RO} > \Delta b^{RE}$ and $\Delta \beta^{RO} > \Delta \beta^{RE} > 0$. Therefore, along this boundary, (14) implies that the upstream party will work harder on both tasks under relational outsourcing than relational employment: $a_1^{RO} > a_1^{RE}$ and $a_2^{RO} > a_2^{RE} = 0$. Intuitively, in this unproductive-multitasking example, setting $\Delta \beta > 0$ to encourage the unproductive action a_2 reduces total surplus on the right side of (16′), but also reduces the reneging temptation on the left side of (16′). At $a_2 = 0$, the former is second-order, but the latter is first-order, so Δb can be increased to increase the productive action a_1.

RESULT 3. The optimal integration decision can depend on the discount rate. Formally, there exist parameters q_1, q_2, p_1, p_2, ΔQ, ΔP such that at intermediate discount rates the first-best can be achieved by relational employment but not by relational outsourcing, but at high discount rates no relational contract is feasible and spot outsourcing yields higher total surplus than does spot employment.

Given (18), first-best relational contracts require $\Delta b = \Delta Q$ and $\Delta \beta = 0$. Conditions (19) and (20) show that the first-best is always achievable under either ownership structure at sufficiently low discount rates, and also that the first-best contract generates higher (or lower) reneging temptation under relational outsourcing than under relational employment when $\Delta P > \Delta Q$ or $(\Delta P < \Delta Q)$.

The arrow labeled $R3$ in Figure II illustrates how the discount rate can affect the optimal organizational form. At sufficiently low discount rates, both relational outsourcing and relational employment can achieve the first-best. But because $\Delta P > \Delta Q$ in this region of the figure, as the discount rate increases the first-best becomes infeasible under relational outsourcing but is still feasible under relational employment. At still higher discount rates, relational employment still dominates relational outsourcing but neither can achieve the first-best. Finally, at sufficiently high discount rates, the optimal organizational form switches to outsourcing—initially to second-best relational outsourcing and then to spot outsourcing.

RESULT 4. Holding all marginal incentives constant, the optimal integration decision can depend on the payoff levels. Formally, holding $q_i \Delta Q + p_i \Delta P$ constant for $i = 1, 2$ fixes the choice between spot employment or spot outsourcing, but changing ΔP or ΔQ (with corresponding changes in p_i or q_i to keep $q_i\Delta Q + p_i\Delta P$ constant) affects the reneging temptations and hence the choice between relational employment and relational outsourcing.

Changes in ΔP or ΔQ have two effects in our model. First, these changes affect the reneging temptations in (10′) and (16′) because the bargaining position of the upstream party after reneging depends on who owns the asset. Second, (17) shows that changes in ΔP or ΔQ affect the optimal upstream action choices under spot outsourcing and so affect the comparison between spot outsourcing and spot employment. In developing Result 4, we neutralize the second effect by holding marginal incentives constant; that is, we allow ΔP or ΔQ to vary while holding constant $q_1\Delta Q + p_1\Delta P$ and $q_2\Delta Q + p_2\Delta P$. As an example, think of doubling the potential increase in alternative-use value, $\Delta P \equiv P_H - P_L$, while halving the probability of obtaining P_H for any vector of actions (that is, reducing p_1 and p_2 by half). This change has no effect on spot-market outcomes but does affect the reneging temptations and therefore the optimal asset ownership structure.

Result 4 is perhaps our most striking point of departure from static theories of asset ownership in the tradition of Grossman and Hart, in which everything is determined by marginal incentives and payoff levels are irrelevant.[17] Intuitively, the level of total surplus is critical in our repeated-game model, because this surplus must be sufficient to deter reneging. Marginal incentives also matter in our theory, but for roughly the same reasons as in the static models.

RESULT 5. A mediocre spot market may prevent the existence of *any* firm, including a firm that would be more efficient than the spot market. Formally, suppose that q_1, q_2, p_1, p_2, ΔQ, and ΔP imply that spot outsourcing dominates spot employment ($S^{SO} > S^{SE}$). Then there exists r^* such that if $r > r^*$, then no values of Δb and $\Delta\beta$ satisfy the reneging constraint (10′).[18]

17. We thank a referee for noting that not all static theories of asset ownership share the feature that payoff levels are irrelevant. For example, DeMeza and Lockwood [1998] change the bargaining game in the Grossman-Hart model and reverse this result.

18. In Appendix 2 we not only prove this result but state and prove the analogous result for employment: mediocre spot employment can prevent the existence of any outsourcing (see Result 6).

Result 5 extends the corollary in Section III: we have already shown that a firm cannot mimic the spot-market outcome after it brings a transaction inside the firm; we now show that the firm may also be unable to improve upon the spot-market outcome, because the availability of spot-market outcome as a fallback after reneging may render infeasible any desirable relational-employment contract.

To sketch the proof of Result 5, we can extend the proof of the corollary by a continuity argument, as follows. Suppose that spot outsourcing dominates spot employment, $S^{SO} > S^{SE}$, and recall that a relational contract paying bonuses $\Delta b = \frac{1}{2}\Delta Q$ and $\Delta\beta = \frac{1}{2}\Delta P$ will reproduce the spot-market outcome, $S^{RE}(\Delta b, \Delta\beta) = S^{SO}$. Now consider bonuses $\Delta b'$ and $\Delta\beta'$ that are near $\Delta b = \frac{1}{2}\Delta Q$ and $\Delta\beta = \frac{1}{2}\Delta P$ but generate slightly higher surplus, $S^{RE}(\Delta b', \Delta\beta') > S^{SO}$. Then the left side of (10′) is near $\frac{1}{2}\Delta Q + \frac{1}{2}\Delta P$ but the right side is only slightly above zero, so (10′) fails. Thus, small improvements on the spot-market outcome will not be feasible (where the definition of "small" depends on the discount rate). It remains to show that large improvements on the spot-market outcome are not feasible, which we do in Appendix 2.[19]

V. Discussion

This paper integrates two prominent strands of the literature on the theory of the firm: asset ownership and relational contracting. Because others have explored asset ownership (e.g., Grossman and Hart), relational contracts within firms (e.g., Bull), and relational contracts between firms (e.g., Klein and Leffler), we focus on comparing relational contracts within firms to those between. Our main proposition is that asset ownership affects the parties' temptations to renege on a relational contract, so the integration decision is determined in part by the different rela-

19. Baker, Gibbons, and Murphy [1994] establish a similar result involving compensation contracts: relational contracts are feasible only if formal contracts are sufficiently inferior. MacLeod and Malcomson [1989] anticipated part of this result, by showing that surplus is necessary for a relational contract to exist. Relative to their result, there are two innovations in our two papers. First, we endogenize the performance of the spot-governance alternative to a relational contract. That is, rather than taking the payoffs from spot governance to be exogenous, we derive these payoffs in the same economic environment in which we analyze relational contracts. Second, we show that in our models surplus is necessary but not sufficient.

tional contracts facilitated by asset ownership. As a corollary, we show that firms cannot replicate spot-market outcomes, because the reneging temptation is too great once the transaction is brought inside the firm. We also derive five related results: (1) vertical integration is an efficient response to widely varying supply prices; (2) high-powered incentives create bigger reneging temptations under integration than under nonintegration; (3) the discount rate may affect optimal asset ownership; (4) the level of payoffs, not just the marginal incentives, can affect the integration decision; and (5) firms cannot improve on the spot-market outcome if that outcome offers too tempting a fallback after reneging.

In this section we consider four additional issues: the sociological literature on the formal and informal aspects of organizational design, how our approach might be applied to understanding other organizational forms, the implications of our analysis for internal organizational processes, and a role for managers in the economic theory of the firm.

A. *Formal versus Informal Aspects of Organizational Structure*

Organizational sociologists have long emphasized the distinction between formal and informal aspects of organizational structure. Formal aspects include official job descriptions and reporting relationships, as well as formal contracts (i.e., contracts that can be enforced by a court). Informal aspects include norms and mutual understandings, as well as network structures among individuals (i.e., who you know in the organization besides the people to whom you have formal reporting ties). Roughly speaking, the formal structure is the organization chart, whereas the informal structure is the way things really work. As Granovetter [1985, p. 502] notes: "The distinction between the 'formal' and the 'informal' organization of the firm is one of the oldest in the literature, and it hardly needs repeating that observers who assume firms to be structured in fact by the official organization chart are sociological babes in the woods." Blau and Scott [1962, p. 6] go further, asserting that formal and informal aspects not only coexist but interact: "It is impossible to understand the nature of a formal organization without investigating the networks of informal relations and the unofficial norms as well as the formal hierarchy of authority and the official body of rules, since the formally instituted and the informal emerging patterns are inextricably intertwined."

Asset ownership is a formal aspect of organizational structure; relational contracts are informal. By integrating the two in a single economic model, we are catching up with the sociologists. Yet there is value added by our economic approach: because ownership and relational contracts interact (rather than just coexist), we can choose the former to facilitate the latter, thereby optimizing overall organizational performance. As we describe in the next two subsections, there are many potential applications of this idea.[20]

B. Other Organizational Forms

In this paper we analyze the four organizational forms shown in Figure I, devoting most of our attention to the two on the bottom row: relational employment and relational outsourcing. While these four organizational forms expand and clarify the traditional distinction between markets and firms, they only hint at the variety of forms now much discussed in the business and organizational literatures, including joint ventures, strategic alliances, networks, business groups, clans, and virtual organizations.[21] Unlike the business and organizational literatures, however, the economics literature has not had much to say about these nonstandard organizational forms. Furthermore, where these forms have received theoretical attention from economists, the focus has typically been on asset ownership and other formal aspects of organizational structure, such as in Rey and Tirole [1999].

We suspect that informal aspects, especially relational contracts, are important to the success of these nontraditional organizational forms. We also suspect that the formal and informal aspects not only coexist but also interact, creating another opportunity to choose the former to facilitate the latter. Although the model in this paper has only two stages of production with one party at each stage, richer models could add both parties and

20. The broader statement of this idea is that one should choose all formal aspects (not just ownership) by taking into account their consequences for all informal aspects (not just relational contracts). For other applications of this idea, see Williamson [1985, Chapter 7 and 8] on hostages, Kahn and Huberman [1988] on up-or-out rules, and Bernheim and Whinston [1998] on strategic ambiguity.

21. See, for instance, Chesborough and Teece [1996], Dyer [1996], Gerlach [1991], Granovetter [1995], Gulati and Singh [1998], Kogut [1989], Miles and Snow [1992], Pisano [1989], and Powell [1990].

stages. For example, one could begin to model a joint venture as two parties at one stage who create an asset at the other stage, which they control by both formal and informal means. Similarly, one could begin to model a business group as several parties at several stages of production, with both cross-ownership and relational contracts linking the parties, possibly through a central party. We expect that formal structures such as 50–50 ownership in joint ventures or minority stock holdings in business groups will be better understood using models that study the interplay between these formal structures and the informal relational contracts between the parties. See Bragelien [2000] for a promising start along these lines.

C. Internal Organizational Processes

Of course, the interplay between formal and informal organizational structures is not limited to relationships between firms; there are many applications of this idea within firms. We argue that one particular form of informal structure—subjective judgments whose force depends on parties' reputations—plays a crucial role in organizational processes such as transfer pricing, capital budgeting, compensation, and corporate governance. These organizational processes are not simple exercises in formal contracting, as they often appear in the economics literature, but rather have important informal aspects. We suspect that these informal aspects can be hampered or facilitated by formal organizational structures, such as whether the firm is organized by function versus division, whether its jobs are defined for individuals or teams, and so on. As above, we envision a class of models in which formal organizational structures interact with informal relational contracts.

To conserve space, we discuss only transfer pricing and corporate governance.[22] Early research on transfer pricing (e.g., Hirshleifer [1956] and Gould [1964]) treated this problem as one of trying to re-create the market inside the firm, so that decentralized agents will face incentives that produce efficient resource allocation. But Eccles [1985] conducted an extensive field study of transfer pricing practices and found that transfer prices are rarely used to allocate resources. Instead, the rights to allocate

22. See Bower [1970] on the role of subjectivity, judgment, and reputation in the determination of divisional capital allocations, and Lawler [1971] on how compensation rarely relies exclusively on objective measures of performance, instead relying heavily on managerial subjectivity and judgment.

resources are held centrally, with the transfer-pricing scheme serving as part of the performance measurement and incentive system for the divisions. Our model is consistent with Eccles' findings. Under relational employment, the transfer payment does not serve to allocate resources or transfer ownership in the good produced, because the good is already owned by the downstream party. Rather, the purpose of the transfer payment is to provide incentives for the upstream party to take actions that make the good more valuable downstream.

As another example of subjectivity in organizational processes, consider corporate governance. One of the original motivations for agency theory was to model the relationship between managers and investors. Yet the relationship between managers and shareholders is seldom mediated entirely, or even largely, by formal contracts. Executive compensation contracts in corporations almost always give significant discretion to the board of directors in determining both the size and timing of payouts (see Kole [1997]). We argue that the role of the board is to design and implement a relational contract between management and the shareholders. Using a variety of objective and subjective measures of performance, the board attempts to disentangle the effects of management's actions from those of luck [Lorsch and McIver 1994] and to eliminate distortions induced by accounting-based measures of performance [Dechow, Huson, and Sloan 1994]. Thus, corporate governance is again an interaction between formal and informal systems.

D. Conclusion: Management and the Nature of the Firm

We find it curious that most of the literature on the theory of the firm makes little reference to (nonowner) managers. By emphasizing the importance of relational contracts, our model highlights a role for managers: the development and maintenance of relational contracts, both within and between firms. In our model, this role involves designing the relational contract (that is, determining what the observable but noncontractible Q's and P's should be, as well as determining the optimal b_{ij}'s), communicating this to employees, assessing outcomes (that is, observing the Q's and P's), and deciding whether to honor the relational contract (that is, properly evaluating the reneging constraints). In our model these tasks are trivial; in reality each requires judgment and knowledge of the specifics of complex situations. Furthermore, hard as these tasks are in practice, much evidence suggests that *changing* a relational contract is harder still: managers must end one relational contract but preserve enough credibility to begin another, and the new contract they seek to begin often looks suspiciously like reneging on the old one they seek to end!

We are not arguing that such management of relational contracts occurs only in firms. To the contrary, we have emphasized that management is crucial in ongoing supply relationships. Nor are we arguing that firms cannot occur without management. That is, we can imagine firms that fit the Grossman-Hart model, in which all noncontractible rights of control are held by a single individual ("spot employment" in Figure I). But if these rights become too numerous and complex to be held by a single individual, the firm must have some mechanism to coordinate their exercise, and because these rights are not contractible, their exercise cannot be controlled by formal contracts. Rather, the exercise of noncontractible rights must be coordinated by relational contracts. In short, the firm must have managers ("relational employment" in Figure I). We conclude that understanding the role of managers, who design and implement the relational contracts that underpin informal organizational processes, is essential to understanding firms.

Appendix 1: Necessary and Sufficient Conditions for Self-Enforcing Relational Contracts When Payments Are $b_{ij} = b_i + \beta_j$

Relational Employment

Equation (10) provides the necessary and sufficient condition for the relational-employment contract $(s,\{b_{ij}\})$ to be self-enforcing:

$$\max(b_{ij}) - \min(b_{ij}) \leq \tfrac{1}{r}(S^{RE} \max[S^{SO}, S^{SE}]). \tag{10}$$

When $b_{ij} = b_i + \beta_j$, there are four cases to consider.

1. $b_H > b_L$, $\beta_H > \beta_L$. Then $\max(b_{ij}) = b_{HH}$, $\min(b_{ij}) = b_{LL}$, and the reneging temptation is $\Delta b + \Delta\beta$, where $\Delta b \equiv b_H - b_L > 0$ and $\Delta\beta \equiv \beta_H - \beta_L > 0$.
2. $b_H > b_L$, $\beta_H < \beta_L$. Then $\max(b_{ij}) = b_{HL}$, $\min(b_{ij}) = b_{LH}$, and the reneging temptation is $\Delta b - \Delta\beta$, where $\Delta b > 0$ and $\Delta\beta < 0$.
3. $b_H < b_L$, $\beta_H > \beta_L$. Then $\max(b_{ij}) = b_{LH}$, $\min(b_{ij}) = b_{HL}$,

and the reneging temptation is $-\Delta b + \Delta\beta$, where $\Delta b < 0$ and $\Delta\beta > 0$.

4. $b_H < b_L$, $\beta_H < \beta_L$. Then $\max(b_{ij}) = b_{LL}$, $\min(b_{ij}) = b_{LL}$, and the reneging temptation is $-\Delta b - \Delta\beta$, where $\Delta b < 0$ and $\Delta\beta < 0$.

These four reneging temptations can be summarized as $|\Delta b| + |\Delta\beta|$, yielding

$$(10') \qquad |\Delta b| + |\Delta\beta| \leq \tfrac{1}{r}(S^{RE} - \max[S^{SO}, S^{SE}]).$$

Relational Outsourcing

Equation (16) provides the necessary and sufficient condition for the relational-outsourcing contract $(s, \{b_{ij}\})$ to be self-enforcing:

$$(16) \quad \max(b_{ij} - \tfrac{1}{2}(Q_i + P_j)) - \min(b_{ij} - \tfrac{1}{2}(Q_i + P_j)) \leq \tfrac{1}{r}(S^{RO} - \max[S^{SO}, S^{SE}]).$$

Define $Z \equiv b_L + \beta_L - \tfrac{1}{2}(Q_L + P_L)$, and note that

$$(HH) \quad b_{HH} - \tfrac{1}{2}(Q_H + P_H) = (\Delta b - \tfrac{1}{2}\Delta Q) + (\Delta\beta - \tfrac{1}{2}\Delta P) + Z$$

$$(HL) \quad b_{HL} - \tfrac{1}{2}(Q_H + P_L) = (\Delta b - \tfrac{1}{2}\Delta Q) + Z$$

$$(LH) \quad b_{LH} - \tfrac{1}{2}(Q_L + P_H) = (\Delta\beta - \tfrac{1}{2}\Delta P) + Z$$

$$(LL) \quad b_{LL} - \tfrac{1}{2}(Q_L + P_L) = Z.$$

Again, there are four cases to consider.

1. $\Delta b > \tfrac{1}{2}\Delta Q$, $\Delta\beta > \tfrac{1}{2}\Delta P$. Then $\max(\cdot) = HH$, $\min(\cdot) = LL$, and the reneging temptation is $(\Delta b - \tfrac{1}{2}\Delta Q) + (\Delta\beta - \tfrac{1}{2}\Delta P)$.
2. $\Delta b > \tfrac{1}{2}\Delta Q$, $\Delta\beta < \tfrac{1}{2}\Delta P$. Then $\max(\cdot) = HL$, $\min(\cdot) = LH$, and the reneging temptation is $(\Delta b - \tfrac{1}{2}\Delta Q) - (\Delta\beta - \tfrac{1}{2}\Delta P)$.
3. $\Delta b < \tfrac{1}{2}\Delta Q$, $\Delta\beta > \tfrac{1}{2}\Delta P$. Then $\max(\cdot) = LH$, $\min(\cdot) = HL$, and the reneging temptation is $-(\Delta b - \tfrac{1}{2}\Delta Q) + (\Delta\beta - \tfrac{1}{2}\Delta P)$.
4. $\Delta b < \tfrac{1}{2}\Delta Q$, $\Delta\beta < \tfrac{1}{2}\Delta P$. Then $\max(\cdot) = LL$, $\min(\cdot) = HH$, and the reneging temptation is $-(\Delta b - \tfrac{1}{2}\Delta Q) - (\Delta\beta - \tfrac{1}{2}\Delta P)$.

These four reneging temptations can be summarized as $|\Delta b - \tfrac{1}{2}\Delta Q| + |\Delta\beta - \tfrac{1}{2}\Delta P|$, yielding

$$(16') \quad |\Delta b - \tfrac{1}{2}\Delta Q| + |\Delta\beta - \tfrac{1}{2}\Delta P| \leq \tfrac{1}{r}(S^{RO} - \max[S^{SO}, S^{SE}]).$$

APPENDIX 2: PROOFS OF RESULTS 1 THROUGH 5

RESULT 1. Vertical integration is an efficient response to widely varying supply prices. Formally, given q_1, q_2, p_1, p_2, ΔQ, and r, there exists ΔP^* such that if $\Delta P > \Delta P^*$, then the downstream party owns the asset in the efficient governance structure.

Proof. Given Lemmas 1 and 3 below, Result 1 follows by setting $\Delta P^* = \max\{\Delta P', \Delta P''\}$: because $\Delta P > \Delta P'$, spot outsourcing is not efficient; because $\Delta P > \Delta P''$, relational outsourcing is not feasible.

LEMMA 1. For sufficiently large ΔP, spot employment dominates spot outsourcing. That is, given q_1, q_2, p_1, p_2, and ΔQ, there exists $\Delta P'$ such that if $\Delta P > \Delta P'$ then $S^{SE} > S^{SO}$.

Proof. $2(S^{SO} - S^{SE}) = (3/4)(q_1^2 + q_2^2)\Delta Q^2 + (1/2)(p_1q_1 + p_2q_2)\Delta Q\Delta P - (1/4)(p_1^2 + p_2^2)\Delta P^2$, so choose $\Delta P'$ to be the larger root of the quadratic.

LEMMA 2. Too strong an incentive based on the alternative-use value makes relational outsourcing inferior to spot employment. That is, given q_1, q_2, p_1, p_2, and ΔQ, there exists $\Delta\beta'$ such that, for any Δb, if $\Delta\beta > \Delta\beta'$ then $S^{RO} - S^{SE} < 0$.

Proof. $2(S^{RO} - S^{SE}) = (q_1^2 + q_2^2)\Delta b(2\Delta Q - \Delta b) + 2(p_1q_1 + p_2q_2)(\Delta Q - \Delta b)\Delta\beta - (p_1^2 + p_2^2)\Delta\beta^2$. Maximize the first term with respect to $\Delta b \geq 0$ (at $\Delta b = \Delta Q$); maximize the second term with respect to $\Delta b \geq 0$ (at $\Delta b = 0$). Now choose $\Delta\beta'$ to be the larger root of the resulting quadratic, with the maximized versions of the first and second terms replacing the originals.

LEMMA 3. Too large a variation in the alternative-use value makes relational outsourcing infeasible. That is, given q_1, q_2, p_1, p_2, ΔQ, and r, there exists $\Delta P''$ such that if $\Delta P > \Delta P''$ then the reneging constraint (16′) for relational outsourcing fails.

Proof. Choose $\Delta P''$ such that $1/2\Delta P'' > \Delta\beta' + (S^* - S^{SE})/r$, where S^* is the first-best surplus. If $\Delta\beta > \Delta\beta'$, then Lemma 2 implies that $S^{RO} - S^{SE} < 0$, so $S^{RO} - \max\{S^{SO}, S^{SE}\} < 0$, so (16′) fails. But $\Delta\beta' \geq \Delta\beta$ implies that $1/2\Delta P'' > \Delta\beta$, so the second term on the left-hand side of (16′) is at least $\frac{1}{2}\Delta P'' - \Delta\beta \geq \frac{1}{2}\Delta P'' - \Delta\beta' > (S^* - S^{SE})/r \geq (S^{RO} - S^{SE})/r \geq (S^{RO} - \max\{S^{SO},S^{SE}\})/r$, so (16′) fails.

RESULT 2. High-powered incentives create bigger reneging temptations under integration than under nonintegration, with the consequence that performance payments in relational incentive contracts will be smaller in firms than in (otherwise equivalent) markets. Formally, given q_1, q_2, p_1, p_2, ΔQ, ΔP, and r, if the most efficient employment contract yields $a_1^{RE} < a_1^{FB}$ and $a_2^{RE} < a_2^{FB}$, then either the most efficient outsourcing contract yields $a_1^{RO} > a_1^{RE}$ and $a_2^{RO} > a_2^{RE}$, or no relational-outsourcing contract exists.

Proof. Because relational employment yields actions below the first-best, the reneging constraint (10′) must bind. Consider implementing the same incentives, Δb and $\Delta\beta$, through relational outsourcing instead of employment. Given the same incentives, the same actions would result, but the reneging constraint (16′) would differ. If $\Delta b \geq \frac{1}{2}\Delta Q$ and $\Delta\beta \geq \frac{1}{2}\Delta P$, then the left-hand side of (16′) is smaller than the left-hand side of (10′), but the right-hand sides are identical, so (16′) is slack, so the actions in the efficient relational-outsourcing contract can be increased from those in the efficient relational-employment contract. Alternatively, if $\Delta b < \frac{1}{2}\Delta Q$ or $\Delta\beta < \frac{1}{2}\Delta P$, then it may be that no relational-outsourcing contract is feasible. But if relational outsourcing is feasible, then a small increase in Δb (if $\Delta b < \frac{1}{2}\Delta Q$) or $\Delta\beta$ (if $\Delta\beta < \frac{1}{2}\Delta P$) increases the actions while reducing the left-hand side of (16′). Hence, it will not be efficient for the incentives in the relational-outsourcing contract to be as weak as those under relational employment.

RESULT 3. The optimal integration decision can depend on the discount rate. Formally, there exist parameters q_1, q_2, p_1, p_2, ΔQ, ΔP such that at intermediate discount rates the first-best can be achieved by relational employment but not by relational outsourcing, but at high discount rates no relational contract is feasible, and spot outsourcing yields higher total surplus than does spot employment.

Proof. The elements of the proof have already been given in various places in the text. As noted just after (19) and (20), if $\Delta P > \Delta Q$, then there exist discount rates at which the first-best is feasible under relational employment but not under relational outsourcing. But as noted in the second paragraph of subsection IV.B, in our unproductive-multitasking example, spot outsourcing dominates spot employment if $p\Delta P > \sqrt{3}q\Delta Q$. Thus, for $\Delta Q < \Delta P < \sqrt{3}(q/p)\Delta Q$, an increase in r can move the efficient organizational form from first-best relational employment to spot outsourcing, as shown by the arrow labeled $R3$ in Figure II.

RESULT 4. Holding all marginal incentives constant, the optimal integration decision can depend on the payoff levels. Formally, holding $q_i\Delta Q + p_i\Delta P$ constant for $i = 1, 2$ fixes the choice between spot employment or spot outsourcing, but changing ΔP or ΔQ (with corresponding changes in p_i or q_i to keep $q_i\Delta Q + p_i\Delta P$ constant) affects the reneging temptations and hence the choice between relational employment and relational outsourcing.

Proof. Given $q_1, q_2, p_1, p_2, \Delta Q$, and ΔP, define r^* such that (19) holds with equality. For $r = r^*$, if $\Delta P > \Delta Q$, then (16) fails, but if $\Delta P < \Delta Q$, then (20) holds strictly. Suppose that $\Delta P > \Delta Q$. (The proof for $\Delta P < \Delta Q$ is analogous.) Choose some $\Delta P' < \Delta Q$, and define $p_i' = p_i\Delta P/\Delta P'$ for $i = 1, 2$, so that $q_i\Delta Q + p_i\Delta P = q_i\Delta Q + p_i'\Delta P'$ for $i = 1, 2$. Then (20) fails for $(q_1, q_2, p_1, p_2, \Delta Q, \Delta P, r^*)$ but holds strictly for $(q_1, q_2, p_1', p_2', \Delta Q, \Delta P', r^*)$. Now consider r^{**} just above r^*, so that (19) just fails at $(q_1, q_2, p_1, p_2, \Delta Q, \Delta P, r^{**})$, but the second-best relational employment contract at $(q_1, q_2, p_1, p_2, \Delta Q, \Delta P, r^{**})$ is only slightly worse than first-best. In particular, for r^{**} sufficiently close to r^*, the second-best relational employment contract at $(q_1, q_2, p_1, p_2, \Delta Q, \Delta P, r^{**})$ will generate higher surplus than the second-best relational outsourcing contract at $(q_1, q_2, p_1, p_2, \Delta Q, \Delta P, r^{**})$ because $\Delta P > \Delta Q$. Thus, at $(q_1, q_2, p_1', p_2', \Delta Q, \Delta P', r^{**})$ the first-best can be achieved under relational outsourcing but not under relational employment, but at $(q_1, q_2, p_1, p_2, \Delta Q, \Delta P, r^{**})$ relational outsourcing is strictly worse than first-best while relational employment is arbitrarily close to first-best.

RESULT 5. A mediocre spot market may prevent the existence of any firm. Formally, suppose that $q_1, q_2, p_1, p_2, \Delta Q$, and ΔP imply that spot outsourcing dominates spot employment ($S^{SO} > S^{SE}$). Then there exists r^* such that if $r > r^*$ then no values of Δb and $\Delta\beta$ satisfy the reneging constraint (10′).

Proof. Given Lemma 4 below, Result 5 follows because $S^{SO} > S^{SE}$.

LEMMA 4. For sufficiently high r, the only possible relational-employment contract is the trivial case of $\Delta b = \Delta\beta = 0$ (i.e., replication of spot employment). That is, given $q_1, q_2, p_1, p_2, \Delta Q$, and ΔP, there exists r^*_D such that if $r > r^*_D$ then no values of Δb and $\Delta\beta$ satisfy the reneging constraint (10′) except perhaps $\Delta b = \Delta\beta = 0$.

Proof. The reneging constraint (10′) holds only if $|\Delta b| + |\Delta\beta| \leq (S^{RE} - S^{SE})/r$. But this inequality can be written as

$$\text{(A1)}\quad 2r(\Delta b + \Delta\beta) + (a_j^{RE} - q_1\Delta Q)^2 + (a_2^{RE} - q_2\Delta Q)^2 \leq (q_1^2 + q_2^2)\Delta Q^2,$$

where $a_i^{RE} = q_i\Delta b + p_i\Delta\beta$. Note that at $\Delta b = \Delta\beta = 0$ we have $a_1^{RE} = a_2^{RE} = 0$, so (A1) holds with equality. We will show that for sufficiently high values of r, values of Δb or $\Delta\beta$ other than zero increase the left-hand side of (A1), but the right-hand side is constant, so the reneging constraint (10′) fails unless $\Delta b = \Delta\beta = 0$.

Let $L_D(\Delta b, \Delta\beta)$ denote the left-hand side of (A1). Then $\partial L_D/\partial\Delta b = 2r + 2(a_1^{RE} - q_1\Delta Q)q_1 + 2(a_2^{RE} - q_2\Delta Q)q_2$. Because a_1^{RE} and $a_2^{RE} \geq 0$, we have that if $r > (q_1^2 + q_2^2)\Delta Q$, then $\partial L_D/\partial\Delta b > 0$. Similarly, $\partial L_D/\partial\Delta\beta = 2r + 2(a_1^{RE} - q_1\Delta Q)p_1 + 2(a_2^{RE} - q_2\Delta Q)p_2$, so if $r > (p_1q_1 + p_2q_2)\Delta Q$, then $\partial L_D/\partial\Delta\beta > 0$. Let $r^*_D = \max\{(q_1^2 + q_2^2)\Delta Q, (p_1q_1 + p_2q_2)\Delta Q\}$. Then for $r > r^*_D$, we have that (A1) fails and hence that (10′) fails, except perhaps at $\Delta b = \Delta\beta = 0$.

RESULT 6. Mediocre spot employment may prevent the existence of any outsourcing. Formally, suppose that q_1, q_2, p_1, p_2, ΔQ, and ΔP imply that spot employment dominates spot outsourcing ($S^{SE} > S^{SO}$). Then there exists r^* such that if $r > r^*$ then no values of Δb and $\Delta\beta$ satisfy the reneging constraint (16′).

Proof. Given Lemma 5 below, Result 6 follows because $S^{SE} > S^{SO}$.

LEMMA 5. For sufficiently high r, the only possible relational-outsourcing contract is the trivial case of $\Delta b = ½\Delta Q$ and $\Delta\beta = ½\Delta P$ (i.e., replication of spot outsourcing). That is, given $q_1, q_2, p_1, p_2, \Delta Q$, and ΔP, there exists r^*_U such that if $r > r_U^*$ then no values of Δb and $\Delta\beta$ satisfy the reneging constraint (16′) except perhaps $\Delta b = ½\Delta Q$ and $\Delta\beta = ½\Delta P$.

Proof. The reneging constraint (16′) holds only if $|\Delta b - ½\Delta Q| + |\Delta\beta - ½\Delta P| \leq (S^{RO} - S^{SO})/r$. But this inequality can be written as

$$\text{(A2)}\quad 2r|\Delta b - ½\Delta Q| + 2r|\Delta\beta - ½\Delta P| + (a_1^{RO} - q_1\Delta Q)^2 + (a_2^{RO} - q_2\Delta Q)^2 \leq (a_1^{SO} - q_1\Delta Q)^2 + (a_2^{SO} - q_2\Delta Q)^2,$$

where $a_i^{RO} = q_i\Delta b + p_i\Delta\beta$ and $a_i^{SO} = ½q_i\Delta Q + ½p_i\Delta P$. Note that at $\Delta b = ½\Delta Q$ and $\Delta\beta = ½\Delta P$, we have $a_i^{RO} = a_i^{SO}$, so (A2) holds with equality. We will show that for sufficiently high values of r, values of Δb other than $½\Delta Q$ or values of $\Delta\beta$ other than $½\Delta P$ increase the left-hand side of (A2), but the right-hand-side is constant, so the reneging constraint (16′) fails except perhaps at $\Delta b = ½\Delta Q$ and $\Delta\beta = ½\Delta P$.

Let $L_U(\Delta b,\Delta\beta)$ denoted the left-hand side of (A2). For $\Delta b > ½\Delta Q$, we have $\partial L_U/\partial\Delta b = 2r + 2(a_1^{RO} - q_1\Delta Q)q_1 + 2(a_2^{RO} - q_2\Delta Q)q_2$. Because a_1^{RO} and $a_2^{RO} \geq 0$, we have that if $r > (q_1^2 + q_2^2)\Delta Q$, then $\partial L_U/\partial\Delta b > 0$ for $\Delta b > ½\Delta Q$. For $\Delta b < ½\Delta Q$, we have $\partial L_U/\partial\Delta b = -2r + 2(a_i^{RO} - q_1\Delta Q)q_1 + 2(a_2^{RO} - q_2\Delta Q)q_2$. We wish to show that if r is sufficiently high, then $\partial L_U/\partial\Delta b < 0$ for $\Delta b < ½\Delta Q$. It therefore suffices to establish an upper bound on $q_1a_1^{RO} + q_2a_2^{RO}$. Because $a_i^{RO} = q_i\Delta b + p_i\Delta\beta$ and $\Delta b < ½\Delta Q$, it suffices to establish an upper bound on $\Delta\beta$. This is done in Lemma 6.

Similarly, for $\Delta\beta > ½\Delta P$ we have $\partial L_U/\partial\Delta\beta = 2r + 2(a_1^{RO} - q_1\Delta Q)p_1 + 2(a_2^{RO} - q_2\Delta Q)p_2$. Because a_1^{RO} and $a_2^{RO} \geq 0$, we have that if $r > (p_1q_1 + p_2q_2)\Delta Q$ then $\partial L_U/\partial\Delta\beta > 0$ for $\Delta\beta > ½\Delta P$. For $\Delta\beta < ½\Delta P$ we have $\partial L_U/\partial\Delta\beta = -2r + 2(a_1^{RO} - q_1\Delta Q)p_1 + 2(a_2^{RO} - q_2\Delta Q)p_2$. We wish to show that if r is sufficiently high then $\partial L_U/\partial\Delta\beta < 0$ for $\Delta\beta < ½\Delta Q$. It therefore suffices to establish an upper bound on $p_1a_1^{RO} + p_2a_2^{RO}$. Because $a_i^{RO} = q_i\Delta b + p_i\Delta\beta$ and $\Delta\beta < ½\Delta P$, it suffices to establish an upper bound on Δb. This is done in Lemma 7.

Let r_U^* be the maximum of $(q_1^2 + q_2^2)\Delta Q$, $(p_1q_1 + p_2q_2)\Delta Q$, and the two other values of r determined above. Then for $r > r_U^*$ we have that (A2) fails and hence that (16′) fails, except perhaps at $\Delta b = ½\Delta Q$ and $\Delta\beta = ½\Delta P$.

LEMMA 6. Too strong an incentive based on the alternative-use value makes relational outsourcing inferior to spot outsourcing. That is, given q_1, q_2, p_1, p_2, and ΔQ, there exists $\Delta\beta''$ such that, for any Δb, if $\Delta\beta > \Delta\beta''$ then $S^{RO} - S^{SO} < 0$.

Proof. $2(S^{RO} - S^{SO}) = K(\Delta b) + 2(p_1q_1 + p_2q_2)(\Delta Q - \Delta b)\Delta\beta - (p_1^2 + p_2^2)\Delta\beta^2$. As in the proof of Lemma 2, maximize $K(\Delta b)$ with respect to $\Delta b \geq 0$, and maximize the second term with respect to $\Delta b \geq 0$ (at $\Delta b = 0$). Now choose $\Delta\beta''$ to be the larger root of the resulting quadratic, with the maximized versions of the first and second terms replacing the originals.

LEMMA 7. Too strong an incentive based on the downstream value makes relational outsourcing inferior to spot outsourcing. That is, given q_1, q_2, p_1, p_2, and ΔQ, there exists $\Delta b''$ such that, for any $\Delta\beta$, if $\Delta b > \Delta b''$ then $S^{RO} - S^{SO} < 0$.

Proof. $2(S^{RO} - S^{SO}) = M(\Delta\beta) + 2\{(q_1^2 + q_2^2)\Delta Q - (p_1q_1 + p_2q_2)\Delta\beta\}\Delta b - (q_1^2 + q_2^2)\Delta b^2$. As in the proof of Lemma 2, maximize $M(\Delta\beta)$ with respect to $\Delta\beta \geq 0$, and maximize the second term with respect to $\Delta\beta \geq 0$ (at $\Delta\beta = 0$). Now choose $\Delta b''$ to be the larger root of the resulting quadratic, with the maximized versions of the first and second terms replacing the originals.

HARVARD BUSINESS SCHOOL AND NBER
MASSACHUSETTS INSTITUTE OF TECHNOLOGY AND NBER
UNIVERSITY OF SOUTHERN CALIFORNIA

REFERENCES

Arrow, Kenneth, "Vertical Integration and Communication," *Bell Journal of Economics,* VI (1975), 173–183.

Baker, George, Robert Gibbons, and Kevin J. Murphy, "Subjective Performance Measures in Optimal Incentive Contracts," *Quarterly Journal of Economics,* CIX (1994), 1125–1156.

Baker, George, Robert Gibbons, and Kevin J. Murphy, "Bringing the Market Inside the Firm?" *American Economic Review,* XCI (2001), 212–218.

Barnard, Chester, *The Functions of the Executive* (Cambridge, MA: Harvard University Press, 1938).

Bernheim, Douglas, and Michael Whinston, "Incomplete Contracts and Strategic Ambiguity," *American Economic Review,* LXXXVIII (1998), 902–932.

Blau, Peter, *The Dynamics of Bureaucracy* (Chicago, IL: University of Chicago Press, 1955).

Blau, Peter, and Richard Scott, *Formal Organizations: A Comparative Approach* (San Francisco, CA: Chandler Publishing, 1962).

Blumenstein, Rebecca, and Gabriella Stern, "UAW, Auto Makers Find Some Things Better Left Unsaid," *Wall Street Journal,* November 25, 1996.

Bower, Joseph, *Managing the Resource Allocation Process* (Boston, MA: Harvard Business School Press, 1970).

Bragelien, Iver, "Asset Ownership and Implicit Contracts," Unpublished manuscript, Norwegian School of Business, 2000.

Bull, Clive, "The Existence of Self-Enforcing Implicit Contracts," *Quarterly Journal of Economics,* CII (1987), 147–159.

Carlton, Dennis, "Vertical Integration in Competitive Markets under Uncertainty," *Journal of Industrial Economics,* XXXVII (1979), 189–209.
Che, Yeon-Koo, and Seung-Weon Yoo, "Optimal Incentives for Teams," *American Economic Review,* XCI (2001), 525–41.
Chesbrough, Henry, and David Teece, "When Is Virtual Virtuous? Organizing for Innovation," *Harvard Business Review* (January–February 1996), 65–73.
Coase, Ronald, "The Nature of the Firm," *Economica,* IV (1937), 386–405.
Cusumano, Michael, and Akira Takeishi, "Supplier Relations and Management: A Survey of Japanese, Japanese-Transplant, and U. S. Auto Plants," *Strategic Management Journal,* XII (1991), 563–588.
Dalton, Melville, *Men Who Manage* (New York: Wiley, 1959).
Dechow, Patricia, Mark Huson, and Richard Sloan, "The Effect of Restructuring Charges on Executives' Cash Compensation," *Accounting Review,* LXIX (1994), 138–156.
DeMeza, David, and Ben Lockwood, "Does Asset Ownership Always Motivate Managers? Outside Options and the Property Rights Theory of the Firm," *Quarterly Journal of Economics,* CXIII (1999), 361–386.
Dore, Ronald, "Goodwill and the Spirit of Market Capitalism," *British Journal of Sociology,* XXXIV (1983), 459–482.
Dyer, Jeffrey, "How Chrysler Created an American Keiretsu," *Harvard Business Review* (July–August 1996), 32–46.
Eccles, Robert, *The Transfer Pricing Problem* (Lexington, MA: D. C. Heath, 1985).
Garvey, Gerald, "Why Reputation Favors Joint Ventures over Vertical and Horizontal Integration: A Simple Model," *Journal of Economic Behavior and Organization,* XXVIII (1995), 387–397.
Gerlach, Michael, *Alliance Capitalism: The Social Organization of Japanese Businesses* (Berkeley, CA: University of California Press, 1991).
Goldberg, Victor P., and John R. Erickson, "Quantity and Price Adjustment in Long-Term Contracts: A Case Study of Petroleum Coke," *Journal of Law and Economics,* XXX (1987), 369–398.
Gould, J. R., "Transfer Pricing in Firms When There Are Costs of Using an Outside Market," *Journal of Business,* XXXVII (1964), 61–67.
Gouldner, Alvin, *Patterns of Industrial Bureaucracy* (New York, NY: The Free Press, 1954).
Granovetter, Mark, "Economic Action and Social Structure: The Problem of Embeddedness," *American Journal of Sociology,* XCI (1985), 481–510.
——, "Coase Revisited: Business Groups in the Modern Economy," *Industrial and Corporate Change,* IV (1995), 93–130.
Grossman, Sanford, and Oliver Hart, "The Costs and Benefits of Ownership: A Theory of Vertical and Lateral Ownership," *Journal of Political Economy,* XCIV (1986), 691–719.
Gulati, Ranjay, and Harbir Singh, "The Architecture of Cooperation: Managing Coordination Costs and Appropriation Concerns in Strategic Alliances," *Administrative Science Quarterly,* XLIII (1998), 781–814.
Hart, Oliver, *Firms, Contracts, and Financial Structure* (Oxford: Clarendon Press, 1995).
Hart, Oliver, and John Moore, "Property Rights and the Nature of the Firm," *Journal of Political Economy* XCVIII (1990), 1119–1158.
Halonen, Maija, "Reputation and Allocation of Ownership," Working Paper, Helsinki School of Economics, 1994.
Hirshleifer, Jack, "On the Economics of Effective Intracompany Pricing," *Journal of Business,* XXIX (1956), 172–184.
Holmstrom, Bengt, "The Firm as a Subeconomy," *Journal of Law, Economics, and Organization,* XV (1999), 74–102.
Holmstrom, Bengt, and Paul Milgrom, "Multitask Principal-Agent Analyses: Incentive Contracts, Asset Ownership, and Job Design," *Journal of Law, Economics, and Organization,* VII (1991), 24–52.
Holmstrom, Bengt, and Jean Tirole, "Transfer Pricing and Organizational Form," *Journal of Law, Economics, and Organization,* VII (1991), 201–228.
Kahn, Charles, and Gur Huberman, "Two-sided Uncertainty and 'Up-or-Out' Contract," *Journal of Labor Economics,* VI (1988), 423–444.

Klein, Benjamin, "Why Hold-ups Occur: The Self-Enforcing Range of Contractual Relationships," *Economic Inquiry,* XXXIV (1996), 444–463.

——, "Fisher-General Motors and the Nature of the Firm," *Journal of Law and Economics,* XLIII (2000), 105–141.

Klein, Benjamin, Robert Crawford, and Armen Alchian, "Vertical Integration, Appropriable Rents and the Competitive Contracting Process," *Journal of Law and Economics,* XXI (1978), 297–326.

Klein, Benjamin, and Keith Leffler, "The Role of Market Forces in Assuring Contractual Performance," *Journal of Political Economy,* LXXXIX (1981), 615–641.

Klein, Benjamin, and Kevin M. Murphy, "Vertical Restraints as Contract Enforcement Mechanisms," *Journal of Law and Economics,* XXXI (1988), 265–297.

Klein, Benjamin, and Kevin M. Murphy, "Vertical Integration as a Self-Enforcing Contractual Arrangement," *American Economic Review,* LXXXVII (1997), 415–420.

Kogut, Bruce, "The Stability of Joint Ventures: Reciprocity and Competitive Rivalry," *Journal of Industrial Economics,* XXXVIII (1989), 183–198.

Kole, Stacey, "The Complexity of Compensation Contracts," *Journal of Financial Economics,* XLIII (1997), 79–104.

Kreps, David, "Corporate Culture and Economic Theory," in J. Alt and K. Shepsle, eds., *Perspectives on Positive Political Economy* (Cambridge University Press, 1990).

Lawler, Edward, *Pay and Organizational Effectiveness: A Psychological View,* (New York, NY: McGraw-Hill, 1971).

Levin, Jonathan, "Relational Incentive Contracts," Working Paper, Stanford University, 2000.

Lorsch, Jay, and Elizabeth McIver, *Pawn and Potentates: The Reality of America's Corporate Boards* (Boston, MA: Harvard Business School Press, 1994).

Macaulay, Stewart, "Non Contractual Relations in Business: A Preliminary Study," *American Sociological Review,* XXVIII (1963), 55–67.

MacLeod, Bentley, and James Malcomson, "Implicit Contracts, Incentive Compatibility, and Involuntary Unemployment," *Econometrica,* LVII (1989) 447–480.

MacLeod, Bentley, and James Malcomson, "Motivation and Markets," *American Economic Review,* LXXXVIII (1998), 388–411.

Macneil, Ian, "Contracts: Adjustments of Long-Term Economic Relations under Classical, Neoclassical, and Relational Contract Law," *Northwestern University Law Review,* LCCII (1978), 854–906.

Maskin, Eric, and Jean Tirole, "Two Remarks on Property Rights," *Review of Economic Studies,* LXVI (1999), 139–149.

Miles, Raymond, and Charles Snow, "Causes of Failure in Network Organizations," *California Management Review,* XXXIV (1992), 53–72.

Nishiguchi, Toshihiro, *Strategic Industrial Sourcing: The Japanese Advantage* (New York, NY: Oxford University Press, 1994).

Pisano, Gary, "Using Equity Participation to Support Exchange: Evidence from the Biotechnology Industry," *Journal of Law, Economics, and Organization,* V (1989), 109–126.

Podolny, Joel, and Karen Page, "Network Forms of Organization," *Annual Review of Sociology,* XXIV (1998), 57–76.

Powell, Walter, "Neither Market nor Hierarchy: Network Forms of Organization," *Research in Organizational Behavior,* XII (1990), 295–336.

Rey, Patrick, and Jean Tirole, "Divergence of Objectives and the Governance of Joint Ventures," Working Paper, IDEI, 1999.

Sako, Mari, and Susan Helper, "Determinants of Trust in Supplier Relations: Evidence from the Automotive Industry in Japan and the United States," *Journal of Economic Behavior and Organization,* XXXIV (1998), 387–417.

Selznick, Philip, *TVA and the Grass Roots* (Berkeley, CA: University of California Press, 1949).

Simon, Herbert, "A Formal Theory Model of the Employment Relationship," *Econometrica,* XIX (1951), 293–305.

——, *Administrative Behavior* (New York, NY: The Free Press, 1947, 1976).

Telser, Lester, "A Theory of Self-Enforcing Agreements," *Journal of Business*, LIII (1981), 27–44.

Whinston, Michael, "On the Transaction Cost Determinants of Vertical Integration," unpublished manuscript, Northwestern University, 2000.

Williamson, Oliver, *Markets and Hierarchies: Analysis and Antitrust Implications* (New York, NY: Free Press, 1975).

——, *The Economic Institutions of Capitalism* (New York, NY: Free Press, 1985).

——, *The Mechanisms of Governance* (New York, NY: Oxford University Press, 1996).

Part II
Vertical Integration

[8]

The Vertical Integration of Production: Market Failure Considerations*

By Oliver E. Williamson
University of Pennsylvania

The study of vertical integration has presented difficulties at both theoretical and policy levels of analysis. That vertical integration has never enjoyed a secure place in value theory is attributable to the fact that, under conventional assumptions, it is an anomaly: if the costs of operating competitive markets are zero, "as is usually assumed in our theoretical analysis" (Arrow, 1969, p. 48), why integrate?

Policy interest in vertical integration has been concerned mainly with the possibility that integration can be used strategically to achieve anticompetitive effects. In the absence of a more substantial theoretical foundation, vertical integration, as a public policy matter, is typically regarded as having dubious if not outright antisocial properties. Technological interdependencies or, possibly, observational economies, constitute the principal exceptions.

The technological interdependency argument is both the most familiar and the most straight-forward: successive processes which, naturally, follow immediately in time and place dictate certain efficient manufacturing configurations; these, in turn, are believed to have common ownership implications. Such technical complementarity is probably more important in flow process operations (chemicals, metals, etc.) than in separable component manufacture. The standard example is the integration of iron and steel-making, where thermal economies are said to be available through integration. It is commonly held that where "integration does not have this physical or technical aspect —as it does not, for example, in integrating the production of assorted components with the assembly of those components— the case for cost savings from integration is generally much less clear" (Bain, 1968, p. 381).

There is, nevertheless, a distinct unease over the argument. This is attributable, probably, to a suspicion that the firm is more than a simple efficiency instrument, in the usual scale economies and least-cost factor proportions senses of the term, but also possesses coordinating potential that sometimes transcends that of the market. It is the burden of the present argument that this suspicion is warranted. In more numerous respects than are commonly appreciated, the substitution of internal organization for market exchange is attractive less on account of technological economies associated with production but because of what may be referred to broadly as "transactional failures" in the operation of markets for intermediate goods. This substitution of internal organization for market exchange will be referred to as "internalization."

The two principal prior contributions on which the argument relies are Coase's seminal discussion on "The Nature of The Firm" (1937) and Arrow's more recent review of market versus nonmarket allo-

* Research on this paper has been supported by a grant from the Brookings Institution. It is part of the larger study referred to in footnote 1. Helpful comments from Noel Edelson, Stefano Fenoaltea, Julius Margolis, and Almarin Phillips are gratefully acknowledged.

cation (1969). As will be evident, I agree with Malmgren (1961) that the analysis of transaction costs is uninteresting under fully stationary conditions and that only when the need to make unprogrammed adaptations is introduced does the market versus internal organization issue become engaging.

But while Malmgren finds that the advantage of the firm inheres in its capacity to control information and achieve plan consistency among interdependent activities, which may be regarded as an information processing advantage, I mainly emphasize the differential incentive and control properties of firms in relation to markets. This is not to suggest that information processing considerations are unimportant, but rather that these incompletely characterize the distinctive properties of firms that favor internal organization as a market substitute.

I. *Internal Organization: Affirmative Aspects*

A complete treatment of vertical integration requires that the limits as well as the powers of internal organization be assessed. As the frictions associated with administrative coordination become progressively more severe, recourse to market exchange becomes more attractive, *ceteris paribus*. It is beyond the scope of this paper, however, to examine the organizational failure aspect of the vertical integration question.[1] Rather it is simply asserted that, mainly on account of bounded rationality and greater confidence in the objectivity of market exchange in comparison with bureaucratic processes, market intermediation is generally to be preferred over internal supply in circumstances in which markets may be said to "work well."[2]

The properties of the firm that commend internal organization as a market substitute would appear to fall into three categories: incentives, controls, and what may be referred to broadly as "inherent structural advantages." In an incentive sense, internal organization attenuates the aggressive advocacy that epitomizes arms length bargaining. Interests, if not perfectly harmonized, are at least free of representations of a narrowly opportunistic sort; in any viable group, of which the firm is one, the range of admissable intraorganizational behavior is bounded by considerations of alienation. In circumstances, therefore, where protracted bargaining between independent parties to a transaction can reasonably be anticipated, internalization becomes attractive.[3]

Perhaps the most distinctive advantage of the firm, however, is the wider variety and greater sensitivity of control instruments that are available for enforcing intrafirm in comparison with interfirm activities (Williamson, 1970). Not only does the firm have the constitutional authority and low-cost access to the requisite data which permit it to perform more precise own-performance evaluations (of both a contemporaneous and *ex post* variety)

[1] I discuss the organizational failure dimension of this issue in *Aspects of Monopoly Theory and Policy* (forthcoming). Policy implications of the argument are also examined there.

[2] An intermediate market will be said to work well if, both presently and prospectively, prices are non-monopolistic and reflect an acceptable risk premium, and if market exchange experiences low transaction costs and permits the realization of essential economies. To the extent that the stipulated conditions do not hold, internal supply becomes relatively more attractive, *ceteris paribus*.

[3] Common ownership by itself, of course, does not guarantee goal consistency. A holding company form of organization in which purchaser and supplier are independent divisions, each maximizing individual profits, is no solution. Moreover, merely to stipulate joint profit maximization is not by itself apt to be sufficient. The goal needs to be operationalized, which involves both rulemaking (with respect, for example, to transfer pricing) and the design of efficacious internal incentives. For a discussion, see Williamson (1970).

than can a buyer, but its reward and penalty instruments (which include selective use of employment, promotion, remuneration, and internal resource allocation processes) are more refined.

Especially relevant in this connection is that, when conflicts develop, the firm possesses a comparatively efficient conflict resolution machinery. To illustrate, fiat is frequently a more efficient way to settle minor conflicts (say differences of interpretation) than is haggling or litigation. *Inter*organizational conflict can be settled by fiat only rarely, if at all. For one thing, it would require the parties to agree on an impartial arbitrator, which agreement itself may be costly to secure. It would also require that rules of evidence and procedure be established. If, moreover, the occasion for such interorganizational settlements were to be common, the form of organization converges in effect to vertical integration, with the arbiter becoming a manager in fact if not in name. By contrast, *intra*organizational settlements by fiat are common (Whinston, 1964, pp. 410–14).

The firm may also resort to internalization on account of economies of information exchange. Some of these may be due to structural differences between firms and markets. Others, however, reduce ultimately to incentive and control differences between internal and market organization. It is widely accepted, for example, that communication with respect to complex matters is facilitated by a common training and experience and if a compact code has developed in the process. Repeated interpersonal interactions may permit even further economies of communication; subtle nuances may come through in familiar circumstances which in an unfamiliar relationship could be achieved only with great effort. Still, the drawing of an organizational boundary need not, by itself, prevent intensely familiar relations from developing between organizations. Put differently, but for the goal and control differences described above, the informational advantages of internal over market organization are not, in this respect, apparent. Claims of informational economies thus should distinguish between economies that are attributable to information flows *per se* (structure) and those which obtain on account of differential veracity effects (see Part D, Section II).

II. *Market Failure Considerations*

What are referred to here as market failures are failures only in the limited sense that they involve transaction costs that can be attenuated by substituting internal organization for market exchange. The argument proceeds in five stages. The first three are concerned with characterizing a successively more complex bargaining environment in which small numbers relations obtain. The last two deal with the special structural advantages which, either naturally or because of prevailing institutional rules, the firm enjoys in relation to the market.

A. *Static Markets*

Consider an industry that produces a multicomponent product, assume that some of these components are specialized (industry specific), and assume further that among these there are components for which the economies of scale in production are large in relation to the market. The market, then, will support only a few efficient sized producers for certain components.

A monopolistic excess of price over cost under market procurement is commonly anticipated in these circumstances—although, as Demsetz (1968) has noted, this need not obtain if there are large numbers of suppliers willing and able to bid at the initial contract award stage. Assume, however, that large numbers bidding is not feasible. The postulated conditions then afford an "apparent" incentive for assemblers to integrate backward or suppliers to integrate forward. Two different cases can be distinguished: bilateral monopoly (oligopoly) and competitive assembly with monopolistic supply. The former is considered here; the latter is treated in Part C.

Bilateral monopoly requires that both price and quantity be negotiated. Both parties stand to benefit, naturally, by operating on rather than off the contract curve—which here corresponds to the joint profit maximizing quantity (Fellner, 1947). But this merely establishes the amount to be exchanged. The terms at which this quantity will be traded still need to be determined. Any price consistent with nonnegative profits to both parties is feasible. Bargaining can be expected to ensue. Haggling will presumably continue until the marginal private net benefits are perceived by one of the parties to be zero. Although this haggling is jointly (and socially) unproductive, it constitutes a source of private pecuniary gain. Being, nevertheless, a joint profit drain, an incentive to avoid these costs, if somehow this could be arranged, is set up.

One possible adaptation is to internalize the transaction through vertical integration; but a once-for-all contract might also be negotiated. In a perfectly static environment (one that is free of disturbances of all kinds), these may be regarded with indifference: the former involves settlement on component supply price while merger requires agreement on asset valuation. Bargaining skills will presumably be equally important in each instance (indeed, a component price can be interpreted in asset valuation terms and conversely). Thus, although vertical integration may occur under these conditions, there is nothing in the nature of the problem that requires such an outcome.

A similar argument in these circumstances also applies to adaptation against externalities: joint profit considerations dictate that the affected parties reach an accommodation, but integration holds no advantage over once-for-all contracts in a perfectly static environment.

Transforming the relationship from one of bilateral monopoly to one of bilateral oligopoly broadens the range of bargaining alternatives, but the case for negotiating a merger agreement in relation to a once-for-all contract is not differentially affected on this account. The static characterization of the problem, apparently, will have to be relaxed if a different result is to be reached.

B. *Contractual Incompleteness*

Let the above conditions be enriched to include the stipulation that the product in question is technically complex and that periodic redesign and/or volume changes are made in response to changing environmental conditions. Also relax the assumption that large numbers bidding at the initial contract award stage is infeasible. Three alternative supply arrangements can be considered: a once-for-all contract, a series of short-term contracts, and vertical integration.

The dilemma posed by once-for-all contracts is this: lest independent parties interpret contractual ambiguities to their own advantage, which differences can be resolved only by haggling or, ultimately, litigation, contingent supply relations ought exhaustively to be stipulated. But exhaustive stipulation, assuming that it is feasible, is itself costly. Thus although, if production functions were known, appropriate responses to final demand or factor price changes might be deduced, the very costliness of specifying the functions and securing agreement discourages the effort. The problem is made even more severe where a changing technology poses product redesign issues. Here it is doubtful that, despite great effort and expense, contractual efforts reasonably to comprehend the range of possible outcomes will be successful. An adaptive, sequential decision process is thus indicated. If, however, contractual revisions or amendments are regarded as an occasion to bargain opportunistically, which predictably they will be, the purchaser will defer and accumulate adaptations, if by packaging them in complex combinations their true value can better be disguised; some adaptations may be foregone altogether. The optimal sequential decision-making process can in these respects be distorted.

Short-term contracts, which would facilitate adaptive, sequential decision-making, might therefore be preferred. These pose problems, however, if either (1) efficient supply requires investment in special-purpose, long-life equipment, or (2) the winner of the original contract acquires a cost advantage, say by reason of "first mover" advantages (such as unique location or learning, including the acquisition of undisclosed or proprietary technical and managerial procedures and task-specific labor skills).

The problem with condition (1) is that optimal investment considerations favor the award of a long-term contract so as to permit the supplier confidently to amortize his investment. But, as indicated, long term contracts pose adaptive, sequential decision-making problems. Thus optimal investment and optimal sequential adaptation processes are in conflict in this instance.

It might be argued that condition (2) poses no problems since initial bidders will fully reflect in their original bids all relevant factors. Thus, although anticipated downstream cost advantages (where downstream is used both here and subsequently in the sense of time rather than place) will give rise to small numbers competition for downstream supply, competition at the initial award stage is sufficient to assure that only competitive returns will be realized over the entire supply interval. One might expect, therefore, that the low bidder would come in at a price below cost in the first period, set price at the level of alternative supply price in later periods, and earn normal returns over-all. Appropriate changes can be introduced easily at the recontracting interval.

A number of potential problems are posed, however. For one thing, unless the total supply requirements are stipulated, "buying in" strategies are risky. Also, and related, the alternative supply price is not independent of the terms that the buyer may subsequently offer to rivals. Moreover, alternative supply price is merely an upper bound; an aggressive buyer may attempt to obtain a price at the level of current costs on each round. Haggling could be expected to ensue. Short-term contracts thus experience what may be serious limitations in circumstances where nontrivial first-mover advantages obtain.

In consideration, therefore, of the problems that both long and short-term contracts are subject to, vertical integration may well be indicated. The conflict between efficient investment and efficient sequential decision-making is thereby avoided. Sequential adaptations become an occasion for cooperative adjustment rather than opportunistic bargaining; risks may be attenuated; differences between successive stages can be resolved more easily by the internal control machinery.

It is relevant to note that the technological interdependency condition involving flow process economies between otherwise separable stages of production is really a special case of the contractual incompleteness argument. The contractual dilemma is this: On the one hand, it may be prohibitively costly, if not infeasible, to specify contractually the full range of contingencies and stipulate appropriate responses between stages. On the other hand, if the contract is seriously incomplete in these respects but, once the original negotiations are settled, the contracting parties are locked into a bilateral exchange, the divergent interests between the parties will predictably lead to individually opportunistic behavior and joint losses. The advantages of integration thus are not that technological (flow process) economies are unavailable to nonintegrated firms, but that integration harmonizes interests (or reconciles differences, often by fiat) and permits an efficient (adaptive, sequential) decision process to be utilized. More generally, arguments favorable to integration that turn on "supply reliability" considerations commonly reduce to the contractual incompleteness issue.[4]

C. *Strategic Misrepresentation Risk*

Contractual incompleteness problems develop where there is *ex ante* but not necessarily *ex post* uncertainty. Strategic misrepresentation risks are serious where there is uncertainty in both respects. Not only is the future uncertain but it may not be possible, except at great cost, for an outside agency to establish accurately what has transpired after the fact. The advantages of internalization reside in the facts that the firm's *ex post* access to the relevant data is superior, it attenuates the incentives to exploit uncertainty opportunistically, and the control machinery that the firm is able to activate is more selective.

1. Affirmative Occasions for Integration. Three affirmative occasions to integrate on account of strategic misrepresentation risk and two potentially anticompetitive consequences of integration can be identified.

(a) Moral Hazard. The problem here arises because of the conjoining of inharmonious incentives with uncertainty—or, as Arrow puts it (1969, p. 55), it is due to the "confounding of risks and decisions." To illustrate, consider the problem of contracting for an item the final cost and/or performance of which is subject to uncertainty. One possibility is for the supplier to bear the uncertainty. But, he will undertake a fixed price contract to deliver a specified result the costs of which are highly uncertain only after attaching a risk premium to the price. Assume that the buyer regards this premium as excessive and is prepared on this account to bear the risk himself. The risk can easily be shifted by offering a cost-plus contract. But this impairs the incentives of the supplier to achieve least-cost performance; the supplier may reallocate his assets in such a way as to favor other work to the disadvantage of the cost-plus contract.

Thus, although, if commitments were self-enforcing, it might often be institutionally most efficent to divide the functions of risk bearing and contract execution (that is, cost-plus contracts would have ideal properties), specialization is discouraged by interest disparities. At a minimum, the buyer may insist on monitoring the supplier's work. In contrast therefore to a fixed-price contract, where it is sufficient to evaluate end-product performance, cost-plus contracts, because

[4] It is sometimes suggested that breach of contract risk affords an additional reason for integration: the small supplier of a critical component whose assets are insufficient to cover a total damage claim leaves the purchaser vulnerable. But this is an argument against small suppliers, not contracting quite generally; the large, diversified supplier might well have superior risk pooling capability to that of the integrated firm. The risks of contractual incompleteness, however, remain and may discourage purchasing from large, diversified organizations. For a discussion of "ideal" contracts in this connection, see Arrow (1965, pp. 52–53).

they expose the buyer to risks of inefficient (high cost) contract execution, require that *both* inputs and outputs be evaluated.

Internalization does not eliminate the need for input evaluation. Rather, the advantage of internalization, for input monitoring purposes, resides in the differential ease with which controls are exercised. An external agency, by design, lacks recourse to the internal control machinery: proposed remedies require the consent of the contractor and then are highly circumscribed; unrestricted access by the buyer to the contractor's internal control machinery (including selective use of employment, promotion, remuneration, and internal resource allocation processes) is apt to be denied. In consideration of the costs and limitations of input monitoring by outsiders, the buyer may choose instead to bear the risk and perform the work himself. The buyer thus internalizes, through backward vertical integration, a transaction which, but for uncertainty, would move through the market. A cost-type contract for *internal procurement* is arranged.

(b) Externalities/Imputation. The externality issue can be examined in two parts. First, has a secure, unambiguous, and "appropriate" assignment of property rights been made? Second, are the accounting costs of imputing costs and benefits substantial? If answers to these questions are affirmative and negative respectively, appropriability problems will not become an occasion for vertical integration. Where these conditions are not satisfied, however, integration may be indicated.

The assignment aspect of this matter is considered in Part E below. Here it is assumed that an efficacious assignment of property rights has been made and that only the expense of imputing costs and benefits is at issue. But indeed this is apt often to be the more serious problem. High imputation expenses which discourage accurate metering introduce ambiguity into transactions. Did party A affect party B and if so in what degree? In the absence of objective, low cost standards, opposed interests can be expected to evaluate these effects differently. Internalization, which permits protracted (and costly) disputes over these issues to be avoided, may on this account be indicated.

(c) Variable Proportions Distortions. Consider the case where the assembly stage will support large numbers; fewness appears only in component supply. Whether monopolistic supply prices provide an occasion for vertical integration in these circumstances depends both on production technology and policing expense. Variable proportions at the assembly stage afford opportunities for nonintegrated assemblers to adapt against monopolistically priced components by substituting competitively priced factors (McKenzie, 1951). Although conceivably the monopolistic component supplier could stipulate, as a condition of sale, that fixed proportions in assembly should prevail, the effectiveness of such stipulations is to be questioned—since, ordinarily, the implied enforcement costs will be great. Where substitution occurs, inefficient factor proportions, with consequent welfare losses, will result. The private (and social) incentives to integrate so as to reduce total costs by restoring efficient factor combinations are evident.

2. Anticompetitive Consequences. Anticompetitive effects of two types are commonly attributed to integration: price discrimination and barriers to entry (cf. Stigler, 1968, p. 303).

(a) Price Discrimination. The problem here is first to discover differential demand elasticities, and secondly to arrange for sale in such a way as to preclude reselling. Users with highly elastic demands which purchase the item at a low price must not be able to service inelastic demand customers by acting as a middleman; all sales must be final. Although vertical integration may facilitate the discovery of differential elasticities, it is mainly with respect to the non-resale condition that it is regarded as especially efficacious.

Integration, nevertheless, is a relatively extreme response. Moreover, price discrimination is clearly practiced in some commodities without recourse to vertical integration (witness electricity and telephone service). What are the distinguishing factors? Legality considerations aside, presumably it is the cost of enforcing (policing) terms of the contract that are at issue. Some commodities apparently have self-enforcing properties—which may obtain on account of high storage and repacking costs or because reselling can not be arranged inconspicuously. The absence of self-enforcing (policing) properties is what makes vertical integration attractive as a means of accomplishing discrimination.

(b) Entry Barrier Effects. That the vertical integration of production might be used effectively to bar entry is widely disputed. Bork (1969, p. 148) argues that "In general, if greater than competitive profits are to be made in an industry, entry should occur whether the entrant has to come in at both levels at once or not. I know of no theory of imperfections in the capital market which would lead suppliers of capital to avoid areas of higher return to seek areas of lower return." But the issue is not one of profit avoidance but rather involves cost incidence. If borrowers are confronted by increasingly adverse rates as they increase their finance requirements, which Hirshleifer suggests is a distinct possibility (1970, pp. 200–1), cost may not be independent of vertical structure.

Assuming that vertical integration has the effect of increasing capital requirements, the critical issues are to what extent and for what reasons the supply curve of finance behaves in the way postulated. The following conjecture is offered as a partial explanation: unable to monitor the performance of *large, complex* organizations in any but the crudest way or to effect management displacement easily except on evidence of seriously discreditable error, investors demand larger returns as finance requirements become progressively greater, *ceteris paribus*. Thus the costs of policing against the contingency that managers will operate a rival enterprise opportunistically are, on this argument, at least partly responsible for the reputed behavior of the supply curve of capital. In consideration of this state of affairs, established firms may use vertical integration strategically to increase finance requirements and thereby to discourage entry if potential entrants feel compelled, as a condition of successful entry, to adopt the prevailing structure —as they may if the industry is highly concentrated.

D. *Information Processing Effects*

As indicated in Section I, one of the advantages of the firm is that it realizes economies of information exchange. These may manifest themselves as information impactedness, observational economies, or what Malmgren (1961) refers to as the "convergence of expectations."

1. Information Impactedness. Richardson illustrates the problems of information impactedness by reference to an entrepreneur who was willing to offer long-term contracts (at normal rates of return, presumably) but which contracts others were unprepared to accept because they were not convinced that he had "the ability, as well as the will, to fulfill them. He may have information sufficient to convince himself that this is the case, but others may not" (Richardson, 1960, p. 83). He goes on to observe that the perceived

risks of the two parties may be such as to make it difficult to negotiate a contract that offers commensurate returns to each; objective risks are augmented by contractual risks in these circumstances. Integration undertaken for this reason is akin to self-insurance by individuals who know themselves to be good risks but are priced out of the insurance market because of their inability, at low cost, to "reveal" this condition to insurers.

2. Observational Economies. As Radner indicates, "the acquisition of information often involves a 'set-up cost'; i.e., the resources needed to obtain the information may be independent of the scale of the production process in which the information is used" (Radner, 1970, p. 457). Although Radner apparently had horizontal firm size implications in mind, the argument also has relevance for vertical integration. If a single set of observations can be made that is of relevance to a related series of production stages, vertical integration may be efficient.

Still, the question might be raised, why common ownership? Why not an independent observational agency that sells information to all comers? Or, if the needed information is highly specialized, why not a joint venture? Alternatively, what inhibits efficient information exchange between successive stages of production according to contract? In relation, certainly, to the range of intermediate options potentially available, common ownership appears to be an extreme response. What are the factors which favor this outcome?

One of the problems with contracts is that of specifying terms. But even if terms could be reached, there is still a problem of policing the agreement. To illustrate, suppose that the common information collection responsibilities are assigned by contract to one of the parties. The purchasing party then runs *a veracity risk:* information may be filtered and possibly distorted to the advantage of the firm that has assumed the information collection responsibility. If checks are costly and proof of contractual violation difficult, contractual sharing arrangements manifestly experience short-run limitations. If, in addition, small numbers prevail so that options are restricted, contractual sharing is subject to long-run risks as well. On this argument, observational economies are mainly to be attributed to strategic misrepresentation risks rather than to indivisibilities.

3. Convergence of Expectations. The issue to which the convergence of expectations argument is addressed is that, if there is a high degree of interdependence among successive stages of production and if occasions for adaptation are unpredictable yet common, coordinated responses may be difficult to secure if the separate stages are operated independently. March and Simon (1958, p. 159) characterize the problem in the following terms:

> Interdependence by itself does not cause difficulty if the pattern of interdependence is stable and fixed. For, in this case, each subprogram can be designed to take account of all the subprograms with which it interacts. Difficulties arise only if program execution rests on contingencies that cannot be predicted perfectly in advance. In this case, coordinating activity is required to secure agreement about the estimates that will be used as the basis for action, or to provide information to each subprogram unit about the activities of the others.

This reduces, in some respects, to a contractual incompleteness argument. Were it feasible exhaustively to stipulate the appropriate conditional responses, coordination could proceed by contract. This is ambitious, however; in the face of a highly variable and uncertain environment, the attempt to program responses is apt to be inefficient. To the extent that an unprogrammed (adaptive, sequential) decision process is employed instead, and in consideration of the severe incentive and control limitations that long-term contracts experience in these circumstances (See Part B above), vertical integration may be indicated.

But what of the possibility of short-term contracts? It is here that the convergence of expectations argument is of special importance. Thus assume that short-term contracts are not defective on account either of investment disincentives or first-mover advantages. It is Malmgren's (1961) contention that such contracts may nevertheless be vitiated by the absence of structural constraints. The costs of negotiations and the time required to bring the system into adjustment by exclusive reliance on market (price) signals are apt to be great in relation to that which would obtain if successive states were integrated and administrative processes employed as well or instead.

E. *Institutional Adaptations*

Institutional adaptations of two types are distinguished: simple economic and extra-economic.

1. Simple Economic. As has been noted by others, vertical integration may be a device by which sales taxes on intermediate products are avoided, or a means by which to circumvent quota schemes and price controls (Coase, 1937, pp. 338–39; Stigler, 1968, pp. 136–37). But vertical intergration may also be undertaken because of the defective specification of property rights.

Although the appropriate assignment of property rights is a complex question, it reduces (equity considerations aside) to a simple criterion: What assignment yields maximum total product (Coase, 1960, p. 34)? This depends jointly on imputation and negotiation expenses and on the incentives of the compensated party. So as to focus on the negotiation expense aspect, assume that imputation expenses are negligible and set the incentive question aside for the moment.[5] An "appropriate" assignment of property rights will here be defined as one which automatically yields compensation in the amount of the external benefit or cost involved, while an "inappropriate" assignment is one that requires bargaining to bring the parties into adjustment. Thus if A and B are two parties and A's activity imposes costs on B, the appropriate assignment of property rights is to require A to compensate B. If instead property rights were defined such that A is not required to compensate B, and assuming that the externality holds at the margin, efficient adaptation would occur only if B were to bribe A to bring his activity into adjustment—which entails bargaining. Only if the costs of such bargaining are neglected can the alternative specifications of property rights be said to be equivalent. For similar reasons, if A's activity generates benefits for B, the appropriate specification of property rights will be to require B fully to compensate A. Harmonizing the otherwise divergent interests of the two parties by internalizing the transaction through vertical merger

[5] As Coase has emphasized (1960, pp. 32–33, 41), compensation can impair the incentives of the compensated party that experiences an external cost to take appropriate protective measures. Parties that are assured of compensation will be content to conduct business as usual. Such a practice easily contributes to greater social cost than would obtain were compensation denied. A sensitivity to what, in a broad sense, might be regarded as contributory negligence is thus required if the system is to be brought fully into adjustment. Clairvoyance with respect to contributory negligence would of course permit the courts to supply those who experience the external cost with requisite incentives to adapt appropriately. Since, however, such clairvoyance (or even unbiasedness) cannot routinely be presumed, internalizing the transaction through vertical integration may be indicated for this reason as well. (Interestingly, a symmetrical problem is not faced where the externality is a benefit. Stipulating that compensation shall be paid induces Meade's (1952) orchard grower not merely to extend his production appropriately, but also to shift from apples to peaches if this is socially advantageous.)

promises to overcome the haggling costs which result when property rights are left either undefined or inappropriately specified.

2. OTHER. Risk aversion refers to the degree of concavity in the utility valuation of pecuniary outcomes. Decision-makers who are risk averse will be concerned not merely with the expected value, but also with the dispersion in outcomes associated with alternative proposals: the greater the dispersion, the lower the utility valuation. *Ceteris paribus,* decision-makers who are the less risk averse will presumably assume the risk bearing function. Even, however, if attitudes toward risk were identical—in the sense that every individual (for any given set of initial endowments) would evaluate a proposal similarly —differing initial asset positions among the members of a population could warrant a specialization of the risk-bearing function, with possible firm and market structure effects (Knight, 1965).

Arrow calls attention to norms of social behavior, including ethical and moral codes. He observes in this connection that "It is useful for individuals to have some trust in each other's word. In the absence of trust, it would become very costly to arrange for alternative sanctions and guarantees, and many opportunities for mutually beneficial cooperation would have to be foregone" (1969, p. 62). One would expect, accordingly, that vertical integration would be more complete in a low-trust than a high-trust culture, *ceteris paribus.*

III. *Conclusions*

That product markets have remarkable coordinating properties is, among economists at least, a secure proposition. That product markets are subject to failure in various respects and that internal organization may be substituted against the market in these circumstances is, if somewhat less familiar, scarcely novel. A systematic treatment of market failure as it bears on vertical integration, however, has not emerged.

Partly this is attributable to inattention to internal organization: the remarkable properties of firms that distinguish internal from market coordination have been neglected. But the fragmented nature of the market failure literature as it bears on vertical integration has also contributed to this condition; the extensive variety of circumstances in which internalization is attractive tends not to be fully appreciated.

The present effort attempts both to address the internal organization issue and to organize the market failure literature as it relates to vertical integration in a systematic way. The argument, however, by no means exhausts the issues that vertical integration raises. For one thing, the discussion of market failures may be incomplete in certain respects. For another, a parallel treatment of the sources and consequences of the failures of internal organization as they relate to vertical integration is needed. Third, the argument applies strictly to the vertical integration of production; although much of it may have equal relevance to backward vertical integration into raw materials and forward integration into distribution, it may have to be delimited in significant respects. Fourth, game theoretic considerations, which may permit the indicated indeterminacy of small numbers bargaining situations to be bounded, have been neglected. Finally, nothing in the present analysis establishes that observed degrees of vertical integration are not, from a social welfare standpoint, excessive. It should nevertheless be apparent that a broader a priori case for the vertical integration of production exists than is commonly acknowledged.

REFERENCES

Kenneth J. Arrow, *Aspects of the Theory of Risk-Bearing,* Helsinki, 1965.

———, "The Organization of Economic Activity: Issues Pertinent to the Choice of Market versus Nonmarket Allocation," in *The Analysis and Evaluation of Public Expenditures: The PPB System,* Vol. 1, Joint Economic Committee, Washington, D.C., 1969 pp. 47–64.

Joe S. Bain, *Industrial Organization,* New York, 1968.

Robert H. Bork, "Vertical Integration and Competitive Processes," in J. Fred Weston and Sam Peltzman, eds., *Public Policy Toward Mergers,* Pacific Palisades, Calif., 1969, pp. 139–49.

Ronald H. Coase, "The Nature of the Firm," *Economica,* Nov. 1937, *4,* 386–405; reprinted in George J. Stigler and Kenneth E. Boulding, eds., *Readings in Price Theory,* Homéwood, Ill., 1952, pp. 331–51.

———, "The Problem of Social Cost," *Journal of Law and Economics,* 1960, *3,* 1–44.

Harold Demsetz, "Why Regulate Utilities?" *Journal of Law and Economics,* April 1968, *11,* 55–66.

William Fellner, "Prices and Wages under Bilateral Oligopoly," *Quarterly Journal of Economics,* August 1947, *61,* 503–32.

J. Hirshleifer, *Investment, Interest and Capital,* Englewood Cliffs, N.J.,1970.

Frank H. Knight, *Risk, Uncertainty and Profit,* New York, 1965.

Lionel McKenzie, "Ideal Output and the Interdependence of Firms," *Economic Journal,* December 1951, *61,* 785–803.

H. B. Malmgren, "Information, Expectations and the Theory of the Firm," *Quarterly Journal of Economics,* August 1961, *75,* 399–421.

James E. Meade, "External Economies and Diseconomies in a Competitive Situation," *Economic Journal,* March 1952, *62,* 54–67.

Roy Radner, "Problems in the Theory of Markets under Uncertainty," *American Economic Review,* May 1970, *60,* 454–60.

G. B. Richardson, *Information and Investment,* London, 1960.

George J. Stigler, *The Organization of Industry,* Homewood, Ill., 1968.

Andrew Whinston, "Price Guides in Decentralized Organizations," in W. W. Cooper, H. J. Leavitt, and M. W. Shelly, II, eds., *New Perspectives in Organization Research,* New York, 1964, pp. 405–48.

Oliver E. Williamson, *Corporate Control and Business Behavior,* Englewood Cliffs, N.J., 1970.

[9]

VERTICAL INTEGRATION, APPROPRIABLE RENTS, AND THE COMPETITIVE CONTRACTING PROCESS*

BENJAMIN KLEIN
University of California, Los Angeles

ROBERT G. CRAWFORD
Brigham Young University

and

ARMEN A. ALCHIAN
University of California, Los Angeles

MORE than forty years have passed since Coase's fundamental insight that transaction, coordination, and contracting costs must be considered explicitly in explaining the extent of vertical integration.[1] Starting from the truism that profit-maximizing firms will undertake those activities that they find cheaper to administer internally than to purchase in the market, Coase forced economists to begin looking for previously neglected constraints on the trading process that might efficiently lead to an intrafirm rather than an interfirm transaction. This paper attempts to add to this literature by exploring one particular cost of using the market system—the possibility of post-contractual opportunistic behavior.

Opportunistic behavior has been identified and discussed in the modern analysis of the organization of economic activity. Williamson, for example, has referred to effects on the contracting process of "*ex post* small numbers opportunism,"[2] and Teece has elaborated:

Even when all of the relevant contingencies can be specified in a contract, contracts are still open to serious risks since they are not always honored. The 1970's are replete with examples of the risks associated with relying on contracts . . . [O]pen displays of

* We wish to acknowledge useful comments on previous drafts by Harold Demsetz, Stephen Friedberg, Victor Goldberg, Levis Kochin, Keith Leffler, Lynne Schneider, Earl Thompson, and participants at a seminar at the Center for the Study of American Business at Washington University and at Law and Economics Workshops at UCLA and the University of Chicago. Financial assistance was provided by a grant of the Lilly Endowment Inc. for the study of property rights and by the Foundation for Research in Economics and Education. The authors are solely responsible for the views expressed and for the remaining errors.

[1] R. H. Coase, The Nature of the Firm, 4 Economica 386 (1937), reprinted in Readings in Price Theory 331 (George J. Stigler & Kenneth E. Boulding eds. 1952).

[2] Oliver E. Williamson, Markets and Hierarchies: Analysis and Antitrust Implications 26-30 (1975).

opportunism are not infrequent and very often litigation turns out to be costly and ineffectual.[3]

The particular circumstance we emphasize as likely to produce a serious threat of this type of reneging on contracts is the presence of appropriable specialized quasi rents. After a specific investment is made and such quasi rents are created, the possibility of opportunistic behavior is very real. Following Coase's framework, this problem can be solved in two possible ways: vertical integration or contracts. The crucial assumption underlying the analysis of this paper is that, as assets become more specific and more appropriable quasi rents are created (and therefore the possible gains from opportunistic behavior increases), the costs of contracting will generally increase more than the costs of vertical integration. Hence, *ceteris paribus*, we are more likely to observe vertical integration.

I. Appropriable Quasi Rents of Specialized Assets

Assume an asset is owned by one individual and rented to another individual. The quasi-rent value of the asset is the excess of its value over its salvage value, that is, its value in its next best *use* to another renter. The potentially appropriable specialized portion of the quasi rent is that portion, if any, in excess of its value to the second highest-valuing *user*. If this seems like a distinction without a difference, consider the following example.

Imagine a printing press owned and operated by party A. Publisher B buys printing services from party A by leasing his press at a contracted rate of $5,500 per day. The amortized fixed cost of the printing press is $4,000 per day and it has a current salvageable value if moved elsewhere of $1,000 (daily rental equivalent). Operating costs are $1,500 and are paid by the printing-press owner, who prints final printed pages for the publisher. Assume also that a second publisher C is willing to offer at most $3,500 for daily service. The current quasi rent on the installed machine is $3,000 (= $5,500 − $1,500 − $1,000), the revenue minus operating costs minus salvageable value. However, the daily quasi rent from publisher B relative to use of the machine for publisher C is only $2,000 (= $5,500 − $3,500). At $5,500 revenue daily from publisher B the press owner would break even on his investment. If the publisher were then able to cut his offer for the press from $5,500 down to almost $3,500, he would still have the press service available to him. He would be appropriating $2,000 of the quasi rent from the press owner. The $2,000 difference between his prior agreed-to daily rental of $5,500 and the next best revenue available to the press once the machine is purchased and installed is less than the quasi rent and therefore is potentially appropriable. If no second party were available at the

[3] David J. Teece, Vertical Integration and Divestiture in the U.S. Oil Industry 31 (1976).

present site, the entire quasi rent would be subject to threat of appropriation by an unscrupulous or opportunistic publisher.

Our primary interest concerns the means whereby this risk can be reduced or avoided. In particular, vertical integration is examined as a means of economizing on the costs of avoiding risks of appropriation of quasi rents in specialized assets by opportunistic individuals. This advantage of joint ownership of such specialized assets, namely, economizing on contracting costs necessary to insure nonopportunistic behavior, must of course be weighed against the costs of administering a broader range of assets within the firm.[4]

An appropriable quasi rent is not a monopoly rent in the usual sense, that is, the increased value of an asset protected from market entry over the value it would have had in an open market. An appropriable quasi rent can occur with no market closure or restrictions placed on rival assets. Once installed, an asset may be so expensive to remove or so specialized to a particular user that if the price paid to the owner were somehow reduced the asset's services to that user would not be reduced. Thus, even if there were free and open competition for entry to the market, the specialization of the installed asset to a particular user (or more accurately the high costs of making it available to others) creates a quasi rent, but no "monopoly" rent. At the other extreme, an asset may be costlessly transferable to some other user at no reduction in value, while at the same time, entry of similar assets is restricted. In this case, monopoly rent would exist, but no quasi rent.

We can use monopoly terminology to refer to the phenomenon we are discussing as long as we recognize that we are not referring to the usual monopoly created by government restrictions on entry or referring to a single supplier or even highly concentrated supply. One of the fundamental premises of this paper is that monopoly power, better labeled "market power," is pervasive. Because of transaction and mobility costs, "market power" will exist in many situations not commonly called monopolies. There may be many potential suppliers of a particular asset to a particular user but once the investment in the asset is made, the asset may be so specialized to a particular user that monopoly or monopsony market power, or both, is created.

A related motive for vertical integration that should not be confused with our main interest is the optimal output and pricing between two successive monopolists or bilateral monopolists (in the sense of marginal revenue less

[4] Vertical integration does not completely avoid contracting problems. The firm could usefully be thought of as a complex nonmarket contractual network where very similar forces are present. Frank Knight stressed the importance of this more than 50 years ago when he stated: "[T]he internal problems of the corporation, the protection of its various types of members and adherents against each other's predatory propensities, are quite as vital as the external problem of safeguarding the public interests against exploitation by the corporation as a unit." Frank H. Knight, Risk, Uncertainty, and Profit 254 (1964).

than price). A distortion arises because each sees a distorted marginal revenue or marginal cost.[5] While it is true that this successive monopoly distortion can be avoided by vertical integration, the results of the integration could, for that purpose alone, be achieved by a long-term or a more detailed contract based on the true marginal revenue and marginal costs. Integrated ownership will sometimes be utilized to economize on such precontractual bargaining costs. However, we investigate a different reason for joint ownership of vertically related assets—the avoidance of postcontractual opportunistic behavior when specialized assets and appropriable quasi rents are present. One must clearly distinguish the transaction and information costs of reaching an agreement (discovering and heeding true costs and revenues and agreeing upon the division of profits) and the enforcement costs involved in assuring compliance with an agreement, especially one in which specialized assets are involved. It is this latter situation which we here explore as a motivation for intrafirm rather than interfirm transactions.

We maintain that if an asset has a substantial portion of quasi rent which is strongly dependent upon some other particular asset, both assets will tend to be owned by one party. For example, reconsider our printing press example. Knowing that the press would exist and be operated even if its owner got as little as $1,500, publisher B could seek excuses to renege on his initial contract to get the weekly rental down from $5,500 to close to $3,500 (the potential offer from publisher C, the next highest-valuing user at its present site). If publisher B could effectively announce he was not going to pay more than, say, $4,000 per week, the press owner would seem to be stuck. This unanticipated action would be opportunistic behavior (which by definition refers to unanticipated nonfulfillment of the contract) if the press owner had installed the press at a competitive rental price of $5,500 anticipating (possibly naively) good faith by the publisher. The publisher, for example, might plead that his newspaper business is depressed and he will be unable to continue unless rental terms are revised.

Alternatively, and maybe more realistically, because the press owner may have bargaining power due to the large losses that he can easily impose on the publisher (if he has no other source of press services quickly available), the press owner might suddenly seek to get a higher rental price than $5,500 to capture some newly perceived increase in the publisher's profits. He could do this by alleging breakdowns or unusually high maintenance costs. This type of opportunistic behavior is difficult to prove and therefore litigate.

[5] This matter of successive and bilateral monopoly has long been known and exposited in many places. See, for example, Robert Bork, Vertical Integration and the Sherman Act: The Legal History of an Economic Misconception, 22 U. Chi. L. Rev. 157, 196 (1954); and the discussion in Fritz Machlup & Martha Taber, Bilateral Monopoly, Successive Monopoly, and Vertical Integration, 27 Economica 101 (1960), where the problem is dated back to Cournot's statement in 1838.

As we shall see, the costs of contractually specifying all important elements of quality varies considerably by type of asset. For some assets it may be essentially impossible to effectively specify all elements of quality and therefore vertical integration is more likely. But even for those assets used in situations where all relevant quality dimensions can be unambiguously specified in a contract, the threat of production delay during litigation may be an effective bargaining device. A contract therefore may be clearly enforceable but still subject to postcontractual opportunistic behavior. For example, the threat by the press owner to break its contract by pulling out its press is credible even though illegal and possibly subject to injunctive action. This is because such an action, even in the very short run, can impose substantial costs on the newspaper publisher.[6]

This more subtle form of opportunistic behavior is likely to result in a loss of efficiency and not just a wealth-distribution effect. For example, the publisher may decide, given this possibility, to hold or seek standby facilities otherwise not worthwhile. Even if transactors are risk neutral, the presence of possible opportunistic behavior will entail costs as real resources are devoted to the attempt to improve posttransaction bargaining positions in the event such opportunism occurs. In particular, less specific investments will be made to avoid being "locked in."[7] In addition, the increased uncertainty of quality and quantity leads to larger optimum inventories and other increased real costs of production.

This attention to appropriable specialized quasi rents is not novel. In addition to Williamson's[8] pathbreaking work in the area, Goldberg's[9] percep-

[6] While newspaper publishers generally own their own presses, book publishers generally do not. One possible reason book publishers are less integrated may be because a book is planned further ahead in time and can economically be released with less haste. Presses located in any area of the United States can be used. No press is specialized to one publisher, in part because speed in publication and distribution to readers are generally far less important for books than newspapers, and therefore appropriable quasi rents are not created. Magazines and other periodicals can be considered somewhere between books and newspapers in terms of the importance of the time factor in distribution. In addition, because magazines are distributed nationally from at most a few plants, printing presses located in many different alternative areas are possible competitors for an existing press used at a particular location. Hence, a press owner has significantly less market power over the publisher of a magazine compared to a newspaper and we find magazines generally printed in nonpublisher-owned plants. (See W. Eric Gustafson, Periodicals and Books, in Made in New York 178, 190 (Max Hall ed. 1959).) But while a magazine printing press may be a relatively less specific asset compared to a newspaper printing press, appropriable quasi rents may not be trivial (as possibly they are in the case of book printing). The magazine printing contract is therefore unlikely to be of a short-term one-transaction form but will be a long-term arrangement.

[7] The relevance for private investments in underdeveloped, politically unstable, that is, "opportunistic," countries is painfully obvious. The importance for economic growth of predictable government behavior regarding the definition and enforcement of property rights has frequently been noted.

[8] Oliver E. Williamson, The Vertical Integration of Production: Market Failure Consid-

tive analysis of what he calls the "hold up" problem in the context of government regulation is what we are discussing in a somewhat different context. Goldberg indicates how some government regulation can usefully be considered a means of avoiding or reducing the threat of loss of quasi rent. (Goldberg treats this as the problem of providing protection for the "right to be served.") He also recognizes that this force underlies a host of other contractual and institutional arrangements such as stockpiling, insurance contracts, and vertical integration. Our analysis will similarly suggest a rationale for the existence of particular institutions and the form of governmental intervention or contractual provisions as alternatives to vertical integration in a wide variety of cases.

II. Contractual Solutions

The primary alternative to vertical integration as a solution to the general problem of opportunistic behavior is some form of economically enforceable long-term contract. Clearly a short-term (for example, one transaction, non-repeat sale) contract will not solve the problem. The relevant question then becomes when will vertical integration be observed as a solution and when will the use of the market-contracting process occur. Some economists and lawyers have defined this extremely difficult question away by calling a long-term contract a form of vertical integration.[10] Although there is clearly a continuum here, we will attempt not to blur the distinction between a long-term rental agreement and ownership. We assume the opportunistic behavior we are concentrating on can occur only with the former.[11]

For example, if opportunism occurs by the owner-lessor of an asset failing to maintain it properly for the user-lessee and hence unexpectedly increasing the effective rental price, legal remedies (proving contract violation) may be very costly. On the other hand, if the user owned the asset, then the employee who failed to maintain the asset properly could merely be fired.[12] If the employee

erations, 61 Am. Econ. Rev. 112 (Papers & Proceedings, May 1971); and Oliver E. Williamson, Markets and Hierarchies: Analysis and Antitrust Implications (1975).

[9] Victor P. Goldberg, Regulation and Administered Contracts, 7 Bell J. Econ. & Management Sci. 426, 439-41 (1976).

[10] See, for example, Friedrich Kessler & Richard H. Stern, Competition, Contract, and Vertical Integration, 69 Yale L.J. 1 (1959).

[11] It is commonly held that users of assets that can be damaged by careless use and for which the damage is not easy to detect immediately are more likely to own rather than rent the assets. However, these efficient maintenance considerations apply to short-term contracts and are irrelevant if the length of the long-term rental contract coincides with the economic life of the asset. Abstracting from tax considerations, the long-term contract remains less than completely equivalent to vertical integration only because of the possibility of postcontractual opportunistic reneging. These opportunistic possibilities, however, may also exist within the firm; see note 4 *supra*.

[12] We are abstracting from any considerations of a firm's detection costs of determining proper maintenance. Ease of termination also analytically distinguishes between a franchisor-

could still effectively cheat the owner-user of the asset because of his specific ability to maintain the asset, then the problem is that vertical integration of a relevant asset, the employee's human capital, has not occurred. For the moment, however, we will concentrate solely on the question of long-term rental versus ownership of durable physical assets.[13]

Long-term contracts used as alternatives to vertical integration can be assumed to take two forms: (1) an explicitly stated contractual guarantee legally enforced by the government or some other outside institution, or (2) an implicit contractual guarantee enforced by the market mechanism of withdrawing future business if opportunistic behavior occurs. Explicit long-term contracts can, in principle, solve opportunistic problems, but, as suggested already, they are often very costly solutions. They entail costs of specifying possible contingencies and the policing and litigation costs of detecting violations and enforcing the contract in the courts.[14] Contractual provisions specifying compulsory arbitration or more directly imposing costs on the opportunistic party (for example, via bonding) are alternatives often employed to economize on litigation costs and to create flexibility without specifying every possible contingency and quality dimension of the transaction.

Since every contingency cannot be cheaply specified in a contract or even known and because legal redress is expensive, transactors will generally also rely on an implicit type of long-term contract that employs a market rather than legal enforcement mechanism, namely, the imposition of a capital loss by the withdrawal of expected future business. This goodwill market-enforcement mechanism undoubtedly is a major element of the contractual alternative to vertical integration. Macauley provides evidence that relatively informal, legally unenforceable contractual practices predominate in business relations

franchisee arrangement and a vertically integrated arrangement with a profit-sharing manager. If cheating occurs, it is generally cheaper to terminate an employee rather than a franchisee. (The law has been changing recently to make it more difficult to terminate either type of laborer.) But the more limited job-tenure rights of an employee compared to a franchisee reduce his incentive to invest in building up future business, and the firm must trade off the benefits and costs of the alternative arrangements. A profit-sharing manager with an explicit long-term employment contract would essentially be identical to a franchisee.

13 The problems involved with renting specific human capital are discussed below.

14 The recent Westinghouse case dealing with failure to fulfill uranium-supply contracts on grounds of "commercial impossibility" vividly illustrates these enforcement costs. Nearly three years after outright cancellation by Westinghouse of their contractual commitment, the lawsuits have not been adjudicated and those firms that have settled with Westinghouse have accepted substantially less than the original contracts would have entitled them to. A recent article by Paul L. Joskow, Commercial Impossibility, the Uranium Market, and the Westinghouse Case, 6 J. Legal Stud. 119 (1977), analyzes the Westinghouse decision to renege on the contract as anticipated risk sharing and therefore, using our definition, would not be opportunistic behavior. However, the publicity surrounding this case and the judicial progress to date are likely to make explicit long-term contracts a less feasible alternative to vertical integration in the situations we are analyzing.

and that reliance on explicit legal sanctions is extremely rare.[15] Instead, business firms are said to generally rely on effective extralegal market sanctions, such as the depreciation of an opportunistic firm's general goodwill because of the anticipated loss of future business, as a means of preventing nonfulfillment of contracts.

One way in which this market mechanism of contract enforcement may operate is by offering to the potential cheater a future "premium," more precisely, a price sufficiently greater than average variable (that is, avoidable) cost to assure a quasi-rent stream that will exceed the potential gain from cheating.[16] The present-discounted value of this future premium stream must be greater than any increase in wealth that could be obtained by the potential cheater if he, in fact, cheated and were terminated. The offer of such a long-term relationship with the potential cheater will eliminate systematic opportunistic behavior.[17]

The larger the potential one-time "theft" by cheating (the longer and more costly to detect a violation, enforce the contract, switch suppliers, and so forth) and the shorter the expected continuing business relationship, the higher this premium will be in a nondeceiving equilibrium. This may therefore partially explain both the reliance by firms on long-term implicit contracts with particu-

[15] Stewart Macaulay, Non-Contractual Relations in Business: A Preliminary Study, 28 Am. Soc. Rev. 55 (Feb. 1963).

[16] The following discussion of the market enforcement mechanism is based upon the analysis of competitive equilibrium under costly quality information developed in Benjamin Klein & Keith Leffler, The Role of Price in Guaranteeing Quality, J. Pol. Econ. (forthcoming 1979), which formally extends and more completely applies the analysis in Benjamin Klein, The Competitive Supply of Money, 6 J. Money, Credit, & Banking 423 (1974). It is similar to the analysis presented in Gary S. Becker & George J. Stigler, Law Enforcement, Malfeasance, and Compensation of Enforcers, 3 J. Legal Stud. 1 (1974), of insuring against malfeasance by an employer. This market-enforcement mechanism is used in Benjamin Klein & Andrew McLaughlin, Resale Price Maintenance, Exclusive Territories, and Franchise Termination: The Coors Case (1978) (unpublished manuscript), to explain franchising arrangements and particular contractual provisions such as resale price maintenance, exclusive territories, initial specific investments, and termination clauses.

[17] Formally, this arrangement to guarantee nonopportunistic behavior unravels if there is a last period in the relationship. No matter how high the premium, cheating would occur at the start of the last period. If transactors are aware of this, no transaction relying on trust (that is, the expectation of another subsequent trial) will be made in the penultimate period, because it becomes the last period, and so on. If some large lump-sum, final-period payment such as a pension as part of the market-enforcement scheme, as outlined by Gary S. Becker & George J. Stigler, *supra* note 16, this last-period problem is obvious. One solution to this unrecognized last-period problem is the acceptance of some continuing third party (for example, escrow agents or government enforcers) to prevent reneging on the implicit contracts against reneging we are outlining. Alternatively, the potential loss of value of indefinitely long-lived salable brand-name assets can serve as deterrents to cheating even where the contract between two parties has a last period. If one party's reputation for nonopportunistic dealings can be sold and used in later transactions in an infinite-time-horizon economy, the firm that cheats in the "last" period to any one buyer from the firm experiences a capital loss. This may partially explain the existence of conglomerates and their use of identifying (not product-descriptive) brand names.

lar suppliers and the existence of reciprocity agreements among firms. The premium can be paid in seemingly unrelated profitable reciprocal business. The threat of termination of this relationship mutually suppresses opportunistic behavior.[18]

The premium stream can be usefully thought of as insurance payments made by the firm to prevent cheating.[19] As long as both parties to the transaction make the same estimate of the potential short-run gain from cheating, the quantity of this assurance that will be demanded and supplied will be such that no opportunistic behavior will be expected to occur.[20] If postcontractual reneging is anticipated to occur, either the correct premium will be paid to optimally prevent it or, if the premium necessary to eliminate reneging is too costly, the particular transaction will not be made.

We are not implicitly assuming here that contracts are enforced costlessly and cannot be broken, but rather that given our information-cost assumptions, parties to a contract know exactly when and how much a contract will be broken. An unanticipated broken contract, that is, opportunistic behavior, is therefore not possible in this particular equilibrium. In the context of this model, expected wealth maximization will yield some opportunistic behavior only if we introduce a stochastic element. This will alter the informational equilibrium state such that the potential cheater's estimate of the short-run gain from opportunistic behavior may be at times greater than the other firm's estimate. Hence, less than an optimal premium will be paid and opportunistic behavior will occur.

The firms collecting the premium payments necessary to assure fulfillment of

[18] Although it may not always be in one's narrow self-interest to punish the other party in such a reciprocal relationship since termination may impose a cost on both, it may be rational for one to adopt convincingly such a reaction function to optimally prevent cheating. R. L. Trivers, The Evolution of Reciprocal Altruism, 46 Q. Rev. Bio. 35, 49 (March 1971), discusses similar mechanisms such as "moralistic aggression" which he claims have been genetically selected to protect reciprocating altruists against cheaters. Similarly, throughout the discussion we implicitly assume that cheating individuals can only cheat once and thereafter earn the "competitive" rate of return. They may, however, be forced to earn less than the competitive wage if they are caught cheating, that is, take an extra capital loss (collusively, but rationally) imposed by other members of the group. This may explain why individuals may prefer to deal in business relations with their own group (for example, members of the same church or the same country club) where effective social sanctions can be imposed against opportunistic behavior. Reliance on such reciprocal business relationships and group enforcement mechanisms is more likely where governmental enforcement of contracts is weaker. Nathaniel H. Leff, Industrial Organization and Entrepreneurship in the Developing Countries: The Economic Groups, 26 Econ. Dev. & Cultural Change 661 (1978), for example, documents the importance of such groups in less-developed countries. Industries supplying illegal products and services would likely be another example.

[19] It is, of course, an insurance scheme that not only pools risks but also alters them.

[20] As opposed to the analysis of Michael R. Darby & Edi Karni, Free Competition and the Optimal Amount of Fraud, 16 J. Law & Econ. 67 (1973), the equilibrium quantity of opportunistic behavior or "fraud" will be zero under our assumptions of symmetrical information.

contractual agreements in a costly information world may appear to be earning equilibrium "profits" although they are in a competitive market. That is, there may be many, possibly identical, firms available to supply the services of nonopportunistic performance of contractual obligations yet the premium will not be competed away if transactors cannot costlessly guarantee contractual performance. The assurance services, by definition, will not be supplied unless the premium is paid and the mere payment of this premium produces the required services.

Any profits are competed away in equilibrium by competitive expenditures on fixed (sunk) assets, such as initial specific investments (for example, a sign) with low or zero salvage value if the firm cheats, necessary to enter and obtain this preferred position of collecting the premium stream.[21] These fixed (sunk) costs of supplying credibility of future performance are repaid or covered by future sales on which a premium is earned. In equilibrium, the premium stream is then merely a normal rate of return on the "reputation," or "brand-name" capital created by the firm by these initial expenditures. This brand-name capital, the value of which is highly specific to contract fulfillment by the firm, is analytically equivalent to a forfeitable collateral bond put up by the firm which is anticipated to face an opportunity to take advantage of appropriable quasi rents in specialized assets.

While these initial specific investments or collateral bonds are sometimes made as part of the normal (minimum-cost) production process and therefore at small additional cost, transaction costs and risk considerations do make them costly.[22] We can generally say that the larger the appropriable specialized quasi

[21] A more complete analysis of market equilibrium by the use of specific capital in guaranteeing contract enforcement is developed in Benjamin Klein & Keith Leffler, *supra* note 16.

[22] An interesting example of the efficient creation of such a specific collateral investment is provided in *In re* Tastee-Freeze International, 82 F.T.C. 1195 (1973). In this case the franchisor required the franchisee to purchase all the equipment to make soft ice cream except the final patented feeder mechanism which they would only rent at the nominal price of one dollar per month. This, we believe, served the function of substantially reducing the salvage value of the equipment upon termination and therefore was part of the enforcement mechanism to prevent cheating (for example, intentionally failing to maintain quality) by franchisees. If the feeder were sold, the equipment plus the feeder would have a substantial resale value and would not serve the purpose of assuring contract compliance. Similarly, if the equipment were rented along with the feeder the franchisee would not experience a capital loss if terminated. Since the assets of the franchisee are contractually made specific, a situation is created where the assets are now appropriable by an opportunistic franchisor. Generally, a franchisor will lose by terminating a franchisee without cause since that will produce poor incentives on the remaining franchisees to maintain quality and will make it more difficult for the franchisor to sell franchises in the future. But what prevents the franchisor from an unanticipated simultaneous termination of all franchisees, especially after growth of a chain is "complete"? This is logically equivalent to the last-period problem discussed at note 17 *supra* and is restrained in part by its effects on the salable value of the brand name of the franchisor. While we do not know of any evidence of such systematic franchisor cheating, an analysis of this problem which merely asserts that franchisees voluntarily sign contracts with knowledge of these short-term termina-

rents (and therefore the larger the potential short-run gain from opportunistic behavior) and the larger the premium payments necessary to prevent contractual reneging, the more costly this implicit contractual solution will be. We can also expect the explicit contract costs to be positively related to the level of appropriable quasi rents since it will pay to use more resources (including legal services) to specify precisely more contingencies when potential opportunities for lucrative contractual reneging exist.

Although implicit and explicit contracting and policing costs are positively related to the extent of appropriable specialized quasi rents, it is reasonable to assume, on the other hand, that any internal coordination or other ownership costs are not systematically related to the extent of the appropriable specialized quasi rent of the physical asset owned. Hence we can reasonably expect the following general empirical regularity to be true: the lower the appropriable specialized quasi rents, the more likely that transactors will rely on a contractual relationship rather than common ownership. And conversely, integration by common or joint ownership is more likely, the higher the appropriable specialized quasi rents of the assets involved.

III. Example of Appropriable Specialized Quasi Rent

This section presents examples of specialized quasi rents where the potential for their appropriation serves as an important determinant of economic organization. A series of varied illustrations, some quite obvious and others rather subtle, will make the analysis more transparent and provide suggestive evidence for the relevance of the protection of appropriable quasi rents as an incentive to vertically integrate. It also suggests the direction of more systematic empirical work that obviously is required to assess the significance of this factor relative to other factors in particular cases. Where this force towards integration (that is, the economizing on contracting costs necessary to assure nonopportunistic behavior in the presence of appropriable quasi rents) does not appear to dominate, important insights regarding the determinants of particular contracting costs and contract provisions are thereby provided.[23]

---

tion provisions is certainly incomplete (see, for example, Paul H. Rubin, The Theory of the Firm and the Structure of the Franchise Contract, 21 J. Law & Econ. 223 (1978)).

This example and much of this section of the paper is based upon a more complete theoretical and empirical analysis of actual contractual relationships developed for an ongoing study by Benjamin Klein of FTC litigation in the area of vertical-distribution arrangements.

[23] It is important to recognize that not only will contracting and enforcement costs of constraining opportunistic behavior determine the form of the final economic arrangement adopted by the transacting parties, but they will also influence the firm's production function. That is, the level of specific investment and therefore the size of the potentially appropriable quasi rent is not an independent "technological" datum in each of these following cases, but is economically determined in part by transaction costs.

A. *Automobile Manufacturing*

An illustrative example is the ownership by automobile-producing companies of the giant presses used for stamping body parts. The design and engineering specifications of a new automobile, for example Mustang for Ford, create value in Ford auto production. The manufacture of dies for stamping parts in accordance with the above specifications gives a value to these dies specialized to Ford, which implies an appropriable quasi rent in those dies. Therefore, the die owner would not want to be separate from Ford. Since an independent die owner may likely have no comparable demanders other than Ford for its product and to elicit supply requires payment to cover only the small operating costs once the large sunk fixed cost of the specific investment in the dies is made, the incentive for Ford to opportunistically renegotiate a lower price at which it will accept body parts from the independent die owner may be large. Similarly, if there is a large cost to Ford from the production delay of obtaining an alternative supplier of the specific body parts, the independent die owner may be able to capture quasi rents by demanding a revised higher price for the parts. Since the opportunity to lose the specialized quasi rent of assets is a debilitating prospect, neither party would invest in such equipment. Joint ownership of designs and dies removes this incentive to attempt appropriation.[24]

In this context, it is interesting to study in some detail the vertical merger that occurred in 1926 of General Motors with Fisher Body. The original production process for automobiles consisted of individually constructed open, largely wooden, bodies. By 1919 the production process began to shift towards largely metal closed body construction for which specific stamping machines became important. Therefore in 1919 General Motors entered a ten-year contractual agreement with Fisher Body for the supply of closed auto bodies.[25] In order to encourage Fisher Body to make the required specific investment, this contract had an exclusive dealing clause whereby General Motors agreed to buy

[24] The argument also applies to die inserts which can be utilized to make slight modifications in original dies. The value of die inserts is largely an appropriable quasi rent, and so they will also be owned jointly with the designs and basic dies. Aside from the engineering design of the car, the engine blocks, the exterior shell (and possibly the crankshafts, camshafts, and gearing), no other part of the automobile would appear to possess specialized appropriable quasi rents and therefore necessarily be made exclusively by the automobile company. The integration of Ford into the manufacture of spark plugs—a part which seems to be easily standardizable among different autos—by their merger with Autolite, therefore must be explained on other grounds. See Ford Motor Co. v. United States, 405 U.S. 562 (1972).

[25] The manufacturing agreement between General Motors and Fisher Body can be found in the minutes of the Board of Directors of Fisher Body Corporation for November 7, 1919.

In addition to this long-term contract General Motors also purchased a 60% interest in Fisher at this time. However, as demonstrated by future events, the Fisher brothers clearly seem to have maintained complete control of their company in spite of this purchase.

substantially all its closed bodies from Fisher. This exclusive dealing arrangement significantly reduced the possibility of General Motors acting opportunistically by demanding a lower price for the bodies after Fisher made the specific investment in production capacity. Since exclusive dealing contractual conditions are relatively cheap to effectively specify and enforce, General Motor's postcontractual threat to purchase bodies elsewhere was effectively eliminated.

But large opportunities were created by this exclusive dealing clause for Fisher to take advantage of General Motors, namely to demand a monopoly price for the bodies. Therefore, the contract attempted to fix the price which Fisher could charge for the bodies supplied to General Motors. However, contractually setting in advance a "reasonable" price in the face of possible future changes in demand and production conditions is somewhat more difficult to effectively accomplish than merely "fixing" required suppliers. The price was set on a cost plus 17.6 per cent basis (where cost was defined exclusive of interest on invested capital). In addition, the contract included provisions that the price charged General Motors could not be greater than that charged other automobile manufacturers by Fisher for similar bodies nor greater than the average market price of similar bodies produced by companies other than Fisher and also included provisions for compulsory arbitration in the event of any disputes regarding price.

Unfortunately, however, these complex contractual pricing provisions did not work out in practice. The demand conditions facing General Motors and Fisher Body changed dramatically over the next few years. There was a large increase in the demand for automobiles and a significant shift away from open bodies to the closed body styles supplied by Fisher.[26] Meanwhile General Motors was very unhappy with the price it was being charged by its now very important supplier, Fisher. General Motors believed the price was too high because of a substantial increase in body output per unit of capital employed. This was an understandable development given the absence of a capital cost pass-through in the original contract.[27] In addition, Fisher refused to locate their body plants adjacent to General Motors assembly plants, a move General Motors claimed was necessary for production efficiency (but which required a large very specific and hence possibly ap-

[26] By 1924 more than 65% of automobiles produced by General Motors were of the closed body type. See Sixteenth Annual Report of the General Motors Corporation, year ended December 31, 1924.

[27] Deposition of Alfred P. Sloan, Jr. in United States v. DuPont & Co., 366 U.S. 316 (1961), from complete set of briefs and trial records in custody of General Motors, 186-90 (April 28, 1952). Also see direct testimony of Alfred P. Sloan, Jr. in United States v. DuPont & Co., vol. 5 trial transcript, 2908-14 (March 17, 1953). (The government was attempting to demonstrate in this case that General Motors vertically integrated in order to get Fisher to purchase its glass requirements from DuPont.)

propriable investment on the part of Fisher).[28] By 1924, General Motors had found the Fisher contractual relationship intolerable and began negotiations for purchase of the remaining stock in Fisher Body, culminating in a final merger agreement in 1926.[29]

B. *Petroleum Industry*

Appropriable quasi rents exist in specialized assets of oil refineries, pipelines, and oil fields. This leads to common ownership to remove the incentive for individuals to attempt to capture the rents of assets owned by someone else.

Suppose several oil wells are located along a separately owned pipeline that leads to a cluster of independently owned refineries with no alternative crude supply at comparable cost. Once all the assets are in place (the wells drilled and the pipeline and refineries constructed) the oil-producing properties and the refineries are specialized to the pipeline. The portion of their value above the value to the best alternative user is an appropriable specialized quasi rent. The extent of the appropriable quasi rent is limited, in part, by the costs of entry to a potential parallel pipeline developer. Since pipelines between particular oil-producing properties and particular refineries are essentially natural monopolies, the existing pipeline owner may have a significant degree of market power.

These specialized producing and refining assets are therefore "hostage" to the pipeline owner. At the "gathering end" of the pipeline, the monopsonist pipeline could and would purchase all its oil at the same well-head price regardless of the distance of the well from the refinery. This price could be as low as the marginal cost of getting oil out of the ground (or its reservation value for future use, if higher) and might not generate a return to the oil-well owner sufficient to recoup the initial investment of exploration and drilling. At the delivery-to-refinery end of the pipeline, the pipeline owner would be able to appropriate the "specialized-to-the-pipeline quasi rents" of the refineries. The pipeline owner could simply raise the price of crude oil at least to the price of alternative sources of supply to each refinery that are specialized to the pipeline. Given the prospects of such action, if the pipeline owner were an independent monopsonist facing the oil explorers and a

[28] *Id.* It is obvious that long-term exclusive dealing contracts are necessary if such investments are to be made by nonvertically integrated firms. See *In re* Great Lakes Carbon Corp., 82 F.T.C. 1529 (1973), for an example of the government's failure to understand this. Great Lakes Carbon Corporation built plants highly specific to particular refineries to process petroleum coke (a by-product of the refining process) for these refineries and was prosecuted for requiring long-term exclusive dealing contracts with refineries.

[29] United States v. DuPont & Co., vol. 1, defendants trial exhibits numbers GM-32, GM-33, GM-34.

monopolist to the refinery owners, everyone (explorers and refiners) would know in advance their vulnerability to rent extraction. Therefore oil-field owners and refinery owners would, through shared ownership in the pipeline, remove the possibility of subsequent rent extraction.[30]

The problem would not be completely solved if just the oil field or the refineries (but not both) were commonly owned with the pipeline, since the local monopoly (or monopsony) would persist vis-à-vis the other. Prospectively, one would expect the common ownership to extend to all three stages. If several refineries (or oil fields) were to be served by one pipeline, all the refinery (or oil field) owners would want to jointly own the pipeline. A common practice is a jointly owned company which "owns" the pipeline with the shares by producers and refiners in the pipeline company corresponding roughly to the respective shares of oil to be transported.[31]

[30] Our argument is distinct from the traditional argument in the oil-business literature that vertical integration occurs to achieve "assurance" of supplies or of markets in the face of implicitly or explicitly assumed disequilibrium conditions. See, for example, P. H. Frankel, Integration in the Oil Industry, 1 J. Indus. Econ. 201 (1953); Melvin G. de Chazeau & Alfred H. Kahn, Integration and Competition in the Petroleum Industry 102-04 (1959); and Michael E. Canes, A Theory of the Vertical Integration of Oil Firms (Oct. 1976) (unpublished manuscript, Amer. Petroleum Inst.). Jerry G. Green, Vertical Integration and Assurance of Markets (Oct. 1974) (Discussion Paper No. 383, Harvard Inst. of Econ. Research), similarly argues more formally that price inflexibility in an intermediate market which causes shortages and overproduction is an incentive for vertical integration.

It is also important to distinguish between this risk-reducing reason for joint ownership (that is, the reduction in the risk of appropriation of user-associated specialized quasi rents) and the possible risk reduction from joint ownership when there is negative correlation of changes in values of nonappropriable generalized quasi rents. Joint ownership of assets whose value fluctuations are negatively correlated so that gains in one are offset by losses in the other is said to provide a form of insurance against total value changes of the resources used in the manufacturing process. These changes are not the result of any postcontractual opportunistic behavior but of general economic forces outside the control of the immediate parties. For example, a refinery and an oil-producing property fluctuate in value in opposite directions if a new oil field is discovered. The price of oil will fall but the price of refined products will not fall until additional refineries can process larger amounts of oil into more refined products at essentially constant production costs. Then, some of the oil-field owner's losses in value of crude oil are gained by his refinery. This reduces the fluctuation in values caused by factors unrelated to the efficiency of oil producing, refining, and distributing abilities.

However, diversification can also be achieved by methods other than vertical integration. One way is for the investor to buy stocks in the separate unintegrated firms—in effect integrating their ownership by joint holding of common stocks. Although individual action may not always be as cheap or effective as action through intermediaries, financial intermediaries are available such as mutual funds rather than direct diversification by integrated firms. One possible reason why negatively correlated assets could be worth more combined in a single firm is the reduction in the probability of bankruptcy and hence the probability of incurring bankruptcy costs (such as legal fees). An integrated firm with negatively correlated assets could increase its debt to equity ratio while keeping the probability of bankruptcy constant and therefore decrease the taxes on equity without any additional risk. This may be one of the gains of many conglomerate mergers.

[31] Jane Atwood & Paul Kobrin, Integration and Joint Ventures in Pipelines (Sept. 1977) (Research Study No. 5, Am. Petroleum Inst.), find an extremely high positive correlation

Consider other inputs in the production process. The oil tanker, for example, is specialized to crude oil transportation. But since it is essentially equivalued by many alternative users, the appropriable quasi rent is near zero. So we would expect oil tankers not to be extensively owned by refiners or producers. Similarly, the assets used for refinery construction are not specialized to any single refiner or refinery and they should also not be commonly owned with the refinery.

Preliminary examination of the development of the American petroleum industry in the nineteenth century reveals numerous examples that appear consistent with the hypothesis that as technological change leads to assets involved in production, transportation, refining, and marketing becoming more specialized to other specific assets, joint ownership became efficient as a means of preventing opportunistic behavior.

For example, Rockefeller recognized the importance of the pending technological change implied by the substitution of highly specific long-distance pipelines for the somewhat more general capital of the railroads as the efficient mode of transporting oil and took advantage of it. First, before long-distance pipelines were clearly economical, Rockefeller used his dominant oil-refining position to obtain a price reduction on oil he shipped by rail and also rebates from the railroads on oil shipped by competitive oil producers. We conjecture that Rockefeller obtained these price reductions by threatening to build a pipeline parallel to the railroad. He was therefore able to extract the appropriable quasi rents of the railroads. This explains why the rebates were solely a function of oil shipped and not related to nonoil products such as agricultural goods. It also explains why the discount and rebate to Rockefeller were often of the same magnitude. The payment should be a function of total demand for transporting oil.

The obvious question is why some small oil producer or even a nonoil-producing firm did not similarly threaten the railroads with building a pipeline early (before it was cheaper than rail transport) and demand a payment as a function of total oil shipped. The answer, we believe, is that only a dominant oil

between a firm's crude production and its share of ownership in the pipeline. On the other hand, natural gas pipelines, although apparently economically similar in terms of potentially appropriable quasi rents, do not appear to be vertically integrated. Rather than joint-ownership arrangements with the gas producers, these pipelines are often independently owned. The difference may be due to more effective FPC (and now the Federal Energy Regulatory Commission) regulation (of the wellhead and citygate gas prices and the implied pipeline tariff) compared to the direct Interstate Commerce Commission regulation of oil pipelines as common carriers. Regulation of oil pipeline tariffs could, for example, be easily evaded by opportunistic decreases in the wellhead prices paid for oil. More complete government regulation of gas prices may effectively prevent opportunistic behavior by the natural gas pipeline owners, and thereby serve as an alternative to vertical integration. (See Victor P. Goldberg, *supra* note 9.) Edmund Kitch informs us that the evidence does indicate a much greater degree of vertical integration of natural gas pipelines in the period before FPC regulation.

producer would have credible bargaining power with the railroads in this situation because only a dominant producer would be able to make such a highly specific investment. If a small producer or nonoil-producing firm made such an investment, it could easily be appropriated by the oil-producing firms, especially with an alternative means of transportation available. It was therefore necessary for Rockefeller to gain a dominant oil-producing and refining position in order to make a credible threat to the railroads. Appropriating the quasi rents of the railroads by discounts and rebates not only effectively metered the demand for oil transportation but also made it easier for Rockefeller to gain a monopolistic position in the industry without being forced to buy out rivals at prices that would completely reflect future-discounted monopoly profits.[32]

C. *Specific Human Capital*

The previous analysis has dealt with examples of physical capital. When specific human capital is involved, the opportunism problem is often more complex and, because of laws prohibiting slavery, the solution is generally some form of explicit or implicit contract rather than vertical integration.

For example, consider the following concrete illustration from the agricultural industry. Suppose someone owns a peach orchard. The ripened peaches, ready for harvest, have a market value of about $400,000. So far costs of $300,000 have been paid and the remaining harvesting and shipping costs will be $50,000 ($5,000 transport and $45,000 labor), leaving $50,000 as the competitive return on the owner's capital. Assume the laborers become a union (one party to whom the crop is now specialized) and refuse to pick unless paid $390,000. That would leave $5,000 for transport and only $5,000 for the owner

[32] Although our preliminary investigation indicates that control of the transportation system and vertical integration of it with the oil fields and refineries were significant, there were many other factors in Rockefeller's success. For example, the unpredictability of the life of oil fields raised the risks of a substantial investment in an integrated pipeline transportation system from one field. That Rockefeller correctly or luckily surmised that the Bradford field in 1874 would be long-lived was surely a source of his success. Also his skill in discovering consumer-preferred retailing methods, achieving lower-cost refining, and correctly assessing the ability to refine sulphurous Ohio crude undoubtedly were additional factors. See, for example, Ralph W. Hidy & Muriel E. Hidy, History of Standard Oil Company (New Jersey): Pioneering in Big Business 1882-1911 (1955); 1 & 2 Allan Nevins, John D. Rockefeller: The Heroic Age of American Enterprise (1940); and Harold F. Williamson & Arnold R. Daum, The American Petroleum Industry (1959).

This oil-pipeline analysis of appropriable specific capital may be applicable in many other situations. It should hold, for example, for ore mines and refineries which are specialized to each other. We predict that copper smelters specialized to a single mine will tend to be jointly owned, as will a cement quarry and its nearby smelter (mill). Railroad spur lines (and the land on which the track runs) from ore mines to smelters should likewise be owned by the mine-smelter owner. In addition, we would expect television program producers in an area with a single transmitter tower to be joint owners of the tower.

of the peach orchard, instead of the $350,000 necessary to cover incurred costs and the cost of capital. If the union had power to exclude other pickers, it could extract all the appropriable quasi rent of that year's crop specialized to that particular labor union's service. The union would be extracting not just the usual monopoly rents involved in raising wages, but also the short-run appropriable quasi rents of the farmer's specific assets represented by the ripened peaches. This gain to the union is a one-period return because obviously the farmer will not make any additional specific investments in the future if he knows it will be appropriated by the union.

To reduce this risk of appropriation, the farmer may have a large clan family (or neighbors of similar farms) do his picking. Because of diseconomies of scale, however, this "cooperative" solution is not generally the lowest-cost arrangement and some reliance on market contracting will be necessary. The individual farmer, for example, may want the labor union to put up a forfeitable bond to compensate him in the event the union under threat of strike asks for more wages at harvest time. Alternatively, but equivalently, the collateral put up by the union could be the value of the brand-name capital of the union, a value which will depreciate if its leaders engage in opportunistic behavior. The farmer would then make a continuing brand-name payment to the union (similar to the premium payment noted above) for this collateral.[33]

The market value of the union's reputation for reliability of contract observance is the present-discounted value of these brand-name payments which will be greater than any short-run opportunistic gain to the union leaders that could be obtained by threats at harvest time. These payments which increase the cost to the union of opportunistic behavior would be substantial for a perishable product with a large appropriable quasi rent. It is therefore obvious why producers of highly perishable crops are so antagonistic to unionization of field labor. They would be especially hostile to unions without established reputations regarding fulfillment of contract and with politically motivated (and possibly myopic) leaders.[34]

[33] If the premium is a payment to the union per unit time, then the arrangement is identical to a collateral-bond arrangement where the union collects the interest on the bond as long as no opportunistic behavior occurs. Because of possible legal difficulties of enforcing such an arrangement, however, the premium may be reflected in the price (that is, a higher wage).

[34] It is interesting to note in this context that California grape farmers preferred the established Teamsters Union to the new, untried, and apparently more politically motivated fieldworkers union organized by Cesar Chavez.

Since unions are not "owned," union leaders will not have the proper incentive to maximize the union's value; they will tend more to maximize returns during their tenure. If, however, union leadership (ownership) were salable, the leaders would have the optimal incentive to invest in and conserve the union's brand-name capital. They therefore would not engage in opportunistic actions that may increase current revenue while decreasing the market value of the union. "Idealistic" union leaders that do not behave as if they own the union may, in fact, produce less wealth-maximizing action than would "corrupt" leaders, who act as if they person-

In addition to implicit (brand-name) contracts, opportunistic union behavior may be prevented by use of explicit contracts, often with some outside arbitration as an element of the contract-enforcement mechanism. Although it is difficult for an outsider to distinguish between opportunistic behavior and good-faith modifications of contract, impartial arbitration procedures may reduce the necessity of explicitly specifying possible contingencies and thereby reduce the rigidity of the explicit long-term contract.[35]

When the problem is reversed and quasi rents of firm-specific human capital of employees may be opportunistically appropriated by the firm, implicit and explicit long-term contracts are also used to prevent such behavior. Because of economies of scale in monitoring and enforcing such contracts, unions may arise as a contract cost-reducing institution for employees with investments in specific human capital.[36]

In addition to narrow contract-monitoring economies of scale, a union creates a continuing long-term employment relationship that eliminates the last-period (or transient employee) contract-enforcement problem and also creates bargaining power (a credible strike threat) to more cheaply punish a firm that violates the contract. Even when the specific human-capital investment is made by the firm, a union of employees may similarly reduce the contract-enforcement costs of preventing individual-worker opportunism. There are likely to be economies of scale in supply credibility of contract fulfillment, including the long-term continuing relationship aspect of a union. The existence of a union not only makes it more costly for a firm to cheat an individual worker in his last period but also makes it more costly for an individual worker in his last period to cheat the firm, because the union has the incentive (for example, withholding pension rights) to prevent such

---

ally own the union. Alternatively, the current members of the union may have control, not in the sense of having directly salable shares, but in the sense that the valuable union asset can be transferred to their children or relatives. If government regulations force union members to give away these rights to future rents (for example, by forcing them to admit minorities and eliminate nepotism), we can expect them to intentionally depreciate or not create the reputation capital of the union by opportunistic strikes. See Benjamin Klein, *supra* note 16, where similar problems with regard to the supply of money by nonprivately owned, nonwealth-maximizing firms are discussed.

[35] An interesting legal case in this area is Publishers' Ass'n v. Newspaper & Mail Del. Union, 114 N.Y.S.2d, 401 (1952). The union authorized and sanctioned a strike against the New York Daily News although the collective bargaining agreement had "no-strike" and arbitration clauses. The Daily News took the union to arbitration, and the arbitrator found actual damages of $2,000 and punitive damages of $5,000 if the union again violated the contract. (The court, however, overturned the punitive damages for technical reasons.) See David E. Feller, A General Theory of the Collective Bargaining Agreement, 61 Calif. L. Rev. 663 (1973), for a discussion of the flexibility obtained with arbitration provisions in labor contracts.

[36] We should explicitly note that we are not considering unions as cartelizing devices, the usually analyzed motivation for their existence. This force is obviously present in many cases (for example, interstate trucking) but is distinct from our analysis.

an externality on the continuing workers. Therefore unions are more likely to exist when the opportunistic cheating problem is greater, namely, when there is more specific human capital present.[37]

The first Becker analysis of the specific human-capital problem[38] ignored opportunistic bargaining difficulties and implicitly assumed arbitrary contracting costs in particular situations to determine a solution. Becker initially assumed that the firm would cheat the employee if the employee made the specific investment. He then argued that the only reason the firm would not make the entire specific investment is because the quit rate of employees, which is a negative function of wages, would then be greater than optimal. Becker did not consider the completely reciprocal nature of the possibilities for cheating. The opportunistic behavior we are emphasizing suggests the possibility of the employee threatening to quit after the firm makes the specific investment unless the wage rate is readjusted upward. Becker's solution of a sharing of the costs and benefits of the specific investment via an initial lump-sum payment by the employee and a later higher-than-market wage does not eliminate the bilateral opportunistic bargaining problem because the employer may later decrease the wage back to the competitive level (or the employee may demand a higher wage to appropriate the partial specific investment by the employer). If it is assumed that employers will not cheat or break contracts in this way, then the efficient solution would be to merely have the employee make the entire specific investment (and therefore have the optimal quit rate) because the employer can costlessly "guarantee" (by assumption) a higher wage reflecting the increased productivity of the firm. But, more generally, to obtain an equilibrium solution to the problem, the costs of creating credibility of contract fulfillment and the costs of enforcing contracts must be explicitly considered.

One of the costs of using an explicit contract which relies on governmental or other outside arbitration for enforcement—rather than on an implicit contract which relies on depreciation of the value of a firm's brand-name (that is, the loss of future premium payments)—is the likely increase in rigidity. For example, the difficulty of specifying all contingencies in labor contracts and of adjusting to unanticipated conditions is likely to lead to wage rigidity. Because contractual changes tend to create suspicion regarding the purpose of the contract alteration and, in particular, raise the ques-

[37] When allowing for this "reverse" effect of employee-specific capital, and therefore higher wages, on the formation of unions, the usual positive effect of unions on wages appears to vanish. See, for example, O. Ashenfelter & G. Johnson, Unionism, Relative Wages, and Labor Quality in U.S. Manufacturing Industries, 13 Int'l Econ. Rev. 488 (Oct. 1972); and Peter Schmidt & Robert P. Strauss, The Effect of Unions on Earnings and Earnings on Unions: A Mixed Logit Approach, 17 Int'l Econ. Rev. 204 (Feb. 1976).

[38] Gary S. Becker, Human Capital 18-29 (1964).

tion of whether a firm is using the changed conditions as an opportunity to seize some of the specific quasi rents, long-term labor contracts may consist of rigid wages and layoff provisions. If in the face of declining demand, a firm must keep wages fixed and lay off workers rather than merely reduce wages, the incentive for it to opportunistically claim a false reduction in demand is substantially reduced.[39]

The fear of opportunistic behavior leads to price (and often also output) rigidity in all kinds of long-term explicit contracts where specific capital is present. This, in turn, leads to the creation of institutions to encourage increased flexibility in the face of changing market conditions. For example, the prime-rate convention, an announced benchmark in terms of which interest rates of corporate bank loans are stated, may be partially rationalized as a cheap means by which the bank can convey information to borrowers that the bank is not opportunistically raising interest fees to a particular customer. A corporate client who has made a specific investment in the supply of information to the bank regarding its credit worthiness (including its financial record of transactions with the bank) creates some appropriable quasi rents. However, when the price of the loan is stated as, say, prime plus one per cent, unless the bank decides to cheat all customers simultaneously and thereby limit new business, an individual customer can clearly distinguish between general market movements in interest rates and any changes the bank decides to make in the particular customer's credit rating. "Price protection" clauses in contracts, where a price decrease to any customer is guaranteed to be given to all customers, may be explained on similar grounds.

These information-cost-reducing institutions, including the use of impartial arbitrators, are highly imperfect. Therefore contracts involving specific assets, even where a price is not explicitly fixed long term, will consequently involve some price rigidity. The macroeconomic implications of this observation (for example, the employment effects of aggregate nominal demand shocks) are obvious.[40] But the interaction of macroeconomic considerations and industrial

[39] This argument is distinct from the recent argument for the existence of rigid long-term implicit labor contracts as a means of bearing risk. See, for example, D. F. Gordon, A Neo-Classical Theory of Keynesian Unemployment, 12 Econ. Inquiry 431 (Dec. 1974); and Costas Azariadis, Implicit Contracts and Underemployment Equilibria, 83 J. Pol. Econ. 1183 (1975). We should also note that although Masamori Hashimoto, Wage Reduction, Unemployment, and Specific Human Capital, 13 Econ. Inquiry 485 (Dec. 1975), has correctly argued that cyclically flexible wages are more likely when specific human capital is present because both workers and employers will want to minimize the likelihood of job separation and thereby protect future returns on the specific human-capital investment, he ignores the contrary effect of increased specific human capital increasing the potential for opportunistic cheating and therefore increasing wage rigidity. The net theoretical effect is indeterminate. One possible reason that high-ranking corporate executives with a great deal of specific human capital appear to have highly flexible wages is because of the large amount of information about the firm they possess and therefore the shorter lag in detecting opportunism.

[40] The recent "rational-expectations" approach to business cycles, which relies on consumer

organization may not be that obvious. In particular, an increase in the variance of price-level movements, which increases the expected costs to both parties of price rigidity and thereby increases the acceptable degree of price flexibility, also makes it easier for a firm to cheat by opportunistically raising its price. Increased price uncertainty is therefore likely to lead to increased vertical integration.

Where more trust is present and implicit rather than explicit contracts are used, contract prices including wages are likely to be more flexible. If the variance of the price level increases—which makes it more difficult to detect opportunistic behavior and therefore the short-run gains from such cheating—the equilibrium implicit contract will imply a larger premium stream. The interesting question is what are the economic determinants of the implicit relative to explicit contracting costs which will in turn determine the degree of price flexibility.

One determinant of implicit contracting costs is the anticipated growth of demand for the firm's product. The more rapidly demand is expected to grow, the more likely a firm will rely on an implicit contract with its customers. Creating trust is cheaper for firms facing rapid demand growth compared to firms with stable or declining demand because the loss of future business by customer termination if the firm is found to be cheating implies a relatively larger cost. Therefore a smaller current premium payment is necessary to assure nonopportunistic behavior. Hence the higher the anticipated growth in demand for a firm, the lower the contracting cost of using implicit relative to explicit contracts and the more flexible prices and other contract terms set by the firm can be expected to be.[41]

---

and producer uncertainty regarding whether a particular demand shock is a relative or an aggregate shift (see, for example, Robert E. Lucas, Jr., Some International Evidence on Output-Inflation Tradeoffs, 63 Am. Econ. Rev. 326 (1973)), implicitly assumes economic agents do not observe current movements of money supply and price level. A more realistic assumption is that economic agents are not "fooled," especially over long periods, about the nature of the shock but rather are bound, either explicitly or implicitly, by long-term contracts that have previously fixed prices.

[41] A crucial determinant of economic organization is therefore the anticipated demand growth compared to the actual demand growth, or the demand growth anticipated at the time of contract and the demand growth actually experienced and therefore anticipated at some later time. For example, one possible reason for the recent movement by oil-refining companies towards vertically integrated retail-marketing operations may be the increased cost of controlling franchised dealers due to the large decrease in the anticipated growth of demand for gasoline in the period since the large OPEC-initiated price increase of crude oil. With demand growing slower than originally anticipated, the initial equilibrium "premium" earned by dealers will now be less than necessary to assure their noncheating behavior. The anticipated decrease in the total number of dealers (that is, the fact that future demand is anticipated to be zero for many dealers in the new equilibrium) will create last-period problems for particular locations that can be largely avoided by employee-operated outlets. See Benjamin Klein & Keith Leffler, *supra* note 16, for a more complete discussion of these issues.

The cost to a growing firm of cheating on laborers, for example, would be higher in terms of the future increased wages (of increased employment) it would have to pay if it cheated. The penalty for not relying on the firm's brand name is then more effective. This may explain why firms such as International Business Machines appear to have highly flexible labor compensation arrangements that are, in fact, quite similar to Japanese wage payments which consist of large, highly variable, biannual bonuses. Our analysis suggests that it is not because of different cultural values that Japanese labor relations rely on much trust, but because the high growth rate of future demand makes it relatively cheap for firms to behave in this way.[42]

D. *Leasing Inputs and Ownership of the Firm*

Examination of leasing companies should reveal that leases are less common (or too expensive) for assets with specialized quasi rents that could be appropriated by the lessee or lessor. Leasing does not occur in the obvious cases of elevators or the glass of windows in an office building where postinvestment bilaterally appropriable quasi rents are enormous, while the furniture in the building is often rented. In banks, the safe is owned by the bank, but computers (though not the memory discs) are sometimes rented.[43] Though this may seem like resorting to trivialities, the fact that such leasing arrangements are taken for granted merely corroborates the prior analysis.

The standard example of leasing arrangements occurs with transportation capital, such as the planes, trucks, or cars used by a firm. This capital is generally easily movable and not very specific. But leasing arrangements are far from universal because some of this capital can be quite specific and quasi rents appropriated. For example, early American steam locomotives were specialized to operating conditions such as high speed, hill climbing, short hauls, heavy loads, sharp corners, as well as types of coal for fuel. Slight differences in engines created significant differences in operating costs. High specialization made it desirable for the rail companies to own locomotives (as well as the land on which water was available for steam). The advent of the more versatile, less specialized, diesel locomotive enabled

42 Walter Galenson & Konosuke Odaka, The Japanese Labor Market, in Asia's New Giant 587 (Hugh Patrick & Henry Rosovsky eds. 1976); and Koji Taira, Economic Development and the Labor Market in Japan (1970), both documented the fact that this highly flexible wage feature of Japanese labor contracts did not become widespread until the postwar period, a time of extremely rapid growth.

43 In addition to computers being less specific and hence possessing smaller appropriable quasi rents than elevators, firms (for example, IBM) that supply computers generally possess extremely valuable brand names per unit of current sales due to a large anticipated growth in demand. Since there are some quasi rents associated with the use of a computer by a bank that could possibly be appropriated by threat of immediate removal, we would expect that if rental contracts existed they would more likely be with highly credible firms with high anticipated demand growth.

more leasing and equipment trust financing. Similarly, Swift, the meat packer and innovator of the refrigerator car for transporting slaughtered beef, owned the specialized refrigerator cars it used.[44]

On the other hand, some capital may be quite specific to other assets in a firm's productive process and yet leased rather than owned. These cases provide useful insights into the nature of the contracting costs underlying our analysis. For example, consider the fact that agricultural land, a highly specific asset, is not always owned but often is rented. Land rented for farming purposes is typically for annual crops, like vegetables, sugar beets, cotton, or wheat, while land used for tree crops, like nuts, dates, oranges, peaches, apricots, or grape vines—assets that are highly specialized to the land—is usually owned by the party who plants the trees or vines.[45] However, long-term rental arrangements even for these "specialized asset" crops are not entirely unknown.

It is instructive to recognize why land-rental contracts, rather than vertical integration, can often be used without leading to opportunistic behavior. The primary reason is because it is rather cheap to specify and monitor the relevant contract terms (the quality of the good being purchased) and to enforce this particular rental contract. In addition, the landowner generally cannot impose a cost on the farmer by pulling the asset out or reducing the quality of the asset during the litigation process. Note the contrast with labor rental where it is essentially impossible to effectively specify and enforce quality elements (for example, all working conditions and the effort expended by workers) and where the possibility of withdrawal by strike or lockout is real and costly. Therefore, we do observe firms making highly specific investments in, for example, trees or buildings on land they do not own but only rent long term.[46] This is because credible postcontractual opportunistic threats by the landowner are not possible. However, if the landowner can vary the quality of the land, for example, by controlling the irrigation system to the crops or the electricity supply to a building, then a

[44] The great bulk of all refrigerator cars are not owned by the railroads, but rather by shipper-users such as packers and dairy companies. See Robert S. Henry, This Fascinating Railroad Business 247 (1942).

[45] While 25% of vegetable and melon farms in California in 1974 were fully owned by the farm operator, 82% of fruit and nut tree farms were fully owned, a significantly different ownership proportion at the 99% confidence interval. Similarly, the ownership proportions of cash grain and cotton farms were 40% and 39%, respectively, both also significantly different at the 99% confidence interval from the proportions of fruit and nut tree farm ownership. See 1 U.S. Dep't of Commerce, Bureau of the Census, 1974 Census of Agriculture, State and County Data, pt. 5, at tab. 28. Summary by Tenure of Farm Operator and Type of Organization, *id.*, 1974, California, pp. 1-29 to 1-30.

[46] Rental terms may be related to sales of the firm using the land in order to share the risk of real-value changes and to reduce the risk of nominal land-value changes involved with a long-term contract.

significant possibility of postinvestment opportunistic behavior exists and we would therefore expect vertical integration.[47]

One specific asset that is almost always owned by the firm is its trade-name or brand-name capital and, in particular, the logo it uses to communicate to consumers. If this asset were rented from a leasing company, the problems would be obvious. The firm would be extremely hesitant to make any investments to build up its goodwill, for example, by advertising or by successful performance, because such investments are highly specific to that "name." The quasi rents could be appropriated by the leasing company through increases in the rental fee for the trade name. Not only would the firm not invest in this specific asset, but there would be an incentive for the firm to depreciate a valuable rented brand name. Although these problems seem insurmountable, rental of the capital input of a firm's brand name is not entirely unknown. In fact, franchisors can be thought of as brand-name leasing companies. A franchisee is fundamentally a renter of the brand-name capital (and logo) owned by the franchisor. Because of the specific capital problems noted above, direct controls are placed on franchisee behavior. The rental payment is usually some form of profit-sharing arrangement and, although the franchisee is legally considered to be an independent firm, the situation is in reality much closer to vertical integration than to the standard contractual relationship of the independent market.

Finally, the analysis throws light on the important question of why the owners of a firm (the residual claimants) are generally also the major capitalists of the firm.[48] As we have seen, owners may rent the more generalized capital, but will own the firm's specific capital. This observation has implications for recent discussions of "industrial democracy," which fail to recognize that although employees may own and manage a firm (say, through their union), they will also have to be capitalists and own the specific capital. It will generally be too costly, for example, for the worker-owners to rent a plant because such a specific investment could be rather easily appropriated from its owners after it is constructed. Therefore it is unlikely to be built. A highly detailed contractual arrangement together with very large brand-name premium payments by the laborers would be neces-

[47] Coase's example of a monopolist selling more of a durable good, say land, after initially selling a monopoly quantity at the monopoly price is analytically identical to the problem of postcontractual opportunistic behavior. Existing contractual relationships indicate, however, that the land case may be relatively easy to solve because it may not be expensive to make a credible contract regarding the remaining land. But, one of Coase's indicated solutions, the short-term rental rather than sale of the land is unlikely because it would discourage specific (to land) investments by the renter (such as building a house, developing a farm, and so forth) for fear of appropriation. See R. H. Coase, Durability and Monopoly, 15 J. Law & Econ. 143 (1972).

[48] We are grateful to Earl Thompson for discerning this implication.

sary to assure nonopportunistic behavior. This is generally too expensive an alternative and explains why capitalists are usually the owners of a firm.[49]

E. *Social Institutions*

Much of the previous analysis has dealt with tangible capital. Contractual arrangements involving such assets are often cheaper than complete vertical integration, even when the assets are highly specific (for example, the land-rental case.) As the discussion on human capital suggests, however, when the specific assets involved are intangible personal assets, the problems of contract enforcement become severe. In addition, when the number of individuals involved (or the extent of the specific capital) becomes very large, ownership arrangements often become extremely complex.

For example, consider country clubs. Golf country clubs are social, in addition to being golfing, organizations. Sociability of a country club involves substantial activities away from the golf course: dinners, dances, parties, cards, games, and general social activities with friends who are members of the club. However, some golf courses are operated with very few social activities for the set of members and their families. The social clubs (usually called "country clubs") are mutually owned by the members, whereas golf courses with virtually no off-course social activity often are privately owned with members paying daily golf fees without owning the golf course.

Mutual ownership is characteristic of the social country club because the specialized quasi rent of friendship is collected by each member whose friendship is specialized to the other members. The members' behavior toward one another constitutes an investment in forming valuable friendships, a congenial milieu, and rapport among the members. Each member has invested in creating that congenial milieu and atmosphere specialized to the other members. And its value could be stolen or destroyed by opportunistic behavior of a party authorized to admit new members.

[49] Armen A. Alchian & Harold Demsetz, Production, Information Costs, and Economic Organization, 62 Am. Econ. Rev. 777 (1972), claim that if the owner of the firm also owns the firm's capital it supplies evidence that he can pay for rented inputs, including labor. This appears to be incorrect since the owner could supply credibility by using some of his assets completely unrelated to the production process, such as treasury bonds, for collateral. Michael C. Jensen & William H. Meckling, On the Labor-Managed Firm and the Codetermination Movement (unpublished manuscript, Feb. 1977), emphasize the costs of monitoring managerial performance and the maintenance of rented capital, and the problems of efficiently allocating risks in a pure-rental firm. They also note that it is "impossible" for a firm to rent all the productive capital assets because many of them are intangible and therefore "it is impossible to repossess the asset if the firm refused to pay the rental fee" (*id.* at 20). This argument is similar to our analysis of opportunistic behavior. However, rather than asserting that such rentals are impossible, we would merely recognize the extremely high contracting costs generally present in such situations. More importantly, we claim that such an argument also extends to the rental of tangible specific capital.

To see how, suppose the club were owned by someone other than the members. Once the membership value is created by the interpersonal activities of the members, the owner of the club could then start to raise the fees for continuing members. Assuming some costs of the members moving away en masse and forming a new club, the owner could expropriate by higher fees some of the specialized quasi-rent value of the sociability created by the members' specialization to each other in their own group. Alternatively, the owner could threaten to break the implicit contract and destroy some of the sociability capital by selling admission to "undesirable" people who want to consort with the existing members.

Similarly, if the social country club were owned by the members as a corporation with each member owning a share of stock salable without prior approval of existing members (as is the case for the business corporation), a single member could, by threatening to sell to an "undesirable" potential member, extract some value of congeniality from the current members, as a payment for not selling.[50]

An extreme case of this general problem is a marriage. If each mate had a transferable share salable to a third party, there would be far fewer marriages with highly specific investments in affection and children. If a relationship is not one of specialized interest (specialized to a particular other party) or if it required no investment by any member, then the marriage relationship would be more like a corporation. As it is one of highly specific investments, marriages have historically been mutually owned entities, with permission of both parties generally required for alteration of membership. Government arbitration of this relationship to prevent postinvestment opportunistic behavior by either party can contribute toward lower bargaining costs and investments of resources (recoverable dowries) by both parties to improve their respective postinvestment bargaining positions, and, most importantly, create confidence that opportunistic behavior will not be successful. The legislative movement to "no-fault" divorce suggests that modern marriages may have less specific assets than formerly.[51]

[50] The "free-rider" problems of bribing an opportunistic member to prevent sale to an "undesirable" member are obvious. This analysis could be applied to social clubs such as Elks, Masonic Order, and so forth.

[51] Similarly, people whose work is highly specialized to each other will be partners (common ownership). For example, attorneys that have become highly specialized to their coattorneys will become partners, whereas new associates will at first be employees. A small team of performers (Laurel and Hardy, Sonny and Cher) who were highly specialized to each other would be "partners" (co-owners) rather than employee and employer. While it is still difficult to enforce such contracts and prevent postcontractual opportunistic behavior by either party, joint ownership creates an incentive for performance and specific investment not present in an easily terminable employer-employee contract that must rely solely on the personal brand-name reputation of contracting parties. Trust, including the reputation of certifying institutions such as

The importance of mobility costs when many individuals in a group must jointly decide to take action, as in the case of an opportunistic country-club owner, and the importance of government intervention are clearly reflected in the case of the money-supply industry.[52] The decision regarding what is used as the dominant money (medium of exchange) in society, like many other social agreements and customs, entails a large degree of rigidity on the individual level. A decision to change a social institution, in this case what is used as money, must involve a large subset of the population to be effective. Given this natural monopoly, the cost to an individual or a new entrant of attempting change may be prohibitively costly. Therefore, once a dominant money supplier is established, the potential wealth gain that can be realized through opportunistic behavior by the money issuer (that is, by unanticipated inflation) is enormous. The private implicit contractual solution would therefore entail an extremely high brand-name "premium" payment (seigniorage return) to guarantee that a wealth-maximizing, unregulated, private, dominant money supplier will not cheat by increasing the money supply faster than anticipated. Because this premium payment and therefore the rental price of money will be so high, it is unlikely that a private, implicit contractual solution is the cheapest arrangement.[53] Traditional vertical integration would also be extremely costly in this case of a consumer asset used by so many individuals (in fact it is difficult to even understand exactly what it would mean). Some form of government intervention is obviously likely, either in the form of regulation by enforcing an explicit contractual guarantee, or in the form of outright nationalization. Government ownership of the monetary unit is actually close to what one may consider vertical integration on the part of consumers in this particular case.

---

theatrical agents, law schools, and so on, and the presence of social sanctions against opportunistic partners remain important.

[52] The following discussion extends the analysis in Benjamin Klein, *supra* note 16.

[53] The alternative cost of holding money will be significantly above the marginal cost of producing cash balances (where costs are defined exclusive of the costs necessary to guarantee nonopportunistic behavior), thereby leading to less than "the optimum" quantity of cash balances. See, for example, Milton Friedman, The Optimum Quantity of Money, in The Optimum Quantity of Money and Other Essays 1 (1969), for the original statement of this supposed inefficiency.

An alternative solution analytically equivalent to the "premium" solution would be the putting up by the dominant money supplier of a large forfeitable collateral bond equal to the value of the possible short-run wealth gain from cheating. This bond would be held in part by each of the demanders of the firm's money in proportion to each particular individual's money holdings and interest received on the bond by each individual would be paid to the firm if cheating did not occur. While this would not create any inefficiencies of price greater than marginal cost as implied by the premium solution, the transaction costs of enforcing such an arrangement among such a large and changing number of individuals would be extremely high. If the government acted as the consumers' agent, the solution would now be similar to a regulated industry, with the potential for opportunistic expropriation of the bond by the government.

IV. Concluding Comment

We should emphasize in conclusion that most business relationships are neither likely to be as simple as the standard textbook polar cases of vertical integration or market contract nor as easily explained as some of the above examples. When particular examples are examined in detail, business relationships are often structured in highly complex ways not represented by either a simple rental contract or by simple vertical integration. A timely example is the ownership rights of common services supplied in condominium or "new-town" projects. One solution often adopted is joint ownership of common assets, similar to the joint ownership by petroleum producers and refiners of oil pipeline as noted above. In the condominium case, however, the number of shareowners is sometimes equal to hundreds or even thousands of individuals and the resulting contractual arrangements are closer to a constitution for a local "government" than to the simple paradigm of a two-person market transaction. When governing costs are high, individuals have often opted for a long-term management contract (often with the builder of the housing project) for maintaining the common assets. The possible problems associated with the opportunistic appropriation by the manager of the quasi rents in specialized assets of the individual owners (including specific assets used to furnish each apartment such as carpeting and any specific "friendship capital" from association with other owner occupants) are obvious. The fact that there has been a great deal of litigation in this area is not surprising. The difficulty may be partially due to what appears to be significant economies of scale in supplying confidence concerning contract performance and diseconomies of scale in the actual production and management of housing. Some insurance or franchising arrangement may therefore evolve in this area.

There is a continuing search in this difficult area using market and governmental (regulatory, legislative, and judicial) processes to produce institutional and private contractual innovation that will lead to more economical contractual relations and ownership rights. We have little idea why one solution appears to have been efficient for one condominium project and another solution for another project. This merely indicates that as we move toward more complex ownership relationships the problem of efficiently structuring the economic relationship, either within the firm or via contracts, also becomes highly complex. Stating that the world is complicated is another way of admitting our ignorance. However, explicitly recognizing that contracting costs are not zero, as they are often implicitly assumed to be in economic analysis, and explicitly considering the determinants of these costs (such as the presence of appropriable quasi rents) is the first step in explaining the large variety of contractual and ownership arrangements we observe in the real world.

More generally, we have seen that once we attempt to add empirical detail to Coase's fundamental insight that a systematic study of transaction costs is necessary to explain particular forms of economic organization, we find that his primary distinction between transactions made within a firm and transactions made in the marketplace may often be too simplistic. Many long-term contractual relationships (such as franchising) blur the line between the market and the firm. It may be more useful to merely examine the economic rationale for different types of particular contractual relationships in particular situations, and consider the firm as a particular kind or set of interrelated contracts.[54] Firms are therefore, by definition, formed and revised in markets and the conventional sharp distinction between markets and firms may have little general analytical importance. The pertinent economic question we are faced with is "What kinds of contracts are used for what kinds of activities, and why?"

[54] If we think of firms as collections of interrelated contracts rather than the collection of goods operative in the contracts, the question of who "owns" the firm (the set of contracts) appears somewhat nonsensical. It may be useful to think solely of a set of claimants to various portions of the value consequences of the contractual coalition, with no "owner" of the firm.

[10]

Supplier switching costs and vertical integration in the automobile industry

Kirk Monteverde*

and

David J. Teece**

This article tests a transactions cost theory of vertical integration with data from the U.S. automobile industry. Existing theory is first refined to take into account industrial know-how and the cost of transferring such know-how. A testable model is then developed, which is estimated by using probit techniques. The results support the view that transactions cost considerations surrounding the development and deepening of human skills have important ramifications for delineating efficient organizational boundaries.

1. Introduction

■ In recent years, economists have begun the systematic exploration of transactions cost issues, for example, see Williamson (1975, 1979). Research has also been initiated on know-how and its relationship to the nature of the firm. Although commonly ignored in economic theory, specialized know-how has important ramifications for organizational design. In particular, vertical integration issues arise when industrial know-how, including skills, becomes deepened and specialized to a particular firm. This article attempts to draw together the literatures on transactions cost and industrial know-how, and it brings them to bear on the analysis of efficiency incentives for backward vertical integration in the U.S. automobile industry.

2. Vertical integration by U.S. automakers

■ In the context of the U.S. automobile industry, we are interested in explaining why firms take parts production in-house. We hypothesize that assemblers will vertically integrate when the production process, broadly defined, generates specialized, nonpatentable know-how. When production processes are of this kind, both assembler and supplier are exposed to the possibility of opportunistic recontracting. Even if the title to specialized equipment used by the supplier is held by the assembler, this need not provide protection against rent appropriation if transaction-specific know-how has been generated. The existence of transaction-specific know-how and skills and the difficulties of skill transfer mean that it will be costly to switch to an alternative supplier. (Teece, 1977, 1980). An assembler will tend to choose vertically integrated component production

---

* Stanford University.

** Stanford University.

We would like to thank Charles Holloway, Paul Kleindorfer, and the referees and editors for many useful comments.

when high switching costs would otherwise lock the assembler into dependence upon a supplier and thereby expose that assembler to opportunistic recontracting or to the loss of transaction-specific know-how.

Within the vehicle manufacturing industry, supplier switching costs appear to be associated principally with development activities for new automotive parts. The design of a new vehicle model is a complex, five-year-long undertaking. Some components cannot be procured by simply announcing to suppliers performance and design requirements. The "specs" are often unknown *ex ante*. Consequently, preproduction heuristic development is critically important to the evolution of many vehicle parts. This process generates production as well as design knowledge. A suppler working in cooperation with the assembler on preproduction development gains a first-mover advantage because of knowledge acquired during development. This suggests the following testable hypothesis:

> The greater is the applications engineering effort associated with the development of any given automobile component, the higher are the expected appropriable quasi rents and, therefore, the greater is the likelihood of vertical integration of production for that component.

We shall test this hypothesis. The dependent variable we construct is dichotomous: each sample component is coded as being predominantly manufactured either in-house or by an external supplier. We next define a set of independent variables that may be expected to influence the choice between in-house production and external purchase, with our primary interest centering upon the influence of applications engineering. We then employ probit analysis to estimate the relationship between the independent variables and our measure of vertical integration.

To form the dependent variable, a list of 133 automotive components was obtained from an assembler. For each of the components, we ascertained the extent of vertical integration by General Motors and Ford for U.S. production in 1976. Each of the 133 components was recorded as either produced internally or sourced externally. For proprietary reasons, data about the exact percentage of each item in our sample that was manufactured in-house were not divulged. Hence, we took internal production of 80 percent or more of a component as an operational definition of integrated production. Taken together, the 133 component groupings include most of the major items that go into a complete vehicle.[1] Thus, the sample provides a representative picture of vertically integrated production for Ford and General Motors in 1976. The data are presented in Table 1.

Consider the independent variables. An excellent operational measure of applications engineering effort is the cost of developing a given component. Firms in the industry have these data on a component-by-component basis, but because of the data's proprietary nature, we were not able to gain direct access to them. However, a source within the industry who is privy to the data provided an engineering cost rating for our sample of automotive components.[2] This yielded a surrogate measure of relative engineering

[1] One conspicuous absence, however, is that of tires, none of which are produced by either Ford or General Motors. It should also be noted that two items, steel and vinyl, which are included in the sample, might better be classed as "basic materials" rather than components, as both are further upstream in the production process than most of the other items in the sample. However, the list submitted by our sources was accepted without alteration except for the elimination of "miscellaneous" categories and unidentifiable part names.

[2] The source was the design engineer for one of the major U.S. automakers who had responsibility for supervising development of a new generation of small, fuel-efficient vehicles to be manufactured in the United States. The reliability of his ratings was tested by obtaining a separate set of ratings from another automotive engineer. The two sets of ratings shared a correlation coefficient of .8, adding confidence that our ratings were a meaningful surrogate for the underlying construct.

TABLE 1 The Backward Vertical Integration of Ford and General Motors
("1" denotes 80 percent or more of component requirements produced in-house as of 1976.)

Part Category	Ford	GM
• <u>BODY</u>		
Body Sheet Metal	1	1
Exterior Ornamentation		
Paint (Topcoat)		
Primer		
Bumpers	1	1
Body Lamps	1	1
Sealed Beam Bulbs		1
Weatherstrip		
Mirrors—Outside		
Mirrors—Inside		1
Interior Trim	1	1
Interior Ornamentation		1
Carpeting & Mats		
Headlining	1	1
Safety Belts		
Inertia Locks		
Lock—Cylinders		
Door Handles		1
Hinges (Door, Hood, Decklid)	1	1
Window Regulator (Power)		1
Window Regulator (Manual)	1	1
Glass	1	
Windshield Wiper Motor	1	1
Windshield Washer System	1	1
Crash Pad		1
Seat Frame & Springs		
Seat Pad		1
Seat Tracks (Man. & Elec.)		1
Lamp Bulbs		1
Head Restraints	1	1
Headlamp Assembly	1	1
Sealers & Insulation		
Armrests		1
Grill		
Frame		
Jack & Wrench		
Engine Mounts		
• <u>ENGINE</u>		
Engine Stampings	1	1
Cylinder Head	1	1
Block	1	1
Manifold (Intake & Exhaust)	1	1
Crankshaft	1	1
Camshaft	1	1
Piston	1	N/A
Piston Ring		
Valves (Intake & Exhaust)	1	N/A
Radiator	1	1
Fan		
Air Cleaner	1	1
Air Cleaner Element		1
Carburetor		1
Fuel Pump		1
Starter	1	1
Distributor	1	1
Spark Plug		1
Ignition Coil	1	1
Oil Filter	1	1
• <u>EMISSION COMPONENTS</u>		
Catalytic Converter		1
Air Pump		1
Carbon Cannister	1	1
Substrate & Coating		
PCV, EGR, etc. Valves		
• <u>CHASSIS</u>		
W.C., H.C. (Optional)		
Wheel Covers & Hub Caps (Std.)		1
Coil Springs	1	1
Leaf Springs		1
Shock Absorbers	1	1
Upper & Lower Arms	1	1
Spindle Assembly	1	1
Driveshaft Assembly	1	1
Wheels	1	
Wires		
Rear Axle	1	1
Drums		
Master Brake Cylinder		
Power Brake Booster		1
Parking Brake		
Muffler		
Tailpipe/Inletpipe		
Brakes		
Disc Caliper & Rotor		1
Front Suspension	1	1
Rear Suspension	1	1
• <u>TRANSMISSION</u>		
Auto. Transmission Assy.	1	1
Auto. Transmission Cases	1	1
Manual Trans. Assembly		1
• <u>STEERING</u>		
Manual Steering Gear	1	1
Power Steering Gear	1	1
Steering Linkage		1
Steering Column	1	1
Steering Wheel		1
Power Steering Pump		1
Steering Assembly	1	1
• <u>FUEL</u>		
Fuel Tank	1	1
Gas Cap		
• <u>VENTILATION</u>		
A/C Assembly	1	1
Evaporator	1	1
Expansion Valve		1
Vacuum Motors		1
Blower Wheels		
Blower Motors	1	1
Heater Assembly	1	1
Heater Core	1	1
Compressor		1
Clutch		1
ATC Components		1
Condensor	1	1
Dehydrator/Receiver		N/A
Hose Assemblies		N/A

continued overleaf

TABLE 1 *(Continued)*

Part Category	Ford	GM	Part Category	Ford	GM
• <u>ELECTRICAL</u>			Antenna		1
Instrument Cluster & Panel	1	1	Speed Control System	1	1
Speedometer Cable Assembly		1	Clock		
Fuel Sender	1	1	Switches		
Alternator	1	1	• <u>OTHER</u>		
Regulator	1	1	Tubing (Brake/Fuel Lines)		
Battery		1	Antifreeze		
Horn	1	1	Oils & Grease		
Battery Cables		1	Steel		
Wiring Harness		1	Standard Parts, Fasteners		
Radio	1	1	Vinyl	1	
Tape Player		1	Water Pump Assembly	1	1
Speakers		1	Oil Pump	1	

effort. The rating was done on a 10-point scale with each component considered to require from "none" to "a lot" of engineering investment. We assume that such a rating scale provides a reasonable enough approximation to interval scaled data to allow use of parametric procedures.

To avoid misspecifications of the model, three sets of control variables are introduced. The first control variable distinguishes components that are specific to a company from those that are generic. Some of the components included in the sample (e.g., fasteners) are not designed specifically for any single automaker. These are items for which traditional spot market contracting may be expected to operate quite well; and for these components there would appear to be no incentive to integrate. However, components that are not specific to a single assembler's product may be expected to be among those rated as requiring the least applications engineering. To ensure that the engineering variable does not indicate a statistical relationship with integration that actually arises because nonspecific components will not be attractive integration candidates, a "component specificity" variable is introduced into the model.

The determination as to which sample components represent assembler-specific parts and which do not was accomplished with the cooperation of a replacement parts wholesaler. Company officials were asked to isolate those components for which identification of the manufacturer, make, and model of the automobile was not necessary to procure a replacement unit.[3] We assume that those components for which make and model information is not critical are not company-specific in original assembly. Using this procedure, a group of 30 items was identified as non-company-specific.

The second control variable relates to the identity of the sample firms. Because we developed a combined cross sectional model aggregating both Ford and General Motor's data, we include a dummy variable to control for systematic differences between these two firms with regard to vertical integration.

The third set of control variables relate to systems effects. The automobile represents not simply an assemblage of parts, but a "system"—a set of objects with relationships between the objects and their attributes (Hall, 1973, p. 103). In the vehicle "system," the "objects" are the individual components, and the relationships between components

[3] The actual question was: "Please examine the following list of 133 automotive components and indicate which of the noncaptive items on the list could be procured as replacement units without necessarily having to know the manufacturer, make, and model of the vehicle for which the replacement is sought. That is, which of the following categories of parts may be expected to be largely common across several manufacturers' vehicles."

consist principally of their mechanical or electrical interrelations and their "packaging"—the latter being the industry's term for physically fitting all components within the dimensions of the body. Clearly, design and implementation for any system as complex as an automobile must be tightly coordinated.[4] Because of the superior coordinating properties of vertical integration,[5] the degree to which any given component's design affects the performance or packaging of other components is a potentially important consideration in explaining the likelihood of vertically integrated production of the given component (Armour and Teece, 1980).

As shown in Table 1, the components were first grouped into nine categories (body, engine, emission components, chassis, transmission, steering, fuel, ventilation, electrical) and a tenth miscellaneous category. These categories were subsequently collapsed into six subsystems by merging emissions with engine, transmission and steering with chassis, and fuel tank and cap with body. The aggregation was based on expert evaluation of the degree of technical interrelatedness among the components. Vertical integration is predicted for components with large systems effects. Since we are unable to rank the subsystems according to the degree of interrelatedness, we simply posit that different subsystems will display different levels of vertical integration. Thus, a set of dummy variables was introduced into the model to represent each component's membership in a subsystem.

The predictor variables were combined into a single model estimated by probit techniques. A vector of parameter estimates for β was derived to maximize the log likelihood function:

$$L = \sum_{i=1}^{n} y_i \ln F(x_i'\beta) + \sum_{i=1}^{n} (1 - y_i) \ln [1 - F(x_i'\beta)],$$

where y_i is 1 if the ith component is integrated in production and zero otherwise; x_i is the vector of values of the independent variables for the ith observation; and $F(x_i'\beta)$ takes the specific form:

$$F(x_i'\beta) = \frac{1}{\sqrt{2\pi}} \int_{-\infty}^{x_i'\beta} e^{-u^2/2} du.$$

The x_i vector contains, for each sample point i, the values of the eight independent variables defined below:

$ENGINEERING_i$ = rating of the ith observation on the amount of engineering effort required in designing the part;

$SPECIFIC_i$ = 1 if the ith observation corresponds to a part specific to a single assembler; 0 otherwise;

$COMPANY_i$ = 1 if the ith observation was from General Motors; 0 if the ith observation was from Ford;

[4] White observes that: "The complex process of designing, producing, testing, and modifying an automobile requires a high degree of coordination. Engine, transmission, frame, body, brakes, windshield, and other components all have to perform well with each other and have to be in the right place at the right time in the right quantities" (White, 1971, p. 78).

[5] Vertical integration permits executive fiat to be used to achieve the requisite coordination in a timely fashion (Williamson, 1975). Scherer also notes the coordination benefits of integration and offers an example from the auto industry: "The benefits from integration also increase with the complexity of product component interrelationships. It is easier to make the various parts of an automobile fit together when all parties to the coordination effort work for the same boss than when design changes must be processed through a purchasing office" (Scherer, 1980, p. 90).

$$ENGINE_i = \begin{cases} 1 & \text{if the } i\text{th observation corresponds to an engine and emissions subsystem part;} \\ 0 & \text{otherwise;} \end{cases}$$

$$CHASSIS_i = \begin{cases} 1 & \text{if the } i\text{th observation corresponds to a chassis, transmission, and steering subsystem part;} \\ 0 & \text{otherwise;} \end{cases}$$

$$VENTILATION_i = \begin{cases} 1 & \text{if the } i\text{th observation corresponds to a ventilation subsystem part;} \\ 0 & \text{otherwise.} \end{cases}$$

$$ELECTRICAL_i = \begin{cases} 1 & \text{if the } i\text{th observation corresponds to an electrical subsystem part;} \\ 0 & \text{otherwise;} \end{cases}$$

$$BODY_i = \begin{cases} 1 & \text{if the } i\text{th observation corresponds to a body, fuel tank and cap subsystem part;} \\ 0 & \text{otherwise.} \end{cases}$$

The parameter estimates for β_1 through β_8, the asymptotic t-statistics corresponding to these eight predictor variables, and the model summary statistic are given in Table 2.

Recall that in-house production of 80% or more of a component's output was selected as the operational definition of vertical integration. To establish the robustness of the

TABLE 2 **Probit Coefficients, Asymptotic t-Statistics (in parentheses), and χ^2-Statistic in Equation to Explain Vertical Integration**
(Defined upon three thresholds for percentage of in-house parts production.)

Coefficient Estimated	Related Variable	Vertical Integration Defined as In-house Production of: ≥70%	≥80%	≥90%
β_1	*ENGINEERING*	0.1319 (3.24)*	0.1461 (3.57)*	0.1453 (3.54)*
β_2	*SPECIFIC*	0.8773 (3.64)*	0.8186 (3.33)*	0.7902 (3.15)*
β_3	*COMPANY*	0.7388 (4.22)*	0.7125 (4.05)*	0.9010 (5.08)*
β_4	*ENGINE*	0.5521 (1.21)	0.5348 (1.17)	0.7168 (1.47)
β_5	*CHASSIS*	0.0615 (0.138)	0.0003 (0.001)	0.03051 (0.637)
β_6	*VENTILATION*	0.3620 (0.733)	0.4903 (0.983)	0.6552 (1.25)
β_7	*ELECTRICAL*	0.6861 (1.48)	0.6905 (1.49)	1.085 (2.18)†
β_8	*BODY*	0.0857 (0.201)	−0.2293 (−0.532)	0.1152 (0.248)
χ^2 Value		110.064*	111.291*	126.676*

* Indicates significance beyond the .001 level.
† Indicates significance beyond the .05 level.

results, we also obtained a listing of those items which would be considered integrated were the cutoff changed to 70% and then to 90%.

The principal point to note about the results in Table 2 is that regardless of the threshold chosen, the variable used as a proxy for transaction-specific skills ("engineering") is highly significant. The development effort associated with the design of any given automotive component is shown to be positively related to the likelihood of vertically integrated production of that component, thereby confirming the central hypothesis of this article.

Second, the coefficient on the "*SPECIFIC*" variable is also positive and statistically significant, which lends support to the hypothesis that only components specific to a single assembler will be candidates for vertical integration. It can also be seen that the coefficient for the "*COMPANY*" variable is positive and statistically significant, thereby indicating that General Motors is more integrated into component production than is Ford.

Finally, the systems-effects hypothesis is only mildly supported by the probit analysis. With the exception of the "*ELECTRICAL*" variable in the ≥90% integration threshold case, none of the coefficients on the five dummy variables taken alone indicates a significant relationship with backward integration. Nevertheless, the set of five systems effect dummies, taken together, significantly contributed to the explanatory power of the model.

In general, the change in magnitude of the coefficients was minor as the definition of vertical integration was altered. The variation was the greatest among the individual subsystem variables that, with the one exception of the electrical subsystem variable, were not found to be significantly different from zero.

3. Conclusion

■ Transactions cost considerations surrounding the development and deepening of human skills appear to have important ramifications for vertical integration in the automobile industry, thereby supporting the transactions cost paradigm advanced by Williamson. GM and Ford are more likely to bring component design and manufacturing in-house if relying on suppliers for preproduction development service will provide suppliers with an exploitable first-mover advantage. We posit that this is a result of the high switching costs entailed if the supplier acquires transaction specific know-how at the assembler's expense. Since know-how cannot simply be transferred from supplier to supplier like a book of blueprints (Winter, 1980), backward integration is the more prudent course of action. General Motors and Ford also have a preference for backward vertical integration when the components are firm-specific and their design must be highly coordinated with other parts of the automobile system.

Hence, the vertical structure of GM and Ford appears to be based at least in part on efficiency considerations. Specifically, the structure appears to be designed to take advantage of the coordinating properties of hierarchies as well as the ability of internal organization to reduce the exposure of the automakers to opportunism from suppliers—a hazard which is apparently absent in the less integrated Japanese industry[6] where "the relationship between the major auto firm and its satellite suppliers is one of total cooperation" (Ouchi, 1981, p. 19).

References

Armour, H.O. and Teece, D.J., "Vertical Integration and Technological Innovation." *Review of Economics and Statistics* (August 1980), pp. 470–474.

[6] We posit that cooperation between the auto companies and remaining suppliers will also characterize the U.S. industry because the integrated and "quasi-integrated" (Monteverde and Teece, 1982) structure of the industry has eliminated most occasions for opportunistic rent appropriation.

FINNEY, D.J. *Probit Analysis.* Cambridge, England: The University Press, 1952.

HALL, A.D. "Some Fundamental Concepts of Systems Engineering" in S.L. Optner, ed., *Systems Analysis*: Middlesex, U.K.: Penguin, 1973.

MONTEVERDE, K.A. AND TEECE, D.J. "Appropriable Rents and Quasi-Vertical Integration." *Journal of Law and Economics* (forthcoming, 1982).

OUCHI, W. *Theory Z: How American Business Can Meet the Japanese Challenge.* Reading, Ma.: Addison-Wesley, 1981.

SCHERER, F.M. *Industrial Market Structure and Economic Performance*, 2nd ed. Chicago: Rand McNally, 1980.

TEECE, D.J. "Technology Transfer by Multinational Firms: The Resource Costs of Transferring Technological Know-How." *Economic Journal* (June 1977), pp. 242–261.

———. "Economies of Scope and the Scope of the Enterprise." *Journal of Economic Behavior and Organization* (September 1980), pp. 223–247.

WHITE, L.J. *The Automobile Industry since 1945.* Cambridge: Harvard University Press, 1971.

WILLIAMSON, O.E. *Markets and Hierarchies: Analysis and Antitrust Implications.* New York: Free Press, 1975.

———. "Transactions-Cost Economics: The Governance of Contractual Relations." *Journal of Law and Economics* (October 1979), pp. 233–261.

WINTER, S.G. "An Essay on the Theory of Production." Yale School of Organization and Management, Working Paper Series A #39, June 1980.

[11]

THE ORGANIZATION OF PRODUCTION: EVIDENCE FROM THE AEROSPACE INDUSTRY*

SCOTT E. MASTEN
University of Michigan

THE interface between successive stages of production is frequently governed by contractual agreements, and the efficiency of such arrangements has been the subject of considerable attention in the economic literature. But production is organized administratively within firms as well as contractually between them, and given the practical limitations of bureaucratic organization, the relevant question can be seen to be not merely whether contractual deficiencies exist but how severe such deficiencies may be relative to the alternative costs of organizing production internally. The important issue from an institutional choice perspective thus becomes how the particular details of a transaction affect the *differential* efficiency of alternative organizational forms.

Recent theoretical work has sought to identify such relationships.[1] In particular, the choice between internal and external organization and, in the event of the latter, the choice of contract terms have been related to several critical parameters of the transaction. This paper presents some

* I would like to thank Oliver Williamson and Roger Sherman for helpful comments. The cooperation of the General Electric Company is also gratefully acknowledged. Support for this research was received from the Center for the Study of Organizational Innovation and from Sloan and National Science Foundation grants for the study of Transaction Cost Economics at the University of Pennsylvania. The paper was completed while I was at the University of Virginia.

[1] See, in particular, Benjamin Klein, Robert G. Crawford, & Armen A. Alchian, Vertical Integration, Appropriable Rents, and the Competitive Contracting Process, 21 J. Law & Econ. 297 (1978); and Oliver E. Williamson, Transaction-Cost Economics: The Governance of Contractual Relations, 22 J. Law & Econ. 233 (1979). A formal model treating the make-or-buy decision as part of a producer's overall optimization problem may be found in Scott E. Masten, Transaction Costs, Institutional Choice and the Theory of the Firm (1982) (unpublished Ph.D. dissertation, Univ. Pennsylvania); *id.*, Institutional Choice and the Organization of Production: the Make-or-Buy Decision (January 1984) (unpublished manuscript Univ. Virginia, Dept. Economics).

[*Journal of Law & Economics*, vol. XXVII (October 1984)]

evidence of the practical import of those relationships, based on a study of input procurement practices in the aerospace industry.

The administration of procurement in this industry is two tiered. On the first level, the government chooses a prime contractor who is assigned overall responsibility for a particular program; and on the second, the contractor manages the production of the system itself, including what is of particular interest here—the administration of subcontracts. This paper considers procurement practices at both levels. To begin, the essential elements of the theory will be briefly reviewed in Section I. Section II then presents the results of an examination of input procurement for an aerospace system containing nearly two thousand component specifications. Tests are based on a probit model of the dichotomous choice between internal and external procurement of supplies. The estimated coefficients provide indirect measures of the relative costs of internal and external procurement with respect to several qualitative variables. Following this, the procurement policies of the federal government are reviewed and interpreted in light of the theory, with particular emphasis on the form of the relationship between the government and the prime contractor. Conclusion and additional comments appear in the final section.

I. The Make-or-Buy Decision

Having selected an end-product line, a producer must decide which in the stream of intermediate products and processes successively combining to form his eventual output he will administer within the organization and which he will delegate to outside suppliers, along with the terms under which any external procurements would take place. In practice, this series of procurement decisions—sometimes referred to as a producer's make-or-buy program—involves a large number of considerations including design requirements; inventory needs; quality control; production, overhead, and transportation costs; and the capabilities, capacities, and negotiating strength of potential suppliers relative to those of the producer himself.[2]

Transaction cost economics has sought to place these concerns within an economic context and relate the outcome of individual make-or-buy decisions to details of the transaction. According to that view, the choice among alternative organizational arrangements is part of an agent's over-

[2] These concerns and many others are evident in E. Raymond Corey, Procurement Management: Strategy, Organization, and Decision-Making (1978), and were also present in internal memoranda and discussions with company representatives.

all optimization problem, and the net value of a transaction organized in a particular manner depends not only on the losses due to potential misallocations of resources but also on the costs of conducting the transaction itself. Hence, a manager choosing a procurement mode will consider, in addition to the value of the goods and services actually procured, both the opportunity costs of the additional demands that would be placed on his time and attention by internalizing a transaction and the various "organizational" expenses that would be involved in dealing with outside suppliers. The latter include the costs of negotiating the terms under which exchange is to take place and, oftentimes, the various expenses associated with adopting and upholding formal contractual agreements.

In general, the organizational costs associated with market exchange increase, the more specialized, profitable, and durable are the investments associated with a given transaction. Idiosyncratic assets, because of their specialized and durable nature, imply that parties to a transaction face only imperfect exchange alternatives for an extended period. The more specialized those assets, the larger will be the quasi-rents at stake over that period and hence the greater the incentive for agents to attempt to influence the terms of trade through bargaining or other rent-seeking activities once the investments are in place.

The role of contracts is to prevent such activities from dissipating too large a portion of the gains from trade by stipulating acceptable behavior at the outset of a transaction-specific relationship. But contracts incur expenses in both specification and enforcement that limit their usefulness. First, because contingent performance is costly to stipulate and even more difficult for courts to administer, contracts typically contain few provisions and, as a result, tend to be inflexible mechanisms for governing exchange. The greater the complexity of the transaction and the level of uncertainty associated with it, the greater the likelihood of being bound to an inappropriate action, and hence the greater the implicit costs of contractual organization. This inflexibility, in turn, tends to constrict the time span of contractual agreements. Because confidence that any given state of the world will obtain decreases the more distant the relevant horizon, committing yourself to a particular activity becomes less desirable the more remote the specified date of performance. A trade-off therefore exists between the opportunity costs of being bound to an inflexible agreement and the hazards of negotiating follow-on procurements in a condition of bilateral monopoly. In sum, the more idiosyncratic are the investments associated with a particular transaction, the greater are the incentives to incur the costs of writing more detailed and longer term contracts. Greater uncertainty or complexity of a transaction, however, implies, on the one hand, an incentive to write more detailed agreements and, on the other, a disincentive to commit to long term contractual relationships.[3]

Greater complexity would also, of course, put additional strain on decision makers under internal organization, which is intended to eliminate rent seeking by internalizing the quasi-rents that are the object of that behavior.[4] But the possibility of rendering decisions in an adaptive, sequential fashion under internal organization reduces the need relative to contracting of exploring and enumerating the full contingency tree ex ante.[5] Nevertheless, the expediency of internalizing successive transactions is limited by the bureaucratic inefficiencies that inevitably develop as organizations get large.

II. Input Procurement in the Aerospace Industry

There is an abundance of supportive, if informal, evidence illustrating the relationships discussed above. A recent article on the semiconductor industry, for example, revealed the existence of a correlation between design specificity and the internal procurement of supplies in the production of electronic components: "Most major chip buyers, after trying but failing to get the big producers to serve their needs for low volumes of custom circuits, have launched chip-production lines of their own and today turn out almost all of the custom chips made as well as two-thirds of such semi-custom products as gate arrays."[6]

In addition, the article contended that the reason that downstream producers found it necessary to develop in-house production capabilities for these products, despite the expertise of the established chip manufacturers and "the high cost of maintaining internal production," was to avoid the "frictions between vendors and customers" encountered in a market where specialized designs are highly profitable and increasingly complex.[7]

Although accounts of this type can be illuminating, they lack the au-

[3] The trade-offs involved here are discussed at greater length in Masten, Transaction Costs, Institutional Choice and the Theory of the Firm, *supra* note 1.

[4] In the case of specialized human capital, quasi-rents cannot be eliminated by internalization in the same way that they can with physical capital. Rather, hierarchical organization seeks to substitute internal for third-party adjudication of conflicting interests. Thus, from this perspective, the firm becomes a quasi-judicial body entrusted by its members to resolve disputes and enforce cooperative behavior.

[5] Oliver E. Williamson, Markets and Hierarchies: Analysis and Antitrust Implications 25 (1975).

[6] The 80's Look in Chips: Custom, Not Standard, Business Week, January 18, 1982, at 36H.

[7] *Id.* at 36D-L.

thority often accorded formal tests of hypotheses. Unfortunately, the level of detail at which the theory operates has made rigorous applications difficult. One way in which the information requirements can be moderated, however, is to restrict attention to a single industry. This reduces the need for absolute measures for such variables as design specificity and complexity and permits qualitative tests based on ordinal rankings of inputs by their characteristics. Recently, this strategy has been employed by Kirk Monteverde and David Teece to analyze vertical integration in the automobile industry and by Thomas Palay in a study of railroads.[8] The present paper examines related issues in the context of defense-related production, an area in which specialized designs are common and the alternative values of investments often limited.

The model I wish to test is the following: Let G_i be the institution chosen by the producer to govern the acquisition of product or process i, and let G_i^* represent internal organization of that activity and $\tilde{G}_i$ external or "market" procurement. Then the outcome of the producer's make-or-buy decision can be summarized as

$$G_i = G_i^* \quad \text{if } L_i^*(\omega_i) < \tilde{L}(\lambda_i, \omega_i),$$

and

$$G_i = \tilde{G}_i \quad \text{if } L_i^*(\omega_i) \geqslant \tilde{L}(\lambda_i, \omega_i),$$

where L_i^* is the cost of maintaining production internally and $\tilde{L}_i$ is the cost of market-mediated exchange, depicted as a function of the specificity (λ) and complexity (ω) of the transaction.

The aerospace system studied contained 1,887 component specifications, each of which was identified as either a "make" or "buy" item by a team of company representatives made up of the managers of the material systems and manufacturing engineering departments and members of their staffs. The disposition of the entire make-or-buy program is summarized by generic category in Table 1.

The procurement team was asked to complete questionnaires designed to elicit information about the attributes of the items and associated investments. Each of the items within several of the cells in Table 1 shared similar characteristics, permitting completion of a single questionnaire for the entire cell. The remaining cells were randomly sampled in approximate proportion to the ratio between the size of the cell and the total

[8] Kirk Monteverde & David J. Teece, Supplier Switching Costs and Vertical Integration in the Automobile Industry, 13 Bell J. Econ. 206 (1982); Thomas Palay, Comparative Institutional Economics: The Governance of Rail-Freight Contracting, 13 J. Legal Stud. 265 (1984).

TABLE 1
THE MAKE-OR-BUY PROGRAM

Category	Quantity	Make	Buy
Top and major subassemblies	17	17	...
Components assembly	185	114	71
Structure machining	11	5	6
Structure forgings	8	...	8
Mechanical detail parts	138	53	85
Connectors	180	...	180
Printed wire board assembly	80	80	...
Flexible/hard printed wire boards	151	147	4
Electrical piece parts	971	11	960
Heat shields	4	...	4
Insulating materials	62	10	52
Harness/coax	80	80	...

number of components in the system. The result was thirty-four individual observations, which can be statistically weighted to reflect their actual distribution in the program.[9]

From this information, two measures of specificity were developed. The first, corresponding to design specificity, was based on whether an item was identified as used exclusively by this company (highly specialized), used or easily adaptable for use by other aerospace firms (somewhat specialized), or used in other industries (relatively standard). "Electrical piece parts" such as transistors and resistors, for example, would be standard items, while hybrid circuits designed to individual specifications would be considered highly specialized.[10]

A second variable was created to reflect site specificity based on whether colocation or grouping of facilities or processes was considered to be an important factor in production. Various economies may arise from positioning successive operations side by side. But if associated assets are costly to reposition, their alternative use value may be low. Such was the case in this system with the computerized lathes and other machinery used to bore and mill nose cones. The machinery itself has a

[9] Since the data for this study were generated from a choice based sample, weighted exogenous sampling maximum likelihood estimation was employed. For a discussion of the properties of these estimators see Charles F. Manski & Steven R. Lerman, Estimation of Choice Probabilities from Choice Based Samples, 45 Econometrica 1977 (1977).

[10] Although *asset* design would be preferable to *input* design as a measure of specificity, it is difficult, even at this level of disaggregation, to separate the specialized from standard assets used in the manufacture of a given input. The fact that specialized inputs may at times be produced using standardized assets, however, merely implies that input design measures will have lower *t*-statistics than would asset design; hence, information on the latter would only improve the explanatory power of the model. See *infra*.

number of uses. However, because of transfer and control costs between operations, the configuration and geographical location of the equipment is important. Meanwhile, installation and removal costs make relocation impractical. Consequently, once the assets have been positioned, they are more or less committed to a particular use.

Since this study focused on a single system, it was not possible to test the effects of demand uncertainty on the internalization decision using these data alone. Complexity, however, may be used as a proxy for the degree of uncertainty on the production side; the more complex a component, the more details to be accounted for and the more dimensions in which something can go wrong. To determine the relative complexity of the components, a ranking system used internally by the company was adopted. In that three-way classification scheme, "A-items" were the most and "C-items" the least complex.

For estimation purposes, the following specification of the model was employed:

$$L_i^* = \bar{B} + b \cdot \omega_i + u_i,$$

and

$$\tilde{L}_i = a \cdot \lambda_i + c \cdot \omega_i + v_i,$$

where u_i and v_i are random errors assumed to have independent normal distributions, and a, b, and c are coefficients. $\bar{B}$ represents the "administrative burden" of internalizing a transaction and would be expected to be positive. Since complexity increases the costs associated with organizing production both administratively within firms and contractually between them, both b and c should be positive. But because flexibility in contracting demands prior anticipation of potential problems while internal organization permits adaptation to changing circumstances in a sequential fashion, the differential effect of complexity on the costs of alternative organizational arrangements favors internal organization over contractual exchange.[11] Hence, we would expect $c - b > 0$. Finally, the coefficient on item specificity, a, is also expected to be positive reflecting the greater potential for opportunistic behavior in idiosyncratic transactions.

Since L^* and $\tilde{L}$ are not actually observed, the estimation is based on the disposition of the dichotomous make-or-buy choice. The probability that input j will be produced inside the firm is

$$\begin{aligned} \text{pr}(L_j^* < \tilde{L}_j) &= \text{pr}(u_j - v_j < a\lambda_j + (c - b)\omega_j - \bar{B}) \\ &= F(a\lambda_j + (c - b)\omega_j - \bar{B}), \end{aligned}$$

[11] See Williamson, *supra* note 5.

TABLE 2
ESTIMATED COEFFICIENTS FOR THE MAKE-OR-BUY DECISION

Variable	Coefficient	t-Ratio	Mean of Variable
CONSTANT	−3.8657	−6.8064	1.00000
COMPLEX	1.8865	5.4444	.84208
SPECI	3.3696	6.5486	.34605
STANDARD	−2.7775	−.1724	.50874
COLOC	5.1120	.1269	.09433
χ^2: 32.0788, 4 *df**			
Pseudo R^2: .610734†			
Proportion of observations for which $y = 1$: .2729.			

*Indicates that the equation is significant beyond the .001 level.
†This measure is analogous to standard R^2s. Its properties are discussed in Takeshi Amemiya, Qualitative Response Models: A Survey, 19 J. Econ. Literature 1483 (1981).

where $F(\cdot)$ is the normal distribution. The likelihood function of the model is

$$\Lambda = \prod_{i=1}^{n} F(a\lambda_i + (c - b)\omega_i - \bar{B})^{y_i} [1 - F(a\lambda_i + (c - b)\omega_i - \bar{B})]^{(1 - y_i)},$$

where $y_i = 1$ if item i is produced internally and zero if acquired outside the firm. The actual explanatory variables used in the estimations were

COMPLEX_i	= 1	if the item is rated as complex (A- and B-items),[12]
	= 0	otherwise (C-items);
SPECI_i	= 1	if the item is highly specialized,
	= 0	otherwise;
STANDARD_i	= 1	if the item is relatively standard,
	= 0	otherwise;[13]
COLOC_i	= 1	if colocation of assets or processes is considered important,
	= 0	otherwise.

Maximum likelihood estimates for the weighted observations and corresponding statistics are presented in Table 2. The column on the far

[12] No significant difference was found in the coefficients on A- and B-items in any of the various specifications of the model experimented with.

[13] The variables SPECI_i and STANDARD_i were derived from the same ordinally measured construct; see text at note 10 *supra*. "Somewhat specialized" items are the omitted category.

		SPECI	
		0	1
COMPLEX	0	< .01	.31
	1	.02	.92

FIGURE 1

right-hand side of the table, "mean of variable," indicates the proportion of inputs possessing that characteristic.

The coefficients on both COMPLEX and SPECI are highly significant and positive as expected, indicating that the probability of internalization is higher for complex and highly specialized inputs. But although the coefficients for COLOC and STANDARD have the expected signs, statistical confidence in these estimates is low.[14]

Note also that the constant term in this equation has a large effect on the probability of internalization. This coefficient reflects the predisposition of management toward external procurement and, given the specification of the model, can be interpreted as an indirect measure of the administrative burden incurred by internalizing an additional transaction. Each of the remaining coefficients provides an estimate of the implicit costs of contracting *relative* to this burden for transactions possessing the corresponding characteristic.

The matrix in Figure 1 presents the estimated probabilities that components possessing the corresponding characteristics will be produced internally.[15] As is apparent from these estimates, the degree of specialization is by far the most important determinant of organizational form in this system. The lack of alternative uses for a component increases the probability that it will be procured internally from less than 1 percent to 31 percent for relatively uncomplex items and from 2 percent to 92 percent for more complex components. Since the omitted category includes those inputs

[14] The insignificant coefficient on STANDARD implies that there is no significant difference between the effects of "standard" items and the omitted category, "somewhat specialized" items, on the internalization decision. In other words, "standard" items are at least as likely to be procured externally as are "somewhat specialized" components.

[15] Specifically, the probability that component *i* will be procured internally is $F(-3.8657 + 1.8865\text{COMPLEX}_i + 3.3696\text{SPECI}_i)$ where F is the cumulative normal distribution.

used only in other aerospace applications, these estimates suggest that the existence of alternative uses for a component, even in a fairly highly concentrated industry such as this, warrants reliance on external procurement.

The complexity of an item also increases the probability that it will be "sourced in-house." Moreover, as expected, the hazards of incomplete contracts in complex environments appear to be much greater when specialized designs are involved, increasing the likelihood of internalization from 31 percent to 92 percent (as compared with less than 1 percent to only about 2 percent for items which are only "somewhat specialized"). Thus, as predicted by the theory, the need to employ specialized designs appears to be a necessary condition for the breakdown of market-mediated exchange and the subsequent internalization of production, especially where fairly complex products are involved.

Additional detail missed in the surveys but obtainable case by case further supports the hypothesized relationships. For instance, the system design called for both rigid and flexible printed wire boards. Although both types involved specialized designs, the flexible boards could be produced using standard equipment and were procured externally. The hard boards, on the other hand, were unique items that could not be produced using existing facilities. Not having an expertise in this area, the company sought to establish outside sources but found that manufacturers were "unwilling" to take on the business. The fact that the company was obliged to develop its own production capability suggests that the "organizational savings" from sourcing outside the company were not adequate to compensate potential suppliers for the hazards to which they would be exposed by incurring such specialized costs. However, the components that, although specially designed, could be produced with standard assets were not subject to those hazards. Such evidence supports the contention that asset design is a more powerful predictor of organization form than is input design.

The survey also indicated other factors of concern to procurement managers in deciding whether to internalize production. Among the more important were the existence of preexisting production capability or capacity and the perception of a need for "control" over the production process. But each of these concerns is itself explained in large part by the degree of complexity and specificity of the item: the company was more likely to have previously developed a capability or capacity for the production of more specialized and complex components, and the perception of a need for control arose primarily in those cases in which the market or the courts were least likely to regulate transactions effectively, again when production was highly specialized and complex.

III. Government Procurement Policies

Although data sufficiently detailed to permit evaluation of all the hypotheses of the transaction-cost paradigm are not yet available, it is possible at least to compare the concerns identified in these theories with the procedures adopted by procurement managers. This section selectively examines several of the federal government's procurement policies to see how well they conform to the theory presented in Section I.

A. *Make-or-Buy Policies*

Although in defense-related production the basic responsibility for procurement decisions, as with all management functions, remains with the firm, the government reserves the right to review a prospective contractor's make-or-buy program.[16] Of particular interest from the standpoint of the present analysis is that proposed make-or-buy programs need only be submitted for review "where the work is complex, the dollar value substantial, and there is not adequate price competition."[17] More specifically, information on a prospective contractor's make-or-buy program is *not* required by the government:

i) when a proposed contract has total estimated value of less than $1,000,000 . . . ;
ii) in research and development contracts, unless the contract is for prototypes or hardware and it can reasonably be anticipated that significant follow-up quantitites of the product will be procured;
iii) when the contracting officer determines that the price is based on adequate price competition, or established catalog or market prices of commercial items sold in substantial quantities to the general public . . . ; or
iv) when the contracting officer determines that the work is not complex.[18]

What is notable about this passage is that each of the stipulations contained in it has a direct correlate in transaction-cost theory: special attention or precautions are unnecessary for transactions which (i) are low in value, (ii) are not likely to generate first-mover advantages in follow-on production, (iii) are accompanied by price competition or involve standard products, or (iv) are not complex. If the value of the contract is

[16] The government defines a contractor's make-or-buy program as "that part of a contractor's written plan which identifies the major subsystems, assemblies, subassemblies, and components to be manufactured, developed, or assembled in his own facilities, and those which will be obtained elsewhere by subcontract." Defense Acquisition Regulations, Gov't Cont. Rep. (CCH) ¶ 32,888. The objective of such reviews is to assure that the contractor has applied "sound business and technical judgement" and that his decisions will not "adversely affect the government's interests," *id.* ¶ 32,888.15.

[17] *Id.* ¶ 32,887.

[18] *Id.* ¶ 32,888.

small, the potential losses to an inappropriate make-or-buy program will also be small and therefore will not generally justify the cost of review. Where large amounts are at stake, however, an improper make-or-buy decision can have more serious consequences. Review is also desirable where research and development activities will bestow extended advantages on the agent; a contractor's decision to subcontract some part of this work to another firm may leave both the prime contractor and the government open to extortion in subsequent dealings. In contrast, items which are generally available pose relatively few such hazards. Finally, when work is not complex, an agent has fewer opportunities to deceive the government about his costs and is therefore less likely to be successful in obtaining unwarranted price adjustments.

B. *Procurement Hazards and Remedies*

The government's policies for administering its own acquisitions further reveal its awareness of the potential for opportunistic behavior on the part of contractors and of the conditions under which such behavior is most likely to emerge. "Buying in" is one manifestation explicitly recognized as a potential hazard. " 'Buying in' refers to the practice of attempting to obtain a contract award by knowingly offering a price or cost estimate less than anticipated costs with the expectation of either (i) increasing contract price or estimated cost during the period of performance through change orders or other means, or (ii) receiving future 'follow-on' contracts at prices high enough to recover any losses on the original 'buy-in' contract."[19]

Contracting officers are advised to be particularly alert to this possibility when performance of the contract involves substantial "preproduction engineering, special tooling, special plant rearrangement, training programs and such nonrecurring costs as initial rework, initial spoilage, and pilot runs,"[20] all of which represent specialized investments in the transaction. Where such investments are at stake, the government provides several policy options directed at preventing the incidence of buying in at the outset of the relationship.

1. *Acquisition of Special Tooling.* One option, applicable at least in cases where first-mover advantages are embedded in specialized physical capital, is for the government to take title to specialized assets.[21] Oppor-

[19] *Id.* ¶ 32,069.

[20] *Id.* ¶ 32,866.

[21] This alternative is referred to as quasi-vertical integration by Kirk Monteverde & David J. Teece, Appropriable Rents and Quasi-Vertical Integration, 25 J. Law & Econ. 321 (1982).

tunism by the original contractor can then be countered by transferring the assets to more cooperative suppliers. The government's policies covering the acquisition of special tooling and special test equipment address this alternative in detail, clearly indicating a sensitivity to the trade-offs between the hazards of leaving title to specialized tooling with contractors and the costs of internal administration.

Policy. It is the policy of the Department of Defense that contractors provide and retain title to special tooling required for the performance of defense contracts to the maximum extent consistent with sound procurement objectives. Government acquisition of title or the right to title in special tooling creates substantial administrative burden, encumbers the competitive procurement process and frequently results in the retention of special tooling without advantage commensurate with such burden. In certain instances, however, the acquisition of special tooling or rights thereto may help the Government obtain fair prices, recover the residual value of special tooling paid for by the Government, and increase competition in subsequent procurements by increasing the number of sources, where tooling is susceptible of use by more than one contractor, considering its adaptability and all costs of movement.[22]

The instances in which acquisition is likely to be beneficial are precisely those in which buying in is apt to be a problem, namely, where because of "start-up costs or other nonrecurring costs, . . . the successful offeror is likely to become, in effect, a sole source for follow-on procurements."[23]

The data accumulated on the aerospace system discussed in the preceding section indicates that the government frequently employs the option to acquire special tooling. Of the fifty-four investments in special tooling or test equipment covered by the surveys, the government retained title in all but seven instances. Moreover, with one exception involving proprietary technology, each of the latter either was ranked as having a high alternative use value or had a shorter use life than the average for the forty-seven to which the government acquired title.

The expediency of this policy toward special tooling depends heavily on the mobility and adaptability of the assets in question; rents will still accrue to equipment unless it can be removed and reassigned to other uses or users at low cost. In addition, the policy cannot eliminate advantages that arise from specialized know-how acquired through performance of the contract.

[22] Defense Acquisition Regulations, supra note 16, ¶ 34,705. See also the criteria in *id.* ¶ 34,705.10. "*Special tooling* means all jigs, dies, fixtures, molds, patterns, taps, gauges, other equipment and manufacturing aids . . . which are of such a specialized nature that, without substantial modification, their use is limited to the development or production of particular supplies or parts thereof, or the performance of particular services." *Id.* ¶ 34,657. A similar definition applies to special test equipment, ¶ 34,657.35.

[23] *Id.* ¶ 32,866.

2. *Extended Contracting*. Because the latter policy option applies only where specialized investments are easily transferable, the government provides other methods to attempt to forestall buying in. In particular, where specialized investments cannot be internalized for adaptability or administrative reasons, government policy calls for the use of more extensive contracting: "To avoid or minimize the opportunity for 'buying in' on a procurement which is likely to be succeeded by one or more 'follow-on' procurements, the Government should obtain from the contractor a binding price commitment covering as much of the entire program as is practicable. Such a commitment may be secured through employment of one of the following procurement techniques: (i) multi-year procurement . . . ; or (ii) price options for additional quantities. . . ."[24]

Quantity options are intended for use in contracts where "additional requirements are foreseeable but not known and . . . realistic competition for the option is impracticable once the initial contract is awarded."[25] Similarly, multiyear contracting and subcontracting are encouraged where "the item is expected to be obtained only from a sole source during the entire multi-year period."[26] But because of the rigidity of contracting in general, multiyear agreements should only be adopted if "(i) the contract or service is of stable design and specification [and] (ii) the quantity required is reasonably firm and continuing,"[27] that is, where the degree of uncertainty is moderate. Thus, the terms and conditions under which extended contracting is to be employed indicate a perception of the benefits and hazards of the institution that coincide with the arguments outlined in Section I.

IV. Conclusions

Evidence from both stages of the defense procurement process indicates a general reluctance on the part of administrators to internalize transactions: government procurement policies refer explicitly to the "substantial administrative burden" incurred in acquiring and managing equipment and facilities, and estimations of actual contractor procurement practices indicate a strong "predisposition" toward external sourcing. But it is a reluctance that can be overcome by exposure to the hazards of market exchange when components are specialized and complex, as the evidence also attests.

[24] *Id.* ¶ 32,069.

[25] *Id.* ¶ 32,423; also see Use of Options, *id.* ¶ 32,081.

[26] *Id.* ¶ 32,082.

[27] *Id.* ¶ 32,081.

Overall, the data on the aerospace system support the contention that design specificity and complexity are necessary, if not sufficient, conditions for the breakdown of cooperation in market-mediated exchanges and the subsequent integration of production within the firm. In addition, the procurement policies professed by the government provide supportive detail not yet available in the formal analysis, such as the effects of uncertainty on the scope of contractual agreements and the relevance of the absolute value of investments on the need for specialized governance structures. How one views this evidence depends on one's prior assumptions. In a descriptive sense, these excerpts suggest that agents engaged in procurement activities are concerned with the sorts of issues addressed in the transaction-cost paradigm. From a prescriptive standpoint, the model indicates that the government's policies in this regard are appropriate and sensible. Whether or not these policies are actually carried out is, of course, another matter.[28]

Finally, the estimations reported here provide an indication of the relative efficiency of contractual and hierarchical organizational forms. While at a rudimentary level at present, this sort of analysis may eventually permit economists to assess the value of particular contractual arrangements to the parties involved and, subsequently, to evaluate the desirability of adopting alternative legal conventions or of government interference in contractual relationships.

[28] See, for example, Oliver E. Williamson, The Economics of Defense Contracting: Incentives and Performance, in Issues in Defense Economics 229–32 (Roland N. McKean ed. 1979).

[12]

Vertical Integration and Long-term Contracts: The Case of Coal-burning Electric Generating Plants

PAUL L. JOSKOW
Massachusetts Institute of Technology

1. INTRODUCTION

What factors determine the institutional arrangements that govern supply relationships between input suppliers and their customers? Why are some transactions internalized through vertical integration? Why are many market transactions governed by complex long-term contracts? What determines the structure of such contracts and why are they used instead of simple spot market transactions? Over the past several years, a substantial amount of theoretical work has attempted to answer these questions. A much smaller quantity of empirical work devoted to testing alternative theories and expanding our understanding of vertical integration and contracting has appeared. Most of the empirical work has focused on examining the choice between vertical integration and "the market."[1] Empirical analysis of contracts has been minimal. Aside from Macaulay's classic paper and a recent paper by Goldberg and Erickson, most of the empirical analysis of contracts has been limited to examples based on interpretations of facts obtained from court decisions or secondary sources.[2] In this paper I provide a theoretical

I am grateful to Fred Dunbar, Victor Goldberg, Edmund Kitch, Oliver Williamson, Dick Schmalensee, Oliver Hart, and Steve Shavell for help and comments. I also want to thank National Economic Research Associates, Inc. for giving me access to its coal contract library.

1. Monteverde and Teece is an excellent example of this type of empirical work.
2. This is not to say that the examples have not been useful. The example presented by

Journal of Law, Economics, and Organization vol. 1, no. 1, Fall 1985

and empirical analysis of the structure of vertical arrangements governing coal supply transactions between electric utilities and coal suppliers.[3] I examine coal supply arrangements between electric utilities and coal suppliers in general but focus on the structure of these vertical relationships for mine-mouth coal plants.

Theoretical work devoted to the analysis of vertical arrangements has taken a number of different approaches.[4] I am particularly interested in what has been called the "transactions cost approach," which I attribute to Coase, Williamson, Klein, Goldberg, and others working in their tradition.[5] My plan in this paper is to use the transactions cost framework developed by these authors as the theoretical basis for analyzing coal supply arrangements and to make use of the empirical results to "test" the validity of the theory as a framework for understanding the structure of vertical relationships.

1.1. Potential Biases

Before proceeding further it is useful to answer a question likely to be in the reader's mind. Why study coal supply arrangements involving electric utilities? Since the buyers in this case are subject to economic regulation by state and federal regulatory agencies, we are confronted with a potentially complicating set of incentives that would not arise in studying the supply arrangements of unregulated firms. My reasons are quite simple. Detailed knowledge of a variety of characteristics of buyers and sellers seems essential for applying and testing transactions cost theory empirically. I already possess considerable information about electric utilities, power plants, and coal markets as a result of earlier research. Furthermore, in part because they are regulated, there is a lot of information available about particular utilities, their power plants, and their coal supply arrangements. It is even possible to obtain a large set of actual coal supply contracts and related documents. The opportunity to analyze data at this level of microeconomic detail is extremely rare.

Nevertheless, it is necessary to be sensitive to potential biases in supply arrangements that may be caused by economic regulation. It is my belief that economic regulation of electric utilities (including both the incentive created by price regulation and the direct restrictions on mergers and acqui-

---

Klein, Crawford, and Alchian of the evolution of the supply relationship between General Motors and Fisher Body was instrumental in getting me interested in pursuing this project. Empirical studies of contract by Palay and by Masten have been published while this paper was in progress.

3. This is part of a larger project examining vertical relationships between electric utilities and input suppliers.

4. Some of the alternative approaches are discussed in Williamson (1983; 520–21) and Williamson (1984).

5. These papers include Coase (1937, 1972); Williamson (1971, 1975, 1979, 1983, and 1984); Klein, Crawford, and Alchian; Klein; Monteverde and Teece; and Goldberg.

sitions imposed by state and federal law) tends to discourage vertical integration. State regulators tend to be hostile to vertical integration and both state and federal regulators have, especially in recent years, treated the recovery of costs from captive (integrated) mines quite harshly.[6] There may be a similar bias against long-term contracts. The prospect of "automatic" pass-through of fuel costs through fuel adjustment clauses may also make electric utilities less responsive to the kinds of costs that motivate unregulated firms to adopt vertical arrangements that minimize costs.

I argue below that, particularly for mine-mouth plants, transaction cost theory implies that vertical integration or complex long-term contracts will be used to support exchange. Thus, data involving electric utilities are more likely to lead to rejection of the transactions cost theory than might otherwise be the case if one side of the transaction were not regulated. In an effort to at least partially control for any regulatory biases, I try to make comparisons between different types of electric generating plants. By making comparisons between supply arrangements for different types of plants with different transaction characteristics but subject to the same types of regulatory restrictions, I should be able to get a feeling for whether regulation is driving the results (in which case there should be no differences) or whether the transaction cost considerations hypothesized are important.

2. VERTICAL SUPPLY ARRANGEMENTS: AN OVERVIEW OF THE TRANSACTIONS COST APPROACH

In this section I provide a synthesis of what I take to be the primary theoretical foundations and implications of the transaction cost literature that I attribute to Coase, Williamson, Klein, Goldberg, and others. I have integrated ideas developed over time and across commentators and added my own interpretations.[7]

2.1. The Basic Theory

Economic institutions (or governance structures) emerge to minimize the costs of making transactions. These costs include both ordinary production costs (land, labor, capital, materials, and supplies) that make up the components of a neoclassical cost function and certain transactions costs associated with establishing and administering an ongoing business relationship. These transactions costs (which are identified more completely below) are real economic costs that must be taken into account along with ordinary production costs in structuring cost-minimizing economic institutions.

6. See McGraw-Hilll (1981: 371–73), *Electrical Week*, August 23, 1982, and *Electrical Week*, April 5, 1982. Some state commissions and FERC have been paying increasing attention to purchases made from subsidiaries and purchases made under long-term contracts.

7. The primary references are contained in n. 5.

There exists a continuum of *potential* governance structures for vertical relationships. At one extreme we have vertical integration. At the other extreme we have Walrasian auction markets. In between we have a wide array of potential contracting institutions that mediate transactions through the market but involve the use of a variety of specialized contractual provisions that arise as a consequence of efforts by firms to minimize the total cost of transactions over time. The nature, magnitude, and institutional response to transactions costs depends upon particular identifiable characteristics of the transactions involved. Thus, specific combinations of transactional characteristics, as they interact with more conventional production opportunities, lead to predictable cost-minimizing organizational and contractual responses.

2.2. Transactions Costs and Transaction Characteristics

Transactions costs include the following: costs of negotiating and writing contingent contracts; costs of monitoring contractual performance; costs of enforcing contractual promises; and costs associated with breaches of contractual promises. In each case these costs may include the costs of acquiring and processing information, legal costs, organizational costs, and costs associated with inefficient (in the neoclassical sense) pricing and production behavior.

There appear to be four important characteristics of transactions that have been identified as affecting the nature and magnitude of these transactions costs in important ways.[8] These include:

a. the extent to which the contemplated transactions are characterized by uncertainty and complexity;

b. the extent to which cost-minimizing transactions (in the neoclassical cost function sense) require one or both parties to a transaction to make durable transaction-specific (idiosyncratic) sunk investments;

c. the extent to which there are diseconomies associated with vertical integration that must be traded off against transactions costs that arise when market transactions are relied upon (these may include economics of scale, scope, or learning associated with supplying similar inputs in multiple vertical supply relationships; they also include incentive and command and control costs associated with bringing additional activities

8. I believe that information asymmetries can and should be further integrated into this literature and added to the list. The transactions cost literature I focus on here has either ignored or placed in the background both information asymmetries and differences between agents in the costs of bearing risks. The principle-agent literature, which is concerned with related problems, relies on assumptions about information asymmetries and risk aversion, but ignores transaction-specific investments. See Holmstrom, Shavell, and Hart. It would be productive to integrate the two approaches, but this is well beyond the scope of this paper.

inside a firm that would not arise when "market" transactions are relied upon);[9]

d. the "frequency" of transactions or more generally reputational constraints.

As uncertainty and complexity become more important in a vertical relationship the expected costs of writing, administering, and enforcing full contingent contracts increases. When uncertainty and complexity are important it becomes uneconomical to write full contingent contracts, and "market contracts" will tend to be incomplete. A contract is incomplete in the sense that it does not specify unambiguously the obligations of each party in every possible state of nature.

Contractual incompleteness sets the stage for ex post performance problems. When contingencies arise that are not fully and unambiguously covered by formal contractual provisions, one or both parties to the transaction may have incentives to "behave badly" by taking actions that increase the costs or reduce the revenues that will be obtained by the other party. The anticipation at the contract formation stage that "bad behavior" will occur when certain contingencies arise affects the cost-minimizing structure of the initial vertical relationship.

The "bad behavior" that may occur has been termed "opportunism" by Williamson. As I understand it, opportunism refers both to behavior that does not maximize joint profits (and is inefficient) when a particular contingency arises and also behavior that involves the appropriation of wealth of one party by the other in some states of nature without necessarily inducing distortions in supply or demand. In either case, upon realization that opportunistic behavior may occur, the governance structure and the terms and conditions of any arrangement chosen are adjusted ex ante. Contracts that pose more serious hazards are provided with greater safeguards.

The theory generally assumes that markets are competitive ex ante (many buyers and sellers). Opportunism can emerge ex post because certain characteristics of the supply relationship give one or both parties to the transaction some monopoly power when certain contingencies arise. In most of the recent work in this tradition, the primary source of monopoly power is the presence of durable transaction-specific sunk investments (see below). However, there appears to be a natural relationship between opportunism in this sense and more conventional notions of moral hazard that arise because of information asymmetries.[10] In the latter case, incentive problems arise because one party to the transaction both can affect (uncertain) outcomes by his own behavior and has better (less costly) access to information about the

9. Thus there are both costs and benefits associated with internal production. Grossman and Hart provide an interesting analysis of this issue.

10. Holmstrom, Shavell, and Hart are excellent examples of the approach taken in this growing literature.

causes of observed outcomes. The agent can exploit an information monopoly to its advantage.

Following the theoretical and empirical work in this tradition, I focus on durable transaction-specific sunk investments and largely ignore problems associated with information asymmetries and differences in the costs of bearing risk. Williamson (1983: 526) identifies four different types of transaction-specific sunk investments:

a. *Site specificity*: buyer and seller are in a "cheek-by-jowl" relation with one another, reflecting ex ante decisions to minimize inventory and transportation expense.

b. *Physical asset specificity*: when one or both parties to the transaction make investments in equipment and machinery that involves design characteristics specific to the transaction and which have lower values in alternative uses.

c. *Human-capital specificity*: arising as a consequence of learning-by-doing, investment, and transfer of skills (specific human capital) specific to a particular relationship.

d. *Dedicated assets*: general investments that would not take place but for the prospect of selling a significant amount of product to a particular customer. If the contract is terminated prematurely, it would leave the supplier with significant excess capacity.

Given contractual incompleteness due to uncertainty and complexity, as durable transaction-specific investments become more important, the transactions costs associated with mediating vertical relationships using conventional "spot markets" increase. Very simply, the argument is that transaction-specific sunk investments generate a stream of potentially appropriable quasi-rents equal to the difference between the anticipated value in the use to which the investments were committed and the next best use. The presence of transaction-specific investments creates incentives for one party to "hold up" the other ex post and can lead to costly haggling. When transaction-specific investments are important, governance structures will emerge ex ante to reduce the incentives either party has to exploit them ex post. Considerable emphasis has been placed on the proposition that vertical integraion is more likely to emerge when cost-minimizing (in the neoclassical sense) transactions involve durable transaction-specific sunk investments. Williamson's recent work and a great deal of Klein's work, however, consider contractual alternatives to vertical integration where transactions costs are important. If vertical integration is not economical because of diseconomies associated with internal production, contractual arrangements to govern exchange between independent agents will emerge to economize on these transactions costs. The structure of these market contracts will reflect efforts to create incentives and restrictions that reflect anticipted performance problems so that agents will perform as initially promised when different contingencies arise.

The theory also assumes that there is a strong incentive to structure contracts to minimize reliance on the legal system (which is costly and confronts grave difficulties in distinguishing promised behavior from "bad behavior") and therefore to structure vertical arrangements to achieve a "private ordering" that does not rely on legal enforcement. Nevertheless, people do sue one another for breach of contract, and various rules for defining breach and calculating damages exist (Muris). Thus, contractual arrangements should at least evolve in the shadow of the law, with recognition that court enforcement remains an option. Opportunities to specify contractual agreements in a clear and unambiguous way so as to strengthen the credibility and reduce the costs and uncertainty of legal sanctions should be taken advantage of.

The reliance of vertical integration is constrained by any diseconomies that may be associated with it. A supplier of some input that involves transaction-specific investments, for example, may achieve economies as a consequence of engaging in similar types of transactions with other buyers. There may be economies of scale associated with shared inputs across transactions or learning economies associated with repetitive production in many separate relationships. Internal incentive and command and control problems may limit the economic desirability of vertical integration.

Finally, the market may provide a natural deterrent to agents behaving badly and eliminate the need to rely on either vertical integration or complex "non-standard" contracts. There is a potential cost to breaches of written or implied contractual promises: the loss of future business from either this buyer or other buyers. In markets where buyers and sellers frequently engage in similar types of transactions, and where it is possible at low cost to distinguish "bad behavior" from "promised behavior" (perhaps combined with bad luck), reputational constraints will mitigate hold-up incentives and allow agents to more comfortably use simple auction markets, recognizing that the market provides penalties for inefficient behavior. These considerations may help to explain Macaulay's findings regarding the informality of contracts in business.

3. OVERVIEW OF U.S. COAL MARKETS

The primary market for coal today is the electric power industry, which accounts for more than 80 percent of domestic coal consumption. The second most important source of coal demand is coke plants (about 10 percent), which produce coke for the iron and steel industry. All other industrial consumers in the aggregate account for most of the remainder, with a small amount of coal continuing to be used in the residential/commercial sectors (see table 1). Coal is used to generate more than 50 percent of the electricity produced in the U.S. and accounts for more than 70 percent of fossil fuel utilization.

Coal reserves are not distributed uniformly across the country in terms of either quantity or quality. The Bureau of Land Management divides the

Table 1. U.S. Coal Consumption by Sector, 1980 and 1982

	1980		1982	
Sector	Tons (millions)	%	Tons (millions)	%
Electric utilities	569	81	594	84
Coke plants	67	10	41	6
Other industrial	60	9	64	9
Residential/commercial	6	1	8	1
	702		707	

SOURCE: *Quarterly Coal Report*, U.S. Department of Energy (DOE/EIA-0121), September 1983.

country into more than twenty coal-producing districts, but the bulk of the coal supplies are conveniently grouped into a handful of areas: the Appalachian region, the Interior (Midwestern) region, the Western region (often divided into the North Plains and Mountain regions), and Texas. Historically, most of the coal produced came from the Appalachian and Midwestern regions. Coal production in the Western region has increased dramatically in the past decade, reflecting the attractive economics of large strip-mining operations, declining productivity and labor problems in the East that increased costs, and an increasing demand for low-sulfur coal to meet air pollution restrictions.

There are substantial differences between the regions in terms of coal quality and optimal mining techniques and scale. Coal in the Appalachian region generally has a high BTU content, a sulfur content that varies from 1 to 3 percent, and ash content that varies from 10 to 15 percent (see table 2). The coal in the Interior region generally has a lower BTU content and a higher sulfur content. There is relatively little low-sulfur (1 percent or less) coal in the Midwest. Coal in the Western region varies widely in BTU content and ash content, with average BTU content significantly lower than the other regions. But Western coal generally has a very low sulfur content and relatively low mining costs (see below), making it especially attractive in midwestern states subject to sulfur emissions restrictions despite high transport costs. The coal being produced in Texas is almost all lignite, with low BTU content, low sulfur, and high ash content.

Topography and the nature of coal deposits affect the optimal type and scale of mining, and these characteristics also vary significantly among the regions. In Appalachia, underground mining accounts for about 60 percent of production and underground mines are relatively small (see table 3). Underground mines in the East appear to have relatively small minimum efficient scales (MES) (Zimmerman: 17–36), although the observed size distribution is somewhat misleading since it contains a large number of old and marginal mines which are very small. The topography of the Appalachian region makes necessary the use of relatively small mobile machinery for surface mining (Zimmerman: 26) and the MES of a strip-mining operation here is also relatively small.

In the Midwest, surface mining accounts for about 70 percent of coal production and both underground and surface mines are much larger than in the Appalachian area. The topography of the Interior region makes it eco-

Table 2. Regional Coal Characteristics, 1982 Production

Region/state/BLM district	BTU/lb	% sulfur	% ash
Appalachian			
Alabama	12,154	1.3	11.8
Georgia	12,338	1.5	11.7
Ohio	11,565	3.3	12.5
Pennsylvania			
1	12,228	1.9	14.5
2	12,233	2.0	12.1
Tennessee			
8	12,349	1.5	10.9
13	12,293	0.9	12.3
Virginia			
8	12,592	1.0	10.9
West Virginia			
3	12,708	2.3	10.7
6	12,109	3.9	11.4
8	12,213	0.9	11.8
Kentucky/East	12,184	1.1	10.6
Interior			
Illinois	10,959	2.7	10.2
Indiana	10,942	2.6	10.2
Kentucky/West	11,446	3.2	11.2
Missouri	10,276	4.8	17.1
Kansas	10,463	4.7	20.7
Texas	6,445	0.8	15.5
Western			
Wyoming	8,686	0.4	6.2
Montana	8,958	0.6	6.8
New Mexico	9,342	0.7	19.0
North Dakota	6,590	0.6	8.2
Utah	11,643	0.5	10.3
Washington	8,100	0.8	15.7

SOURCE: *Cost and Quality of Fuels for Electric Utility Plants*, U.S. Department of Energy (DOE/EIA-0191(82). August 1983, table 53.

Table 3. Underground and Surface Mining by Region, 1982

Region	% Underground	Annual output per mine	
		Underground	Surface
Appalachian	60	138,900	100,003
Interior	30	760,590	411,650
Western	11	441,810	2,646,040
U.S. total	40	170,040	242,540

SOURCE: Calculated from *Coal Data (1981/82)*, National Coal Association, II–11 and II–12.

nomical to use larger equipment and to better exploit economies of scale in strip mining than in the East. The MES of surface mines is larger in the Midwest as a result. In the Western region almost all of the coal comes from large strip mines (most of the underground mining takes place in Utah and Colorado). The topography and the nature of the deposits permits the use of large draglines and shovels, allowing fuller exploitation of surface-mining scale economies and larger MES (Zimmerman: 24–35). Surface mines are generally substantially more capital intensive than underground mines, and surface-mining technology seems to be characterized by substantial scale economies.

The bulk of the coal produced (about 75 percent) is carried by railroad (sometimes in conjunction with barge transport) (National Coal Association, 1984: 28). Transportation costs account for a large part of the delivered costs of coal on average. About half of the coal transported by rail is shipped by unit trains consisting of 100 or more specialized cars (often owned or leased by the utility buying the coal). Unit train shipments are generally acknowledged to be the most economical way of moving large volumes of coal by train. About 20 percent of the coal transported is carried by inland barges for at least part of the trip. Trucks account for a small part of the "mine-to-market" transportation but are used at both the loading end and the receiving end of the trip to collect and distribute coal (National Coal Association, 1984: 29). Coal slurry pipelines are a fourth transport option, but only one is currently operating.

Transportation opportunities vary from region to region. There appears to be more inter- and intra-mode competition in the East than in the West. For coal produced in the Interior and Western regions, rail transportation is essentially the only alternative to mine-mouth operations. Many of these producing areas must rely on one or perhaps two railroads to move coal out of these areas, and direct rail linkages between coal fields and potential load centers often do not exist.

Overall, most analysts have concluded that the coal supply market is quite competitive in the ex ante bidding sense used by Williamson (Gordon: 67–69). Concentration in mining and reserve ownership is low and entry appears to be relatively easy. Any monopoly problems are generally attributed to the railroads.

4. COAL SUPPLY ARRANGEMENTS FOR ELECTRIC GENERATING PLANTS AND TRANSACTION-SPECIFIC INVESTMENTS

When a utility considers building a new base-load generating plant it must make a number of interrelated decisions.[11] The most important decisions that must be made concern the following:

1. How large should the generating unit(s) be?
2. What type of fuel should they burn?
3. Where should the plant be located?
4. How should the generating unit's boiler be designed to minimize expected fuel costs over the life of the unit?
5. If a coal burning plant is built, what types of coal will the plant utilize, what is it likely to cost, and where is this type of coal likely to come from?
6. How will the coal be transported from the mine to the plant and what are the expected costs of transportation?

For purposes of discussion here we will assume that the optimal size of the generating units has been determined and that a decision has been made to utilize coal as the primary fuel for generating electricity in the plants that are built. In the spirit of transaction cost theory we first consider the cost minimizing options that utilities have in each of the remaining dimensions given the "ordinary" or neoclassical cost opportunities they face. We then discuss the importance of transaction-specific investments associated with four "stylized" cost minimizing investment/coal procurement strategies and the associated implications for the choice of governance structure to support cost minimizing exchange in each case.

A utility considering building a new coal plant can choose between two primary locational strategies. It can build a plant (independently or jointly with other utilities) in or near its own service territory, reflecting the electrical requirements of its system, land and cooling water availability, transportation facilities, etc., and arrange for transportation of the coal from one or more mines to the plant. This has been the approach taken for most operating coal plants. Alternatively, the utility can build (itself or jointly with other utilities) a plant adjacent to coal reserves from which coal will be mined for that plant, with effectively zero coal transportation costs, and then use a high

11. A base-load unit is a unit that is designed to operate at full capacity throughout the year, regardless of variations in total system demand. Demand variations are accommodated with "cycling" or "peaking" units. Almost all coal-burning units are designed to operate as base-load units for a substantial fraction of their useful lives, on the order of twenty years.

voltage transmission system to transport the power from the supply point to load centers. Such plants are referred to as mine-mouth plants. For utilities whose service territories are far from coal-mining areas, the choice between these two alternatives is quite discrete. Obviously, however, a utility whose electric loads are also close to coal-producing areas can take advantage of the best of both alternatives.

The decision to choose one locational strategy rather than another (ignoring transactions costs) depends on the prices of coal at the mine in different locations, the availability and costs of coal transport alternatives, the costs and institutional constraints associated with the transmission of electricity, and any institutional constraints affecting the ownership and operation of coal units in states other than those in which the utility is chartered to provide service.

A generating unit is typically designed optimally to burn coal with particular characteristics (BTU content, sulfur content, ash content, chemical composition, grindability, etc.). The use of coal that differs from the design specifications of a plant can lead to a loss in thermal efficiency or to increases in plant outages and maintenance costs. Exactly how tightly a plant is designed is, within some range, a variable of choice for the utility. The design decision depends on a utility's anticipated fuel procurement strategy, the variation in coal quality in the areas from which the utility is likely to purchase coal, the quantities of different types of coal available in these areas and the number of suppliers producing it, and the costs of building more fuel flexibility into the plant. For a mine-mouth plant, the design is necessarily governed by the characteristics of the coal in the areas adjacent to the plant.

In general, cost-minimizing coal procurement strategies and plant design are intimately related. A utility could plan to buy coal for a plant through spot market purchases or short-term contracts from a wide variety of different suppliers. If this strategy is chosen, boiler design flexibility is likely to be an important consideration, unless coal in the areas where the utility anticipates buying in this way is of fairly uniform quality. At the other extreme a utility could plan to purchase all of its coal requirements from one specific mine over the life of the plant. In this case, the plant could be designed optimally to burn coal with the characteristics expected to be available from this mine. Intermediate strategies involving more or less burning flexibility and more or less flexibility in procurement can also be pursued. A utility can choose to purchase from existing mines that are already supplying coal for other utilities and plants or contract in advance from a mine that has not yet been developed.

The cost-minimizing coal procurement strategy will depend on a number of factors. The expected f.o.b. price of coal in various areas is a primary consideration, along with the expected costs of transporting coal from the mines to the plant. Air pollution restrictions are likely to sharply constrain the kinds of coal that some utilities can burn economically. The economics of mining is likely to affect coal procurement strategies as well. If there are substantial economies of scale in mining, a utility may be able to reduce its coal costs by committing itself to purchase all of its coal from one large mine.[12] If economies of scale in mining are not important, there is little advantage to doing so. The availability of alternative transportation opportunities may also affect the strategy.

If the decision is made to build a mine-mouth plant, the location, design, and coal procurement strategy generally go hand in hand with one another. The plant is consciously located near specific coal reserves, is designed to optimally burn coal of the quality that will be mined there, and the utility expects to acquire coal for the plant from one or more adjacent mines over a large portion of the expected life of the plant.

There are numerous possible combinations of plant design strategies, coal procurement strategies, and transportation strategies that are possible. Let me identify four stylized cases for further discussion.

Case 1: The utility expects to purchase coal from a large number of existing suppliers located at different points in a fairly large geographical area through spot market purchases and simple short-term contracts. The elasticity of supply of coal of like quality from this general area is fairly high and numerous utilities are active in purchasing coal there. The identity of the particular mines from which coal is purchased is not of any importance to the utility. It anticipates making transportation arrangement with a variety of railroads and barge companies, contracting for delivery as it contracts for coal. It designs its plant with enough flexibility to accept coal of the variable quality that would be available from any of the mines in the general area.

Case 2: The utility expects to purchase coal from a relatively small number of existing mines located close to one another and producing similar types of coal. The mines currently supply coal to other utilities. To economically meet the anticipated demand the mines must make modest investments to increase their capacity. The utility expects to rely on these mines for several years but anticipates the possibility of switching suppliers, sub-

12. My reasoning here is related to Williamson's notion of dedicated assets. The development of a mine requires durable investments. The mine operator chooses both an optimal level of capacity and an optimal mining technique to meet expected demand. Mining techniques vary in capital intensity. More capital-intensive techniques are optimal at larger scales, other things equal. Without a long-term commitment by buyers to take specific quantities, the mine operator will treat nominal contract demand as being uncertain with an expected value that is less than the nominal contract demand. Mine capacity and mining technique will be chosen to reflect this expected demand and the unit cost of coal and prices determined based on this expected demand. If a buyer can commit itself to a firm demand equal to the nominal demand, it can induce the mine operator to expand capacity, reducing unit costs. Some of the savings can be passed along as a lower price than would otherwise prevail if the contract demand were treated as being uncertain. The more significant the scale economies, the greater the associated price reduction.

ject to contractual restrictions, if economic opportunities arise to do so. It anticipates relying on two different railroads to transport the coal, but alternative transportation arrangements can be made at a small cost penalty. Other suppliers of coal of this quality in proximate areas exist, but the elasticity of supply in the short run is very low. The longer-run supply elasticity is fairly large, however. The utility designs its boiler to burn coal of the type available from these two mines, applying tighter design specifications than in the case above. It recognizes that switching suppliers may make it difficult to obtain coal with the same characteristics as its initial suppliers but coal quality is sufficiently uniform in the areas where alternative suppliers are likely to be located that coal quality deviations can be accommodated with only small increases in costs.

Case 3: The utility anticipates obtaining supplies from one or two specific mines for the life of the plant. The mines are currently in operation but will make substantial investments to increase capacity in anticipation of these purchases. The quantities of coal that the utility expects to purchase do not exhaust the economic capacity of these mines, and the mine owners eventually anticipate making sales to other utilities at similar prices. There are very limited supplies available in the short run from other mines in this area, and coal quality varies widely from mine to mine in the same general geographical area. The utility anticipates relying on a single railroad to transport the coal and plans to invest in unit trains to carry the coal on this railroad's tracks. The plant is designed with tight specifications to optimally burn the coal from these mines including specific investments in pollution control equipment.

Case 4: The utility builds a mine-mouth plant and anticipates obtaining all supplies from one or two adjacent mines. The plant is designed specifically to optimally burn coal from these mines. The mine would not be built but for the existence of the plant, and opportunities to sell coal at the same price to other buyers is uncertain. The utility makes extensive investments in transmission capacity to move the power from mine to load centers.

These four cases involve very different degrees of transaction-specific investments. In the first case, the buyer makes specific investments to design its plant to burn coal of the quality produced in a fairly large geographical area, but the value of the investments would not be reduced by shifting suppliers on short notice since there is an elastic supply of coal of similar quality available from this area. Multiple transport options combined with ease of shifting suppliers does not make the value of the plant economically dependent on the behavior of a particular railroad. Suppliers have not made investments specific to the purchases of this particular plant or utility. None of the four potential types of transaction-specific sunk investments seem to be important.

In the second case, transaction-specific investments are likely to be somewhat more important. The plant has tighter design specifications. Sudden switching of suppliers could be costly because the elasticity of supply is small, although if appropriate notice is given additional mining capacity can be brought into production to satisfy additional demand at approximately the same price. Only two railroads are utilized, but alternative transport options are available at a small increase in cost. The suppliers have made some investments in direct response to the anticipated demand of this utility, but the associated mines are already operating, and alternative purchasers of the coal would probably emerge with some lag. Thus, the power plant investment is characterized by some physical asset specificity and some of the mining investments may fall into the dedicated assets category.

In the third case, transaction specific investments are much more important. The utility has designed its plant to burn coal from a particular mine. It has invested in unit trains to transport that coal. The mine owners will make investments to increase the capacity of the mine almost completely as a response to the expected demand by this utility. The utility effectively ties itself to a single transport option, although by owning the rail cars that will carry the coal it has some control over the availability of transportation and simplifies the problem of writing a contract for transport services with the railroad. In this case the investment in the plant is characterized by a greater degree of physical asset specificity. The mining investment has the character of a dedicated asset. Although the vertical relationship is not of the "cheek-by-jowl" nature implied by the concept of site specificity, the existence of a single railroad and utility investments in rolling stock to be used on that railroad seem to lead to a similar result.

The fourth case is a mine-mouth plant and is characterized by at least three of the four types of asset specificity identified by Williamson: (a) site specificity—the plant and mine are deliberately located next to one another to minimize costs; (b) physical asset specificity—the plant is designed to burn the particular types of coal located in the adjacent reserves; and (c) dedicated assets—the mine would not be built but for the promise of purchases from the adjacent plant, and the plant would not be built but for the availability of coal from the adjacent mine.[13] Human (or organizational) asset specificity "that arise in a learning-by-doing fashion" as identified by

13. The importance of dedicated assets is made clearly by one of the contracts for a mine-mouth plant that is analyzed below.

> Buyers will construct, own and operate a coal fired steam-electric generating plant . . . adjoining coal lands of Seller, based upon the assurance of a dependable supply of coal of specified quality and characteristics for the useful life of the plant.
>
> The Buyers would not design and construct a plant of this type [at this site] . . . but for the availability of a dependable supply of coal from seller through December 31, 2019. . . .
>
> It is essential to the Seller, because of the substantial capital investment it must make in order to have the capability to supply Buyers' requirements, that buyers purchase all of their coal requirements for said plant from Seller. (From the coal supply agreement between the five joint owners of units 3 and 4 of the Colstrip generating plant in Montana and Western Energy Company, dated July 2, 1980.)

Williamson may also be important especially with regard to coordination between the plant operator and the mine operator, but I will not treat this fourth form of asset specificity in this discussion.

Let us consider the implications of asset specificity for the optimal choice of governance structure in each case, assuming for now that contracts will be incomplete and reputational constraints are not important (we look at these issues in more detail below as part of the detailed analysis of mine-mouth plants). According to transaction cost theory, other things being equal, the potential for opportunism should vary directly with the importance of transaction specific investments. These problems of opportunism should in turn affect the nature of the contractual relationships between buyers and sellers. In case 1 opportunism should be minimal and reliance on spot market purchases and simple contracts should be adequate. In case 2, there is a potential for opportunistic behavior by the buyer and the seller, but this is sharply constrained since transaction-specific investments are modest. Alternatives to spot market transactions and simple short-term contracts are likely to be desirable to provide some protection for buyers and sellers from ex-post hold-up problems. Vertical integration is not a viable option, however, given the procurement strategy of the utility. In case 3, both the buyer and the seller make transaction-specific investments and opportunism is potentially quite serious. The potential for the railroad to act opportunistically is another real complication. Long-term contracts with extensive protection for both the buyer and the seller from opportunistic behavior is suggested. Vertical integration is a possibility, although if the utility also sinks investments in the mine the railroad's incentives to hold it up may be even greater. Long-term coal supply contracts with utility performance contingent on performance of the railroad may be desirable.

Asset specificity appears to be most important for mine-mouth plants and opportunism potentially the most severe. Such plants appear to be prime candidates for the use of complex long-term contracts or vertical integration to support exchange.

In the case of mine-mouth plants we can assume that neoclassical cost considerations led to this locational choice, and we can examine the choice of governance structures that have been made in response to the associated transaction cost considerations. For other plants, we have no easy way of identifying directly the underlying neoclassical cost conditions that might make one of the other strategies economical for particular plants. However, in light of the general characteristics of coal supply and transportation discussed above, we can make at least some qualitative statements about the likely incidence of each of the three cases.

For the strategy covered by case 1 to be economical (transaction cost considerations aside), several characteristics of supply and transportation must prevail. The supply areas where the utility can most economically obtain coal should have coal of fairly uniform quality, should have numerous producing mines, and should be supplying quantities of coal that are very large relative to the demands of any particular plant. Economies of scale in coal mining should not be important, so that it is not advantageous for a plant to commit itself to long-term supplies with a single supplier. In addition, transport cost savings associated with the use of several competing transport alternatives should be greater than the savings associated with the use of unit trains to transport large quantities of coal from a single point to the plant. Alternatively, the mines must be close enough together to economically move the coal to a local point for onward transport by unit trains.

These characteristics of coal supply and transportation do not appear to be satisfied in most areas of the country. To the extent that this extreme case would be an economical coal procurement strategy anywhere, it is likely to be so for some plants located in the East which utilize coal from certain areas in Appalachia and for one reason or another cannot make efficient use of unit trains.[14]

The second case is likely to be more consistent with the supply and transportation opportunities faced by many plants located in the East and especially in the eastern half of the Midwest which secure supplies from Appalachia and the eastern Interior region. This reflects potential benefits associated with making at least limited commitments to particular mines, the costs of efficiently operating plants with variable coal quality, and economies associated with concentrating coal transportation and investments in unit trains. Longer-term contracts with some protection from opportunism would be more likely in this case, although there seems to be little reason for vertical integration.

As we move further west, the advantages of reliance on a small number of mines because of scale economies, transport economies, and variations in coal quality become more important. Potential opportunism becomes more severe and reliance on spot markets or simple contracts more problematical. Long-term contracts with appropriate protective provisions become more likely. Utilities in the Midwest and West that rely on supplies of coal from the West to satisfy air pollution requirements or which take advantage of cheap lignite and subbituminous coal—and must make very specific plant investments to burn it effectively—are likely to have arrangements similar to those suggested in case 3. Procurement strategies that lie between cases 2 and 3 are likely to reflect opportunities faced by other plants in the Midwest.

Overall, this suggests that (excluding mine-mouth plants) as we move

14. The age of the plant is also likely to be relevant. Over time, technological change has made it possible to build more efficient plants that produce steam at higher temperature and pressures. The newer high-pressure units, especially supercritical units, tend to be more sensitive to variations in coal quality. See Joskow and Rose for a discussion of changes in generating-unit technology over time.

from East to West, we should see less reliance on spot market purchases and more reliance on long-term contracts. There should be relatively little reliance on spot market purchases generally since the supply, transportation, and generating technology conditions conducive to cost-minimizing supply strategies that do not involve at least some asset specificity by either the buyer or the seller are likely to exist for a relatively small fraction of all coal-burning power plants. Mine-mouth plants are the prime candidates for complex long-term contracts or vertical integration.

5. VERTICAL INTEGRATION, SPOT MARKETS, AND CONTRACT SALES

The previous discussion suggests that we should observe considerable variation in coal supply arrangements. Spot market transactions and simple short-term contracts will be economical choices for some plants, tending to be older plants located in the East. Vertical integration is most likely for mine-mouth plants, but such plants account for a relatively small fraction of total coal utilization (on the order of 15 percent—see below). If vertical integration is not chosen to govern supply for mine-mouth plants, contracts will have to be structured to mitigate opportunism in the context of a supply relationship governed by complex long-term contracts. Most coal-burning plants are likely to face economic opportunities that fall somewhere between these two extremes and will not rely extensively on either spot markets or vertical integration or the very long and tight contracts that simulate the opportunism-mitigating features of vertical integration.

We now turn to an examination of the extent to which vertical integration, spot markets, and other contractual arrangements are utilized to support exchange between coal-generating plants and their suppliers for the industry as a whole.

Table 4 lists the utilities that are integrated into coal production in one way or another and their coal subsidiaries (where the latter information is available).[15] The table also provides information on the extent of vertical integration (percent of coal requirements provided by coal subsidiaries) for each of these companies. Less than 15 percent of coal consumed by utilities is supplied to plants by a coal company owned by the owner of the plant (or one of the owners in the case of jointly owned plants). Another 3 percent or

15. Exactly what constitutes vertical integration is far from obvious. Some utilities own a plant themselves and have a mining division or subsidiary that operates the mines. Other utilities own plants themselves, own both coal reserves and the mines, but contract with independent operators to produce the coal. Still other utilities own the reserves, but contract with independent contractors to both develop and operate the mines. In other cases, the plant is jointly owned by several utilities, only one of which has an ownership interest in the mines serving the plant. I classify any of these cases as vertical integration and make finer distinctions in the discussion of mine-mouth plants below.

so of U.S. coal consumption is produced by coal companies owned by utilities but supplied to plants not owned by the integrated utility in question. The extent of vertical integration into coal production in the electric utility industry is substantally less than in the coking (iron and steel) industry, where about 65 percent of requirements come from integrated coal suppliers.

About half of the utilities owning coal-producing subsidiaries are fully integrated, supplying all of their coal requirements (and often supplying coal to other utilities as well). The others generally supply only a small fraction of their coal needs. Those utilities that are integrated tend to be relatively large consumers of coal, but more than half of the twenty largest utility consumers of coal are not integrated. A few utilities are currently attempting to divest

Table 4. Vertical Integration into Coal Mining by Electric Utilities

Utility/subsidiaries	1980 production		Extent
	(tons)	(state)	
Texas Utilities	27,590,768	(TX)	100% requirements
Pacific P&L/NERCO			
Bridger Coal (joint owner)	6,453,302	(WY)	100% requirements by
Decker Coal (joint owner)	5,534,429	(MT)	company-owned mines or
Glenrock Coal	3,800,000	(WY)	mines owned by joint-
Sond Mountains Minerals	500,000	(AL)	owners of plants + substan-
Spring Creek Coal	100,000	(MT)	tial third-party sales.
Bankhead Coal	390,000	(AL)	
Total	16,777,331		
American Electric Power			~30% of requirements
Windsor Power House			
Southern Ohio Coal			
Central Ohio Coal			
Southern Appalachian Coal			
Cedar Coal			
Central Appalachian			
Simco/Peabody (joint owner)			
Price River Coal		(UT)	
Total	16,057,181		
Montana Power			
Western Energy	10,448,000	(MT)	100% of requirements + third-party sales.
Washington Water Power	5,140,000	(WA)	Requirements of Centralia, system's only coal plant.
Utah P&L	4,600,000	(UT)	~65% of requirements; mines operated by contractor.
Montana/Dakota Utilities			100% of requirements +
Knife River Coal	4,788,967	(MT, ND)	third-party sales.

Table 4. Vertical Integration into Coal Mining by Electric Utilities, *continued*

Utility/subsidiaries	1980 production (tons)	(state)	Extent
Pennsylvania P&L			
Pennsylvania Mines	2,928,211	(PA)	~50% of requirements
Greenwich Collieries	1,528,807	(PA)	
Lady Jane Collieries	200,963	(PA)	
Total	4,657,981		
Black Hills P&L			100% of requirements incl.
Wyodak Resources	2,500,000	(WY)	all of Wyodak plant.
Duke Power			
Eastover Mining Co.	2,084,000	(PA)	~15% of requirements. Subsid. up for sale in 1983.
Duquesne L&P	900,000	(PA)	~20% of requirements
Iowa PS Co.			
Energy Dev. Co.	877,631	(WY)	NA
VEPCO			~15% requirements
Laurel Run Mining	619,981	(WV)	(Mt. Storm plant)
Tampa Electric			
Cal-Glo Coal	388,000	(KY)	~10% of requirements
Ohio Edison	188,439	(OH)	~5% of requirements
Carolina P&L			
Leslie Coal (80%)	545,800	(KY)	~5% of requirements
McInnes Coal (80%)	—		
Total production by utility-controlled mines			83,000,000 tons
Sales to third parties (excl. joint plant owners)			13,000,000
Net integrated production			70,000,000
% of total utility coal use (tons):	14		
% of total utility coal use (BTUs):	12		

SOURCE: Compiled from data in 1982 *Keystone Coal Manual*, *Moody's Public Utility Manual* (various years), annual reports, and 10-K filings.

themselves of coal subsidiaries, largely as a consequence of unfavorable regulatory treatment of coal obtained from captive mines.[16]

Thus, about 85 percent of the coal used to generate electricity is supplied through some type of market transaction mechanism. Readily available data on coal supply arrangements breaks utility coal transactions down into spot transactions and contract transactions (see table 5). Generally, spot transactions involve coal supply agreements for relatively small fixed quantities of coal with delivery schedules extending for less than a year. Transactions that involve deliveries extending over a period of more than a year generally fall in the contract category. The proportion of spot transactions varies consider-

16. Duke Power has been actively seeking a buyer for its coal subsidiary. Carolina Power and Light and Pennsylvania Power and Light are also considering selling their coal subsidiares. See, for example, *Electrical Week*, August 23, 1982.

Table 5. Spot and Contract Transactions

Year	% spot	% contract
1974	23.8	76.2
1975	18.2	81.8
1976	14.0	86.0
1977	19.4	80.6
1978	21.2	78.8
1979	12.8	87.2
1980	11.5	88.5
1981	13.1	86.9
1982	9.6	90.4

Regional Breakdown: 1982

Region	% spot
Appalachian	17.4
Interior	7.4
Texas	8.1
Western	1.6
Total	9.6

SOURCE: Calculated from *Cost and Quality of Fuels for Electric Utility Plants*, U.S. Department of Energy (DOE/EIA-0191(82)). August 1983, table 53.

ably from year to year. The relatively high values from 1974–75 and 1977–78 appear to reflect coal strikes that took place during portions of these periods. There is also substantial regional variation in the volume of coal made available through spot market transactions. The spot market accounts for a much larger fraction of transactions in the East than elsewhere, and there is essentially no spot market for coal in the West.

The contract category includes everything from one-year contracts to fifty-year contracts, and individual contracts vary widely in the annual tonnage provided for. There is probably relatively little difference from a transactional perspective between spot sales and contract sales with deliveries spread over one or two years, so it would be useful to break down the contract category further by duration and volume. Additional information on contract deliveries by duration and annual quantities is not as easily obtained from standard government sources as the initial breakdown between spot and contract. However, I have analyzed a sample of more than 200 coal contracts that accounted for more than 30 percent of contract coal deliveries in 1979 (see table 6).[17] Over 80 percent of the coal sold under these contracts involved delivery commitments for more than five years and more than 70 percent involved commitments extending over a period of more than ten

17. The contract information was obtained from Pasha Publications, *1980 Guide to Coal Contracts*, for another project. Data on 270 contracts was collected but only 205 contained both information on duration and delivered quantities for 1979.

years. This breakdown is roughly equivalent to the survey information Gordon (55–58) obtained for 1969. Longer contract periods are generally associated with larger annual volumes of coal as well.

These results are broadly consistent with the previous discussion. About 60 percent of the coal supplied to electric utilities involves relatively long-term contracts (more than five years). The spot market is not a significant governance mechanism for coal supply arrangements between utilities and coal producers. It is most important in the East and essentially nonexistent in the West. Vertical integration is not particularly important either, accounting for a somewhat smaller fraction of coal supplied.

Table 6. Distribution of 205 Contracts by Duration and Annual Tonnage

Duration	% of coal deliveries	Tons/year/contract
less than or 5 years	17	267,000
6-10 years	12	556,000
11-20 years	37	885,000
21–30 years	17	1,309,000
more than 30 years	17	2,411,000

SOURCE: See text and n. 17.

6. COAL SUPPLY ARRANGEMENTS FOR MINE-MOUTH PLANTS IMPLIED BY TRANSACTION COST CONSIDERATIONS

I argued above that coal supply transactions for mine-mouth plants are characterized by at least three of the four types of asset specificity identified by Williamson (1983: 26). From a transactional perspective, these plants are distinguished from the "typical" coal plant primarily by the unusual importance of durable transaction-specific investments. Transaction cost theory suggests that mine-mouth plants should be much more likely to be integrated or make use of complex long-term contracts than the typical generating plant. Before proceeding further it is worth considering briefly the other characteristics of transactions that are likely to affect the governance structure for coal plants generally and mine-mouth coal plants in particular:

Uncertainty/complexity: There is no easy way to measure the extent to which a particular type of transaction is subject to uncertainty or complexity. Indeed, it is not at all obvious from the literature how one even would conceptualize either a cardinal or ordinal measurement procedure. Precise measurement is not critical, however. Uncertainty and complexity are important to the extent that buyers and sellers cannot write unambiguous and easily enforceable full contingent claims contracts. When full contingent claims contracts cannot be written, contracts are necessarily incomplete. Contractual incompleteness is not the source of transactional difficulties, but rather sets the stage for contractual difficulties in the presence of transaction-specific investments or information asymmetries.

From the perspective of a utility considering investment in a coal plant with an expected life of thirty-five years or more, it is certainly reasonable to assume that there is enough uncertainty about coal demand in the short run and over the life of the plant to make it difficult to write a full contingent claims contract. Coal demand will vary with the utilization rate of the plant and the thermal efficiency of the plant. Both of these vary over time in a nondeterministic way. As a plant ages and moves higher in the dispatch profile, plant utilization will also vary with total electrical load and with the prices of fuels burned by other plants on a utility's system. Air pollution restrictions and cooling water availability may limit plant utilization and affect both the quantity and the types of coal required. Furthermore, because coal quality is very important and numerous coal characteristics are relevant for plant design and plant performance, the "simple" product *coal* is a much more complex product than first appears.

From the perspective of a mine owner considering investing in a new mine or expanding an existing mine, there is also likely to be considerable uncertainty about mining costs and coal quality over the life of the mine. Ex ante, there is at least some uncertainty about mining costs, cleaning requirements, and reserves given prevailing input prices. Over time, the nominal and real costs of mining are inherently uncertain, depending not only on the physical characteristics of the reserves, but also on changes in input prices, contract work rules, government regulations affecting mining costs, and technologies.

For the purposes of examining governance structures for coal supplied to electric utilities, I think that it is fair to assume that contracts will necessarily be incomplete. This is especially true for mine-mouth plants, where both parties make long-term reliance investments contingent on the performance of the other over many years.

Reputational constraints: Is it likely that the threat of losing future purchases (in the case of the mining company) or the prospect that buyers will have to pay higher transactions prices in future contracts (reflecting a price for anticipated breaches on the part of the buyer) will deter the kinds of "bad behavior" that the transactions cost literature is concerned with? Reputational constraints depend primarily on the importance of repeat purchase activity and the ability to distinguish bad (good) outcomes (such as high mining costs or failures to deliver promised quantities) that arise because of inefficient (efficient) behavior from bad (good) outcomes that arise simply because of bad (good) luck. Reputational constraints are likely to be most important when utilities find it economical (in the neoclassical sense) to adopt procurement strategies such as those outlined in case 1 and case 2 above. There is extensive repeat purchase activity, sales are made to many sellers from the same mines, and the utility buys from several different sellers. These constraints are not likely to be significant in the case of mine-mouth operations, however.

Individual mine-mouth operations have many idiosyncrasies that make it difficult for third parties to distinguish poor performance due to actions by either party from poor performance resulting from exogenous factors that are not subject to control by either party. Especially in the last ten or fifteen years, regulatory changes and labor problems have had profound effects on mining costs and production. Many generating units built over the past twenty years have experienced much poorer heat rates and availabilities than had been anticipated. It is likely to be difficult to determine how much of this change was due to exogenous factors and how much can be associated with suboptimal levels of effort by either party. Overall, it seems unlikely that reputational constraints can provide protection from opportunistic behavior in the case of mine-mouth plants.

Diseconomies of internal production: I have no way of evaluating objectively whether there are important economies that a large coal producer with production activity and experience from other supply arrangements would bring to a transaction that a utility embarking on coal production itself would not be able to take advantage of. I suspect that there are some economies of scale or experience in this sense that utilities would not be able to take advantage of, but I have seen no evidence that would allow me to make a definitive statement.[18] Nor is there any way to estimate empirically internal incentive and command and control problems that might increase costs from integrated production compared to the costs of market procurement and necessarily limit the economic extent of vertical integration. There is little reason to believe, however, that these considerations are more important for mine-mouth plants than they are for other types of plants.

In summary, these observations suggest the following. The assumption of incomplete contracts is probably a good one for all types of generating plants. This sets the stage for opportunism if transaction-specific investments are necessary for structuring a minimum cost supply relationship. Transaction-specific sunk investments are considerably more important for mine-mouth plants than for other types of plants. Reputational constraints are not likely to be particularly effective in the case of mine-mouth plants. Diseconomies of internal production are likely to affect the economics of vertical integration equally, regardless of the particular type of plant involved.

18. The utility owners of Western Coal (formed to supply the San Juan plant) did apparently consider taking over mining responsibilities from Utah-International, the developer and operator of the adjacent mine. Among other things they concluded that Utah could take advantage of some economies associated with its mining operations at Four Corners. See letter from Western Coal Co. to Tucson Gas and Electric and Public Service of New Mexico regarding negotiations between Western (jointly owned by the two utilities) and Utah-International (dated February 21, 1978, on file).

This all implies that coal supply transactions for a mine-mouth operation are prime candidates for the choice of vertical integration as a transaction cost-minimizing governance structure. Regulatory considerations, coal supplier economies, and other diseconomies of vertical integration may make vertical integration less attractive than alternative contractual governance structure, or even impossible. If vertical integration is not chosen, some type of long-term contractual arrangement containing provisions that anticipate performance difficulties and designed to effectuate a smooth and efficient relationship between the buyer and the seller should be forthcoming. Reliance on a spot market or even relatively short-term contracts are not likely to prove to be a cost-minimizing alternative.

Let's assume that for one reason or another a mine-mouth plant operator chooses to secure supplies through contract rather than vertical integration. What are the characteristics of an efficient contractual relationship? What contractual provisions will emerge as the parties negotiate a mutually acceptable supply agreement in response to anticipated transactions costs and contract execution difficulties? Are the resulting arrangements efficient?

From a normative (efficiency) perspective we would expect a coal supply arrangement to emerge with these desirable features:

a. The contemplated mine-mouth operation will go forward if it is the cost-minimizing way for the utility to generate electricity; the parties will be able to strike a deal.

b. Once a plant and mine are built, the plant operator will continue to take supplies from the adjacent mine as long as this is the least cost source of supply, without the buyer switching to a (socially) uneconomical supplier.

c. The seller will produce coal efficiently.

d. The seller will continue to supply the quantities and quality of coal promised as long as it represents the least cost source of supply for the plant. The seller will not uneconomically shift supplies to other buyers.

e. The agreement will be flexible enough to allow supply and demand by the supplier/purchaser to adjust to changes in economic conditions. If the current supplier is not the minimum cost producer, the agreement should provide a mechanism to shift suppliers, reduce production, etc.

f. Minimization of haggling over price and production levels that may disrupt efficient supply arrangements but may be a natural outcome of the bilateral monopoly situation that emerges once each party sinks costs in reliance on the agreement.

g. Avoidance of litigation and litigation costs.

The actual provisions that emerge will reflect efforts by each party to maximize profits with due recognition of the costs of writing, monitoring, and enforcing contractual promises. A variety of price and nonprice provisions are potentially available to support exchange and mitigate opportunism. The optimal price and nonprice provisions are likely to be related to one another and it is difficult to discuss them independently. It is even more difficult to discuss them together.

Let me assume, to begin, that the costs of producing coal do not change over time due to changes in input prices, technological change, government regulation, contractual changes in work rules, and so on, and that a price (level and structure) is negotiated at the start of the contract and is *anticipated* to be fixed over the term of the contract, although either party is free to try to exploit any ex post monopoly power to force the other to agree to a higher or lower price after production begins. I assume that other changes in market conditions may take place over time which affect the value of the coal to the buyer and the opportunity cost to the seller of supplying to the adjacent plant. Given these assumptions, I can suggest the kinds of nonprice terms that we should expect to find in these contracts to mitigate opportunism and then relax the assumptions about the costs of producing coal to examine alternative patterns for determining prices over the life of the contract.

6.1. Nonprice Provisions

Given the three types of investment specificity that characterizes this type of production, neither the utility nor the coal supplier will want to be the first mover. The utility is not going to start building a power plant on this site without some supply agreement because it would be subject to hold-up by the owner(s) of adjacent reserves. The same is true of the coal supplier vis-à-vis the utility. Furthermore, effective design of the mine-mouth operation requires cooperation between both the utility and the coal supplier. Thus, a firm governance structure is likely to be in place before any substantial plant investments are made by either party.

I expect to see very long-term contracts negotiated which specify purchasing (take) and supply obligations for the plant and the mine over a substantial fraction of the life of the plant—at least twenty years. Neither the power plant owner nor the supplier is likely to want to enter into a relationship which involves frequent renegotiation of terms after each incurs transaction-specific sunk investments.

I would expect to see extensive use of requirements contracts. The quantity of coal to be delivered under the contract must be specified somehow. Coal requirements will vary from month to month and year to year. Some of this variation can be dealt with through a coal inventory accumulation, although one of the desirable features of a mine-mouth plant is the ability to minimize inventories that might otherwise be necessary to insure against transportation problems. Ideally, the power plant owner would simply like the mine to deliver enough coal to satisfy the requirements of the plant. Since requirements vary, the easiest way to specify quantities from the viewpoint of the plant operator is simply to write the contract as a requirements contract.

There are strategic reasons for the utility to write the contract as a requirements contract as well and to include provisions to restrict sales to third parties. Reducing promised deliveries during the anticipated term of the contract may be perceived as a supplier-credible threat as part of an effort to hold up the utility, because the utility's initial investment is larger, longer-lived, and less easily redeployed than those of the mining company. The mine operator could credibly reduce supplies over time by ceasing to make replacement and expansion investments and use this threat to extract better terms from the utility. Furthermore, depending on the pricing provisions in the contract, changing market conditions could make it profitable for the mining company to breach the contract to supply even if it is not efficient to do so. Clear language that the contract is for plant requirements over a specified period of time makes court enforcement easier if disputes arise between the plant owner and the mine owner that cannot be resolved otherwise. It also suggests that provisions for dealing with sales to third parties and the dedication of specific reserves to the agreement along with the requirements provisions will protect the utility from the threat and potential costs of diverting supplies to other buyers.[19]

A requirements contract serves to protect the seller in similar ways. Threats by the buyer to switch to alternative suppliers are made less credible both because comparable suppliers will not be waiting in the wings to take up the slack and because breach is easier to detect and penalize through legal sanctions.

Coal quality is of particular importance to the utility, and the mining company is in a position to affect coal quality by its mining practices. The mining company may be able to reduce its costs by mining low-quality deposits, shirking on cleaning, and increase effective prices (especially in per ton priced contracts) by increasing the quantity of "junk" in the coal. The utility may have difficulty distinguishing coal quality problems that arise because of poor mining practices and coal quality problems that arise because the reserves are of generally lower quality than had been anticipated when the contract was negotiated. The supplier may also have an interest in the precise definition of the expectations about coal quality ex ante since claims of poor coal quality may be used by a utility as an excuse to breach the contract. One would expect substantial ex ante investigation of reserve characteristics to verify that the promised quality specifications can be achieved. I would also expect the contract itself not only to specify minimum acceptable coal quality but also to define clearly the specific reserves on which ex ante

19. This is especially true if the pricing provisions of the contract have a significant cost plus component.

quantity/quality evaluations were made and to provide for the dedication of these reserves to production for this plant. To the extent that variations in coal quality can be easily "priced," I would expect pricing provisions expanded to do so.

Williamson (1983) discusses the desirability of "protective governance structures" to deal with potential hold-up problems when "hostage arrangements" cannot be structured to eliminate expropriation incentives possessed by one or both parties. Contractual incompleteness and the potential for haggling are a serious potential problem in unintegrated mine-mouth operations. While court enforcement remains an option and coal contract disputes do occasionally lead to litigation, arbitration clearly represents an opportunity to provide a dispute resolution system that does not entail the costs (broadly defined) of litigation. Thus, I expect to see arbitration provision contained in these contracts as well as other cooperative arrangements that allow for the smooth functioning of a complex agreement and the settlement of disputes without resorting to litigation.

6.2. Pricing Provisions

Establishing a pricing formula to govern compensation arrangements for contracts lasting many years that provide incentives to both the buyer and the seller to perform as promised without leading to serious inefficiencies itself is not an easy task. Dealing with the kinds of ex post performance problems addressed in the transactions cost literature and providing mechanisms for smooth adjustments in obligations as various contingencies arise is complicated by the uncertainty governing future costs and market conditions that are inherent in this relationship. Input prices are likely to change over time, technological developments may reduce the current and expected future costs of mining from similar reserves, labor agreements may change work rules and increase or decrease productivity, new government regulations may increase mining costs, unanticipated mining problems may emerge, new property and severence taxes may be applied, and so on. General changes in supply and demand are likely to lead to changes in the value of the coal at the mine-mouth operation both from the buyer's perspective and the seller's perspective.

The compensation arrangements should reflect two interrelated objectives. First, they should be structured to eliminate the incentives either party has to behave opportunistically. Second, the pricing provisions should be structured in such a way that efficient demand and supply decisions are made by both the buyer and the seller. It would, for example, be undesirable if a pricing formula gave one or both parties the incentive to reach their purchase and supply promises if this would increase the social costs of supplying coal or producing electricity. Let us examine four different methods for establishing prices over time.

1. *Market price contracts.* If the product under consideration were a homogeneous product sold in a competitive auction market and carrying a clear market price, the simplest way of determining prices might be just to stipulate that payments would be made at some fraction of an appropriate market price indicator. This is not likely to be a particularly attractive alternative as the sole determinant of prices for coal supplied for a mine-mouth operation, however.

Coal is not a homogeneous commodity with regard to the characteristics of the coal or the location of the coal. The mine-mouth supply price includes both the cost of coal and (implicitly) the cost of transportation. There simply will not be any meaningful market price for coal of this particular type delivered to the plant. This is especially problematical in the West, where there is essentially no spot market to tie anything to. Market price contracts may make a lot of sense for a homogeneous commodity like uranium, or even for coal in some areas of the country and when other types of plants are involved, but not for mine-mouth plants.

2. *Fixed price contracts:* An alternative to a market price contract is a simple fixed price contract (as I assumed above). Risk allocation problems aside, this contract has poor incentive properties with regard to continuing performance. The primary problem is that if the supplier's actual costs rise significantly above the fixed price when certain contingencies arise, the supplier will have strong incentives to breach (reduce quantities provided in the short run, cease making investments to expand its capacity to continue to supply, run down the value of the equipment, etc.) even if such behavior is inefficient. Similarly, if the expected price of coal available from alternative suppliers falls below the fixed price (due to cost reductions generally, changing market conditions, etc.) the plant operator may find it profitable to breach even if it is inefficient to do so.

Expectations of secular increases in input prices, reserve depletion, and changes in work rules and government regulations that are likely to reduce productivity make these problems worse. A long-term fixed price contract must assure that the present discounted value (PDV) of expected revenues is greater than or equal to the PDV of expected costs or the supplier will not agree to enter into the supply arrangement. Given expectations of nominal cost increases over time, this implies a fixed price that will "front load" the cash flow so that in early years the supplier is getting revenues substantially above current costs, while in later years he may receive revenues substantially below the then current cost. At some point the fixed contract price may fall below current incremental costs, and the supplier will have an incentive to abandon the mine, substantially reduce production, cease making investments, and so on.[20] Fixed prices in long-term contracts do not appear to me

20. This depends on the length of the contract, the capital output ratio, the durability of the investments, the expected rate of inflation, and the discount rate used. I have performed some simulations of the relationship between the fixed price and the incremental costs for a variety of

to be credible because the specification of a fixed price is so likely to provide incentives to one or both parties to threaten to breach and to trigger renegotiation.

3. *Cost plus profit contracts:* A third alternative is to negotiate a cost plus profit contract in which the supplier is compensated for all of the costs incurred in production, including the cost of capital. Risk allocation considerations aside, if it could be assured that the supplier would produce efficiently, such a contract has some desirable properties. It is unlikely that the buyer would have a strong incentive to breach, because it is unlikely that he could get the coal more cheaply elsewhere over the duration of the contract, unless the market value of the coal increases or decreases faster than production costs, since the mine-mouth supplier is presumably facing the same changes in input prices, regulations, technological change, etc., as are other comparable suppliers.

A cost-based price also ensures that prices are high enough so that the supplier does not have an incentive to walk away from the supply arrangement when costs increase due to input price changes, productivity changes due to changes in health and safety regulation, land reclamation costs, and so on, as might occur with a fixed price contract. A cost-based price of course does not eliminate the incentives a supplier might have to ship supplies to buyers if there is a large unanticipated increase in the value of the coal, for example, as a result of an increase in the demand for low-sulfur coal, making it more valuable in the market than it is under the contract (i.e., the long-run supply function for low-sulfur coal is upward sloping and the economic rent associated with an assumed inframarginal reserve rises). And it is unlikely that it would be efficient for the supplier to shift to another buyer if such a contingency arose. Similar inefficient responses by buyers can be expected if the value of coal falls and the "costs" used in the pricing formula reflect generated rents based on ex ante expectations.

An important problem with a cost plus contract is that it has poor incentive properties with regard to the supplier's incentives to minimize costs. Without more, the supplier has little incentive to produce efficiently. If costs rose high enough the buyer would have incentives to switch to other suppliers, but there is likely to be a potentially large wedge for inefficiency, since the next best alternative would on average be more costly to the buyer than an efficiently operated mine-mouth facility.

4. *Indexed contracts*: The fourth and final type of contract that I consider is an indexed contract. This is a natural alternative to a fixed price contract. Rather than try to set a fixed price that rolls in revenues for anticipated fu-

reasonable assumptions. Reasonable assumptions about expected input price inflation suggests that the abandonment problem becomes serious for contracts that are longer than fifteen or twenty years. The mines at mine-mouth plants are often organized as separate subsidiaries of larger coal companies and it is possible that a utility would have difficulty making a claim against the parent company.

ture changes in input prices, costs of government regulations, changes in union work rules, and so on, we can set a base price that is adjusted over time as input prices rise. For example, the base price can be broken down into components (labor, materials and supplies, depreciation, profit, property taxes) and then each component escalated according to an appropriate input price and productivity index. This type of contract seems to deal with some of the undesirable properties of both the fixed price and cost plus contracts. Prices now rise over time as input prices rise and productivity opportunities change, and we do not have to front-load cash flow. Prices rise as the supplier's input prices rise and production opportunities change but are independent of the actual production decisions made by the supplier. If the supplier can increase productivity more than provided for by the index, his actual costs will rise by less than the indexed price. If his costs rise—because of bad mining practices, for example—his net revenues are reduced as a result. This type of contract provides incentives for the supplier to minimize costs (given coal quantity and quality). Furthermore, the increases in input prices, technological change, and so forth will have similar effects on the costs of proximate alternative suppliers as well. Although this type of pricing provision cannot guarantee that contract prices will move in lockstep with the prices that might be charged by competing suppliers over time, it does account for several important causes of changing supply prices. An indexed contract therefore appears to dominate either a fixed price or cost plus contract.

An indexed contract is not without problems, however. It may be difficult to index some components of mining cost that will affect the costs of producing from this mine and "comparable" mines (actual and potential). New labor contracts may change work rules, increasing labor costs. New mining regulations may increase costs substantially. Technological change may reduce costs and substantially alter the cost-minimizing weights used to index the price. This kind of adjustment mechanism can also get very complicated if we try to break down the base price into numerous components. The indexed price could move far away from the economic costs of production, giving either the buyer or the seller increased incentives to breach the agreement. Complexity would encourage haggling and litigation.

In addition to general provisions for adjusting the *level* of prices, the price *structure* could be adapted to provide additional financial protection against expropriation and uneconomic buyer/supplier switching. For example, Williamson (1983) and Goldberg and Erickson suggest that nonlinear prices may be used as a device to help to insure that the buyer performs. A seller concerned that a buyer will shift to other suppliers might find a fixed annual payment (to cover sunk costs) plus a commodity charge attractive or include minimum take or pay provisions in the contract. We should recognize, however, that optimally adjusting nonlinear price schedules over time may be even more complicated than adjusting simple (linear) unit prices.

None of the price adjustment mechanisms is ideal, in the sense that the method of setting the level and structure of prices alone can deal effectively with all of the performance problems that can arise in a long-term coal supply arrangement. Thus, whatever method is used to determine prices, I also expect to see substantial reliance for protection on the kinds of nonprice provisions discussed above.

Finally, there is the problem of "surprises" that affect either the price or nonprice terms of a contract, events that were not anticipated with positive probability by either party to the contract when the contract was negotiated. The expected effects of surprises are not reflected in the terms of the contract. As I have argued elsewhere (1977: 157), "bounded rationality" suggests that there are some contingencies that are simply not contemplated by the parties when they negotiate a supply arrangement. These contingencies may involve the effects of unexpected changes in government regulation, dramatic changes in supply or demand in the market, or other changes that would impose a large financial burden on one of the parties if it performed as required by literal interpretation of the contract—a burden that was not reflected, for example, in the base price or adjustment provisions. Both parties to the contract should recognize ex ante that surprises will occur and I would expect to find general provisions in contracts, such as force majeur or gross inequity clauses, that specify a process for dealing with such unspecified contingencies if they arise.

7. COAL SUPPLY ARRANGEMENTS FOR MINE-MOUTH COAL PLANTS: GENERAL CHARACTERISTICS

Table 7 lists all of the mine-mouth coal plants with first units that began operating no earlier than 1960 (with one exception) that I was able to identify.[21] The method used to identify these plants is discussed in the appendix.There are twenty-one plants, which accounted for about 15 percent of electric utility coal deliveries. Most of the plants are multiunit facilities and more than half are jointly owned by at least two utilities. Only two of the plants used any coal purchased on the spot market and in both cases spot sales accounted for only a small fraction of total consumption.

Table 8 provides general information on the coal supply arrangements that have been made for each plant. In 1982, ten of the plants obtained all of their coal supplies from either a coal-mining division or a subsidiary of one of the utilities owning the plant (i.e., coal supply arrangements involved some form of vertical integration). One plant (Mt. Storm) obtained part of its supplies from a coal-mining subsidiary of the utility (but this accounted for 100

21. The initial source I used to date the units at different plant sites gave the wrong date for the first unit of the Montrose plant (1960 rather than 1958). I decided to leave it on the list. There are two or three other utilities with mine-mouth plants which predate the sample period.

Table 7. Mine-Mouth Coal Plants

Unit names	Utility/state	Joint owners	Units (yrs)	Capacity (MWE) 1982	Coal deliveries (tons)
Big Brown	Texas Util. (TX)	No	71, 72	1186	5,963,000
Martin Lake	Texas Util. (TX)	No	77, 78, 79	2379	11,413,000
Monticello	Texas Util. (TX)	No	74, 75	1980	9,797,000
Hunter	Utah P&L (UT)	No	78, 80 (83, 85)	892	2,525,000
Huntington	Utah P&L (UT)	No	74, 77	892	2,492,000
Naughton	Utah P&L (WY)	No	63, 68, 71	707	2,040,000
Wyodak	Pacific P&L (WY)	Yes	78	331	1,812,000
Centralia	Pacific P&L (WA)	Yes	72, 72	1329	4,400,000
Bridger	Pacific P&L (WY)	Yes	74, 75, 76, 77	2034	6,025,000
San Juan	Pub. Serv. NM (NM)	Yes	73, 76, 79, 82	1708	5,071,000
Colstrip	Montana Power (MT)	Yes	75, 76 (84, 85)	716	2,103,000
Four Corners[a]	Arizona PS (NM)	Yes	63, 63, 64, 69, 70	2269	7,291,000
Young	Minkotta Coop (ND)	Yes	70, 77	673	2,983,850
Coyote	Mont./Dakota (ND)	Yes	81	450	1,669,000
Montrose	Kan. City P&L (MO)	No	58, 60, 64	536	1,326,700
Craig	Col.-Ute Coop (CO)	Yes	79, 80 (83)	894	2,303,000
Asbury	Emp. Dist. (MO)	No	70	212	707,000
Keystone[b]	Penn. Elec (PA)	Yes	67, 68	1872	3,543,000
Homer City	Penn. Elec (PA)	Yes	69, 71, 77	2012	3,811,000
Conemaugh[b]	Penn. Elec (PA)	Yes	70, 71	1872	2,668,000
Mt. Storm	VEPCO (WV)	No	65, 66, 73	1662	3,100,000

a. Units 4 and 5 jointly owned.
b. Pennsylvania Electric operates plant for joint owners but has no direct ownershhip interest. Other GPU subsidiaries own part of the plants along with other utilities.
SOURCE: See appendix.

percent of mine's capacity). In the case of jointly owned plants with coal supplied by a coal subsidiary of one of the plant owners, there is typically a formal contract written between the owners of the plant and the coal subsidiary. I have noted these in table 8 by using the term *integrated/contract* to reflect this state of affairs.

Together, mine-mouth power plants account for about 50 million tons of "integrated" coal supplies per year. This is about 60 percent of all coal supplied to utilities by coal companies owned by one of the owners of a plant. In other words, mine-mouth plants account for about 15 percent of total coal utilization but 60 percent of all coal supply arrangements governed by some form of vertical integration. A mine-mouth plant is thus about six times more likely to rely on vertical integration to support exchange than is any other type of coal-burning power plant.

The remaining ten plants all rely primarily on long-term contracts for the supply of coal.[22] The contracts vary in duration from twenty years to fifty years, with thirty-five years being typical. The "integrated/contract" supply

22. Note that the Huntington and Hunter plants were initially supplied under long-term contracts, but the utility eventually acquired the mines. Coal supply arrangements for the San Juan plant moved in the opposite direction.

arrangements generally involve long-term contracts with thirty-five-year durations as well. Referring back to table 6 it is clear that very long contracts are far more likely to emerge to govern coal supply arrangemenuts for mine-mouth plants than they are to govern supply arrangements generally in the electric utility industry. On average less than 20 percent of the coal supplied under the 200 sample contracts had durations of greater than thirty years (and most of this is accounted for by mine-mouth plants). Both the extensive reliance on vertical integration and very long-term contracts are quite consistent with the predictions of transaction cost theory.

8. NONPRICE PROVISIONS OF LONG-TERM CONTRACTS FOR MINE-MOUTH PLANTS

I was able to obtain the actual contracts governing transactions between the coal supplier and the power plant owners for sixteen of the twenty-one mine-mouth plants on the list.[23] Since some plants have more than one contract, either because separate contracts were written for different units or (in one case) contracts were written with two adjacent mining companies, I have twenty-one contracts in all, plus amendments and revisions, covering sixteen plants. These contracts may be "incomplete," but many of them are very complicated. These were not just documents dashed off because the companys' lawyers said they should have a legal document to "confirm their orders."

Table 9 summarizes the incidence of various nonprice provisions of the coal supply contracts reflecting the discussion above.

Duration: As indicated above, most of the contracts have durations of thirty years or more, with thirty-five years being most typical. And these are real long-term contracts. Sixteen of the contracts have no scheduled renegotiation provisions. Three contracts provide for price renegotiation (subject to certain constraints) after twenty years. One provides for renegotiation of the escalation weights only. One contract allows the buyer to terminate after six years but obligates him to reimburse the mining company for all fixed costs. Short-term renegotiation provisions and options to terminate on short notice are generally not provided for, as they sometimes are in other coal contracts (McGraw-Hill, 1981: 352–53). It is also clear from reading the contracts that are available that these supply agreements are generally negotiated several years before the initial units for which the coal is to be supplied are placed in service. Neither party moves first; they move together.

Requirements contracts/dedication of reserves: Almost all of the contracts are full requirements contracts. Of those that are not, one contract simply

23. This includes the initial contracts and amendments for Hunter and Huntington.

Table 8. Coal Supply Arrangements for Mine-Mouth Plants

Unit	Supply Arrangements	Initial contract	Duration
Big Brown	Integrated	None	NA
Martin Lake	Integrated	None	NA
Monticello	Integrated	None	NA
Huntington	Initially long-term contract; util. acquired mines in 1977	1971	35 yrs
Hunter	Initially long-term contract; util. acquired mines in 1977	1974	35 yrs
Naughton	Long-term contract	1957	40 yrs
Wyodak	Integrated/contract	1977	35 yrs
Centralia	Integrated/contract	1970	35 yrs
Bridger	Integrated/contract	1974	35 yrs
San Juan	Initially coal subsidiary contracted with mining co. to build and operate mine on util. sub. reserves. Reserves later sold to mining co. and supplies now provided under long-term contract.	1972, 1980	37 yrs
Colstrip	Integrated/contract (units 1, 2)	1971	35 yrs
	(unit 3)	1980	36 yrs
Four Corners	Long-term contracts (units 1, 2, 3)	1960, 1963	35 yrs
	(units 4, 5)	1966	35 yrs
Young	Long-term contract	1966	50 yrs
Coyote	Integrated contract	1978	35 yrs
Montrose	Long-term contracts (units 1, 2)	1956	~30 yrs
	(unit 3, different mine)	1959	~35 yrs
Craig	Long-term contract	1973	35 yrs
Asbury	Long-term contract + some spot	1966	20 yrs
Keystone	Long-term contract	1964	~30 yrs
Homer City	Long-term contracts (2)	1966	~30 yrs
Conemaugh	Long-term contracts	196?	~30 yrs
Mt. Storm	Initial supply arrangements unknown; currently coal comes from adjacent company-owned mine (100% of output plus contract purchases from other suppliers with different durations, plus some spot purchases.	NA	NA

SOURCE: See appendix.

specifies annual supplies for each of twenty years, one contract specifies annual quantities (plus or minus 10 percent) for each of thirty-five years, one 90 percent requirements contract, and one plant that has two contracts each for 50 percent of requirements (with flexibility to go down to 40 percent). In all but one case specific reserves are dedicated to fulfilling the contract as well. Most of the contracts also have explicit restrictions on sales to third parties which require the approval of the plant operator, or most favored nations clauses.

Coal quality: Coal quality is handled in one or both of two ways. Most of the contracts include "contract" coal quality characteristics and "minimum" coal quality characteristics, often along with various bonus/penalty provisions if certain coal quality specs (usually BTU content) fall above or below those specified in the contract. BTU content of coal, sulfur content, size, moisture, and ash content are the most frequently specified characteristics. If coal quality specifications are not included, the contract provides for "run-of-mine" deliveries free of certain impurities from specified reserves. Some contracts have as many as sixteen coal quality characteristics specified.

Maximum delivery commitments: In addition to providing requirements obligations for the buyer and seller, the contracts typically specify maximum monthly and annual quantities that the suppliers are committed to deliver. These are often adjustable within some range if the purchasers give adequate notice to the supplier. These provisions sometimes get very complicated, especially when a sequence of generating units is planned. Even if a utility claims its requirements are greater than the maximum, the supplier has no contractual obligation to supply more than the maximum.

Arbitration: All but three of the contracts have specific arbitration provisions to deal with disputes arising under the contracts. Two of the

Table 9. Summary of Selected Nonprice Provisions of Contracts (21 contracts)

Duration	
Mean:	35 yrs
Median:	35 yrs
Mode:	35 yrs
Min:	20 yrs
Max:	50 yrs
Requirements contracts	
Full requirements:	16
Partial (%) req.:	3
Annual quantities:	2
Min take/min payment	
Yes:	16
Not mentioned:	5 (2, cost plus or two-part tariff; 1, added by amendment)
Arbitration	
Yes:	18
Not mentioned:	3
Scheduled renegotiation	
Yes:	5 (3, after 20 years; 1, escal. weights only; 1, buyer pays fixed costs on termination)
No:	16
Coal quality specs	
Yes:	14
No:	7 (run of mine for specified reserves)
Specification/dedication of reserves	
Yes:	20
Not mentioned:	1
Specific restrictions on third-party sales	
Yes:	13
Not mentioned:	8
Gross inequity	
Yes:	12
Not mentioned:	9 (3, cost plus; 3, integrated/contract; 1, "fair profit" provision)

SOURCE: See appendix.

three contracts without these provisions were eventually terminated after utility acquisition of the mines. A few of the contracts also provide for a joint utility/supplier committee to facilitate the smooth operation of the coal supply arrangements and to avoid disputes.

9. PRICING PROVISIONS IN LONG-TERM CONTRACTS

There are two general types of formulas used to determine prices in the actual coal contracts that I have reviewed. The predominant form (fourteen of twenty-one contracts) of pricing involves the specification of a base price (either per ton or per million BTUs) which is broken down into several different components (labor, materials, depreciation, profit, taxes, etc.) with an escalation provision specified for each. Usually some of the components are indexed in some way, while other components are adjusted for changes in actual cases. There is some variation among contracts in this regard. These contracts thus represent a mixture of the indexed and cost plus contracts discussed above. They recognize explicitly that prices will have to be adjusted over time (up or down) to reflect changes in input prices and several categories of real cost changes that are not subject to the control of the mining company. Prices are not, however, formally tied to market prices, nor do changes in the relationship between contract prices and market prices automatically trigger renegotiation. The older contracts tend to have a fraction of the price which is not escalated, and it is quite clear that uncertainty due to inflation and unanticipated exogenous events affecting real mining costs have been of increasing importance in structuring long-term contracts between utilities and independent suppliers over time.

The second primary type of compensation arrangement (seven contracts plus one indexed contract with a cost plus option) is a cost plus profit contract. These contracts normally specify that the buyer will pay all operating costs, depreciation, amortization, property and severence taxes, plus an allowance for profit (normally per ton or per BTU with a couple of exceptions). These contracts generally recognize explicitly that pure cost plus arrangements raise incentive problems and include specific incentive provisions.

Table 10 summarizes a number of the key provisions governing price adjustments over time.

9.1. Base Price Escalation Contracts (14 contracts)

Wages and benefits: Labor costs are normally broken down into several categories to reflect wages, benefits, employment taxes, etc. A base hourly wage rate is typically indexed to changes in wage rates (including benefits, taxes, etc.) as specified in collective bargaining agreements applicable to the area in which the mine is located (if it is unionized and sometimes if it is not) or

Table 10. Summary of Pricing Provisions in Contracts

General pricing provisions: Base price plus escalation: 14
Cost plus profit: 7 and 1 with option

ESCALATION PROVISIONS IN BASE PRICE PLUS ESCALATION CONTRACTS

- Components of base price
- Wages/benefits
  - Indexed: 11
  - Actual costs: 3
- Materials and supplies
  - Indexed: 13
  - Actual costs: 1
- Depreciation/amortization
  - Indexed: 4 (2 partial, 1 full)
  - Actual costs: 3
  - Fixed: 2
  - Aggregated with other components: 4
  - Other: 1
- Profit
  - Indexed: 5
  - ROI: 1
  - Fixed: 3
  - Aggregated with other components: 4
  - Other: 1
- Residual aggregate
  - Indexed: 4
  - Fixed: 2
  - None: 8
- Taxes/royalties
  - Actual costs: 14
- Costs due to changes in gov't regulations
  - Actual costs: 12
  - Not mentioned: 2 (subsequently added by amendement)
- Changes in contract/union work rules
  - Actual costs: 13
  - Fixed: 1 (contract has cost plus option)

COST PLUS PROFIT CONTRACTS

- Treatment of base profit per unit
  - Indexed: 6
  - ROI: 2 (includes contract with cost plus option)
- Incentive Provisions
  - Bonus/penalty based on "standard cost" comparisons: 3
  - Bonus/penalty based on market price comparions: 3
  - Option to rebid mining agreement: 1
  - Contractual promise to develop incentive provision: 1

NONLINEAR RATE STRUCTURE (in addition to/along with minimum take): 5 of 21

to the average wage rate actually paid to workers at the mine, including changes in government-mandated tax and benefit payments. I have identified the treatment of wages and benefits as indexed if the wage component had a fixed weight in the base price, excluding adjustments for contractual or legal changes in work rules, and was adjusted only for changes in prevailing wage rates. Several contracts have manning tables attached to indicate how the average wage rate is to be determined. In three of the contracts all increases in labor costs per unit output were passed through, so that changes in labor costs due to both input price changes and changes in realized productivity were reflected in transactions prices. These are denoted as adjustments based on "actual cost."

Materials and supplies (M&S): The M&S component of the base price is almost always indexed using a weighted average of several components of the wholesale price index (WPI). As many as nine separate components of the WPI are sometimes used. One contract contains a pass-through for changes in actual M&S costs. Two contracts adjust M&S costs using the same index used to adjust wages (one contract was written in 1957 and the other has an unusual cost plus option). Explosives and electricity are often indexed separately.

The fraction of the base price attributable to labor costs and materials and supplies varies considerably but generally falls within the range of 50 to 70 percent of the base price.

Depreciation/amortization: This capital cost component is treated in a variety of ways. In about half the cases it is indexed directly (one case partially indexed and one case fully indexed), using either the WPI or the consumer price index (CPI), or aggregated with a profit component and residual costs and then indexed. In three cases actual costs were passed through and in two cases this component was fixed. One contract had a more complicated treatment of depreciation and profits, which used a fixed component unless profits fell below some lower boundary, in which case prices would be adjusted upward.

Profit: In five cases a specific profit component was indexed either by the WPI or the CPI. In one case prices were adjusted upward or downward if the rate of return on sales fell above or below some range specified in the contract. In three cases the profit component was fixed. In four cases it was aggregated with depreciation and other residual costs and then indexed in three cases and was fixed in the other.

Costs due to changes in government regulations: Costs associated with complying with new government regulaions are generally treated as a cost to be passed on to the buyer. The provisions for calculating these costs are sometimes quite vague and are often subject to arbitration. The two contracts which did not contain such a provision were subsequently amended to include it. Both of these contracts were written in the 1960s.

Changes in taxes (excluding income) and royalties: These cost changes are generally simply passed through. Since they are usually changes in tax rates it is as if they were indexed.

Changes in contract/union work rules: In all but one of the contracts, provisions were made to adjust the labor component for changes in contract working hours, overtime pay, vacation time, etc. Several contracts contain detailed examples of the computations that should be made to implement this provision.

9.2. COST PLUS CONTRACTS (8 contracts)

Seven of the twenty-one contracts were primarily cost plus contracts and an additional contract gave the seller the option to switch from an indexed contract to a cost plus arrangement on six months' notice (it is counted twice in the totals). In six of these contracts the profit component is indexed to the CPI or the WPI. In two contracts the profit is based on a fair rate of return on investment.

Seven of the eight contracts (including the contract with the cost plus option) have formal incentive provisions. The eighth has vague language in the contract indicating that an incentive plan would be developed through negotiation after three years (the mine involved was subsequently acquired by the utility, before the date which would have triggered this provision). In three of the contracts there is a bonus/penalty provided for, in the form of an adjustment to the profit component based on a comparison with market prices. In one of these contracts the incentive payment is tied to a comparison between the unit cost increase under the contract and the increase in a weighted average of local, regional, and national coal prices. The other two contracts provide for a reward if the coal produced is the lowest cost of any comparable mine in the state.

Three of the contracts provide for a bonus/penalty based on the relationship between the actual costs and an indexed "standard cost." The indexed standard cost is constructed in a way similar to the construction of the base price plus escalation prices in the first set of contracts. Components are specified and then either indexed (mostly) or adjusted for some actual cost changes. The indexed standard cost is then compared to the actual cost per ton. There is a sliding scale that adjusts the profit component upward if the actual cost is below the standard cost and vice versa. The sliding scale bonus/penalty adjustment has a minimum and maximum. In each of these contracts explicit provisions are made as well for the utility to acquire the assets of the mines at net book value. In at least two of the three contracts, the utilities financed the initial development of the mines and hold mortgages on the property.[24]

The contract which gives the mining company the option to change from an indexed contract to a cost plus contract also gives the buyers the option to put the mining contract up for competitive bids if the cost plus option is exercised. The contract provides that a new mining company can acquire the assets at depreciated book cost or fair market value, whichever is lower.

24. This is probably true of Keystone as well, although I was unable to find documents indicating that utility financing had been provided.

In these cost plus contracts, the utility frequently has the contractual right not only to audit the books and submit the reasonableness of costs incurred to arbitration, but also to approve mining plans, capital expenditures, and budgets. Indeed, the distinction between vertical integration and "contract" in several of these cost plus contracts becomes almost a matter of semantics rather than a sharp distinction given the joint control, the presence of utility financing, and the cost plus nature of the pricing provisions.

9.3. Other Provisions

Nonlinear pricing/minimum take or pay: five of the contracts had nonlinear price schedules (although one had ten components with prices *increasing* as aggregate production increased). Most of the contracts have minimum take or pay provisions. Of the five contracts without minimum take or pay provisions, one was a cost plus contract, one had a two-part tariff, and one had a minimum take or pay provision added by amendment.

Gross inequity/force majeur: Many of the contracts recognize explicitly that the pricing provisions specified can track the "prudent" costs incurred by the mining company only imperfectly. While the contracts intend both parties to bear some price/cost risk, it is not the intent of the contract to impose inequitable losses on the mining company or (in fewer cases) allow it to earn inequitable profits as a result of "surprises." These contracts contain a fairly vague provision that allows one or both parties to reopen the contract by asserting that its continuance constitutes a gross inequity. Thirteen of the contracts have gross inequity provisions and in at least a few cases these provisions were used to reopen the contracts. All of the contracts recognize that certain contingencies may arise that make it impossible for the plant to continue to operate or that make it impossible for it to continue to burn coal from this mine. Fairly standard force majeur provisions are included in all of the contracts. In a few cases considerable detail regarding what does and what does not constitute force majeur and how compensation will be made during force majeur periods is contained in the contracts.

10. EXPERIENCE WITH CONTRACT EXECUTION OVER TIME

A complete analysis of coal supply arrangements for mine-mouth plants would ideally include a detailed discussion of how these supply arrangements worked out over time. Did one party to the contract try to hold up the other? Were there haggling problems? Was there uneconomical supplier switching? Did the contractual provisions allow for smooth adjustments in obligatons? Did the parties continue to perform as economic conditions changed? Did the parties resort to litigation to get contractual promises enforced?

Most of the information that one would need to do such an in-depth analysis is not publicly available. I will discuss the fragments of evidence that I have been able to put together, however.

Most of the initial supply arrangements that were made at the time the construction of a mine-mouth plant was planned have continued to govern supply arrangements up until the present time, despite fairly dramatic changes in coal prices, mining costs, and air pollution restrictions. However, many of the contracts have been amended, in several cases numerous times, for a variety of reasons. The contracts negotiated in the 1960s and early 1970s often had pricing provisions that did not provide adequate protection to the mining company for the kinds of cost increases that occurred in the 1970s. Amendments revising the base price and escalation provisions appear to be quite common. Sometimes these amendments are made in the course of negotiating a new supply agreement to accommodate additional generating units on the site. The gross inequity provisions have also been used to adjust prices. In several cases initial provisions for annual price adjustments were amended to provide for semi-annual, quarterly, or monthly base price adjustments as the inflation rate increased in the 1970s. In a few cases there were amendments clarifying the operation of the pricing provisions contained in the contracts, no doubt following a dispute between the parties. I was surprised at how enduring these relationships have been and how few modifications there have been made to the initial supply arrangements, given the many changes that have occurred in coal markets over the last twenty years.

Two of the twenty-one plants identified experienced significant changes in their initial supply arrangements. The owners of the San Juan plant initially created a jointly owned coal subsidiary (Western Coal Company), which owned the reserves and coal cleaning facilities.[25] They contracted with a subsidiary of Utah-International to build and operate a mine to produce coal from these reserves in 1972. The mining contract gave either party the option to terminate the agreement after six years, in which case the plant owners would have to acquire the mining assets. The contract price (apparently) contained a large fixed component. Utah notified the owners that it would exercise its option to terminate after six years since it was losing money. It offered to renegotiate the supply arrangement and preferred a cost plus contract. After determining that they could not produce the coal any cheaper and that an alternative fixed price contract offered by Utah was too expensive, the joint owners of the plant signed a new mining agreement with a cost plus profit pricing formula. Subsequently, Western Coal sold the

25. See letter from Western Coal Co. to Tucson Gas and Electric and Public Service of New Mexico regarding negotiations with Utah-International (dated February 21, 1978, on file).

reserves to the mine operator as well, and the utilities signed a revised thirty-seven year cost plus contract with Utah-International.

Utah Power & Light initially secured coal supplies for the Hunter and Huntington units under two long-term contracts with Peabody Coal. The first contract signed in 1971 provided for the requirements of the first two units of the Huntington plant. The second contract signed in 1974 (involving a second mine) provided for supplying the requirements of the first two units of the Hunter plant. Both contracts were for thirty-five years. The first used a base price plus escalation formula. The second used a cost plus formula with no explicit incentive provision. They both also contain unusually wide ranges in acceptable coal quality and no bonus/penalty payments tied to coal quality. Both mines were acquired by Utah Power & Light in 1977 and are operated by an independent operator under a thirty-year agreement.[26] The mining agreement does not contain coal quality specs or a bonus/penalty system. The plants encountered serious operating problems due to poor coal quality and wide variations in coal quality both before *and* after the acquisition of the mines. The utility never rejected any coal under the agreements.

I could find only one supply arrangement in the group where a dispute led to litigation. In 1973 Colorado-Ute Electric Cooperative signed a long-term requirements contract with Utah-International to supply coal for the first two units of the Craig generating station. The contract specified that the units would each have a capacity of 350 MWE. The requirements contract specified both a minimum take (and associated minimum payments) by the utility and a maximum monthly and yearly delivery obligation by the supplier. Deliveries above the maximum were at the discretion of the seller. Without telling the supplier, Colorado-Ute subsequently increased the actual size of each generating unit by about 20 percent. The year before deliveries were to commence the supplier sued for breach of contract, requesting that it be obligated only to deliver the minimum takes specified in the contract. Colorado-Ute argued that it was entitled to deliveries up to the maximum specified in the contract. The federal district court (425 F.Supp. 1093 [D. Colo. 1976]) found for the supplier, allowing him to rescind part of the agreement. Deliveries are being made under the contract, but only at the minimum take levels. A commentary on the case suggests that market conditions had changed after the contract was negotiated, that the seller could get higher prices by selling the additional coal to others, and perhaps that it could extract a higher price from Colorado-Ute.[27]

26. McGraw-Hill (1981: 392). This publication does not identify the utility and plants by name, but it is clear from the information provided that the utility is Utah Power and Light and the plants are Hunter and Huntington.

27. McGraw-Hill (1981: 486). Additional coal was eventually purchased from another supplier.

11. DISCUSSION

The empirical results are quite consistent with the predictions of the transactions cost theory. Spot markets and short-term contracts account for a relatively small fraction of coal supply transactions for electric utilities. For the utility industry as a whole, long-term contracts rather than vertical integration is the preferred governance structure. Vertical integration is much more prevalent for mine-mouth plants than it is for other coal-fired generating stations, however. Although mine-mouth plants account for only 15 percent of total coal consumption by electric utilities, they account for more than half of the supplies governed by some form of vertical integration. When contracts are chosen in lieu of vertical integration (or, in a sense, in addition to it for jointly owned generating plants) for mine-mouth plants, the parties rely on very long-term contracts to support exchange. These contracts, while certainly "incomplete," are often quite complex, containing numerous price and nonprice provisions to protect both parties from breach and to help ensure the smooth operation of the supply relationship over time.

Although my research examining coal supply arrangements for non-mine-mouth generating plants is not yet complete, preliminary results suggest that there are important differences, on average, between contracts governing exchange for mine-mouth plants compared to other types of generating plants. The contractual duration of coal supply agreements for mine-mouth plants is substantially longer than for other types of plants and involves substantially larger annual delivery commitments (compare table 6 and table 8). Preliminary analysis of about sixty contracts for other coal plants suggests that these figures may understate the differences in length of commitment. Several of the non–mine-mouth contracts contain renegotiation and termination provisions that specifically allow one or both parties to terminate the agreement without paying damages long before the stated term of the contract is reached. This is not generally the case for mine-mouth plants. Contracts for mine-mouth plants are generally written as requirements contracts. This is rarely the case for the other contracts that I have examined.[28]

Although long-term contracts establish pricing provisions ex ante, this does not mean that prices are rigid. The pricing formulas used allow for frequent price adjustments based on input price changes and other cost changes that are attributable to exogenous events. While prices will not gen-

28. I have performed a preliminary analysis of 60 contracts that do not involve mine-mouth plants. The average duration of the contracts is about thirteen years. Only four are requirements contracts. Only three involved mines that had not been developed at the time the contract was signed. Eighteen of these contracts provide for scheduled price renegotiation during the term of the contract.

erally track short-term movements in market prices, they do respond in the long run to changes in the costs of producing coal. Recent contracts often provide for quarterly or monthly adjustments, and some older contracts have been amended to do so.

The pricing provisions, along with certain nonprice provisions, also reflect an interest by buyers that their suppliers produce efficiently. Two-thirds of the contracts make extensive use of indexing provisions to adjust prices so that the price the seller receives is partially independent of his production decisions. If the seller can beat the index he can increase his profits, and if the seller does not mine efficiently his profits will fall. All of the cost plus profit contracts recognize explicitly that pure cost plus pricing has bad incentive properties with regard to efficient production. All but one of these contracts contains additional provisions to give suppliers incentives to produce efficiently.

Overall, I have found the transactions cost framework to be an extremely powerful vehicle for gaining a better understanding of the nature of vertical supply relationships between power plant owners and their coal suppliers.

APPENDIX

This appendix summarizes the methods used for collecting the information on vertical integration and contracts that is discussed in the text.

Vertical Integration

I started with lists of captive coal mines contained in the McGraw-Hill *Keystone Coal Manual* and Gordon. Individual utility entries in *Moody's Public Utilities Manual* were reviewed to verify the information provided there and to resolve differences between the two lists. Next, Pasha Publications' *Guide to Coal Contracts* was searched for additional information on utility ownership of mines. Then, the entries for the 25 largest utility consumers of coal in *Moody's* were reviewed in an effort to identify additional utility-owned mines. Finally, the ownership of all suppliers identified in the contracts with mine-mouth plants was determined from another listing in the *Keystone Coal Manual*.

Annual production figures by mines and consumption figures for utilities were obtained from the *Keystone Coal Manual*, the Department of Energy's *Cost and Quality of Fuels for Electric Utilities*, *Moody's* and annual reports.

Mine-Mouth Plants

The definition of a mine-mouth plant is at least partially subjective and no general list of such plants appears to exist. I searched for plants that were deliberately located adjacent to specific coal reserves in order to exploit these reserves to generate electricity and where the adjacent mining facilities were built in reliance on these plants. The *Guide to Coal Contracts* has extensive information on coal transportation modes used to serve many plants. Mine-mouth plants are frequently noted explicitly. In a few cases, mine-mouth plants were identified when conveyor belts or short-haul rail spurs were designated as the coal transportation mode. Gordon contains a discussion of mine-mouth plants and identifies a few. The *Keystone Coal Manual* also provides information to identify mine-mouth plants. These sources were supplemented by searches of annual reports and various government publications. I identified more plants than appear on the list but eliminated plants which had first units which began operating before 1960, since I thought that it would be difficult to obtain information on initial supply arrangements for plants that began operating so long ago. One plant (Montrose) that began supplying electricity before 1960 is on the list because the start-date that I initially identified turned out to be incorrect. I left it on the list since I had already collected the information on coal supply arrangements. Almost all of the older plants that were dropped from the list obtain at least some of their coal from utility-owned coal subsidiaries. In several cases these plants were greatly expanded with large units built in the 1960s or 1970s and rely on contracts for a large fraction of their supplies. It is possible that this selection process did not capture all mine-mouth plants in existence.

Contracts

General information on the contract characteristics for each plant was obtained from the *Guide to Coal Contracts*. Individual contracts, amendments, etc., were obtained from the *Washington Service Bureau*. These contracts in turn were obtained primarily from SEC files. National Economic Research Associates gave me access to their coal contract library, where these contracts are filed. In a few cases I was able to obtain additional information by making telephone calls to individual utilities and reviewing 10-K filings.

The contracts are sometimes long and complicated. Just reading them is not very productive. I used a coding sheet which contained entries for a variety of contract characteristics based on the discussion of the implications of transactions cost theory contained in the text. Each contract was read to fill in the relevant characteristics that had been identified. In several cases it is necessary to make interpretations of provisions which are unclear or ambiguous, so the coding of the contracts involves some subjective evaluations as well. I read every contract, amendment, and any associated correspondence myself.

REFERENCES

Coase, Ronald H. 1937. "The Nature of the Firm," 4 *Economica* 386–405.

———. 1972. "Industrial Organization: A Proposal for Research," in Victor R. Fuchs, ed., *Policy Issues and Research Opportunities in Industrial Organization*, vol. 3. New York: National Bureau of Economic Research.

Goldberg, Victor P. 1976. "Regulation and Administered Conracts," 7 *Bell Journal of Economics* 426–48.

——— and John E. Erickson. Undated. "The Law and Economics of Long-Term Contracts: A Case Study of Petroleum Coke," mimeo.

Gordon, Richard L. 1975. *U.S. Coal and the Electric Power Industry*. Washington, D.C.: Resources for the Future, Johns Hopkins University Press.

Grossman, Sanford J., and Oliver Hart. 1984. "The Cost and Benefits of Ownership: A Theory of Vertical Integration," London: London School of Economics, mimeo.

Hart, Oliver D. 1983. "Optimal Labour Contracts under Asymmetric Information: An Introduction," 50 *Review of Economic Studies* 3–36.

Holmstrom, Bengt. 1979. "Moral Hazard and Observability," 10 *Bell Journal of Economics* 74–91.

Joskow, Paul L. 1977. "Commercial Impossibility, The Uranium Market and the Westinghouse Case," 6 *Journal of Legal Studies* 119–76.

———and Nancy Rose. 1984. "The Effects of Technological Change, Experience and Environmental Regulation on the Construction Costs of Coal-Burning Generating Units," MIT Department of Economics Discussion, paper.

Klein, Benjamin. 1980. "Transaction Cost Determinants of 'Unfair' Contractual Relations," 70 *American Economic Review* 356–62.

———, R. A. Crawford and A. A. Alchian. 1979. "Vertical Integration, Appropriable Rents, and the Competitive Contracting Process," 21 *Journal of Law and Economics* 297–326.

Macaulay, Stewart. 1963."Non-Contractual Relations in Business," 28 *American Sociological Review* 55–70.

Masten, Scott E., 1984. "The Organization of Production: Evidence from the Aerospace Industry," 23 *Journal of Law and Economics* 403–19.

McGraw-Hill, Inc. 1981. *How to Negotiate and Administer a Coal Supply Agreement.* New York.

———. 1982. *Keystone Coal Industry Manual.* New York.

Monteverde, Kirk, and David J. Teece 1982. "Supplier Switching Costs and Vertical Integration in the Automobile Industry," 13 *Bell Journal of Economics* 206–13.

Moody's Investors Services. (Various Years.) *Moody's Public Utility Manual,* New York.

Muris, Timothy J. 1981. "Opportunistic Behavior and the Law of Contracts," 65 *Minnesota Law Review* 521–90.

National Coal Association. 1983. *Coal Data.(1981/82).* Washington, D.C.

———. 1984. *Facts about Coal (1984/85).* Washington, D.C.

———. (Various years.) *Steam Electric Plant Factors.* Washington, D.C.

Palay, Thomas M. 1984. "Comparative Institutional Economics: The Governance of Freight Rail Contracting," 13 *Journal of Legal Studies* 265–88.

Pasha Publications. (1981, 1983). *Guide to Coal Contracts.* Arlington, VA.

Shavell, Steven. 1979. "Risk Sharing and Incentives in the Principal and Agent Relationship," 10 *Bell Journal of Economics* 55–73.

U.S. Department of Energy. (Various years.) *Inventory of Power Plants in the United States,* DOE/EIA-0095. Washington, D.C.: Government Printing Office.

———. (Various years.) *Cost and Quality of Fuels for Electric Utility Plants,* DOE/EIA-0191. Washington, D.C.: Government Printing Office.

———. (Various issues.) *Quarterly Coal Report,* DOE/EIA-0121. Washington, D.C.: Government Printing Office.

———. 1983. *Coal Production–1982,* DOE/EIA-0118(82). Washington, D.C.: Government Printing Office.

Williamson, Oliver E. 1971. "The Vertical Integration of Production: Market Failure Considerations," 61 *American Economic Review* 112–23.

———. 1975. *Markets and Hierarchies: Analysis and Antitrust Implications,* New York: Free Press.

———. 1979. "Transaction Cost Economics: The Governance of Contractual Relations," 22 *Journal of Law and Economics* 233–61.

———. 1983. "Credible Commitments: Using Hostages to Support Exchange," 73 *American Economic Review* 519–40.

———. 1984. *The Economic Institutions of Capitalism*. Draft manuscript.

Zimmerman, Martin. 1981. *The U.S. Coal Industry: The Economics of Policy Choice*. Cambridge: MIT Press.

[13]

ELSEVIER

Journal of Economic Behavior and Organization
Vol. 26 (1995) 431–443

JOURNAL OF
Economic Behavior
& Organization

Specific investment, economies of scale, and the make-or-buy decision: A test of transaction cost theory

Bruce R. Lyons

School of Economic & Social Studies, University of East Anglia, Norwich, NR4 7TJ, UK

Received September 1992, final version received February 1994

Abstract

This paper develops empirical tests of three hypotheses arising from transaction cost theory, as developed by Oliver Williamson. Evidence is provided from a new dataset on 178 inputs gathered from UK engineering firms. The probability of buying-in specialised inputs is higher if the production technology is non-specific, but only if there are economies of scale or scope. Furthermore, the economies of scale/scope effect is much reduced in the presence of specific assets. This interactive hypothesis has not been formally tested before. We also believe this to be the first cross-section empirical test of transaction cost make-or-buy theory using European data.

Keywords: Contracts; Specific assets; Transaction costs

JEL classification: L14; L22

1. Introduction

A variety of methodologies have been used to test transaction cost theory [1]. The key focus of attention has been almost exclusively on asset specificity, that is

[1] Useful early reviews can be found in Joskow (1988), and chapters 3 and 4 of Schmalensee and Willig (eds) (1989), written by Williamson and Perry respectively. *All* of the studies they cite refer to US firms only. Excellent examples include Monteverde and Teece (1982), Masten (1984), and Lieberman (1991).

SSDI 0167-2681(94)00070-0

the degree to which the value of an investment is tied to continuing trade between a particular pair of traders. This is appropriate since it is the key factor that makes transaction cost theory testable. Given that bounded rationality prevents the writing of complete, contingent contracts, in-house production may be the only way to protect transaction specific investments [2] from opportunistic behaviour. However, this focus on specific assets ignores a second important technological characteristic relevant to the make-or-buy decision: economies of scale or economies of scope. A trade-off between asset specificity and economies of scale or scope is central to the transaction cost theory of vertical integration as developed by Oliver Williamson. Until now, however, there appears to be no systematic empirical work that examines its implications. This paper examines the relationship between scale economies and specific assets, and provides the first European empirical study (to my knowledge) which gives cross-section evidence on asset specificity and the make-or-buy decision.

In section 2, Williamson's (1985, 1989) 'heuristic' model of the transaction cost theory of vertical integration is sketched. The model is operationalised as a very simple stochastic optimisation problem, and three testable hypotheses are developed. One relates to specific assets, the second to economies of scale or scope, and the third to the interaction between specificity and scale. Section 3 presents some representative results based on a single definition of economies of scale, and section 4 provides a sensitivity analysis using different definitions of scale and scope. Section 5 concludes.

2. Williamson's heuristic model

Williamson (1985, 1989) develops what he calls a 'heuristic' model for understanding the vertical boundaries of the firm. This simplified model examines the make-or-buy decision for a fixed output of a component used in fixed proportions and made with a technology of exogenous asset specificity, k. First, consider the governance costs of external procurement as compared with in-house production. $k = 0$ would imply that the investments required to manufacture a bought-in component could be costlessly transferred to production for an alternative customer should the original transaction not continue. Relevant investments include geographic location and human capital as well as physical assets, though the empirical work reported in this paper concentrates on the latter. In the absence

[2] Transaction specific investments result in assets that have greater value when used to service a particular transaction, than they would have if that relationship broke down. For example, building a factory near to a big customer, or buying a machine or die that is fully efficient only for a specific design of product, or spending a great deal of time and effort to understand a customer's particular needs and requirements, or simply investing in an expensive piece of capital equipment that would lie idle for some time before an alternative customer could be found.

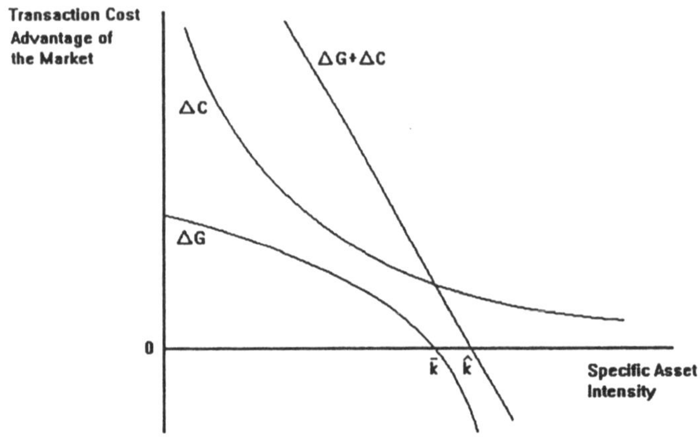

Fig. 1. Williamson's 'heuristic' model.

of specific assets, Williamson argues that market based organisation is favoured because high powered (profit) incentives, necessary to minimise costs and optimise innovation, cannot be fully preserved within a unified firm. On the other hand, if $k > 0$, then assets are specific and, once such investments have been made, suppliers leave themselves vulnerable to opportunistic recontracting. This may result in a risk premium being added to the price, or a failure to make the appropriate investments. Either way, as the costs of using the market rise, the organisational balance is moved in favour of in-house production. As Williamson (1985, p.91) puts it: 'market procurement is the preferred supply mode where asset specificity is slight – because of the incentive and bureaucratic disabilities of internal organization in production and cost control respects. But internal organization is favoured where asset specificity is great, because a high degree of bilateral dependency exists in those circumstances and high-powered incentives impair the ease with which adaptive, sequential adjustments to disturbances are accomplished'. Defining ΔG as the difference between the bureaucratic costs of internal governance and the corresponding governance costs of markets, the relationship with asset specificity is shown in Fig. 1. This reproduces Williamson's (1985) Fig. 4-2. In the absence of economies of scale or scope, the make-or-buy decision is simple: produce in-house if optimal asset specificity exceeds k, and buy-in otherwise.

A second line in Williamson's argument is that the market is able to aggregate demands, and so achieve economies of scale or scope which are unavailable within the firm. In-house production of quantities large enough to achieve full economies of scale, with external sale of output surplus to requirements, can lead to transactional problems since potential purchasers are also likely to be downstream rivals. Importantly, this advantage for the market is related to k. In the absence of specific assets, there is no constraint on demand aggregation and this gives external production a considerable edge in achieving lower production costs. However, as technologies become more specific, the aggregation of demands from different firms generates fewer savings. [3] Defining ΔC as the unit production cost difference for a given demand by the downstream firm, ΔC is a positive, decreasing function of k, asymptotically approaching zero. The net cost of in-house production in the presence of economies of scale or scope is $\Delta G + \Delta C$, and the critical level of asset specificity determining the make-or-buy decision rises to $\hat{k}$.

In order to operationalise this basic model, it must be recognised that rational, optimising firms may have imperfect information and make errors. Furthermore, we cannot measure all the detailed technological, historical and environmental factors that influence an individual firm's decision with respect to a particular input. Define π_i as the perceived difference in profitability between subcontracting (i.e. buying-in) and integrated production for input i. Then,

$$\pi_i = \beta X_i + u_i \tag{1}$$

where X_i is a vector of exogenous technology variables representing asset specificity, k, and scale or scope economies; β is a vector of coefficients; and u_i is an error term with cumulative density function F(u). It might well be argued that asset specificity is endogenous to organisational choice, with specific technologies more likely to be chosen if production is in-house. As will be seen below, however, our measure of asset specificity is based on the response to a question about *ideal* technology, as opposed to technology in use, and so should be exogenous to organisational choice.

The make-or-buy decision is dichotomous: either the input is subcontracted, $SUBCON_i = 1$, or it is made in-house, $SUBCON_i = 0$. Ignoring ties, we observe $SUBCON_i = 1$ if $\pi_i > 0$ and $SUBCON_i = 0$ otherwise. Thus,

$$\begin{aligned} \text{Prob}(SUBCON_i = 1) &= \text{Prob}(\pi_i > 0) = \text{Prob}(u_i > -\beta X_i) \\ &= 1 - F(-\beta X_i) \end{aligned} \tag{2}$$

[3] This brief analysis begs the question of why firms do not produce in-house and sell their excess supplies into the market. This would be straightforward if customers could be found outside the industry. However, the problem is that the market may consist of downstream rivals, who fear opportunistic manipulation of their supplies. In such cases, downstream rivals may still not worry about potential opportunism as long as the production technology is so general that alternative suppliers from outside the industry can be found with ease. Thus, the market benefit of demand aggregation may be greatest when there is some industry specificity, but no firm specificity in the assets in question. These arguments serve to illustrate the fact economies of scale (or scope) affect organisation fundamentally because of fear of opportunism (i.e. transaction costs).

Assuming a logistic cumulative distribution F(u), the appropriate estimation procedure is a simple logit model. [4]

The vector X_i remains to be specified. Linearising, [5] we can write for input i,

$$\Delta G_i = \alpha_0 + \beta_0 k_i \text{ where } \alpha_0 > 0 \text{ and } \beta_0 < 0 \quad (3)$$

and if i is subject to economies of scale or scope,

$$\Delta C_i = \alpha_1 + \beta_1 k_i \text{ where } \alpha_1 > 0 \text{ and } \beta_1 < 0 \quad (4)$$

Suppose we observe whether production of an input is subject to economies of scale or scope only as a dichotomous variable. If such economies exist, $S_i = 1$, the transaction cost advantage of the market is

$$\Delta G_i + \Delta C_i = [\alpha_0 + \alpha_1] + [\beta_0 + \beta_1] k_i \quad (5)$$

while if there are no such economies, $S_i = 0$, equation (3) holds. Substitution of (3) and (5) into (1) yields,

$$\pi_i = S_i \{[\alpha_0 + \alpha_1] + [\beta_0 + \beta_1] k_i\} + [1 - S_i] \{\alpha_0 + \beta_0 k_i\} + u_i \quad (6)$$

Rearranging,

$$\pi_i = \alpha_0 + \beta_0 k_i + \alpha_1 S_i + \beta_1 k_{ii} S_i + u_i \quad (7)$$

The stochastic formulation suggests three testable hypotheses, each associated with the estimated coefficients in (7): [6]

H1: Inputs requiring a specific production technology are more likely to be produced in-house (i.e. both ΔG and $\Delta G + \Delta C$ are negative functions of k). In terms of equation (7), $\beta_0 < 0$ and $[\beta_0 + \beta_1] < 0$.

H2: Inputs requiring a technology which exhibits economies of scale or scope are less likely to be produced in-house (i.e. $\Delta C > 0$ so $\alpha_1 > 0$).

H3: Economies of scale or scope have a *greater impact* on the make-or-buy decision in the absence of specific assets (i.e. ΔC is decreasing in k so $\beta_1 < 0$).

As stated earlier, there is now a substantial body of US evidence supporting H1. H2 has also received attention, if not systematic testing, as the traditional, production cost based story of the boundary of firms. [7] But the interactive hypothesis H3 appears to have received no attention at all.

[4] Our results are almost identical if we assume F(u) is cumulative normal and estimate by probit.

[5] In our empirical work, the specific investment and scale/scope economies variables are all dichotomous, so 'linearisation' is not additionally restrictive in this case.

[6] Since α_0 is estimated as the intercept, and so includes the average influence of unobserved variables represented in the error term, it would be inappropriate to claim $\alpha_0 > 0$ as a test of a fourth hypothesis proposed by Williamson, that the market has advantages in the absence of both scale economies and specific assets.

[7] In his survey, Joskow (1988, p.108) suggests one possible example. He interprets Monteverde and Teece's (1982) finding that GM are more likely to produce in-house than are Ford as possibly 'a very imperfect proxy for the role of scale economies as a potential cost of vertical integration'.

3. The 'make-or-buy' tradeoff: a first look

A postal questionnaire asking a wide range of questions about subcontracting behaviour was sent to 1,326 establishments in the UK mechanical engineering, motor vehicle, electronics and metal processing industries. The survey was conducted in early March 1991. [8] We used an address list which named the executives in charge of purchasing, and which was targeted at sites that were expected to be employing at least 100 people. This form of approach allowed us to gather a relatively large number of useable responses, but at the expense of being able to ask only relatively simple questions. Our final questionnaire was developed following two pilot studies (one postal and the other by telephone).

The basic methodology was to ask firms first about the production technology of a specialised input they currently subcontract to another firm to produce, and then also to report on the technology of an input currently produced in-house (but which it might be possible to buy-in). Both inputs were self-selected, subject to the constraint that they had to be of *a design or specification which was specific to the responding firm's own product*. Such inputs could be components, sub-assemblies or processed materials. [9] In selecting the in-house input, respondents were instructed: 'As far as possible, your chosen input should be of comparable significance to your final product as is the subcontracted input'. We are thus able to focus as clearly as possible on the influence of technological characteristics on the organization of production. By scrutinizing marginal make-or-buy decisions, this makes it as difficult as possible for the transaction cost theory to predict correctly. [10]

We received 102 completed questionnaires. The reason for this apparently low response rate was almost certainly due to our requirement that the subcontracted input should be specialised, and many firms will only buy-in more standard inputs. [11] Firms not buying-in a specific input were asked at an early stage in the

[8] These postal questionnaires have since been followed up with a sample of twenty face-to-face interviews. The interviews followed the same schedule as the postal, and focused on clarifying the interpretation of questions and answers, as well as allowing a wider ranging discussion.

[9] The examples we gave were: shaped metal casing, but not standard sheet steel; customised computer software, but not standard microchips; customised electronic controls, but not standard electric motors; specialised ceramics, but not off-the-shelf chemicals.

[10] 5 firms in the sample chose to report on inputs bought-in from a sucontractor with whom they had (typically very minor) ownership connections. Excluding these observtions from the analysis reported below has no effect on our results.

[11] The questionnaire was also quite lengthy, with 134 coded responses plus a number of open answers. More positively, the 102 returns were quite comprehensively filled in, with 93 complete responses to the questions on the subcontracted input; though this fell to 85 on the in-house questions. This drop may have been because respondents were more sensitive to in-house issues, but it may also have been because the questions came later in a questionnaire which was also perceived as an investigation of subcontracting. The reported results are insensitive to the exclusion of non-matched pairs of inputs.

questionnaire not to continue filling it in (many of the subsequent questions would have been meaningless for standardised inputs). For each input, questions were asked about the specificity of technology, and production economies of scale and scope.

For both inputs, the firms were asked: 'does the ideal input production technology involve significant investment in *specialised capital equipment* that has little alternative use?' [12] The variable IDEAL was created such that IDEAL = 1 for affirmative answers and zero for negatives. IDEAL is our proxy for k_i. [13]

For the in-house input, we asked: if your demand for this input was twice what it is now, would the average production cost be reduced by nil, 1-4%, 5-9%, 10-24%, 25-49%, or at least 50%? Following the pilot telephone interviews, we realised that a similar quantitative question could not be sensibly asked about the subcontracted input. Such detailed information is not normally available to respondents in the purchasing firm. However, we did find that the purchasing firm could answer true or false to the following proposition about the subcontracted input: 'production involves economies of scale and our requirements are not large enough to exhaust them'. [14] The zero-one dummy variable ES10L was constructed such that ES10L = 1 for the subcontracted input if costs could be reduced by at least 10%, and for the in-house input if the economies of scale statement was true. Thus, ES10L reflects the existence of significant *economies of scale*, and is our proxy for S_i in this section. Section 4 examines the sensitivity of our results to alternative specifications of the presence of economies of scale or scope.

A first look at the data suggests support for H1: while 54% of the in-house inputs possessed an ideal specific technology, only 25% of the subcontracted inputs did. This difference between proportions is statistically highly significant ($z = 4.02$). It will be convenient for comparative purposes to express this result slightly differently. Pooling the 178 observations on the 93 subcontracted inputs

[12] In the question relating to the subcontracted input, the last four words were replaced by 'the subcontractor would have difficulty in efficiently utilising if you cancelled your order'. A referee raised the concern that the question asked about the in-house input might be answered in the affirmative for equipment that is specialised but not firm-specific. While it is possible that respondents might assume the question only relates to alternative uses in-house, we believe that the natural interpretation for businessmen would be to include potential uses outside the firm (e.g. they would not label as specialised a fork-lift truck used in their own factory only for warehouse operations). Our interpretation was confirmed both in examples firms provided in the questionnaire, and in the follow up face-to-face interviews.

[13] We also asked questions about specific investments in time and effort, but these turned out to be poor discriminators. Almost without exception, production of the inputs under consideration required significant investment in specific human assets.

[14] This proposition was the fourth of seven statements (*not* mutually exclusive) offered as reasons why they chose to subcontract rather than produce in-house. The alternatives included access to superior technology, cheap labour, economies of scope, and flexibility in the face of fluctuating demand.

(SUBCON = 1) and the 85 in-house inputs (SUBCON = 0) for which answers were completed on all the relevant questions, maximum likelihood logit estimation gives (t-statistics in parenthesis):

$$\text{(R1) SUBCON} = \underset{(3.24)}{0.641} - \underset{(-4.11)}{1.313} * \text{IDEAL} \quad \text{Log Likelihood (LL)} = -118.2$$

However, this apparent support for the role of specific assets requires important modification when we estimate the more complete specification given in Equation (7). Defining INT10L as the interaction term IDEAL * ES10L,

$$\text{(R2) SUBCON} = \underset{(-0.91)}{-0.238} \underset{(-1.58)}{-0.742} * \text{IDEAL} + \underset{(4.39)}{2.231} * \text{ES10L} \underset{(-2.34)}{-1.702} * \text{INT10L} \quad \text{LL} = -102.2$$

Of course, such a regression using four RHS variables (including the constant) must exactly predict the proportions of subcontracted inputs in each of the four IDEAL = 0,1 and ES10L = 0,1 combinations. The interest lies in the significance of individual coefficients as direct tests of the three hypotheses derived in section 2.

Economies of scale are shown to significantly favour subcontracting (the coefficient on ES10L, $\alpha_1 > 0$), thus supporting H2. However, the estimate of β_0 (i.e. the coefficient on IDEAL) is not significantly different from zero. [15] Only in conjunction with economies of scale (i.e. adding the coefficients on IDEAL and INT10L) does H1 receive significant support. [16] It appears that, in the absence of scale economies, in-house production is preferred whether or not specific assets are required for production. [17] Thus, the role of specific assets is closely tied to the existence of economies of scale. H3 receives significant support (the coefficient on INT10L, $\beta_1 < 0$) and, in the presence of scale economies, specific assets are revealed to play a substantial part in bringing production in-house (i.e. $\beta_0 + \beta_1 < 0$). In fact, the evidence is that economies of scale have no significant residual influence on the make-or-buy decision when IDEAL = 1. [18] Overall, in the absence of economies of scale, specific assets do not significantly affect organisation, and in the presence of specific assets, economies of scale have no influence.

[15] Except, miserably, at the 10% level on a 1-tail test!

[16] An F-test on the null hypothesis of $\beta_0 + \beta_1 = 0$ yields calculated F = 19.52, which comfortably rejects the null at all conventional levels of significance.

[17] It is important to recall that all the inputs under investigation are idiosyncratic, and this conclusion would not necessarily apply to standard inputs.

[18] For the 109 inputs without specific equipment, the difference between the subcontracted proportions with and without economies of scale is 44% points (z = 4.77), while for the 69 inputs requiring an ideal specific technology, the difference is only 12% points (z = 1.00).

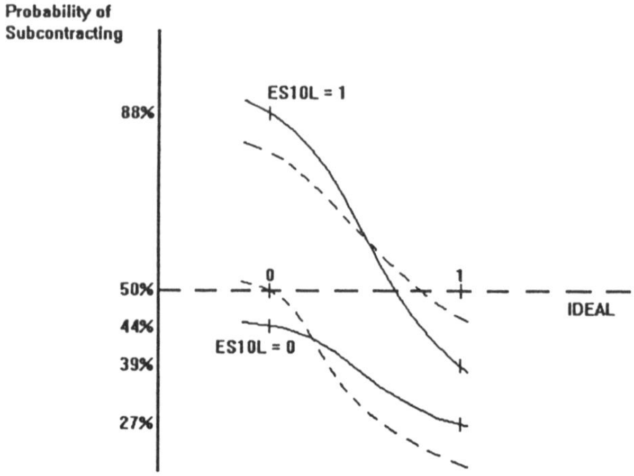

Fig. 2. Heuristic representation of the ES10L results.

These results are represented in Fig. 2, which is linked to Fig. 1 through Eqs. (2) and (7). The solid lines join points from (R2) (which are also the actual proportions). The dotted lines come from the misspecified model:

$$\text{(R3) SUBCON} = \underset{(-0.06)}{-0.013} \underset{(-4.31)}{-1.553} * \text{IDEAL} + \underset{(4.24)}{1.489} * \text{ES10L} \quad \text{LL} = -105.0$$

The significance of the coefficient on IDEAL in (R3) demonstrates the importance of a correctly specified model.

Finally, as with all institutional structures, it is possible that current subcontracting arrangements are in disequilibrium. In the questionnaire, we asked firms if they would be willing to subcontract on a larger scale. 68% gave a positive answer, including all of the 6 firms producing in-house despite economies of scale and no specific equipment. Furthermore, only 3 of the 9 who were subcontracting despite an ideal specific technology and no economies of scale, indicated that they might subcontract further. In fact, each of these reported economies of *scope* in the subcontracted input (see next section), so the potential dynamics lend further support to our cross-section findings.

4. Sensitivity analysis

As explained in the previous section, we were unable to ask identical questions about the extent of scale economies for in-house and subcontracted inputs. Unfortunately, this raises the question of comparability of the economies of scale

Table 1
Alternative definitions of economies of scale and scope

	Non specific equipment	Ideal specific equipment	χ^2	θ
(A) Subcontracted input (N = 93)				
Subcontactor has advantage including:				
economies of scale: Yes	**44**	14		
No	26	*9*	0.029	62%
economies of scope: Yes	**54**	14		
No	16	*9*	2.332	73%
either scale or scope or both: Yes	**61**	17		
No	9	*6*	2.240	84%
(B) In-house input (N = 85)				
Average cost reduction from doubled output:				
at least 1%	*22*	37		
nil	17	**9**	5.738	69%
at least 5%	*18*	35		
0–4%	21	**11**	8.056	62%
at least 10%	*6*	22		
0–9%	33	**24**	10.056	33%
at least 25%	*1*	4		
0–24%	38	**42**	1.433	6%
at least 50%	*0*	2		
0–49%	39	**44**	1.737	2%

Bold highlights results clearly supporting Williamson's transaction cost model.
Italics highlight results clearly contrary to Williamson's transaction cost model. Critical values of χ^2 are: $\chi^2_{.1} = 2.706$ $\chi^2_{.05} = 3.841$ $\chi^2_{.02} = 5.412$ $\chi^2_{.01} = 6.636$ and $\chi^2_{.001} = 10.827$. θ is the proportion of inputs with economies of scale or scope as defined.

variable for each source of input. Table 1 summarises the additional information we were able to collect on the extent of both scale and scope economies.

The top half of the table reports on the subcontracted input. Apart from the economies of scale statement, respondents were offered the following economies of scope true/false option: 'the subcontractor is able to produce more cheaply because he supplies a range of related products'. Given that we are discussing idiosyncratic inputs, scope will often be a more appropriate dimension than scale, and this is borne out by the larger number of respondents acknowledging the former. Also, a number of respondents claimed that particular inputs were subject to both economies of scale and of scope. This overlap is consistent with the expectation that scale and scope are not easily separable for specific inputs. Taken together, two-thirds of subcontracted inputs had no ideal specific technology, but an advantage in scale or scope; and only 7% had a specific technology with no scale or scope advantage.

Table 2
Regression sensitivity analysis using different definitions of economies of scale and scope

n	i	CONSTANT	IDEAL	ESni	INTni	Log Lik.	F
1	LP	−0.636	0.231	1.656	−2.028	−108.50	21.9 **
		(−1.54)	(0.34)	(3.44) **	(−2.63) **		
5	LP	−0.847	−0.241	2.072	−2.184	−104.62	23.7 **
		(−2.13)*	(−0.37)	(4.31) **	(−2.88) **		
10	LP	−1.299	−0.087	3.618	−2.490	−83.75	23.2 **
		(−3.46) **	(−0.15)	(6.36) **	(−3.12) **		
1	P	−0.061	0.061	0.977	−1.949	−111.37	22.0 **
		(−0.17)	(0.59)	(2.27)*	(−2.74) **		
5	P	−0.272	0.071	1.389	−2.105	−109.16	23.8 **
		(−0.819)	(0.13)	(3.24) **	(−3.02) **		
10	P	−0.724	−0.257	2.939	−2.411	−93.96	23.6 **
		(−2.38) *	(−0.52)	(5.59) **	(−3.26) **		
1	L	0.425	−0.425	0.268	−1.240	−113.32	16.6 **
		(1.36)	(−0.75)	(0.66)	(−1.78)		
5	L	0.214	−0.414	0.680	−1.396	−112.74	18.4 **
		(0.73)	(−0.77)	(1.68)	(−2.04)*		
10	L	−0.238	−0.742	2.231	−1.702	−102.22	19.5 **
		(−0.91)	(−1.58)	(4.39) **	(−2.34) **		

Notes: n is the minimum average cost reduction (expected for the in-house input if output was doubled) required for ESni = 1. For i = L, if the subcontractor has an advantage in achieving economies of scale, then ESiL = 1; for i = P, if she has an advantage in economies of scope, then ESiP = 1; and for i = LP, if the advantage is in either or both, then ESiLP = 1. All regressions have 178 observations. F is the F-test for the null hypothesis that $\beta_0 + \beta_1 = 0$. t-statistics are given in brackets under logit regression coefficients. ** significant at the 1% level (2-tail test). * significant at the 5% level (2-tail test).

Part B of Table 1 gives more detail on economies of scale for the in-house input. Using the most encompassing definition (i.e. if output was doubled, average cost need decrease by only 1%) there are only 9 observations which clearly support the transaction cost view, and 22 which run counter to expectation. Obviously, these numbers improve as the scale criterion becomes more stringent and, with scale economies defined as requiring an average cost elasticity of 10% or more, the transaction cost story looks very good. Moreover, even using the most encompassing 1% definition, in-house production is more likely to sacrifice scale economies if there is a specific technology. Only 56% of in-house inputs with non-specific technologies exhibited scale economies, compared with 80% of those with a specific technology. The χ^2 statistic shows that this trade-off is most clear when scale economies are defined at the 10% cost elasticity.

For the purpose of the current exercise, a crucial question is what percentage in-house cost reduction is comparable with an affirmative answer to the economies of scale or scope propositions in relation to the subcontracted input. Unfortunately, there is no accurate way of answering this on the basis of the questionnaire returns, though it seems unlikely that the 10% mark would not be considered as a cost advantage. Table 2 reports logit regressions similar to (R2), but using different cut-offs for the in-house scale effect, combined with either scale or scope or one-or-both [19] advantages for the subcontracted input. Our earlier results are revealed to be robust, indeed strengthened using the combined scale/scope advantage for the subcontracted input. The transaction cost theory receives strong support, with the important exception that specific investments only affect the make-or-buy decision in the presence of economies of scale or scope. [20]

5. Conclusion

The purpose of this paper has been to test some predictions of transaction cost theory using a new dataset on the make-or-buy decision by UK firms in the engineering industry. Particular emphasis has been placed on the role of economies of scale or scope, and the interaction with specific assets. Economies of scale and scope are a significant motivation behind the decision to buy-in, but only in the absence of specific assets. Specific assets are the overriding influence when scale or scope economies exist. However, in the absence of such economies, specific assets are found to have little influence on the make-or-buy decision largely because most such inputs are made in-house anyway. This may be because all the inputs under investigation are idiosyncratic.

Acknowledgements

I would like to thank two very constructive referees, whose comments have much improved this paper, but who bear no responsibility for remaining errors. This work was funded by the UK Economic and Social Research Council (Grant Number W108251011), in conjunction with Barclays Bank, Commission of the European Communities (DGXXIII), Department of Employment and Rural Development Commission.

References

Joskow, Paul, 1988, Asset specificity and the structure of vertical relationships: empirical evidence, Journal of Law, Economics and Organisation 4, 95–117.

Lieberman, Marvin, 1991, Determinants of vertical integration: an empirical test, Journal of Industrial Economics XXXIX, 451–466.

[19] 'One-or-both' means the input is subject to either economies of scale or economies of scope or both advantages.

[20] The one serious sensitivity to the definition of scale is the influence of economies of scale or scope on the extent of subcontracting, given that an ideal, specific technology exists. Using the 10% cut-off, there is no significant difference in the subcontracted proportions with and without economies of either scale only or scope only, but there is for ES10LP ($z = 2.06$). However, at the 1% and 5% cut-offs, the subcontracted proportion is actually smaller with economies of scale than without.

Masten, Scott, 1984, The organisation of production: evidence from the aerospace industry, Journal of Law and Economics 27, 403–417.

Monteverde, K. and David Teece, 1982, Supplier switching costs and vertical integration in the automobile industry, Bell Journal of Economics 13, 206–213.

Schmalensee, Richard and Willig, Robert (Eds.), 1989, Handbook of Industrial Organization: Vol. 1, Amsterdam: North-Holland.

Williamson, Oliver, 1985, The Economic Institutions of Capitalism, New York: Free Press.

Williamson, Oliver, 1989, Transaction cost economics, Chapter 3 in Schmalensee and Willig (1989).

[14]

Rand Journal of Economics
Vol. 15, No. 3, Autumn 1984

Integration of the sales force: an empirical examination

Erin Anderson*

and

David C. Schmittlein*

This article develops and tests a model of integration of a marketing function, personal selling. The model, derived from transaction cost analysis as developed principally by Williamson, is formulated as a logistic function, which is estimated with data from the electronic components industry. As expected, integration is associated with increasing levels of asset specificity, difficulty of performance evaluation, and the combination of these two factors. Contrary to the transaction cost model, neither frequency of transactions nor interaction of specificity and environmental uncertainty is significantly related to integration. The transaction cost model improves significantly upon the fit of a simple model relating integration to company size alone. These results suggest that for studying transactions of this kind, it is fruitful to view the firm as a governance structure.

1. Introduction

■ In recent years considerable attention has been paid to the question of when vertical integration takes place (Williamson, 1979; Klein, Crawford, and Alchian, 1978; Holmstrom, 1979). These approaches consider contracts in far more detail than their predecessors did; and, at least implicitly, they recognize the behavioral phenomena of bounded rationality and opportunism and make allowances for the environmental phenomenon of uncertainty. But these and other recent treatments have been subject to little empirical testing other than by selected case studies.[1]

Discussions of vertical integration typically focus on manufacturing. This leads to emphasis on the valuation of physical assets, which may or may not be specialized to the user. Although it has been recognized that human assets are also relevant (Williamson, 1981b; Monteverde and Teece, 1982), less attention has been paid to their role. We focus on the integration of a particular marketing function, personal selling (as opposed to

* University of Pennsylvania.

This research was supported by the Marketing Science Institute, the Wharton Center for Marketing Strategy Research, and the University of California, Los Angeles.

The authors would like to thank Oliver Williamson, Barton Weitz, Stanley Ornstein, and Vijay Mahajan for helpful comments. We also appreciate the detailed and insightful comments of an anonymous reviewer and of Alvin Klevorick.

[1] Two exceptions are Monteverde and Teece (1982) and Teece (1980).

mass communications). The issue is whether to use a manufacturers' representative or a "direct" (employee) salesperson to sell a product line. The resolution of this issue turns on human assets, if only because differences in physical assets are negligible in this setting.

Section 2 further develops this issue and presents a transaction-cost explanation based on the work of Williamson (1975, 1979, 1981a,b), from which we develop a theoretical model. Section 3 discusses collection of field data from 172 sales managers for 16 electronic component manufacturers. Estimation of the logistic function is the subject of Section 4, and the results are presented in Section 5. Section 6 discusses the implications of these exploratory findings.

2. Relevant transaction costs

■ A manufacturers' representative ("rep") is an independent business entity that offers selling services to a manufacturer ("principal") in return for a commission on any sales realized. A typical rep agency consists of several salespeople and office staff and operates like the sales department of a firm. The agency, however, represents a number of noncompeting manufacturers whose products fit to form a sales package (e.g., office supplies from one maker, typewriters from another). Reps usually bear all sales expenses and are the principal's exclusive salespeople for a defined set of customers (e.g., office products stores in Southern California). Thus, reps are what we shall refer to as the market governance mode. In contrast, "direct" sales people are employees of one manufacturer, typically paid by salary or salary plus incentives. Hence, direct salespeople are the integrated (hierarchical) governance mode.[2]

As of 1974, 50% of all U.S. manufacturers used reps, either alone or in conjunction with a direct sales force (Research Institute of America, 1975). Yet, as of 1977, only 10% of U.S. dollar volume in 15 major industrial categories was conducted through reps (Taylor, 1981). Apparently, the market mode is less often used than the integrated mode, although this varies considerably across product categories.

Williamson (1975, 1979, 1981a,b) has developed a transaction-cost theory of integration. Klein, Crawford, and Alchian (1978) offer a closely related treatment. The logic and concepts of Williamson's approach are readily transferable to the rep/direct choice and provide a framework for our exploratory analysis of this issue.

Asset specificity arises when durable assets become customized to the user. When assets are fungible, market contracting is preferable since the agent pooling several firms' demands more fully exhausts scale economies and risk-pooling benefits. At the same time, the threat of ready replacement disciplines performance. In contrast, if assets become specialized to a relationship, the parties are locked into bilateral exchange. The result is that opportunism and maladaptation are unchecked by market forces.[3] In such circumstances, integration enables the firm to dampen opportunism and inflexibility because integration carries with it access, audit, and incentive advantages. Other things equal, reps should be more efficient (and presumably chosen more often) when assets are nonspecific and direct salespeople should be more efficient and chosen more often when assets are highly specific.

A salesperson or sales force possesses physical and human assets. Physical assets (cars, offices, etc.) are unspecialized, and hence may be disregarded in our analysis. Of

---

[2] Markets and hierarchies are really endpoints on a continuum from a completely independent external entity to a completely dependent internal entity. Rep and direct sales forces may fall at different points along the continuum; however, for purposes of exploratory analysis, we simplify into rep (external) and direct (internal).

[3] Although in theory a sufficiently complex contingent claims contract might produce the same effect, in practice bounded rationality, uncertainty, and the derivative condition of information impactedness render this solution infeasible.

the human assets (knowledge/ability and relationships), those which are specialized relate to the principal (company) and the customer. The relevant specialized knowledge and relationships can be described as follows.

Consider the salesperson experienced in a given industry who begins to represent Company *A*. The salesperson's industry skills are all that is necessary—unless *A* is a distinctive firm. Suppose that Company *A* has its own particular operating procedures, formal and informal, which our salesperson must learn. To get Company *A* to act effectively (e.g., to rectify a customer complaint quickly), our salesperson must have built relationships within the firm (e.g., with production personnel or design engineers). Further, if *A*'s products are not standard, it is necessary to learn their distinctive features and applications. Finally, our salesperson may acquire sensitive information to perform his tasks. The knowledge and relationships our salesperson eventually acquires about *A* are assets specific to *A*. The more these assets affect the salesperson's performance, the higher their value and the more the selling task is characterized by asset specificity.

This scenario may be repeated on the customer side. *A*'s customers may be distinctive in their ways of doing things and in their orientations and needs. The importance of these features is magnified when *A*'s sales are concentrated in critical "key" accounts: for these accounts it pays to learn every customer idiosyncracy. Further, with some accounts relationships cultivated may become so important that the customer exhibits loyalty to the salesperson—not to the principal.[4] Thus, where customers are distinctive, where sales are concentrated in key accounts, and where relationships matter (especially where loyalty to the salesperson may arise), asset specificity is high.

A major proposition follows: the greater the total value of company-specific assets (on the company and customer sides), the greater the likelihood of vertical integration in the form of a direct sales force.

□ **Uncertainty.** Williamson (1979) highlights one form of environmental uncertainty, that of environmental unpredictability. This complicates writing and enforcing contingent claims contracts since the environment shifts in unforeseen ways. The market mode is still advantageous, but transactions will be completed less smoothly than in more certain environments. Thus, the presumption of market superiority is undisturbed—*unless* assets are specific to a nontrivial degree.

The shifting environment forces renegotiation, which may lead to delays. This poses a fundamental problem under the market mode because even the best contracts are incomplete. The integrated firm is better able to cope because adaptations can be made as needed without revising formal agreements between independent parties (Williamson, 1979). Hence, the likelihood of integration is expected to increase, given nontrivial asset specificity, with increasing uncertainty.

Williamson's later writings (1981a) recognize a second form of uncertainty, which he calls "internal." Alchian and Demsetz (1972) highlight the same concept, which they call the difficulty with which individual productivity can be metered. We refer to this second form of uncertainty as the difficulty of evaluating performance. It occurs in the selling function for three reasons. First, it may be infeasible to record each salesperson's results accurately. For example, in selling air freight services, records are kept at the warehouse level, while salespeople operate at the customer level. Second, responsibility for a sale may not be assignable to an individual. This occurs when team sales are involved or when customers may place an order with someone other than the salesperson

[4] This asset is especially potent. It is specific in that it grows while the salesperson represents that principal and is particularly beneficial to the principal while the transaction continues. But this asset may be transferred to another principal should the transaction end, which makes the threat of opportunism acute.

who makes the presentation. Third, "performance" may not be a simple, readily measurable scalar. It may be a vector of indicators, the relative importance of each being hard to ascertain and the value of each being difficult to measure (e.g., satisfaction of prospects approached, value of market intelligence provided).

When performance is difficult to evaluate, imperfect input measures and a manager's subjective judgment are preferable to defective (simple, observable) output measures. Integration is not essential, since monitoring and judgmental evaluation of individual performance can be done by managers of a firm that contracts to provide service to another. Nevertheless, the evaluators must be evaluated themselves, and simple output measures of the contractor's performance are often inadequate when underlying individual results are difficult to assess.

Accordingly, the likelihood of integration should increase with the difficulty of monitoring performance.

□ **Making the tradeoff: frequency.** The transaction costs imposed by specific assets (especially in combination with environmental unpredictability) and by monitoring difficulty make vertical integration more appealing. But a specialized governance mechanism involves significant setup and maintenance costs. For rarely occurring transactions, losses from opportunism and inflexibility are likely to be lower than the integrated firm's incremental overhead. As a transaction recurs more frequently, however, integration becomes more desirable since potential losses from not integrating outweigh the overhead costs of integration.

The issue is whether a firm can at least break even on the fixed cost of an integrated function. Although the idea is logically appealing, it is difficult to express empirically. Fixed costs are difficult to estimate and the breakeven point (over an arbitrary time span) is unclear. Nonetheless, one does see rules of thumb used to approximate this minimum scale notion. For example, we were told by two sales managers in the electronic components industry that a common heuristic involves drawing a geographical territory that a salesperson could physically cover and estimating its maximum attainable sales potential. If less than $1,000,000 is at stake, the territory is too "sparse" or "thin" to be covered by a direct salesperson. Density, then, is an analogue of frequency in the selling setting and may be thought of as the ratio of attainable potential to required travel in a territory. Since the desirability of integration increases as density increases (though the breakeven point is unascertainable), we expect to see more use of a direct sales force as density increases.

Scherer (1980, p. 84) suggests that firm size is also a very important factor. Since large firms achieve economies of scale in finding, holding, and utilizing management skills, a large firm "may be able to get more mileage out of its expenditures on a field sales force and other marketing instruments." Scale economies are likely to play an important role in virtually all integration decisions. More generally, size is widely regarded as a pervasive influence on firm behavior (Miles, 1980) and on firm and industry performance for reasons of scale and scope economy, market power aspirations, and the ability to aggregate inputs (Scherer, 1980). Thus, our model includes company size, in addition to asset specificity, uncertainty, and frequency.

3. Data from the electronic components industry

■ The above hypotheses were tested on survey data from the electronic components industry. We selected one industry, rather than several, to detect real differences in practice that might otherwise be confounded with industry-specific effects. This limits the generalizability of results, but does allow us to establish internal validity. The electronic components industry was chosen because its variety makes it a microcosm of American business, as can be seen in the following industry description (Electronic Industries Association, 1981).

Electronics concerns the conduction of electricity through a material such that the electrons' flow is influenced. The ability to influence electron flows (rather than simply to carry them) is what distinguishes electronic equipment from electrical equipment. In 1980, the electronic components industry posted factory sales in the United States of over 25 billion dollars. The many component producers (including some non-American companies) cover a broad spectrum. Generally, they sell to original equipment manufacturers (OEM's), though many OEM's (e.g., Texas Instruments) are themselves integrated backward into production of certain components.

Most components are categorized as "active" or "passive." Active components (such as semiconductors) contribute to signal energy in a circuit, whereas passive components do not. This distinction is important because the passive sector is more mature ("low tech"), with less product differentiation and more intense price competition. A capacitor (passive component) may sell for a few cents a pound and be treated as a commodity, whereas an integrated circuit (active component) may be engineering intensive, customized to the user's application, and treated as a highly differentiated product. Component producers vary not only in their products, but also in their strategies (e.g., low-cost producer vs. high-cost innovator), sizes, management styles, and distribution methods.

Component distribution proceeds through three different channels. The first two, company salespeople and manufacturers' representatives, involve no transfer of title to goods. Of these, reps are becoming increasingly popular. The third option is industrial distributors, independent wholesalers who purchase components for resale. Because distributors take title, they are less subject to the manufacturers' influence (particularly on pricing) than either direct salespeople or reps. Nonetheless, distributors are also becoming more popular. Many firms use all three, restricting each mode to certain product lines and customers. For example, a full line manufacturer may use distributors to sell passive components to small customers; reps to sell passive and active components to medium customers and active components to small customers; and direct salespeople to sell passive and active components to large customers. This study tests a transaction cost explanation for these assignments in cases where title stays with the manufacturer (i.e., reps vs. direct salespeople).

Sixteen recognized electronic component manufacturers participated in the study. Only recognized firms were included to permit a contrast between what might be presumed to be well-run direct sales forces and well-run reps.[5] The unit of analysis was the product line of a given company in a given territory or set of territories. A "territory" (defined by the firm) is a subset of customers covered by a sales force (rep or direct) reporting to a sales manager. Since most companies keep records and assign managers at the product-line-in-territory level, this unit of analysis facilitates data gathering.

[5] A list of recognized firms was generated from the *1980 Audit of Brand Recognition*, a survey in which purchasers of a given electronic component (e.g., switching diodes) listed the three manufacturers they would consider as suppliers. For all major categories of components, we selected every manufacturer mentioned by at least 10% of the purchasers. This procedure generated a very long list of recognized firms, many of which were on the West Coast. For convenience, non-West Coast firms were eliminated. With the endorsement of the EIA (Electronic Industries Association), the vice presidents of sales of 21 firms were contacted. Eleven have participated. In addition, nine recognized firms (none from the West Coast) suggested by EIA were contacted and five have participated. In total, 16 of 30 companies cooperated. To assess the seriousness of nonresponse bias, the 16 respondents and 14 nonrespondents were compared as to size, the sophistication of their product line, and whether they were rep or direct. The nonparticipants have little in common on these grounds. Since these three variables are important descriptors of electronic component manufacturers, the threat of nonresponse bias does not appear serious, although doubtless it is present.

The survey respondents were territory sales managers, who are in an excellent position to know both the selling environment and the firm's environment. Each manager is a boundary spanner, a person on both sides of the boundary between the firm and the customer in a particular territory. To be a sales manager, especially in this industry, one needs to have been a salesperson. Managers also know their territories, since the median length of time served in the territory is six years.[6]

Each sales manager was directed by top sales management to fill out a questionnaire and to return it directly to the research team. This questionnaire was extensively pretested and in total, 145 completely usable responses (of 172 questionnaires returned) are available.[7] The response rate per company is virtually 100% because company personnel followed up missing questionnaires.

4. The logistic response function

■ This section describes our specific model for the decision to use reps vs. a direct salesforce. Following the order in which the concepts described in Section 2 were introduced, the variables listed below are hypothesized to affect the likelihood of using a direct salesforce.

□ Measurement of variables.

Transaction specificity of assets (TSA). This is the average of six (standardized) variables representing managers' perceptions of:

(i) nature of the company: difficulty of a salesperson's learning the ins and outs of their company which are needed for success. Managers indicated their perception by circling a number from 1 to 7 on the following semantic differential scale:

1	2	3	4	5	6	7
Disagree						Agree

in response to the statement, "It's difficult to learn all the ins and outs of our company that a salesperson needs to know to be effective."

(ii) nature of the product: amount of extra training needed in this firm by a new salesperson who has experience in the product class (answer indicated in number of weeks of training).

(iii) confidential information: measured as a semantic differential in response to the statement, "An experienced salesperson's inside information could do us a lot of damage if it got out."

(iv) nature of the customer: measured as a semantic differential in response to the statement, "To be effective, the salesperson has to take a lot of time to get to know our accounts."

(v) importance of key accounts: percent of accounts given special attention.

(vi) customer loyalty: influence of personal relationships between salespeople and accounts on sales. Greater loyalty is measured as disagreement with the statement, "Personal relationships between our salespeople and accounts have little influence on sales of our product line."

---

[6] The median manager spends 35% of working time in the field, observing first-hand how the territory operates. Of the managers who supervise reps, one of every five has a representative's council, a forum for regular exchange between reps and managers. Such a forum increases the likelihood that managers know well the territories for which they report.

[7] The questionnaire itself was designed in accordance with the guidelines of the "key informant" literature (Campbell, 1955; Seidler, 1974). All questions that were not answered by at least 95% of the respondents were eliminated as having been overly difficult. The result, we believe, is a data set of high quality.

Uncertainty as environmental unpredictability (UEU). Expected deviation between forecast and actual sales in the next year, expressed as a percentage (plus or minus).

Uncertainty as difficulty of evaluating performance (UDEP). Perceived difficulty of measuring the results of individual salespeople equitably. Measured as semantic differential in response to "It is very difficult to measure equitably the results of individual salespeople."

Territory density (TD). Negative of the percentage of salespersons' time spent driving or flying, i.e., the less time spent traveling, the more dense the territory.

Company size (SIZE). 1980 company assets in dollars (Gupta, 1980).

On the basis of the motivation in Section 2, all of the variables above are hypothesized to have a positive effect on the likelihood of using a direct sales force. To account for differences in scale—semantic differential, percentages, dollars—each of these variables was standardized before estimating the response function. Specifically, each observation was transformed by subtracting the variable's mean and then by dividing by the standard deviation. Thus, standardized variables have a mean of zero and a standard deviation of one, and the magnitudes of response function coefficients may be directly compared.

In addition to these main effects, two interactions were also considered. As noted earlier, the effects of both types of uncertainty—environmental unpredictability and the difficulty of evaluating performance—are expected to be greater when transaction specificity of assets is high. This necessitates using multiplicative interaction terms.[8] The specificity/unpredictability interaction is denoted *ZUEUTSA*, and the specificity/difficulty of evaluating performance interaction is *ZUDEPTSA*.

Because of the binary dependent variable, the logistic response function is used to represent the impact of the five main effects and two interactions on the probability of going direct. Letting $X_{1j}, X_{2j}, \ldots, X_{7j} \equiv X_j$ stand for the seven factors described above for subject j, we have

$$P[D_j = 1|X_j] = \frac{e^{\beta_0 + \sum_{i=1}^{7} \beta_i X_{ij}}}{1 + e^{\beta_0 + \sum_{i=1}^{7} \beta_i X_{ij}}}, \tag{1}$$

where

$$D_j \equiv \begin{cases} 0 \text{ if manufacturers' reps are used, or} \\ 1 \text{ if a direct sales force is used,} \end{cases}$$

and $P[D_j = 1|X_j]$ is the probability that a firm with company and market characteristics X_j uses a direct sales force. Taking the natural logarithm of both sides in (1) yields the (linear) relation between the factors and the logit or log odds ratio:

$$\ln\left(\frac{P[D_j = 1|X_j]}{1 - P[D_j = 1|X_j]}\right) = \beta_0 + \sum_{i=1}^{7} \beta_i X_{ij}. \tag{2}$$

[8] Since all three of these variables are standardized, the interactions cannot logically be formed by simply multiplying two of them. Cooper and Nakanishi (1982) provide a solution to this problem using the zeta-squared transform:

$$\zeta^2(X) = \begin{cases} 1 + X^2 & \text{if} \quad X \geq 0 \\ (1 + X^2)^{-1} & \text{if} \quad X \leq 0. \end{cases}$$

Then the two desired interaction terms can be meaningfully constructed as

$$ZUEUTSA \equiv \zeta^2(UEU)\zeta^2(TSA)$$

and

$$ZUDEPTSA \equiv \zeta^2(UDEP)\zeta^2(TSA).$$

After being computed by these definitions, *ZUEUTSA* and *ZUDEPTSA* were also standardized before the response function was estimated.

The coefficients were estimated by maximizing the likelihood function:

$$L(D_j|X_j;\beta) = \prod_{j=1}^{N} P[D_j = 1|X_j]^{D_j}(1 - P[D_j = 1|X_j])^{1-D_j}, \tag{3}$$

where N is the number of subjects on which data have been collected. Maximization of (3) was accomplished with the Gauss-Newton nonlinear least squares method used by the BMD program BMDPLR (Dixon, 1981). The next section reports the results when this model (1) and measurement method were applied to the sales force integration data.

5. Empirical results

■ **Parameter estimates.** Case 1 of Table 1 gives the parameter estimates and their asymptotic standard errors for the seven hypothesized determinants of sales force integration. The most significant factors, based on the ratio of coefficient ÷ standard error, are difficulty of evaluating performance (*UDEP*), company size (*SIZE*), and transaction specificity of assets (*TSA*). All three have the hypothesized (positive) effect on the probability of using a direct sales force. With our sample of 145, the remaining four variables are not significant and have negative coefficients, which are inconsistent with the hypotheses.

The instantaneous rate of change of the probability of going direct with respect to a variable X_{ij} is

$$\frac{\partial P[D_j = 1|X_j]}{\partial X_{ij}} = \beta_i P[D_j = 1|X_j](1 - P[D_j = 1|X_j]) \tag{4}$$

(Domencich and McFadden, 1975, p. 84). Examining this derivative for the values of β_i in Table 1 leads to two conclusions. First, the variables that, at the mean (i.e., for $X_j = 0$) have the largest estimated effect on the probability of going direct, are *UDEP*, *TSA*, and *SIZE*. Second, in the neighborhood of the mean, each variable's impact on the probability of using a direct sales force is reasonably linear.

TABLE 1 Parameter Estimates for Logistic Response Function

Effect	Coefficient	Asymptotic Standard Error	Coefficient ÷ Standard Error
Case 1: All Hypothesized Effects			
TSA	.616	.285	2.159
UEU	−.053	.276	−.193
UDEP	.782	.287	2.728
TD	−.172	.198	−.871
ZUEUTSA	−.027	.282	−.097
ZUDEPTSA	−.381	.295	−1.292
SIZE	.470	.204	2.307
Constant β_0	−.434	.188	−2.306
Case 2: Transaction Cost Effects Omitted			
SIZE	.547	.174	3.140
Constant β_0	−.405	.176	−2.302

l^* = logarithm of maximized likelihood.
Case 1: $l^* = -85.60$.
Case 2: $l^* = -92.87$.

□ **Importance of transaction-cost variables.** To evaluate the contribution of the set of transaction-cost variables over and above the results that could be obtained by using company size alone, we performed a logit analysis using only the latter factor. The estimated coefficients are listed as Case 2 in Table 1.[9]

The incremental benefit from including transaction costs in the analysis can be evaluated in two ways: statistical significance and predictive effectiveness. The logarithm of the maximized likelihood function is reported in Table 1 for the two models—the one including transaction cost effects and the one excluding them. The likelihood ratio test statistic is $c = 2(-85.60 + 92.87) = 14.54$. Under the null hypothesis that $\beta_i = 0$ for all of the transaction-cost variables, c has the χ^2 distribution with 6 degrees of freedom. Since the critical value for χ^2 at the .05 level is

$$\chi^2_{(6)} = 12.6,$$

the null hypothesis is rejected.

Alternately, the contribution of the transaction-cost variables can be examined in terms of predictive effectiveness. One index of effectiveness for comparing models estimated by maximum likelihood is Akaike's Information Criterion (Akaike, 1974):

$$AIC = -2(l^* - n), \tag{5}$$

where l^* is the logarithm of the maximized likelihood and n is the number of estimated parameters. This approach penalizes models having a large number of parameters, since the model with the smallest value of *AIC* is preferred.[10] In our application, the values of *AIC* for the two and eight parameter models are 189.74 and 187.20, respectively. Hence, the more complex model is again preferred. This result shows that the set of transaction-cost variables are not just statistically significant; one would also expect them to aid in predicting the degree of sales force integration for firms which are not included in the estimation sample.

6. Conclusion

■ Our estimated logistic function, with three significant parameters, provides support for our model of the appearance of integrated and nonintegrated sales forces. The significant predictor variables have the expected sign, which indicates support for the theoretical rationales underlying them. Although several expected effects were not observed, those transaction-cost effects that do appear improve upon a simple company-size model of integration.

Williamson (1979) argues that transaction-specific assets are the single most important determinant of vertical integration, followed by uncertainty. In our results, however, the order is reversed. Internal uncertainty, i.e., how difficult it is to evaluate individual performance, is strongly associated with the use of a direct sales force. Specificity, although strongly associated, has somewhat less of an effect. A likely explanation is that in this setting, the provision of a marketing service, the specificity of three of the four categories of assets—physical, site, and dedicated—is either minor or implausible. Where human

[9] Since the β-values have the same sign here as they did in Case 1, there is some evidence that multicollinearity between the set of transaction-cost variables and company size is not overly high.

[10] The statistic has been used for measuring predictive ability in a wide variety of settings including regression, time series analysis, multidimensional scaling, and cluster analysis (Rust and Schmittlein, 1982). Stone (1977) showed that using *AIC* to compare models is asymptotically equivalent to using the cross-validated likelihood function. For the logistic response function, Rust and Schmittlein (1982) also found *AIC* and cross validation to be very close in small samples (i.e., 10–12 observations per estimated parameter).

assets assume a prominent role, internal uncertainty is likely to assume considerable importance (Ouchi, 1979).

Contrary to the implications of Williamson's framework, the expected specificity/uncertainty interactions were not found; in this setting it appears that specificity and uncertainty have no incremental effect when they appear in combination. Further, frequency (density) appears to have no impact. Considerable difficulties are associated with measuring variables related to territorial density, e.g., workload, concentration of accounts, geographical dispersion, potential (Ryans and Weinberg, 1979). We suggest that measurement error might account for the weakness of our density measure. Recall that our measure of travel time is intended as a proxy for the ratio of potential to geographical dispersion. Had we been able to measure both potential and dispersion directly, the likelihood of error would have been much smaller.

Size of firm, the only nonterritory level variable, proves to be a powerful covariate. As expected, the larger the firm, the more likely it is to fill a territory with direct personnel.

These findings are for one type of integration (a marketing service) and one industry; hence, their generality remains to be established. Nonetheless, the results are encouraging, particularly to those who view the firm as an intendedly but imperfectly rational governance structure. Traditionally, economists have focused on production costs to the exclusion of transaction costs. Consequently, technological costs are viewed as the principal determinant of integration. The dominance of this paradigm led Coase (1972) to lament the state of affairs in industrial organization research at that date and to call for a more direct approach focusing on governance features. Our model is such an approach, and our results suggest that transaction-costs considerations are important determinants of integration.

References

AKAIKE, H. "A New Look at the Statistical Model Identification." *IEEE Transactions on Automatic Control*, Vol. 19 (1974), pp. 716–723.

ALCHIAN, A. AND DEMSETZ, H. "Production, Information Costs, and Economic Organization." *American Economic Review*, Vol. 62 (December 1972), pp. 777–795.

CAMPBELL, D.T. "The Informant in Quantitative Research." *American Journal of Sociology*, Vol. 60 (1955), pp. 339–342.

COASE, R.H. "Industrial Organization: A Proposal for Research" in U.R. Fuchs, ed., *Policy Issues and Research Opportunities in Industrial Organization, Economic Research, Retrospect and Prospect*, New York: Columbia University Press, 1972.

COOPER, L.G. AND NAKANISHI, M. "Standardizing Variables in Multiplicative Choice Models." *Journal of Consumer Research*, Vol. 10 (June 1983), pp. 96–108.

DIXON, W.J., ED. *BMDP Statistical Software*. Berkeley: University of California Press, 1981.

DOMENCICH, T.A. AND MCFADDEN, D. *Urban Travel Demand: A Behavioral Analysis*. Amsterdam: North-Holland, 1975.

Electronic Design, Audit of Brand Recognition by the Electronic Original Equipment Market. Rochelle Park, N.J.: Hayden Publishing Company, 1980.

ELECTRONIC INDUSTRIES ASSOCIATION. *Electronic Market Data Book*. Washington, D.C.: Electronic Industries Association, 1981.

GUPTA, N. "Some Alternative Definitions of Size." *Academy of Management Journal*, Vol. 23 (1980), pp. 759–766.

HOLMSTROM, B. "Moral Hazard and Observability." *Bell Journal of Economics*, Vol. 10 (Spring 1979), pp. 74–91.

KLEIN, B., CRAWFORD, R.A., AND ALCHIAN, A.A. "Vertical Integration, Appropriable Rents, and the Competitive Contracting Process." *Journal of Law and Economics*, Vol. 21 (October 1978), pp. 297–326.

MILES, R.H. *Macro Organizational Behavior*. Santa Monica: Goodyear Publishing Co., 1980.

MONTEVERDE, K. AND TEECE, D.J. "Supplier Switching Costs and Vertical Integration in the Automobile Industry." *Bell Journal of Economics*, Vol. 13 (Spring 1982), pp. 206–213.

OUCHI, W.G. "A Conceptual Framework for the Design of Organizational Control Mechanisms." *Management Science*, Vol. 25 (1979), pp. 833–848.

RESEARCH INSTITUTE OF AMERICA. "When, Where, and How to Use Manufacturers' Representatives." Staff Report, 1975.

RUST, R.T. AND SCHMITTLEIN, D.C. "A Bayesian Cross-Validated Likelihood Method for Comparing Alternative Specifications of Quantitative Models." *Marketing Science*, forthcoming.

RYANS, A.B. AND WEINBERG, C.B. "Territory Sales Response." *Journal of Marketing Research*, Vol. 16 (November 1979), pp. 453–465.

SCHERER, F.M. *Industrial Structure and Economic Performance*. Chicago: Rand-McNally, 1980.

SEIDLER, J. "On Using Informants: A Technique for Collecting Quantitative Data and Controlling Measurement Error in Organization Analysis." *American Sociological Review*, Vol. 39 (December 1974), pp. 816–831.

STONE, M. "An Asymptotic Equivalence of Choice of Model by Cross Validation and Akaike's Criterion." *Journal of the Royal Statistical Society*, Vol. 39 (1977), pp. 44–47.

TAYLOR, T.C. "A Raging 'Rep' idemic." *Sales and Marketing Management*, Vol. 127 (June 8, 1981), pp. 33–35.

TEECE, D.J. "Economics of Scope and the Scope of the Enterprise." *Journal of Economic Behavior and Organization*, Vol. 1 (1980), pp. 223–247.

WILLIAMSON, O.E. "The Economics of Organization: The Transaction-Cost Approach." *American Journal of Sociology*, Vol. 87 (1981a), pp. 548–577.

———. "The Modern Corporation: Origin, Evolution, Attributes." *Journal of Economic Literature*, Vol. 19 (December 1981b), pp. 1537–1568.

———. "Transaction-Cost Economics: The Governance of Contractual Relations." *Journal of Law and Economics*, Vol. 22 (October 1979), pp. 233–262.

———. *Markets and Hierarchies: Analysis and Antitrust Implications*. New York: Free Press, 1975.

[15]

Forward Integration into Distribution: An Empirical Test of Transaction Cost Analysis

GEORGE JOHN
University of Minnesota

BARTON A. WEITZ
University of Florida

1. INTRODUCTION

The issue of forward vertical integration has attracted a good deal of attention from researchers in several disciplines, including economics, marketing, and law. Many explanations have been offered for this phenomenon, including technological interrelationships involving economies of scale and scope (Chandler), uncertainty and risk considerations (Arrow, 1969), information externalities (Green), and strategic purposes. Blair and Kaserman (1983) offer an extensive survey of the extant literature in this area.

Of particular note, however, is the recent rise in prominence of the transaction costs analysis (TCA) of vertical integration. This approach consists of a blend of institutional economics, organizational theory, and contract law, and has been developed primarily by Oliver Williamson (1979, 1985). He views vertical integration as a response to the inability of arms-length market relationships to govern exchange efficiently under particular circumstances. The level of specialized assets[1] required to support the exchange, the uncertainty[2] surrounding the exchange, and the frequency[3] of exchange are

The authors are in alphabetical order. The financial support provided to the first author by the Graduate School Research Committee, University of Wisconsin is gratefully acknowledged. The comments of the *JLEO* reviewer are greatly appreciated.

1. Specialized assets are those investments in physical and/or human assets that have very limited salvage value outside the focal exchange.
2. Uncertainty refers to the condition of being unable to predict relevant contingencies.
3. Frequency refers to the distinction between one-shot exchange and recurrent exchange. We shall not deal with this variable here since we are interested only in recurrent exchange.

Journal of Law, Economics, and Organization vol. 4, no. 2 Fall 1988
 ISSN 8756–6222

identified as the principal factors that make market-mediated exchange inefficient.

Despite the increasing use of the transaction cost approach to explain forward integration, empirical tests of this line of reasoning are few. Some of the more prominent include make versus buy decisions in component sourcing (Monteverde and Teece), integration of the selling function (Anderson and Schmittlein), shipper-carrier relations (Palay), integration in the aluminum industry (Stuckey), and aerospace contracting relations (Masten). For a summary of these and other empirical TCA studies of long-term contracting, see Joskow. Clearly, there is a need to assess the validity of the particular propositions offered by TCA concerning vertical integration. Such evidence would advance our conceptual models by pinpointing areas of needed refinement, as well as begin to shed light on the diverse choices made by firms regarding forward integration.[4]

In this paper we present an empirical test of TCA propositions concerning forward integration by surveying a sample of industrial goods manufacturers. The variables implicated by the theory are measured via a questionnaire directed at a key informant within each firm. The resulting data are subjected to multiple regression and multinomial logit analysis to assess the degree of support for the predictions.

The remainder of the paper is divided into five sections. In section 2 we describe some of the institutional detail regarding industrial marketing channels and distinguish the principal alternative configurations. In section 3 we develop the link between forward integration and each of the key variables in transaction cost analysis. In section 4 the measures and data collection procedures are described. In section 5 we report the results of the analysis, and section 6 closes the paper with a discussion of the implications of the study.

2. DISTRIBUTION CHANNELS FOR INDUSTRIAL GOODS

One of the principal requirements for conducting an empirical investigation of TCA predictions is a high level of microanalytic detail concerning the alternative institutional arrangements. We begin by describing the organizational forms of distribution channels found in industrial goods markets.

The classification of channel structures in industrial markets is made difficult by the overlapping structures and inconsistent terminology found in the literature; see Stern and El-Ansary for a general discussion of distribution channels. Nevertheless, following Haas, Diamond, and Sutton, we can isolate

4. With respect to this diversity of choices, the available data (U.S. Bureau of the Census) show that industries vary considerably in their degree of forward integration. Further, casual observation reveals that such diversity extends to firms within industries as well.

two categories of channel organizations that differ with respect to the degree of forward integration. These researchers generally classify the various alternatives into direct and indirect channels. In the direct channel, the firm does not employ an independent reseller. Rather, it retains ownership of the product until it passes to the end-user. All of the downstream tasks are undertaken directly by company employees or else by such commission agents as manufacturers' representatives. The key attribute is that only the firm has any claim to residual profits.

The indirect channel classification comprises a bewildering array of institutional structures. The firm sells to independent resellers (such as distributors, wholesalers, retailers), who in turn resell the product to end-users or other resellers. These indirect channels vary by the type of intermediaries involved and the number of levels present within a particular system. Indirect channels are often "referred to collectively as distributors" (Sutton). Stern and El-Ansary provide a detailed description of several different types of distributors within the channel. All these indirect channels involve downstream firms that actually purchase the product and resell it. Since they take title to the product, residual profits are not claimed exclusively by the manufacturer.

From the standpoint of TCA, it is evident that direct channels represent relatively more forward integration than indirect channels. Thus, TCA predictions about vertical integration essentially speak to the choices made by manufacturers regarding direct versus indirect channels. As a recent survey of industry practice (Sutton) found, most firms can and indeed do use both direct and indirect channels simultaneously. A good illustration of multiple channels is IBM's using Computerland (a reseller) as a channel intermediary while making direct sales to end-users. Marketing specialists consider the multiplicity of channels and the management of these systems to be a critical managerial task (Stern and El-Ansary).

Multiple channel usage makes it infeasible to adopt the basic research design used in previous TCA studies. These studies typically have focused on only two disjunct categories representing the integrated and nonintegrated options. For instance, Anderson studied the internalization of the selling function in electronics firms by comparing sales territories serviced by sales branches with those serviced by commission agents. Overlapping territories where employee sales forces and commissioned agents operate concurrently were consciously excluded from the estimation sample. Likewise, when Monteverde and Teece and Walker and Weber compared the make versus buy decision for components, they excluded components that are both purchased and manufactured at the same time from their data. By contrast, we will examine indirect and direct channels used by industrial manufacturers, allowing for the possibility that these channels may be used simultaneously by some firms.

3. TRANSACTION COST ANALYSIS OF RESELLERS IN DISTRIBUTION CHANNELS

According to TCA, the firm's decision to use resellers is made on the basis of comparative institutional efficiency, In particular, it ascertains which of the alternatives constitutes the transaction-cost-minimizing condition. Such costs are distinct from production costs and are the "costs of running the system" (Arrow, 1969). Searching for information, bargaining, monitoring, and contract enforcing are all instances of these costs.

To some degree, transaction costs have earned the reputation of being capable of explaining anything in a post-hoc fashion because they have not been defined in an operational fashion. This state of affairs has been alleviated, however, by Williamson's (1979, 1985) elaboration of this approach. He provides testable implications of transaction-cost-minimizing analysis by elaborating the links between key attributes of transactions and institutional structures. Based on transaction costs logic, one can then match attributes of transactions with institutional structures that minimize these costs. Each of these attributes of transactions is discussed in turn below.

3.1. Asset Specificity

This significant attribute of transactions refers to the extent to which specialized or nonredeployable investments are needed to support an exchange. Example of such investments include railcars specialized to haul one brand of automobile (Palay), refrigerated trucks needed to ship unpasteurized beer, specialized software that communicates only with one firm's computers (Jackson), and dedicated production equipment (Monteverde and Teece).

Specialized human assets are also present to varying degrees in distribution channels. The time and effort employed to acquire firm-specific knowledge needed for downstream activities is perhaps the most common form of these investments found in distribution channels (Heide and John). Notice that such knowledge becomes largely useless if the relationship terminated.

A high level of specific assets has profound implications for forward vertical integration. The primary consequence is to expose the transaction in question to opportunistic behavior. Because nonredeployable specific assets make it costly to switch to a new relationship, the market safeguard against opportunism is no longer effective. The other party can expropriate the value of quasi-rents associated with these assets. Presumably, rational firms would not invest in them unless they could be safeguarded.

According to TCA, the ultimate safeguard for specific assets is to internalize the transaction in question. Vertical integration provides a safeguard because of (a) the better monitoring and surveillance properties of organizations relative to markets, and (b) the reduction of profits from opportunistic behavior since employees do not ordinarily have claims to profit streams. In the context of forward integration into wholesaling and/or retailing, the safeguarding of specific assets will involve internalizing the functions of independent resellers. We can summarize this as the following testable proposition:

Proposition 1. As the levels of specific assets needed to support distribution activities are increased, industrial firms will rely more heavily on direct channels.

3.2. Uncertainty

Williamson (1985) implicates uncertainty as the other principal factor involved in forward vertical integration decisions. Fundamentally, an inability to predict contingencies creates problems in writing contracts because these agreements are incomplete in some important respects. When unforeseen contingencies arise, market contracts experience strain in adapting to the changed circumstances because opportunistically inclined parties can try to interpret unspecified clauses to their own advantage. (It is important to note that contractual incompleteness is attributable to the limited cognitive capabilities of human actors.)

In a distribution channel it is evident that *environmental uncertainty* can exist with respect to many marketing activities, such as sales targets and promotional activities to support the introduction of new products. Clearly, institutional structures that permit sequential, adaptive decision making are needed when such uncertainty increases. Marketing specialists (Shapiro, Anderson and Weitz) have argued that one of the principal drawbacks of dealing with independent intermediaries is the difficulty of renegotiating agreements in light of changed circumstances. Similarly, organizational researchers (Stinchcombe) have shown that relationships incorporate more elements of hierarchy in response to increrases in uncertainty.

Transaction cost analysis posits that an appropriate response to increased environmental uncertainty is to internalize the transaction. First, vertically integrated structures permit sequential, adaptive decision making to proceed more smoothly because of administrative mechanisms. Authority structures permit quicker resolution of conflicts arising from differing interpretations of evolving circumstances. They enhance the information flow between the parties, thus enabling them to react better to the uncertainties. To summarize this as a testable proposition, we have:

Proposition 2. As downstream environmental uncertainties increase in industrial goods markets, manufacturers will rely more heavily on direct channels.

In addition to environmental uncertainty, Williamson (1985) introduces the notion of *behavioral uncertainty.* Unlike environmental uncertainty, which is exogenously imposed on the exchange, behavioral uncertainty arises within the context of the exchange itself due to the opportunistic inclinations of the transacting parties. Behavioral uncertainty refers to the difficulty of ascertaining the actual performance or adherence to contractual agreements. Stinchcombe has discussed in some detail the impact of such performance assessment difficulties on the structure of commercial relationships.

Behavioral uncertainty can take the form of false claims by downstream resellers that they have executed faithfully some agreed-upon channel activity (such as shelf stocking or cooperative advertising) while they simply pocket the remuneration for the activity or else save the costs of undertaking it. In such circumstances, greater control over reseller activities is desirable. While (costly) supervision can effectively reduce such blatant opportunism, a subtler problem arises when there are long lags between actions and market responses. Such lags in the downstream selling environment make it difficult to infer which actions were responsible for the observed outcomes. Related as such behavioral uncertainty is to performance issues, we advance the following proposition:

Proposition 3. As performance assessment difficulties in downstream activities increase, manufacturers will rely more heavily on direct channels.

3.3 Production Costs

Although TCA tends to downplay the significance of production costs and related technological effects on forward integration, the object, nonetheless, is to minimize the sum of transaction and production costs in making forward integration decisions. Following Williamson's (1985) treatment of these effects, we argue that larger firms will tend to integrate their channels more readily than smaller firms when economies of scale or scope are substantial. Summarizing, we have the following testable proposition:

Proposition 4. Industrial manufacturers who can exhaust economies of scale will rely more heavily on direct channels.

It should be noted that the above prediction is identical to that proposed by marketing specialists (Haas; Stern and El-Ansary). Their reasoning is quite different, however. Rather than relying on the assumption that firms strive to minimize transaction and production costs, they argue that firms will generally prefer to internalize activities wherever possible. Since larger firms are better able to afford the set-up costs involved, they will use direct channels more often. As the leading marketing channels textbook notes, independent resellers "exist only by virtue of the fact that suppliers and/or customers . . . cannot afford to integrate, and therefore must rely on such intermediaries. . . ." (Stern and El-Ansary: 129). TCA maintains that what matters is not whether the firm can afford to integrate but whether there is an incentive to integrate. In contrasting the two explanations, we would argue that the TCA reasoning is more appealing since it does not assume that firms are motivated to internalize activities as a general tendency. The justification for such an assumption derives from the power-oriented perspective on firm behavior developed by organization theorists. Since we are concerned with firm behavior in competitive markets, it seems more reasonable to invoke an efficiency perspective. Nevertheless, it should be stressed that the present study cannot rule out either explanation, should a firm size effect be found in the data.

4. EMPIRICAL STUDY

4.1. Research Design

A principal consideration in testing the TCA predictions advanced in the previous sections involves the operationalization of the dependent variable, vertical integration. Since the theory predicts that increasing levels of asset specificity and uncertainty result in greater forward integration, it becomes important to isolate a set of structures that can be unambiguously ordered with respect to the presence of forward integration. We accomplish this by examining industrial manufacturers and classifying their downstream channels into direct and indirect systems. The direct channel represents forward vertical integration. Since firms often utilize both kinds of channels, a quantified measure of the extent of forward integration is provided by assessing the fraction of that firm's sales going through the direct channel.

It should be stressed that this test involves a semi-microanalytic level of detail. We have ignored the institutional variation that exists within the indirect channel itself. Resellers can vary greatly in the degree to which vertical control is imposed on them by the upstream firm. For instance, an authorized dealer of a firm is likely to have far less discretion than a merchant wholesaler. Nevertheless, since they are both resellers who take title to the product and claim residual downstream profits, they are considered equivalent in our classification scheme.

To summarize, we intend to test the TCA predictions involving forward integration by examining industrial marketing channels. We focus on the use of direct versus indirect channels and classify those firms that use both types simultaneously as using "mixed" channels. The fraction of sales going through the direct channel is a quantified measure of the firm's position on the continuum of internalizing downstream activities.

4.2 Sample

The data reported here are obtained from a sample of industrial firms with sales over $50 million. The sample was drawn from a list of firms maintained by a commercial vendor. The responses of eighty-seven industrial goods firms constitute the data for estimating our models. An examination of the sample characteristics (table 1) reveals that there is substantial variation in the type(s) of channels used, ranging from exclusively direct to exclusively indirect, with the majority of firms drawing to some extent on both direct and indirect channels. The variety of products sold is very broad, including equipment, components, and operating supplies. This sample appears quite comparable to recently published marketing studies of channel types (Lilien, Coughlan). Despite the diversity of this sample, it should be emphasized that it is a nonrandom sample. The commercially available list used as our sampling frame may contain biases of unknown magnitude. We stress the need to cumulate evidence from multiple studies.

4. 3. Method

As the study concerns organizational-level decisions, a key informant survey was used to gather data. In this approach, the researcher uses one individual in each organization who is knowledgeable about the issues at hand and reports on behalf of the organization. These individuals are not selected at random from each organization. Rather, they are deliberately selected to be key informants by virtue of their position within the firm; see John and Reve for a detailed discussion of this approach.

The informants in this survey were sales managers. We can justify their choice on the following grounds. Decisions about channels typically reside at a reasonably high level within the sales function of a firm since the sales staff is the locus of contact between the focal firm and the downstream intermediaries. Further, channels decisions are not made for individual prod-

Table 1. Sample Characteristics

Measure	Average
Percentage of sales through direct channel	61%
Specific assets (Time required for new hire with prior experience to become familiar)	8.4 months
Environmental uncertainty (Average across 5 items on a 5-point scale response format)	3.0
Behavioral uncertainty (Typical time from initial contact to order placement)	4.6 months
Territory sparseness (Percentage of salesperson's time spent on travel)	23.0%
Annual sales	$133.4 million

ucts; rather, they are made for a line of related products. With these considerations in mind, it was felt that an appropriate key informant would be the sales manager in charge of a product line. Individuals in these positions are likely to be extremely knowledgeable about the downstream distribution function.

As described earlier, a commercial list of sales managers in firms with annual sales over $50 million was purchased and was used as the mailing list for the study.[5] A postcard was mailed to each of the individuals on the mailing list asking the firm to participate in the study. As an incentive to participate, the sales managers were told that a summary of the results would be provided to them. The survey instrument was developed with the assistance of on-site interviews with sales managers in about a dozen firms, who responded to an initial version of the questionnaire and gave us feedback that enabled us to identify potential problems with the questionnaire. After making the necessary changes, the final questionnaire was mailed to all the individuals in the sample who agreed to participate.

4.4. Measures

Each sales manager was asked to complete the questionnaire for a distinct self-selected product line; all the questions were answered at the level of this product line. The specific questions used to measure each of the variables involved in the propositions are described below.

4.5. Channel

The use of resellers was captured by responses to the following question:

What percentages of sales are made to the following types of customers?
________ end users
________ channel members (wholesalers, distributors, retailers)
100% total

The percentage sold to end-users (% DIRECT) constitutes the amount going through a direct channel. Sales to channel members represent the use of resellers.

4.6. Specific Assets

In order to measure this variable, we capitalize on the notion that products requiring a good deal of training and experience specific to the line represent situations where specific assets are present. This was measured with the following item:

5. The list included both industrial and consumer goods firms. Only the responses of the industrial goods manufacturers are analyzed here.

How much time is required for a newly hired salesperson with ***experience in the industry*** to become adequately familiar with your products and customers?
_______months.

This measure (SPSKILLS) does not measure the overall level of skill needed; rather, only the nontransferable component is measured. It specifies a person with prior experience in the industry. To the extent that the skills are transferable, such an individual would not need much time to adapt to this situation. This measure is similar to one used by Anderson.

4.7. Environmental Uncertainty

The inability to predict relevant contingencies is measured with the rating scale items described below. These items capture the extent to which the downstream marketing environment is volatile and turbulent.

How would you describe these products compared to other products in general?

Stable market shares	1	2	3	4	5	Volatile market shares
Easy to monitor trends	1	2	3	4	5	Difficult to monitor trends
Stable industry volume	1	2	3	4	5	Volatile industry volume
Sales forecasts are quite accurate	1	2	3	4	5	Sales forecasts are quite inaccurate
Predictable	1	2	3	4	5	Unpredictable

The measure (ENVUNCT) was formed by computing the average response to these five items. Social science researchers use this summated scale strategy to enhance the reliability of measures. Such a summation is reasonable only if the items are unidimensional in a factor-analytic sense and are internally consistent. Evidence of unidimensionality is provided by extracting all the principal components in these data. The results showed that only the first principal component had an eigenvalue greater than one, which indicates that one factor adequately describes the variance in the items. Evidence of internal consistency was provided by computing Cronbach's alpha, and this estimate (0.73) is well above the suggested 0.6 cutoff for basic research.[6]

4.8. Behavioral Uncertainty

The second aspect of uncertainty addressed here is the difficulty of assessing performance. We measure this variable by capitalizing on the notion that it is more difficult to ascertain adherence to contractual agreements by downstream actors when critical points in the selling cycle are separated by relatively longer periods of time. When transactions are performed instantaneously, the performance of each party is more readily observable. If the

6. See Churchill for a discussion of these issues related to summated scales. The appendix describes an alternative measurement model for this scale. The substantive results were robust across these procedures.

market reacts with a lag to actions taken, however, it becomes more difficult to attribute output to efforts. Each survey respondent answered the following question:

What is the typical time between an initial contact concerning the product and the ultimate placement of an order? ________months.

This measure (BEHUNCT) measures the length of the selling cycle and indexes the difficulty of assessing downstream performance.

4.9 Scale Variables

There are two scale variables included in the study. In the first of these, we asked the informant to report the sales volume of the product line in question (SALES).

What is the annual sales volume of this product line? $________

The second scale variable described the density of sales territories. The density of a sales territory refers to the geographic concentration of customers. Denser territories make it possible to assign a company employee to that territory and to use that person's time efficiently. In relatively sparser territories, it may not be possible to exhaust the available time of company personnel assigned to that area. By contrast, independent resellers are better able to exhaust scale economies by aggregating the products of different firms. We measure territory sparseness as follows:

What percent of the typical field salesperson's time is spent on the following activities?

________ face-to-face selling
________ service, after sales support
________ paper work
________ travel time
________ other
100%

Our measure of (lack of) density (SPARSE) is the fraction of time reported for travel. Obviously, more time is spent on the road when the density of the territory is lower. This is the same indicator of density used by Anderson.

5. RESULTS

The first model estimated from the data is a multiple regression model with the fraction of sales made through the direct channel (% DIRECT) as the dependent variable. The results are displayed in table 2. Since all the propositions specify the expected sign of the coefficient,[7] their significance is tested via 1-tail tests at the usual 0.05 level.

7. The dependent variable was first transformed using a logistic function, $ln\left[\frac{P}{1-p}\right]$, in order to constrain the range of predictions to lie between 0 and 100 on the original scale.

Table 2. Regression Model of Channel Configuration

Dependent variable: $LN \frac{\% \text{ DIRECT}}{(1 - \% \text{ DIRECT})}$

Independent Variable	Coefficient	T-value
Constant	−1.061	0.203
SPSKILLS	0.147	2.608*
ENVUNCT	0.773	1.806*
BEHUNCT	0.218	3.001*
LNSALES	−0.057	−0.204
SPARSE	−0.059	−1.988*

R^2adj = 0.281.
*sig. at $p \leq .05$ (1-tail).

The model explains about 28 percent of the variation in sales volume through the direct channel. As the F-ratio indicates, this is a significant amount of explained variance. Turning to the individual coefficients, we see that specific assets (SPSKILLS) increase significantly the fraction of sales made directly to end-users (b = 0.147, t = 2.608). This result lends support for Proposition 1.

Regarding the uncertainty variables involved in Propositions 2 and 3, we see that the environmental uncertainty coefficient (ENVUNCT) is significant in the direction posited in Proposition 2 (b = 0.773, t = 1.806). The behavioral uncertainty coefficient (BEHUNCT) exhibits a similar result (b = 0.218, t = 3.001), which supports Proposition 3.

The final set of independent variables are the scale effects variables. Sales volume (LNSALES) has no significant effect on the dependent variable (b = −0.057, t = −0.204). The other scale variable (SPARSE) indicates that sparser territories are related to significantly lower levels of direct channel sales (b = −0.059, t = −1.988). Thus, only mixed support is found for Proposition 4.

Sales volume excepted, the above results appear to provide considerable support for the TCA predictions. It is quite possible, however, that the linear model does not describe the organizational decision very well. Suppose these channel decisions were made in a relatively "lumpy" fashion where the firm chooses a direct, indirect, or mixed channel. The continuous dependent variable would not capture such a decision very well. Since the theoretical model is not sufficiently refined as to permit us to exclude either possibility, it would seem necessary to verify the robustness of the results. To achieve this, we estimated another model with these data. This consisted of a maximum-likelihood estimation of a multinomial logit model. The independent variables remain the same, while the dependent variable is respecified as a qualitative measure to represent the (possibly) discrete decision.

We placed the firms in the sample into three classifications; direct, mixed, and indirect channels based on a 90 percent rule. If a firm sold more than

90 percent of its volume through either a direct or an indirect channel, we classified that firm into the direct and indirect channel categories respectively. The remaining firms were classified into the mixed channel category. The 90 percent cutoff was established by inspecting the distribution of the dependent variable for natural breaks. This is the same classification rule used by Lilien.

This classification yielded 15 firms in the indirect channel category (17 percent), 39 firms in the mixed channel category (44 percent), and 33 firms in the direct channel category (38 percent). The following multinomial logit model describing the probability that a firm will fall into the ith category was estimated:

$$Prob\ (i/\bar{x}) = \frac{e^{\bar{x}\phi_i}}{\sum_{j=1}^{3} e^{\bar{x}\phi_j}}$$

where $\bar{x}$ is the vector of independent variables describing each firm and ϕ_i is the vector of coefficients associated with the i_{th} category.

Note that there is a set of ϕ_i coefficients associated with each category. Since these coefficients are determined only up to an arbitrary normalization, we have chosen the normalization $\phi_3 = 0$, where $i = 3$ describes the indirect channel. Each set of coefficients can now be interpreted as the effect of the independent variables on the probability of choice of that channel category relative to our chosen reference option (that is, the indirect category).

Table 3 displays the results of a maximum-likelihood estimation of this model. The Chi-square statistic displayed tests the hypothesis that the estimated coefficients (except the constant) are all zero. This is rejected at the 0.05 level.

Examining the significance of the ϕ_1 coefficients, we can see that SPSKILLS is significantly positive ($\phi = 0.187$, $t = 1.56$). Thus, as specific asset levels increase, the probability of using the direct channel increases relative to the probability of using the indirect channel. The environmental uncertainty measure displays a similar effect ($\phi = 1.66$, $t = 2.39$). The behavioral uncertainty measure is also significant in the expected directioin ($\phi = 0.553$, $t = 1.92$).

Turning to the scale-related variables, we see that sales (LNSALES) has no significant effect ($\phi = -0.011$, $t = -0.029$). Territory sparseness displays the anticipated significant negative coefficient, though ($\phi = -0.082$, $t = -1.78$).

As for the ϕ_2 coefficients, which assess the probability of the mixed channel category versus the indirect category, the specific assets coefficient is insignificant ($\phi = 0.097$, $t = 0.82$). The environmental uncertainty measure displays an expected positive coefficient, which is also significant ($\phi = 1.17$, $t = 1.80$). Similarly, the behavioral uncertainty measure displays a signifi-

Table 3. Multinomial Logit Model of Channel Configuration

Dependent variable: Direct, mixed, indirect channels
Reference category: indirect channel

Parameter ($\phi_{i=1}$)	Estimate	T-value
Constant	−4.446	−0.620
SPSKILLS	0.187	1.562*
ENVUNCT	1.660	2.394*
BEHUNCT	0.553	1.922*
LNSALES	−0.011	−0.029
SPARSE	−0.082	−1.781*
Parameter ($\phi_{i=2}$)		
Constant	−6.904	−1.062
SPSKILLS	−0.097	0.820
ENVUNCT	1.167	1.799*
BEHUNCT	0.480	1.686*
LNSALES	0.274	0.809
SPARSE	−0.075	−1.771*

Chi-Square (10 d.f.) = 31.64.
*sig. at $p \leq .05$ (1-tail).

Table 4. Independent Variable Derivatives

Variable	Direct	Mixed	Indirect
Constant	0.506	−0.688	0.182
SPSKILLS	0.023	−0.019	−0.004
ENVUNCT	0.137	−0.093	−0.043
BEHUNCT	0.024	−0.008	−0.016
LNSALES	−0.066	0.071	−0.005
SPARSE	−0.003	0.0003	0.002

cant, positive coefficient (ϕ = 0.48, t = 1.69). The scale variable describing sales volume is insignificant (ϕ = 0.274, t = 0.81), but the territory sparseness measure displays the expected significant negative effect (ϕ = −0.075, t = −1.77).

The substantive results implied by these coefficients are more readily interpreted by examining the estimates in table 4. These estimates are derivatives that show how a change in any of the independent variables would affect the distribution of channel choices. Looking at the results of SPSKILLS, we see that as specific assets increase, the probability of the direct channel increases (d_1 = 0.023), while the probability of the mixed channel option decreases (d_2 = −0.019) as does the probability of the indirect channel (d_3 = −0.043). With respect to environmental uncertainty, increases in this variable result in more direct channels (d_1 = 0.136), fewer mixed channels (d_2 = −0.093), and fewer indirect channels (d_3 = −0.043). Behavioral uncertainty displays a similar pattern of results (d_1 = 0.024, d_2 = −0.008, d_3 = −0.016).

Turning to the scale variable, we find that larger volumes decrease direct channels ($d_1 = -0.066$), increase mixed channels ($d_2 = 0.071$), and decrease indirect channels ($d_3 = -0.004$). These effects are not statistically significant, though. With respect to territory density, we see that increased sparseness decreases direct channels ($d_1 = -0.0028$) but increases mixed channels ($d_2 = 0.003$) and indirect channels ($d_3 = -0.002$).

Taken together, the results of the two models are remarkably consistent. They increase our confidence in the robustness of the effects found in the data. Specific assets and uncertainty consistently increased the use of direct channels. As for the scale variables, territory sparseness consistently decreased direct channel use, while the sales volume measure had no effect in either model.

6. DISCUSSION

To the best of our knowledge, this is the first empirical test of TCA predictions involving forward integration into distribution. Aside from Anderson's study of manufacturers' agents versus employee sales forces, no other empirical results concerning downstream integration have been reported. The results obtained here are supportive of the basic refutable predictions made form the TCA perspective. We saw that firms were less likely to use reseller channels when specific assets levels were higher. Similar shifts were observed for higher levels of environmental uncertainty and behavioral uncertainty.

Our study has several methodological and theoretical implications. From a methodological standpoint, it is the first study that has accounted for the possibility that firms do not use a single means of reaching the end-user. Integration is a matter of degree rather than a binary choice. Along these lines, Stinchcombe has argued persuasively that the continuous nature of these shifts should not be underestimated. In fact, his analysis would suggest an even more microanalytic approach with explicit measures of the actual hierarchical mechanisms involved.

The design of an empirical test of TCA predictions rests on developing sufficient information about the institutional forms present in the context of interest. It would appear that empirical studies of TCA propositions are best conducted at a semi-microanalytic level of detail. Accounting data are probably unlikely to suit the needs of such research. Rather, researchers will have to rely on the organizational and sociological tradition of using questionnaires and rating scale data. Large sample sizes and "representative" selection have to be sacrificed in order to obtain the requisite detailed information. Consequently, it becomes important to cumulate results across a series of smaller studies.

From the standpoint of theory development, we have already noted that the basic refutable propositions of the TCA approach are supported in this study. Nevertheless, the causal mechanisms underlying these results still await direct testing. For instance, it is presumed that the firm's response to environmental uncertainty is prompted by the desire to make decision adaptively and sequentially. No direct evidence of this mechanism is currently available in the literature. Similarly, the effects of specific assets on the integration decision is presumed to be a reaction to the firm's vulnerability to opportunism. If, however, an exchange were governed by a norm of non-opportunism, then the model would become much more complex. Integration would presumably be a response only if the normative restraint were inadequate. Such an extension of the basic model rests on uncovering the conditions governing the appearance and maintenance of such normative restraints on opportunism.

Finally, with respect to the variables relating to the production cost, the present results contrast with the only other previous study that included production costs (Walker and Weber). They concluded that "comparative production costs" were responsible for most of the explanatory power of their model. Further, transaction costs variables received only "mixed" support in their study.

By contrast, the transaction cost variables were responsible for most of the explanatory power of the current models. Only one of the two production cost variables proved significant. One reason for insignificant results involving the sales volume measure of scale may be due to variance in the minimum efficient scale (MES) of distribution-related activities across the industries represented in our sample. Since we do not have a measure of minimum efficient scale to adjust the sales variable, our measure must be viewed with some skepticism. This possibility appears even more likely when one considers the significant supportive results obtained with the other scale variable. Unlike sales volume, the territory sparseness measure is not affected by interindustry differences in efficient scale. Time spent traveling is always an unproductive use of resources. On balance, it appears that both production and transaction costs are implicated in firms' decisions to integrate into the downstream channel. Nevertheless, the differences in results between the two studies suggest that further attention needs to be directed to the role of production costs in TCA models.

APPENDIX

Computing an average rating for five items described in section 4.7 to form the ENVUNCT measure assumes that these data are scaled intervally. Although this assumption has been used in the previous empirical studies of TCA propositions involving questionnaire data (Anderson and Schmittlien; Walker and Weber) and is standard practice in many disciplines, it is sometimes argued that rating scales provide only rank-order data. In order to assess the robustness of our results with respect to this assumption, an alternative measurement model was fitted and the vertical integration models were reestimated. This alternative was the Rasch latent trait model described by Wright and Stone.

Rather than assuming that the observed responses are intervally scaled, the Rasch model assumes that the probability of a response to a rating scale item i is a function of the amount of the trait β_j presents in the subject j and a parameter δ_i that indexes the amount of the trait reflected in the item. Specifically,

$$Prob[x_{ji} = 1 \mid \beta_j, \delta_i] = exp(\beta_j - \delta_i)/[1 + exp(\beta_j - \delta_i)]$$

where $x_{ji} = 1$ when subject j responds favorably, and
0 when subject j responds unfavorably to item i.

Using a maximum-likelihood estimator (Wilkinson), one can obtain estimates of the amount of the trait present in each subject from the observed responses of all the subjects to all the items. These estimates of the trait are scaled intervally although the observed data are only categorical.

To apply this model to our data, we first dichotomize the responses to each of the five items. Responses above the midpoint on the scale were given the value 1 while responses below the midpoint were coded as 0. These represent the high and low uncertainty categories of responses. Then maximum likelihood estimates of the latent trait being measured were obtained for each subject. The resulting intervally scaled estimate of the trait for each subject β_j was used in place of the previously used measure (ENVUNCT) in the regression and multinomial logit models.

These reestimated models show no substantive differences compared to the originally estimated models shown in tables 2 and 3. All previously significant variables remain significant and retain their sign. Likewise, all previously insignificant variables remain insignificant. Thus, it appears that our assumption of interval data arising from the rating scale items does not affect the conclusions drawn from the study.

REFERENCES

Anderson, Erin. 1985. "The Salesperson as Outside Agent or Employee: A Transaction Cost Analysis," 4 *Marketing Science* 234–54.

Anderson, Erin, and David Schmittlein. 1984. "Integration of the Sales Force: An Empirical Investigation," 15 *Rand Journal of Economics* 385–95.

Anderson, Erin, and Benton Weitz. 1986. "Make or Buy Decisions: Vertical Integration and Marketing Productivity," 27 *Sloan Management Review* 3–20.

Arrow, Kenneth. 1969. "The Organization of Economic Activity: Issues Pertinent to the Choice of Market Versus Nonmarket Allocation," in *The Analysis and Evaluation of Public Expenditure: The PPB System*. Vol. 1. U.S. Joint Economic

Committee, 91st Cong., 1st Sess., Washington, D.C.: U.S. Government Printing Office 59–73.
———. 1971. *Essays in the Theory of Risk-Bearing*. Chicago: Markham.
Blair, Richard, and David Kaserman. 1983. *Law and Economics of Vertical Integration and Control*. New York: Academic Press.
Chandler, Alfred. 1977. *The Visible Hand: The Managerial Revolution in American Business*. Cambridge: Harvard University Press.
Churchill, Gilbert. 1979. "A Paradigm for Developing Better Measures of Marketing Constructs," 16 *Journal of Marketing Research* 64–73.
Coughlan, Anne. 1985. "Competition and Cooperation in Marketing Channel Choice: Theory and Application," 4 *Marketing Science* 110–29.
Diamond, William. 1963. *Distribution Channels for Industrial Goods*. Columbus: Ohio State University.
Green, Jerry. 1984. "Information in Economics," in K. Arrow and S. Honkapohja, eds., *Frontiers of Economics*. London: Basil Blackwell.
Haas, Robert. 1976. *Industrial Marketing Management*. New York: Petrocelli / Charter.
Heide, Jan, and George John. 1988. "The Role of Dependence Balancing in Safeguarding Transaction-Specific Assets in Conventional Channels," 52 *Journal of Marketing* 20–35.
Jackson, Barbara Bund. 1985. *Winning and Keeping Industrial Customers: The Dynamics of Customer Relationships*. Lexington, Mass.: Lexington Books.
John, George, and Torger Reve. 1982. "The Reliability and Validity of Key Informant Data from Dyadic Relationships in Marketing Channels," 19 *Journal of Marketing Research* 517–24.
Joskow, Paul. 1988. "Asset Specificity and the Structure of Vertical Relationships: Empirical Evidence," 4 *Journal of Law, Economics, and Organization* 95–117.
Lilien, Gary. 1979. "ADVISOR 2: Modeling the Marketing Mix Decision for Industrial Products," 25 *Management Science* 191–204.
Masten, Scott. 1984. "The Organization of Production: Evidence from the Aerospace Industry," 27 *Journal of Law and Economics* 403–18.
Monteverde, Kirk, and D. Teece. 1982. "Supplier Switching Costs and Vertical Integration in the Automobile Industry," 13 *Bell Journal of Economics* 206–13.
Palay, Thomas. 1984. "Comparative Institutional Economics: The Governance of Rail Freight Contracting," 13 *Journal of Legal Studies* 265–88.
Shapiro, Benson. 1977. *Sales Program Management: Formulation and Implementation*. New York: McGraw-Hill.
Stern, Louis, and Adel El-Ansary. 1982. *Marketing Channels*. Second Edition. Englewood Cliffs, N.J.: Prentice-Hall.
Stinchcombe, Arthur. 1985. "Contracts as Hierarchical Documents," in *Organization Theory and Project Management*, A. L. Stinchcombe and C. A. Heimer. Oslo: Norwegian University Press.
Stuckey, John. 1983. *Vertical Integration and Joint Ventures in the Aluminum Industry*. Cambridge: Harvard University Press.
Sutton, Harold. 1986. *Rethinking the Company's Selling and Distribution Channels*. Report No. 885. Conference Board.
U.S. Bureau of the Census 1980. *1977 Census of Wholesale Trade*. Geographic Area Services, Report No. WC77–A–52.
Walker, Gordon, and David Weber. 1984. "A Transaction Cost Approach in Make-or-Buy Decisions," 29 *Administrative Science Quarterly* 373–91.
Wilkinson, Leland. 1986. *SYSTAT: The System for Statistics*. Evanston, Ill.: SYSTAT.

Williamson, Oliver. 1979. "Transaction Cost Economics: The Governance of Contractual Relations," 22 *Journal of Law and Economics* 233–62.

———. 1985. *The Economic Institutions of Capitalism: Firms, Markets, Relational Contracting*. New York: Free Press.

Wright, Benjamin, and Michael Stone. 1979. *Best Test Design: Rasch Measurement*. Chicago: MESA Press.

[16]

Asset Specificity and the Structure of Vertical Relationships: Empirical Evidence

PAUL L. JOSKOW
Massachusetts Institute of Technology

A meeting to celebrate the fiftieth anniversary of "The Nature of the Firm" could not take place at a more appropriate time. Theoretical and empirical research into the kinds of issues raised by Professor Coase in his 1937 paper has increased substantially in recent years. It is a good time to take stock of where we are, how we got here, and where we are going in this area.

I have been asked to do two things in this paper. First, to discuss the theoretical research that has had an important influence on my own thinking and research on issues related to the nature of the firm. I will use this opportunity to reminisce about my own intellectual enlightenment to provide a historical survey of the conceptual developments that I feel have been of most importance. Second, to review recent empirical research that has been stimulated by this theoretical work. Since my recent research interests in this area have focused primarily on issues associated with the structure of vertical relationships, and, in particular, the role of asset specificity, transactions costs, and incomplete contracts, it is this strand of the literature that I will focus on here.

1. TRANSACTIONS COSTS, INCOMPLETE CONTRACTS, AND ASSET SPECIFICITY

I first read the paper whose anniversary we are here to celebrate when I was in my first year of graduate school here at Yale. When I arrived at Yale

Journal of Law, Economics, and Organization vol. 4, no. 1 Spring 1988

in the fall of 1968, I chose the industrial organization course (140a) as my one free elective. The course was taught by Richard Nelson, who had recently returned to Yale from Rand. I recall arriving early for the first meeting of the course along with a couple of other students. Dick Nelson arrived early too. We chatted with Dick in the nervous way that first-year students are apt to do, and it soon became clear that our professor had never taught an industrial organization course before. We were lucky. Rather than concentration ratios, profit rates, measurement of scale economies, and interindustry regressions of these variables on one another, the course focused on the structure and behavior of firms and related organizations. It was a very exciting course.

In a more recent paper Professor Coase (1972) discussed the state of industrial organization at that time. While his characterization and criticisms of what the field was like then reflects my own views very well, Dick Nelson's course was nothing like that at all. We read papers by Coase, Alchian, Simon, Cyert and March, Marschak and Radner, Chandler, Williamson, Winter, Arrow, Downs, Niskanen, and others. The industrial organization field to which we were introduced included discussions of manufacturing firms and nonmanufacturing firms, for-profit and nonprofit firms, government bureaucracies and other political institutions. We were asked to explore questions about the boundaries between firms and markets, the internal organization of firms, the costs of obtaining, processing, and communicating information, information flows and decisionmaking within firms, organizational objectives, and organizational behavior. I am fairly sure that we never learned what a concentration ratio was or why it might be of interest.

My interest in the nature of firms and other organizations can be traced directly to Economics 140a at Yale. This exposure to the literature on firm and organizational structure and behavior, combined with my interests in empirical applications and public policy that brought me to Yale, have largely defined the kinds of problems that I find interesting to work on as well as my approach to these problems.

At that time I had not yet focused on "transactions costs" as being of central importance to my understanding of the boundary between firms and markets, the structure of firms, and the nature of contractual relationships between firms at different levels of the production chain. As a new Ph.D. in 1972 I was still very much influenced by the psychological and sociological perspective developed by Herbert Simon and his students. Indeed, I think that it is fair to say that I was suspicious of the use of vague notions of transactions costs for explaining economic institutions that did not fit neatly into the model of perfect competition. I did not find a clear and consistent body of theoretical work that carefully identified what the relevant transactions costs were, why they were important in some contexts but not in others, and how institutional arrangements should be expected to respond to them. My concern was that one could always invent a specification of transactions costs that could rationalize almost anything.[1] By rationalizing everything we might really be explaining nothing.

My interest in transactions costs was stimulated considerably by the work that Oliver Williamson was doing about the time that I began teaching at MIT. After I came to MIT in 1972, Williamson sent me drafts of a manuscript that was to be published as *Markets and Hierarchies* in 1975. I still remember reading those drafts. It was hard going. I was confronted with a whole new language plus an older language used in new ways; information impactedness, opportunism, small-numbers bargaining, bounded rationality, etc.[2] I felt that there was something important there, however, and worked hard to understand what Williamson was saying. I understood that uncertainty, adverse selection problems, moral hazard problems, the costs of writing, monitoring, and enforcing contracts, sequential bargaining over the distribution of benefits associated with sunk investments, and so on were all somehow important. However, I don't think that I understood how it all fit together or how these considerations could be related systematically to variations in institutional arrangements.

The most important thing that I took away from *Markets and Hierarchies* was the "comparative institutional" perspective. That is, a general recognition that there is a wide range of institutional arrangements that can be used to govern transactions between economic agents. Specific institutional arrangements emerge in response to various transactional considerations in order to minimize the total cost of making transactions. The boundary between a firm and a market provides a very rough distinction between the two primary institutional mechanisms for allocating resources, but this is the beginning, not the end, of the inquiry. Firms can take on many different organization structures. Market transactions can take many different forms ranging from simple spot market transactions to complex long-term contracts. The specific set of institutional arrangements chosen would represent the governance structure that minimized the total cost of consummating the transactions of interest.

Markets and Hierarchies also had important implications for antitrust policy, around which so much of contemporary industrial organization had evolved. Many of the institutional arrangements that conventional economic theory could not explain as natural outcomes of a model of perfect competition—vertical integration, contractual vertical restraints, joint ventures, and certain other horizontal agreements—were viewed as being suspect within the Bain-Mason branch of industrial organization and were often presumed to be a consequence of monopoly power or efforts to obtain it. This

1. This concern was shared by my colleague Stanley Fischer (1977).

2. I think that I am the anonymous colleague expressing some difficulty with the exposition whom Williamson (1975:xii) quotes in the preface. Alas, my correspondence files are not nearly as complete as are Professor Coase's.

view provided the intellectual basis for antitrust policies that are now in disrepute and have, to a great extent, been reversed.[3]

One can of course find these same themes in Coase's 1937 paper and certainly in his 1972 paper. And of course, the Chicago branch of industrial organization had a very different perspective on antitrust policy. But for me, it is *Markets and Hierarchies* that put needed structure on this perspective. It provided the foundation for a theory of institutional choice and design that had the prospect of yielding clear causal relationships between transactional characteristics and institutional arrangements. This in turn began to give us a theoretical framework that could be subjected to empirical verification. However, as of 1975 I think that it is fair to say that I found what was now the Coase/Williamson view in my own mind to be interesting, but I did not know what to do with it or have much interest in doing something with it myself.

Several papers that appeared after 1975 helped to improve my understanding of the transactions cost framework and how it could be used to explain the choice and structure of institutional arrangements designed to minimize the costs of transacting. The first paper was Williamson's (1976) paper on franchise bidding for monopoly franchises. This paper included a case study of the franchising process for the cable television franchise in Oakland, California. The paper is in a sense a reply to the franchise bidding solution to the natural monopoly problems advanced by Demsetz (1968). Williamson uses the transactions cost framework to provide an alternative analysis of bidding for monopoly franchises.[4] He argues quite convincingly that in the real world characterized by uncertainty, changing input prices, changing technology, multiple products, long-lived investments specific to a particular buyer/seller relationship, there are significant costs associated with writing, monitoring, and enforcing the different types of contracts between a supplier and a municipality that are the outcome of a franchise bidding scheme. The characteristics of the product at issue—a cable television system offering a variety of service—led Williamson to conclude that the least cost governance structure emerging from a franchise bidding process in this case will be an incomplete long-term contract that has adaptive properties with many similarities to public utility regulation.

The analysis of franchise bidding through the transactions cost lens does not necessarily mean that franchise bidding is inferior to state commission regulation of franchised monopolies either in general or with regard to cable television circa 1970, but rather that the two modes of control may not be

3. It should be recalled that the full title of Williamson's 1975 book is *Markets and Hierarchies: Analysis and Antitrust Implications*.

4. As Demsetz (57, n. 7) recognizes, the franchise bidding approach can be traced back at least to a paper by Chadwick published in 1859. Municipal franchising and regulation also characterized the provision of electricity, telephone, and gas service in the United States prior to the rapid diffusion of state commission regulation after 1907.

as different as first meets the eye.[5] Williamson (1976:74) argues that both modes of organization must confront a variety of command and control problems because of the characteristics of the transaction, both are imperfect compared to some abstract ideal, and that they differ "mainly in degree, rather than in kind." The comparative institutional perspective comes out very clearly. What is the best that we can do in an imperfect world? The analysis can usefully be guided by theory, but the answer to the public policy question is inherently an empirical matter. It cannot be resolved "in theory."

Victor Goldberg's (1976) paper further develops the relational contracting paradigm contained in Williamson's paper and applies it more broadly to the economic analysis of public utility regulation.[6] Goldberg's primary point is that traditional economic analysis of the benefits and costs of regulation implicitly assumes that the alternative to regulation is a perfectly competitive market or a frictionless, transactions-cost-free franchise bidding system. This type of comparison will necessarily make administrative regulation look bad because it necessarily has imperfections. But Goldberg argues convincingly, as does Williamson, that this is the wrong comparison to make. "Many of the problems associated with regulation lie in what is being regulated, not in the act of regulation itself" (Goldberg, 1976:426). Public utility regulation is an administrative contract that must be compared to contractual arrangements that are realistic alternatives to the regulatory status quo. Williamson and Goldberg make it clear that we must start our analysis of institutional choice, whether the analysis is normative or positive, with a complete understanding of the characteristics of the transactions that buyers and sellers are seeking to consummate. We can then identify the problems that must be confronted to provide for an efficient trading relationship and compare alternative institutional arrangements in terms of their ability to cope efficiently with these problems. Thus, in evaluating traditional public utility regulation we must carefully and completely articulate the nature and expected performance of the institutions that we anticipate will replace it given the characteristics of the services being regulated and the transactional problems associated with these characteristics that must be confronted.

The Williamson and Goldberg papers had an important effect on my own understanding of the importance of the economic characteristics that characterize specific buyer and seller relationships and the role of transactions costs in determining the cost-minimizing governance structure for exchange. My thinking is always stimulated by a concrete example and Williamson

5. Indeed, two recent MIT Ph.D. theses have examined the performance of cable TV franchising using comprehensive data bases (Prager and Zupan). They find that, with some exceptions, reneging on franchise agreements and renegotiation problems at the refranchising stage have not been a serious problem in practice. There are other inefficiencies associated with franchise bidding for cable TV franchises, however.

6. While Goldberg's paper appeared after Williamson's, I believe that the two papers were written at about the same time.

provided one. Furthermore, my general interests in regulation meant that these papers had focused transactions cost considerations on issues of central concern to me. The combination of durable relationship-specific investments, uncertainty about future demand and cost realizations, and contractual incompleteness arising from the costs of writing, monitoring, and enforcing full contingent claims contracts began to emerge as the key elements of this theoretical approach to understanding institutional choice and design.

Two additional papers helped to crystallize these ideas for me. Klein, Crawford, and Alchian's (1978) paper was certainly very influential in clarifying my thinking on the broad challenge raised by Coase and advanced by Williamson. They focus very clearly on the importance of relationship-specific investments, combined with incomplete contracts, as the critical factors that lead simple spot market transactions to be plagued by transactional difficulties. Klein, Crawford, and Alchian argue that more complex long-term contracts may be an attractive alternative to spot markets, but that incomplete long-term contracts can run into performance problems as well. They argue that coordination problems arising from specific investments will be less severe if the transaction is internalized. As a result, they hypothesize that internal organization (vertical integration) is more likely to become the preferred governance structure the more important are specific investments by the buyer and/or the seller. The exposition in this paper was clear and it was backed up with several interesting examples, the relationship between General Motors and Fisher Auto Body being the one that I found most interesting.[7]

Williamson's (1979) contemporaneous paper focuses much more attention on the importance of asset specificity and idiosyncratic investments than does his early book and papers.[8] It also focuses more on the structure of vertical relationships between firms, independent of the internal structure of the organization, internal labor markets, and so forth. The paper develops a clear mapping between three dimensions of transactions—the degree of asset specificity, the importance of uncertainty,[9] and the frequency of transactions—and the cost-minimizing governance structure for transactions between different levels in the supply chain. The paper also concludes with some concrete predictions about the nature of the institutional arrangements that are likely to emerge with different combinations of these three variables.

7. Coase's lectures indicate that he identified asset specificity as being of potential importance in an unpublished letter more than forty years earlier. He also studied the GM/Fisher Body relationship at that time. His third lecture suggests, however, that he no longer believes that asset specificity is of great importance for understanding vertical integration and long-term contracts.

8. *Markets and Hierarchies* focuses much more on ex-ante and ex-post information asymmetries, although the opportunism problem is developed clearly in this context. Long-lived assets specific to the relationship play a more important role in Williamson's 1976 paper.

9. Uncertainty is treated in the text (253–54), but not in the tables and figures included in the paper.

For example, as investments become more specific to the buyer/seller relationship, Williamson anticipates that cost-minimizing institutional choice will respond by moving from simple anonymous (spot) market contracting (classical contract law), to more complex long-term contractual arrangements with protective provisions (neoclassical contract law), and ultimately to internal organization. Williamson defines transaction- or relationship-specific investments more completely in a subsequent paper (Williamson, 1983).

By 1980, this body of research had moved us from a general understanding of the importance of transactions costs in explaining the choice between firms and markets and issues associated with the internal organization of the firm, to a fairly specific theory for explaining the structure of vertical relationships based on variations in the importance of asset specificity, uncertainty, product complexity, and the constraints of repeat purchase activity.[10] Asset specificity means that hold-up or opportunism problems must be confronted by the transacting parties at the contract execution stage. Full contingent claims contracts become more costly to write, monitor, and enforce when uncertainty and complexity increase (that is, there are more contingencies). Incomplete long-term contracts are a potentially attractive alternative to sequential spot market trade, but such contracts will necessarily be imperfect governance mechanisms. The more costly it is to contract on all contingencies and the greater the ex-ante incentive effects of potential ex-post hold-ups, the more imperfect long-term contracts are likely to be. Internal organization has costs, but as the costs of incomplete long-term contracts increase, internal control is likely to become more attractive. This suggests that if we can find a way to measure variations in the choice of governance structure and can match these choices with measures of the associated degree of asset specificity, uncertainty, and complexity, we are on our way to being able to test this theory empirically.

I do not want to suggest that by 1980 this theory of the determinants of the structure of vertical relationships was all neatly tied down. The theory did not have a rigorous mathematical foundation and, it is my perception, was not taken very seriously at that time by those who call themselves theorists.[11] How this all related to the evolving theory of agency which relied so heavily on information asymmetries and risk aversion was elusive (and still is).[12] Of more concern, exactly why internal organization should be expected to yield outcomes superior to imperfect market transactions was not, in my mind, developed very well. Rather, there was an implicit reliance on

10. I have not emphasized the role of reputation in this discussion, but it plays a role in both Williamson's and Klein's work.

11. This never concerned me too much since so much of what passes as "theory" is little more than toy models with no obvious value in explaining real economic phenomena. Really good theory is too rare but is of fundamental importance to our understanding of these phenomena.

12. It should be emphasized, however, the information asymmetries, moral hazard, and adverse selection problems were central to Williamson's discussion in *Markets and Hierarchies*.

the power of the master-servant relationship to resolve disputes that would otherwise arise when independent firms deal with each other through a market. Many of these gaps have been explored in more depth since then, as theorists have come to recognize the importance of the ideas advanced by Coase, Williamson, Goldberg, Klein, and others and have turned their attention to the development of a more complete theoretical structure.[13] In any event, things had moved far enough by 1980 or so that the stage was set for more systematic empirical work, going beyond individual examples, aimed at testing the causal relationships suggested by this theoretical framework.

2. VERTICAL INTEGRATION IN THE ELECTRIC POWER INDUSTRY

Before proceeding with a discussion of this recent empirical work and my own efforts to contribute to it, I would like to detour slightly to discuss my first effort to apply what I had learned from this body of research to a particular problem. Beginning in 1978 or so, several sectors of the economy that had been subject to pervasive price and entry regulation for many years were fully or partially deregulated. These sectors included airlines, trucking, railroads, telecommunications, cable television, etc. After President Reagan took office, the pressure to extend the deregulation movement to other industries and aspects of economic activity increased. Sometime in late 1981 or early 1982, Richard Schmalensee and I were asked by the Department of Energy to do a study of the prospects and problems associated with deregulation for the electric utility industry. This study eventually became a book entitled *Markets for Power: An Analysis of Electric Utility Deregulation* (Joskow and Schmalensee, 1983).

I will not go into the details of our analysis of the many proposals for restructuring and deregulation that were being discussed, but I do want to emphasize the contribution of what we had learned from the transactions cost research that was maturing at about that time. The traditional analysis of restructuring and partial deregulation of the electric utility industry assumed implicitly that there were no benefits from vertical integration. Indeed it implicitly took the posture that vertical integration, long-term requirements contracts, and the like were sinister instruments to monopolize the business. The "irrelevant complications" that Williamson (1976) and Goldberg (1976) found to be so important for comparing alternative control mechanisms were ignored. The books called certain functions (for example, generation, transmission, distribution) by different names so it was simply assumed that they could be costlessly separated into independent firms and that "the market" could be relied upon to govern efficiently exchange relationships between them. There were many generating plants, so "in theory"

13. See, for example, Hart and Holmstrom and the references they cite, and Grossman and Hart.

a competitive generation market which relied on simple spot market transactions to govern trade would result.

Schmalensee and I observed that the nature of generation, transmission, and distribution technology and the physical operating characteristics of an integrated AC electric power system suggested that the "irrelevant complications" that were being ignored were likely to be of considerable potential importance. Long-lived investments specific to individual geographical areas, transmission nodes, fuel supply, and transportation opportunities were the norm. Planning of generation and transmission were intimately related to one another and were as much substitutes as complements. Power flowed according to the laws of physics, not according to the terms of contracts, and it moved very fast. The efficient and reliable operation of the system was quite complex. Following Williamson and Goldberg, we recognized that these realities had important implications for the structure of electricity supply entities and the kinds of governance structure that would emerge in the absence of vertical integration. We went on to discuss the kinds of contractual relationships that might emerge with different degrees of government-mandated vertical disintegration and with different assumptions about the nature of electric power technology.

The purpose of our analysis was not to show that restructuring and deregulation was necessarily a bad idea. Indeed, we concluded that some restructuring and deregulation of certain aspects of electricity supply might be a very good idea. What we did try to show was that the model against which the existing system was being compared was unrealistic and would not work well if it were imposed. Many of the problems perceived with the electric power industry were inherent problems associated with the characteristics of electricity supply, not problems that were simply a consequence of public utility regulation. These problems would have to be confronted by any institutional alternative to the status quo. As a result, we argued that the analysis of alternative public policies toward competition and regulation in the electric power industry should carefully incorporate the important transactional characteristics associated with the efficient production of electricity.

I think that we succeeded in elevating the discussion of restructuring, deregulation, and competition to a higher plain. Gradual restructuring is now taking place in this industry, and more reliance on competition in just those areas we identified as being most conducive to it is taking place today (Joskow, 1986). The role of long-term contracts and the benefits and costs of vertical integration have become central to the debate.

3. ASSET SPECIFICITY, VERTICAL INTEGRATION, AND LONG-TERM CONTRACTS: EMPIRICAL EVIDENCE

I think that Schmalensee and I would have been much happier with our analysis if there had been more (any!) empirical support available for the transactions cost perspective that we found so intuitively appealing and so consistent with the historical evolution of the electric power industry. At about the time we finished our book more empirical analysis of and support for the transactions cost perspective to vertical integration and long-term contracts finally began to emerge. I will now proceed to discuss this recent empirical work. I start with work that focuses on vertical integration and then go on to discuss empirical work that examines "nonstandard" contractual relationships between buyers and sellers.

3.1. Vertical Integration

As I suggested above, by roughly 1980 the theoretical discussion of the role of transactions costs in determining the nature of the firm and the structure of "nonstandard" market relationships between firms had been refined considerably. From the broad set of issues regarding the structure of firms and markets raised by Coase (1937, 1972) and Williamson (1975), the discussion had come to focus on the determinants of vertical integration (internal organization) and the nature of contractual relationships between firms at different levels of the production process.[14] The importance of asset specificity had become the key factor used to explain departures from governance by simple spot market transactions. Indeed, things had moved far enough along that we had a theory that was conducive to empirical verification.

For useful empirical work to proceed several conditions must be satisfied. First, we need a theory that provides us with clear structural relationship between a set of dependent variables and a set of independent variables. Second, we need to be able to measure empirically variations in the key independent and dependent variables. Finally, ideally, we should have one or more alternative and observationally distinct theories that explain variations in the independent variables of interest so that the competing theories can be compared to one another.[15]

The bare-bones theory that has evolved from this literature appears to be something like the following: when specific investments represent a significant fraction of the costs of consummating an efficient vertical supply arrangement, the reliance on simple anonymous spot market transactions is

14. This is not to suggest that issues associated with horizontal integration and the internal organization of firms are not important. Transactions cost theory has just not developed as far in exploring these issues.

15. Let me emphasize that I do not believe that there is a single general theory that will ever provide a unified explanation of vertical integration and the structure of long-term contracts. There are a variety of economic characteristics that will influence firm decisions to organize and contract in different ways. At least some of the alternative theories need to be developed further so that they can yield hypotheses that can be subjected to empirical verification. Stigler, Warren-Boulton, and Perry offer theories that are not necessarily in conflict with transactions cost theories, but rather suggest that there are situations where vertical integration will be relied upon even in the absence of asset specificity and the like.

likely to be an unsatisfactory governance mechanism for inducing the parties to make the specific investments necessary to yield a least-cost supply relationship. Anonymous spot markets fail because the sinking of relationship-specific investments transforms a large-numbers bargaining situation ex ante into a small-numbers bargaining situation ex post in which one or both parties have an opportunity to extract a portion of the quasi-rent stream associated with the specific investments. To induce the parties to make optimal investments ex ante, some method must be found to constrain the ex-post hold-up and haggling problems that would emerge if the parties relied on repeated bargaining over the terms of trade ex post. In principle this can be accomplished if the parties can costlessly contract on the specific investments that they agree to make, the quantities they agree to deliver, and the prices that they agree to pay when various contingencies arise as the contractual relationship plays out over time.[16] They are likely to be able to do so only imperfectly, however. This is because there are costs associated with writing, monitoring, and enforcing contracts and because there are likely to be information asymmetries. Furthermore, long-term contracts themselves may introduce costs and performance problems of their own. Internal organization or vertical integration is viewed as a method for overcoming some of the problems associated with imperfect long-term contracts, although vertical integration may confront costs of its own as well. The ultimate choice of governance structure requires balancing the costs and benefits of these alternative governance systems.

The theory suggests that we think of the primary dependent variable here as being a limited dependent variable that indicates what mode of organization will be chosen by the parties to the transactions: vertical integration, long-term contracts, or spot market trade. Finer distinctions within each of these three categories could also be made. Other things equal, we expect the parties more frequently to choose vertical integration or a long-term contract as the quasi-rents associated with specific investments become more important and the associated benefits of precommitment increase. Some measure of asset specificity is therefore a necessary independent variable to consider in any empirical analysis. There are likely to be different transactions and organization costs associated with vertical integration and long-term contracts that are not present with simple spot markets. Difficulties in writing, monitoring, and enforcing a long-term contract that can respond efficiently to changing market conditions over time may impose costs that tip the balance toward vertical integration. Internal organization costs, scale economies, experience, and so forth may tip the balance back toward contract

16. The implication of Fudenberg, Holmstrom, and Milgrom appears to be that if we assume that there is no private information (common knowledge), only the ability to contract on the specific investments is necessary. If the parties can contract on the specific investments and there is common knowledge, then the parties can rely on sequential renegotiation to determine prices and quantities at each point in time. These are strong assumptions.

or spot market mechanisms. Ideally, we should also include independent variables measuring these costs as well.[17]

Given this structural framework, we are left with the task of measuring the choices among alternative vertical structures (the dependent variables), measuring variations in the importance of asset specificity, and measuring the transactions costs of the various alternatives to simple spot market transactions. These measurement tasks are not trivial. At least in principle we should be able to determine whether specific types of transactions involve internal production, long-term contracts, or simple spot market transactions. We can in principle distinguish important differences between long-term contracts such as the extent of precommitment, the use of financial hostages (Williamson, 1983), and various other protective measures. In practice, this kind of very disaggregated firm and input-specific data can be very difficult to obtain. Relying on industry level data and inter-industry comparisons, as has been typical in empirical work in industrial organization (Schmalensee, 1987), is not likely to be at all satisfactory.

Even if we can get satisfactory measures of variations in the structure of vertical relationships, we must, at the very least, find some way to measure variations in the importance of asset specificity. This is even a more difficult task. How do we know whether a particular investment has the specificity characteristics of interest? How do we measure how important the ex-post performance problems would be if repeated bargaining were relied upon? How do we measure the nature and costs of the agents' production decisions if denied the opportunity to rely on nonstandard arrangements to minimize ex-post performance problems? We are certainly not going to find these numbers written down neatly in a book of industry statistics. The best that we can hope for is more qualitative information on variations in the importance of asset specificity.

Williamson's (1983) discussion of four distinct types of relationship-specific investment is very helpful for identifying and measuring variations in the importance of asset specificity. Very briefly, they are:

(a) Site specificity: The buyer and seller are in a "cheek-by-jowl" relationship with one another, reflecting ex-ante decisions to minimize inventory and transportation costs. Once sited, the assets in place are highly immobile.

(b) Physical asset specificity: When one or both parties to the transaction make investments in equipment and machinery that involves design characteristics specific to the transaction and which have lower values in alternative uses.

(c) Human asset specificity: Investments in relationship-specific human capital that often arise through a learning-by-doing process.

17. Leaving these variables out may not be a serious problem in certain circumstances. See the approach taken by Masten (1984).

(d) Dedicated assets: General investments by a supplier that would not otherwise be made but for the prospect of selling a significant amount of product to a particular customer. If the contract were terminated prematurely it would leave the supplier with significant excess capacity.

With this framework in mind, let me turn to a discussion of the empirical evidence.[18]

Monteverde and Teece (1982) (henceforth, M-T) is the first systematic effort to try to examine empirically the role of asset specificity in determining the structure of vertical relationships. They focus on the choice between internal production (vertical integration) and market procurement of automobile components by Ford and General Motors (GM). They work with a list of 133 automotive components and determine whether each is produced internally or purchased through the market.[19] In this way, they measure variations in the choice of vertical integration or market procurement using a dichotomous dependent variable that takes on a value of one if the component is manufactured internally and zero otherwise. They are concerned only about the choice between vertical integration and market procurement and not about intermediate contractual forms.

The focus of the M-T paper is on applications engineering effort as a measure of the degree of asset specificity. This would appear to fall into Williamson's (1983) category of "human asset specificity." They state their hypothesis as follows: "The greater is the applications engineering effort associated with the development of any given automobile component, the higher are the expected appropriable quasi rents, and therefore, the greater is the likelihood of vertical integration of production for that component" (Monteverde and Teece, 1982:207). To measure variations in applications engineering effort an index of its importance was developed with the help of an automobile design engineer. The expectation is that where applications engineering is more important, vertical integration will be more prevalent. A dummy variable is also used to identify components as either "specific" to a particular company or "generic" to all auto companies. M-T expect to find that "specific" components will have a higher probability of being vertically integrated. Finally, a dummy variable is used to distinguish between observations for GM and Ford. This variable may pick up idiosyncratic differences

18. It is not my intention to survey all of the empirical evidence. I will discuss my favorite papers.

19. In fact this is not an all-or-nothing decision. Internal production *and* market procurement takes place for many components. M-T choose an arbitrary cutoff value for the proportion of each component's supply that is attributable to internal production to define whether it is "integrated" or "not integrated" based on this cutoff value. The results are not sensitive to certain variations in the cutoff, however. It is not clear why a continuous variable measuring the proportion of production attributed to vertical integration was not used, perhaps in conjunction with a switching regressions technique.

between Ford and GM or serve as a very imperfect proxy for the role of scale economies as a potential cost of vertical integration. In the latter case we would expect GM to be more integrated than Ford, other things equal.[20]

A natural question that arises at this point is: What is the alternative explanation for variations in make or buy decisions? An alternative theory is not provided here. Furthermore, the simultaneous comparison of many models can be methodologically very difficult. Instead, as is quite common in this line of work and economics more generally, hypothesis testing pertains to a single model which is either consistent or inconsistent with the data. If it is inconsistent with the data it is rejected. If it is consistent with the data it is implicitly accepted until new hypothesis or data can be examined. In M-T, the null hypothesis is simply that asset specificity is not important for explaining variations in vertical integration. The alternative hypothesis is that vertical integration is more likely when asset specificity is more important.

M-T's results lead to the rejection of this null hypothesis. The coefficient estimates obtained are consistent with the predictions of the asset specificity/transactions cost theory. More applications effort, more specificity, and a large firm (GM) make vertical integration more likely. This empirical work therefore provides support for the view that variations in asset specificity affect the choice between vertical integration and market procurement as hypothesized.

Scott Masten (1984) provides a related empirical analysis of make or buy decisions by an aerospace firm for the components of a large system that it had contracted to provide to the government. Masten's analysis takes more explicit account of the comparative institutional choice aspect of the problem, by explicitly setting up the empirical analysis as an expected cost-minimizing problem involving the choice between two alternative governance mechanisms, and by attempting to incorporate directly considerations reflecting the costs of internalization versus market procurement.

The empirical analysis proceeds in the following way. A sample of components is drawn and a dichotomous variable indicating whether the component is produced internally or purchased in the market is the dependent variable. A questionnaire was given to the firm's procurement team to obtain their rankings of the various components in terms of their "specificity" and "complexity." Two measures of specificity are utilized. One is a measure of design specificity based on questionnaire responses as to whether the components were "specific," "somewhat specific," or "standard" vis-à-vis this system.[21] The second is a measure of site specificity or colocation. A third variable measures the complexity of the component and is designed to cap-

20. M-T also group components into systems, using system-specific dummy variables, but have no prior expectations about which systems are characterized by greater asset specificity.

21. Two dummy variables are used. The first indicates whether the component is highly specific or not. The second indicates whether the component is standard or not. The "somewhat specialized" category is the comparison group.

ture the costs of writing complete contracts. The more important are these variables, Masten hypothesizes, the higher are the costs of market contracting compared to internal organization. Masten, following Williamson, assumes that as complete contracting becomes more costly, vertical integration is more likely. A maximum likelihood model is specified in which the probability of the firm choosing vertical integration is equal to the probability that the costs of governance through vertical integration are lower than the costs of trading through the market.

Masten finds that variations in the importance of asset specificity affect the choice between vertical integration and market procurement as hypothesized. The specificity and complexity variables have the expected signs and are very significant, while the other variables generally have the expected signs. This is further evidence that asset specificity considerations are important for understanding the structure of vertical relationships. It also suggests that contractual "complexity" as well as asset specificity leads vertical integration to be chosen over contracting.

Anderson and Schmittlein look at a different dimension of internalization. They examine firm decisions to integrate the marketing function as measured by their reliance on employee sales personnel (direct sales people) or independent sales agents (manufacturer's representatives) to market products to customers. Direct sales people are employees of a single firm and are paid a salary or salary plus incentive payment. Manufacturer's representatives are organized as separate firms and represent many manufacturers. The use of direct sales people is the integrated governance structure. The focus of the analysis is on the role of asset specificity, the difficulty in monitoring the performance of sales personnel (as a measure of asymmetric information problems), and scale economies (a potential source of internalization costs), in the choice between organizational modes. The asset specificity in question here is related to Williamson's notion of "human asset specificity."

Anderson and Schmittlein make use of a data base they develop for firms in the electronic components industry. The unit of analysis is the product line of individual firms sold into specific sales territories. An index of asset specificity based on the results of a questionnaire is developed which takes account of variations in service territory characteristics and company size. The authors find that as asset specificity becomes more important, vertical integration is more likely. They also find that vertical integration is more likely when it is more difficult to evaluate the performance of sales personnel. Finally, larger firms are more likely to utilize employees to market their products. The results are quite consistent with the predictions of transactions cost theory.

Stuckey provides a very interesting, though rarely cited, study of vertical integration in the aluminum industry. Unlike the previous studies, this is a more traditional empirical industry study that does not rely extensively on econometric analysis. Nevertheless, Stuckey has put together a great deal of information on vertical integration, contractual relationships, and the characteristics of the firms and products involved at all stages of the aluminum industry. He argues quite convincingly that the extensive reliance on vertical integration between bauxite mines and alumina refineries is a consequence of physical asset specificity and site specificity considerations. These considerations are also important for transactions between alumina refineries and smelters, although they are less important and have declined over time. Stuckey argues that integration between smelting and fabrication is likely to be more a consequence of the desire of aluminum firms to engage in downstream price discrimination (Perry) than a consequence of transactions cost considerations. These results serve to remind us that there are many possible reasons for vertical integration rather than a single one which will necessarily apply in all circumstances.[22]

My paper (Joskow, 1985) on vertical integration by electric utilities into coal production takes a similar approach to Stuckey's.[23] My interest in doing some empirical work in this area was stimulated by Williamson's discussion of "site-specificity." An example of site specificity near and dear to my heart is a mine-mouth coal burning generating plant. I thought that it would be interesting to see whether there were significant organizational and contractual differences for coal supply between mine-mouth plants and other types of electric generating plants burning coal.

I decided to examine the extent of vertical integration between electric utilities and coal suppliers, as well as the reliance on long-term contracts and spot market purchases. I discovered that there are wide variations in coal supply relationships. Roughly 15 percent of utility coal is supplied by utility subsidiaries. Another 15 percent is purchased in a spot market. The rest is purchased under contracts that vary in duration from one year to fifty years. Unlike aluminum, where upstream vertical integration is pervasive, the variations in the structure of vertical relationships between electric utilities and coal suppliers provided an opportunity to see if intra-industry variations in asset specificity and transactions costs could explain variations in the vertical governance structure chosen.

I proceeded to identify a set of mine-mouth plants and put together detailed information on coal supply arrangements for each of them. In those cases where long-term contracts are used to govern coal trade, I was generally able to obtain the actual contracts. If Williamson's site specificity story was correct, I hypothesized that I would find vertical integration to be much more prevalent for mine-mouth plants than for other plants. If market procurement was relied upon by a mine-mouth plant, I hypothesized that long-term contracts would be used and that they would carefully specify the terms

22. Stuckey also examines Stigler's "life-cycle" theory of vertical integration and finds, at best, only limited support for it in the time series patterns of vertical integration.

23. I had not read his book until I prepared the present paper.

of future trade when various contingencies arose and contain protective provisions to guard against opportunistic behavior. This is just what I found. Vertical integration is much more likely for a mine-mouth plant than other coal-burning plants. When vertical integration is not chosen, unusually long detailed contracts are used to support exchange. These contracts usually involve thirty-five-year commitments by the buyer and the seller to the terms of future trade.

The studies that I have discussed so far all focus on a specific industry and use firm level, plant level, and transaction level data to examine empirically the factors that determine intra-industry variations in the structure of vertical relationships. An alternative approach is to use inter-industry data to try to explain variations in the structure of vertical relationships across industries. This approach would require finding some meaningful way to measure differences in the extent of vertical integration across industries, to measure variations in asset specificity across industries, and control for other inter-industry characteristics that might be correlated with these independent variables.

The use of inter-industry data has a long tradition in industrial organization (Schmalensee, 1987). As Schmalensee suggests, it is an approach for testing hypotheses in industrial organization that has significant limitations. I believe that good empirical work aimed at testing theories such as those I have been discussing here *requires* that we know a lot about the characteristics of the firms and products that we are relying on in the empirical work. The use of industry-level aggregate values for the relevant variables, drawn for hundreds of industries, precludes doing so. Measurement of the degree of vertical integration, using the kinds of inter-industry data that are readily available, is itself a very difficult problem. The traditional use of the ratio of value added to sales seems to me to have too many problems to be used with great credibility (Scherer 79). More meaningful measures of vertical integration can be developed for a cross-section of industries (Scherer 79, and Bradburd and Caves), but it is a lot of work. In any case, I am not aware of any contemporary studies that have taken the inter-industry approach to examine the role of asset specificity or transactions costs more generally in explaining variations in the extent of vertical integration.[24]

3.2. Long-term Contracts

Whereas the earliest empirical work focused on the choice between vertical integration and market procurement, there is now a growing body of empirical evidence which examines the structure of contractual relationships from a transactions cost perspective. This work focuses on the role of asset spec-

24. Many of these same problems emerge if we rely on a cross-section of *firms* drawn from different industries.

ificity and contracting hazards in explaining variations in the use and structure of long-term contracts. Most of this work has either been published in the last few years or is still unpublished.

Goldberg and Erickson (1987) analyze the characteristics of ninety contracts for petroleum coke written between 1946 and 1973. The contracts were produced in the course of a Federal Trade Commission investigation which charged that the long-term contracts between eight oil refiners and Great Lakes Carbon Corporation violated the antitrust laws. Goldberg and Erickson compile and analyze the provisions of the contracts and certain characteristics of the transactions. They argue that the price and quantity provisions of the contracts are best understood from a "relational contracting" perspective. The provisions of the contracts reflect the interest of the parties in guarding against the expropriation of idiosyncratic investments and contain provisions to mitigate contracting hazards.

Mulhern (1986) examines the relationship between specific "protective" features and price adjustment provisions contained in a large sample of preregulatory era natural gas contracts and variables that measure variations in ex-post bargaining problems.[25] He also discusses and analyzes alternatives to the transactions cost explanations for the use of these provisions. The empirical results suggest that transactions cost considerations play a significant role in explaining variations in contractual provisions. Furthermore, the transactions cost approach explains these variations better than the competing hypotheses that Mulhern examines.[26]

Palay (1984, 1985) has done an extremely interesting study of the evolution of informal contracts between railroads and shippers. During the period he studied, railroad rates were regulated by the Interstate Commerce Commission. However, the provisions of the regulated tariffs available to shippers were not sensitive to the desire of certain shippers to have "specialized services" made available to them that would require the railroads to make idiosyncratic investments.

Regulated firms typically are subject to a broad but vague "obligation to service" all demand at prevailing regulated rates. Exactly how far these obligations to provide service on demand extend is not always clear, but generally they do not extend to specialized and nonstandard services. These same tariffs impose no explicit long-term obligations on shippers to take or pay for service. As a result, the railroads were reluctant to make durable investments specific to a particular service pursuant to a traditional tariff

25. He also examines the relationship between the ownership of gathering lines which are durable, site-specific investments, and potential ex post bargaining problems associated with asset specificity.

26. Masten and Crocker (1985) examine take-or-pay provisions in post-regulatory era natural gas contracts. They obtain results similar to those reported by Mulhern but also find that price regulation has a significant effect on variations in take-or-pay obligations.

which did not protect these investments.[27] Palay demonstrates how a system of informal contracts between railroads and shippers emerged "underneath" the standard regulated tariffs, to support relationship-specific investments.[28]

Palay's study has important implications for the growing trend in some regulated industries to increase the opportunities buyers have to switch suppliers while continuing to regulate rates using generally available tariffs that do not recognize the importance of specific investments, and which place no long-run obligations on buyers. Informal contracts may emerge to fill in the gaps created by imperfect regulation, but a formal contract negotiation system is likely to be superior to simplistic regulated tariffs. Providing for more opportunities for buyers to search among competing regulated suppliers while continuing to regulate rates and service obligations is bound to lead to inefficiencies.

Stuckey's study of vertical relationships in the aluminum industry also examines the use and structure of long-term contracts. He focuses his discussion on examples of contracting problems and contractual failures that have emerged between smelters and upstream mining and refining operations in the relatively rare circumstances when they relied on contracts rather than vertical integration. The contractual failures he discusses are associated with ex-post coordination and haggling problems that arise when relationship-specific investments are important. The prevalence of contracting problems is probably why vertical integration is so pervasive at these levels in the aluminum industry. Gallick performs a similar type of analysis of contracts and vertical integration between the fishing and processing segments of the U.S. tuna industry. Complex contracts appear to emerge to cope with a variety of vertical coordination problems identified in the transactions cost literature. Co-ownership of vessels (vertical integration) is also a factor in some cases. Contracts seem to deal with contracting hazards better in the tuna industry than in the upstream segments of the aluminum industry.

In a recent paper (Joskow, 1987) I analyze the relationship between the duration of contracts between electric utilities and coal suppliers, agreed to by the parties at the contract execution stage, and several variables designed to capture variations in the importance of relationship-specific investments associated with each contract. The empirical work relies on a sample of about 300 coal contracts written between 1960 and 1979. Contract duration is used to measure the extent to which the parties to the contract are willing to precommit to the terms of future trade ex ante rather than relying on repeated negotiation. I argue that when relationship-specific investments are

27. In theory of course regulators could design the terms and conditions of suitable contracts to match variations in transactional characteristics, but this is asking much more of regulators than even the best-intentioned are likely to be able to deliver.

28. In my work on coal supply relationships I have found that utilities requiring specialized rail cars to transport coal purchased under a long-term contract sometimes own or lease the cars themselves, rather than relying on the railroad to provide them on an as-available basis.

more important the parties will be more likely to tie down the terms of future trade ex ante by specifying contracts with longer durations. I use several variables to serve as proxies for physical asset specificity, dedicated assets, and site specificity (Williamson, 1983) measured on a contract-by-contract basis. I find that these variables explain variations in contract duration quite well.[29]

In a subsequent paper (Joskow, 1988), I went on to examine price adjustment provisions and actual price adjustment behavior in long-term coal contracts. The average duration of the contracts in my sample (adjusted for truncation bias) is about fifteen years. How does one go about setting prices in advance for deliveries over such a long period of time which will not lead to ex-post adaptation problems? Since long-term contracts are used extensively to govern transactions between coal suppliers and electric utilities the parties have presumably found a way to adjust prices over time that does not seriously distort the incentives of either party to perform as promised under the agreement. How well have these contractual provisions worked? I found that the vast majority of contracts rely on a pricing *formula* that adjusts prices for changes in input prices and certain other contingencies. I argue that this approach is designed to track changes in prevailing market conditions arising from general changes in the costs of producing coal, although they can do so only imperfectly. These provisions are likely to track changes in prevailing market conditions due to market demand shocks, compared to cost-side shocks, much less well.

The paper examines the determinants of the initial base prices in these contracts as well as the subsequent prices that are observed for deliveries in 1979, 1980, and 1981. By looking at the prices charged in 1979, 1980, and 1981 pursuant to contracts written in many different years, we can determine whether there are any significant systematic ex-post price rigidities associated with the economic conditions prevailing at the time the contracts were written. Base prices (controlling for coal characteristics and production region) appear generally to reflect prevailing average market prices at the time the contract is written. There is no evidence of hostages or front-loading of payments for other reasons. The basic structure of the price equation is similar for subsequent transactions prices to that observed for base prices. Transactions prices pursuant to these long-term contracts move along reasonably closely with changes in prevailing market conditions during the period studied. However, I do find some price rigidities that are associated with differences in economic conditions at the time the contracts were signed. At least for the period studied, the rigidities are not so large, *on average*, as to

29. Crocker and Masten (1986) have written a related paper that looks at the duration of natural gas contracts, making use of the data in Masten and Crocker (1985). My paper emphasizes the benefits of long-term contracts. Their paper tries to capture both the costs and the benefits.

suggest that they would lead to serious performance failures.[30] Some contracts do very poorly at tracking prevailing market conditions, however, and serious contracting disputes have arisen as a result.

4. CONCLUSIONS

We have come a long way since 1937. The nature of the firm and the nature of market relationships between firms has attracted a lot of recent theoretical interest. Relationship-specific investments, asymmetric information, and the costs of writing, monitoring, and enforcing contractual relationships have emerged as the key factors explaining "nonstandard" vertical relationships. The development of more specific theories of the firm and contractual relationships between firms is now being followed by more and more empirical work. This work generally provides strong empirical support for the importance of transactions cost considerations, especially the importance of asset specificity, in explaining variations in vertical relationships. Clearly there is more theoretical and empirical work to be done. I hope that theoretical and empirical work will continue to have a closer relationship to one another in this area than is typical in industrial organization. Both the theoretical and empirical analysis can go forward with greater assurance that there is indeed a pot of gold to be found at the end of the rainbow if we continue to look for it.

REFERENCES

Anderson, Erin, and David Schmittlein. 1984. "Integration of the Sales Force: An Empirical Examination," 15 *Rand Journal of Economics* 385.

Bradburd, Ralph E., and Richard Caves. 1986. "Transactional Influences on the Adjustment of Industries' Prices and Outputs." Unpublished mimeo.

Coase, Ronald H. 1937. "The Nature of the Firm," 4 *Economica N.S.* 386.

———. 1972. "Industrial Organization: A Proposal for Research." In V. R. Fuchs, ed., *Policy Issues and Research Opportunities in Industrial Organization*. New York: National Bureau of Economic Research.

Crocker, Keith J., and Scott E. Masten. 1986. "Mitigating Contractual Hazards: Unilateral Options and Contract Length," Working paper no. 449, Graduate School of Business Administration, University of Michigan, March 1986 (revised June 1986, April 1987).

Demsetz, Harold. 1968. "Why Regulate Utilities," 11 *Journal of Law and Economics* 55.

30. Remember the parties always can rely on vertical integration or spot market transactions (or very short contracts), if performance problems are likely to be associated with long-term contracts. Further research on pricing behavior when coal markets became very soft in 1984 and 1985 is ongoing.

Fischer, Stanley. 1977. "Long-term Contracting, Sticky Prices, and Monetary Policy: Comment," 3 *Journal of Monetary Economics* 317.

Fudenberg, Drew, Bengt Holmstrom, and Paul Milgrom. 1987. "Short-term Contracts and Long-term Agency Relationships." Unpublished mimeo.

Gallick, Edward C. 1984. "Exclusive Dealing and Vertical Integration: The Efficiency of Contracts in the Tuna Industry." Washington, D.C.: Bureau of Economics Staff Report, U.S. Federal Trade Commission.

Goldberg, Victor. 1976. "Regulation and Administered Contracts," 7 *Bell Journal of Economics* 426.

———, and John R. Erickson. 1987. "Quantity and Price Adjustment in Long-term Contracts: A Case Study of Petroleum Coke," 30 *Journal of Law and Economics* 369.

Grossman, Sanford J., and Oliver D. Hart. 1986. "The Costs and Benefits of Ownership: A Theory of Vertical Integration," 76 *Journal of Political Economy* 691.

Hart, Oliver, and Bengt Holmstrom. 1987. "The Theory of Contracts." In T. Bewley, ed., *Advances in Economic Theory,* Fifth World Congress. Cambridge: Cambridge University Press.

Joskow, Paul L. 1985. "Vertical Integration and Long-term Contracts: The Case of Coal-Burning Electric Generating Plants," 1 *Journal of Law, Economics, and Organization* 33.

———. 1986. "Competition and Deregulation in the Electric Power Industry." Paper presented to the International Association for Energy Economists, October 1986.

———. 1987. "Contract Duration and Transactions Specific Investment: Empirical Evidence from Coal Markets," 77 *American Economic Review* 168.

———. 1988. "Price Adjustment in Long-term Contracts: The Case of Coal." MIT Department of Economics Working paper no. 444, March 1987(b). 31 *Journal of Law and Economics* (forthcoming).

———, and Richard Schmalensee. 1983. *Markets for Power: An Analysis of Electric Utility Deregulation*. Cambridge: MIT Press.

Klein, Benjamin, Robert A. Crawford, and Armen A. Alchian. 1978. "Vertical Integration, Appropriable Rents, and the Competitive Contracting Process," 21 *Journal of Law and Economics* 297.

Masten, Scott. 1984. "The Organization of Production: Evidence from the Aerospace Industry," 27 *Journal of Law and Economics* 403.

———, and Keith J. Crocker. 1985. "Efficient Adaptation in Long-term Contracts: Take-or-Pay Provisions for Natural Gas," 75 *American Economic Review* 1083.

Monteverde, Kirk, and David Teece. 1982. "Supplier Switching Costs and Vertical Integration in the Automobile Industry," 13 *Bell Journal of Economics* 206.

Mulhern, J. Harold. 1986. "Complexity in Long-term Contracts: An Analysis of Natural Gas Contract Provisios," 2 *Journal of Law, Economics, and Organization* 105.

Palay, Thomas. 1984. "Comparative Institutional Economics: The Governance of Rail Freight Contracting," 13 *Journal of Legal Studies* 265.

———. 1985. "Avoiding Regulatory Constraints: Contracting Safeguards and the Role of Informal Agreements," 1 *Journal of Law, Economics, and Organization* 155–76.

Perry, Martin K. 1978. "Price Discrimination and Forward Integration," 9 *Bell Journal of Economics* 209.

Prager, Robin Ann. 1986. "Firm Behavior in Franchise Monopoly Markets: The Case of Cable Television." Unpublished Ph.D. dissertation, MIT.

Scherer, F. M. 1980. *Industrial Market Structure and Economic Performance*. Chicago: Rand McNally.

Schmalensee, Richard. 1987. "Interindustry Studies of Structure and Performance." Sloan School of Management, working paper no. 1874–87.
Stigler, George. 1951. "The Division of Labor Is Limited by the Extent of the Market," 59 *Journal of Political Economy* 185.
Stuckey, John. 1983. *Vertical Integration and Joint Ventures in the Aluminum Industry.* Cambridge: Harvard University Press.
Warren-Boulton, Frederick R. 1967. "Vertical Control with Variable Proportions," 75 *Journal of Political Economy* 123.
Williamson, Oliver. 1975. *Markets and Hierarchies: Analysis and Antitrust Implications.* New York: Free Press.
———. 1976. "Franchise Bidding for Natural Monopolies—In General and with Regard to CATV," 7 *Bell Journal of Economics* 73.
———. 1979. "Transactions-Cost Economics: The Governance of Contractual Relations," 22 *Journal of Law and Economics* 3.
———. 1983. "Credible Commitments: Using Hostages to Support Exchange," 73 *American Economic Review* 519.
———. 1985. *The Economic Institutions of Capitalism.* New York: Free Press.
Zupan, Mark. 1987. "Three Essays on the Efficacy of Cable Franchise Bidding Schemes." Unpublished Ph.D. dissertation, MIT.

Part III
Non-Standard Agreements

Markets, Bureaucracies, and Clans

William G. Ouchi

Evaluating organizations according to an efficiency criterion would make it possible to predict the form organizations will take under certain conditions. Organization theory has not developed such a criterion because it has lacked a conceptual scheme capable of describing organizational efficiency in sufficiently microsopic terms. The transactions cost approach provides such a framework because it allows us to identify the conditions which give rise to the costs of mediating exchanges between individuals: goal incongruence and performance ambiguity. Different combinations of these causes distinguish three basic mechanisms of mediation or control: markets, which are efficient when performance ambiguity is low and goal incongruence is high; bureaucracies, which are efficient when both goal incongruence and performance ambiguity are moderately high; and clans, which are efficient when goal incongruence is low and performance ambiguity is high.•

THE NATURE OF ORGANIZATIONS

What is an organization, and why do organizations exist? Many of us would answer this question by referring to Barnard's (1968) technological imperative, which argues that a formal organization will arise when technological conditions demand physical power, speed, endurance, mechanical adaptation, or continuity beyond the capacity of a single individual (1968: 27–28). Yet when the stone is too large or the production facility too complex for a single person, what is called for is cooperation, and cooperation need not take the form of a formal organization. Indeed, grain farmers who need a large grain elevator do not form corporations which take over the farms and make the farmers into employees; instead, they form a cooperative to own and operate the elevator.

Others would refer to March and Simon's (1958) argument that an organization will exist so long as it can offer its members inducements which exceed the contributions it asks of them. While this position explains the conditions under which an organization may continue to exist, it does not explain how an organization can create a whole which is so much greater than the sum of its parts that it can give them more than they contribute.

Most of us, however, would refer to Blau and Scott's (1962) definition of a formal organization as a purposive aggregation of individuals who exert concerted effort toward a common and explicitly recognized goal. Yet we can hardly accept this definition whole, suspecting as Simon (1945: 257–278) has that individuals within organizations rarely have a common understanding of goals.

Another point of view on the question of why organizations exist began with an inquiry by Coase (1937) and has recently been developed by Williamson (1975). In this view, an organization such as a corporation exists because it can mediate economic transactions between its members at lower costs than a market mechanism can. Under certain conditions, markets are more efficient because they can mediate without paying the costs of managers, accountants,

0001-8392/80/2501-0129$00.75

•

I am indebted to many colleagues for their constructive criticisms of this paper, particularly to Chris Argyris, Peter Blau, Larry Cummings, Charles Horngren, Joanne Martin, John Meyer, Jerry Porras, Edgar Schein, W. Richard Scott, Arnold Tannenbaum, Richard Walton, and Oliver Williamson.

or personnel departments. Under other conditions, however, a market mechanism becomes so cumbersome that it is less efficient than a bureaucracy. This transactions cost approach explicitly regards efficiency as the fundamental element in determining the nature of organizations.

MARKETS, BUREAUCRACIES, AND CLANS

Transactions costs are a solution to the problem of cooperation in the realm of economic activity. From the perspective of Mayo (1945) and Barnard (1968), the fundamental problem of cooperation stems from the fact that individuals have only partially overlapping goals. Left to their own devices, they pursue incongruent objectives and their efforts are uncoordinated. Any collectivity which has an economic goal must then find a means to control diverse individuals efficiently.

Many helpful ideas have flowed from this definition of the problem of cooperation. Some (e.g., Etzioni, 1965; Weick, 1969) have emphasized the tension between individual autonomy and collective interests which must attend cooperative action, while others (e.g., Simon, 1945) have emphasized the impossibility of achieving a completely cooperative effort. Our interest is in the efficiency with which transactions are carried out between individuals who are engaged in cooperative action.

Cooperative action necessarily involves interdependence between individuals. This interdependence calls for a transaction or exchange in which each individual gives something of value (for example, labor) and receives something of value (for example, money) in return. In a market relationship, the transaction takes place between the two parties and is mediated by a price mechanism in which the existence of a competitive market reassures both parties that the terms of exchange are equitable. In a bureaucratic relationship, each party contributes labor to a corporate body which mediates the relationship by placing a value on each contribution and then compensating it fairly. The perception of equity in this case depends upon a social agreement that the bureaucratic hierarchy has the legitimate authority to provide this mediation. In either case, individuals must regard the transaction as equitable: it must meet the standards of reciprocity which Gouldner (1961) has described as a universal requirement for collective life.

It is this demand for equity which brings on transactions costs. A transactions cost is any activity which is engaged in to satisfy each party to an exchange that the value given and received is in accord with his or her expectations.

Transactions costs arise principally when it is difficult to determine the value of the goods or service. Such difficulties can arise from the underlying nature of the goods or service or from a lack of trust between the parties. When a company is being sold by one corporation to another corporation, for example, it may not be unambiguously clear what the true value of that company is. If firms similar to the company are frequently bought and sold, and if those transactions occur under competitive conditions, then the market process will be accepted as a legitimate estimator of the true value. But if the company is unique, and there is only one potential buyer, then market forces are absent. How will the buyer and seller determine a fair price? They may call upon a third party to estimate the value of the company. Each party may in addition call upon other experts who will assist them in evaluating both the value of the company and the adequacy of the judgment of the third party. Each side may also require an extensive and complete contract which will describe exactly what is being bought and sold. Each of these activities is costly, and all of them are regarded here as transactions costs: they are necessary to create a perception of equity among all parties to the transaction.

This same argument applies to transactions in which a service, such as the labor of an individual, is the object of exchange. If one individual sells his or her services to another, it may be difficult to assess the true value of that labor. In particular, if the labor is to be used in an interdependent technology, one which requires teamwork, it may be difficult to assess the value contributed by one worker as opposed to another, since their joint efforts yield a single outcome in this case, or in a case where it is likely that task requirements will change, then the auditing and complex contracting required to create the perception of equity can become unbearably costly.

We have identified two principal mechanisms for mediating these transactions: a market and a bureaucracy. These alternatives have received the greatest attention from organization theorists (e.g., Barnard, 1968; Weber, 1968) and economists (e.g., Coase, 1937; Arrow, 1974). However, the paradigm also suggests a third mechanism: If the objectives of individuals are congruent (not mutually exclusive), then the conditions of reciprocity and equity can be met quite differently.

Both Barnard and Mayo pointed out that organizations are difficult to operate because their members do not share a selfless devotion to the same objectives. Mayo (1945) argued that organizations operated more efficiently in preindustrial times, when members typically served an apprenticeship during which they were socialized into accepting the objectives of the craft or organization. Barnard (1968: 42–43) posed the problem thus:

> A formal system of cooperation requires an objective, a purpose, an aim. . . . It is important to note the complete distinction between the aim of a cooperative effort and that of an individual. Even in the case where a man enlists the aid of other men to do something which he cannot do alone, such as moving a stone, the objective ceases to be personal.

While Barnard, like Arrow, views markets and bureaucracies as the basic mechanisms for achieving the continued cooperation of these individuals, he also allowed (1968: 141) for the possibility of reducing the incongruence of goals in a manner consistent with Mayo's view of the preindustrial organization:

> An organization can secure the efforts necessary to its existence, then, either by the objective inducement it provides or by changing states of mind. It seems to me improbable that any organization can exist as a practical matter which does not employ both methods in combination.

If the socialization of individuals into an organization is complete, then the basis of reciprocity can be changed. For example, Japanese firms rely to a great extent upon hiring inexperienced workers, socializing them to accept the company's goals as their own, and compensating them according to length of service, number of dependents, and other nonperformance criteria (see Abegglen, 1958; Dore, 1973; Nakane, 1973). It is not necessary for these organizations to measure performance to control or direct their employees, since the employees' natural (socialized) inclination is to do what is best for the firm. It is also unnecessary to derive explicit, verifiable measures of value added, since rewards are distributed according to nonperformance-related criteria which are relatively inexpensive to determine (length of service and number of dependents can be ascertained at relatively low costs). Thus, industrial organizations can, in some instances, rely to a great extent on socialization as the principal mechanism of mediation or control, and this "clan" form ("clan" conforms to Durkheim's meaning of an organic association which resembles a kin network but may not include blood relations, 1933: 175) can be very efficient in mediating transactions between interdependent individuals.

Markets, bureaucracies, and clans are therefore three distinct mechanisms which may be present in differing degrees, in any real organization.[1] Our next objective is to specify the conditions under which the requirements of each form are most efficiently satisfied.

THE MARKET FAILURES FRAMEWORK

We can approach this question most effectively by examining the markets and hierarchies approach provided by Williamson (1975), which builds upon earlier statements of the problem by Coase (1937) and others (for a more detailed description of the functioning of each mechanism, see Ouchi, 1979).

Market transactions, or exchanges, consist of contractual relationships. Each exchange is governed by one of three types of contractual relations, all of which can be specified completely. That is, because each party is bound only to deliver that which is specified, the contract must specify who must deliver what under every possible state of nature. The simplest form of contract is the "spot" or "sales" contract. This is what occurs when you walk up to a candy counter, ask for a candy bar, and pay the amount the salesperson asks. In such a transaction, all obligations are fulfilled on the spot. However, the spot market contract is, by definition, incapable of dealing with future transactions, and most exchange relationships involve long-term obligations.

A common device for dealing with the future is the "contingent claims contract," a document that specifies all the obligations of each party to an exchange, contingent upon all possible future states of nature. However, given a future that is either complex or uncertain, the bounded rationality of individuals makes it impossible to specify such a contract completely. Leaving such a contract incompletely specified is an alternative, but one that will succeed only if each party can trust the other to interpret the uncertain future in a

1
In the broader language necessary to encompass both economics and organization theory, an organization may be thought of as any stable pattern of transactions. In this definition, a market is as much an organization as is a bureaucracy or a clan. The only requirement is that, for the purposes of this discussion, we maintain a clear distinction between the idea of "bureaucracy" and the idea of "organization." Bureaucracy as used here refers specifically to the Weberian model, while organization refers to any stable pattern of transactions between individuals or aggregations of individuals.

manner that is acceptable to him. Thus, given uncertainty, bounded rationality, and opportunism, contingent claims contracting will fail.

Instead of trying to anticipate the future in a giant, once-and-for-all contract, why not employ a series of contracts, each one written for a short period within which future events can confidently be foreseen? The problem with such "sequential spot contracting" is that in many exchange relationships, the goods or services exchanged are unique, and the supplier requires specialized knowledge of how to supply the customer best and most efficiently. The supplier acquires this knowledge over time and in doing so gains a "first mover advantage," which enables him to bid more effectively on subsequent contracts than any potential competitor can. Knowing this, potential competitors will not waste their time bidding, thus producing a situation of "small numbers bargaining" or bilateral monopoly, in which there is only one buyer and seller. Under this condition, competitive pressures are absent, and each party will opportunistically claim higher costs or poor quality, whichever is in his or her interest. In order to maintain such an exchange, each party will have to go to considerable expense to audit the costs or performance of the other. If these transactions costs are too high, the market relationship will fail due to the confluence of opportunism with small numbers bargaining, even though the limitations of uncertainty and bounded rationality have been overcome.

Thus, under some conditions no completely contractual market relationship is feasible. Table 1 summarizes the conditions which lead to market failure. According to the paradigm, no one of the four conditions can produce market failure, but almost any pairing of them will do so.

The idea of market failure is an analytical device. Economists do not agree on a specific set of conditions that constitute the failure of a market; indeed one point of view argues that even monopolistic conditions may be competitive. However, the idea of market failure as expressed by Williamson (1975) is useful as a conceptual framework within which to compare the strengths of markets as opposed to bureaucracies. The technique is to contend that all transactions can be mediated entirely by market relations, and then ask what conditions will cause some of these market mechanisms to fail and be replaced by bureaucratic mechanisms. In this sense, every bureaucratic organization constitutes an example of market failure.

The bureaucratic organization has two principal advantages over the market relationship. First, it uses the employment relation, which is an incomplete contract. In accepting an employment relation, a worker agrees to receive wages in

Table 1

The Market Failures Framework*

Human factors		**Environmental factors**
Bounded rationality	←——→	Uncertainty/Complexity
Opportunism	←——→	Small numbers

*Adapted from Williamson (1975: 40).

exchange for submitting to the legitimate right of the organization to appoint superior officers who can (1) direct the work activities of the employee from day to day (within some domain or zone of indifference), thus overcoming the problem of dealing with the future all at once and (2) closely monitor the employee's performance, thus minimizing the problem of opportunism.

Second, the bureaucratic organization can create an atmosphere of trust between employees much more readily than a market can between the parties to an exchange. Because members of an organization assume some commonality of purpose, because they learn that long-term relationships will reward good performance and punish poor performance, they develop some goal congruence. This reduces their opportunistic tendencies and thus the need to monitor their performance.

Bureaucracies are also characterized by an emphasis on technical expertise which provides some skill training and some socialization into craft or professional standards. Professionals within a bureaucratic setting thus combine a primary affiliation to a professional body with a career orientation, which increases the sense of affiliation or solidarity with the employer and further reduces goal incongruence.[2]

In summary, the market failures framework argues that markets fail when the costs of completing transactions become unbearable. At that point, the inefficiencies of bureaucratic organization will be preferred to the relatively greater costs of market organization, and exchange relationships move from one domain into the other.

Consider one example. The 10,000 individuals who comprise the workforce of a steel mill could be individual entrepreneurs whose interpersonal transactions are mediated entirely through a network of market or contractual relationships. Each of them could also have a market relation with yet another combine which owned the capital equipment and facilities necessary to produce steel. Yet steel mills are typically bureaucratic in form and each worker is in an employment, not market, relation with the corporation. Market forces have failed because the determination of value contributed by one worker is highly ambiguous in the integrated steelmaking process, which makes the transactions cost attendant upon maintaining a market too high.

EXTENDING THE MARKET FAILURES FRAMEWORK: CLANS

Bureaucracies can fail when the ambiguity of performance evaluation becomes significantly greater than that which brings about market failure. A bureaucratic organization operates fundamentally according to a system of hierarchical surveillance, evaluation, and direction. In such a system, each superior must have a set of standards to which he can compare behavior or output in order to provide control. These standards only indicate the value of an output approximately, and are subject to idiosyncratic interpretation. People perceive them as equitable only as long as they believe that they contain a reasonable amount of performance information. When tasks become highly unique, completely integrated, or ambiguous for other reasons, then even bu-

2
Despite these desirable properties, the bureaucratic type has continually been under attack and revision. As Williamson points out, the move from U-form (functional) to M-form (divisional) organization among many large firms has been motivated by a desire to simulate a capital market within a bureaucratic framework because of its superior efficiency. By regrouping the parts of the organization, it is possible to create subentities that are sufficiently autonomous to permit precise measurement and the determination of an effective price mechanism. Although each division may still operate internally as a bureaucracy, the economies which accrue from this partial market solution are often large, offsetting the diseconomies of functional redundancy which often accompany the separation of the organization into divisions.

reaucratic mechanisms fail. Under these conditions, it becomes impossible to evaluate externally the value added by any individual. Any standard which is applied will be by definition arbitrary and therefore inequitable.

If we adopt the view that transactions costs arise from equity considerations, then we can interpret Table 1 in a different light. Simon's work on the employment relation (1957: 183-195) shows that Table 1 contains some redundancy. He emphasized that under an employment contract, the employer pays a worker a premium over the "spot" price for any piece of work. From the point of view of the worker, this "risk premium" compensates him for the likelihood that he will be asked to perform duties which are significantly more distasteful to him than those which are implied in the employment contract. The uncertainty surrounding the likelihood of such tasks and the expectation that the employer will or will not ask them determines the size of the risk premium. If the employee agreed with all the employer's objectives, which is equivalent to completely trusting the employer never to request a distasteful task, then the risk premium would be zero.

The employment relation is relatively efficient when the measurement of performance is ambiguous but the employer's goals are not. In an employment relation, each employee depends on the employer to distribute rewards equitably; if employees do not trust the employer to do so, they will demand contractual protections such as union representation and the transactions cost will rise.

Thus, the critical element in the efficiency of market versus employment relations has to do with (1) the ambiguity of the measurement of individual performance, and (2) the congruence of the employees' and employer's goals. We can now reformulate the transactions cost problem as follows: in order to mediate transactions efficiently, any organizational form must reduce either the ambiguity of performance evaluation or the goal incongruence between parties. Put this way, market relations are efficient when there is little ambiguity over performance, so the parties can tolerate relatively high levels of opportunism or goal incongruence. And bureaucratic relations are efficient when both performance ambiguity and goal incongruence are moderately high.

What form of mediation succeeds by minimizing goal incongruence and tolerating high levels of ambiguity in performance evaluation? Clearly, it is one which embodies a strong form of the employment relation as defined by Simon (1945), which is a relationship in which the risk premium is minimized. The answer is what we have referred to as the clan, which is the obverse of the market relation since it achieves efficiency under the opposite conditions: high performance ambiguity and low opportunism.

Perhaps the clearest exposition of the clan form apears in what Durkheim (1933: 365) refers to as the case of organic solidarity and its contrast with contractual relations:

> For organic solidarity to exist, it is not enough that there be a system of organs necessary to one another, which in a general way feel solidarity, but it is also necessary that the way in which they should come together, if not in every kind of meeting, at least

> in circumstances which most frequently occur, be predetermined. . . . Otherwise, at every moment new conflicts would have to be equilibrated. . . . It will be said that there are contracts. But, first of all, social relations are not capable of assuming this juridical form. . . . A contract is not self-sufficient, but supposes a regulation which is as extensive and complicated as contractual life itself. . . . A contract is only a truce, and very precarious, it suspends hostilities only for a time.

The solidarity to which Durkheim refers contemplates the union of objectives between individuals which stems from their necessary dependence upon one another. In this sense, any occupational group which has organic solidarity may be considered a clan. Thus, a profession, a labor union, or a corporation may be a clan, and the professionalized bureaucracy may be understood as a response to the joint need for efficient transactions within professions (clan) and between professions (bureaucracy). Goal congruity as a central mechanism of control in organizations also appears repeatedly in Barnard:

> The most intangible and subtle of incentives is that which I have called the condition of communion. . . . It is the feeling of personal comfort in social relations that is sometimes called solidarity, social integration. . . . The need for communion is a basis of informal organization that is essential to the operation of every formal organization (1968: 148; see also pp. 89, 152, 169, 273).

Descriptions of organizations which display a high degree of goal congruence, typically through relatively complete socialization brought about through high inclusion (Etzioni, 1965), are also found in Lipset, Trow, and Coleman (1956: 79–80), Argyris (1964: 10, 175), Selznick (1966), and Clark (1970). In each case, the authors describe the organization as one in which it is difficult to determine individual performance. However, such organizations are not "loosely coupled" nor are they "organized anarchies" simply because they lack market and bureaucratic mechanisms. A clan, as Durkheim points out, provides great regularity of relations and may in fact be more directive than the other, more explicit mechanisms. That clans display a high degree of discipline is emphasized by Kanter (1972) in her study of utopian communities, some of which were successful businesses such as Oneida and Amana. According to Kanter, this discipline was not achieved through contractualism or surveillance but through an extreme form of the belief that individual interests are best served by a complete immersion of each individual in the interests of the whole (1972: 41).

More recently, Ouchi and Jaeger (1978) and Ouchi and Johnson (1978) have reported on modern industrial organizations which closely resemble the clan form. In these organizations, a variety of social mechanisms reduces differences between individual and organizational goals and produces a strong sense of community (see also Van Maanen, 1975; Katz, 1978). Where individual and organizational interests overlap to this extent, opportunism is unlikely and equity in rewards can be achieved at a relatively low transactions cost. Moreover, these organizations are typically in technologically advanced or closely integrated industries, where teamwork is common, technologies change often, and therefore individual performance is highly ambiguous.

When a bureaucracy fails, then due to excessively ambiguous performance evaluation, the sole form of mediation remaining is the clan, which relies upon creating goal congruence. Although clans may employ a system of legitimate authority (often the traditional rather than the rational-legal form), they differ fundamentally from bureaucracies in that they do not require explicit auditing and evaluation. Performance evaluation takes place instead through the kind of subtle reading of signals that is possible among intimate coworkers but which cannot be translated into explicit, verifiable measures. This means that there is sufficient information in a clan to promote learning and effective production, but that information cannot withstand the scrutiny of contractual relations. Thus, any tendency toward opportunism will be destructive, because the close auditing and hard contracting necessary to combat it are not possible in a clan.

If performance evaluation is so ambiguous and goals so incongruent that a clan fails, what then? We can only speculate, but it seems that this final cell may be the case discussed by Meyer and Rowan (1977) in which control is purely ceremonial and symbolic. School systems, like other organizations, do employ a variety of mechanisms. Yet if there is no effective mechanism of mediation between individuals, the perception of equity may be purely superstitious, based on a broad, community-based acceptance of the legitimacy of the institution.

MARKETS, BUREAUCRACIES, AND CLANS: AN OVERVIEW

Having distinguished three mechanisms of intermediation, we can now summarize them and attempt to set out the general conditions under which each form will mediate transactions between individuals most efficiently. Table 2 discriminates markets, bureaucracies, and clans along two dimensions: their underlying normative and informational requirements.

Table 2

An Organizational Failures Framework

Mode of control	Normative requirements	Informational requirements
Market	Reciprocity	Prices
Bureaucracy	Reciprocity Legitimate authority	Rules
Clan	Reciprocity Legitimate authority Common values and beliefs	Traditions

Normative requirements refer to the basic social agreements that all members of the transactional network must share if the network is to function efficiently, without undue costs of performance auditing or monitoring. A norm of reciprocity, according to Gouldner (1961), is one of only two social agreements that have been found to be universal among societies across time and cultures (the other is the incest taboo). If no such norm were widely shared, then a potential trader would have to consume so much energy in setting the contractural terms of exchange in advance and in auditing the performance of the other party afterwards that the potential transaction would cost too much. Under such conditions, a division of labor is unthinkable and social existence impossible. Therefore, a norm of reciprocity underlies all exchange mechanisms.

A norm of legitimate authority is critical for two reasons. As discussed above, it permits the assignment of organizational superiors who can, on an ad hoc basis, specify the work assignments of subordinates, thus obviating the need for a contingent claims employment contract which would be either so complex as to be infeasible or so simple as to be too confining or else incomplete. Legitimate authority also permits organizational superiors to audit the performance of subordinates more closely than is possible within a market relationship. In a bureaucracy, legitimate authority will commonly take the "rational/legal" form, whereas in a clan it may take the "traditional" form (see Blau and Scott, 1962: 27–38). Legitimate authority is not ordinarily created within the organization but is maintained by other institutions such as the church or the educational system (Weber, 1947; Blau and Scott, 1962; Barnard, 1968: 161–184). While the legitimacy of a particular organization may be greater or smaller as a result of its managerial practices, it is fundamentally maintained within a society generally.

Common values and beliefs provide the harmony of interests that erase the possibility of opportunistic behavior. If all members of the organization have been exposed to an apprenticeship or other socialization period, then they will share personal goals that are compatible with the goals of the organization. In this condition, auditing of performance is unnecessary except for educational purposes, since no member will attempt to depart from organizational goals.

A norm of reciprocity is universal, legitimate authority is accepted, though in varying degree, in most formal organizations, and common values and beliefs are relatively rare in formal organizations. Etzioni (1965) has described this last form of control as being common only to "total organizations" such as the military and mental hospitals, and Light (1972) describes its role in ethnically bound exchange relationships. However, we have also noted that a partially complete form of socialization, accompanied by market or bureaucratic mechanisms, may be effective across a wider range of organizations. Mayo (1945) contended that instability of employment, which upsets the long socialization period necessary, is the chief enemy of the development of this form of control.

The informational prerequisites of each form of control are prices, rules, and traditions. Prices are a highly sophisticated form of information for decision making. However, correct prices are difficult to arrive at, particularly when technological interdependence, novelty, or other forms of ambiguity obscure the boundary between tasks or individuals. Rules, by comparison, are relatively crude informational devices. A rule is specific to a problem, and therefore it takes a large number of rules to control organizational responses. A decision maker must know the structure of the rules in order to apply the correct one in any given situation. Moreover, an organization can never specify a set of rules that will cover all possible contingencies. Instead, it specifies a smaller set of rules which cover routine decisions, and refers exceptions up the hierarchy where policymakers can invent rules as needed. As Galbraith (1973) has pointed out, under conditions of uncertainty or complexity the number of exceptions becomes so great that the hierarchy becomes overloaded and the quality of decision making suffers.

Traditions are implicit rather than explicit rules that govern behavior. Because traditions are not specified, they are not easily accessible, and a new member will not be able to function effectively until he or she has spent a number of years learning them (Van Maanen and Schein, 1978). In terms of the precision of the performance evaluation they permit, traditions may be the crudest informational prerequisite, since they are ordinarily stated in a general way which must be interpreted in a particular situation. On the other hand, the set of traditions in a formal organization may produce a unified, although implicit philosophy or point of view, functionally equivalent to a theory about how that organization should work. A member who grasps such an essential theory can deduce from it an appropriate rule to govern any possible decision, thus producing a very elegant and complete form of control. Alternatively, a disruption of the socialization process will inhibit the passing on of traditions and bring about organizational inefficiency.

SOME CONCLUDING THOUGHTS

Under conditions of extreme uncertainty and opportunism, transactions cost may rise. Indeed, Denison (1978) has observed that net productivity declined in the United States between 1965 and 1975 due to changes in "the industrial and human environment within which business must operate" (1978:21). According to Denison, output per unit of input has declined for two reasons: 78 percent of the decline is due to increased costs of air, water, and safety on the job, and the remaining 22 percent is attributable to increased needs for surveillance of potentially dishonest employees, customers, contractors, and thieves. The resources put into improvements in air, water, and safety are not a net loss to society although they may reduce corporate profitability. The increased need for surveillance in business, however, may represent the fact that the cost of monitoring transactions has risen. Mayo (1945) might have predicted this change as an inevitable result of the instability which accompanies industrialization. In our framework, we could advance the following explanation: exchange relationships are generally subject to so much informational ambiguity that they can never be governed completely by markets. Consequently, they have been supplemented through cultural, clan mechanisms. As instability, heterogeneity, and mobility have intensified in the United States, however, the effectiveness of these cultural mechanisms has been vitiated and bureaucratic mechanisms of surveillance and control have increased. Although bureaucratic surveillance may be the optimal strategy under present social conditions, it is nonetheless true that the United States is devoting more of its resources to transactional matters than it did ten years ago, and that represents a net decline in its welfare.

The degree of uncertainty and opportunism that characterize American society may be such that no mechanisms of control ever function very well. We have already observed that the conditions necessary for a pure market, bureaucracy, or clan are rare. Even a combination of these control mechanisms may be insufficient in many cases, however. In organizations using new technologies or in the public sector, the rate of change, instability of employment, or ambiguity of performance evaluation may simply overwhelm all rational control attempts.

In these cases, exchange becomes institutionalized. Meyer and Rowan's (1977) central thesis is that school systems, by their nature, evade any form of rational control. They have no effective price mechanism, no effective bureaucratic control, and no internally consistent cultures (see also Meyer et al., 1978). Thus school systems (as distinguished from education, which need not be done by large organizations) continue to grow and survive because the objectives which they are believed to pursue have been accepted as necessary by society. Since rational control is not feasible within the school, no one knows whether it is actually pursuing these goals, but an institutionalized organization (the church is another example) need not give evidence of performance (see also Ouchi, 1977: 97–98).

All work organizations are institutionalized in the sense that fundamental purposes of all viable organizations must mesh at least somewhat with broad social values (Parsons and Shils, 1951). This institutionalization permits organizations to survive even under conditions that severely limit their capacity for rational control. Ultimately, organizational failure occurs only when society deems the basic objectives of the organization unworthy of continued support.

What is an organization? An organization, in our sense, is any stable pattern of transactions between individuals or aggregations of individuals. Our framework can thus be applied to the analysis of relationships between individuals or between subunits within a corporation, or to transactions between firms in an economy. Why do organizations exist? In our sense, all patterned transactions are organized, and thus all stable exchanges in a society are organized. When we ask "why do organizations exist," we usually mean to ask "why do bureaucratic organizations exist," and the answer is clear. Bureaucratic organizations exist because, under certain specifiable conditions, they are the most efficient means for an equitable mediation of transactions between parties. In a similar manner, market and clan organizations exist because each of them, under certain conditions, offers the lowest transactions cost.

REFERENCES

Abegglen, James C.
1958 The Japanese Factory: Aspects of Its Social Organization. Glencoe, Il: Free Press.

Argyris, Chris
1964 Integrating the Individual and the Organization. New York: Wiley.

Arrow, Kenneth J.
1974 The Limits of Organization. New York: Norton.

Barnard, Chester I.
1968 The Functions of the Executive, 30th anniversary ed. Cambridge: Harvard.

Blau, Peter M., and W. Richard Scott
1962 Formal Organizations. San Francisco: Scott, Foreman.

Clark, Burton R.
1970 The Distinctive College: Antioch, Reed, and Swarthmore. Chicago: Aldine.

Coase, R. H.
1937 "The nature of the firm." Economica, new series, 4: 386–405.

Denison, Edward F.
1978 Effects of Selected Changes in the Institutional and Human Environment upon Output Per Unit of Input. Brookings General Series Reprint #335. Washington: Brookings.

Dore, Ronald
1973 British Factory-Japanese Factory. Berkeley: University of California.

Durkheim, Emile
1933 The Division of Labor in Society. G. Simpson, trans. New York: Free Press.

Etzioni, Amitai
1965 "Organizational control structure." In James G. March (ed.), Handbook of Organizations: 650–677. Chicago: Rand McNally.

Galbraith, Jay
1973 Designing Complex Organizations. Reading, MA: Addison-Wesley.

Gouldner, Alvin W.
1961 "The norm of reciprocity." American Sociological Review, 25: 161–179.

Kanter, Rosabeth Moss
1972 Commitment and Community. Cambridge: Harvard.

Katz, Ralph
1978 "Job longevity as a situational factor in job satisfaction." Administrative Science Quarterly, 23: 204–223.

Light, Ivan H.
1972 Ethnic Enterprise in America. Berkeley: University of California.

Lipset, Seymour M., Martin A. Trow, and James S. Coleman
1956 Union Democracy. Glencoe, Il.: Free Press.

March, James G., and Herbert A. Simon
1958 Organizations. New York: Wiley.

Mayo, Elton
1945 The Social Problems of an Industrial Civilization. Boston: Division of Research, Graduate School of Business Administration, Harvard University.

Meyer, John W., and Brian Rowan
1977 "Institutionalized organizations: Formal structure as myth and ceremony." American Journal of Sociology, 83: 340–363.

Meyer, John W., W. Richard Scott, Sally Cole, and Jo-Ann K. Intili
1978 "Instructional dissensus and institutional consensus in schools." In Marshall W. Meyer and Associates (eds.), Environments and Organizations: 233–263. San Francisco: Jossey-Bass.

Nakane, Chie
1973 Japanese Society, rev. ed. Middlesex, England: Penguin.

Ouchi, William G.
1977 "The relationship between organizational structure and organizational control." Administrative Science Quarterly, 22: 95–113.
1979 "A conceptual framework for the design of organizational control mechanisms." Management Science, 25: 833–848.

Ouchi, William G., and Alfred M. Jaeger
1978 "Type Z organization: Stability in the midst of mobility." Academy of Management Review, 3: 305–314.

Ouchi, William G., and Jerry B. Johnson
1978 "Types of organizational control and their relationship to emotional well-being." Administrative Science Quarterly, 23: 293–317.

Parsons, Talcott, and Edward A. Shils
1951 "Values, motives, and systems of action." In Talcott Parsons and Edward A. Shils (eds.), Toward a General Theory of Action: 47–275. Cambridge: Harvard.

Selznick, Philip
1966 TVA and the Grass Roots (orig. ed., 1949). New York: Harper Torchbooks.

Simon, Herbert A.
1945 Administrative Behavior. New York: Free Press.
1957 Models of Man. New York: Wiley.

Van Maanen, John
1975 "Police socialization: A longitudinal examination of job attitudes in an urban police department." Administrative Science Quarterly, 20: 207–228.

Van Maanen, John, and Edgar H. Schein
1978 "Toward a theory of organizational socialization." Manuscript, Sloan School of Industrial Administration, Massachusetts Institute of Technology.

Weber, Max
1947 The Theory of Social and Economic Organization (orig. ed., 1925). A. M. Henderson and T. Parsons, trans. New York: Free Press.
1968 Economy and Society (orig. ed., 1925). G. Roth and C. Wittich, eds. New York: Bedminster Press.

Weick, Karl E.
1969 The Social Psychology of Organizing. Reading, MA: Addison-Wesley.

Williamson, O. E.
1975 Markets and Hierarchies: Analysis and Antitrust Implications. New York: Free Press.

[18]

Journal of Economic Behavior and Organization 2 (1981) 335–357. North-Holland

THE QUASIFIRM IN THE CONSTRUCTION INDUSTRY

Robert G. ECCLES*

Harvard Business School, Boston, MA 02163, USA

Received May 1981, final version received March 1982

Construction projects are executed by general contractors who retain the services of special trade subcontractors. This form of organization is preferable to vertically integrating these trades because of the transaction cost implications of construction technology. The general contractor and special trade subcontractors can form a stable organizational unit when conditions permit. This organizational form, called here the 'quasifirm', is analogous to the 'inside contracting system' discussed by Williamson (1975). This paper uses Williamson's (1975, 1979) transaction cost approach to argue the theoretical existence of the quasifirm in the construction industry. Empirical evidence from a field study of homebuilders is presented in support of this argument.

1. Introduction

A fundamental question of economic organization is the extent to which a firm is directly responsible for producing all of the inputs required for its products. This is the general question of vertical integration. Should the firm decide to vertically integrate, it is then faced by the question of how to organize to complete the work. If the firm chooses to obtain certain inputs from other firms it faces the question of how to manage these relationships.

Williamson (1975) addressed this issue of the division of labor between and among firms and markets in terms of a transaction cost approach. In a more recent paper he (1979) elaborated this approach through a framework of governance structures developed out of contract law. His transaction cost approach makes it possible to examine both intrafirm and interfirm organization with some common concepts. This paper argues that his approach can be used to explain the organization of work in the construction industry given certain conditions. It also asserts that a contracting mode intermediate between the relational contracting modes of bilateral governance (obligational contracting) and unified governance (internal organization) is the preferred mode for construction work given

*I would like to thank Professor Harrison White of Harvard University for some very helpful comments on earlier drafts of this paper. Discussions with Professor Paul Lawrence of Harvard Business School have also been helpful.

0167–2681/81/0000–0000/$02.75

certain conditions. I call this mode or form the 'quasifirm'. This organization form, based on a set of stable relationships between a general contractor and special trade subcontractors, is analogous to the inside contracting system in manufacturing. Williamson (1975) located this form between markets and vertically integrated hierarchies in his continuum of alternative contracting modes.

In this paper I will argue theoretically for the existence of the quasifirm, an organizational form with characteristics of both markets and hierarchies, in two related ways. First, I will show that Williamson's (1979) framework of governance structures needs to be modified to include an intermediate structure for the relational contracting mode given characteristics of the construction industry. Second, I will show that Williamson's (1975) treatment of the inside contracting system fulfills this need. This re-emphasizes the notion of a continuum of contracting modes, which was explicit in his earlier statement of the transaction cost approach, within the context of governance structures. Finally, I will present empirical data supporting the existence of the quasifirm from a study of 26 residential homebuilders in eastern Massachusetts. Secondary sources confirm the existence of this organizational form in this and other countries for a variety of general contractor types.

2. The quasifirm as a governance structure

Williamson used three dimensions for characterizing transactions to develop his framework of governance structures for commercial transactions. The three dimensions are '(1) uncertainty, (2) the frequency with which transactions recur, and (3) the degree to which durable transaction specific investments are incurred' [Williamson (1979, p. 239)]. His criterion for organizing commercial transactions was that of economizing on the sum of production and transaction costs. Transactions of recurrent frequency with mixed or highly idiosyncratic investments make market contracting hazardous and permit the cost recovery of specialized governance structures.

In the case of mixed transactions, since asset specialization is incomplete, bilateral structures may be favored for several reasons. Scale economies may favor outside procurement. Outside procurement is also advantageous for cost control, especially under steady-state supply conditions. This organizing mode has problems, however, in terms of adaptability and contractual expense. Quantity adjustments have better incentive-compatibility properties than do price adjustments.

As transactions become increasingly idiosyncratic in terms of investment requirements, economies of scale can be as easily realized by the buyer as by outside suppliers. Vertical integration, the unified governance structure, becomes advantageous. With this form 'adaptations can be made in a sequential way without the need to consult, complete, or revise interfirm agreements' [Williamson (1979, p. 253)].

For mixed investments, as the degree of uncertainty increases so does the necessity for contractual adaptability. If special design features of the purchased component are to be preserved an elaborated governance structure will be required, perhaps resulting in a unified structure. The alternative is to forego valued design features and resort to market governance.

Technical characteristics of construction result in a preferred contracting mode intermediate between bilateral and unified governance structures when certain environmental conditions exist. Using Woodward's (1965) classification of production technologies into unit and small batch, large batch and mass, and process, Thompson (1967) classified construction as an intensive (unit) or job shop technology. Construction projects require a unique combination of labor and material inputs, performed and coordinated on-site. This results in transaction implications different from mass assembly and process technologies typically found in manufacturing.

Construction projects require a large number of labor specialties such as carpenters, bricklayers, plumbers, pipefitters, electricians, painters, roofers, drywallers, sheet metal workers, glaziers, and laborers. These trades differ in terms of work activities, training, skill level, and assessed value in the labor market. Coordinating the work of these labor specialties over the course of a project is a complex task. At any point in time a number of these specialties will be simultaneously involved on the project and often the work of one cannot proceed until a phase of work has been completed by several others.

There are some important differences between job shop and mass assembly or continuous process technologies. In the typical mass assembly process raw materials are progressively transformed over a series of separable steps into the final product. Between each separate step are buffer inventories that absorb fluctuations in output at one stage in order to avoid ripple effects further down the production line. These inventories permit a decoupling of a serially related set of tasks where the input of one task is the output of the preceding task. A major problem of vertical integration is in balancing capacities at each step in the process when scale economies are sought at each step. The balancing problem is essentially that of obtaining integer relationships among input factor proportions since scale economies result in discrete additions to capacity.

In construction the various trades do not have this serial relationship in as rigid a form, although it does exist to a large extent. Some trades cannot proceed or begin until others have completed a task, e.g., carpenters cannot build the walls until the foundation has been completed. Mechanical trades (plumbing, heating and cooling, and electrical) have to complete various tasks before carpenters, masons, and painters can proceed. Between these serial relationships is a certain degree of flexibility, however, which is not a result of buffer inventories. The equivalent in construction to manufacturing inventories (apart from raw materials which are inventories in the true sense) is work in progress.

The loose coupling of some tasks gives trades a range of time within which they need to complete a task. Although the various trades use the work of other trades, they do not incorporate this work into an intermediate product which is then moved on to the next stage of production. In construction the intermediate products are fixed and the men move; the reverse is true of manufacturing. This, combined with the unique nature of construction, eliminates the existence of buffer inventories both within and between trades.

The organization of construction projects involves relationships among the owner, the general contractor, and various special trade contractors. Most typically, the owner writes a general contract with a general contractor who assumes total responsibility for accomplishing the project. Often these projects are for a fixed price on a total or unit of work basis and have time deadlines and financial incentives and penalties. Other forms include cost plus contracts which can also have incentives and penalties. For fixed price contracts general contractors are usually selected by competitive bidding among a group of firms who have been qualified to bid for the project.

The major alternative to the owner-general contractor arrangement is when the owner and general contractor are the same party. This is called 'operative' or 'speculative' building. The owner-general contractor uses his own and borrowed funds to construct a building which is then sold (e.g., a house) or rented (e.g., apartments and office space). Operative building is especially prevalent in the construction of single-family homes.

One of the basic decisions which must be faced by the general contractor is which trades will be performed by workers directly employed by the general contractor and which will be performed by special trade subcontractors. These special trade subcontractors directly hire workers in one or a few related trades and write subcontracts with the general contractor for certain portions of the project. Usually these special trade subcontractors perform work for a number of general contractors. The terms and conditions of these subcontracts are similar to those in the general contract. All contracts and subcontracts are based on terms and conditions established by the owner with the assistance of architects and engineers.

The plans and specifications, which describe the project, its location and characteristics, methods of construction to be used, standards and performance tests which must be met, and raw material suppliers to be used, determine the unique combination of input factors required to complete the project. The uniqueness of the required set of input factors (trades) characterizes both total factor requirements and these requirements as a function of time. Furthermore, site conditions can be unpredictable and on-site production exposes the production process to environmental conditions, especially the weather. As a result of these characteristics of construction's production technology, the general contractor faces a high degree of uncertainty about what resources will be required in the future. Demand volatility exacerbates this uncertainty.

I have argued [Eccles (1979)] that there are strong reasons for the general contractor to make extensive use of subcontractors, based on a theory of subcontracting using concepts borrowed from Stigler (1951), Thompson (1967), and Williamson (1975). Table 1 shows data on the amount of subcontracting by eight basic types of general contractors. These data demonstrate extensive subcontracting. This theory of subcontracting predicts positive relationships between amount of subcontracting and project complexity, project size, and extent of the market. These relationships have been confirmed empirically using census data [Eccles (1981)]. The argument underlying this theory is somewhat complex but the essence is that given bounded rationality of the general contractor in highly uncertain conditions, market contracting for input resources is preferred over vertical integration. The larger amounts of subcontracting for the first four types of general contractors in table 1 is a result of greater project complexity due to the larger number of trades involved and the greater variance in the set of resource requirements over time.

When construction projects are not subject to institutional regulations which require competitive bidding (as in projects funded by federal, state, and municipal agencies), relations between the general contractor and his

Table 1

Annual subcontracting expenditures by eight types of general contractors.[a]

Type of general contractor	Amount subcontracted[b]
Single-family and operative builders	0.386
Residential — other than single-family	0.539
Industrial buildings and warehouses	0.429
Other non-residential	0.543
Highway and street	0.183
Bridge, tunnel, and elevated highway	0.219
Water, sewer, pipeline, communication and power line	0.087
Heavy construction, not elsewhere classified	0.198

[a]*Source*: 1972 Census of Construction Industries (U.S. Government Printing Office, Washington, DC).

[b]Subcontracting expenditures as a ratio of construction receipts.

subcontractors are stable and continuous over fairly long periods of time and only infrequently established through competitive bidding. This type of 'quasi-integration' results in what I call the 'quasifirm'. It is a preferred mode to either pure market transactions or formal vertical integration. On a project basis the relationship resembles neoclassical contracting since both parties have strong incentives to complete the project. As these parties continue to work together from project to project the relational contracting mode appears.

For most construction trades physical capital investment requirements are quite low and not highly idiosyncratic. Human capital investments are more important and a special trade contractor, who focuses on one trade and works for a number of general contractors, can obtain production economies. By working for a number of general contractors the special trade contractor is able to maintain a more constant work force level, thereby economizing on transactions costs which would result from the hiring and firing of workers in response to demand volatility. This transaction cost problem would be especially acute for a general contractor who directly employed a number of trade specialties. Uncertainty about future projects and their resource requirements would create a severe balancing problem for a general contractor employing many trades directly. This problem is eliminated through the use of subcontractors to whom a commitment is made only for the duration of the project. The use of subcontractors with fixed price contracts also facilitates cost control and reduces supervision responsibilities. Clearly, market contracting modes have desirable characteristics when compared to the vertical integration alternative.

But the use of subcontractors through a pure market governance structure has its own attendant problems. Transaction costs would be high if, for every new project, a general contractor solicited bids from a number of subcontractors for each trade. A similar argument can be made for subcontractors, always bidding for projects against a large number of competitors. The necessity to maintain quality under fixed price contracts, with obvious incentives for shirking performance requirements, and the high degree of cooperation required on a project can result in severe consequences if problems develop with the general contractor–subcontractor relationship. Through a continuing association both parties can benefit from the somewhat idiosyncratic investment of learning to work together. Yet since this investment is not *highly* idiosyncratic, both parties have as a viable alternative ending the relationship at the completion of any project. The large numbers of general contractors and special trade subcontractors make this a real alternative, although both parties are able to reduce uncertainty about future business relationships by maintaining a continuing association. Furthermore, the project nature of construction enhances adaptability since the terms of the relationship are renegotiated for every new project.

Thus, the characteristics of construction technology enable recurrent transactions between a general contractor and subcontractors. Both parties benefit from a bilateral structure over a market structure. However, a pure bilateral structure is not required since the market alternative can be invoked without jeopardizing the specificity of component design, i.e., subcontract terms and conditions, by the very nature of construction projects. Although there are advantages to a bilateral structure, the costs of the market structure alternative are not prohibitive. The actual preferred mode is intermediate between these two alternatives. It is also intermediate between bilateral and unified structures. This argument is developed in the following two sections.

3. The quasifirm as inside contracting system

3.1. The transaction cost approach

Williamson's (1975) formulation of the new institutional economics in terms of transactions can be used to demonstrate the existence of quasi-integration by the general contractor. His effort is valuable for two reasons. First, it conceptualizes the study of the division of labor among firms and markets in terms of pairs of factors, one human and one environmental; one pair is bounded rationality and uncertainty/complexity. Thus, not only is bounded rationality in uncertain and complex conditions an important determinant of the structure and management of the firm [Burns and Stalker (1961), Chandler (1962), Lawrence and Lorsch (1967), and Thompson (1967)], but these two factors are also important in determining from the firm's perspective which tasks it will perform and which it will allocate in the market. The other pair, opportunism and small numbers, refers to the degree to which an external resource is a contingency for the firm. For example, if there are only a few suppliers of a good or service in the task environment and the demand for their output is strong, the firm may find supplies unavailable or available only on undesirable terms of cost and/or delivery.

A second value in his approach is that it can be used to study various organizational (hierarchical) forms as well as the market versus hierarchy question. Williamson identified a number of basic forms roughly ordered in terms of increasing internal complexity and vertical integration: markets, peer groups, simple hierarchies, inside contracting systems (unified ownership of plant and equipment), U-form enterprises (centralized–functional), and M-form enterprises (autonomous divisions having operating responsibility with a central office performing strategic planning and offering staff support). This sequence is not a strict unidimensional ordering; the M-form enterprise is both more internally complex and more similar to market organization than the U-form enterprise. Greater internal complexity is reflected in the fact that the M-form enterprise is composed of a number of U-form enterprises (the autonomous divisions) and a corporate headquarters. These autonomous divisions function in many ways like independent firms. Often they compete unsuccessfully with firms in the market for business with each other. Thus, internal transactions in these firms can have similar characteristics to market transactions. In contrast, the inside contracting system is a set of market transactions with similar characteristics to hierarchical transactions. Most generally, pure markets and pure hierarchies are at opposite ends of a continuum of contracting modes.

I will show that the construction equivalent of manufacturing's inside contracting system is viable. To do this, an analogy must be made from the factory to the project. First, I will show that Williamson's general approach argues for subcontracting vs. integration. Second, I will show that these subcontracting relationships can be advantageously organized analogous to the inside contracting system.

3.2. The advantages of subcontracting

Each of the two pairs can be examined for the construction industry. Consider the first pair, opportunism and small numbers. Certainly opportunism exists in the construction industry. Critics of the industry and disgruntled members would say it exists to an excessive degree. But in most cases the small numbers condition does not obtain. Except on very specialized, large jobs or in particular local circumstances there are usually a large number of special trade contractors and general contractors competing for work. This work is often obtained through competitive bidding, one project at a time. Because projects are temporary, limitations are put on the length of time opportunistic behavior has to be suffered by the general contractor (or the subcontractor, for that matter). The uniqueness of projects also helps limit first-mover advantages when it comes time to collect bids for the next job. And because jobs are performed at different sites, explicit reaffirmation of contract renewal for the next job is necessary since the relationship is automatically 'dissolved'.

Self-interest itself helps curb opportunism in light of the temporary nature of construction projects. In some cases the general contractor chooses to negotiate with a subcontractor rather than obtain competitive bids. The desire for future work is an incentive to the subcontractor to establish a good working relationship with the general contractor.

Thus, the temporary nature of projects, their uniqueness, and large numbers of tradesmen substantially reduce the problems of first-mover advantages; sequential spot contracting is a viable contracting mode in construction.

The second pair of factors, bounded rationality and uncertainty/complexity, certainly exists for construction. The factors that reduce first-mover advantages also result in a high degree of uncertainty.

Bounded rationality is especially acute for small firms. There are two possible relationships between small size and subcontracting: (1) subcontracting may be necessary due to small size, or (2) small size may be a result of extensive subcontracting. In the first case, subcontracting is necessary because the bounded rationality of the firm makes it impossible to directly supervise all of the trades. Use of subcontractors reduces the administrative burden on the firm of hiring, supervising, and firing workers in all of the trades. Limited administrative capacity is conserved. Here subcontracting is a consequence of small size which is in turn a result of other factors. These include demand volatility, low entry costs, and the geographical distribution of projects which must be performed on site. Without the constraints of these other factors, the general contractor could alleviate bounded rationality by increasing administrative capacity, thereby permitting direct employment of workers.

Alternatively, small size may be a consequence of the fact that extensive use is made of subcontractors, and subcontractors are used for reasons other than bounded rationality due to small size. Evidence that this is at least partially the case is suggested by the fact that large contractors, with smaller bounded rationality constraints, actually subcontract more than small contractors [Eccles (1981)].

While the relationships among characteristics of construction technology, subcontracting, and firm size are complex, the predominant causality is in the direction of firm size as a consequence of subcontracting. Factors which favor subcontracting, such as the balancing problem and demand volatility, also act as constraints on increasing the administrative component to alleviate bounded rationality problems in order to obtain greater vertical integration. The widely held view that general contractors make extensive use of subcontractors because they are too small grossly oversimplifies the situation. In the construction industry bounded rationality and uncertainty/complexity are both partially a result of a common set of factors. Their simultaneous existence argues for the advantages of subcontracting over vertical integration.

There are other incentives to contract for functional inputs from the market. Fixed price contracts when input costs are uncertain create risk which can be reduced through writing fixed price subcontracts that reduce potential cost over-runs. Since small numbers is not a problem, these required inputs can be obtained at competitive prices. Williamson emphasized how hierarchical transactions can reduce risk, but paid less attention to how market transactions can reduce risk since he approached the problem largely from the perspective of 'market failure'. As a result, most of his argument implies that integration is the response to bounded rationality and uncertainty/complexity.

Whether the response to this pair of factors is integration or disintegration (subcontracting) depends at least partially upon whether it is uncertainty of output (price) because of uncertainty of demand or uncertainty of input (cost) because of unique projects in variable conditions. When demand and prices are uncertain but the firm is relatively sure of obtaining the necessary resource inputs no incentive exists for backward integration. This is the case for construction and here subcontracting is preferred. However, when demand and prices are more certain but uncertainty exists about the availability, cost, and terms of input resources, backward integration is preferred when bounded rationality makes contingent claims contracting prohibitive. The argument here follows Williamson's (1979) discussion of when bilateral structures are replaced with unified ones. A similar argument can be made for forward integration. Most generally, whether or not vertical integration is preferred to some form of market contracting depends upon the relative consequences of bounded rationality under uncertainty/ complexity on the firm's input and output transactions.

3.3. The inside contracting system

The subcontracting of trades can be effectively handled by the construction analogue of the inside contracting system. Under the inside contracting system, one firm contracts with other individuals or firms on a fixed-price or piece-rate basis to perform a certain task, using plant, equipment, materials, and semi-finished goods supplied by the major contractor. These inputs supplied by the major contractor make this an intermediate form between bilateral and unified structures. Buttrick (1952) discussed this system and its disappearance at the Winchester Repeating Arms Company in the early 1900s. It was replaced by an integrated complex hierarchy.

The construction equivalent of the manufacturing plant is the *project*, which is built on-site for a specific owner. With some exceptions (e.g., materials handling machinery), equipment is relatively unimportant in construction, and there is no plant other than the project itself. But just as the manufacturer has the choice of the inside contracting system or directly hiring foremen and workers, so does the general contractor have the choice to integrate or subcontract trades. Most of the five advantages Williamson attributes to the inside contracting system exist in construction. And most of the eight disadvantages attributed by Williamson do *not* exist in construction. Two of the most important reasons for their non-existence are (1) all parties are located on-site and are directed and coordinated by the general contractor only (a wheel network) since (2) construction production is not completely characterized by the technological form of serial, separable stages.

Consider first Williamson's attractive attributes of the inside contracting system. First, 'it provide[s] for the aggregation at a single location of a series of primary work groups that [are] involved in successive manufacturing processes' (1975, p. 96). All parties to the construction project are already on-site because of project immobility. Furthermore, the process is not one of successive stages. Thus, transportation expenses are not even an issue. The 'cheek-by-jowl association . . . with corresponding economies of communication' (1975, p. 96) is inevitable given on-site production. Second, the general contractor has little physical capital which he needs to be concerned about using productively. The inside contracting system relieves the general contractor, with little technical knowledge but who owns the capital equipment, from the responsibility for using it efficiently. What little capital equipment that is required in construction is usually owned by subcontractors. Equipment used directly by the general contractor is often rented. Third, special trade subcontractors, like inside contractors (first-level supervisors) have incentives for efficient labor performance in both supervisory and process innovation respects because of fixed-price contracts and the desire to remain competitive in the market. Fourth, although unlike manufacturing in which the firm's ownership of the plant and equipment limits the monopoly powers of various subcontractors, construction projects are temporary and their completion solves any monopoly problems. Finally, since all parties are at the same site, information impactedness is less of a problem. Therefore, the characteristics of construction and the use of subcontractors result in the same organizational advantages as the inside contracting system does for manufacturing.

But Williamson (1975, pp. 96–97) listed five difficulties and three defective incentives of the inside contracting system:

(1) A bilateral monopoly position, albeit restrained, developed between the parties.
(2) The periodic renegotiation of rates induced the contractor to hoard information and to delay process innovations.
(3) The flow of components was difficult to regulate.
(4) Work-in-progress inventories were excessive and, since each stage incurred only its own direct labor costs, later stage processes were wasteful of components on which early stage work was completed.
(5) Contractor incomes were sometimes excessive in relation to those of the capitalist, endangering the status of company officials.
(6) Equipment was not utilized and maintained with appropriate care.
(7) Process innovations were biased in favor of labor-saving, as against materials-saving, innovations.
(8) Incentives for product innovation were insufficient.

These difficulties contribute to the replacement of the inside contracting system with a complex hierarchy. Instead of having inside contractors, the firm has employees who are foremen in charge of various stages of the production process. If similar advantages of integration do not exist in construction, then some strong incentives for further hierarchical emphasis also do not exist.

All eight disadvantages can be resolved: (1) temporary projects that require the general contractor to reselect subcontractors on the next job prevent bilateral monopoly problems except in peculiar local circumstances where there are a limited number of firms capable of performing work of a given type or magnitude; (2) the contract price (rate) is re-established for each new job, which reduces problems of information hoarding and process innovation delays; (3) there is no flow of components in an intensive technology as in the serial, separable technology assumed by Williamson; (4) the fact that construction is not a series of separable stages with the output of one trade serving as the input for another reduces work-in-progress inventory problems although trades can damage the work of others; (5) excessive incomes are simply not a problem. Data from the *1970 U.S. Census of the Population* reveal under 'Other Managers and Administrators — Self-Employed' (a good approximation of owners of construction firms): In 1969 the mean salary (males only) was $11,900 for Total Construction (General Building, General Except Building, and Special Trade) and $11,747 for Special Trade alone. For females, these figures were $9,010 and $6,201, respectively. There are no large salary differences in favor of special trade contractors; (6) in regard to equipment use, subcontractors own or rent whatever equipment they need and *transport it to the site*, which they can do as easily as the general contractor; (7) subcontractors work according to the plans and specifications of architects, who identify the materials to be used; hence, materials innovation is out of the hands of both the general contractor and the subcontractor and all that the subcontractor *can* do is find labor-saving process innovations; and (8) again, product innovation is the responsibility of the architect so there are no advantages of integration over subcontracting. Therefore, the difficulties that contributed to the inside contracting system being replaced in manufacturing by a complex hierarchy do not exist as strongly in construction.

One other interesting comparison between the inside contracting system and subcontracting in construction can be made. Buttrick (1952, p. 16) noted that a variation of the inside contracting system existed in the machine shop 'long after the system was discarded elsewhere in the plant'. He also noted that there is evidence that many machine shops operated in this fashion considerably past the First World War. A machine shop, working with 'plans and specifications of a new tool, jig, or machine part, "presented" to the machinist for bidding . . . [who] made a profit if the amount paid in wages to others and to himself was less than the amount the company paid him for the finished jig or tool' [Buttrick (1952, p. 216)] very closely approximates the temporary, unique, project nature of construction. One of the major differences noted by Buttrick between the machine shop and the rest of the company was that 'each contract job differed from the next . . . [so] there was not much chance he [the machinist] would become "indispensable"' [Buttrick (1952, p. 217). Here is evidence that technological conditions are an important determinant of organizational form. Although the inside contracting system was a 'stage' in the organization of production it lasted longer for the job shop technology than for the mass assembly technology.

4. Field study evidence of the quasifirm

I have argued that the quasifirm, as the construction analogue to the inside contracting system, is an advantageous governance structure which is intermediate between the bilateral and unified structures. It is also intermediate between relational and neoclassical contracting. The neoclassical aspects arise from the lack of complete continuity in the general contractor–subcontractor relationship. If a subcontractor is not used on every project, contracting relations will take on a more occasional frequency. The frequency becomes more recurrent as a subcontractor is used on all projects. Locating the quasifirm within Williamson's (1979) governance structure matched with commercial transactions simply requires replacing his discrete categories for frequency and investment characteristics with continua. In this section I will (1) review the research design for a study of homebuilders, (2) demonstrate that the firms studied conform to the pattern of extensive subcontracting and discuss the reasons why, (3) use data from this study to demonstrate the existence of the quasifirm, and (4) discuss five categories of relationships in the quasifirm by which the 17 trades can be classified.

4.1. Research design

I conducted interviews with 38 homebuilders in the summer of 1978. Although care should be taken in generalizing these findings since the interviews were restricted to builders in eastern Massachusetts — and a state with a severely depressed housing industry at the time of these interviews — they do provide some insights into the nature of the quasifirm. Secondary sources corroborate the existence of this contracting mode.

Six of the 38 interviews were pilot interviews to test the two questionnaires used. One questionnaire collected data on the firm (years in business, number of units built, etc.) and the other questionnaire collected data on 17 types of subcontractors. Of the 32 remaining interviews it was possible to use 26. The others were excluded either because it turned out that the firm was not in homebuilding (several were remodelers and rehabilitators only) or did not apply for other reasons (e.g., the person interviewed was not able to give me the necessary data). Finally, of the 26 usable interviews, persons at two firms refused to answer the questionnaire on characteristics of the firm and two

Table 2
Characteristics of 22 residential builders eastern Massachusetts. Summer 1978.

	Single family only	Multifamily only	Both	Total
Number of builders	12.0	4.0	6.0	22.0
Average number of units started 1978	22.1	112.2	53.7	69.0
Average years in business	25.1	16.8	24.8	22.9

firms did not start units in 1978. Nearly all of the data discussed here, however, is from the second questionnaire on subcontracting practices.

Table 2 shows the basic characteristics of the builders who were interviewed. Most of them were either single-family only or single- and multifamily builders. There were no very large tract builders in this sample. (In fact, there were very few in all of Massachusetts.) The average builder had been in business almost 23 years.

4.2. Extensive subcontracting

As expected, most of the trades were subcontracted most of the time, although there was substantial variation by trade (table 3). Drywall, electrical, heating and cooling, plaster, plumbing, and tile were nearly always subcontracted. The trades most frequently performed 'in-house' were finish carpentry, finish landscaping, landscaping/rough grading, roofing, rough carpentry, and siding.

For all trades combined the aggregate responses for all trades of why subcontracting was used were: (1) keep overhead costs low (29.6%), (2) lower construction costs (26.6%), (3) insufficient amount of work (16.4%), (4) supervision problems (10.5%), (5) keep equipment investment cost low (0.1%), (6) volatility in workload (0.1%), and (7) miscellaneous, such as need for license, not 'own trade', and faster construction time (15.3%). In only a few instances did homebuilders indicate even a slight possibility of integrating a trade currently being subcontracted within the next five years. Both production and transaction costs were important reasons for subcontracting. Overhead costs and supervision problems are related to transaction costs, and to a certain extent production costs. Similarly, insufficient amount of work is related to both production economies but also the transaction costs involved in hiring and firing workers.

The low figure for keeping equipment investment costs low is not surprising but the same low figure for volatility in workload is quite surprising. Because of this I discussed this issue with the homebuilders in

Table 3

Subcontractors: Amount, type, number, length of relationship with 26 homebuilders in Eastern Massachusetts (1978).

Type of contractor	Subcontract 75–100% of the time	Work always performed by general contractor	Average number of subcontractors	Average length of longest subcontractor relationship in years	Use of labor only subcontractors[a]
Drywall	96.2%	0.0%	2.2	7.6	23.1%
Electrical	100.0	0.0	1.8	11.8	7.7
Finish carpentry	50.0	30.8	2.4	5.3	83.3
Finish landscaping	57.7	38.5	2.0	6.7	43.8
Flooring	88.5	3.8	1.9	8.4	60.0
Foundations	84.6	3.8	2.0	9.9	76.0
Heating and cooling	96.2	3.8	1.9	11.1	4.0
Insulation and caulking	80.8	3.8	1.9	9.6	4.0
Landscaping/ rough grading	46.2	50.0	1.8	11.5	38.5
Masonry	76.9	7.7	2.0	9.5	29.2
Painting	76.9	15.4	2.1	10.7	27.3
Plaster	96.2	0.0	1.9	10.2	0.0
Plumbing	96.2	3.8	1.9	11.1	3.9
Roofing	69.2	26.9	2.6	6.2	89.5
Rough carpentry	61.5	34.6	2.8	7.7	94.1
Siding	65.4	30.8	2.9	6.5	94.4
Tile	100.0	0.0	1.7	9.5	38.5
Average	79.0	14.9	2.1	9.2	41.1

[a]As a percent of builders who subcontract this trade 75–100% of the time.

some depth. Nearly all of them insisted that volatility due to seasonality or business cyclicality was an insignificant factor in their decision to subcontract. They maintained that if volatility due to these two factors were eliminated this would have no effect on the degree of trade integration. It is the nature of construction technology which determines the preferred contracting mode, not market conditions. Further evidence of this is given in the lack of a positive relationship between seasonal variability and extent of subcontracting based on a study using U.S. census data [Eccles (1981)].

Data on type of contracts written with subcontractors support the claim that cost control is facilitated by market-like transactions. The homebuilders were asked to indicate what type of contracts were written for each type of subcontractor. In the aggregate 71.6% were fixed price contracts for the total job. Another 25.1% were fixed price contracts on a unit of work basis such as a certain amount per lineal foot. Hourly rates and time and material contracts, the least effective for cost control, accounted for the remaining 3.3%. Little variation existed in these percentages across the individual trades.

A major potential disadvantage with the use of outside suppliers is that coordination becomes especially difficult. This is an especially serious concern in construction. However, data show that coordinating the work of these subcontractors is not a serious problem. On a five point scale (1 = not difficult, 2 = slightly difficult, 3 = somewhat difficult, 4 = difficult, and 5 = very difficult) the homebuilders were asked to indicate how difficult it was to schedule and coordinate the work of each type of subcontractor. The average for all trades was 1.9, with a range of 1.6 to 2.4, which indicates that subcontractors can be effectively scheduled and coordinated. This is substantiated by the response to the question of how frequently the progress of the job was delayed by each type of subcontractor (1 = never, 2 = rarely, 3 = sometimes, 4 = often, and 5 = very often). The average for all trades was 2.4, with a range of 2.0 to 2.9. Given the uncertainty of construction's production technology and the many problems that can occur, it appears that using subcontractors does not materially interfere with the progress of the job.

4.3. Evidence of the quasifirm

Evidence for the existence of the quasifirm is found in the number of subcontractors used in each trade, the length of general contractor–subcontractor relationships, the use of labor-only subcontractors, and procedures used for selecting subcontractors for a project. These data reveal a governance structure with some market characteristics which is intermediate between bilateral and unified structures.

As shown in table 3, the average number of subcontractors for all trades combined was only 2.1. Some special forms of two-subcontractor relationships included geographical location (one electrical contractor for north, one for south), subspecialties (tar and gravel roofing, for example, is a distinct roofing specialty), a regular subcontractor and a fill-in, and two subcontractors in duopolistic competition. Given the large number of available subcontractors and the number of projects started in the course of a year, it is highly unlikely that only two subcontractors would be used if pure market contracting modes were used.

It is clear that general contractors recurrently do business with a small number of subcontractors. The range was only 1.7 to 2.9 which shows that this practice holds for all trades. There were four or more subcontractors in only 9.7% of the cases. The largest number was six and occurred in only three cases, less than 1.0%. In 37.8% of the cases there was only one subcontractor. General contractor–subcontractor relations for each trade can be characterized as a recurrent series of transactions with a small number of subcontractors.

Further evidence of the stability of general contractor–subcontractor relations is found in the average length of the longest relationships for each trade. As shown in table 3, the average for all trades was 9.2 years. The range was from 5.3 years to 11.8 years. In 11.2% of these cases the subcontractors had been with the builder for 20 years or more. The longest relationship was 37 years (an electrical subcontractor). Two electrical subcontractors were also next with 30 and 27 years, and another tied with several other types for 25-year relationships. These recurrent relationships involving a few subcontractors in each trade can exist for substantial periods of time.

Others have noted the practice of general contractors using a selected group of subcontractors for long periods of time. In his comprehensive study of homebuilding firms in the San Francisco area Maisel (1953) noted that the same subcontractors were used from project to project and that often these subcontractors worked only for one builder. 'Together, the builder and his subcontractors form an organizational unit, albeit an informal one' [Maisel (1953, p. 142)]. Hutton (1970) noted this practice in Australia, as did Sansom (1959) in a cross-national study (Denmark, Norway, Belgium, Austria, Holland, Italy, France, Great Britain, and West Germany) involving 26 firms and 50 building sites. He (1959, p. 42) noted:

> 'It was quite frequently found, for example, that a main contractor always sublet the same work to the same one or two subcontractors (often painting, plumbing, electrical work or glazing), or that a small subcontractor, particularly one for labor only, might work almost entirely for one main contractor. In some cases connections of 30 years' duration or more existed, and a main contractor would even assist in finding men for a subcontractor if a shortage occurred on a particular job.'

For relationships to continue this long both parties must find it beneficial. The small number of subcontractors and the length of the relationships characterize a fairly stable set of bilateral structures, centered on the general contractor, which performs a large number of projects over a period of time. The quasifirm, not a completely vertically integrated firm, not a collection of firms determined by pure market transactions, and not a bilateral structure involving only one subcontractor in each trade (a set of monopolistic relationships) moves from project to project, at each move balancing the advantages of market, bilateral and unified governance structures.

The existence of a substantial amount of labor-only subcontracting demonstrates that the quasifirm is intermediate between bilateral and unified governance structures. The builders' average use of labor-only subcontractors was 41.1% (table 3). Labor-only subcontractors work with material purchased by the general contractor. They are very similar to employees working on a piece rate basis, especially given the small size of most subcontracting firms. According to census data [U.S. Bureau of the Census (1975)], 61.9% of all special trade construction firms have no employees and 22.8% have one to four employees. The average for all special trade firms is 3.3 and for those with employees 8.8. In many cases the distinction between employees and subcontractors can be a very fuzzy one indeed. This is especially true given the fact that the builders indicated that some of their subcontractors worked almost exclusively for them. It is in these cases where general contractor–subcontractor relationships most resemble the inside contracting system in which the major contractor supplies the plant, equipment, and materials.

The quasifirm contracting mode is intermediate between bilateral and unified structures. When materials are purchased by the general contractor, the relationship is recurrent and stable, and the subcontractor works almost exclusively for one general contractor, it is only fixed price contracts on a total or unit basis which formally distinguish between a bilateral and a unified structure. For all practical purposes integration exists except for the fact neither party would describe it as an employer–employee relationship. The practice of labor-only subcontracting appears to be prevalent. Abrams (1946), Colean (1947), Foster (1974), Haber (1930), Haber and Levinson (1956), and Meyerson et al. (1962) discussed this practice in the United States. Hillebrandt (1971) noted this practice in Great Britain, Hutton (1970) noted its existence in Australia, and Sansom (1959) reported its use in his cross-national study. The existence of this practice in many countries over a long period of time must be a result of common factors of construction technology which makes it a contracting mode that economizes on production and transaction costs.

The builders were asked which of five basic methods they used for selecting subcontractors for each trade and establishing the contract price. Results were similar for all types of subcontractors. For all trades combined, formal competitive bidding, in which the lowest bidder is automatically awarded the contract, was used in only 19.6% of the cases. Formal competitive bidding is the market contracting mode in its purest form. All other methods used involve some form of negotiation: 24.5% negotiated selection and price on a project basis, 23.4% negotiated fixed unit prices which would apply for a set period of time with selected subcontractors, 18.5% used competitive bidding while retaining discretion to select a subcontractor other than the lowest bidder, and 14.0% simply accepted the price given to them by the subcontractor. Maisel (1953) reported similar results with 85% of the firms in his study using direct negotiation rather than formal competitive bidding. Sansom (1959) also reported that competitive bidding was not the predominant contracting mode.

Nearly all of the contractors who used some form of negotiation periodically 'tested the market', either through formal competitive bidding or simply by asking other builders what prices they were paying for subcontractors. Sansom (1959) also reported this practice in his cross-national study. Sometimes this was done proactively. Other times a builder accepted a subcontractor's prices until they started to 'feel out of line'. Most builders evinced confidence in knowing what the 'going rate' was for the different types of work. This information seems to be efficiently transmitted in the market. The builders, especially the larger ones, also spoke of being approached by subcontractors who would offer very low prices as an incentive to the builder to give them an opportunity to work for him and establish a relationship. Builders were cautious in accepting these offers, however, due to concerns about quality and experiences in the past when a subcontractor had started to raise his prices once he thought he was firmly established.

Many builders found that even when they resorted to competitive bidding, their usual subcontractors submitted the lowest bids. Sansom (1959) found evidence of this as well. Presumably, some efficiencies (first-mover advantages) accrue to subcontractors who gain experience in working with a builder. These gains are both in terms of familiarity with the builder's own work methods and experience with a certain type of building. Of course, there are undoubtedly cases where the subcontractor is simply clever enough to submit a bid he is fairly confident will be lowest, knowing that this is only a 'market test'. His ability to do this, however, is limited if future work is of an identical variety and the same prices would be expected to hold.

Data from this study can be used to summarize the quasifirm contracting mode. The quasifirm is centered on a general contractor who makes extensive use of subcontractors. In each trade only a few subcontractors are used. With them the general contractor has recurrent transactions which continue over long periods of time. In many cases they are labor-only subcontractors who work with materials supplied by the general contractor. Various forms of negotiation are used in about 80% of the cases and formal competitive bidding in the remaining 20% to select subcontractors and establish contract prices for a project. These prices are almost always either fixed total prices or fixed unit prices. This fairly stable collection of firms, with some variation in the subset of subcontractors used on each project, contains both market and hierarchical transaction characteristics. It contains aspects of classical contracting (with some elements of neoclassical contracting) and is intermediate between bilateral and unified governance structures.

4.4. *Relationships in the quasifirm*

The 17 types of subcontractors can be grouped into five categories on the basis of similarities in contracting relationships. Two criteria define these categories: extent of vertical integration and similarity to the inside contracting system. These categories make it possible to make a more detailed examination of the quasifirm than the general description derived above without treating every trade as a unique case. The five categories are: (1) basic trades — finish carpentry, roofing, rough carpentry, and siding, (2) labor specialties — flooring and foundations, (3) labor and material specialties — drywall, insulation and caulking, masonry, painting, plaster, and tile, (4) unskilled trades — finish landscaping and landscaping/rough grading, and (5) technical specialties — electrical, heating and cooling, and plumbing. Table 4 shows the important characteristics for each of these categories. The basic and unskilled trades categories are distinguished by being more often integrated. In these two categories it is less clear which contracting mode is preferable. The other three categories are comprised of trades which are nearly always subcontracted.

The basic trades category is comprised of the carpentry-based aspects of a project. These tasks are essential for controlling the progress of the job. This helps explain the lesser degree of subcontracting of 61.5%. In 30.8% of the firms studied these trades had always been performed directly by the firm. When asked why these tasks were performed in-house, 51.2% cited better coordination and control as the primary reason, 25.6% cited better quality work, and 18.6% cited faster job completion. Only 2.3% of the builders cited lower construction cost as a reason for vertical integration. For the basic trades, integration versus subcontracting is often a trade off between lower costs, on the one hand, and coordination and quality, on the other. This is not always an easy decision as reflected in the fact that about a third of the firms used to subcontract but have integrated and vice versa. Relationships with subcontractors in the basic trades closely resemble employees working

Table 4
A typology for contracting relationships in the quasifirm.

	Basic trades	Labor specialties	Labor and material specialties	Unskilled trades	Technical specialties
Subcontract 75–100% of the time[a]	61.5%	86.6%	87.8%	52.0%	97.5%
Always integrated[b]	30.8%	3.8%	4.5%	44.3%	2.5%
Formerly integrated[c]	35.6%	13.5%	17.3%	13.5%	3.8%
Formerly subcontracted[d]	30.8%	3.8%	4.5%	44.3%	2.5%
Use of labor-only subcontractors[e]	90.3%	68.0%	20.4%	41.2%	5.2%
Average number of subcontractors	2.7	2.0	2.0%	1.9%	1.9
Average length of longest subcontractor relationship	6.4	9.2	9.5	8.1	11.3
Skill level[f]	3.6	3.2	3.4	2.4	4.2

Basic trades — finish carpentry, roofing, rough carpentry, siding.
Labor specialties — flooring, foundations.
Labor and material specialties — drywall, insulation and caulking, masonry, painting, plaster, tile.
Unskilled trades — finish landscaping, landscaping/rough grading.
Technical specialties — electrical, heating and cooling, plumbing.

[a]Percent of builders who subcontract 75–100% of the time.
[b]Percent of builders who have always performed trade in-house.
[c]Percent of builders who used to perform trade in-house but now subcontract.
[d]Percent of builders who used to subcontract but now perform trade in-house.
[e]Percent of labor-only subcontractors by builders who subcontract trade.
[f]Average skill level on scale of 1 (=low skill) to 5 (=high skill).

on fixed price contracts of some form. Thus, 90.3% are labor-only subcontractors. The more transient nature of these relationships is shown by the lowest average length of longest relationship (6.4 years) and the highest average number of subcontractors (2.7). Relationships with these trades most closely resemble the inside contracting system.

A somewhat surprising finding of this study was the large amount of integration of the unskilled trades category comprised of finish landscaping and landscaping/rough grading (48.0%). These tasks are usually performed by unskilled laborers as reflected in the low average skill level rating the builders gave these phases of the job (2.4). Not only had 44.3% of the builders always performed these trades themselves, but 44.3% used to subcontract and are now integrated. Nearly all of the change in both directions had been for finish landscaping, with twice as many deciding to integrate as deciding to shift to subcontractors.

As with the basic trades, the decision of what is the preferred contracting mode is not an easy one. Better coordination and control is about equally important a reason for integration (41.7%) as is better quality of work (20.8%). Lower construction costs are a more important reason (25.5%). It is easy to obtain scale economies since these workers can be used for many other tasks such as helping the more skilled trades. This facilitates integration. These relationships are also similar to employer/employee relationships in the 41.2% of the cases using labor-only subcontractors. To a lesser extent than the basic trades, relationships with the general contractor resemble the inside contracting system, but bilateral structures are more common when subcontractors are used.

The labor specialties category is distinguished by these tasks nearly always been subcontracted but with substantial use of labor-only subcontractors. These trades are less critical to the progress of the project than the basic trades. Economies are obtained by subcontracting these trades but the materials needed, largely wood and concrete, can be easily purchased by the general contractor. These trades closely resemble the inside contracting system in their relationship with the general contractor.

The labor and material specialties category has the largest number of trades and is the most heterogenous category. While all of these trades are nearly always subcontracted, there is some variation in use of labor–only subcontractors (from 4.0% to 38.5%) and in skill level (from 2.3 to 3.9). Typically these subcontractors buy their own materials. These relationships are very stable (the longest averaging 9.5 years) but more closely resemble a bilateral structure rather than the inside contracting system.

The final category of technical specialties is comprised of the mechanical trades of electrical, heating and cooling, and plumbing. It is characterized by the highest average skill level (4.2), nearly total use of subcontractors, almost no use of labor-only subcontractors, and stable relationships (11.3 years). The only case of vertical integration was a heating, cooling, and plumbing contractor who had diversified into homebuilding and still performed these trades. Even he commented that he wished he had decided to subcontract this work from the start. These trades are most distinctly separable from the rest of the project in terms of the training and types of skills required and their coordination with the rest of the trades. For these trades the relationship is almost a pure bilateral structure.

References

Abrams, Charles, 1946, The future of housing (Harper & Row, New York).
Bennigson, Lawrence, 1971, The strategy of running temporary projects, Innovation 24, 32–41.
Burns, Tom and G.M. Stalker, 1961, The management of innovation (Tavistock, London). Republished as Social Science Paperback, 1966.
Buttrick, John, 1952, The inside contract system, The Journal of Economic History 12, 205–221.
Chandler, Alfred D., Jr., 1962, Strategy and structure (MIT Press, Cambridge, MA).
Colean, Miles L., 1947, American housing, problems and prospects (Twentieth Century Fund, New York).
Eccles, Robert G., 1979, Organization and market structure in the construction industry: A study of subcontracting, Unpublished doctoral dissertation (Harvard University, Cambridge, MA).
Eccles, Robert G., 1981, Bureaucratic and craft administration revisited: The impact of market structure on the nature of the construction firm, Administrative Science Quarterly 26, 449–469.
Foster, Howard G., 1974, Manpower in homebuilding: A preliminary analysis (University of Pennsylvania Press, Philadelphia, PA).
Haber, William, 1930, Industrial relations in the building industry (Harvard University Press, Cambridge, MA).
Haber, William and Harold M. Levinson, 1956, Labor relations and productivity in the building trades (University of Michigan Press, Ann Arbor, MI).
Hillebrandt, Patricia M., 1971, Small firms in the construction industry (Her Majesty's Stationery Office, London).
Hutton, John, 1970, Building and construction in Australia (University of Melbourne, Melbourne).
Lawrence, Paul R. and Jay W. Lorsch, 1967, Organization and environment (Harvard Business School Division of Research, Boston, MA).
Maisel, Sherman J., 1953, Housebuilding in transition (University of California Press, Berkeley, CA).
Meyerson, Martin, Barbara Terrett and William L.C. Wheaton, 1962, Housing, people, and cities (McGraw-Hill, New York).
Sansom, P.C., 1959, Organization of building sites (Her Majesty's Stationery Office, London).
Stigler, George J., 1951, The division of labor is limited by the extent of the market, The Journal of Political Economy 3, 185–193.
Thompson, James D., 1967, Organizations in action (McGraw-Hill, New York).
U.S. Bureau of the Census, 1972, 1970 Census of the population (U.S. Government Printing Office, Washington, DC).
U.S. Bureau of the Census, 1975, 1972 Census of construction industries (U.S. Government Printing Office, Washington, DC).
Williamson, Oliver E., 1975, Markets and hierarchies: Analysis and antitrust implications (Free Press, New York).
Williamson, Oliver E., 1979, Transaction cost economics: The governance of contractual relations, Journal of Law and Economics 22, 233–261.
Woodward, Joan, 1965, Industrial organization: Theory and practice (Oxford University Press, Oxford).

[19]

Neither Market Nor Hierarchy: Network Forms of Organization

Walter W. Powell

Network forms of organization – typified by reciprocal patterns of communication and exchange – represent a viable pattern of economic organization. Networks are contrasted with market and hierarchical governance structures, and the distinctive features of networks are highlighted. Illustrative examples of network arrangements – in craft and high-technology industries, in regional economies, and in formerly vertically integrated fields – are presented. The paper concludes with a discussion of the conditions that give rise to network forms.

In recent years, there has been a considerable amount of research on organizational practices and arrangements that are network-like in form. This diverse literature shares a common focus on lateral or horizontal patterns of exchange, interdependent flows of resources, and reciprocal lines of communication. Yet this rich vein of work has had much impact on students of organizational behavior. This is not particularly surprising, given the many divergent strands of this work. One would need to have followed the fields of international business, technology strategy, industrial relations, organizational sociology, and the new institutional economics, as well as interdisciplinary work on such themes as cooperation, the embeddedness of economic life in social structure, and the proliferation of small business units to have kept abreast. The purpose of this chapter is to render this literature more accessible to scholars in the organizational behavior field. I do so by arguing that relational or network forms of organization are a clearly identifiable and viable form of economic exchange under certain specifiable circumstances.

I begin by discussing why the familiar market-hierarchy continuum does not do justice to the notion of network forms of organization. I then contrast three modes of organization – market, hierarchy, and network – and stress the salient features of each. The logic of network forms is explored systematically in order to demonstrate how networks differ from other forms. I cull the literature in a number of social science and management fields and provide examples of a wide range of organizational arrangements that can be characterized as networks. This review affords considerable insight into the etiology of network forms, and allows me to develop a number of empirically disconfirmable arguments about the circumstances that give rise to networks and allow them to proliferate. I close with some thoughts on the research agenda that follows from these arguments.

Markets and Firms

In his classic article on the nature of the firm, the economist Ronald Coase (1937) conceived of the firm as a governance structure, breaking with orthodox accounts of the firm as a 'black box' production function. Coase's key insight was that firms and markets were alternative means for organizing similar kinds of transactions. This provocative paper, however, lay fallow, so to speak, for nearly four decades, until it was picked up by Williamson and other proponents of transaction costs economics in the 1970s. This work took seriously the notion that organizational form matters a great deal, and in so doing moved the economics of organization much closer to the fields of law, organization theory, and business history.

The core of Williamson's (1975; 1985) argument is that transactions that involve uncertainty about their outcome, that recur frequently and require substantial 'transaction-specific investments' – of money, time or energy that cannot be easily transferred – are more likely to take place within hierarchically organized firms. Exchanges that are straightforward, non-repetitive and require no transaction-specific investments will take place across a market interface. Hence, transactions are moved out of markets into hierarchies as knowledge specific to the transaction (asset specificity) builds up. When this occurs, the inefficiencies of bureaucratic organization will be preferred to the relatively greater costs of market transactions. There are two reasons for this: (1) bounded rationality – the inability of economic actors to write contracts that cover all possible contingencies; when transactions are internalized, there is little need to anticipate such contingencies since they can be handled within the firm's 'governance structure'; and (2) 'opportunism' – the rational pursuit by economic actors of their own advantage, with every means at their disposal, including guile and deceit; opportunism is mitigated by authority relations and by the stronger identification that parties presumably have when they are joined under a common roof.

This dichotomous view of markets and hierarchies (Williamson, 1975) sees firms as separate from markets or more broadly, the larger societal context. Outside the boundaries of firms are competitors, while inside managers exercise authority and curb opportunistic behavior. This notion of sharp firm boundaries was not just an academic view. A good deal of management practice as well as antitrust law shared the belief that, in Richardson's (1972) colorful language, firms are 'islands of planned co-ordination in a sea of market relations.'

But just as many economists have come to view firms as governance structures, and are providing new insights into the organization of the employment relationship and the multidivisional firm (to cite only two examples), firms appear to be changing in significant ways and forms of relational contracting have assumed much greater importance. Firms are blurring their established boundaries and engaging in forms of collaboration that resemble neither the familiar alternative of arms-length market contracting nor the former ideal of vertical integration.

Some scholars respond to these changes by arguing that economic changes can be arrayed in a continuum-like fashion, with discrete market transactions located at one end and the highly centralized firm at the other. In between these poles, we find various intermediate or hybrid forms of organization.[1] Moving from the market pole, where prices capture all the relevant information necessary for exchange, we find putting-out systems, various kinds of repeated trading, quasi-firms, and subcontracting arrangements; toward the hierarchy pole, franchising, joint ventures, decentralized profit centers, and matrix management are located.

Is this continuum view satisfactory? Can transaction costs logic meet the task of explaining this rich array of alternative forms? Williamson clearly thinks that it can. Shifting gears somewhat, he remarks that he is 'now persuaded that transactions in the middle range are much more common' than he previously recognized (Williamson, 1985, p. 83).[2] But, he avers, the distribution of transactions are such that the tails of this continuum from market to hierarchy are 'thick.'

I do not share the belief that the bulk of economic exchange fits comfortably at either of the poles of the market–hierarchy continuum. The legal theorist Ian Macneil (1985, p. 485) also disputes this view, arguing that, 'discrete exchange can play only a very limited and specialized function in any economy.'[3] Moreover, although I was earlier of the view that nonmarket, nonhierarchical forms represented hybrid modes (Powell, 1987), I now find that this mixed mode or intermediate notion is not particularly helpful. It is historically inaccurate, overly static, and it detracts from our ability to explain many forms of collaboration that are viable means of exchange.[4]

The view that transactions are distributed at points along a continuum implies that markets are the starting point, the elemental form of exchange out of which other methods evolve. Such a view is, obviously, a distortion of historical and anthropological evidence. As Moses Finley (1973) tells us so well, there was no market in the modern sense of the term in the classical world, only money in the nature of free booty and treasure trove. Nor did markets spring full blown with the Industrial Revolution. Economic units emerged from the dense webs of political, religious and social affiliations that had enveloped economic activity for centuries. Agnew (1986) documents that the word market first enters the English language during the twelfth century to refer to specific locations where provisions and livestock were sold. The markets of medieval England had a highly personal, symbolic, and hierarchical flavor. E.P. Thompson (1971) used the term 'the moral economy' to characterize the intricate pattern of symbolic and statutory expectations that surrounded the eighteenth century marketplace. It was not until the latter part of the eighteenth century that among the British educated classes the term market became separated from a physical and social space and came to imply a boundless and timeless phenomenon of buying and selling (Agnew, 1986).[5]

By the same token, hierarchies do not represent an evolutionary end-point of economic development. A long view of business history would suggest that firms with strictly defined boundaries and highly centralized operations are quite atypical.[6] The history of modern commerce, whether told by Braudel, Polanyi, Pollard, or Wallerstein, is a story of family businesses, guilds, cartels, and extended trading companies – all enterprises with loose and highly permeable boundaries.

Recent work on the growth of small firms also casts doubt on the utility of a continuum view of economic exchange. Larson (1988) and Lorenzoni and Ornati (1988) draw similar portraits from very different settings – high tech start-ups in the United States and craft-based firms in Northern Italy – which do not follow the standard model of small firms developing internally through an incremental and linear process. Instead, they suggest an entirely different model of externally-driven growth in which preexisting networks of relationships enable small firms to gain an established foothold almost overnight. These networks serve as conduits to provide small firms with the capacity to meet resource and functional needs.[7]

The idea that economic exchanges can be usefully arrayed along a continuum is thus too quiescent and mechanical. It fails to capture the complex realities of exchange.[8] The continuum view also misconstrues patterns of economic development and blinds us to the role played by reciprocity and collaboration as alternative governance mechanisms. By sticking to the twin pillars of markets and hierarchies, our attention is deflected from a diversity of organizational designs that are neither fish nor fowl, nor some mongrel hybrid, but a distinctly different form.

To be sure, there are a number of social scientists who question whether the distinction between market and hierarchy is particularly useful in the first place.[9] They contend that no sharp demarcation exists and that the argument is more a matter of academic pigeon-holing than of substantive operational differences. These analysts are united, however, more by their dislike of stylized models of economic exchange than by any shared alternative perspective.

One group of critics emphasizes the embeddedness of economics in social and cultural forces. Markets, in this view, are structured by a complex of local, ethnic, and trading cultures, and by varying regimes of state regulation (Gordon, 1985). Historians and sociologists contend that the market is not an amoral self-subsistent institution, but a cultural and social construction (Agnew, 1986; Reddy, 1984; Zelizer, 1988).[10] Others maintain that markets cannot be insulated from social structure because differential social access results in information asymmetries, as well as bottlenecks, thus providing some parties with considerable benefits and leaving others disadvantaged (Granovetter, 1985; White, 1981).

Another chorus of skeptics point to the intermingling of various forms of exchange. (See Bradach and Eccles, 1989, for a good review of this literature.) Stinchcombe (1985) shows that there are strong elements of hierarchy and domination in written contracts. Goldberg (1980, p. 338) notes that many market exchanges have been replaced by interorganizational collaborations. He contends that much economic activity 'takes place within long-term, complex, multiparty contractual (or contract-like) relationships; behavior is in various degrees sheltered from market forces.' Similarly, much of the observed behavior in hierarchical firms seems unrelated to either top management directives or the logic of vertical integration. For example, a firm's relationships with its law, consulting, accounting, and banking firms may be much more enduring and personal than its employment relationship with even its most senior employees.[11] The introduction of market processes into the firm also appears to be widespread. Eccles (1985) observes that large firms commonly rely on such market-like methods as transfer pricing and performance-based compensation schemes, while Eccles and Crane (1987) report that dual reporting relationships, internal competition, and compensation based on services provided to clients are the current norm in investment banking.

Markets, Hierarchies, and Networks

I have a good deal of sympathy regarding the view that all economic exchange is embedded in a particular social structural context. Yet it is also the case that certain forms of exchange are more social – that is, more dependent on relationships, mutual interests, and reputation – as well as less guided by a formal structure of authority. My aim is to identify a coherent set of factors that make it meaningful to talk about networks as a distinctive form of coordinating economic activity. We can then employ these ideas to generate arguments about the frequency, durability, and limitations of networks.

When the items exchanged between buyers and sellers possess qualities that are not easily measured, and the relations are so long-term and recurrent that it is difficult to speak of the parties as separate entities, can we still regard this as a market exchange? When the entangling strings of obligation and reputation reach a point that the actions of the parties are interdependent, but there is no common ownership or legal framework, do we not need a new conceptual tool kit to describe and analyze this relationship? Surely this patterned exchange looks more like a marriage than a one-night stand, but there is no marriage license, no common household, no pooling of assets. In the language I employ below, such an arrangement is neither a market transaction nor a hierarchical governance structure, but a separate, different mode of exchange, one with its own logic, a network.

Many firms are no longer structured like medieval kingdoms, walled off and protected from hostile outside forces. Instead, we find companies involved in an intricate latticework of collaborative ventures with other firms, most of whom are ostensibly competitors. The dense ties that bind the auto and biotechnology industries, discussed below, cannot be easily explained by saying that these firms are engaged in market transactions for some factors of production, or by suggesting that the biotechnology business is embedded in the international community of science. At what point is it more accurate to characterize these alliances as networks rather than as joint ventures among hierarchical firms?

We need fresh insights into these kinds of arrangements. Whether they are new forms of exchange that have recently emerged or age-old practices that have gained new prominence (more on the etiology of networks below), they are not satisfactorily explained by existing approaches. Markets, hierarchies, and networks are pieces of a larger puzzle that is the economy. The properties of the parts of this system are defined by the kinds of interaction that take place among them. The behaviors and interests of individual actors are shaped by these patterns of interaction. Stylized models of markets, hierarchies, and networks are not perfectly descriptive of economic reality, but they enable us to make progress in understanding the extraordinary diversity of economic arrangements found in the industrial world today.

Table 1 represents a first cut at summarizing some of the key differences among markets, hierarchies, and networks. In market transactions the benefits to be exchanged are clearly specified, no trust is required, and agreements are bolstered by the power of legal sanction. Network forms of exchange, however, entail indefinite, sequential transactions within the context of a general pattern of interaction. Sanctions are typically normative rather than legal. The value of the goods to be exchanged in markets is much more important than the relationship itself; when relations do matter, they are frequently defined as if they were commodities. In hierarchies, communication occurs in the context of the employment contract. Relationships matter and previous interactions shape current ones, but the patterns and context of intraorganizational exchange are most strongly shaped by one's position within the formal hierarchical structure of authority.

The philosophy that undergirds exchange also contrasts sharply across forms. In markets the standard strategy is to drive the hardest possible bargain in the immediate exchange. In networks, the preferred option is often one of creating indebtedness and reliance over the long haul. Each approach thus devalues the other: prosperous market traders would be viewed as petty and untrustworthy shysters in networks, while successful participants in networks who carried those practices into competitive markets would be viewed as naïve and foolish. Within hierarchies, communication and exchange are shaped by concerns with career mobility – in this sense, exchange is bound up with considerations of personal advancement. At the same time, intraorganizational communication takes place among parties who generally know one another,

Table 1 Stylized Comparison of Forms of Economic Organization

	Forms		
Key Features	Market	Hierarchy	Network
Normative Basis	Contract– Property Rights	Employment Relationship	Complementary Strengths
Means of Communication	Prices	Routines	Relational
Methods of Conflict Resolution	Haggling– resort to courts for enforcement	Administrative fiat–Supervision	Norm of reciprocity– Reputational concerns
Degree of Flexibility	High	Low	Medium
Amount of Commitment Among the Parties	Low	Medium to High	Medium to High
Tone or Climate	Precision and/or Suspicion	Formal, bureaucratic	Open-ended, mutual benefits
Actor Preferences or Choices	Independent	Dependent	Interdependent
Mixing of Forms	Repeat transactions (Geertz, 1978)	Informal organization (Dalton, 1957)	Status Hierarchies
	Contracts as hierarchical documents (Stinchcombe, 1985)	Market-like features: profit centers, transfer pricing (Eccles, 1985)	Multiple Partners Formal rules

have a history of previous interactions, and possess a good deal of firm-specific knowledge, thus there is considerable interdependence among the parties. In a market context, it is clear to everyone concerned when a debt has been discharged, but such matters are not nearly as obvious in networks or hierarchies.

Markets, as described by economic theory, are a spontaneous coordination mechanism that imparts rationality and consistency to the self-interested actions of individuals and firms. One need not go as far as Polanyi (1957) did, when he argued that market transactions are characterized by an 'attitude involving a distinctive antagonistic relationship between the partners,' but it is clear that market exchanges typically entail limited personal involvement. 'A contract connects two people only at the edges of their personalities' (Walzer, 1983, p. 83). The market is open to all comers, but while it brings people together, it does not establish strong bonds of altruistic attachments. The participants in a market transaction are free of any future commitments. The stereotypical competitive market is the paradigm of individually self-interested, noncooperative, unconstrained social interaction. As such, markets have powerful incentive effects for they are the arena which each party can fulfill its own internally defined needs and goals.

Markets offer choice, flexibility, and opportunity. They are a remarkable device for fast, simple communication. No one need rely on someone else for direction, prices alone determine production and exchange. Because individual behavior is not dictated by a supervising agent, no organ of systemwide governance or control is necessary. Markets are a form of noncoercive organization, they have coordinating but not integrative effects. As Hayek (1945) suggested, market coordination is the result of human actions but not of human design.

Prices are a simplifying mechanism; consequently they are unsuccessful at capturing the intricacies of idiosyncratic, complex, and dynamic exchange. As a result, markets are a poor device for learning and the transfer of technological know-how. In a stylized perfect market, information is freely available, alternative buyers or sellers are easy to come by, and there are no carry-over effects from one transaction to another. But as exchanges become more frequent and complex, the costs of conducting and monitoring them increase, giving rise to the need for other methods of structuring exchange.

Organization, or hierarchy, arises when the boundaries of a firm expand to internalize transactions and resource flows that were previously conducted in the marketplace. The visible hand of management supplants the invisible hand of the market in coordinating supply and demand. Within a hierarchy, individual employees operate under a regime of administrative procedures and work roles defined by higher level supervisors. Management divides up tasks and positions and establishes an authoritative system of order. Because tasks are often quite specialized, work activities are highly interdependent. The large vertically-integrated firm is thus an eminently social institution, with its own routines, expectations, and detailed knowledge.

A hierarchical structure – clear departmental boundaries, clean lines of authority, detailed reporting mechanisms, and formal decision making procedures – is particularly well-suited for mass production and distribution. The requirements of high volume, high speed operations demand the constant attention of a managerial team. The strength of hierarchical organization, then, is its reliability – its capacity for producing large numbers of goods or services of a given quality repeatedly – and its accountability – its ability to document how resources have been used (DiMaggio and Powell, 1983; Hannan and Freeman, 1984). But when hierarchical forms are confronted by sharp fluctuations in demand and unanticipated changes, their liabilities are exposed.

Networks are 'lighter on their feet' than hierarchies. In network modes of resource allocation, transactions occur neither through discrete exchanges nor by administrative fiat, but through networks of individuals engaged in reciprocal, preferential, mutually supportive actions. Networks can be complex: they involve neither the explicit criteria of the market, nor the familiar paternalism of the hierarchy. The basic assumption of network relationships is that one party is dependent on resources controlled by another, and that there are gains to be had by the pooling of resources.[12] In essence, the parties to a network agree to forego the right to pursue their own interests at the expense of others.

In network forms of resource allocation, individual units exist not by themselves, but in relation to other units. These relationships take considerable effort to establish and sustain, thus they constrain both partners' ability to adapt to changing circumstances. As networks evolve, it becomes more economically sensible to exercise voice rather than exit. Benefits and burdens come to be shared. Expectations are not frozen, but change as circumstances dictate. A mutual orientation – knowledge which the parties assume each has about the other and upon which they draw in communication and problem solving – is established. In short, complementarity and accommodation are the cornerstones of successful production networks. As Macneil (1985) has suggested, the 'entangling strings' of reputation, friendship, interdependence, and altruism become integral parts of the relationship.

Networks are particularly apt for circumstances in which there is a need for efficient, reliable information. The most useful information is rarely that which flows down the formal chain of command in an organization, or that which can be inferred from shifting price signals. Rather, it is that which is obtained from someone whom you have dealt with in the past and found to be reliable. You trust best information that comes from someone you know well. Kaneko and Imai (1987) suggest that information passed through networks is 'thicker' than information obtained in the market, and 'freer' than that communicated in a hierarchy. Networks, then, are especially useful for the exchange of commodities whose value is not easily measured. Such qualitative matters as know-how, technological capability, a particular approach or style of production, a spirit of innovation or experimentation, or a philosophy of zero defects are very hard to place a price tag on. They are not easily traded in markets nor communicated through a corporate hierarchy. The open-ended, relational features of networks, with their relative absence of explicit quid pro quo behavior, greatly enhance the ability to transmit and learn new knowledge and skills.

Reciprocity is central to discussions of network forms of organization. Unfortunately, it is a rather ambiguous concept, used in different ways by various social science disciplines. One key point of contention concerns whether reciprocity entails exchanges of roughly equivalent value in a strictly delimited sequence or whether it involves a much less precise definition of equivalence, one that emphasizes indebtedness and obligation. Game theoretic treatments of reciprocity by scholars in political science and economics tend to emphasize equivalence. Axelrod (1984) stresses that reciprocal action implies returning ill for ill as well as good for good. As Keohane (1986) notes, the literature in international relations 'emphatically' associates reciprocity with equivalence of benefits.[13] As a result, these scholars take a view of reciprocity that is entirely consistent with the pursuit of self-interest.

Sociological and anthropological analyses of reciprocity are commonly couched in the language of indebtedness. In this view, a measure of imbalance sustains the partnership, compelling another meeting (Sahlins, 1972). Obligation is a means through which parties remain connected to one another. Calling attention to the need for equivalence might well undermine and devalue the relationship.[14] To be sure, sociologists have long emphasized that reciprocity implies conditional action (Gouldner, 1960). The question is whether there is a relatively immediate assessment or whether 'the books are kept open,' in the interests of continuing satisfactory results. This perspective also takes a different tack on the issue of self-interest. In his classic work *The Gift*, Marcel Mauss (1967 [1925]), attempted to show that the obligations to give, to receive, and to return were not to be understood simply with respect to rational calculations, but fundamentally in terms of underlying cultural tenets that provide objects with their meaning and significance, and provide a basis for understanding the implications of their passage from one person to another. Anthropological and sociological approaches, then, tend to focus more on the normative standards that sustain exchange; game theoretic treatments emphasize how individual interests are enhanced through cooperation.

Social scientists do agree, however, that reciprocity is enhanced by taking a long-term perspective. Security and stability encourage the search for new ways of accomplishing tasks, promote learning and the exchange of information, and engender trust. Axelrod's (1984) notion of 'the shadow of the future' – the more the immediate payoff facing players is shaped by future expectations – points to a broadened conception of self-interest. Cooperation thus emerges out of mutual interests and behavior is based on standards that no one individual can determine alone. Trust is thereby generated. Trust is, as Arrow (1974) has noted, a remarkably efficient lubricant to economic exchange. In trusting another party, one treats as certain those aspects of life which modernity rendered uncertain (Luhmann, 1979). Trust reduces complex realities far more quickly and economically than prediction, authority, or bargaining.

It is inaccurate, however, to characterize networks solely in terms of collaboration and concord. Each point of contact in a network can be a source of conflict as well as harmony. Recall that the term alliance comes from the literature of international relations where it describes relations among nation states in an anarchic world. Keohane (1986) has stressed that processes of reciprocity or cooperation in no way 'insulate practitioners from considerations of power.' Networks also commonly involve aspects of dependency and particularism.[15] By establishing enduring patterns of repeat trading, networks restrict access (Powell, 1985). Opportunities are thus foreclosed to newcomers, either intentionally or more subtly through such barriers as unwritten rules or informal codes of conduct. In practice, subcontracting networks and research partnerships influence who competes with whom, thereby dictating the adoption of a particular technology and making it much harder for unaffiliated parties to join the fray. As a result of these inherent complications, most potential partners approach the idea of participating in a network with trepidation. In the various examples presented below, all of the parties to network forms of exchange have lost some of their ability to dictate their own future and are increasingly dependent on the activities of others.

Illustrative Cases of Network Forms

It is time to add some flesh to these stylized models. Substantive details enable us to see how these abstractions operate in economic life. I provide examples of networks from a diversity of industries, ranging from highly traditional sectors to the most technologically advanced ones. These disparate examples share some important commonalities. They all involve intricate, multifaceted, durable relationships in which horizontal forms of exchange are paramount. My argument is based on the Simmelian notion that similar patterns of exchange are likely to entail similar behavioral consequences, no matter what the substantive context.

I begin this section with craft industries, a setting where network forms have long been dominant. I turn next to a discussion of industrial districts, where network forms have made a resurgence. I then move to high technology fields; here, networks are a much more novel phenomenon.

They are being established for strategic purposes because neither market nor hierarchical forms have delivered the goods. Networks, in this case, are very much associated with the early stages of product life cycles. I conclude with the case of vertical disaggregation, where networks represent an effort to introduce collaboration into well-established contexts in which trust and cooperation have long been absent. The logic is to move from arenas in which networks are common and easy to form to settings where they are developed almost as a last resort.

Networks in Craft Industries

The distinction between craft-based work and formal organization revolves around not only the dissimilar way in which work is organized in the two settings, but also on a different set of expectations about where authority is located. Craft work tends to be project-based, while in bureaucratic organizations a product moves through a series of functional departments where different activities are performed. In craft work each product is relatively unique, search procedures are non-routine, and the work process depends to a considerable degree on intuition and experimentation (Perrow, 1967). The examples presented below represent well-researched cases that highlight the many network features associated with craft production.

Construction. Robert Eccles (1981), in his research on the construction industry, found that in many countries the relations between a general contractor and his subcontractors are stable and continuous over long time periods, and only rarely established through competitive bidding. This type of quasi-integration results in what Eccles calls the 'quasi-firm.' Although most contracts are set under fixed price terms, no hierarchical organization arises, even though there are clear 'incentive for shirking performance requirements.' Instead, long-term and fairly exclusive association obviates the need for costly organizational monitoring. In an empirical study of residential construction in Massachusetts, Eccles found that it was unusual for a general contractor to employ more than two or three subcontractors in a given trade. This relationship obtained even when a large number of projects were done in the same year, and despite the fact that a number of alternative subcontractors were available.

Publishing. The book industry is, to a considerable extent, based on network relationships (Coser, Kadushin and Powell, 1982). One effort to recognize and profit from these linkages is the establishment of personal imprint lines within large trade publishing houses. Under these arrangements, successful editors enjoy freedom from corporate constraints, and authors enjoy the intimacy and closeness associated with a small company. These extended networks allow an editor to rely on his or her own judgment and not have to appeal for higher level approval. The large firm is able to keep top-flight editors content and, at the same time, give them a greater financial stake in the books they bring in. Personal imprint editors are on their own as far as acquiring and nurturing authors, yet retain corporate clout for financing, sales, and distribution. Other publishers, in a related effort to hold on to key personnel, have 'spun off' subsidiaries that operate in an autonomous fashion within the loose boundaries of the larger company. These 'boutique' operations permit, in the words of the head of one such company, 'the intimacy of a small operation with no committee meetings and no bureaucracy' (Coser et al., 1982, p. 53).

But these developments are merely reflections of a general phenomenon that is characteristic of certain sectors of the book trade. In trade and scholarly publishing, much of the time editors behave as if they are optimizing not their organization's welfare, but the welfare of the social networks to which they belong. In scholarly publishing, editorial research and evaluation relies extensively on personal networks, which are based on loyalty and friendship, cemented over time. Bonds of allegiance shape the processes of access and discovery. These personal relationships are also vital to economic success. While competition among firms does, to some extent, influence the success or failure of particular publishing houses, these selection pressures are dampened by the dense associational ties and personal relations that support all publishing transactions. The fortunes of a scholarly publishing house often depend more on the rise and fall of various academic paradigms than on the efficiency of a firm's internal operations. In a sense, companies do not so much compete with one another as hitch their fate to the success or failure of different academic networks and intellectual fashions.

Both the spinoff arrangements and the quasi-organizations based on personal networks reflect the fact that editors are located in structurally ambivalent positions: loyalty to their authors and their craft often outweighs allegiance to the firm that employs them. From the employer's perspective, the only means of responding to circumstances in which the most valued assets of the organization – the editor and his or her contacts – are highly mobile is to either allow the editor to set up shop on their own within the corporate boundaries or to try to influence editorial behavior in an unobtrusive manner (Powell, 1985, pp. 144–57).

Film and Recording Industries. Sociologists who study popular culture have long known that the music and movie businesses were external economy industries in which there was heavy reliance on subcontracting and freelance talent. But recent research has shed new light on this particular method of matching investment capital and human capital. These industries thrive on short-term contracts, minimization of fixed overhead, mutual monitoring of buyers and sellers, and a constant weaving and interweaving of credits, relationships, and successes or failures. But the ostensibly open competition that one might expect to pervade these markets is minimal (Peterson and White, 1981). Instead, recurrent small-numbers contracting appears to be the norm.

Cultural industries are characterized by high variance and great unpredictability; conditions which breed high rates of social reconstruction or reproduction (Faulkner and Anderson, 1987). These 'project markets' are complex, dynamic, and uncertain. The participants in the film industry – producers, directors, cinematographers, actors, and musicians – appear at first glance to be highly mobile. They move from studio to studio, from one project to another, with few stable ties to any formal organization. But as Faulkner and Anderson (1987) show, in their analysis of participation in 2430 films over a fifteen-year period (1965–1980), considerable stability and recurrent contracting among the participants is the norm. It is the networks of participants, however, that are stable and enduring, not the film studios, where employees come and go and ownership changes frequently.

Not surprisingly, the key players in the film industry trust others with whom they have worked in the past and found to be reliable. What is striking about Faulkner's and Anderson's analysis is how dramatic the patterns of inclusion and exclusion are. Reproduction persists within film genres and between big money and small money films. They observe (p. 907) that 'distinct networks crystallize out of a persistent pattern of contracting when particular buyers of expertise and talent (film producers), with given schedules of resources and alternatives, settle into self-reproducing business transactions with distinct (and small) sets of sellers (directors, cinematographers, and fashionable actors and actresses).' Commercial results feedback and then historically shape the next round of contracting.

These network patterns are interesting in their own right; but Peterson and White (1981) point out that even though they are powerful and long-lasting, they tend to be invisible to most observers. Instead of long-term rates of reproduction, most participants observe individual acts of ranking, favors, and contacts.

These craft-based examples are not particularly unique. Network forms of social organization are found in many cultural industries, in research and knowledge production, and in various industrial districts – such as the diamond trade (Ben-Porath, 1980), the garment and fashion business in Milan and New York, the Lyonese silk industry (Piore and Sabel, 1984), or the 'Third Italy,' discussed below. And many of the professions exhibit some network-like features. Architecture is a prime example; but so apparently is engineering where, to judge from one recent study (Von Hippel, 1987), the informal trading of proprietary know-how among technical professionals in competing firms is extensive.[16] What these different activities share in common is a particular kind of skilled labor force, one with hands-on experience with production and the strategic ability to generate new products to keep pace with changing market demands. The people who perform the work have a kind of knowledge that is fungible, that is, not limited to an individual task but applicable to a wide range of activities. The organizations that complement these human capital inputs are highly porous – with boundaries that are ill-defined, where work roles are vague and responsibilities overlapping, and where work ties both across teams and to members of other organizations are strong.

Regional Economies and Industrial Districts

Recent economic changes have created, or perhaps recreated is a more apt description, new forms of collaboration among for-profit firms. In the previous century, a number of regions and industries were closely identified because both the social life and the economic health of such areas as Lyon and Sheffield were closely linked to the fate of the silk and cutlery trades, respectively (see Piore and Sabel, 1984; Sabel, 1989). This rediscovery or reinvigoration of the 19th century industrial districts points to the advantages of agglomeration, in which firms choose to locate in an area not because of the presence of an untapped market, but because of the existence of a dense, overlapping cluster of firms, skilled laborers, and an institutional infrastructure (for a good discussion of the economics of agglomeration, see Arthur, 1987).

German textiles. Charles Sabel et al. (1987) describe the German textile industry, centered in the prosperous state of Baden-Wurttemberg in southwestern Germany, as an 'association of specialists, each with unmatched expertise and flexibility in a particular phase or type of production.' This flourishing traditional craft industry employs a highly refined system of production that links small and medium-size firms with a wide range of institutional arrangements that further the well-being of the industry as a whole. These support services include industry research institutes, vocational training centers, consulting firms, and marketing agencies. Most textile producers are highly specialized; and, as Sabel et al. (1987) argue, the more distinctive each firm is, the more it depends on the success of the other firms' products that complement its own. This production system depends on an extensive subcontracting system in which key technologies are developed in a collaborative manner. The subcontractors are also connected to overlapping inter-industry supplier networks. These linkages allow textile makers to benefit from the subcontractors' experiences with customers in other industries, and the suppliers are, in turn, buffered from downturns in any one industry. All of these arrangements serve to strengthen the social structure in which textile firms are embedded and to encourage cooperative relations that attenuate the destructive aspects of competition.

The Emilian Model. Perhaps nowhere have socially integrated, decentralized production units had more of an impact than in Italy, where the economy has outgrown Britain's and is catching up to France's.[17] Modena, the microcosm of Latin Europe's renaissance, is the center of Emilia-Romagna, in north central Italy, and it is here that Italy's economic performance has been most exceptional. Behind this success is both a set of unusual, to an American eye, political and social institutions, and a size distribution of firms that seem more suited to the nineteenth century than the late twentieth.[18]

Firms employing fewer than 50 employees engaged 49 per cent of the Italian labor force, and the average manufacturing firm has only 9.19 employees (Lazerson, 1988, p. 330). The proportion of the labor force grouped in smaller units of employment is greater in Emilia than in Italy as a whole (Brusco, 1982). The success of these small enterprises rests on a different logic of production than found in a typical vertically-integrated firm.

These small firms are frequently grouped in specific zones according to their product, and give rise to industrial districts in which all firms have a very low degree of vertical integration (Brusco, 1982). Production is conducted through extensive, collaborative subcontracting agreements. Only a portion of the firms market final products, the others execute operations commissioned by the group of firms that initiate production. The owners of small firms typically prefer subcontracting to expansion or integration (Lazerson, 1988). The use of satellite firms allows them to remain small and preserve their legal and organizational structure as a small company. Often satellite firms outgrow the spawning firms. Though closely related and highly cooperative, the firms remain strictly independent entities.

These industrial districts embrace a wide range of consumer goods and engineering components and machines: knitwear in Modena, clothes and ceramic tiles in Modena and Reggio, cycles, motorcycles and shoes in Bologna, food processing machinery in Parma, and woodworking machine tools in Capri, to name but a few (see Brusco, 1982, pp. 169–70).

Why is production so widely decentralized and so spatially concentrated? The answer appears to be rather idiosyncratic to the Italian case. It is partly a response to labor union power in large firms, where union influence has proved to be a disincentive to job expansion. The small firms exhibit high wage dispersion, with highly skilled workers who have registered as artisans in order to make more than is standard in large-firm industrial relations agreements, and unskilled, temporary employees – students, the elderly, immigrants, who work off the books for much less than they would receive in a large factory, if they could find employment. The districts are also a response to changing tastes and technology, in particular the emerging popularity of custom rather than the standardized goods and the availability of high quality, flexible technologies that are compatible with the needs and budgets of small firms.

These decentralized organizational arrangements depend on a unique set of political and social institutions, most notably the fact that almost all local political authorities are controlled by the Communist party (Brusco, 1982; Lazerson, 1988). A combination of familial, legislative, ideological, and historical factors buttress Emilia-Romagna's economic progress. The continued existence of the extended family provides for economic relations based on cooperation and trust, and facilitates the search for new employees through family and friendship networks (Lazerson, 1988). The CNA, a national organization with close ties to the Italian Communist party, represents some 300 000 artisanal firms and provides them with a rich array of administrative services. These artisanal associations prepare pay slips, keep the books, and pay the taxes, as well as establish consulting, marketing, and financial services (Brusco, 1982). By coordinating these various administrative activities, the associations establish on a cooperative basis the conditions for achieving economies of scale.

Brusco (1982) and Sabel (1989) make a persuasive case that the Emilian model fosters the skills and initiative of artisanal entrepreneurs. The number of entrepreneurs previously employed by large firms, particularly as foremen, is very high. By tapping both initiative and detailed production knowledge, the small firms are able to offer a vast array of new products. And these small firms, through their multitude of collaborative networks, are able to give shape to new ideas with a speed unimaginable in larger enterprises.

Extended Trading Groups. The kind of collaboration that obtains in the industrial districts of southwestern Germany or north central Italy is based in part on a set of local circumstances, but the principles of mutual organization on which the districts are based are more widely applicable. Interfirm cooperation is often found in economic activities based in a particular region, such as in Japan or Scandinavia, or in locales where firms from similar industries are spatially concentrated, such as Silicon Valley or Route 128 in the United States. The extended trading relationships that develop under these circumstances of physical proximity may vary considerably in their details, but their underlying logic is constant.

Ronald Dore (1983) argues that networks of preferential, stable trading relationships are a viable alternative to vertical integration. His work on the regionally concentrated Japanese textile industry, particularly its weaving segment, aptly illustrates this point. The industry was dominated in the 1950s by large mills, most of which were vertically integrated enterprises with cotton-importing, spinning and finishing operations. By 1980 the larger mills had closed and the integrated firms had divested and returned to their original base in spinning. This 'devolution' has led to a series of stable relationships among firms of different sizes. The key to this system is mutual assistance. Dore (1983) gives the example of a finisher who re-equips with a more efficient process, which gives him a cost advantage. This finisher, however, does not win much new business by offering a lower price. The more common consequence is that merchants go to their own finishers and say: 'Look how X has got his price down. We hope you can do the same bccause we really would have to reconsider our position if the price difference goes on for months. If you need bank financing to get the new type of vat we can probably help by guaranteeing the loan.' This type of relationship is, of course, not limited to the Japanese textile industry; similar patterns of reciprocal ties are found in many other sectors of the Japanese economy.[19]

What are the performance consequences of these kinds of trading relationships? Dore suggests that the security of the relationship encourages investment by suppliers, as the spread of robotics among Japan's engineering subcontractors amply attests. Trust and mutual dependency result in a more rapid flow of information. In textiles, changes in consumer markets are passed quickly upstream to weavers, and technical changes in production also flow downstream rapidly. There is, Dore asserts, a general emphasis on quality. One would not terminate a relationship when a party cannot deliver the lowest price, but it is perfectly proper to terminate a relationship when someone is not maintaining quality standards.

More recently, Dore (1987) has maintained that Japanese economic relations in general do not have the properties (i.e., opportunism, short-term profit-maximization, and distrust) that we commonly associate with capitalist enterprise and on which we build our theories of economic organization (in particular, transaction cost economics). He contends that the costs of doing business in Japan are lower than in Britain or the United States because of concerns for reputation and goodwill and considerations of trust and obligation. Moreover, he argues, this embedding of business relations in moral and social concerns does not reduce economic vitality, it sustains it and provides Japan with a considerable edge (for further discussion on this point, see the chapter by Lincoln).

But is Japan all that unique? Perhaps it is true, as Dore (1987) suggests, that as a nation, Japanese industry is organized more along the principles of an extended network (see also, Imai and Itami, 1984), but it does not appear to have a monopoly on these practices. Hagg and Johanson (1983), in an analysis of the industrial markets which comprise the core of the Swedish economy, describe a series of long term, stable relationships among industrial producers who share R&D resources and personnel. They suggest that the companies are actually investing in their connections with other companies, and in the process, losing their own identity to some extent. Instead of a competitive environment, there is a sharing of risks and resources and a pooling of information. Hagg and Johanson argue that these arrangements eliminate costly safeguards and defensive measures and are better adapted to uncertainty. Competition in intermediate producer markets is not eliminated, rather coalitions of firms compete with other coalitions, not on the basis of price, but in terms of product development and knowledge accumulation.

Swedish researchers have chronicled numerous such collaborative projects, principally among large manufacturing companies (Hakansson, 1987; Johanson and Mattson, 1987). Most of the ventures involve at least one firm with a home base in Sweden, but the researchers do not speculate whether Swedish industry has a particular proclivity for coordinating product development activities with suppliers, consumers, and producers of complementary products. These 'network forms of interorganizational relations' tend to be long-term, costly, project-based efforts at product development or technological innovation (Hakansson, 1987). They differ, however, in a number of respects from some of the examples discussed above. They usually involve very large firms, such as Volvo, Saab-Scandia, Ericsson, and Fairchild, and are typically heavy manufacturing projects in fields such as aerospace, metallurgy, mining, and marine engines. Unlike many of the subcontracting relationships, in which one firm serves as a principal and various satellite firms as agents, these production ventures bring companies together as co-contractors. In the language of agency theory, they are both principals and agents: risk-takers who allocate tasks and share in the gains or losses and contributors to the final product.

It was not all that long ago that notions of industrial districts and spatially concentrated production were largely ignored – both intellectually and geographically.[20] Now, every municipality seems busy at work trying to create their own Route 128 or Modena.[21] The success of these forms of extended trading networks has several key ramifications:

1. One of the main consequences has been to blur the boundaries of the firm – boundaries are being expanded to encompass a larger community of actors and interests that would previously have either been fully separate entities or absorbed through merger;
2. A new constellation of forces is being recognized as crucial to economic success: whether in the Third Italy or Silicon Valley, spatially concentrated production involves the cooperation of local government, proximity to centers of higher education, a highly skilled

labor pool, extensive ties to research institutes and trade associations, and cooperation among firms with specialized skills and overlapping interests;

3. The spread of technologically advanced, smaller units of enterprise – a growth that comes at the expense of larger companies and is not explained solely by the shift from manufacturing to services (Loveman, Piore and Sengenberger, 1987), and occurs without notable direct investment or significant employment increase, but rather as a result of expansion through various cooperative interorganizational relationships (Lorenzoni and Ornati, 1988).

Strategic Alliances and Partnerships

In many respects, partnerships and joint ventures are not new developments. They have been common among firms involved in oil extraction and petroleum refining as a means of spreading risks. Chemical and pharmaceutical firms have long conducted basic research jointly with university scientists. And some of the most complex partnerships have taken place in the commercial aircraft industry. Three major global players – Boeing, McDonnell Douglas, and Airbus Industrie – construct their planes via complex joint ventures among firms from many nations (Mowery, 1987). Boeing and Rolls Royce teamed up to produce the Boeing 757, and much of the construction of the Boeing 767 is done, through joint ventures, in Japan and Italy. Airbus Industrie is a four nation European aircraft consortium, supported in part through loans (or subsidies, if you take the competition's view) from European governments.[22]

There is widespread evidence, however, that experimentation within various new kinds of interfirm agreements, collaborations, and partnerships have mushroomed in an unprecedented fashion (Friar and Horwitch, 1985; Teece, 1986; Zagnoli, 1987; Hergert and Morris, 1988; Mowery, 1988). Firms are seeking to combine their strengths and overcome weaknesses in a collaboration that is much broader and deeper than the typical marketing joint ventures and techhnology licensing that were used previously. These new ventures may take the form of novel cooperative relationships within suppliers, or collaboration among several small firms to facilitate research and new product development. More generally, internally generated and financed research is giving way to new forms of external R&D collaboration among previously unaffiliated enterprises. Indeed, in some industries, there appears to be a wholesale stampede into various alliance-type combinations that link large generalist firms and specialized entrepreneurial start-ups. Nor are these simply new means to pursue research and development; the new arrangements also extend to production, marketing, and distribution. And, in some circumstances, large firms are joining together to create 'global strategic partnerships' (Perlmutter and Heenan, 1986) that shift the very basis of competition to a new level – from firm vs. firm to rival transnational groupings of collaborators.[23]

In the past, the most common way in which large companies gained expertise or products that they were unable to develop on their own was to acquire another company with the needed capability. Mergers and acquisitions in high technology fields have not disappeared, but their track record is generally poor (Doz, 1988). Partnerships are more frequent now because of growing awareness that other options have serious drawbacks. Recent efforts at various kinds of more limited involvement represent an important alternative to outright takeover. Equity arrangements – deals that combine direct project financing and varying degrees of ownership – are an example. A larger firm invests, rather than purchases, primarily for reasons of speed and creativity. The movement in large companies away from in-house development to partial ownership reflects an awareness that small firms are much faster at, and more capable of, innovation and product development. General Motors explained its 11 per cent investment in Teknowledge, a maker of diagnostic systems that use a type of artificial intelligence, by noting that 'if we purchased the company outright, we would kill the goose that laid the golden egg.' Equity arrangements can be quite complex. Some small companies have several equity partners, and large companies find themselves in the novel position of negotiating product development contracts and licensing arrangements with companies that they partly own. Equity investments are typically 'complemented by various agreements, such as research contracts from the larger firm to the smaller one, exclusive licensing agreements to the larger firm, and often loan and other financial agreements provided by the larger firm to the smaller one' (Doz, 1988, p. 32).

These developments, not surprisingly, are particularly common in technology-intensive industries (Mariti and Smiley, 1983; Zagnoli, 1987; Contractor and Lorange, 1988). Both the motivations for collaboration and the organizational forms that result are quite varied. Firms pursue cooperative agreements in order to gain fast access to new technologies or new markets, to benefit from economies of scale in joint research and/or production, to tap into sources of know-how located outside the boundaries of the firm, and to share the risks for activities that are beyond the scope or capability of a single organization. The ensuing organizational arrangements include joint ventures, strategic alliances, equity partnerships, collaborative research pacts of large scale research consortia, reciprocity deals, and satellite organizations. There is no clear cut relationship between the legal form of cooperative relationships and the purposes they are intended to achieve. The form of the agreement appears to be individually tailored to the needs of the respective parties, and to tax and regulatory considerations. The basic thrust, however, is quite obvious: to pursue new strategies of innovation through collaboration without abrogating the separate identity and personality of the cooperating partners.

In these process-oriented fields, knowing how to make a product and how to make it work is absolutely critical to success. In recent years, as product life cycles shorten and competition intensifies, timing considerations and access to know-how have become paramount concerns. Teece and Pisano (1987) suggest that, increasingly, the most qualified centers of excellence in the relevant know-how are located outside the boundaries of the large corporation. Fusfeld and Haklisch (1985) argue that corporations are becoming less self-sufficient in their ability to generate the science and technology necessary to fuel growth. The larger and more technology-intensive the firm, the greater the amount of technical expertise it requires to maintain its position. Whether it is the case that one firm's technological competence has outdistanced the others, or that innovations would be hard to replicate internally, as suggested by the growing reliance on external sources of research and development (see Friar and Horwitch, 1985; Graham, 1985; and Hamilton, 1985), network forms of organization represent a fast means of gaining access to know-how that cannot be produced internally. The network-like configurations that have evolved in high technology can process information in multiple directions. They create complex webs of communication and mutual obligation. By enhancing the spread of information, they sustain the conditions for further innovation by bringing together different logics and novel combinations of information.

Collaborative agreements involve a wide variety of organizations. While the joining together of small firms that possess entrepreneurial commitment and expertise in technology innovation with large scale corporate organizations that have marketing and distribution power represents the prototypical example, these arrangements are certainly not the only option. Many large firms are linking up with other large companies, particularly in international joint ventures.[24] These partnerships are unusual in that they involve the creation of dependencies and linkages among very large firms, such as Toyota and General Motors.

Porter and Fuller (1986) suggest that such coalitions seem well suited to the process of industry and firm globalization, as evidenced by AT&T's alliances with Olivetti, Phillips, NTT, Toshiba and Ricoh. Large telecommunications companies have been very active participants in collaborative international research efforts. Siemens and ICL both have links with Fujitsu, while ICL, Siemens, and Machines Bull have formed a joint research institute in Munich to pool their basic research. Machines Bull is also a partner in a joint venture with Honeywell and N.E.C. Indeed, firms often have stakes in several projects with different partners (and potential competitors) and are engaged in ventures involving several technologies of different stages of development, creating a 'loose network of sometimes interlocking companies' (Contractor and Lorange, 1988, p. 24).

Traditionally, international joint ventures were not regarded favorably by multinational firms, especially those based in the United States. International manufacture and marketing occurred through either direct foreign investment or export, and occasionally international licensing was utilized when a firm wished to exploit a process technology. Joint ventures were sometimes resorted to when political exigencies or protectionist policies prevented operating fully owned subsidiaries. This was the standard reason for joint ventures in Japan, certain third world nations, and socialist countries.

Recent collaborations differ substantially from previous strategies. In these new global partnerships, all of the participants contribute technological and managerial expertise, as well as capital. The relationships are multidimensional and long-term, rather than one-shot transfers of technologies. What has happened to cause firms to prefer cooperation to full ownership, or a 'go-it-alone' approach?

There are numerous factors both pushing and pulling US multinationals into global alliances. On the push side are technological constraints. Much sophisticated technological knowledge is tacit in character (Nelson and Winter, 1982) and cannot easily be transferred by licensing. Indeed, it is the unwritten, intangible character of much firm-specific knowledge that has led US firms, particularly the automakers, to form joint ventures with Japanese manufacturers in an effort to better understand their production processes. Similarly, Japanese companies have been attracted to joint projects with US high tech firms because technological innovation cannot be simply purchased, it requires cumulative knowledge of the linkages among design, production, and sales.

On the pull side are financial concerns and the advantages of risk reduction. In joining a coalition with another firm, both partners may enjoy options that otherwise would not be available to them, ranging from better access to markets, pooling or exchanging technologies, and enjoying economies of scale and scope. Risk-sharing is very attractive in industries where each successive generation of products is expensive to develop, and product life cycles are short.

In some instances, international joint ventures do appear to represent an intermediate position between contracting among independent firms and vertical integration of the entire production chain. This is most common when the venture involves securing complementary inputs representing successive stages of production, or contracting for specific services or distribution arrangements. But this intermediate stage does not appear to be a temporary or unstable arrangement. Indeed, firms in such situations are ceding a good deal of their autonomy and facing considerable interorganizational dependence. Moreover, alliances that involve the pooling of know-how, the ceding of proprietary information, and the sharing of common assets are not intermediate in either an analytical or a developmental sense. They represent a very different form of interorganizational exchange, one in which ongoing vitality rests on continuing mutual dependence.

While US firms have been recently active in international business alliances, collective industrial research is considerably less advanced here than in Japan or Western Europe,[25] where research consortia have proven to be valuable in eliminating costly, duplicative R&D, in achieving economies of scale in research, and in diversifying the search for solutions to technical problems. But it was not until 1984 that Congress passed the National Cooperative Research Act, easing antitrust laws and permitting collaborative research among competing firms. Since then, more than 100 R&D consortiums have been founded, involving more than 500 companies in such fields as biotechnology, telecommunications, automobiles, energy, and steel. Collective industrial research is, nevertheless, still viewed by many in the US industry and government as a form of collusion and as a seedbed for anticompetitive practices.[26]

Despite a growing consensus that the changing nature of technology development encourages collective R&D, firms have been reluctant to share their best scientists and most attractive projects.[27] It may well be the perceived threat of Japan, with its extensive government-sponsored networks of collective research, that is the greatest spur to collaboration among large US firms. Cries of economic nationalism were motivating forces in the establishment of research consortia such as Sematech. This consortium of semiconductor firms may signal a new awareness of the need for collective research. Both IBM and AT&T are, for the first time, surrendering proprietary designs and processes to competitors in hopes of aiding the consortium's efforts at trying to revive the domestic semiconductor industry.

Cooperative arrangements are not necessarily easy to sustain, nor do they always entail success.[28] They can create a host of management problems and they also raise serious questions about effective industrial policy. On the organizational front, Doz (1988) has cautioned that convergence of purpose is often difficult to achieve, consistency of effort can be undermined by parochial subunit goals, and middle managers and technical specialities may not share top management's enthusiasm for cooperation. Similarly, Borys and Jemison (1989) suggest that because partners have not previously worked together, they may misperceive one another's actions. They observe that collaborations often begin with considerable resources, heavy obligations, and lofty expectations. Thus, the pressures to perform successfully may be considerable.

Collaboration can be fraught with other risks. Parties may bring hidden agendas to the venture. There is an ever-present threat that one party will capture the lion's share of the benefits, or defect with the other party's knowledge and expertise.[29] Some analysts worry that US partners to global alliances may provide 'mundane' services such as assembly, distribution, and marketing, which add little value to the product.[30] The key development work and the higher-paying, value-added jobs are taken overseas, and the US firm merely completes the final stages. These issues are far from being resolved, but they point out the complex ways in which collaborative networks may or may not contribute to a country's stock of organizational talents.

Vertical Disaggregation

Evidence is accumulating that many firms are choosing to shrink their operations in response to the liabilities of large-scale organization. For example, Mariotti and Cainarca (1986) describe a 'downsizing' pattern in the Italian textile industry, where there has been a decline in the number of vertically-integrated firms and growth in 'intermediate governance structures.' They attribute this development to three failures that plague vertically-integrated firms: an inability to respond quickly to competitive changes in international markets; resistance to process innovations that alter the relationship between different stages of the production process; and systematic resistance to the introduction of new products.[31] Interestingly, in an earlier era, firms actively pursued a strategy of vertical integration in an effort to reap the benefits of administrative coordination, economies of scale, and risk reduction (Chandler, 1977). Today, these 'strengths' have resulted in various weaknesses: structural inertia, slow response times, and decreased employee satisfaction.

Large organizations are designed to do certain things well over and over again. The more that behaviors are repeated, the more predictable they become; thus, the greater likelihood that these actions will become formalized. Child (1972) found that large organizations tend to be more rule-bound and to require greater documentation of their efforts. For certain kinds of activities, such practices are useful, but for others it can result in informational logjams and a serious mismatch between organizational outcomes and the demands of clients and customers in a changing environment. Thus, the very factors that make a large organization efficient and reliable at some tasks render it cumbersome and resistant to change when it comes to other actions (Nelson and Winter, 1982; Hannan and Freeman, 1984).

The information costs in large organizations are further compounded by motivational difficulties as well. One point that Alchian and Demsetz (1972) and Williamson (1975) implicitly demonstrate is that much of the internal structure of large organizations is designed to prevent collective action by employees. This basic attitude of suspicion may explain the finding by social psychologists that job satisfaction (as measured by turnover, absenteeism, and morale) declines with increases in organizational size and/or centralization (Porter and Lawler, 1965; Berger and Cummings, 1979). The design of organizations can affect the behavior of their members in a number of powerful ways.[32] In large hierarchical organizations, promotions up the career ladder are a key part of the reward structure. You have, then, little incentive to disagree with the operating decisions made by people above you in rank because they are the people who must decide on your promotion. Research suggests that hierarchical design dampens employee motivation because individuals are likely to be more committed when they have participated in a decision, and much less enthusiastic when they have been ordered by superiors to undertake a particular task (Hackman and Oldham, 1980).

When the pace of technological change was relatively slow, production processes were well understood and standardized, and production runs turned out large numbers of similar products, vertical integration was a highly successful strategy. But the disadvantages of large-scale vertical integration can become acute when the pace of technological change quickens, product life cycles shorten, and markets become more specialized. Firms are trying to cope with these new pressures in a variety of ways: by explicitly limiting the size of work units, by contracting work out, or through more collaborative ventures with suppliers and distributors. One route leads firms to a rediscovery of the market, to the hostile world of arms-length relationships. Associated with a greater reliance on external contracts are strong efforts at cost-cutting, and greater managerial freedom in the deployment of resources and personnel. Another route leads firms to try to reorganize production, not so much through eliminating jobs, but by searching for new methods of collaboration among formerly antagonistic and/or competitive parties (Walton, 1985; Weitzman, 1984). Both responses entail some form of vertical disaggregation, or the shrinking of large corporate hierarchies.

The US auto industry provides a good example of the crossroads many firms are at as they encounter the limits of vertical integration. The auto industry has undergone a profound shake-up, but the ultimate consequences of these changes have yet to be determined (see Dyer et al., 1987; Quinn, 1987). Prior to the mid-1970s, the big three automakers operated in a comfortable environment with little competitive pressure and scant customer demands for gas-efficient, high quality cars. The auto companies pursued a strategy of tight integration of production, which provided a means to guarantee supplies during periods of peak demand, as well as to protect the secrecy of annual styling changes. Vertical integration also kept down the prices of the independent parts suppliers with whom the companies traded. There was neither any give and take nor trust between the automakers and the subcontractors. Contracts were lost because a supplier bid .01 cent per item higher than a competitor (Porter, 1983). Automakers rigorously inspected supplier facilities, quality control procedures, stability of raw material sources, cost data, and management quality and depth (Porter, 1983, p. 278). They were reluctant to permit a supplier to manufacture a complete system. Instead, automakers preferred a competitive situation in which several firms supplied various components and the final assembly was done in-house.

Today this old system has crumbled in the face of international competition and fallen prey to the contradictions and short-term logic of the regime of competitive supplier relations. Heightened competition exposed a number of serious defects in this system. Abernathy (1978) has argued that vertical integration in the auto industry led to inflexibility. One consequence of tight technological interdependence is that change in any one part means the entire process must be altered. Pursuit of a cost-minimization strategy also reduced the automakers' ability to innovate. Susan Helper (1987), in an excellent analysis of supplier relations in the auto industry, observes that the old methods prevented suppliers from developing expertise, thereby reducing the skill requirements of their employees. This made it hard for them to develop any nonautomotive contracts and kept them dependent on the auto companies. It also had a chilling effect on innovation. There was neither any incentive nor capability for the suppliers to update equipment, suggest technological changes, or make long-range plans.

Because of their declining market share and lower profits, automakers are experimenting with an enormous variety of new approaches. A complex web of ties has developed among US automakers, their Japanese rivals, American labor, and auto parts suppliers. These changes are transforming the way the US auto industry operates, changing the nature of competition worldwide, and sharply blurring the distinction between domestic and imported cars. Joint venture activity is extensive: between Ford and Mazda, General Motors and Toyota, GM and Volvo, and Chrysler and Mitsubishi. Ownership is also held in tandem: Ford owns 25 per cent of Mazda, GM 42 per cent of Isuzu and 5 per cent of Suzuki, Chrysler 12 per cent of Mitsubishi Motors. These relationships involve close collaboration and joint production on some projects, and secrecy and exclusiveness on other models.

Equally extensive tinkering is underway with respect to subcontracting arrangements (Helper, 1987). The length of contracts has been expanded, from one year to three to five. More joint design work is being undertaken and sole-sourcing agreements are becoming more common. These new, more collaborative arrangements involve less monitoring and costly inspections, yet defect rates are much reduced. The automakers are becoming more dependent on the technological expertise of the suppliers, whose long-run health is now a factor in the automakers' profits.

At the same time, however, the automakers are pursuing a second strategy: outsourcing to low wage areas. They are simultaneously deciding which suppliers are worth investing in a long-term relationship with and determining which components can be obtained on the basis of price rather than quality. In these cases, there is little concern for collaboration or supplier design work; instead, the effort is aimed at finding third-world suppliers that can provide parts at the lowest possible price.

These disparate options graphically illustrate how practices such as subcontracting have a double edge to them: they may represent a move toward relational contracting (Macneil, 1978), with greater emphasis on security and quality; or they could be a return to earlier times, a part of a campaign to slash labor costs, reduce employment levels, and limit the power of unions even further. Hence, many of the current downsizing efforts seem, at the first glance, to be illogical. Some firms are seeking new collaborative alliances with parts suppliers while at the same time they are trying to stimulate competition among various corporate divisions and between corporate units and outside suppliers. Firms are proposing new cooperative relationships with labor unions and in the same motion reducing jobs and outsourcing them to foreign producers.

Are companies really as confused as it seems? Are these various actions merely the faulty experimentation of poor and indecisive managements? Not necessarily. Though many of the efforts at vertical disaggregation appear to work at cross purposes, there does appear to be an underlying theme. Strong competitive pressures within an industry reduce the number of levels of hierarchy within firms and push companies to redefine the boundaries of their organizations. Firms are externalizing the production of highly standardized components, and searching for new collaborative methods to produce components that require highly skilled, innovative efforts. These collaborations may entail new relationships with labor, close relationships with 'outsiders' who are no longer viewed merely as providers of a component but rather as sources of technological creativity that large firms cannot duplicate internally, and new cooperative ventures with competitors to pool risks and to provide access to markets.

The Etiology of Network Forms

Examples, as the old adage goes, are never proof. Qualitative data are often vulnerable to charges of being selectively presented. But qualitative materials are very useful for theory generation. The cases presented above are, in my view, much more than anecdotes, because taken together they represent a number of highly competitive and/or resurgent industries, and more importantly, they tell a consistent story that enables us to understand the circumstances under which network forms arise. These examples suggest that non-market, non-hierarchical modes of exchange represent a particular form of collective action, one in which:

- cooperation can be sustained over the long run as an effective arrangement;
- networks create incentives for learning and the dissemination of information, thus allowing ideas to be translated into action quickly;
- the open-ended quality of networks is most useful when resources are variable and the environment uncertain;
- networks offer a highly feasible means of utilizing and enhancing such intangible assets as tacit knowledge and technological innovation.

The examples presented above suggest that the conditions that give rise to network forms are quite diverse. The immediate causes, to the extent that they can be discerned, reveal a wide variety of reasons for the proliferation of network-like arrangements. In only a minority of instances is it sensible to maintain that the genesis of network forms is driven by a concern for minimizing transaction costs. Strategic considerations – such as efforts to guarantee access to critical resources, to obtain crucial skills that cannot be produced internally, to pacify the concerns of professional communities or national governments, or even, as in the case of global partnerships, to remake the very nature of international competition – certainly seem to outweigh a simple concern with cost minimization.

The origins and development of network forms seldom reveal a simple chain of events. The loose informal ties that sustain the Japanese keiretsu – the powerful trading companies such as Mitsui, Mitsubishi, and Sumitomo – developed because in the years immediately following the Second World War the US Occupation Authority dissolved the tightly centralized prewar zaibatsu (Gerlach, 1990). In Italy, the extended trading groups of small firms in the north central region emerged as a consequence of restricted job opportunities available to educated young people, due in part to labor union power and large firm rigidities (Sabel, 1989). Thus in some cases, the formation of networks anticipates the need for this particular form of exchange; in other situations, there is a slow pattern of development which ultimately justifies the form; and in still other circumstances, networks are a response to the demand for a mode of exchange that resolves exigencies that other forms are ill-equipped to handle. The network story, then, is a complex one of contingent development, tempered by an adjustment to the social and economic conditions of the time.

The absence of a clear developmental pattern and the recognition that network forms have multiple causes and varied historical trajectories suggest that no simple explanation ties all the cases together. Economizing is obviously a relevant concern in many instances, especially in infant industries where competitive preserves are strong. But it alone is not a particularly robust story, it is but one among a number of theoretically possible motives for action – all of which are consonant with a broad view of self-interest. Clearly many of the arrangements discussed above actually increase transaction costs, but in return they provide concrete benefits or intangible assets that are far more valuable. The reduction of uncertainty, fast access to information, reliability, and responsiveness are among the paramount concerns that motivate the participants in exchange networks.

My claims about network forms of organization obviously have broader ramifications. To the extent that these arguments are persuasive, they suggest that some of the basic tenets of other approaches to economic organization are problematic. For example, an exclusive focus on the transaction – rather than the relationship – as the primary unit of analysis is misplaced. Similarly, approaches that neglect the role of the state in shaping the context in which exchange is conducted are too narrow. The degree to which economic actors rely on the marketplace, private enterprise, or network forms of relational contracting is determined, to a considerable extent, by state policies. From a sociologist's perspective, it makes little sense to separate organizational behavior from its social, political, and historical context. To make serious progress in understanding the diversity of organizational forms, we need arguments that are much more historically contingent and context dependent.

Rationale for Network Forms

Does the diversity of network arrangements imply that their pattern of development is largely idiosyncratic? Or do the cases have sufficient generality that we can point to specific enabling conditions that foster the formation and proliferation of networks? If we are able to identify these conditions, then it would be possible to make refutable arguments about the circumstances that promote and sustain network forms. My own modest contribution to the theory of network forms highlights three factors – know-how, the demand for speed, and trust – which are critical components of networks.

Know-how. There are a number of jobs that are based, in large measure, on either intellectual capital or craft-based skills, both of which have been honed through years of education, training, and experience. Many of these kinds of knowledge-intensive activities, such as cultural production, scientific research, design work, mathematical analysis, computer programming or software development, and some professional services, require little in the way of costly physical resources. They are based on know-how and detailed knowledge of the abilities of others who possess similar or complementary skills. Know-how typically involves a kind of tacit knowledge that is difficult to codify (Nelson and Winter, 1982; Teece and Pisano, 1987). These assets are both largely intangible and highly mobile. They exist in the minds of talented people whose expertise cannot be easily purchased or appropriated and who commonly prefer to ply their trade in a work setting that is not imposed on them 'from above' or dictated to them by an outside authority. Indeed, markets or hierarchical governance structures may hinder the development of these capabilities because the most critical assets – the individuals themselves – may choose to walk away.

Network forms of organization, with their emphasis on lateral forms of communication and mutual obligation, are particularly well-suited for such a highly skilled labor force, where participants possess fungible knowledge that is not limited to a specific task but applicable to a wide range of activities. Thus, networks are most likely to arise and proliferate in fields in which knowledge and/or skills do not lend themselves to either monopoly control or expropriation by the wealthiest bidder.

Exchange relations vary both in terms of how they are organized, as well with respect to the object of exchange. Transactions can take place in a variety of contexts; but, as Williamson and others have alerted us, certain kinds of goods and services lend themselves more readily to particular forms of exchange. The more general, and more substitutable are resources, the more likely they will be secured through short-term market transactions. Similarly, some kinds of exchanges fit more comfortably under the rubric of networks. Take the case of joint ventures, either domestic or international, which are organized for the purposes of exchanging skills or services between two or more firms. What kind of ventures are more likely to promote long-term collaboration and shared responsibility? Agreements that are based on contracting for the performance of particular services, such as sales or distribution, are not likely to promote cooperation. Indeed, joint ventures of this kind are often discontinued when one party's capabilities 'catch up' with those of the other. In contrast, when partners are involved in ongoing, complementary activities – such as pooling of research staffs or joint production arrangements – the relationship is more likely to lead to the sharing of critical information and the development of some measure of trust in one another. The sharing of information, as Buckley and Casson (1988) suggest, often leads to the emergence of common values. This cooperation is particularly likely to develop either in circumstances that require operational integration or under conditions of uncertainty about how to obtain desired outcomes. In both cases, there is a strong motive for parties to share information with one another (Buckley and Casson, 1988).

Thus, the exchange of distinctive competencies – be they knowledge or skills – is more likely to occur in networks. The transfer of resources – tangible items, such as equipment, services, patents, and the like – more commonly occurs through a market transaction or among organizational units, depending on the frequency and the distinctiveness of the items that are exchanged.

The *demand for speed* is based on a compelling economic logic. A regime of intense technological competition robs incumbents of their clout and brings upstarts to the fore. Firms join forces with other companies and/or with university scientists to reduce the risks and to share the expense of developing costly products that have very short life spans. Porter and Fuller (1986) argue that partnerships and coalitions are a more rapid means of repositioning than internal development and are less costly, less irreversible, and more successful than mergers. This view suggests that the business environment has changed in such a manner that it now rewards many of the key strengths of network forms of organization: fast access to information, flexibility, and responsiveness to changing tastes. Networks, then, possess some degree of comparative advantage in coping with an environment that places a premium on innovation and customized products.

What is it about networks that makes them more adaptive and well-suited to coping with change? One of the key advantages of network arrangements is their ability to disseminate and interpret new information. Networks are based on complex communication channels. Kaneko and Imai (1987) emphasize this dynamic property of networks, noting that they are particularly adept at generating new interpretations; as a result of these new accounts, novel linkages are often formed. This advantage is seen most clearly when networks are contrasted with markets and hierarchies. Passing information up or down a corporate hierarchy or purchasing information in the marketplace is merely a way of processing information or acquiring a commodity. In either case the flow of information is controlled. No new meanings or interpretations are generated. In contrast, networks provide a context for learning by doing. As information passes through a network, it is both freer and richer; new connections and new meanings are generated, debated, and evaluated.

Thus, to the extent that competition is based on such factors as the ability to innovate and translate ideas into products quickly, network forms of organization are more likely to proliferate. When competition occurs on the basis of price or manufacturing intensity, networks are likely to be less in evidence.

Trust. Several of the examples, particularly the cases of craft-based networks and industrial districts, suggest that certain social contexts encourage cooperation and solidarity, or a sense of generalized reciprocity. In these situations, exchange relations have been long-term and continuous, hence there is scant need to formalize them. What are the specific attributes that create circumstances in which collaboration is so easily accomplished? Axelrod (1984) has demonstrated the powerful consequences of repeated interaction among individuals. When there is a high probability of future association, persons are not only more likely to cooperate with others, they are also increasingly willing to punish those who do not cooperate. When repeat trading occurs, quality becomes more important than quantity. The reputation of a participant is the most visible signal of their reliability. Reputation bulks large in importance in many network-like work settings because there is little separation of formal business statuses and personal social roles. One's standing in one arena often determines one's place in the other. As a result, there is limited need for hierarchical oversight because the desire for continued participation successfully discourages opportunism. Monitoring is generally easier and more effective when done by peers than when done by superiors. Consensual ideologies substitute for formal rules and compliance procedures.

Networks should be most common in work settings in which participants have some kind of common background – be it ethnic, geographic, ideological, or professional. The more homogeneous the group, the greater the trust, hence the easier it is to sustain network-like arrangements. When the diversity of participants increases, trust recedes, and so does the willingness to enter into long-term collaborations. Calculative attitudes replace cooperative ones, and formal agreements – either contractual or bureaucratic – supplant informal understandings.

It also stands to reason that certain kinds of institutional contexts, that is, particular combinations of legal, political, and economic factors, are especially conducive to network arrangements as well as interorganizational collaborations. Yet we know very little about what kinds of political and economic conditions support network forms. As a result, I hold this discussion for the next section on unresolved issues. It is, however, worth noting that networks appear to involve a distinctive combination of factors – skilled labor, some degree of employment security, salaries rather than piece rates, some externally-provided mechanisms for job training, relative equity among the participants, a legal system with relaxed antitrust standards, and national policies that promote research and development and encourage linkages between centers of higher learning and industry – which seldom exist in sufficient measure without a political and legal infrastructure to sustain them.

A Research Agenda

The discussion thus far points to a number of key issues that require more sustained attention, as well as suggests several new topics for the research agenda. We need to know a good deal more about the factors that explain the ecology of network forms. Why is there such considerable cross-national variation in the frequency of network forms? Why are network arrangements so common in some nations and some sectors and not others? The evidence that I have presented suggests that state policies make a difference in the ease with which collaborative arrangements are formed and are sustained, but we have only begun to investigate the relationship between governance structures and state policies. Similarly, network forms are found in a diverse set of industries – craft-based occupations and professions, high technology sectors, and even mature ones such as auto. Can we make sense of this diversity? Do rates of formation vary across industries? Some early research (Friar and Horwitch, 1985; Hamilton, 1985; Hergert and Morris, 1988; Mariti and Smiley, 1983; Zagnoli, 1987) suggests that alliances are much more common in high technology fields, but we do not yet know whether this is a function of a youthful stage in an industry's life cycle or of basic structural features of activities that are highly dependent on the creation of new forms of knowledge.

A good deal more research is needed on the durability of networks. I have suggested above that the distinction between very specific resources and intangible assets might account for divergent patterns. The need to acquire resources may lead to network arrangements that are an interim step, either a half way point between market procurement and outright merger or a transitional move until internal capability is built up. Tacit knowledge, however, is inherently difficult to exchange; it may well lead to repeated, reciprocal interactions, transforming what was initially a relationship approached with some caution and fear into one that is institutionalized and enduring. In these circumstances, collaboration would be expected to shift from a means to an end in itself. Careful comparative research along these lines would be highly useful.

We know very little about the phenomenology of work under different governance structures. Do participants 'experience' networks as qualitatively different from market transactions or careers in hierarchical firms? If the argument that markets, hierarchies, and networks are distinctive forms, with their own logic and procedures, is correct, then we should find important behavioral differences among them. Do members of networks exhibit greater loyalty or commitment? Do participants in network arrangements face novel problems of control? How do people cope with relationships that are both collaborative and competitive, with circumstances in which control is not direct and immediate, and conformity to well-established administrative routines not guaranteed?

What are the performance liabilities of networks? There are, in all likelihood, certain tasks for which networks are poorly suited. When do networks create new levels of complexity that are incommensurate with their intended benefits? Are the gains from network relationships appropriated asymmetrically due to differences in the learning capacity of the participants? Some researchers (Cole, 1985; Pucik, 1988) suggest that much of the imbalance between Western and Japanese partners to joint ventures can be attributed to disparities in learning. Many Japanese firms have in place systematic methods that encourage the transfer of information and know-how from a joint venture throughout their organization (Imai, Nonaka and Takeuchi, 1985). More work is needed to understand how information is processed through networks and how learning is sustained.

Does participation in a network arrangement alter one's orientation toward future collaboration? Do the partners to a successful network relationship change their calculus and decide to act in different ways because of this experience? Does a reputation for being a fair-minded and successful exchange partner translate into clear economic benefits? These are fundamental questions and they suggest that much work remains to be done. This is not a daunting prospect, however. Indeed, one of my goals in this paper has been to suggest that students of organizational behavior are particularly well-equipped to study and explain the circumstances under which cooperation and collaboration proceed with only limited reliance on contracts and the legal system on the one hand, and on administrative fiat and bureaucratic routines on the other.

Acknowledgments

This paper has had a long gestation period. It began as a talk to the Industrial Relations Workshop at MIT's Sloan School of Management. The comments and encouragement of Mel Howitch and Mike Piore are greatly appreciated. A second iteration was presented at the Law, Economics, and Organization Workshop at Yale Law School and at the 1986 meetings of The American Sociological Association. The suggestions of Mitch Abolafia, Wayne Baker, Dick Nelson, Oliver Williamson, and Sid Winter were most helpful. An earlier draft of the paper was prepared while I was a fellow at the Center for Advanced Study in the Behavioral Sciences. The writing of the final draft was supported by funds from the Karl Eller Center for the Study of the Private Market Economy at the University of Arizona. I have benefited from comments by a great many people. Space limitations preclude me from thanking everyone properly, but several people who provided yeoman's help should be singled out: Michael Gerlach, Dave Jemison, Bob Keohane, Andrea Larson, Claus Offe and Charles Perrow. I also profited from comments by members of the audience at seminars at the Berkeley, Stanford, and UCLA business schools and the sociology departments at Arizona, Chicago, and Santa Barbara. Of course, I remain responsible for any errors or omissions.

Notes

1. See Koenig and Thietart (1988) on intermediate forms in the aerospace industry, Thorelli (1986) on industrial marketing networks, Eccles and White (1986) on transfer pricing, and Powell (1987) on hybrid forms in craft and high technology industries.
2. This recognition of intermediate forms has not, however, been accompanied by much in the way of concerted analysis. *The Economic Institutions of Capitalism* may include relational contracting in its subtitle, but the index lists a scant four pages of references to the topic. Similarly, Riordan and Williamson (1985) emphasize polar firm and market choices throughout their analysis, and then acknowledge in their last paragraph that 'hybrid modes of organization are much more important than had hitherto been realized.'
3. Transaction costs reasoning borrows freely from legal scholars, such as Macaulay and Macneil, who are noted for the development of ideas regarding relational contracting. Gordon (1985), however, questions whether this assimilation is satisfactory, noting that the price of success by economists is the 'exclusion of the very elements of contract relations to which Macneil and Macaulay have given most prominence: culture, politics, and power' (p. 575).
4. Transaction cost logic involves the comparison of discrete structural alternatives, typically the comparison that is made is that between market and hierarchy. The problem I have with this analysis is that in many cases where transaction cost reasoning predicts internalization, we find other kinds of governance structures, particularly networks. But one can read Williamson (1985) in a different manner, ignoring the argument about the predominance of markets and hierarchies, and focus instead on the highly important role of credible commitments. The book discusses a marvelous array of mechanisms for creating mutually reliant and self-enforcing agreements. If one conceives of production as a chain of activities in which value is added (Porter, 1985), the question is thus posed: which activities does a firm choose to perform internally and which activities are either downplayed or 'farmed out' so members of a network who presumably can carry theirs out more effectively, due to benefits of specialization, focus, or size (see Jarillo, 1988 for an extended discussion of this network value chain). When production is viewed in this manner, Williamson's arguments about credible commitments are quite useful in assessing what kinds of network agreements are likely to prove durable.

5. This does not mean that market forces were of little consequence before the eighteenth century. Braudel (1982) argues that economic history is the story of slowly-evolving mixtures of institutional forms. He suggests that we can speak of a market economy when the prices in a given area appear to fluctuate in unison, a phenomenon that has occurred since ancient times. But this does not imply that transactions between individuals were of a discrete, impersonal nature.
6. I owe this observation to comments made by Jim Robins.
7. What is remarkable about the firms in these two studies is how explicitly the entrepreneurs follow a 'network' strategy, intentionally eschewing internalization for such crucial and recurrent activities as manufacturing, sales, and research and development.
8. On this point, Macneil (1985, p. 496) suggests that 'the transaction costs approach is far too unrelational a starting point in analyzing' relational forms of exchange. Richardson (1972, p. 884) provides an apt example of these densely connected forms of exchange: 'Firm A, . . . is a joint subsidiary of firms B and C, has technical agreements with D and E, subcontracts work to F, is in marketing association with G – and so on. So complex and ramified are these arrangements, indeed, that the skills of a genealogist rather than an economist might often seem appropriate for their disentanglement.'
9. Bob Eccles and Mark Granovetter have repeatedly made this point to me in personal communications, insisting that all forms of exchange contain elements of networks, markets, and hierarchies. Since they are smarter than me, I should listen to them. Nevertheless, I hope to show that there is merit in thinking of networks as an empirically identifiable governance structure.
10. This line of work is both novel and promising, but it has yet to demonstrate how social ties and cultural patterns transform economic exchange in a systematic fashion; nor do we as yet have any clear cut notions about how cultural or historical factors create or introduce comparative variations in economic life. The focus, thus far, has been more on the intriguing question of how are economic motives culturally constructed.
11. Some economists (Alchian and Demsetz, 1972; Klein, 1983) go so far as to regard the firm as merely a set of explicit and implicit contracts among owners of different factors of production.
12. Many other scholars have their own definitions. Jarillo (1985, p. 32) defines strategic networks as 'long-term, purposeful arrangements among distinct but related for-profit organizations that allow those firms in them to gain or sustain competitive advantage vis-à-vis their competitors outside the network.' Kaneko and Imai (1987) conceive of networks as a particular form of multifaceted, inter-organizational relationships through which new information is generated. Johanson and Mattson (1987) regard networks as a method of dividing labor such that firms are highly dependent upon one another. Coordination is not achieved through hierarchy or markets, but through the interaction and mutual obligation of the firms in the network. Gerlach (1990) suggests that alliances among Japanese firms are an important institutional alternative that links Japanese firms to one another in ways that are fundamentally different from US business practices. Alliances, in his view, are coherent networks of rule-ordered exchange, based on the mutual return of obligations among parties bound in durable relationships.

    I find these various definitions very helpful, but also limited. They all describe networks as a form of dense interorganizational relationships. But networks can also evolve out of personal ties, or market relationships among various parties. Many of the arrangements discussed below, commonly found in the publishing, fashion, computer software, construction, and entertainment businesses are among individuals, independent production teams, or very small business units. Thus, my conceptions of networks is closer to Macneil's (1978; 1985) ideas about relational contracts than to the above views.
13. In an illuminating essay, Keohane (1986, p. 8) defines reciprocity as exchanges of roughly equivalent values in which the actions of each party are contingent on the prior actions of the others in such a way that good is returned for good, and bad for bad.
14. For example, successful reciprocal ties in scholarly book publishing – between authors and editors or between editors in competing houses – were highly implicit, of long-standing duration, and not strictly balanced (Powell, 1985). It was widely believed that the open-ended quality of the relationship meant that the goods being exchanged – advice, recommendations, or manuscripts – were more valuable and reliable.

15. Parties are, of course, free to exit from a network. But the difficulty of abandoning a relationship around which a unit or a company has structured its operations and expectations can keep a party locked into a relationship that it experiences as unsatisfactory. This problem of domination in networks obviously lends itself to transaction costs discussions of credible commitments.
16. In his study of the US steel minimill industry, Von Hippel (1987) found the sharing of know-how to be based on professional networks, which develop among engineers with common research interests. When a request for technical assistance is made, the person being asked typically makes two calculations: (1) is the information being requested vital to the health of the firm or just useful, but not crucial? and (2) how likely is the requester to reciprocate at a later date? Even though no explicit accounting is made, assistance is commonly offered. Von Hippel argues that this 'economically feasible and novel form of cooperative R&D' is probably found in many other industries as well.
17. For useful reports on Italy's economy, see 'Europe's sun belt also rises,' *U.S. News and World Report*, 7/18/88, pp. 27–29; and 'The Italian Economy: A Special Survey,' *The Economist*, 2/27/88, pp. 3–34. Both surveys point to the remarkable transformation of Italian industry, led by vast battalions of small firms, but caution that huge government budget deficits, inefficient public services, and an antiquated financial system could hold back further progress.
18. While the organizational structure of Italian firms may not seem modern, they are decidedly successful and high-tech in their operations. Benetton, the fashionable clothing company, is an oft-cited example. With some 2000 employees, the company orchestrates relations backward with more than 350 subcontractors throughout western Europe and forward with some 100 selling agents and over 4000 retail stores worldwide. The company's spectacular growth from small family business to far-flung empire has not been built on internalization or economies of scale, but on external relations for manufacturing, design, distribution and sales. These extended networks have both advantages in terms of speed and flexibility and liabilities with regard to maintaining quality standards. See Jarillo and Martinez (1987) and Belussi (1986) for detailed case studies of the company.
19. For more discussion of the interfirm networks that pervade the Japanese economy, see Okumura (1982), Shimokawa (1985), and Gerlach (1990).
20. For a thoughtful analysis of regional economies and changes in the scale of production, see Sabel (1989).
21. Such efforts, alas, will be hard pressed to succeed. See Dorfman (1983) on the largely idiosyncratic, hard-to-duplicate origins of the Route 128 technology corridor.
22. The commercial aircraft industry is unusual with respect to the very active role played by governments in insuring that their countries maintain a major presence in the industry. In this case, coalitions and joint ventures are driven as much by political factors and pressures for economic nationalism as by organizational and economic logic. See several of the chapters in Porter (1986) for a discussion of the political aspects of international alliances.
23. Competition over the marketing of tissue plasminogen activator (TPA), an enzyme many expect to be a major drug in treating heart attacks, is the most severe and complicated in biotechnology today. This competitive struggle illustrates how rival transnational alliances race for global market share. The US firm Genentech is allied with Mitsubishi Chemical and Kyowa Ilakko in Japan, while another American firm, Biogen, is collaborating with Fujisawa. Numerous other Japanese and European pharmaceutical alliances, ignoring Genentech's claims for patent priority for TPA, are busy with their own TPA research. This contest shows the intensity of transnational alliance competition, but at the same time that Genentech and Fujisawa are at odds over TPA, they are collaborating in the marketing of another biotech drug, tumor necrosis factor (TNF). Yoshikawa (1988) offers a good road map to the complex, crosscutting terrain of biotechnology strategic alliances.
24. The label 'joint venture' implies the creation of a separate organization, but this need not be the case. Rather than form a new entity, partners can agree to a co-production arrangement. This is common in manufacturing, particularly aerospace, where each partner produces a section of the final product. Or firms may agree to a research partnership in which scientists and laboratories are shared. Similarly, exploration consortia in extractive industries need not create a new firm, but rather pool the costs and risks of existing activities.
25. The founding chairman of Sematech (a research consortium of 14 semiconductor firms), Charles Sporck, bemoaned that, 'We are trailing a pack of nations that are far ahead of us in forming

consortiums. We're especially trailing the Japanese.' Quoted in Peter Lewis, 'Are US Companies Learning to Share?' *New York Times*, 2/1/88, Week in Review, p. 5.

26. Ouchi and Bolton (1988) provide a good summary of the factors that account for the present stage of mixed support in the US for collective industrial research.
27. For a detailed discussion of the origins, development, and initial problems of one large cooperative R&D venture, the Microelectronics and Computer Technology Corporation (MCC) in Austin, Texas, see Peck (1986).
28. Ed Zajac has emphasized to me that the termination of a relationship does not necessarily imply failure. Collaboration is often intended as a means for the transfer of knowledge. Once this process is realized, termination may well be a sign of success.
29. Analysts have cautioned against alliances that involve a relative power imbalance, in which either one partner receives undue benefits or where one partner becomes so dependent on another that they may have no option other than to continue a relationship in which their share is increasingly inferior (see Teece, 1986). This fear, along with the worry that the partner will not perform according to expectations, explains why most potential partners approach an agreement with trepidation. These are typical and well-founded misgivings about any asymmetric exchange relationship.
30. Many commentators have voiced particular concerns about global partnerships, issues that are contested in the current 'manufacturing matters' debate (see Cohen and Zysman, 1987). Reich and Mankin (1986) warn that friendly colleagues often revert to hostile competitors. In the Pentax-Honeywell and Canon-Bell & Howell alliances, Japanese partners took advantage of valuable US technology and know-how only to later discard their American partners. *Business Week*, in its well-known March 3, 1986 issue, cautioned against the growth of 'hollow corporations,' that is, firms that have disaggregated so radically that they are left without any core expertise.
31. Wilkinson (1983) details related developments in Britain, where retailing, clothing, shoemaking, printing, and foodstuffs have undergone vertical disintegration, with the subsequent rise of small firms and numerous subcontracting relationships.
32. Top-down controls create distance between supervisors and subordinates, between powerful executives and less powerful employees. A vertical chain of command, and its accompanying layers of administration, undercuts management's ability to see its directives implemented and creates an environment in which employees see their work as but a tiny cog in a large impersonal machine. The diffuse control structure in large firms both dampens management's ability to move quickly and labor's sense of commitment to the enterprise.

References

Abernathy, W. (1978), *The Productivity Dilemma*, Baltimore: Johns Hopkins University Press.

Agnew, J. (1986), *Worlds Apart: The Market and the Theater in Anglo-American Thought, 1550–1750*, New York: Cambridge University Press.

Alchian, A. and H. Demsetz (1972), 'Production, information costs, and economic organization', *American Economic Review*, **62** (5), 777–95.

Arrow, K. (1974), *The Limits of Organization*, New York: Norton.

Arthur, B. (1987), 'Urban systems and historical path-dependence', to appear in R. Herman and J. Ansubel (eds), *Urban Systems and Infrastructure*, NAS/NAE, forthcoming.

Axelrod, R. (1984), *The Evolution of Cooperation*, New York: Basic Books.

Belussi, F. (1986), 'New technologies in a traditional sector: The Benetton case', Berkeley Roundtable on the International Economy working paper no. 19.

Ben-Porath, Y. (1980), 'The F-connection: Families, friends, and firms in the organization of exchange', *Population and Development Review*, **6**, 1–30.

Berger, C. and L.L. Cummings (1979), 'Organizational structure, attitudes and behavior', in Barry Staw (ed.), *Research in Organizational Behavior*, **1**, 169–208.

Borys, B. and D.B. Jemison (1989), 'Hybrid organizations as strategic alliances: Theoretical issues in organizational combinations', *Academy of Management Review*, **14** (2), 234–49.

Bradach, J.L. and R.G. Eccles (1989), 'Markets versus hierarchies: From ideal types to plural forms', *Annual Review of Sociology*, **15**, 97–118.
Braudel, F. (1982), *The Wheels of Commerce*, New York: Harper and Row.
Brusco, S. (1982), 'The Emilian model: Productive decentralization and social integration', *Cambridge Journal of Economics*, **6**, 167–84.
Buckley, P.J. and M. Casson (1988), 'A theory of cooperation in international business', in P. Contractor and P. Lorange (eds), *Cooperative Strategies in International Business*, Lexington, MA: Lexington Books, pp. 31–53.
Chandler, A.D. (1977), *The Visible Hand*, Cambridge, MA: Harvard University Press.
Child, J. (1972), 'Organizational structure and strategies of control: A replication of the Aston Study', *Administrative Science Quarterly*, **18**, 168–85.
Coase, R. (1937), 'The nature of the firm', *Economica*, **4**, 386–405.
Cohen, S. and J. Zysman (1987), *Manufacturing Matters*, New York: Basic Books.
Cole, R. (1985), 'The macropolitics of organizational change: A comparative analysis of the spread of small-group activities', *Administrative Science Quarterly*, **30**, 560–85.
Contractor, F.J. and P. Lorange (1988), *Cooperative Strategies in International Business*, Lexington, MA: Lexington Books.
Coser, L., C. Kadushin and W.W. Powell (1982), *Books: The Culture and Commerce of Publishing*, New York: Basic Books.
Dalton, M. (1957), *Men Who Manage*, New York: Wiley.
DiMaggio, P. and W.W. Powell (1983), 'The iron cage revisited: Institutional isomorphism and collective rationality in organizational fields', *American Sociological Review*, **48**, 147–60.
Dore, R. (1983), 'Goodwill and the spirit of market capitalism', *British Journal of Sociology*, **34** (4), 459–82.
Dore, R. (1987), *Taking Japan Seriously*, Stanford, CA: Stanford University Press.
Dorfman, N. (1983), 'Route 128: The development of a regional high-tech economy', *Research Policy*, **12**, 299–316.
Doz, Y. (1988), 'Technology partnerships between larger and smaller firms: some critical issues', *International Studies of Management and Organization*, **17** (4), 31–57.
Dyer, Davis, M.S. and A. Webber (1987), *Changing Alliances*, Boston, MA: Harvard Business School Press.
Eccles, R. (1981), 'The quasifirm in the construction industry', *Journal of Economic Behavior and Organization*, **2**, 335–7.
Eccles, R. (1985), *The Transfer Pricing Problem: A Theory for Practice*, Lexington, MA: Lexington Books.
Eccles, R.G. and D. Crane (1987), 'Managing through networks in investment banking', *California Management Review*, **30** (1), 176–95.
Eccles, R.G. and H.C. White (1986), 'Firm and market interfaces of profit center control', in S. Lindenberg, J.S. Coleman and S. Novak (eds), *Approaches to Social Theory*, New York: Russell Sage, pp. 203–20.
Faulkner, R.R. and A. Anderson, (1987), 'Short-term projects and emergent careers: Evidence from Hollywood', *American Journal of Sociology*, **92** (4), 879–909.
Finley, M. (1973), *The Ancient Economy*, Berkeley: University of California Press.
Friar, J. and M. Horwitch (1985), 'The emergence of technology strategy: A new dimension of strategic management', *Technology in Society*, **7** (2/3), 143–78.
Fusfeld, H. and C. Haklisch (1985), 'Cooperative R&D for competitors', *Harvard Business Review*, **85** (6), 60–76.
Geertz, C. (1978), 'The bazaar economy: Information and search in peasant marketing', *American Economic Review*, **68** (2), 28–32.
Gerlach, M.L. (1990), *Alliances and the Social Organization of Japanese Business*, Berkeley: University of California Press.
Goldberg, V.P. (1980), 'Relational exchange: Economics and complex contracts', *American Behavioral Scientist*, **23** (3), 337–52.
Gordon, R.W. (1985), 'Macaulay, Macneil, and the discovery of solidarity and power in contract law', *Wisconsin Law Review*, **3**, 565–80.

Gouldner, A. (1960), 'The norm of reciprocity: A preliminary statement', *American Sociological Review*, **25**, 161–78.

Graham, M. (1985), 'Corporate research and development: The latest information', *Technology in Society*, **7** (2/3), 179–96.

Granovetter, M. (1985), 'Economic action and social structure: A theory of embeddedness', *American Journal of Sociology*, **91** (3), 481–510.

Hackman, R. and G. Oldham (1980), *Work Redesign*, Reading, MA: Addison-Wesley.

Hagg, I. and J. Johanson (1983), *Firms in Networks: A New View of Competitive Power*, Stockholm: Business and Social Research Institute.

Hakansson, H. (ed.) (1987), *Industrial Technological Development: A Network Approach*, London: Croom Helm.

Hamilton, W.F. (1985), 'Corporate strategies for managing emerging technologies', *Technology in Society*, **7** (2/3), 197–212.

Hannan, M. and J.H. Freeman (1984), 'Structural inertia and organizational change', *American Sociological Review*, **49**, 149–64.

Hayek, F. (1945), 'The use of knowledge in society', *American Economic Review*, **35**, 519–30.

Helper, S. (1987), *Supplier Relations and Technical Change*, Ph.D. dissertation, Dept. of Economics, Harvard University.

Hergert, M. and D. Morris (1988), 'Trends in international collaborative agreements', in F. Contractor and P. Lorange (eds), *Cooperative Strategies in International Business*, Lexington, MA: Lexington Books, pp. 99–109.

Imai, K. and H. Itami (1984), 'Interpenetration of organization and market', *International Journal of Industrial Organization*, **2**, 285–310.

Imai, K., I. Nonaka and H. Takeuchi (1985), 'Managing the new product development process: How Japanese companies learn and unlearn', in Kim B. Clark et al. (eds), *The Uneasy Alliance*, Boston, MA: Harvard Business School Press, pp. 337–75.

Jarillo, J.-C. (1988), 'On strategic networks', *Strategic Management Journal*, **9**, 31–41.

Jarillo, J.-C. and J.I. Martinez (1987), 'Benetton S.p.A.: A case study', working paper, Barcelona, Spain: IESE.

Johanson, J. and L.-G. Mattson (1987), 'Interorganizational relations in industrial systems: A network approach compared with the transaction-cost approach', *International Studies of Management and Organization*, **18** (1), 34–48.

Kaneko, I. and K. Imai (1987), 'A network view of the firm', paper presented at first Hitotsubashi–Stanford conference.

Keohane, R. (1986), 'Reciprocity in international relations', *International Organization*, **40** (1), 1–27.

Klein, B. (1983), 'Contracting costs and residual claims: The separation of ownership and control', *Journal of Law and Economics*, **26**, 367–74.

Koenig, C. and R.A. Thietart (1988), 'Managers, engineers and government', *Technology in Society*, **10**, 45–69.

Larson, A. (1988), 'Cooperative alliances: A study of entrepreneurship', Ph.D. dissertation, Harvard Business School.

Lazerson, M. (1988), 'Organizational growth of small firms: An outcome of markets and hierarchies?', *American Sociological Review*, **53** (3), 330–42.

Lorenzoni, G. and O. Ornati (1988), 'Constellations of firms and new ventures', *Journal of Business Venturing*, **3**, 41–57.

Loveman, G., M. Piore and W. Sengenberger (1987), 'The evolving role of small business in industrial economies', paper presented at conference on New Developments in Labor Market and Human Resource Policies, Sloan School, M.I.T.

Luhmann, N. (1979), *Trust and Power*, New York: Wiley.

Macneil, I. (1978), 'Contracts: Adjustment of long-term economic relations under classical, neoclassical, and relational contract law', *Northwestern University Law Review*, **72** (6), 854–905.

Macneil, I. (1985), 'Relational contract: What we do and do not know', *Wisconsin Law Review*, **3**, 483–526.

Mariotti, S. and G.C. Cainarca (1986), 'The evolution of transaction governance in the textile-clothing industry', *Journal of Economic Behavior and Organization*, **7**, 351–74.

Mariti, P. and R.H. Smiley (1983), 'Co-operative agreements and the organization of industry', *Journal of Industrial Economics*, **31** (4), 437–51.

Mauss, M. (1967, 1925), *The Gift*, New York: Norton.

Mowery, D.C. (1987), *Alliance Politics and Economics*, Cambridge, MA: Ballinger.

Mowery, D.C. (ed.) (1988), *International Collaborative Ventures in U.S. Manufacturing*, Cambridge, MA: Ballinger.

Nelson, R. and S. Winter (1982), *An Evolutionary Theory of Economic Change*, Cambridge: Harvard University Press.

Okumura, H. (1982), 'Interfirm relations in an enterprise group: The case of Mitsubishi', *Japanese Economic Studies*, **10** (4), 53–82.

Ouchi, W.G. and M.K. Bolton (1988), 'The logic of joint research and development', *California Management Review*, **30** (3), 9–33.

Peck, M.J. (1986), 'Joint R&D: The case of microelectronics and computer technology corporation', *Research Policy*, **15**, 219–31.

Perlmutter, H. and D. Heenan (1986), 'Cooperate to compete globally', *Harvard Business Review*, **86** (2), 136–52.

Perrow, C. (1967), 'A framework for the comparative analysis of organizations', *American Sociological Review*, **32**, 194–208.

Peterson, R.A. and H. White (1981), 'Elements of simplex structure', *Urban Life*, **10** (1), 3–24.

Piore, M.J. and C.F. Sabel (1984), *The Second Industrial Divide*, New York: Basic Books.

Polanyi, K. (1957), *The Great Transformation*, Boston: Beacon.

Porter, L. and E. Lawler (1965), 'Properties of organization structure in relation to job attitudes and job behavior', *Psychological Bulletin*, **64** (1), 23–51.

Porter, M. (1983), *Cases in Competitive Strategy*, New York: Free Press.

Porter, M. (1985), *Competitive Advantage*, New York: Free Press.

Porter, M. (1986), *Competition in Global Industries*, Boston, MA: Harvard Business School Press.

Porter, M. and M.B. Fuller (1986), 'Coalitions and global strategy', in M. Porter (ed.), *Competition in Global Industries*, Boston, MA: HBS Press, pp. 315–44.

Powell, W.W. (1985), *Getting into Print: The Decision Making Process in Scholarly Publishing*, Chicago: University of Chicago Press.

Powell, W.W. (1987), 'Hybrid organizational arrangements: New form or transitional development?', *California Management Review*, **30** (1), 67–87.

Pucik, V. (1988), 'Strategic alliances with the Japanese: Implications for human resource management', in P. Contractor and P. Lorange (eds), *Cooperative Strategies in International Business*, Lexington, MA: Lexington Books, pp. 487–98.

Quinn, D.P. (1987), 'Dynamic markets and mutating firms: The changing organization of production in automotive firms', working paper presented at APSA meetings, Chicago.

Reddy, W.M. (1984), *The Rise of Market Culture*, New York: Cambridge University Press.

Reich, R.B. and E. Mankin (1986), 'Joint ventures with Japan give away our future', *Harvard Business Review*, **86** (2), 78–86.

Richardson, G.B. (1972), 'The organization of industry', *Economic Journal*, **82**, 883–96.

Riordan, M.H. and O.E. Williamson (1985), 'Asset specificity and economic organization', *International Journal of Industrial Organization*, **3**, 365–78.

Sabel, C.F. (1989), 'Flexible specialization and the re-emergence of regional economies', in P. Hirst and J. Zeitlin (eds), *Reversing Industrial Decline?* Oxford, UK: Berg, pp. 17–70.

Sabel, C., G. Herrigel, R. Kazis and R. Deeg (1987), 'How to keep mature industries innovative', *Technology Review*, **90** (3), 26–35.

Sahlins, M. (1972), *Stone Age Economics*, Chicago: Aldine.

Shimokawa, K. (1985), 'Japan's keiretsu system: The case of the automobile industry', *Japanese Economic Studies*, **13** (4), 3–31.

Stinchcombe, A. (1985), 'Contracts as hierarchical documents', in A. Stinchcombe and C. Heimer (eds), *Organization Theory and Project Management*, Oslo: Norwegian University Press, pp. 121–71.

Teece, D. (1986), 'Profiting from technological innovation: Implications for integration, collaboration, licensing and public policy', *Research Policy*, **15** (6), 785–805.

Teece, D. and G. Pisano (1987), 'Collaborative arrangements and technology strategy', paper presented at conference on New Technology and New Intermediaries, Stanford: Center for European Studies.
Thompson, E.P. (1971), 'The moral economy of the English crowd in the eighteenth century', *Past and Present*, **50**, 78–98.
Thorelli, H.B. (1986), 'Networks: Between markets and hierarchies', *Strategic Management Journal*, **7**, 37–51.
Von Hippel, E. (1987), 'Cooperation between rivals: Informal know-how trading', *Research Policy*, **16**, 291–302.
Walton, R. (1985), 'From control to commitment in the workplace', *Harvard Business Review*, **85** (2), 76–84.
Walzer, M. (1983), *Spheres of Justice*, New York: Basic Books.
Weitzman, M. (1984), *The Share Economy*, Cambridge, MA: Harvard University Press.
White, H.C. (1981), 'Where do markets come from?', *American Journal of Sociology*, **87**, 517–47.
Wilkinson, F. (1983), 'Productive systems', *Cambridge Journal of Economics*, **7**, 413–29.
Williamson, O.E. (1975), *Markets and Hierarchies: Analysis and Antitrust Implications*, New York: Free Press.
Williamson, O.E. (1985), *The Economic Institutions of Capitalism*, New York: Free Press.
Yoshikawa, A. (1988), 'Japanese biotechnology: New drugs, industrial organization, innovation, and strategic alliances', BRIE working paper no. 33.
Zagnoli, P. (1987), 'Interfirm agreements as bilateral transactions?', paper presented at conference on New Technology and New Intermediaries, Stanford: Center for European Studies.
Zelizer, V. (1988), 'Beyond the polemics of the market: Establishing a theoretical and empirical agenda', paper presented at conference on Economy and Society, Santa Barbara: University of California.

[20]

On Clusters, Hybrids, and Other Strange Forms: The Case of the French Poultry Industry

by

CLAUDE MENARD *

This paper explores properties of governance structures identified as "hybrid forms," using a study of the French poultry industry. After an introductory discussion, section 2 emphasizes recent contributions to the analysis of these forms. Section 3 turns to the empirical investigation and raises questions about the coordination process involved, its efficiency, and the coexistence of different organizational structures. Section 4 develops a model focusing on "authority" as the specific mode of adaptation implemented by these forms. The analysis substantiates the idea of "an institutional structure of production" and challenges the dominant view on regulatory policies. (JEL: D 2, D 4, L 1, L 23, L 6, Q 1)

1. Introduction

Hybridization has been a major technological revolution in agriculture, and a major source of gains in productivity in the aviculture industry. But this paper is not about genetics. It is about hybrid "governance structures" such as networks among firms and interfirm contracting, i.e., structures that are neither markets nor hierarchies.

Most recent literature about relationships among firms focuses on the analysis of factors involved in decisions about whether or not to integrate. For example, the industrial organization tradition considers factors related to technological constraints or strategic behavior (TIROLE [1988]). Other recent contributions explain the integration decision in terms of threat of quasi-rents being appropriated opportunistically (KLEIN, CRAWFORD and ALCHIAN [1978]); or of

* While working on this paper, I had extensive discussions with Lee Benham, Ronald H. Coase, Douglass C. North, Oliver E. Williamson, and participants of the workshop on Institutional Economics at Washington University in St. Louis. An earlier version was presented at Université de Paris (Panthéon-Sorbonne), at HEC (Hautes Etudes Commerciales, Paris), and in Wallerfangen. I benefited from detailed comments of Michel Ghertman, Douglas H. Ginsburg, Hans-Bernd Schäfer, Oliver E. Williamson, and several participants. Linda Davenport helped to polish the style. None of them are responsible for any misleading ideas.

the search for an optimal structure of ownership in which rent would be shared in a way that maintains the incentive to invest (GROSSMAN and HART [1986]).

Some authors, though, have emphasized the importance of organizational structures that involve neither pure integration nor pure market relationships. CHEUNG [1983], for example, following COASE [1937], [1988], has described a continuum of contractual arrangements, from spot markets to fully integrated firms, while WILLIAMSON [1985], [1991], [1993b] has developed the concept of a class of discrete structural governances that are neither markets nor hierarchies.

Characterization of these forms, whether they are considered as points on a continuum or as structurally distinct, has been based primarily on their contractual properties. However, much more than contracts is involved (DEMSETZ [1988]; MASTEN [1988]; WILLIAMSON [1993a], [1993b]). This paper will explore both contractual and non-contractual properties, using as illustration a detailed empirical study of the French poultry industry and, more specifically, of the LABEL sector that deals with fresh poultry. I will provide reasons for this choice explicitly in section 3, but I want to emphasize already that the major issues involved apply to other situations as well.

The paper is organized as follows. The following section reviews recent contributions to the analysis of hybrid forms, most of them from the transaction cost perspective. I will use this framework to describe properties of hybrid forms as well as delineate certain limitations of this approach. In section 3, I will present an empirical investigation of the governance structure of the LABEL system in French aviculture in order to provide a new set of data for the analysis of these issues.[1] I will show how this study raises questions about the coordination process involved, its efficiency, and the coexistence of different organizational structures. To clarify these issues, I develop in section 4 a theoretical model that extends the ideas introduced in section 2, with emphasis on "authority" (versus hierarchy or prices) as the specific mode of adaptation of these hybrid forms. I will also substantiate the idea of an "institutional structure of production" (COASE [1992]). My conclusions challenge the dominant view on regulatory policies.

2. *Hybrid Forms: Characteristics and Problems*

Until very recently, most economists have focused their attention on the functioning of the price mechanism, while internal characteristics of formal organizations have been considered as unimportant (KREPS and SPENCE [1985]; for a

[1] The empirical research was conducted in close cooperation with Egizio Valceschini, from the INRA (Institut National de la Recherche Agronomique, France), and benefited very substantially from discussions with Bernard Schaller (also from the INRA) and from the field studies by my research assistants, Benoit Caillet, Eric Chadapaux and Gaelle Garnier. I would like to express to them all my deep gratitude for their help and enthusiasm.

sharp critique of this attitude, see DEMSETZ [1988] [2]). "Institutional arrangements" (DAVIS and NORTH [1971]) that would fall between these two polar structures have received even less attention.

Some influential views even deny the specificity of all these structures. CHEUNG [1983], for instance, concluded his paper on "The Contractual Nature of the Firm" by emphasizing the continuity of contractual arrangements and arguing that contracts, not governance structures, should be economists' main object of investigation. On the opposite, WILLIAMSON [1985], [1991] has strongly promoted the concept of "discrete structural forms," or "governance structures." A brief remark by COASE [1988] can help to reconcile the two approaches; the relevance of each may depend on its object of analysis. Indeed, the fact that blood is found in all mammals cannot be denied; it does not mean that monkeys and humans are all alike!

In the following pages, I adopt a "structuralist view," arguing that "hybrid forms" have identifiable properties that are distinct from those of markets or formal organizations. This section examines these properties. In subsection 2.1, I discuss the nature of hybrid forms, as introduced by WILLIAMSON [1991]. In subsection 2.2, I turn to the most analyzed aspect, that of the contractual arrangements at work in these forms. In subsection 2.3, I discuss the related problems of incentives, modalities of control, and adaptation. Conclusions are drawn, to be compared with the empirical study of the poultry industry in section 3.

2.1 Definition and Discussion

In his paper on "Comparative Economic Organization," WILLIAMSON [1991] suggested that a hybrid form is a specialized governance structure for dealing with bilateral dependence without going as far as integration. The key idea is that of a bilateral dependency strong enough to require close coordination, but not strong enough to induce full integration. The usual explanation for bilateral dependency invokes the existence of specific assets that create some "lock-in" among agents and simultaneously generate appropriable quasi-rents (KLEIN, CRAWFORD and ALCHIAN [1978]). In this view, continuity of the relationship confers added value, but simultaneously invites opportunistic behavior, since the assets are not redeployable, or are redeployable only at very high costs.[3]

But, more precisely, what kind of relationship can address these potentially conflictive purposes? What institutional arrangement can both coordinate efficiently and reduce the risk of opportunism, without the bureaucratic costs

[2] COASE [1972], [1992] has also criticized this bias, but WILLIAMSON [1975] made the real breakthrough. In the following pages, I use the term "formal organization" in place of his "hierarchy," since the latter expression tends to confuse the structure with its mode of adaptation.

[3] Following the slightly different terminology of KLEIN, CRAWFORD and ALCHIAN [1978], assets are very expensive to remove or exchange and/or they are very specialized.

involved in integration? Hybrid forms can be understood as a specific answer to these problems. They will necessarily involve some forms of planning, and of administrative decisions, both within and among the firms concerned (otherwise, the market would suffice). They will develop specific features to maintain long term relationships among the parties to the arrangement, while guaranteeing efficient coordination and acceptable shares of the rent. These features must also be combined so as to define *viable forms*. So far, most of the literature on hybrid forms has emphasized features of the contractual aspect, such as clauses about arbitration, take-or-pay procurement, reciprocity, and measures to create "hostage" positions. But other aspects are also involved, as becomes clear in looking at problems of incentives and controls in interfirm agreements.

2.2 Specific Contractual Arrangements

It is traditional in transaction cost economics to stress the importance and diversity of contractual arrangements (COASE [1937], [1988]; KLEIN, CRAWFORD and ALCHIAN [1978]; CHEUNG [1983]). It is Williamson though who, since 1985, and particularly in his paper of 1991, has provided the most detailed analysis of the differentiated nature of these arrangements and of their relation to governance structures.

Building upon MACNEIL [1974], he has consistently developed a distinction among three classes of contracts, each corresponding to a typical governance structure. Formally, let C be the contractual arrangement characterizing governance structures, p the prices, k the specificity of assets involved, and s the contractual safeguards. C can be expressed as a function of these three variables:

$$C = C(p, k, s)\,.$$

A *classical contract* would be characteristic of *market* relationships, with p the determinant, and k and s very weak if not null. In such contracts, formal clauses specify most characteristics of transactions at stake, with the identity of parties to the contract irrelevant, and transactions highly monetized. In contrast, *forbearance* would be the implicit contract law of *formal organizations*, with prices playing a small role in internal adjustments, while k and s have high values. In these contractual arrangements, adaptability to highly consequential disturbances is crucial, while highly specific assets create risks of opportunism that detailed safeguards are built in to reduce. Hierarchy is at the core of adaptability and operates through "fiat," acting as "its own court of ultimate appeal." In between, *neo-classical contracts* would be characteristic of *hybrid forms*, with prices playing an important role as a factor of adjustment, but one restricted by the presence of specific assets (k is positive), while safeguards are difficult to implement. A neo-classical contract is typically a long-term arrangement, in order to develop a continuing relationship, in which the identity of parties does matter, since bilateral dependency is non-trivial, while adaptation mechanism must be elastic enough to enable parties to adjust to moderately consequential disturbances.

Crucial to our understanding of hybrid forms is the idea that neo-classical contracts define a general framework, within which partners will develop specific features to deal with necessary adjustments. Indeed, classical (spot) contracts are very specific, with prices as the variable of adjustment, and are easy to monitor; courts can implement them. At the other end, forbearance relationships deal with complex situations and, as such, can be only very weakly specified by contracts; "command" is the major mechanism of adjustment, with hierarchy in charge of filling in the blanks left in contracts.

Comparatively, contractual arrangements typical of hybrid forms would define a framework within which specific features have to be developed to implement adjustments required by a long standing relationship among identifiable partners. Comparing several empirical studies,[4] focused mainly on long-term contracts, it is possible to delineate four such features. (*i*) A neo-classical contract defines *adaptation mechanisms* to improve, relative to pure market relationships, the capacity to adjust to unanticipated disturbances. Specific problems (e.g., price adjustments) are usually identified, as are specific procedures for resolving them (e.g., a joint committee). (*ii*) Such contracts also provide *a tolerance zone* within which misalignments can be absorbed (e.g., acceptable fluctuations of prices relative to market prices). Adaptation to disturbances must preserve the relationship; hence, mechanisms in which reciprocity prevails allow for sharing of the risks. (*iii*) These contracts usually require *information disclosure* and substantiation if adaptation is proposed, so that state-contingent claims can be made (e.g., unpredictible changes in costs). (*iv*) Finally, there are provisions for *arbitration*, rather than litigation through courts as in classical contracts, if voluntary agreements fail. Arbitration can operate through relatively "mechanical" clauses, as with "hostage" clauses such as penalties if deadlines are not met; or through more "organic" clauses, as when regulatory clauses among parties are implemented.

Let me emphasize how precise this analysis is, in comparison to most economic references to contracts, which *never* examine specifics. Transaction cost economics represents a real breakthrough from that point of view. Nevertheless, in comparison to our empirical study, the interpretation above raises two intertwined problems. First, it relates neo-classical contracts to an intermediate degree of asset specificity, with associated difficulties in the definition and implementation of safeguards. But as I will show in section 3, arrangements can be devised to discipline participants. Second, WILLIAMSON [1992] shares with KLEIN, CRAWFORD and ALCHIAN [1978] the idea that arbitration in neoclassical

[4] In what follows, I draw ideas mostly from JOSKOW [1985], [1987]; PALAY [1984], [1985]; and WILLIAMSON [1985, ch. 3], [1991].

contracts tends to be very costly, because of the importance of the identity of parties in that type of contract, which makes trust and implicit agreements crucial. When the number of individuals or firms involved becomes large and when assets are specific, "the problems of contract enforcement become severe" (KLEIN, CRAWFORD and ALCHIAN [1978, 322]). However, as we shall see, specific features can be devised to deal with disputes at relatively low costs.

2.3 Incentive Intensity, Modalities of Control, and Adaptation

Though recognized as central to contractual arrangements, issues of incentives, modalities of control, and modes of adaptation specific to hybrid forms have so far barely been studied. Very few theoretical contributions (and even fewer empirical studies) provide valuable insights, but they remain quite general.

The case of *incentives* illustrates these difficulties. When significant disturbances of the environment and bilateral dependency develop, transaction cost economics predicts that delays in responding and increased possibility for opportunistic behavior will considerably reduce the efficiency of the price mechanism. This is exactly why hybrid forms exist; they represent a shift towards cooperation and administrative controls in order to adjust more rapidly and in a more coordinated way to these disturbances. But this shift also weakens the monetary incentives that are the strength of markets, without providing the incentives of hierarchical structures, such as promotions, career path and extended powers of decision. Therefore, is there any incentive advantage to hybrid forms?

The answer provided by recent theories is twofold, and also raises questions. *(i)* Hybrid forms maintain separate ownership and, therefore, involve highly intense incentives that are typical of markets. But since agreements among firms require sharing risks as well as benefits, in a context where actions are not fully observable or verifiable (the *monitorability* of contracts is a problem; ALCHIAN and WOODWARD [1988]), problems of property rights emerge. Who is going to have control over *residual rights* (as opposed to the rights specified by contracts; GROSSMAN and HART [1986])? How will the appropriation of quasi-rent be managed in order to preserve the stability of agreements among participating firms? *(ii)* Because of these flaws in control over residual rights, "concerns for *equity* intrude" (WILLIAMSON [1991, 280]). The equity factor means that cooperative arbitration will interfere with market incentives. OUCHI [1980, 138] has emphasized that: "One principal function of a governance mechanism is to achieve a perception of equity between the parties regarding the division of rewards resulting from the transaction." But this is particularly problematic within a hybrid form; what efficient device can be implemented that will satisfy parties to the agreement?

Because of the limited role of the price mechanism and of the uncertainties surrounding the appropriation of rent, information disclosure will be essential to the existence and stability of hybrid forms. However, how this will happen also remains mysterious, and even more so because of goal incongruence and/or performance ambiguities inherent to the hybrid form (BOWEN and JONES [1986]). Therefore, it is not surprising that some authors have emphasized the role of "dispute-settlement machineries" in such arrangements (e.g., WILLIAMSON [1991]).

In addition, forms of *control* that need to be implemented are very likely to be different in hybrid forms than in other governance structures. In markets, prices discipline participants, eventually with the support of institutions designed to guarantee the observance of classical contracts (e.g., courts). Within formal organizations, rules, procedures of evaluation, and vertical command develop the capacity of parties to measure relative performance. But what about hybrid forms? They share aspects of formal organizations in that they are oriented towards conscious cooperation. But there is no administrative control strictly speaking, since agreements are among firms with distinct ownership (COASE [1988, ch. 5]); therefore, only weak forms of control can be implemented. How is it, then, that these governance structures can be so stable?

Major problems also emerge with respect to the *adaptation mode*. This aspect is crucial, since a fundamental explanation of the existence of hybrid forms is that they enhance the capacity of firms to deal with disturbances that spot markets could not easily meet (or could meet only at prohibitive costs), while maintaining the incentives that pure integration lacks. According to WILLIAMSON [1991], the choice of an adaptation mode depends on: *(i)* whether there is bilateral dependency or not; and *(ii)* whether distribution of gains is well determined or not. Quoting HAYEK [1945] and BARNARD [1938], he proposes a distinction between a A-type of adaptation (where A is for autonomous), operating through prices; and a C-type of adaptation (C for cooperative), with "fiat" at the core. He provides few qualifications, though, of structures between markets and formal organizations, with the exception of one brief remark. Furthermore, he suggested that: *(i)* ownership autonomy will be preserved, thus maintaining some characteristics of the A-type in hybrids, while: *(ii)* contractual safeguards will be implemented in order to preserve cooperative adjustments required by bilateral dependency. Therefore, adaptation mode in hybrid forms would be a compromise of the A-type and the C-type, operating efficiently in both autonomous adaptation and cooperative adaptation, but not as well as markets in the former or as well as hierarchies in the latter.

Other authors have discussed the modalities of adaptation that would characterize hybrid forms, and particularly the role of specific contractual clauses. Adopting the point of view of agency theory, BRICKLEY and DARK [1987] emphasized the role of shared ownership, multi-ownership, or other modalities of mutual control over inputs, illustrated by the franchise system, as devices to adapt. But as I will show in section 3, differences in ownership structures need not involve distinct modes of adaptation. In contrast, ALCHIAN and WOODWARD [1988], emphasized the adaptative role of contractual provisions such as renegotiation or credible commitment clauses (e.g., security deposits). Long-term contracts complemented by standardized procedures based on routines developed among partners or on standards jointly adopted are also viewed as part of the adaptation mode of hybrids (COASE [1937], [1988]; KLEIN, CRAWFORD and ALCHIAN [1978]; PALAY [1984]; JOSKOW [1985], [1987]). While these are certainly pieces of the puzzle, they still need to be integrated into a coherent explanation.

To conclude this section, let me emphasize the importance of these results. First, the contributions under review have clearly identified some major components to be analyzed, a significant advance over the past fifteen years. Second, specific propositions have been made regarding the nature of contractual arrangements involved in hybrid forms and, in a less rigorous form, about their specific mode of adaptation. But I have also pointed out several inadequacies. Too many black holes remain, and their delineation and explanation can best be achieved through the use of empirical studies.

3. Case Study: The French Poultry Industry

I will now turn to such a study, conducted in the French poultry industry during the last two years. With an important role in French agriculture, this industry has performed particularly well over the last twenty years. The industry involves a complex set of arrangements, which makes it of particular interest for the understanding of hybrid forms. It uses perfectly standardized and well-known technologies, so that comparisons are not blurred by changing products or processes as they are in the high tech sector that is often used to illustrate hybrid forms. The institutional environment has also been remarkably stable, and recent changes due to new European regulations make the comparative approach even more significant.

I will develop the analysis in four subsections. In subsection 3.1, I provide basic information and explain the methodology. In subsection 3.2, I describe the institutional environment, particularly that of the fresh poultry sector, on which most of the study focuses. In subsection 3.3, I analyze the specific governance structure of this sector. Finally, in subsection 3.4, I provide a detailed account of the contractual arrangements. In the conclusion, I emphasize crucial points to be interpreted in section 4.

3.1 Methodology and Data: A Short Description

French aviculture is a significant part of the French agro-business, and also of the world production of poultry. In 1992, world production was estimated at 42 million tons, of which 74% was chicken. The rate of growth in this industry has been spectacular; consumption of chicken has more than doubled over the last 30 years, equalling that of beef in 1992, when it amounted to an average of 22 kilos per person, with a record 33 kilos per person in the US (as compared to 4 kilos in 1950!). France is first in European production and second in world exports. Aviculture represented 11% of France's net commercial balance for agriculture in 1992. If we leave aside the relatively small segment oriented towards the production of eggs, the French broiler industry is dominated by 15 groups, totaling 93% of its production. The structure of these groups is somewhat heterogeneous; two relatively integrated firms (DOUX, the European leader; and BOURGOIN) produce most of the standard chicken, while the LABEL system, to be defined below, is more diversified (with LOUE, the leader, supplying over 30% of this category). Also noticeable is the geographical concentration of production; Brittany, with 50% of the total, and more generally the western part of the country which represents over 70% of the production, are to France what the "broiler belt" is to the US.[5] Two-thirds of the French production, and 80% of the LABEL sector, is sold in supermarkets.

A fundamental distinction for the purpose of this study, is that between standard chicken and LABEL chicken. The latter represented only 2.5% of the total production in 1975, but over 30% of the production in 1992. Standard chicken has developed as mass production over the last thirty years; it is based on fast growing breeds (it takes seven weeks nowadays to prepare this kind of chicken for market, compared to fourteen weeks 25 years ago), fattened with grains (half the quantity needed in the early seventies), antibiotics, and animal products; in closed areas, most of the time away from natural light; with the final product either marketed rapidly or, most of the time, cut into sections and frozen. LABEL chickens, on the other hand, must meet high quality standards strictly enforced, among which are the following: *(i)* They are from selected slow growing breeds; *(ii)* food must come mostly from cereals (at least 75%), with no fat or animal proteins added; *(iii)* animals must be at least 81 days old before being slaughtered; and *(iv)* they must have been grown in broilerhouses with enough space to run (no more than 11 animals per square meter, as compared to as many as 24 for standard chicken). *(v)* They must be raised within 100 kilometers, or 2 hours of transportation time from the slaughterhouse; and, most importantly, *(vi)* there must be no more than 9 days between slaughter and final sale to consumers (to be sold with a LABEL, these chicken cannot be frozen). Finally, *(vii)* the product delivered to the market must provide the consumer with very specific information (hence, the name "LABEL"): where the chicken was grown, the composition of its diet, its age in days, the identity of its specific "band,"[6] and the recommended ultimate date of consumption.

Most of our empirical study is about this LABEL sector. We made this choice because the quality and time constraints described above have given rise to a specific institutional arrangement that makes this sector particularly interesting

[5] The American broiler belt stretches from eastern Texas to northern Florida, with Arkansas as its core.

[6] Chickens are grown by "bands;" in the LABEL sector, a band is usually between 400 and 500 animals (as compared to over 1,000 in the standard sector).

for an investigation of hybrid forms; indeed, as I will argue in section 4, lessons from this sector are likely to be *of general significance for all hybrid forms*. On the other hand, a LABEL chicken shares many characteristics with standard ones, as well as with the production of other kinds of poultry. Therefore, I have also used data available for the whole avicultural sector.

My sources of information are twofold. First, there is a very careful and extensive study of the poultry industry made in the early 1980s, with a peak in data collection in 1982, and the publication of the results in 1986.[7] This study was commissioned by the French Ministry of Agriculture, and conducted by researchers from the INRA under the direction of B. Schaller. A decisive source of information for our purposes is a very detailed questionnaire, including several questions on contractual arrangements, filled in by interviewers who visited 21,000 independent chicken growers.[8] I have extensively reviewed this material with B. Schaller. Second, a complementary study has been conducted in 1993–1995, in cooperation with another researcher from the INRA (E. Valceschini) and three research assistants. This study is more qualitative in nature. Data from the 1982–1986 study were revised, completed, and up-dated, particularly in relation to the rapid expansion of the LABEL sector. Also, more specific information was collected on the leading *organizations* in the field, and more extensively on three of them, through compilation of official documents, interviews, and meetings with top managers and with participants of the different organizations involved in the certification process (to be analyzed in subsection 3.3). Preliminary results were produced in the fall of 1994, and presented and discussed with representatives of the profession and of the Ministry of Agriculture, as a double-check of the data.

3.2 The Institutional Environment

Without getting into the details, it is necessary to know some historical facts about the institutional setting to be described.[9]

The LABEL system emerged in the poultry industry in the 1960s, at the time when the European Community implemented its agricultural policy to accompany and stimulate the development of the Common Market. Regulations were progressively introduced to homogenize products and to improve quality control. Although influenced by this context, the LABEL system did not develop as a by-product of new regulations, but, interestingly enough, resulted from the initiative of a group of growers; at the origin, *it is basically the product of self-organization*. These growers were eager to disseminate a more positive image of the poultry industry, at a time when critics were attacking "battery-

[7] SCHALLER [1986].

[8] At that time this represented 10 % of the total number of chicken growers, but much more if one considers that most of the commercial production was then provided by 32,800 growers.

[9] For a more detailed account, see SYLVANDER [1995].

reared" chicken, and, by the same token, to occupy a niche of the market of quality products. To differentiate themselves from the mainstream, and to attract demanding consumers, they wanted an official "certification of quality." The French Government responded rapidly and positively. At a time when agriculture was engaged in extensive changes, with industrialization threatening the traditional way of life of hundreds of thousands of farmers, the possibility of small farmers organizing themselves to modernize their activity, increase their productivity, and develop a specialized niche, appeared as a promising solution from the economic point of view and, moreover, as a very reassuring one from the political point of view. The LABEL system was adopted in the poultry industry in 1965. But results were long to come. In the 1960s, this sector never represented more than 2% of the market; it was only in the mid-seventies that the market boomed, thanks to the development of sales in supermarkets. However, the earlier institutional setting was to remain unchanged until the late 1980s, when the European Community modified the rules of the game.[10]

What does characterize the institutional setting adopted in 1965, which is still largely operational? LABELS in the poultry industry, as other French certifications in areas such as wine production or cheese making, are governed by strict rules concerning production and marketing. A National Committee of Labels and Certifications is in charge of examining and regulating products that are candidates for official certification.[11] This Committee comprises representatives of the government; of the associations of producers, distributors, and consumers; and "independent personalities" such as agricultural experts and economists. To obtain "certification" from the National Committee, producers have to submit their application through a "Certifying Organization," which is an intermediate structure comprising representatives of the firms involved in the industry concerned.[12] In the poultry industry, there were 21 such organizations in 1994, each with representatives from the growers, food suppliers, providers of chicks, and processing plants. These organizations have played a key role. From 1965 to the adoption of standard EN 45011, in 1992, they operated as a planning committee and, at the same time, as the committee to implement and monitor standards defined in agreement with the National Committee. The basic change, since 1992, is that these two functions are now managed by different organizations (at least formally).

The implementation of a LABEL by a "Certifying Organization" is based on a technical document, the *Cahier Des Charges* (literally: "list of specifications"), which is the fundamental contract among the participants in a LA-

[10] New standards were adopted in 1992, bureaucratically labelled "EN 45011."

[11] Note that once approved by the National Committee, demands must still be confirmed ("homologated") by the Ministry of Agriculture. This last step in the procedure seems to be a mere formality.

[12] "Certification" defines the standards to be maintained by producers; but it *does not* determine the specific organizational form to be adopted.

BEL.[13] Five major functions are delegated to the "Certifying Organization," in relation to these specifications:

(i) Production of rules codifying the technical characteristics of the products (e.g., type of breeds, quality of food, duration of growth).
(ii) Definition of modalities of control, for all stages.
(iii) Determination of the specific information to be posted on the final product, in conformity with the certification.
(iv) Establishment of penalties for non-compliance and of procedures for implementation.
(v) Determination of the minimum volume of production to be commercialized (thus providing growers with some guarantee).

These "Certifying Organizations" are themselves represented in a National Council of Producers, the SYNALAF (Syndicat National des Labels Avicoles de France), which operates essentially as a lobby for the "Certifying Organizations" with the National Committee, the Ministry of Agriculture, and the European Commission. To summarize, we have the following institutional structure:

Chain of Producers ---→ Certifying Organizations ⟶ SYNALAF ⟶ National Committee

The fundamental change introduced by the 1992 regulation of the European Community (EN 45011) is that "Certifying Organizations" can no longer both coordinate the partners involved in a specific LABEL product, and control quality and conformity of the product. As a result, the institutional structure is just a little bit more complex; "Certifying Organizations" are now "independent,"[14] while producers have reorganized themselves into Unions of Producers.

In the old as well as in the new system, controls can be and actually are exerted by inspectors from the Government. But most controls are by the "Certifying Organizations," or by an independent organization contracting with them, Quality-France, which operates as a provider of technical services. Costs of these controls are paid to the concerned "Certifying Organization" by fixed contributions for membership and by a commission on transactions among producers involved.

Let me summarize. The institutional setting is organized into three distinct levels: that of individual firms and growers involved in a specific LABEL product; that of the Committee coordinating and controlling complementary firms and growers associated in the production of this specific product; and

[13] In that, a LABEL is more than a brand name since it guarantees very specific characteristics and, as such, commands a premium price.

[14] Which means that at least 50% of the members of the Board must come from outside the groups involved in the LABEL under consideration. They are mostly representatives of consumers, distributors, Chambers of Commerce, and agricultural experts.

that of the National Committee which is the agency in charge of implementing and monitoring laws and regulation, i.e., the concrete expression of the institutional environment.

3.3 The Governance Structures

Grossman and Hart [1986] suggested that the decision to integrate or not should be understood as the search for an optimal structure of property. One puzzling aspect of the LABEL sector, with regard to this idea, is the *diversity of institutional arrangements* involved, each one apparently equally successful. Different structures can apparently attain identical goals with comparable efficiency. In order to explore this problem further, it can be useful to have in mind the set of participants involved in the "Chain of Producers" mentioned above. This can be summarized as follows:

Food Providers (3′)
↓
Selectors ⟶ Incubators ⟶ Growers ⟶ Processing Plants ⟶ Distributors
(1) (2) (3) (4) (5)

"Certifying Organizations" partially or totally coordinate participants (1) through (4). Other more occasional partners (e.g., pharmaceutical companies providing antibiotics or laboratories for quality control) are almost never involved, and will not be considered here. Actually, *two sets of transactions* are at the very core of the industry, on its supply side: the transactions between food providers and growers, and the transactions between growers and processing plants. As a consequence, related agents are the key players, and the *coalition* typical of a specific "Certifying Organization" will be structured by one set of transactions or the other, with growers occupying a very specific position. Moreover, the rapid expansion of the LABEL sector since the mid-seventies has progressively increased the role of the processing plants, at the intersection of production and distribution. This is particularly so considering the time constraint; LABEL chicken cannot be frozen [15] and must be sold within 9 days of being slaughtered, while it takes over 80 days to grow it. Matching these two cycles with a fluctuating demand is therefore a major problem.

Three basic institutional arrangements deal with this problem, *none of them being fully integrated*; they are all *variations of hybrid forms*. Using Williamson [1991], we can represent these different possibilities as follows: [16]

[15] More precisely, frozen chicken cannot be sold as a LABEL product; freezing it means considerable economic losses since the costs of production is significantly higher than for standard chicken.

[16] Williamson suggested to me this representation, which assumes a relationship between specific hybrid forms and degree of assets specificity. *M* is for market, *H* for hybrid, and *O* for formal organization. An ongoing study will test the assumption.

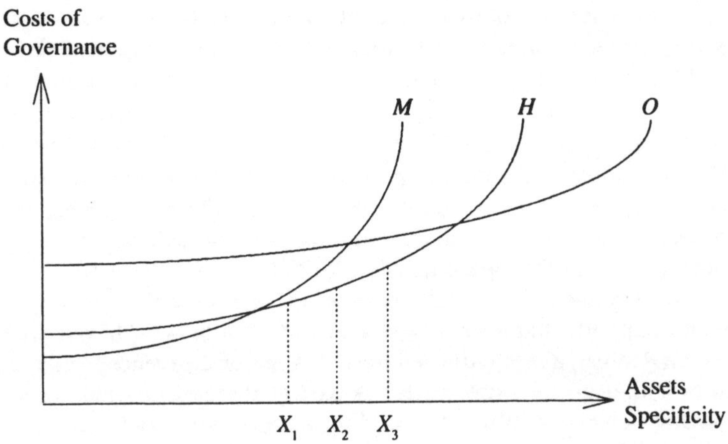

Figure 1

The first arrangement, X_1, is closer to a market arrangement. It involves *a very decentralized structure*, coordinating a network of independent partners. Typical is LOUE, a Union of over 900 growers which initiated the LABEL system for poultry in 1965 and now has 30% of the French market. These growers coordinate themselves through a small and efficient committee, the CAFEL. This Committee negotiates directly with distributors, and then plans the production: it orders chicks from selectors and incubators, at prices negotiated for a whole bunch of transactions (typical contracts are for three years); it establishes contracts (also typically for three years) with food providers determining a price ceiling (under this constraint, growers are free to negotiate specific prices with any of the selected firms). Indeed, growers associated with the CAFEL[17] must buy their supplies only from providers approved by the CAFEL. As part of a "Certifying Organization," they must also meet the "list of specifications" (*Cahier des Charges*, defined in subsection 3.2). Finally the CAFEL contracts with processing plants, with clauses specifying technical controls, prophylactic measures, cutting of chicken, standards for labels to be applied, and prices to be paid to the growers. Several competing plants are involved, so that the CAFEL remains relatively independent, while growers are left with some room to deal with one plant or the other. Hence, the whole structure depends crucially on the coordinating Committee, which negotiates and monitors multilateral contracts and which settles most disputes among participants, reducing transaction costs to the growers while maintaining some competition within the network.

The second structure, X_2, is *a cooperative arrangement*. CANA, which is also a major producer of standard chicken, is representative of that arrangement.

[17] The CAFEL was both a union of producers and a "Certifying Organization" until the adoption of Standard EN 45011. The two functions are now distinct.

This cooperative is much more integrated than the Union of growers described above. It operates both as a food provider[18] and as the owner of processing plants (80% of its current production is processed through its own plants). Growers are independent, but deeply involved in the cooperative, so that it can be described as a multi-ownership structure, the major negotiation being with distributors, almost exclusively supermarkets. In this governance structure, contracts with growers are therefore of a very specific nature, since they are with co-owners. Actually, the most important and difficult contracts are with the distributors, and they are centrally negotiated and monitored.

The third arrangement, X_3, is closer to an *integrated firm*, with a unified ownership, but with characteristics of a hybrid form as well. In our study, we selected ARRIVEE, a family-owned firm.[19] A major difference from the other structures is that growers are much less part of the decision-making process. The firm buys chicks from selectors and incubators with which it has a continuing relationship (contracts are with two firms, with prices negotiated on a yearly basis). It provides growers with these chicks as well as with food (and, eventually, with equipment), and it buys back the grown chicken at prices also negotiated on a yearly basis, through a "cost plus" system. ARRIVEE owns its processing plants, and all of its production is for supermarkets. Therefore, it essentially manages two sets of contracts, those with distributors, that are very similar to "classical contracts," and those with growers. The latter are specific; in order to "motivate" the growers, and very likely to monitor them more easily, the firm has encouraged their organization into a Union of Producers which holds about one-third of the capital of the firm so that, though their "voice" is weak, they have a direct interest in its profitability. Therefore, even in this more classical structure, we have elements of a hybrid form.

These differences in structures naturally raise the important question of their relative performance. Notwithstanding the usual difficulties of obtaining data, the advantage of the institutional environment specific to that sector is that it provides quite extensive information. Indeed, the sector being highly competitive, market prices are well-known. At the same time, the standardized technology involved, paired with the role of the "Certifying Organizations" and the National Committee, which must control quality standards, makes costs of production quite easily observable.[20] A comparison of prices and costs shows

---

[18] Actually, CANA started as a cooperative that provided farmers with food for stock breeding at low prices. In order to sell the food coming from its cooperators, the firm started prospecting growers, then distributors, and finally acquired or built its own processing plants.

[19] ARRIVEE, as well as CANA, is a *late entrant*.

[20] In 1992, the typical cost structure was the following: price of chicks: 11%; price of food: 53%; costs of growing: 36%. This last item can be broken down into: depreciation (38%), heating (8.5%), maintenance (0.9%), water and electricity (3.5%), litter (0.6%), veterinary and medications (1.8%), management (5.7%), and income provided to growers (41%). The average final price paid by processing plants that year was 7.50 French francs per kilo.

no significant difference across the three structures observed. Therefore, *different arrangements within the same family of governance structures,* hybrid forms in this case, operating on the same market, *seem similarly efficient* over a long period of time. This is puzzling, and our study did not provide any adequate explanation for this. A partial factor is historical; the decentralized structure (LOUE) was first implemented, while the others are late entrants, attracted by the high profitability of the sector. But this is hardly a thorough explanation. It may be that transaction costs economics has to be refined in order to go beyond the explanation of the trade-off among governance structures, into the subtleties of specific arrangements within one such structure.

3.4 Contractual Agreements[21]

The previous description shows without ambiguity the essential role of contracts whatever the specific form of the institutional arrangement may be.

Some of these contracts, such as those with incubators, are typically classical market contracts; specified goods (chicks of a certain breed) will be provided under a relatively short term agreement (usually a year), with clauses specifying quantities, dates of delivery, and prices to be paid. Within that framework, adjustments can be negotiated to adapt to changing conditions.

Most contracts, though, particularly those related to the two sets of transactions at the "hard core of the system," i.e., those involving food providers, growers, and processing plants, are much more complex. Two broad situations can be identified: either food providers and processing plants are integrated, with contracts between the integrated firm and the growers on one hand, and the integrated firm and the distributors on the other hand; or partners in the production process all remain distinct, so that complex multilateral contracts have to be implemented.

In both cases, growers are a master piece of the system. This is even more so if one considers *(i)* the number of growers involved (in 1992, 6,368 growers were involved in the LABEL system, as compared to 57 incubators, 117 food providers and 125 processing plants), and *(ii)* that almost all significant variations in productivity come from the growing phase.[22] Technology being standard, chicks and food very much the same, almost all of the variation is due to care from the growers; lack of care in the crucial initial phase, because of benign neglect or because growers are too busy (most of them farm other products), usually results in slower growth, smaller chickens and, most importantly, diseases that spread very rapidly in broilerhouses with thousands of animals. Because of this key role of the growers, and considering the extensive data on

[21] This subsection draws heavily on SCHALLER [1986], and on extensive discussions with him in 1995.

[22] Variations can be as much as two to one.

their contracts made available by the careful investigation of 1982–1986, I will hereafter focus my attention on this class of contractual agreements.[23]

Before identifying and analysing subclasses in this set of contracts, preliminary qualifications are essential. First, the variety of agreements must be emphasized. Most contracts are between individual growers and processing plants or, to a much smaller extent and when the two are not integrated, with food providers. But many contracts are collective, as when a Union of growers is involved. Second, most contracts are purposedly left very incomplete. They usually define a general framework, mostly with technical provisions, tacitly renewed from year to year. Specifics such as prices and quantities are largely managed through verbal agreements. Therefore, "credible commitment" of all parties is crucial, as is the policing of these agreements by the "Certifying Organizations." Third, contractualization is the standard; it concerns over 80% of the growers in Brittany, the main area of production, and is systematic for almost all market-oriented growers, i.e., those able to grow at least 2,000 chickens at a time. Formal contracts may be only a part of the story, but they are an important one.

Three types of contracts can be identified, though exact delineation is not always clear; in the 1982 questionnaire, many growers had difficulty in identifying precisely the type of contracts they were involved in. *(i) Fixed-price contracts* ("contrats à forfait") are agreements in which growers remain fully independent; their commitment is to deliver a certain quantity of chickens at a certain date. Contracts of this type specify characteristics of chicken to be delivered and a fixed amount of money to be paid. They concern few growers, less than 5%, mostly small producers. *(ii) Buy-and-sell contracts* are arrangements in which growers buy chicks and sell chicken, dealing with the same firm (most of the time, a processing plant) at both ends. Growers usually remain in charge of intermediate products, though there may be restrictive clauses (e.g., food must be bought from a predetermined set of providers). In most of these contracts, buying prices are by the piece or by the square meter;[24] but in a non-negligible number of these contracts, payments are based on a "cost plus" system, with a margin added to the costs of production. About one third of the growers operate under such contracts. *(iii)* Last, there are *contracts of the putting-out type* ("contrats à façon"); growers are provided with chicks, food, and equipment, or they must get them from specific firms. Chicken is then bought from them at prices determined long before, usually on a yearly basis; these prices are negotiated to cover expenditures plus a margin. This margin is

[23] In a paper that I was unaware of when I wrote this paper and that Williamson indicated to me, KNOEBER [1989] reached the same conclusion and focused his attention on the same class of contracts, in the case of the American broilers. The purpose of his study is different than mine in that it focuses on the incentive aspects of these contracts. But both our analysis and our conclusions are strongly consistent and complementary.

[24] Convertibility is not an issue, since there is a predetermined number of animals per square meter.

usually flexible,[25] with built-in incentives based on observable indicators such as food consumption (careful growers can significantly reduce quantities by choosing the right time to feed animals according to the period in their life cycle), speed of growth, and final weight. This type of contract dominates (more than 50% of the contractualized growers).[26]

One difficulty with these contracts is that they are part of a more complex network; for example, food providers are involved, and growers may sometime argue about differences in the quality of food delivered. In order to coordinate this complex set of contracts, there is almost always a hierarchy of contracts, with one party acting as *prime contractor*. Comparisons can be suggested with the construction industry (ECCLES [1981]), but with substantial differences (more on this in section 4). In the poultry industry, the prime contractor is most of the time a processing plant or, much less frequently and when the two are distinct, the food supplier. But there are also situations in which a union of growers is the prime contractor (as with LOUE).

The variable duration of these contracts also deserves mention. Short term (less than one year, e.g., the time necessary to grow one band) is predominant: 73% of contracts in 1982; while 13% were for over a year, and 11% of undetermined duration. But this needs to be qualified; as already mentioned, *most contracts are guidelines*, and they are *extended automatically with minor adjustments*, usually about prices, typically on a yearly basis, with the "Certifying Organization" involved. As for long term contracts, they concern almost exclusively very large growers who must invest a significant amount of money in buildings and equipment, i.e., who have to implement specific assets. Such contracts provide these growers a guarantee that at least a minimum of chickens will be regularly bought. This is confirmed by our qualitative study; these contracts usually have specific provisions about "the construction of a new building" or the "financial support of investments."

To conclude this section, I would like to emphasize the complexity of the contractual agreements involved. At the same time, the governance structure is quite straightforward. Contracts provide a general framework (more than 75% of the clauses are about technical aspects). Economic variables such as prices, costs, quantities, are most of the time defined as guidelines (ceilings, minima, etc.), with the specifics to be agreed upon by mutual (verbal) agreement. Prices are not adjusted "spot" (by bands), but on a yearly basis, so that their evolution is "smoothed." Incentives are mostly based on a "cost plus" system, and most of the time are related to observable indicators of relative performance (bonus/malus). They are largely negotiated through the "Certifying Organizations."

---

[25] This can also be implemented in the previous type of contracts, but this is unusual.

[26] This is the type of contracts analyzed by KNOEBER [1989]; he interprets the incentive mechanism involved as a tournament, where growers are ranked according to their relative performances; and he then develops a subtle analysis of the positive effects of this contractual arrangement on productivity and technical progress.

Therefore, the efficiency of this governance structure depends largely on the role of these "Certifying Organizations" and on the related commitment of the partners to do business together. Observability of the conditions of production as well as pressures from a very competitive market facilitate the policing of this system.

4. A Suggested Interpretation

Based on the previous description, the French poultry industry, and more specifically the LABEL sector, are characterized by: *(i)* the diversity of institutional arrangements within the same governance structure; *(ii)* their comparable efficiency; *(iii)* the incompleteness of contracts; and *(iv)* the specificity of coordinating devices involved.

This raises fundamental questions in relation to most explanations provided about hybrid forms. Coase [1937], [1988] emphasized the cost of constant recontracting; in the case study above, short term contracts are continuously renewed, but within an institutional arrangement which seems to considerably reduce transaction costs one would expect. Klein, Crawford and Alchian [1978] explained incentives to integrate, or to negotiate long term contracts, by the necessity of avoiding ex post opportunism when there are appropriable rents; our example shows a stable structure producing significant rents with mostly short term contracts, with opportunism repressed through mutual commitments and an efficient device for sharing rents. Grossman and Hart [1986] centered their explanation of the search for an optimal structure of property; but our case study reveals that several structures can coexist with comparable efficiency.

In this section, I would like to develop a different interpretation, based on ideas suggested in section 2. Emphasis will be put on transactional factors and, even more importantly, on the role of the "institutional structure of production" that the hybrid form under consideration reveals. In subsection 4.1, I come back to the attributes of transactions involved. In subsection 4.2, I complement this analysis by a careful examination of the core of this institutional structure of production, namely: the active role of a governance form based on "authority." In subsection 4.3, I discuss in a comparative mode this specific arrangement in relation to other hybrid forms and to the efficiency issue.

4.1 What do Attributes of Transactions Explain?

The characteristics of hybrid forms analyzed in section 2 were based on the idea of "discrete alignment" suggested by Williamson [1991]: specific governance structures develop to handle specific attributes of transactions. As is now quite well known, Williamson's analysis is based on two behavioral assumptions and three attributes of transactions.

The behavioral assumptions are concerning bounded rationality and opportunism. I suggest that they are not of particular relevance for my case study. Indeed, partners are likely to be bounded rationally; but they operate with a well-known technology[27] in a stable environment with a continuously increasing demand, so that consequences of their limitations are rather weak. Similarly, their opportunism is *strongly constrained* by the observability of key data and by the necessity of credible commitment and honesty in order to remain within a LABEL system operating in a very competitive environment.

Let us turn to the attributes of transactions at stake. My attention here is almost exclusively focused on the set of transactions between growers and processing plants and, to a lesser degree on those between food providers and growers.[28] First, there are *uncertainties* in the LABEL sector. As already mentioned, and notwithstanding an aggregate demand increasing steadily over the last twenty years, short term fluctuations strongly hamper the adjustment of production, considering its cycle. On the supply side, there are also uncertainties related to disease and temperature variations that may affect the output significantly. Moreover, one must take into consideration the increasing competition of new entrants attracted by the profitability of the sector. Therefore, this sector can be qualified as one with moderate but non-negligible disturbances, which favors some form of coordination. Second, the *frequency* of transactions among partners is very high, so that "reputation" contributes to enforce contracts; for a specific grower, bands are traded at least every 12 weeks, and often more. Therefore, characteristics are known to the traders, and this should push in the direction of market arrangements. Third, there is the potential presence of *specific assets*. Although it has been challenged by COASE [1988, ch. 5], this is the factor mostly refered to, as an explanation to specific governance structures, in modern transaction cost economics. Let me review very briefly the different sources of specificity, so as to evaluate their relevance for the analysis of the LABEL system. *(i) Physical assets* are easily redeployable; land can be (and is) used for other purposes, food can be utilized for other breedings, buildings can be shifted to standard chicken or even to other animals at relatively low cost. *(ii) Dedicated assets* are very limited and represent a small fraction of the total costs (less than 10% for the growers). Even special-

[27] Property rights regime may be involved in this though. In the French system, new breeds are mostly developed by scientists working at the INRA, a public agency. They are therefore publicly owned and passed on to all participants. Coordination through "Certifying Organizations" and the National Committee of Certifications facilitates and accelerates this diffusion of technology. In a more "private" regime, as that of the US, differences in technologies may play a much more important role. I am indebted to Sherwin Rosen for having pointed out this aspect.

[28] It must be remembered that food represents 53% of the costs of production of a chicken.

ized equipment used in processing plants can process standard chicken as well, and also ducks etc. *(iii) Human assets* involved are weakly specific too; growers are mostly family farms, with women taking care of poultry and doing so part time. Even for larger growers, quality of care is important, but it requires no specific skills and little know-how.[29] *(iv) Site specificity* plays a more important role, because of regulation constraints on transportation (distances between growers and processing plant). Therefore some mutual dependency develops between growers and processing plants. But these are relatively mild constraints if one considers the geographical concentration of growers and the relatively large number of processing plants available.[30] *(v) "Brand name capital"* is obviously much more crucial for the LABEL system. Indeed, labels not only signal quality (e.g., freshness) to consumers, thus reducing their uncertainty, but also specific breeds, particular conditions of production, area of production etc. In this, connection to a LABEL is a highly specific asset. *(vi) Temporal specificity* is at the core of the LABEL system, since it is a direct consequence of the list of specifications defining a LABEL. Indeed, regulated freshness (9 days between slaughter and final sale) and duration of growth (between 81 and 90 days) make coordination complex; just-in-time production becomes a decisive factor of success.[31] This is a major constraint, which largely explains the necessity of a governance structure much more active than pure market relations.

Weak small number constraint (the number of growers is large and so is that of processing plants, though to a much lesser degree), high frequency of transactions, and weakly specific physical, dedicated and human assets should induce a governance structure of the market type, according to transaction cost economics. On the other hand, the importance of brand name and the related temporal specificity, in an environment with non-negligible factors of uncertainty, should dictate more integrated coordination. Combining the two dimensions, we should obtain a hybrid form with relatively weak internal constraints.

This is *partially* what we have observed in the actual governance of the LABEL system. Hybrid form with contractualization largely predominates; but our empirical analysis has also shown a quite powerful structure of coordination, the "Certifying Organizations," more centralized than what the theory would predict. To understand this aspect, I suggest that we must look at the institutional factor.

[29] The fact that human assets are lowly specific means that it is not an incentive to integrate. *It does not mean* that it does not matter in terms of productivity; indeed, care explains most of the observed variations among growers.

[30] This may be different from the US where because of the distances involved, there is much more dependency between growers and processing plants (see Knoeber [1989]).

[31] This is not so with standard chicken, since it can be frozen.

4.2 An Institutional Structure of Production

Indeed, as shown in section 3, the LABEL system involves a set of multilateral contracts very complex to manage. In a sense, this brings us back to the very central argument of transaction cost economics, as initially developed by COASE [1937], [1988]. The multiplicity and variety of contracts to negotiate and monitor makes pure market arrangements, i.e., contracts of the classical type, inadequate. On the other hand, transaction attributes described above would make integration a costly solution because of the administrative costs involved.

The system of coordination adopted, with a small but powerful structure of coordination, in which contracts are purposedly left incomplete to allow this "government" to adapt, can therefore be viewed as *an efficient governance structure*, with adaptation based on a specific mode, "authority," which depends on a combination of mutual acceptance, threat of termination, and market pressures.

A Partial Subcontracting System...

Networks coordinated through "Certifying Organizations" operate partially as a "subcontracting" system, with the "Certifying Organization" acting as a contractor. Some advantages of this system can be compared with those observed in the construction industry (ECCLES [1981]). A subcontracting system: *(i)* limits bilateral dependency by multiplying the parties to a contract; *(ii)* limits opportunism by exerting a certain control over the income of subcontractors; *(iii)* limits lack of care by having subcontractors providing equipment; *(iv)* reduces the costs of changing prices, since negotiations for adjustments are largely based on risk sharing.

However, there are substantial differences between the LABEL system and the subcontracting system that prevails in the construction industry. First, asymmetries observed in the latter (between general contractor and subcontractors) is not typical of the former. In the construction industry, the contractor has information (about plans etc.) that allows him to outsource services without sharing this information. In the LABEL system, "Certifying Organizations" obtain a significant part of their efficiency, and of their authority, through *information disclosure*. Second, contracts in the LABEL system are of a specific nature; most non-technical clauses concern *rules to govern* relationships among participants. From that point of view, they are closer to "forbearance contracts," while those described by Eccles were more of the neoclassical type. Third, quantities and deadlines, rather than prices, appear to be the major variables of adjustment, defining the "tolerance zone" (see subsection 2.2), so that "Certifying Organizations" have a significant authority over participants in the network in order to coordinate the "cycles." This capacity is less related to contractual provisions, as it is in the construction industry, than to the embeddedness of contracts in a network of relations among participants that are reinforced by their geographical proximity.

... With "Authority" as its Very Active Principle of Governance...
The "Certifying Organization" is clearly the pivotal force in the LABEL system; it implements contracts, selects participants, monitors them, and largely controls adjustments of quantities and prices. It is, indeed, a very active form of governance (GOLDBERG [1976]) and, at the same time, a small and rather inexpensive structure of coordination.

Such an efficient coordination is possible because of the specific mode of adaptation of this governance structure which could well be *typical of all hybrid forms*. This adaptation mode is built on "authority." In previous papers (MENARD [1994], [1995]), I have suggested a distinction between "hierarchy," which is the fundamental principle of coordination in formal organizations, and "authority." Briefly stated, a hierarchical relationship is based on *non-negotiable* asymmetries,[32] in which a "superior" holds the rights to supervise and control; *the capacity to command* is crucial. A superior can discretionarily assign tasks, within certain boundaries; he can designate the position of a member in relation to others; and he can constrain the action of someone else by giving orders. In order to do so, hierarchy requires a formal status, a formal asymmetry; this is why it can operate as "its own court of ultimate appeal" (WILLIAMSON [1985, ch. 3], [1991]). Authority differs substantially in that it is *a delegation of the capacity to decide*; it has a dimension of intentionality, which requires some form of explicit acceptance and reversibility. Indeed, since authority is based on consent, decisions made can always be re-examined. In an authority relationship, one cannot have his views systematically prevail over those of other participants by the very virtue of his position; in order to have decisions accepted and implemented, those with authority must convince their partners, or rely on their trust. This explains the crucial role of *influence* in an authority relationship (for an empirical study, see BRASS [1984]).

This is typically the mechanism at work in the LABEL system. The decision-making capacity of a "Certifying Organization" as well as its role as dispute settler depend entirely on the mutual consent of the partners, which is acknowledged by the presence of their representatives on the Board. Mutual agreements are self-enforcing because of gains expected, but also because this form of government maintains an equilibrium in reducing the possibilities of free-riding and in guaranteeing relative *equity* in the share of appropriable rents by jointly monitoring information. The discipline among members, and the acceptance of authority, are reinforced by market pressures and by the threat of termination of contracts for free-riders.

... Backed by Well-Defined Institutional Rules.
However, the role of the institutional environment is essential to the implementation and stability of the mode of adaptation. As noted by GOLDBERG [1976]

[32] In a market economy, these asymmetries are rooted in the specification and distribution of property rights.

as well as by Coase [1988], [1992], such regulatory devices are an essential part of the functioning of contractual arrangements. This is particularly so in a hybrid form with a large number of participants. With a few participants, authority can be self-enforcing at low costs, with the possible pressure of a third party, as with neoclassical contracts. When number of participants is large, authority requires to be backed by better defined institutional rules.

In the case under examination, it must be kept in mind that in order to be part of the LABEL system, the partners *must* be affiliated with a "Certifying Organization" which gains legitimacy from the National Committee and, therefore, the government. Certification means that a regulatory dimension is involved. Hence, "Certifying Organizations" get their authority from a mixture of private agreements and of public regulation. Indeed, institutionally defined rules determine the composition of these organizations, their functions (e.g., controls of qualities, determination of technical requirements), and the extension of their authority (e.g., acceptance of participants, conditions of penalties). In the LABEL system, the required approval by the National Commission of Certification and Labels operates as a strong incentive for partners to contract *and* to remain within the system. This strong embeddedness into the legal system,[33] backed by the government intervening as an actor into the process, significantly contributes to the stabilization of the authority of "Certifying Organizations."

4.3 A Specific Governance Structure

Having identified the major characteristics of the hybrid form under examination, particularly with regard to contractual arrangements, coordinating devices and mode of adaptation, it is worth comparing this interpretation to some others that have been suggested. This will allow me to discuss aspects of the efficiency issue.

What I would like to argue briefly here is that the LABEL system is *neither a cartel, nor a standard subcontracting arrangement*, but rather a *tightly coordinated network.*

The *cartel* interpretation is suggested by the standard view in Industrial Organization, and has actually been developed by regulators from the European Commission.[34] As it goes on, the argument is that the set of agreements among firms and the role of the "Certifying Organizations" delineate a typical

---

[33] The contractual framework into which the LABEL system is embedded has been defined by a law adopted in 1964. I have already emphasized, in subsection 3.2, the political dimension involved.

[34] The result was the adoption of regulation EN 45011. This regulation can be interpreted as a compromise between proponents of an analysis in terms of "cartel," who claimed that all certification procedures should be dismantled, and the approach developed by representatives of the LABEL system, who emphasized the advantages for consumers of having differentiated products with guarantee of quality.

situation of collusion among producers. The puzzling point, though, in relation to this argument, is that if we look at the data, we do not find the expected effects of a cartel. The goal of this paper being positive (i.e., to analyze characteristics of hybrid forms such as those developed in the LABEL sector) rather than normative (i.e., discussing policy issues), I will merely point out here some inadequacies of the cartel view.

A continuous decline can be observed in the price of LABEL chicken, and, as illustrated by figure 2 below, this evolution is very comparable to that of the prices of standard chicken, a sector in which there are no such arrangements.

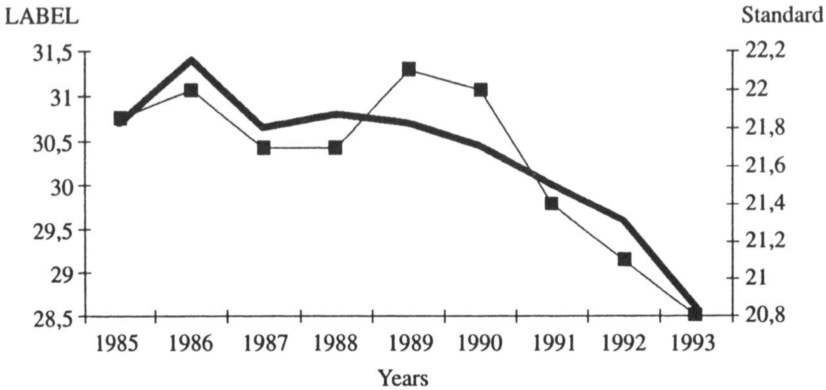

Figure 2

Evolution of Prices of Chicken
Source: SYNALAF

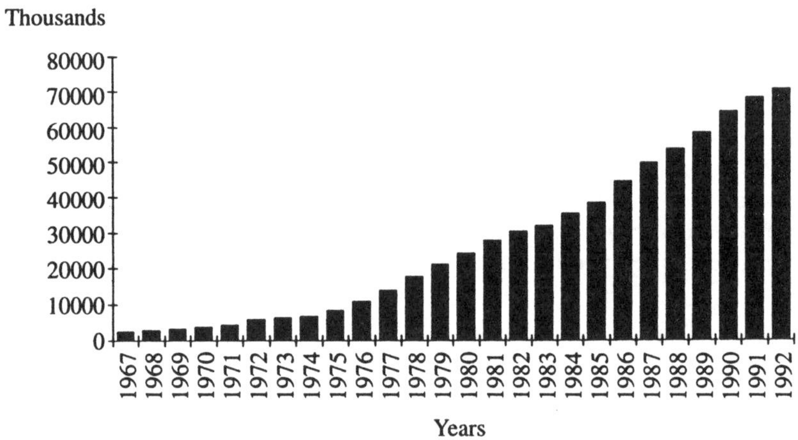

Figure 3

Evolution of Quantities (LABEL Chicken Only)
Source: SYNALAF

Moreover, quantities offered have increased significantly since the mid-seventies, with the market share of LABEL chicken in the poultry industry increasing from less than 2% in 1972 to over 30% in 1992.

This movement has been accompanied by a diversification of products (there are 21 "Certifying Organizations," some with several different labels), so that consumers have more choice in France than in other countries of the European Community. Note also that a LABEL is not required to sell brand name chicken (but it can not be sold as a LABEL chicken). It is also difficult to argue that the LABEL system has operated as a barrier to entry, discriminating against large firms; the expansion and profitability of the LABEL system has attracted new entrants, among which are all major firms of the standard chicken sector. Therefore, competition has intensified over the last 20 years. The conclusion is that either the cartel was a total failure, or the LABEL system was not a cartel. My analysis supports the latter interpretation; the high profitability of the sector has not been the result of a cartel, but of the capacity of a specific institutional arrangement to meet a sustained growth in demand by expanding capacities while reducing prices through gains in productivity and maintenance of low transaction costs.[35]

The *subcontracting* approach to the LABEL system is not satisfying either, as already suggested. One of the best studies of the subcontracting system is that of ECCLES [1981], on the construction industry. He identified the latter as a system of contracts existing "over fairly long periods of time and only infrequently established through competitive bidding" (p. 342). True, the LABEL system involves formally short term contracts that are actually extended over years with no bidding involved. However, it can hardly be described as one of subcontracting. As shown in section 3, it is rather a network of multilateral contracts among partners similarly involved in decision-making. In contrast to the construction industry, there is no loose coupling of tasks to explain the incompleteness of contracts; in the LABEL system, contracts are left incomplete to provide more flexibility in adjusting strictly complementary tasks to the uncertainties of demand. As a result, we do not have the significant asymmetry of the contractor–subcontractors relationship, but a strong incentive to share information and rent in order to maintain the stability of the relationship and its capacity to adapt.

Therefore, the LABEL system is not reducible to a modern version of the putting out system, in which prime contractors would outsource significant parts of their activities to subcontractors. It can be better identified as a *network* (THORELLI [1986]), but with aspects of a *clan* involved (OUCHI [1980]). First, it is built on a complex set of *multilateral contracts*, mixing market incentives with

[35] One may argue that "market-oriented regulators" of the European Commission do not understand the nature of governance structures developed to economize on *both* production and transaction costs. Neglecting the latter may well generate a result opposite to what was intended; the poultry sector will likely become more integrated than before, with less competitors involved, and less variety for consumers.

administrative control, with conflicts and disagreements settled through arbitration procedures *internal* to the network (the "Certifying Organization"). These contracts are on the border between neoclassical and "forbearance" contracts, "Certifying Organizations" acting almost as "their own court of ultimate appeal." Second, this governance structure has a "government" of its own.[36] The "Certifying Organizations" are centralized forms of coordination, with significant power to make decisions; but they have a strictly limited power in that they cannot command. It is also a "government" rather than the hierarchy of a formal organization in that separate ownership is maintained, while redistribution of rents is largely coordinated; equity issues are at the hand of that "government." This role can be observed whatever the specific hybrid structure adopted, be it a quasi-integrated firm, a cooperative, or a network of independent partners. Third, the specific mode of adaptation of that "government" is that of "authority." It operates through mutual consent and commitment among partners. Growers, for example, can always quit a "Certifying Organization" and continue to produce chicken, but without the brand name. From that point of view, they *act as franchisees, but with no franchisor*; the would-be franchisor, the "Certifying Organization," is the emanation of a coalition among the "franchisees!" Last, this structure is stable because it is largely self-enforcing, through this mutual commitment and the accompanying reputation effect, and because it is strongly backed by institutional rules monitored by the National Committee. It is also reinforced by the social embeddedness of these networks; each LABEL is limited to a well-determined geographic area, with growers operating partially as a clan.

5. Conclusion

In this paper, I intended to give a more specific content to what Coase [1992] identified as the institutional structure of production. In order to do so, I have extensively used recent contributions from transactions costs economics, particularly those from Williamson, and I have focused my attention on the analysis of "hybrid" organizational structures, with the example of the LABEL system within the French poultry industry.

It should be clear from this study that neither the technology nor the structure of ownership can be the major determinants of the "hybrid form" that was examined. It is rather a specific institutional arrangement, deliberately developed by partners through a network of contracts, and deeply embedded in the institutional environment. This arrangement is coordinated and conducted by an active form of governance, which emanates from the partners, and which operates through authority. I have also explored the properties of this mode of

[36] I found one similarity in the existing literature, that of the "government" of a condominium (in Klein, Crawford and Alchian [1978]).

adaptation, emphasizing how different it is from hierarchy, which is the adaptation mode of internal organizations. In order for authority to be efficient, it requires mutual consent and commitment. As a result, incentives will have specific characteristics, in that they involve sharing risks and sharing rents among separate owners. But this requires mechanisms of enforcement. The empirical study exhibits such a mechanism; the hybrid form generates its own "government" that has to deal with *equity* problems. Strong support from the institutional environment is crucial to the stability of this "government."

The hybrid structure that I have examined seems *efficient*, according to all usual standards; production has increased continuously over the last twenty years, gains in productivity and low costs of transaction have supported a continuous reduction in relative prices, while the coordination structures have remained remarkably stable within a very competitive environment. This challenges the views of regulators who have argued that this structure is anti-competitive. I suggest that this position may result from a deep ignorance of what a governance structure is, and how it works.

References

ALCHIAN, Armen and Susan WOODWARD [1988], "The Firm is Dead. Long Live the Firm," *Journal of Economic Literature*, 26(1), 65–79.

BARNARD, Chester I. [1938], *The Functions of the Executive*, Harvard University Press: Cambridge, MA.

BOWEN, David E. and Gareth R. JONES [1986], "Transaction Costs Analysis of Service Organization-Customer Exchange," *Academy of Management Review*, 11(2), 428–441.

BRASS, Daniel J. [1984], "Being in the Right Place: A Structural Analysis of Individual Influence in an Organization," *Administrative Science Quarterly*, 29(4), 518–539.

BRICKLEY, James A. and Frederick H. DARK [1987], "The Choice of Organizational Form: The Case of Franchising," *Journal of Financial Economics*, 18(2), 401–420.

CHEUNG, Steven N. S. [1983], "The Contractual Nature of the Firm," *Journal of Law and Economics*, 26(1), 1–22.

COASE, Ronald H. [1937], "The Nature of the Firm," *Economica*, 4, 386–405. Reprinted in WILLIAMSON and WINTER [1991].

–– [1972], "Industrial Organization: A Proposal for Research," pp. 59–73 in: V. R. Fuchs (ed.), *Policy Issues and Research Opportunities in Industrial Organization*, NBER: New York. Reprinted in R. H. Coase, 1988, *The Firm, The Market, and the Law*, Ch. 3, University of Chicago Press: Chicago – London.

–– [1988], "The Nature of the Firm: Origin, Meaning, Influence," *Journal of Law, Economics and Organization*, 4(1), 3–47. Reprinted in WILLIAMSON and WINTER [1991].

–– [1992], "The Institutional Structure of Production," *American Economic Review*, 82(4), 713–719.

DAVIS, Lance E. and Douglass C. NORTH [1971], *Institutional Change and American Economic Growth*, Cambridge University Press: Cambridge.

DEMSETZ, Harold H. [1988], "The Theory of the Firm Revisited," *Journal of Law, Economics and Organization*, 4(1), 141–161. Reprinted in WILLIAMSON and WINTER [1991].

ECCLES, Robert [1981], "The Quasifirm in the Construction Industry," *Journal of Economic Behavior and Organization*, 2(4), 335–357.

GOLDBERG, Victor P. [1976], "Towards an Expanded Economic Theory of Contracts," *Journal of Economic Issues*, 10(1), 45–61.

GROSSMAN, Sanford and Oliver HART [1986], "The Costs and Benefits of Ownership: A Theory of Vertical and Lateral Integration," *Journal of Political Economy*, 94(4), 691–719.

HAYEK, Frederick [1945], "The Use of Knowledge in Society," *American Economic Review*, 35(4), 519–530.

JOSKOW, Paul [1985], "Vertical Integration and Long-Term Contracts: The Case of Coal-Burning Electric Generating Plants," *Journal of Law, Economics and Organization*, 1(1), 33–80.

-- [1987], "Contract Duration and Relationship-Specific Investment: Empirical Evidence From the Coal Market," *American Economic Review*, 77(1), 168–185.

KLEIN, Benjamin, Robert G. CRAWFORD and Armen A. ALCHIAN [1978], "Vertical Integration, Appropriable Rents, and the Competitive Contracting Process," *Journal of Law and Economics*, 21(2), 297–326.

KNOEBER, Charles E. [1989], "A Real Game of Chicken: Contracts, Tournaments and the Production of Broilers," *Journal of Law, Economics and Organization*, 5(2), 271–292.

KREPS, David and Michael A. SPENCE [1985], "Modelling the Role of History in Industrial Organization and Competition," pp. 340–378 in: G. Feiwel (ed.), *Issues in Contemporary Microeconomics and Welfare*, State University of New York Press: Albany.

MACNEIL, Ian R. [1974], "The Many Futures of Contracts," *Southern California Law Review*, 47, 691–816.

MASTEN, Scott E. [1988], "The Legal Basis for the Firm," *Journal of Law, Economics and Organization*, 4(1), 181–198. Reprinted in WILLIAMSON and WINTER [1991].

MENARD, Claude [1994], "Organizations as Coordinating Devices," *Metroeconomica*, 45(3), 224–247.

-- [1995], "Inside the Black Box: The Variety of Hierarchical Forms," pp. 149–170 in: J. Groenewegen (ed.), *Transaction Costs Economics and Beyond*, Kluwer Academic Press: Amsterdam.

OUCHI, William G. [1980], "Markets, Bureaucracies, and Clans," *Administrative Science Quarterly*, 25, 129–141.

PALAY, Thomas M. [1984], "Comparative Institutional Economics: The Governance of the Rail Freight Contract," *Journal of Legal Studies*, 13(2), 265–288.

-- [1985], "Avoiding Regulatory Constraints: Contracting Safeguards and the Role of Informal Agreements," *Journal of Law, Economics and Organization*, 1(1), 155–175.

SCHALLER, Bernard [1986], "Les élevages avicoles français," Collection de Statistiques Agricoles, Etude no. 261, SCEES, Ministère de l'Agriculture, Paris.

SYLVANDER, Bertyl [1995], "Conventions de qualité, concurrence et coopération. Le cas du 'Label Rouge' dans la filière volaille," pp. 72–96 in: G. Allaire and B. Boyer (eds.), *La grande transformation de l'agriculture*, INRA-Economica: Paris.

THORELLI, Hans B. [1986], "Networks: Between Markets and Hierarchies," *Strategic Management Journal*, 7(1), 37–51.

TIROLE, Jean [1988], *The Theory of Industrial Organization*, MIT Press: Cambridge, MA.

WILLIAMSON, Oliver E. [1975], *Markets and Hierarchies*, The Free Press: New York.

-- [1985], *The Economic Institutions of Capitalism*, The Free Press: New York.

-- [1991], "Comparative Economic Organization: The Analysis of Discrete Structural Alternatives," *Administrative Science Quarterly*, 36(2), 269–296.

-- [1992], "Markets, Hierarchies and the Modern Corporation: An Unfolding Perspective," *Journal of Economic Behavior and Organization*, 17(3), 335–352.

-- [1993a], "The Economic Analysis of Institutions and Organizations. In General and With Respect to Country Studies," OECD Working Paper No. 133, OECD, Paris.

-- [1993b], "Transaction Costs and Organization Theory," *Industrial and Corporate Change*, 2(2), 107–156.

-- and Sidney G. WINTER (eds.) [1991], *The Nature of the Firm: Origins, Evolution, and Development*, Oxford University Press: Oxford–New York.

Professor Claude Menard
Centre ATOM
Université de Paris I (Panthéon-Sorbonne)
90 Rue de Tolbiac
75634 Paris Cédex 13
France

[21]

Appropriability Hazards and Governance in Strategic Alliances: A Transaction Cost Approach

Joanne E. Oxley
University of Michigan

Despite the recent proliferation of interfirm alliances designed to govern cooperative efforts in creating or exploiting technology, we have limited understanding of how firms choose among the various alliance types available to them. In this article, I examine the governance properties of different alliance types and develop a simplified market-hierarchy continuum of alliances. This then forms the basis for an empirical examination of appropriability hazards and governance. Strong support for hypotheses derived from transaction cost theory is provided by analysis of a large sample of interfirm alliances. More hierarchical alliances are chosen when appropriability hazards are severe because technology is difficult to specify or because the scope of activities is wider, so that monitoring is hampered.

1. Introduction

A key argument in transaction cost economics (TCE) is that transactions are aligned with governance structures so as to effect a discriminating—mainly transaction cost economizing—match (Williamson, 1991). The archetypal problem in TCE is the vertical integration or "make versus buy" decision, and the focus of transaction cost economizing in this context is on mitigation of "hold-up" problems associated with investments in specific assets (Klein et al., 1978; Williamson, 1985). However, this asset specificity condition is only one example (albeit a significant one) of a more general class of contractual hazards. Indeed, in his most recent discussion of the TCE agenda, Williamson (1996:3) suggests that "identification, explication and mitigation of contractual hazards—which take many forms, many of which long went unremarked—are central to the exercise."

Many thanks for guidance and suggestions go to Oliver Williamson, David Mowery, Bronwyn Hall, Pablo Spiller, Nick Argyres, Emerson Tiller, Francine Lafontaine, Scott Masten, Bernard Yeung, the editors and anonymous reviewers at JLEO, and participants in the seminars and workshops where earlier versions of this article were presented. Research support was generously provided by a Bradley Fellowship through the Center for Research in Management at the University of California, Berkeley and by the Orel Crawford Foundation.

This article examines a form of contractual hazards that previously has been underdeveloped in transaction cost theory—that is hazards related to weak property rights, as they apply to transactions involving technology transfer within interfirm alliances. Many present-day "strategic alliances" are designed to govern cooperative efforts in the creation or exploitation of technology (Hagedoorn, 1993) and firms establishing such alliances must beware the potential for leakage of valuable intellectual property (Teece, 1986). Although these so-called appropriability hazards are a well-accepted characteristic of technology contracts (Levin et al., 1987) there has been little systematic examination of how appropriability hazards can be mitigated within different types of interfirm alliance.

As the number of interfirm strategic alliances exploded in the 1980s, so variety in the types of organizational form adopted grew apace. In addition to equity joint ventures, interfirm linkages run the gamut from fairly simple technology licensing contracts to joint marketing agreements, technology sharing arrangements, research corporations, and consortia. Nonetheless, most previous empirical research has focused only on the choice between contract-based and equity joint ventures (Gulati, 1995; Pisano, 1989, 1990; Pisano et al., 1988), finding that equity arrangements are favored when contracting hazards related to small-numbers bargaining and uncertainty are present to a significant degree.[1]

Although there have been previous attempts to provide useful taxonomies of the large variety of interfirm alliances (e.g., Contractor and Lorange, 1988; Lorange and Roos, 1992), a need remains for a model of interfirm alliances that is tightly connected to underlying theoretical constructs. A contribution of this article is to undertake a closer examination of the governance properties of different alliance types and so provide a systematic way to differentiate among them. A simplified market-hierarchy continuum of alliance forms is proposed which then forms the basis for an empirical analysis of appropriability hazards and governance mode choice.

In choosing among different interfirm alliance types, the logic of transaction cost economics suggests that more "hierarchical" alliances will be chosen for transactions where contracting hazards are more severe. In conducting empirical work we need to maintain the transaction as the unit of analysis, describe transaction characteristics associated with elevated hazards in the particular operational setting, and develop hypotheses that describe how these hazards are mitigated in alliances in the market-hierarchy continuum. In the analysis reported here, the focus is therefore on transaction attributes that determine the level of appropriability hazards, and hence the preferred governance mode,

1. In his later article examining the choice between in-house and external sources of R&D, Pisano discusses transaction costs stemming from both small-numbers bargaining and appropriability concerns (Pisano, 1990). However, as the focus is on leakage to unrelated third parties, the only measure of appropriability hazards used is the number of established companies attempting to develop or commercialize products in the relevant technical area, aggregated over the entire world market.

in technology transfer alliances. Partner firms in such alliances may choose between a unilateral contract (e.g. a simple license), a bilateral contract (such as a cross-license or technology sharing agreement), or an equity joint venture. These alliance forms are ordered along the market-hierarchy continuum with equity joint ventures having governance attributes closest to those of internal organization.

Hypotheses for the empirical study are derived by tracing the source of contracting hazards that arise when firms attempt to transfer technology via a simple unilateral contract. These "appropriability hazards" can be traced to difficulties in adequately specifying payoff-relevant activities, monitoring the execution of prescribed activities, and/or enforcing contracts through the courts. Results from empirical analysis of samples of alliances drawn from the Cooperative Agreement and Technology Indicators (CATI) database provide strong support for the transaction cost hypotheses: more hierarchical alliances are chosen when property rights associated with the technology are difficult to specify in a contract and when the scope of activities is wider, so that monitoring of activities is hampered.

Inclusion of firm-level variables in the empirical model also illuminates a source of confusion in previous empirical studies: In the international management literature, empirical studies of governance choice in inter-firm alliances increasingly rely on the logic of transaction cost economics (e.g., Agarwal and Ramaswami, 1992; Gomes-Casseres, 1989; Hennart, 1991a; Hladik, 1985), but almost without exception, these studies use firm-level characteristics (R&D spending, advertising, firm size, etc.) to proxy for the transaction-level characteristics featured in TCE. This mismatch between the underlying phenomenon and the empirical measures is reflected in inconsistencies in the observed effects of firm-level variables in these previous studies.[2] In the empirical analysis reported here, firm-level effects do not have statistically significant effects. This confirms that, in line with transaction cost theory, it is the attributes of the transaction (i.e., the project), and not those of the firm as a whole, that determine the more efficient mode of governance in alliances.

The remainder of the article is structured as follows: the theoretical framework is presented in Section 2, in which the market-hierarchy continuum of interfirm alliances is introduced, and in Section 3, where appropriability hazards are discussed and the hypotheses are developed. Section 4 details the empirical analysis. Results are presented and discussed in Section 5. Section 6 concludes.

2. The Market-Hierarchy Continuum of Interfirm Alliances

Interfirm alliances for the creation or exploitation of technology come in many varieties. Examples include licensing, cross-licensing and technology sharing

2. Studies of international business arrangements have focused primarily on the choice between autonomous investment and joint venturing. For a discussion of inconsistencies in the observed effects of some of these firm level variables on the propensity to invest autonomously, see Gomes-Casseres (1989).

agreements, international production joint ventures, collaborations in product and process R&D (ranging from R&D contracts to equity joint ventures), and customer-supplier partnerships. The transaction cost view of an interfirm alliance is that of a hybrid governance form, lying between the polar forms of market (i.e., arms-length "spot" contracts) and hierarchy (i.e., organization within the firm). As such, hybrids retain some of the incentive characteristics of markets, while allowing enhanced monitoring and bilateral adaptation. Although these latter governance features are not as well-developed as in the hierarchical governance mode, organizing a transaction within a hybrid avoids some of the bureaucratic and shirking costs associated with hierarchy (Williamson, 1991).

Prior research on interfirm alliances has focused attention on one "hybrid archetype," the equity joint venture (e.g., Geringer and Hebert, 1989; Gomes-Casseres, 1989; Harrigan, 1986; Hennart, 1991b; Killing, 1983; Pisano et al., 1988). This is the classic form of hybrid organization, involving the creation of a new entity jointly owned and operated by two or more collaborating firms. In governance terms, the shared equity in the new venture operates as an effective hostage exchange: because the value of the joint venture depends critically on continued operation, each firm effectively posts a bond equal to its equity share, the value of which is at best only partially redeemable should operations cease. Furthermore, the ongoing returns to each partner are based on the profits of the venture as a whole (usually with distributions in proportion to equity shares), so that the incentives of the "parent" firms are more closely aligned than in the case of an arms-length transaction.

Although the intensity of incentives in a joint venture is not reduced to the same extent as in a fully integrated structure (since parties to the transaction retain a degree of autonomy), the attenuation in incentives nonetheless requires that other administrative controls take the place of the "discipline of the market." These administrative controls include a board of directors, typically comprising members from partner firms in proportion to equity holdings. This provides a direct communication link with senior management of the parent companies, facilitating superior monitoring of partner firms' activities (Kogut, 1988). Furthermore, joint venture owners may be legally entitled to independently verified financial information in addition to information acquired through direct observation (Osborn and Baughn, 1990:505). However, in contrast to directives from senior management or the board of directors in a fully integrated firm, the directives from joint venture parent companies are subject to negotiation and compromise if conflicts between the goals and interests of the firms arise. Indeed, the right of veto over strategic decisions is often explicitly incorporated in the formal agreement accompanying the creation of a joint venture (Geringer and Hebert, 1989; Killing, 1983).

These "veto rights" and other contractual features of joint venture agreements may suggest that the contract law supports of this governance structure approach those of the classical contract law of market transactions (Macneil, 1978). However, because of the need for continued cooperation within the joint venture, the rigid blueprint of classical contract law is rarely applied, and instead is replaced by the highly adjustable framework of "neoclassical" or "relational" contracting, where third-party arbitration may be called for under certain circumstances but access to the courts is reserved as a forum of ultimate appeal (Llewellyn, 1931; Williamson, 1985:70–72).

A simple extension of the transaction cost logic suggests that the many other types of interfirm alliance could be "ranked" by their relative governance attributes, based on the instruments just described—incentive intensity, administrative controls, and contract supports—so rendering the choice of alliance form conceptually straightforward and susceptible to empirical examination using statistical methods. However, any attempt to develop an exhaustive ranking soon runs into significant operational obstacles (see, e.g., Contractor and Lorange, 1988; Lorange and Roos, 1992).[3]

First among these operational difficulties is the extent of microanalytic data required: Making fine-grained assessments of the governance attributes of a particular alliance requires information on a long "list" of features, including formal and informal monitoring or reporting requirements, provisions for third-party arbitration, details of assignments of managerial control rights, and the extent of effective hostage exchanges built into the agreement. Moreover, even with all the necessary data in hand, it is not clear how we compare two alliances in which different combinations of these various governance instruments are present. And finally, different hybrid organizations are often designed to govern quite different types of activities. As such, they may embody idiosyncratic governance features that are as much a feature of the activity itself as a feature of the governance structure per se. This is particularly true in technology sharing or research and development, for example, where pooling of technical resources may have inherent hostage features.

Perhaps as a result of the confusing array of potential combinations of governance instruments available, reported alliance forms tend to cluster into discrete groups, within which there is undoubtedly significant variation, but for which we can identify "step function" differences in governance attributes so that we can assign an ordinal ranking to the alternatives. This allows us to construct a market-hierarchy ordering of organizational forms, with the caveat that we only attempt a ranking of governance structures within broadly comparable activity classes.[4] From available descriptions of technology-related alliance

3. In their original continuum, Contractor and Lorange (1988) rank cooperative ventures from least to most hierarchical, based on the degree of "organizational interdependence," as follows: technical training and start-up assistance; production, assembly and buy-back agreements; patent licensing; franchising; know-how licensing; management or marketing service agreement; nonequity cooperative agreements in R&D, development, or coproduction; equity joint venture. However, in later work, Lorange and Roos (1992) back away from this detailed ordering and present a simplified continuum based on the "degree of vertical integration." The definitions of organizational forms in this new continuum are not entirely transparent and it is not clear how this new continuum maps into the previous one.

4. In the empirical study below, we therefore restrict our attention to horizontal technology transfer arrangements which do not have a significant R&D component.

forms, we can identify three such governance categories (going from least to most hierarchical):

- Unilateral contractual agreements (e.g., unilateral licensing agreements, long-term supply contracts, R&D contracts)
- Bilateral contractual agreements (e.g., technology sharing or cross-licensing agreements, joint research agreements)
- Equity-based alliances (i.e., joint ventures and research corporations)

For the two contract-based hybrid forms, the key distinguishing governance feature is greater incentive alignment in bilateral contractual agreements, based on the ability to effect in-kind hostage exchanges. The variety of administrative controls and monitoring rights found in equity joint ventures, along with the further increase in incentive alignment achieved via shared equity, mean that equity joint ventures lie closest to the hierarchy end of this "market-hierarchy continuum" of alliance forms.

3. Appropriability Hazards in the Market for Know-How: Implications for Governance of Interfirm Alliances

The contracting concern in technology transfer alliances is essentially that payoff relevant activities sometimes cannot be fully specified in a contract, or that prescribed activities cannot be adequately monitored or enforced. When contracts are incomplete because of gaps in specification, the possibility of moral hazard arises on either side of the transaction. For example, the holder of the technology may later find a better partner and so deliver less (or inferior) technology to its partner than promised in the original agreement. On the other hand, the recipient firm may use or modify the technology in ways that were not intended in the contract and which are injurious to the transferor.[5] These are the so-called appropriability hazards associated with technology contracts, the sources of which are rooted in the need to transfer poorly defined tacit "know-how." The transaction-level features leading to elevated appropriability hazards, and their operational corollaries, are explored and summarized in the hypotheses developed below, but first we look at how appropriability hazards may be mitigated within the alliance forms in the market-hierarchy continuum.

A central tenet of TCE is that, absent significant contracting hazards, the "default" low-cost governance mechanism is a simple unilateral contract (Williamson, 1991:279). However, where characteristics of the transaction are such that full specification of the assets to be transferred is infeasible, or monitoring is incomplete, employing a unilateral contract for technology transfer is problematic since either party has incentives to act opportunistically (as suggested above), potentially leading to extensive ex post haggling or complete failure of the agreement. The power of the courts to redress these failures will also be limited, given the associated difficulties of third-party verification.

5. I am indebted to Tracy Lewis for suggesting this framing of the problem.

Foreseeing such problems, both parties to the transaction have incentives to mitigate against the contracting hazards by "moving up" the market-hierarchy continuum of alliance forms.[6] If ex post contract disturbances are not expected to be too severe, then a bilateral contract may suffice: the in-kind hostages inherent in such an arrangement mean that both parties have a continued interest in the maintenance of the arrangement, and ex post haggling will be reduced as a consequence. Furthermore, if disturbances are correlated (e.g., if unexpected external events can be expected to impact the value of the two firms' technology holdings in a similar direction), then monitoring problems are mitigated and opportunities for ex post haggling are further reduced. Nonetheless, defection from the spirit of the contract is likely in the event of highly consequential disturbances. In this instance, the parties are again faced with the problem of resolving disputes in court in the face of difficult third-party verifiability issues. Thus, where severe appropriability hazards are anticipated, a move to an equity joint venture structure is warranted: here the shared equity, additional monitoring rights, and administrative controls make the structure more responsive to even quite large disturbances, and only under extreme "end-game" circumstances will an appeal to third-party adjudication be required.

To understand the governance implications of a particular set of technology transfer activities within an alliance, we now examine, in greater detail, the special contracting problems encountered in such transactions. Appropriability hazards arise out of the unique trading characteristics of information and the consequent failures in the market for "know-how," important aspects of which are captured in Arrow's "fundamental paradox" of information (Arrow, 1971:152)—that the value to the purchaser is not known until he has the information, but then he has in effect acquired it without cost. This paradox provides the rationale for systems of intellectual property protection which exist in various forms throughout the world. Nonetheless, as previous research has amply demonstrated (Levin et al., 1987; Mansfield, 1985, 1986), firms and industries differ significantly in their propensity to patent industrial innovations, as well as in how rapidly new technological information leaks out to rival firms.

Although often characterized as such, it is apparent that "technology" is not synonymous with pure "information," nor does it always share the same public good features as information.[7] Arguments in the literature on interfirm technology transfer, for example, rest on the notion that technology is a complex mix of codified data and poorly defined, tacit "know-how." (Mowery and Rosenberg, 1989:7). This literature emphasizes the difficulties encountered by firms when they try to acquire technology via an arms-length contract because the tacit know-how involved is, by definition, extremely difficult to transfer without intimate personal contact, involving teaching, demonstration, and participation (Polanyi, 1962). In this view, the advantages of hierarchy in reducing the costs

6. Although this discussion is couched in terms of a bilateral transaction, the logic applies equally to a multilateral situation.

7. See Nelson (1990) for an insightful review of the treatment of technological know-how in the economics literature.

of technology transfer hinge on communication, organizational routines, and a necessity for prolonged colocation of participants (Kogut, 1988).[8]

A potential source of confusion concerning the effects of tacit know-how on governance comes from earlier discussions of "appropriability regimes" that refer to leakage of information leading to imitation by rivals (Teece, 1986). There it was argued that a high degree of tacitness in the know-how embodied in a technological innovation reduces appropriability hazards, because inventing around a patent is more difficult in that case (Teece, 1986:287). However, if we consider the effect of tacit know-how on the ease of contracting, it is apparent that the argument does not carry through: if parties attempt to contract for the right to use a technological asset embodying significant tacit know-how, they will face difficulties in adequately specifying the asset and associated property or usage rights to be transferred in a contract. Thus, while the tacitness of know-how reduces appropriability hazards with respect to unrelated parties, hazards in contracting for the transfer of the asset are nonetheless increased.

At the most basic level, if the purpose of a contract (or alliance) is the creation rather than exploitation of technology, adequate specification of property rights will inevitably be problematic, since the contracted assets do not exist at the time the contract is written, and technological innovation is a highly uncertain process (Freeman, 1982; Mowery & Rosenberg, 1989). Even for existing technology, specification is not necessarily straightforward. In addition to the level of tacitness, which may vary across technologies, the age of the technology may be a factor; a contract is more difficult to specify for a novel technology because the buyer and seller share less of the tacit know-how associated with its application than is usual for more "routine" technology transfers (Davidson and McFetridge, 1984).

While it is very difficult to obtain data on aspects of technology transferred in interfirm alliances such as "tacitness" or age, it is possible to make inferences about associated contract specification difficulties based on the type of activities involved in an alliance. For example, in the sample of interfirm alliances used in the empirical analysis described below, alliances may involve the transfer of existing technology to facilitate production and marketing activities in the alliance. Alternatively, product (or process) design activities may be carried out within the alliance, or there may be a mixture of design and production activities. Of these different "transaction types," those which include design activities are most likely to involve the creation or significant modification of technology, so raising the difficulty of adequate specification of

8. Previous empirical studies (Behrman & Wallender, 1976; Robinson, 1988; Teece, 1977) identified several factors that increase the costs of interfirm technology transfer, including the complexity and age of the technology, the recipient firm's "absorptive capacity" (Cohen & Levinthal, 1990), and the amount of previous technology transfer experience. These studies stress the consequent increased need for training, and personnel transfers, but several of these factors also increase contracting hazards associated with transfer—thus the challenge facing firms in such a transaction is to physically organize the project in such a way as to allow effective transfer of the technology while simultaneously designing the governance structure to mitigate associated contractual hazards.

contractual terms. Alliances involving these activities are therefore predicted to present greater appropriability hazards than are "pure" production and marketing agreements, and hence the adoption of a more hierarchical governance structure is hypothesized, ceteris paribus.

Observation 1. A more hierarchical governance mode will be chosen when an alliance involves product or process design than when only production or marketing activities are undertaken.

The amount of monitoring required for partner firms to have confidence that prescribed activities are indeed being adequately undertaken in a technology transfer alliance will also depend on the scope or complexity of the payoff relevant actions. For example, increases in the number of products or technologies included in a contract, or increases in the geographic scope of the transaction, will inevitably increase the difficulty and cost of monitoring activities (as well as possibly exacerbating specification problems). Similarly, if a contract is used to govern a project involving multiple firms, monitoring costs will increase with the number of partners involved, as assigning accountability for pay-off relevant actions taken by multiple partners under uncertainty is problematic (Alchian and Demsetz, 1972). This suggests that the scope of transactions should be limited unless there are compelling reasons to do otherwise, for example, because of the need to bring together diverse elements in a single project. Where increased scope is necessary, a more hierarchical governance structure is indicated. Thus we have

Observation 2. A more hierarchical governance mode will be chosen for transactions involving a broader range of products or technologies.

Observation 3. A more hierarchical governance mode will be chosen for transactions covering a wider geographic area.

Observation 4. A more hierarchical governance mode will be chosen when there are more firms involved in a transaction.

Enforcing technology transfer contracts when a violation of contract terms is detected can be problematic: Particularly in the international arena, differential enforcement of technology contracts can play a large role in governance choices in interfirm alliances as patent laws and their enforcement vary considerably across countries (despite recent efforts at harmonization through the GATT). Where alliance partner firms are all based in a single country (as in the empirical analysis below) there may be differences in the efficacy of patent protection across industries, but these are rooted primarily in the nature of the associated technologies and the subsequent ease or difficulty with which property rights can be specified. Therefore, while we would expect there to be significant cross-national differences in the governance of similar transactions within interfirm alliances, based on enforcement differences, we have no similar expectations regarding interindustry differences in enforcement in the United States.[9]

The relationship between transaction characteristics and the governance structure adopted for an alliance may also be influenced by the presence of alternative safeguards that can act as partial substitutes for more formal governance instruments. One such alternative safeguard is the exchange of hostages involved when firms are linked in multiple ongoing alliances. If the parties to an alliance are involved in other alliances together (whether contractual or equity based), then the payoffs to opportunism within each alliance are lowered, because of the risk that continued gains from cooperation in all of the alliances will be withdrawn (Gulati, 1995; Kogut, 1989). Alternatively, repeat alliances may reduce adverse selection problems in partner choice because of improved information developed over the course of previous cooperative projects (whether ongoing or not), regarding a partner's technological capabilities, assets, and behavior (Balakrishnan & Koza, 1993). Thus, we have:

Observation 5. Less hierarchical governance modes will be chosen if the partners are involved in multiple alliances together.

4. Empirical Analysis

4.1 Data Source

The principal data source for the empirical study is the Cooperative Agreements and Technology Indicators (CATI) information system, a relational database covering over 9000 cooperative agreements involving some 3500 different parent companies in many different industries and countries (Hagedoorn & Schakenraad, 1990). Cooperative agreements in the CATI database are defined as "common interests between independent industrial partners which are not connected through majority ownership," and all involve some arrangement for technology transfer or joint research.

The CATI data is based on systematic examination of secondary reports of alliance formation, primarily during the 1980s. In addition to the organizational form of the alliance, the database includes information on the identity and nationality of the partners, the date of establishment, the type and scope of the transaction involved, and the industry or technology sector in which the cooperative agreement takes place. Coverage of the overall population of global alliances is inevitably incomplete, and there are significant biases in the data, particularly with respect to the geographic and industrial sectors covered.[10] Such biases and omissions arguably render the data unsuitable for analysis of overall alliance activity or of firms' propensity to form strategic alliances. How-

9. A set of industry dummy variables is included in the empirical model, to control for any sectoral differences in patent protection or in the use of different types of alliances that are related to other omitted variables.

10. Hagedoorn and Duysters (1993:1) describe the shortcomings of the data as follows: "... skewness in the distribution of modes of cooperation (i.e., an underestimation of the number of customer-supplier relations and licensing agreements, due to under-reporting in published media), ... some geographic—i.e., Anglo Saxon—bias ... an underestimation of certain technological fields not belonging to modern core technologies and ... some overrepresentation of large firms."

ever, conversations with the originators of the data and independent verification of data on a random sample of alliances confirm that there are no systematic biases in the description and coding of alliance form and activities. Thus the reported biases are not critical here, as we are looking at individual decisions regarding the choice of organizational form.

4.2 Sample and Dependent Variable

The primary sample comprises all horizontal technology transfer alliances between public U.S.-based manufacturing firms in the CATI database established during the period 1980–1989: a total of 165 alliances. Restricting the analysis to public firms undoubtedly introduces some bias into the sample, as many of the smallest firms will be excluded. This is unavoidable, however, since the firm-specific data necessary for analysis of the "complete" model, including control variables (see below), are not readily available for private companies. To assess whether the restricted sample materially affects the results, a simplified model was also estimated for a larger sample of alliances which included private and nonmanufacturing firms. This latter sample comprises 507 alliances, and the model includes only those variables derived from CATI data.

For our sample of horizontal technology transfer alliances, the dependent variable (FORM) takes on one of three values, as discussed earlier:

> FORM = 0 for unilateral contractual agreements (i.e., for second-sourcing and licensing agreements)
> FORM = 1 for bilateral contractual agreements (i.e., for mutual second-sourcing agreements, cross-licensing, and technology sharing agreements)
> FORM = 2 for equity-based alliances (i.e., joint ventures)

The alliances in each of the two samples are fairly evenly distributed among these alliance types: for the "public" sample of 165 alliances and the expanded sample of 507 public and private firm alliances, respectively, 69 (42%) and 244 (48%) are unilateral contractual agreements, 60 (36%) and 135 (27%) are bilateral contracts, and 36 (22%) and 128 (25%) are equity-based alliances.

4.3 Independent Variables

A list of independent variables is shown in Table 1, with the relevant sources, and hypothesized signs. All firm-specific information is derived from Compustat data[11] and Table 2 presents the means, standard deviations, and range of values for the independent variables in the sample of 165 alliances between public U.S.-based firms. None of these variables are highly correlated: the largest correlation coefficient is 0.601, between venture experience and average size of alliance partners.

11. Because Compustat data is based on firm-level observations and many of the firms in the CATI database are actually subsidiaries of larger companies, the first step in obtaining this information was to match subsidiaries with their parent companies in the year the alliance was established. This was accomplished using the *Directory of Corporate Affiliations* for the relevant years.

Table 1. Independent Variable Definitions and Sources

Variable	Definition	Source	Predicted Sign
Transaction type	Activities covered by agreement: product and process design, production and marketing or "mixed."	CATI	+
Technology scope	Range of products or technologies covered by the agreement.	CATI	+
Geographic scope	Geographic scope of alliance: U.S. or North America, or worldwide.	CATI	+
Number of partners	Number of firms in alliance.	CATI	+
Overlapping agreements	Number of previously established alliances linking partner firms.	CATI	–
Control Variables:			
Industry	CATI technology sectors—biotechnology, information technology, new materials and "other."	CATI	n/a
Average firm size	Average size of alliance partners (total assets in millions of 1982 dollars).	Compustat	n/a
Relative size	Ratio of smallest firm to largest firm, measured by total assets.	Compustat	n/a
Average R&D	Combined R&D intensity of alliance partners (total R&D spending/total sales).	Compustat	n/a
R&D gap	Maximum difference among partners' R&D spending/sales.	Compustat	n/a
Same industry	Coded 1 if "main four-digit SIC" is same for all alliance partners.	Compustat	n/a
Alliance experience	Average number of previously established alliances for partner firms.	CATI	n/a

The number of partners was excluded as an independent variable for analysis of the "public firm" sample of 165 alliances, as there were only two alliances in this sample having more than two partners.[12] The number of partners is reintroduced in the model for the full sample of 507 firms, however. The overlapping alliances variable (a measure of alternative safeguards) is the number of alliances in the CATI database established prior to the establishment date of the alliance in question and involving all of the same partner firms.

In addition to the independent variables featured in the hypotheses, the following control variables were included in the model:

- Technology/research field or industry: A series of dummy variables were included, based on the "core technology sectors" identified in the CATI database: "information technology," "new materials," and "biotechnology." Observations without a dummy variable attached are

12. This reflects the large proportion of multipartner alliances with at least one private or nonmanufacturing firm for which the required Compustat data was unavailable.

Table 2. Descriptive Statistics for Independent Variables

	Mean	Standard Deviation	Minimum	Maximum
Design transaction dummy 1 = design 0 = production or mixed	0.078	0.269	0	1
Mixed transaction dummy 1 = mixed 0 = production or design	0.120	0.326	0	1
Technology scope 1 = few or broad range of technologies or products 0 = single technology or product area	0.365	0.483	0	1
Geographic scope 1 = Global Operations 0 = USA or N. America	0.267	0.444	0	1
Overlapping agreements = number of alliances linking partner firms	2.018	1.684	1	9
Information technology dummy	0.491	0.501	0	1
Biotechnology dummy	0.150	0.358	0	1
New materials dummy	0.126	0.333	0	1
Average size = average size of partners (total assets, in $millions)	11.20	14.55	0.036	77.18
Asset ratio = total assets of smallest partner/total assets of largest partner	0.234	0.256	0.001	0.997
Combined R&D intensity = total R&D spending/total sales	0.062	0.041	0.003	0.259
R&D gap = largest difference among partners' R&D spending/sales	0.136	0.371	0.001	2.524
Same industry 1 = all partners have same "main 4-digit SIC" 0 = otherwise	0.120	0.326	0	1
Alliance experience = average total number of alliances of partner firms prior to this alliance date	16.50	13.49	0	65
Time trend 0 = 1980	5.46	2.57	0	9

all other technology sectors represented in the CATI data.[13] This variable controls for significant sectoral differences in the propensity to enter into certain types of alliances that are not captured in the transaction or firm-level independent variables.

- Firm size: Previous studies of the decision to enter joint ventures, and of joint venture performance, have included among the independent variables the absolute size of the firm (e.g., Agarwal & Ramaswami, 1992; Gomes-Casseres, 1990) and/or the asymmetry in the size of participating firms (Harrigan, 1988; Hennart, 1991a). Average size (measured as total assets in 1982 dollars) of the partner firms in the alliance, and the "size ratio" of the firms (i.e., the total assets of the smallest firm in the alliance divided by the total assets of the largest firm) are therefore included in the model.[14]
- R&D intensity: The combined R&D intensity (i.e., total R&D spending/total revenues) of the partner firms is included as a control, since R&D intensity has been a significant (though not consistent) explanatory variable in previous studies of joint venturing versus autonomous international investment (Agarwal & Ramaswami, 1992; Gomes-Casseres, 1989; Hennart, 1991a; Kogut & Chang, 1991).[15]
- R&D gap: A relevant finding from the technology transfer literature is that a large "capabilities gap" between the technology donor and recipient increases the costs of transferring technology across firm boundaries (Teece, 1981). R&D gap, measured as the absolute value of the largest difference in the R&D intensities of partner firms, is therefore included as a proxy to control for the potential impact of such a "capabilities gap."
- Partners in same industry: Also following previous studies (e.g., Balakrishnan and Koza, 1993; Gomes-Casseres, 1989; Hennart, 1991a), a control dummy is included that captures whether both (or all) alliance partners have their primary operations in the same industry (at the four-digit SIC code level).
- Alliance experience: If experience in alliances lowers governance costs

13. The distribution of alliances among the core and other sectors in the CATI database is as follows: information technology, 40%; biotechnology, 15%; new materials, 10%; "other," 35%. "Other" sectors (ordered by share of alliances in the database) are automobiles, engineering, electrical equipment, defense, consumer electronics, instruments, aircraft, food and beverage, mining, medical technology, and space technology.

14. All of the firm-specific information is for the year of establishment of the alliance in question. Firm assets are deflated to 1982 levels based on the capital goods producer price index (U.S. Department of Commerce, 1992).

15. R&D intensity based on the level of sales is an imperfect indicator of R&D efforts as the measure may fluctuate quite widely as sales levels vary. Alternative measures include R&D spending level or R&D intensity based on total assets (which are less variable over time). Using R&D levels introduces additional problems however, as they are strongly correlated with total assets. The analysis was nonetheless repeated with both of these alternative specifications, with no significant impact on the results. Therefore only results using R&D intensity based on total revenues are reported.

more for certain modes than for others, then total alliance experience may affect the choice of mode. A control variable was constructed based on the average number of alliances (in the CATI database) established by each partner firm prior to the establishment date of the alliance in question. Although this measure is inevitably biased over time, this likely reflects the actual experience of firms in the sample, since technology-related alliances were not a common feature of firm strategy prior to the 1980s (Contractor and Lorange, 1988; Hagedoorn and Schakenraad, 1993).

- Time trend: To capture any systematic change in alliance structures adopted over time, an annual time trend variable is included, which takes a value of 0 for alliances established in 1980 to 9 for alliances established in 1989.

4.4 Statistical Methodology

As discussed above, the unit of observation for the analysis is the alliance. Because the categorical dependent variable can take on one of three ordered values, ordered probit is used for the statistical analysis.[16] The model is specified as follows:

$$z_i = \beta X_i + \varepsilon_i, \tag{1}$$

where z_i is an unobservable measure of the position of alliance i in the market-hierarchy continuum, X_i is the vector of characteristics of the transaction and of the participating firms (shown in Table 1), β is the weight attached to each characteristic, and ε_i is a random error term.

Since we only observe the choice of one of three ordered governance modes for each alliance ("FORM_i"), we assume that the unobservable variable z_i can be broken up into discrete intervals that "map" into the categories for FORM_i.

$$\begin{array}{ll} \text{If } z_i < \mu_0 & \text{then FORM}_i = 0 \\ \text{If } \mu_0 \leq z_i < \mu_1 & \text{then FORM}_i = 1 \\ \text{If } \mu_1 \leq z_i & \text{then FORM}_i = 2 \end{array} \tag{2}$$

The underlying model consists of the variables (z_i, X_i) given in Equation (1). The observed variables are X_i and FORM_i, where the observation scheme is given by Equation (2). The objective of the statistical analysis is to estimate β in Equation (1), the parameters which describe the relationship between characteristics of the alliance and participating firms with the position on the market-hierarchy continuum, and how this gets translated into one of the ordered

16. The probit model assumes that the underlying probability distribution is normal. In the common alternative to this model, the logit, the probability distribution is assumed to be logistic. The difference between these cumulative distributions is small (except in the tails), so the results should not be sensitive to the choice between these models, unless there are a large number of observations in the tails (Maddala, 1983). To ensure that this condition was not operable in the samples analyzed here, the models were estimated using both ordered probit and ordered logit. No significant differences in the results were observed, and so only the ordered probit results are reported.

categories of organizational form (FORM_i). We can write the probabilities of falling into the various categories of the dependent variable as

$$\begin{aligned} \Pr(\text{FORM}_i = 0|X_i) &= \Pr[\varepsilon_i < (\mu_0 - \beta X_i)|X_i] = F(\mu_0 - \beta X_i) \\ \Pr(\text{FORM}_i = 1|X_i) &= \Pr[(\mu_0 - \beta X_i) \le \varepsilon_i < (\mu_1 - \beta X_i)|X_i] \\ &= F(\mu_1 - \beta X_i) - F(\mu_0 - \beta X_i) \\ \Pr(\text{FORM}_i = 2|X_i) &= \Pr[\varepsilon_i \ge (\mu_1 - \beta X_i)|X_i] = 1 - F(\mu_1 - \beta X_i) \end{aligned} \tag{3}$$

where $F(.)$ denotes the cumulative normal distribution function corresponding to the distribution of the random variable ε_i—for the ordered probit model, this is a normal distribution, with the normalization that the variance of $\varepsilon_i = 1$.

Some normalization is also necessary on the (unknown) cutoff points, μ_j. Following common practice, we assume that $\mu_0 = 0$. Then, for the ordered probit model,

$$\begin{aligned} \Pr(\text{FORM}_i = 0|X_i) &= \phi(-\beta X_i) \\ \Pr(\text{FORM}_i = 1|X_i) &= \phi(\mu_1 - \beta X_i) - \phi(-\beta X_i) \\ \Pr(\text{FORM}_i = 2|X_i) &= 1 - \phi(\mu_1 - \beta X_i) \end{aligned} \tag{4}$$

where ϕ is the cumulative distribution for a standardized normal variable.

5. Results and Discussion

Estimation results, shown in Table 3, provide support for most of the transaction cost hypotheses. In model 1, based on the sample of 165 "public company alliances," more hierarchical types of alliance were chosen for design and mixed activity transactions than for alliances governing only production or marketing activities. Thus, as hypothesized, firms choose more hierarchical arrangements in situations where specification of the relevant property rights can be expected to be problematic. Furthermore, the positive coefficient on "mixed" (2.947) transactions is significantly higher than for design alone (1.225). This parallels Pisano's findings, that R&D collaborations in the biotechnology industry involving both R&D and other functions were more likely to use equity links than were "pure" R&D agreements (Pisano, 1989).

More hierarchical forms were also chosen when multiple products or technologies were involved in the alliance. The hypothesis links this effect to elevated monitoring difficulties (and hence appropriability hazards) associated with broader transaction scope. However, we have only a dummy variable capturing this aspect of transaction scope, with "Technology Scope" equal to zero for alliances covering a single technology or product area and equal to one for multitechnology/product transactions. This variable is therefore potentially open to alternative explanations: for example, while a unilateral contract may involve activities related to multiple products or technologies and bilateral contracts may involve technology exchanges within a single technology area,[17]

17. This contention is borne out in the data where there are a nontrivial number of cases of multitechnology unilateral contracts and single-technology bilateral contracts.

Table 3. Ordered Probit Estimation Results

	1	2	3	4
Intercept	−0.127	−0.165	0.574*	−0.611*
	(.373)	(.319)	(.326)	(.349)
Design transaction	1.225***	1.185***		1.392***
	(.291)	(.280)		(.192)
Mixed transaction	2.947***	2.966***		2.359***
	(.458)	(.445)		(.160)
Technology scope	1.225***	1.239***		1.113***
	(.286)	(.257)		(.133)
Geographic scope	−0.630	−0.679*		−0.481**
	(.405)	(.391)		(.189)
Overlapping	−0.060	−0.017		0.025
agreements	(.085)	(.080)		(.064)
Number of partners	n/a	n/a	n/a	0.196**
				(.099)
Biotechnology dummy	−0.180	−0.231	0.113	−0.264
	(.503)	(.389)	(.330)	(.197)
Information technology	−0.244	−0.375	−0.211	−0.088
dummy	(.330)	(.295)	(.252)	(.144)
New materials dummy	−0.637	−0.670**	−0.479	−0.344**
	(.325)	(.295)	(.287)	(.174)
Time trend	0.057	0.042	0.011	0.024
	(.055)	(.046)	(.043)	(.064)
Average size (assets)	0.006		0.010	
	(.016)		(.013)	
Asset ratio	−0.194		0.069	
	(.571)		(.394)	
Combined R&D intensity	−1.968		−2.327	
	(4.20)		(3.69)	
R&D gap	0.051		−1.166	
	(.458)		(1.70)	
Same SIC	−0.061		−0.212	
	(.469)		(.324)	
Alliance experience	−0.004		−0.005	
	(.007)		(.006)	
Log of likelihood function	−121.3	−122.3	−172.4	−368.6
χ^2	108.75***	106.67***	10.28	329.26***
Percentage of outcomes predicted correctly	73%	73%	37%	73%
Sample size (*n*)	165	165	165	507

*$p < 0.10$; **$p < 0.05$; ***$p < 0.01$
Standard errors in parentheses

a bilateral agreement may not be a feasible alternative in some instances, if there is only one party with a technological asset to offer.[18] To ensure that

18. I thank one of the anonymous reviewers for this insight.

Table 4. Frequencies of Actual and Predicted Outcomes

	Predicted			
Actual	0	1	2	Total
0	60	6	3	69
1	20	39	1	60
2	5	9	22	36
Total	86	53	26	165

the result on technology scope is not driven solely by such cases, all unilateral arrangements were removed and a binomial model of governance choice was estimated (for the choice between bilateral contracts and equity joint ventures), with similar results in terms of directional effects and levels of significance for all variables.

Overall, model 1 correctly predicts the organizational form of 121 out of the 165 alliances (73.3%). This compares with a random assignment, which would be correct for only 33% of the alliances, or 42% correct if all observations were assigned to the most frequently observed structure, that is, unilateral contract. Furthermore, as shown in Table 4, the "hit rate" is significantly higher than would be expected with random predictions in each of the three organizational form categories.[19]

Although it had the expected negative sign, the coefficient on the overlapping agreements variable was not statistically different from zero, in contrast to the findings in Gulati (1995), discussed earlier. A possible explanation for this inconsistency is that the variable used in the present study is an imprecise proxy for ongoing links between the firms: some agreements between the relevant firms may not be included in the CATI data and there is no data available on alliance dissolution or total project value, which are relevant to a hostage exchange model of overlapping alliances. Taken together these limitations suggest that the coefficient on overlapping alliances should be interpreted with caution.[20]

The estimated coefficient on geographic scope is negative, contrary to the hypothesized sign, and is almost significant at the 10% level. Thus, alliances covering worldwide operations, if anything, tend to be less hierarchical than those covering only North American operations. This finding should again be interpreted cautiously, however, as we do not have complete information about the age and value of the technology in each alliance and it is possible that there are systematic but unobserved differences in the characteristics of technology governed in alliances of differing geographic scope. If firms decline to transfer their newest or most valuable technology in situations where monitoring is particularly problematic—for example, when geographic scope is great—then

19. The ordering of the three categories was also confirmed by estimation of a multinomial logit model which generated results consistent with the findings reported here.

20. Note, however, that Gulati's data also suffers from shortcomings related to a lack of data on alliance dissolution and project value data.

the observed distribution of alliances in these settings may be skewed toward licensing, which is well suited for transfer of older, simpler, more codified technology.[21] More generally, there is a problem of simultaneity in the investment decision: a firm will jointly determine the content and governance of the transaction, that is, what technology will be shared or transferred, and how that transfer will be organized. Although the present study goes further than previous studies in specifying transaction-level variables, we are still unable to completely control for these effects.

An interesting aspect of the estimation results is that none of the control variables is significant—in contrast to previous studies of the choice between internal organization and joint ventures. Here, we see no significant effect on the form of strategic alliances, of firm size (either the average or relative size of the partners), R&D intensity, alliance experience, or the industry in which the alliance operates. This result is also supported in models 2 and 3, which show that a model including only the hypothesized variables performs essentially as well as the full model in accurately predicting the alliance form (72.7% of alliances are correctly predicted), while a model including the control variables alone can predict only 37% correctly.

These results emphasize an important finding of the current study: that it is attributes of the transaction and not firm-level characteristics that determine the type of alliance form chosen. This may also explain the inconsistencies of results in the international business literature that are based on firm-level measures, for example with respect to the effect of R&D intensity on governance mode (Gomes-Casseres, 1989).

Estimation of model 4, on the expanded sample of horizontal technology transfer alliances (still involving U.S.-based firms only), produced very similar results to those in model 2, with essentially the same variables. All the coefficients have the same sign as before, with similar levels of significance.[22] However, since this larger sample includes sufficient alliances with more than two partners to allow inclusion of "number of partners" as an independent vari-

---

21. Previous studies of franchising arrangements suggest an alternative explanation of the negative coefficient on geographic scope. In several studies (Brickley and Dark, 1987; Lafontaine, 1992; Minkler, 1990), measures of geographic dispersion, such as distance from monitoring headquarters or number of states in which the chain has established outlets, are used as proxies for difficulties in direct monitoring of agents' effort. These variables are found to be negatively related to the probability that an outlet will be company owned. The inference is that monitoring difficulties increase the need for high-powered incentives, and thus increase the attractiveness of contractual (versus integrated) solutions. However, in the current study focusing on appropriability hazards in alliances, high-powered incentives have perverse effects, as they increase the probability that technology will be put to uncompensated use outside the scope of the agreement. More hierarchical governance modes are thus the expected response to increased difficulties in monitoring.

22. The robustness of the estimation results suggests that the bias in the "public firm sample" does not have a material effect. This is consistent with the logic of the model, since the theory operates at the level of the transaction rather than at the firm level. Therefore, absent systematic differences in transactions tied to characteristics of the firm, sample biases in firm characteristics should be inconsequential.

able, there is an additional result of interest here: the effect of the number of partners on alliance structure is as hypothesized, suggesting that the increase in anticipated monitoring problems associated with multiple alliance partners induces the partners to choose a more hierarchical alliance structure.

6. Conclusions and Suggestions for Future Research

The empirical results reported above provide strong support for the hypothesis that appropriability hazards are an important consideration when firms establish strategic alliances. When appropriability hazards are severe, because of difficulties in specifying contracts for technology or in monitoring contracting partners' activities, more hierarchical alliance types are chosen. These alliances feature bilateral dependency (hostage exchange) or equity ties which promote monitoring and incentive alignment. Moreover, in contrast to most related studies in the international business arena, the analysis suggests that the form of an alliance depends primarily on the attributes of the transaction itself, rather than on characteristics of the partner firms.

The major limitation of the empirical analysis is the paucity of detailed data on specific technologies transferred in the sample alliances. This means that it is not possible to completely control for simultaneity in the investment decisions. Overcoming this problem would require information on the type of technology in an alliance, in terms of its value and level of advancement relative to the state of the art (which together determine the upper bound on the losses associated with appropriability hazards in a contracting relationship), as well as measures of the tacitness of know-how involved in technology transfers. While this study goes further than most previous work on interfirm alliances in specifying transaction-level variables, development of a more microanalytic data set is clearly a useful undertaking for future work.

The theoretical framework and empirical analysis described in this article nonetheless have important implications for future research. The theory provides a systematic way to differentiate among the many different types of interfirm alliance, and suggests that there is a clear logic to the choice among these different alliance types. Furthermore, the focus on interfirm alliances involving technology transfer provided an ideal setting for exploration of the origins and governance implications of appropriability hazards, or hazards related to weak property rights, that previously have been underdeveloped in transaction cost economics.

There are several avenues for further development of the research, in addition to the one mentioned above. One extension involves testing the hypotheses developed here on a larger sample of alliances involving firms from different countries. This would allow us to examine whether the same logic informs cross-national interfirm organization as it applies to alliances involving only U.S.-based firms. Enforcement issues could also be highlighted in this analysis by examining the added effect of cross-national differences in protection of intellectual property rights (as well as other aspects of the institutional environment) on the choice of organizational form in alliances between firms of different nationalities.

More ambitious extensions to the research would include an examination of the interaction between asset specificity and appropriability hazards over the life of an alliance. The data requirements and complexities of such an undertaking are challenging, as a series of longitudinal studies would be required to facilitate assessment of the evolving relationship between the different contracting concerns. Such a series of studies could address a rich set of questions, however, perhaps including the following: Does the nature of the technology transferred and the scope of projects vary over the course of an alliance? How are governance mechanisms adapted? How do relationship-specific assets develop over the course of an alliance? What is the role (if any) of transaction-specific investments in the equilibration of hazards in the face of appropriability concerns? Can such investments actually reduce contracting hazards in these circumstances?

The prospects for further theoretical and empirical study here are rich and exciting. The challenge is to approach these opportunities in a rigorous and incremental manner, maintaining the strictly comparative institutional approach which is a key advantage of the transaction cost framework.

References

Agarwal, S., and Ramaswami, S. 1992. "Choice of Foreign Market Entry Mode: Impact of Ownership, Location and Internalization Factors." (First Quarter) *Journal of International Business Studies*, 1–27.

Alchian, A. A., and Demsetz, H. 1972. "Production, Information Costs and Economic Organization." 62 *American Economic Review* 777–795.

Arrow, K. J. 1971. *Essays in the Theory of Risk-Bearing*. Chicago: Markham.

Balakrishnan, S., and Koza, M. P. 1993. "Information Assymmetry, Adverse Selection and Joint Ventures." 20 *Journal of Economic Behavior and Organization* 99–117.

Behrman, J., and Wallender, H. 1976. *Transfers of Manufacturing Technology Within Multinational Enterprises*. Cambridge, Mass.: Ballinger.

Brickley, J., and Dark, F. 1987. "The Choice of Organizational Form: The Case of Franchising." 18 *Journal of Financial Economics* 401–420.

Cohen, W. M., and Levinthal, D. A. 1990. "Absorptive Capacity: A New Perspective on Learning and Innovation." 35 *Administrative Science Quarterly* 569–596.

Contractor, F. J., and Lorange, P. 1988. "Why Should Firms Cooperate? The Strategy and Economics Basis for Cooperative Ventures," in F. J. Contractor and P. Lorange, eds., *Cooperative Strategies in International Business*. Lexington, Mass.: Lexington Books.

Davidson, W. H., and McFetridge, D. G. 1984. "International Technology Transactions and the Theory of the Firm." 32 *Journal of Industrial Economics* 253–264.

Freeman, C. 1982. *The Economics of Industrial Innovation*. London: Francis Pinter.

Geringer, J. M., and Hebert, L. 1989. "The Importance of Control in International Joint Ventures." (Summer) *Journal of International Business Studies* 235–254.

Gomes-Casseres, B. 1989. "Ownership Structures of Foreign Subsidiaries: Theory and Evidence." 11 *Journal of Economic Behavior and Organization* 1–25.

———. 1990. "Firm Ownership Preferences and Host Government Restrictions: An Integrated Approach." (First Quarter) *Journal of International Business Studies* 1–22.

Gulati, R. 1995. "Does Familiarity Breed Trust? The Implications of Repeated Ties for Contractual Choice in Alliances." 38 *Academy of Management Journal* 85–112.

Hagedoorn, J. 1993. "Understanding the Rationale of Strategic Technology Partnering: Interorganizational Modes of Cooperation and Sectoral Differences." 14 *Strategic Management Journal* 371–385.

Hagedoorn, J., and Duysters, G. 1993. *The Cooperative Agreements and Technology Indicators CATI Information System*. Unpublished manuscript, MERIT.

Hagedoorn, J., and Schakenraad, J. 1990. "Inter-firm Partnerships and Co-operative Strategies in Core Technologies," in C. Freeman and L. Soete, eds., *New Explorations in the Economics of Technical Change*. London: Frances Pinter.

______. 1993. "Strategic Technology Partnering and International Corporate Strategies," in K. S. Hughes, ed., *European Competitiveness*. Cambridge: Cambridge University Press.

Harrigan, K. 1986. *Managing for Joint Venture Success*. Lexington, Mass.: Lexington Books.

Harrigan, K. R. 1988. "Strategic Alliances and Partner Asymmetries," in F. J. Contractor and P. Lorange, eds., *Cooperative Strategies in International Business*. Lexington, Mass.: Lexington Books.

Hennart, J.-F. 1991a. "The Transaction Costs Theory of Joint Ventures: An Empirical Study of Japanese Subsidiaries in the U.S." (April) *Management Science* 483–497.

______. 1991b. "The Transaction Costs Theory of the Multinational Enterprise," in C. Pitelis and R. Sugden, eds., *The Nature of the Transnational Firm*. London: Routledge.

Hladik, K. 1985. *International Joint Ventures: An Economic Analysis of U.S.-Foreign Business Partnerships*. Lexington, Mass.: Lexington Books.

Killing, J. P. 1983. *Strategies for Joint Venture Success*. London: Croom Helm.

Klein, B., Crawford, R. A., and Alchian, A. A. 1978. "Vertical Integration, Appropriable Rents, and the Competitive Contracting Process." 21 *Journal of Law and Economics* 297–326.

Kogut, B. 1988. "Joint Ventures: Theoretical and Empirical Perspectives." 9 *Strategic Management Journal* 319–332.

______. 1989. "The Stability of Joint Ventures: Reciprocity and Competitive Rivalry." 38 *The Journal of Industrial Economics* 183–198.

______ and Chang, S. J. 1991. "Technological Capabilities and Japanese Foreign Direct Investment in the United States." 73 *Review of Economics and Statistics* 401–413.

Lafontaine, F. 1992. "Agency Theory and Franchising: Some Empirical Results." 23 *Rand Journal of Economics* 263–283.

Levin, R., Klevorick, A., Nelson, R., and Winter, S. 1987. "Appropriating the Returns from Industrial Research and Development." 3 *Brookings Papers on Economic Activity* 783–820.

Llewellyn, K. 1931. "What Price Contract? An Essay in Perspective." 40 *Yale Law Journal* 701–751.

Lorange, P., and Roos, J. 1992. *Strategic Alliances: Formation, Implementation and Evolution*. Cambridge, Mass.: Blackwell.

Macneil, I. R. 1978. "Contracts: Adjustments of Long-Term Economic Relations Under Classical, Neoclassical and Relational Contract Law." 72 *Northwestern University Law Review* 854–906.

Maddala, G. S. 1983. *Limited-Dependent and Qualitative Variables in Econometrics*. New York: Cambridge University Press.

Mansfield, E. 1985. "How Rapidly Does New Industrial Technology Leak Out?" 34 *Journal of Industrial Economics* 217–223.

______. 1986. "Patents and Innovation: An Empirical Study." 32 *Management Science* 173–181.

Minkler, A. 1990. "An Empirical Analysis of a Firm's Decision to Franchise." 34 *Economics Letters* 77–82.

Mowery, D. C., and Rosenberg, N. 1989. *Technology and the Pursuit of Economic Growth*. Cambridge: Cambridge University Press.

Nelson, R. R. 1990. *What is Public and What is Private About Technology?* CCC Working Paper No. 90-9, University of California, Berkeley.

Osborn, R. N., and Baughn, C. C. 1990. "Forms of Interorganizational Governance for Multinational Alliances." 33 *Academy of Management Journal* 503–519.

Pisano, G. 1989. "Using Equity Participation to Support Exchange: Evidence from the Biotechnology Industry." 5 *Journal of Law, Economics, & Organization* 109–126.

______. 1990. "The R&D Boundaries of the Firm: An Empirical Analysis." 35 *Administrative Science Quarterly* 153–176.

______, Russo, M., and Teece, D. 1988. "Joint Ventures and Collaborative Arrangements in the Telecommunications Equipment Industry," in D. Mowery, ed., *International Collaborative*

Ventures in U.S. Manufacturing. Washington, D.C.: American Enterprise Institute.

Polanyi, M. 1962. *Personal Knowledge: Towards a Post-Critical Philosophy*. New York: Harper and Row.

Robinson, R. 1988. *The International Transfer of Technology: Theory, Issues and Practice*. Cambridge, Mass.: Ballinger.

Teece, D. 1977. "Technology Transfer by Multinational Firms: The Resource Costs of Transfering Technological Know-how." (June) *Economic Journal* 242–261.

———. 1981. "The Market For Know-How and the Efficient International Transfer of Technology." 458 *Annals of the American Academy of Political and Social Science* 81–96.

———. 1986. "Profiting from Technological Innovation: Implications for Integration, Collaboration, Licensing and Public Policy." 15 *Research Policy* 285–305.

U.S. Department of Commerce, Bureau of Economic Analysis. 1992. *Business Statistics, 1963–91*. Washington, D.C.: U.S. Government Printing Office.

Williamson, O. E. 1985. *The Economic Institutions of Capitalism*. New York: Free Press.

———. 1991. "Comparative Economic Organization—The Analysis of Discrete Structural Alternatives." 36(4) *Administrative Science Quarterly* 269–296.

———. 1996. *The Mechanisms of Governance*. New York: Oxford University Press.

[22]

The Dynamics of Franchise Contracting: Evidence from Panel Data

Francine Lafontaine

University of Michigan and National Bureau of Economic Research

Kathryn L. Shaw

Carnegie Mellon University and National Bureau of Economic Research

This paper provides the first systematic evidence on how franchisors adjust their royalty rates and franchise fees as they gain franchising experience. This evidence comes from a unique panel data set that we assembled on these monetary contract terms for about 1,000 franchisors each year for the 1980–92 period. We find that there is much persistence, over time, in franchise contract terms within firms. We find this despite sizable across-firm differences in royalty rates and franchise fees. In addition, franchisors do not systematically increase or decrease their royalty rates or franchise fees as they become better established, contrary to predictions from some specific theoretical models. We conclude that variation in contract terms is mostly determined by differences across firms,

We gratefully acknowledge financial support for this research from the National Science Foundation under grant SBR-9312083. An earlier version of this paper was presented at the University of Michigan Business Economics workshop, at the ORSA-TIMS meetings in San Francisco, at the economics workshop at the University of Illinois at Urbana-Champaign, at the winter 1993 meetings of the Econometric Society, at the Georgetown University's economics seminar series, at the Economics Department at Ohio State University, in the economics workshop at University of California at Los Angeles, at the May 1994 Northwestern University summer workshop, at the Département de Sciences Economiques de l'Université Laval, and at the industrial organization workshop at New York University. The current version was presented at the economics departments at the University of Florida, the University of Hawaii, and Columbia University. We thank all the participants at these meetings and workshops, as well as Scott Masten, Andrea Shepard, an anonymous referee, and the editor, Lars Hansen, for all their helpful comments. Finally, we thank Robert Picard for his assistance. The usual caveat applies.

[*Journal of Political Economy*, 1999, vol. 107, no. 5]

not by within-firm changes over time. Finally, we find no negative relationship, within firms, between up-front franchise fees and royalty rates.

I. Introduction

A franchise agreement is typically defined as a contractual arrangement between two legally independent firms, whereby the franchisee pays the franchisor for the right to sell the franchisor's product or the right to use his trademarks in a given location for a specified time period. This form of organization is a well-established business phenomenon: in 1986, the last year for which such data are available, an estimated 35 percent of retailing in the United States took place through franchised chains, and the value of goods sold through these chains represented 13.4 percent of gross domestic product (Kostecka 1988). In a traditional franchise, franchisors sell a finished or semifinished product to franchisees at a markup, as in gasoline stations, car dealerships, and soft drink bottling franchises. In business format franchising, by contrast, the franchisee receives a trade name and a complete business plan in exchange for the payment of a franchise fee and royalties, as in fast-food and automotive repair franchises. In the last few decades, sales through business format franchised chains have grown from a negligible value to about 25 percent of all franchising, or 3.5 percent of GDP. This paper is about the key monetary terms of business format franchise contracts.

Consistent with its economic importance, one now finds in the literature a number of theoretical explanations for the existence of franchising and for the structure of franchise contracts. These models, however, as in much of the theoretical literature on labor and other contracts, have received only a limited amount of empirical attention. In fact, the empirical literature on franchising has followed its own path, focusing mostly on what determines franchisors' decisions to franchise outlets versus operating them directly.[1] The theoretical discussion, meanwhile, has been primarily concerned with the determination of the terms of the optimal contract between franchisor and franchisees given issues of incomplete information and moral hazard. In particular, authors have focused on factors influencing the choice of royalty rates and up-front franchise fees

[1] See Dant, Kaufmann, and Paswan (1992), Dnes (1996), Lyons (1996), and Lafontaine and Slade (1997, 1999) for reviews of this literature. To our knowledge, the only empirical studies of franchise contract terms have been those of Lafontaine (1992*a*, 1993), Sen (1993), Wimmer and Garen (1997), and Gagné, Sigué, and Zaccour (1998). All have relied on cross-sectional data.

in business format franchise contracts. In this paper, we explore empirically the variation in those same variables. Our overall goal is to provide information on contracting patterns that would help sort out existing theories of franchising, but also to suggest avenues for future theoretical work on franchising and on contracting more generally.

We model the determinants of royalty rates and franchise fees using a unique panel data set that we assembled on these monetary contract terms for about 1,000 franchisors each year from 1980 to 1992. These data allow us to address three related questions regarding franchise contract terms. First, how do firms adjust their franchise contract terms as they become established? Second, to what extent are these contract terms characterized by firm-specific fixed differences? And third, what is the relationship between franchise fees and royalty rates?

Our main results are as follows. First, there is a great deal of persistence in franchise contract terms within firms. We find this despite sizable across-firm differences in royalty rates and in franchise fees. Second, franchisors that do change their fees do not systematically increase or decrease their royalty rates as they become better established, contrary to predictions from some existing theoretical models. In fact, we find that variation in royalty rates and franchise fees is almost exclusively explained by across-firm differences, not by within-firm changes in fees over time. Third, despite contrary predictions from theory, there is little apparent trade-off between royalty rates and up-front franchise fees, even within firms. We expect the reason is that franchise fees are a small source of revenue to most franchisors.

The paper is organized as follows. In Section II, we define the franchise contract terms of interest and briefly discuss relevant theories. In Section III, we describe our data, their sources, and characteristics. Our empirical methodology and results are found in Section IV. In Section V, we summarize our results and present conclusions.

II. Franchise Contract Terms: Definitions and Theoretical Framework

A. *Franchise Contract Terms: Definitions*

In business format franchising, royalties, which are usually a constant percentage of the franchised unit's sales, and up-front franchise fees, which are paid only once at the beginning of the contract, are the main sources of revenues to franchisors. Typically, the franchise fee and royalty rate demanded by a franchisor are the same for all franchisees joining a chain at a point in time. Thus one can meaningfully refer to, and examine empirically, the royalty rate and franchise fee offered by a franchisor at a point in time.

From a theoretical perspective, the relevant notion of the royalty rate includes all variable payments—as these payments affect decisions at the margin—whereas the relevant notion of franchise fee captures all fixed payments from the franchisee to the franchisor. Consequently, the "royalty rate" used herein is the percentage of sales paid to the franchisor, including any advertising fee given as a percentage of sales. The "franchise fee" is usually only the fixed up-front fee paid to the franchisor when opening a new outlet. However, when the franchisor requires a fixed payment each week or month (which arises for 700 of our 11,947 observations or 277 of our 3,625 franchisors), these payments are discounted and added to the up-front fee to generate what we call the franchise fee. (See the Appendix for more details.)

Though franchise fees receive a lot of attention in theoretical models, in reality, they usually represent a fairly small proportion of the total amount paid by franchisees to franchisors. In fact, on average, the up-front fee amounts to about 8 percent of the expected value of all payments from franchisee to franchisor (on the basis of our data on average fees and data on expected sales per unit from Kostecka [1988]).

As this paper is concerned with how firms adjust their contract terms over time, it is important to recognize that we are referring to the terms of the contracts offered to new franchisees each year. Contract terms are rarely renegotiated within the contract period. Existing franchisees continue to operate under the terms of their contracts until they are renewed. At that point, they are usually renewed at the "then-current" contract terms. Thus a franchisor that changes the terms of its contract will, after franchising some units under the new contract, have different franchisees operating under different contract terms.

Finally, while the monetary terms of a franchise contract are very central to the agreement, franchise contracts also stipulate many other aspects of the relationship (see Udell [1972] for a compilation of contract clauses), some of which can affect the level of fees. For example, the duration of the agreement, which varies typically between five and 30 years and averages around 15 (Kostecka 1988), will affect the commitment level and investments of both parties and, as such, affect the level of the fees. Similarly, the provision of an exclusive territory (about 60–65 percent of franchisors offer exclusive territories according to various surveys) may make the franchise more attractive to the franchisee and allow the franchisor to charge higher fees. Finally, the franchisor can require franchisees to purchase some inputs from them. If sold at a markup, these purchases can be a substitute for franchise fees and royalties. However, input purchases (voluntary and required) are valued at less than 10 percent of franchisees' sales in most business format franchise sectors (see Lafontaine 1992*a*), largely because U.S. antitrust authorities have not allowed input purchase requirements when "quality" issues can be handled with approved supplier clauses.[2] Thus a number of features of franchising contracts that are typically unmeasured in franchising data can generate across-firm variation in the level of the fees.

B. An Overview of Relevant Theories

Few of the existing models of franchising have direct dynamic implications regarding contract terms. Exceptions include Gallini and Lutz's (1992) signaling model and Mathewson and Winter's (1985) reputation model, both of which imply that franchisors will want to reduce their royalty rates and increase their franchise fees over time. This occurs in the former because information about franchisor quality is revealed over time and in the latter because of the franchisor's increased reputational capital. Rubin (1978), on the other hand, expects franchisors to increase their royalty rates as they become established. This, he argues, must occur to counterbalance the reduction in franchisor incentives that is associated with the lower potential sales of franchised units in a saturated market.

Most other models of franchising do not have any dynamic component. They imply largely that contract terms should be different for different franchisees whose tastes and circumstances vary.[3] But in reality, each franchisor offers the same contract to all franchisees joining at a point in time. Thus if the tastes and circumstances of different franchisees play a role in the contracting decision, they do so only on "average," or because the different contract terms offered by different franchisors allow franchisees to self-select. In this setting, optimal contract terms will differ across chains that face different needs to align franchisee and franchisor incentives (or that

[2] See Hunt and Nevin (1975), Klein and Saft (1985), and Lafontaine (1993) for more on this.

[3] See Cheung (1969), Stiglitz (1974), Reid (1977), and Hallagan (1978) for early sharecropping models that are easily applied to franchising. See also Caves and Murphy (1976), Rubin (1978), Blair and Kaserman (1982), Mathewson and Winter (1985), Brickley and Dark (1987), Martin (1988), Lal (1990), Gallini and Lutz (1992), and Bhattacharyya and Lafontaine (1995) for franchising models.

face different "average" degrees of risk and risk aversion among their franchisees, or that simply want to attract different types of franchisees). In turn, these differences in franchisor needs must relate to the type of businesses they are involved in, the markets they operate in, or their specific monitoring or managerial capabilities. All these considerations imply an important role for sector- and firm-specific effects in the setting of franchise contract terms, but no systematic pattern over time within firms. Furthermore, as noted above, other contract components (such as exclusive territories) offered by franchisors can be complementary to, or substitutes for, the fees. As these other clauses tend to be constant over time within firms, their effect would be captured by dominant firm-specific effects in the data.

While there is no agreement in the theoretical literature as to how royalty rates and franchise fees should change as firms become established, most models agree that, everything else constant, an increase in royalty rate should be accompanied by a decrease in franchise fee, and vice versa. The reason is that the models assume that franchisees are kept at their reservation utility levels. Thus the royalty rates are determined first, on the basis of incentive, information, and risk issues, and then the fixed franchise fee is set equal to the profits left downstream by the royalty rate above those necessary to provide the franchisee with his or her reservation utility.

Finally, because the theories of franchise contracting are fundamentally static, none of them incorporates explicitly dynamic phenomena, such as learning, that could produce systematic changes in contract terms over time. In franchising models in which franchisor quality matters (e.g., signaling), quality is taken as a fixed characteristic that the franchisor knows and simply needs to communicate to franchisees. In reality, firms do not know how successful they will be in franchising before they actually experiment with it. The amount of entry, and even more so exit, in our data suggests that franchisors learn about themselves in the process of franchising. Of course, this learning should affect the terms of the contracts chosen by these firms and how the terms change as the firms become established. For example, if a firm gets a bad signal of its quality at a point in time, it may need to reduce both of its fees to continue to attract franchisees. These issues have not been addressed in the theoretical literature, but our empirical work can help assess their importance.

In what follows, we explore empirically how royalty rates and fixed fees charged to new franchisees each year evolve as franchisors become better established, and how they relate to each other. In keeping with our goal of increasing our understanding of franchising and contracting and to guide future theoretical work, we rely on parametric and nonparametric methods to explore these patterns in our data.

III. The Data

As noted in the Introduction, the data we have access to are quite unique: for the first time, we have information on the contract terms—namely royalty rates, advertising fees, and franchise fees—offered to new franchisees by about 1,000 individual franchisors each year for 13 years, from 1980 to 1992 inclusively. Most of the data used here come from *Entrepreneur* magazine's "Annual Franchise 500" surveys, though some franchisor characteristics were obtained from other data sources (see the Appendix for details).

While the number of franchisors responding to *Entrepreneur*'s survey remains relatively constant over time, one does not find the same franchisors responding to the survey year after year. In fact, we have an average of four and a half years of data for each firm (for firms observed more than once), and we have a complete series of 13 years for only 103 franchisors. Our sample is unbalanced in large part because of entry and exit from franchising. On average, in any given year, about 15 percent of the franchisors covered in the survey have just started franchising. Also, according to Kostecka (1988), between 120 and 180 franchisors stopped franchising or went out of business annually between 1980 and 1986. These high entry and exit rates reflect the low cost of entry into, and fairly low cost of exit from, franchising: firms can get involved in franchising after having established just one pilot unit that is company-owned. According to Dixon (1988), on entry, typical franchisors sell three or four franchises per year, on average, if they do not opt out or go out of business. In our data, firms have seven company units and almost four franchises, on average, in their first year in franchising. The median number of company units and franchises, however, that first year is just one. Moreover, more than 50 percent of the firms we observe the year they start franchising exit franchising within the next five years.[4]

The lack of continuity in our sample also reflects factors specific to the survey we rely on. For many franchisors, responding to this survey is a way to increase their visibility vis-à-vis potential franchise buyers. Thus those franchisors that are not interested in attracting new franchisees may choose not to respond, so that our sample is biased toward new or expanding franchisors. Our sample is also unbalanced because we were fairly conservative in matching franchisors

[4] See Lafontaine and Shaw (1998*a*) for more on franchisor entry and exit.

across survey years. These reasons for the lack of balance in our sample introduce some possibility of sample selection bias, which we return to later. However, much of the variation in the sample also reflects random nonresponses.

Table 1 gives the means, standard deviations, and ranges of our variables, along with the number of observations over which they are calculated. Note that our final sample size of 11,947 observations (from 3,625 different franchisors) falls when the data for a variable were obtained from another source (see the Appendix).

A. *Some Preliminary Data Patterns*

Before we move on to the econometric evidence, it is useful to examine the raw data directly. Given our focus on how contract terms evolve over time, table 2 describes the number of times each fee went up, went down, or stayed the same between two consecutive years. It shows that most firms did not change their royalty rates or nominal fixed fees from one year to the next. For royalty rates, there is no change for 76 percent (or 5,897 of 7,711 in row 1) of all observations. Also, when a change is made, it is as likely to be up as down. However, changes are large when they do occur: the average change in royalty rates is more than two points up or down, representing more than 40 percent of the starting values (see row 1).

Table 2 also shows that in 60 percent (4,621 of 7,711) of the cases, there is no change in nominal franchise fees, despite underlying price inflation in the economy. When there is a change, it is more often up than down; but still one-third of the changes are down. The mean increase when this fee goes up, however, far exceeds the mean inflation rate. This suggests that when these fees are adjusted upward, they are making up for several years of inflation, or they are raised for additional reasons. As for "real" (consumer price index adjusted) franchise fees, they change frequently, but this is simply because the nominal fees do not keep up with inflation.

One possible explanation for the observed lack of change may be that franchisors change their fees regularly, but every few years rather than yearly. Table 3 shows that there is no such pattern of regular changes every few years in the data either. The table displays, for both the royalty rate and the franchise fee, the proportion of all the sequences of length T in which the firm made a change from year $T-1$ to T but had made no change up to $T-1$. For the royalty rate, these data show that the probability that a firm will make a change in the last period goes down as the number of years without a change goes up. For the franchise fee, this probability also goes down as the number of years without a change goes from one to

TABLE 1

DESCRIPTIVE STATISTICS

Variable	Observations	Mean	Standard Deviation	Minimum	Maximum
Royalty rate (%)	11,947	6.4	3.5	.0	30
Advertising fee (%)	11,947	1.5	1.8	.0	30
Franchise fee ($1,000s)	11,947	23.3	36.8	.0	1,118.8
Franchise fee less fixed ($1,000s)	11,947	18.6	16.1	.0	450
Number of outlets*	11,947	153.1	493.8	1.0	8,289
Percentage company-owned outlets	11,947	23.7	29.5	.0	100
Canadian franchisor	11,947	.11	.32	.0	1
Capital required (1992 $1,000s)	11,744	174.8	686.7	.0	38,022
Years franchising	11,947	9.4	9.0	1.0	73
Financing provided (dummy)	11,930	.24	.43	.0	1
Number of states with outlets†	6,514	13.7	14.4	.0	50
Initial training (days)	6,204	16.9	14.3	.0	193.5

* McDonald's had a larger number of units (12,643) than the maximum shown here, but it is excluded from the sample because its reported royalty rate sometimes includes rent for the premises and sometimes does not; the division between the two is too blurred to make the data usable.

† This variable equals zero for the few Canadian franchisors in our data with no units in the United States.

TABLE 2

SUMMARY OF CHANGES FROM YEAR TO YEAR

CHANGES IN	UP			DOWN			NO CHANGE:	TOTAL		
	Observations	Mean Change	Mean Percentage Change	Observations	Mean Change	Mean Percentage Change	OBSERVATIONS	Observations	Mean Change	Mean Percentage Change
Royalty	969	2.21	40.95	845	−2.32	−43.42	5,897	7,711	.02	.39
Franchise fee	2,075	8.64	33.89	1,015	−11.68	−42.13	4,621	7,711	.79	3.57
Franchise fee (real)	1,778	11.65	35.18	5,807	−3.88	−11.60	126	7,711	−.24	−.62

TABLE 3

CHANGE PROBABILITIES

		Royalty Rate (with Advertising Fee)		Nominal Franchise Fee (including Ongoing Fixed Payments)	
Length of Sequence (in Years) (= T)	Number of Sequences	Sequences of Length T with No Change by $T - 1$*	Of These, Percentage with a Change from $T - 1$ to T	Sequences of Length T with No Change by $T - 1$*	Of These, Percentage with a Change from $T - 1$ to T
2	7,711	na	23.52	na	40.07
3	5,159	3,891	17.50	3,051	26.45
4	3,547	2,176	14.02	1,475	23.39
5	2,453	1,272	11.87	745	22.42
6	1,742	776	9.54	382	21.20
7	1,230	491	8.76	201	22.89
8	867	308	7.47	104	27.88
9	614	190	6.84	54	33.33
10	415	117	6.84	26	38.46

* These are sequences of length T in which the value of the royalty rate (franchise fee) has remained constant over all periods to $T - 1$.

five. After that, the likelihood that a firm will change its nominal franchise fee goes up with the number of years since the last change occurred. But for either fee, the probability of a change after any given period without a change is never larger than the probability of change after just one year (shown in the first row of table 3). We conclude that the data are not characterized by a systematic pattern of change every few years for all firms.[5]

Table 4 examines whether there are firms in the data that change their fees all the time whereas others rarely do so. It shows the number of firms that have made x changes in their fees. It does so first for the total sample of 11,947 observations and then for the more balanced sample of firms observed at least 10 times or more. The balanced sample results in particular confirm that there is a fair number of firms (30 out of 139) that made no change in their royalty rates even over 10 years. At the other extreme, 22 firms made five or more changes over the same period. Not surprisingly, firms in general change their franchise fees more often than they do their royalty rates, some of them (10 out of 139 in the last three rows) changing them almost every year. Yet we still find 42 out of the same 139 firms changing their franchise fee two times or less over 10 years or more. We conclude that there is significant heterogeneity across firms in the frequency with which they change the terms of their contracts.

For firms that do make changes, we also examined whether these changes within firms were always positive, always negative, or a mix of the two. Though this is not shown in the table, we found that as soon as firms make at least three changes in royalty rates, these changes almost always include both increases and decreases. Even for the franchise fee, the probability that changes were all positive became quite small (below 20 percent in the overall sample) for firms with four or more changes and continued to decrease significantly thereafter. Thus the data continue to show no sign of systematic pattern up or down in fees over time.

We now turn to the effect of franchisor age on the probability that a firm changes its fees up or down. Figures 1 and 2 illustrate what proportion of all firms with given numbers of years of franchising experience either increase or decrease their royalty rates or franchise fees. These figures show no systematic pattern toward either more or fewer increases in fees as firms become more experienced

[5] We further confirmed the lack of alternative periodicity in the data by differencing over intervals longer than one year (i.e., two- or three-year differences) in our regression analyses. The results we obtained were no different from those reported below for one-year first differences.

TABLE 4

NUMBER OF CHANGES PER FIRM

	ROYALTY RATE (with Advertising Fee)				FRANCHISE FEE (with Fixed Payments)			
	Total Sample		Balanced Sample		Total Sample		Balanced Sample	
NUMBER OF CHANGES	Number of Firms	Observations per Firm*	Number of Firms	Observations per Firm*	Number of Firms	Observations per Firm*	Number of Firms	Observations per Firm*
0	1,097	3.34	30	11.73	756	2.94	3	12.33
1	465	3.89	24	12.04	609	3.35	12	11.92
2	177	5.87	21	11.67	232	5.29	27	11.74
3	77	7.64	23	11.78	126	6.88	29	11.72
4	38	9.39	19	11.63	58	7.84	14	12.43
5	16	10.81	11	12.09	47	8.34	16	11.38
6	8	10.88	6	11.83	23	9.87	12	12.08
7	5	12.00	4	13.00	12	9.67	5	12.00
8	1	13.00	1	13.00	4	12.00	4	12.00
9	0		0		7	11.43	7	11.43
10	0		0		6	11.67	6	11.67
11	0		0		1	12.00	1	12.00
12	0		0		3	13.00	3	13.00

NOTE.—There are 1,288 chains in the data with only one record or no consecutive records, making it impossible to calculate a change. Another 453 firms were excluded because their data were not fully consecutive. Results were not sensitive to whether or not these firms were excluded. When we force 10 or more consecutive observations, we discard all data from 3,486 chains.

* Average number of consecutive observations per firm given the number of changes in contract terms.

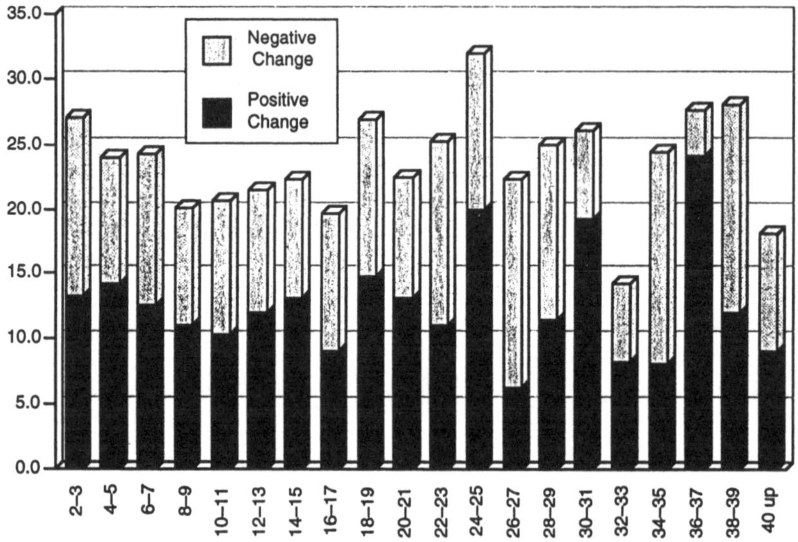

FIG. 1.—Royalty rate: probability of change as a function of years in franchising

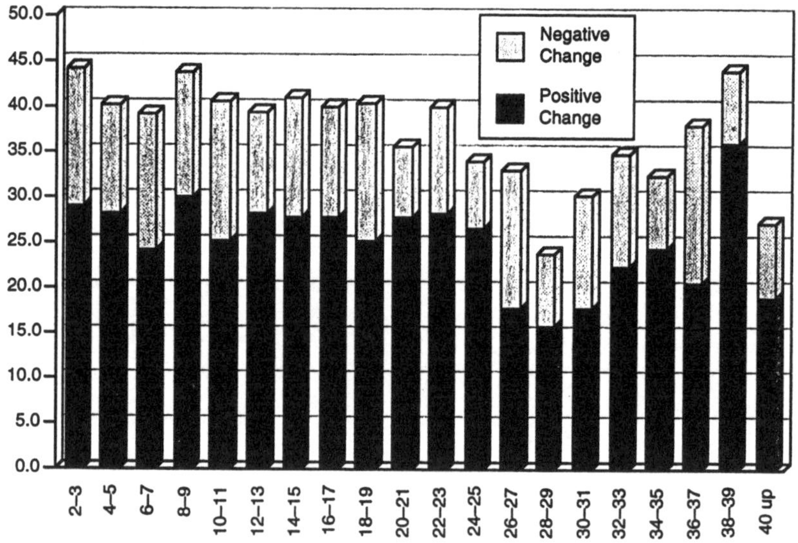

FIG. 2.—Franchise fee: probability of change as a function of years in franchising

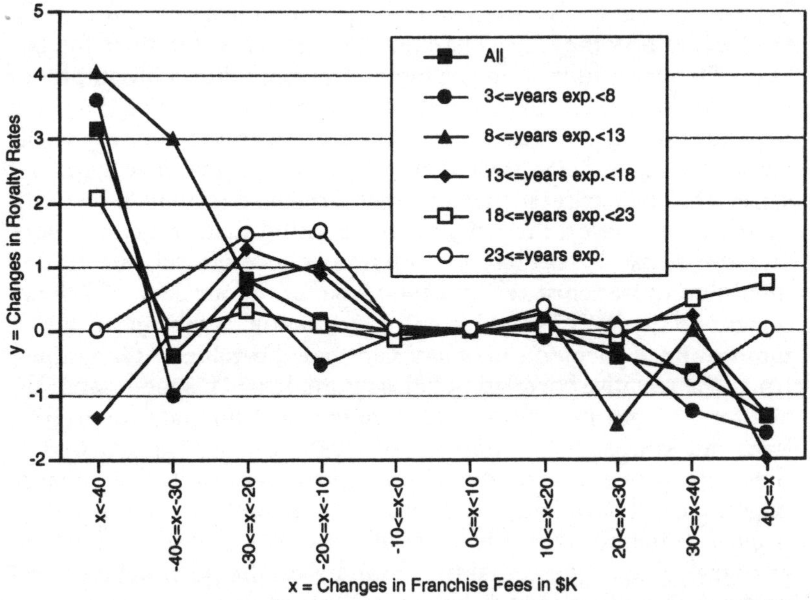

FIG. 3.—Mean changes in royalty rates relative to changes in franchise fees

and no pattern toward more or fewer changes either. Note that at high experience levels, the sample size falls considerably, which explains why there is more volatility. Though the corresponding figures are not shown here, the same lack of systematic effect was found when we examined how fees evolve relative to the number of outlets or, on a yearly basis, relative to inflation rates.

Given the emphasis of the theoretical literature on this relationship, we also want to consider how royalty rates and franchise fees relate to each other. Theory predicts a strong negative correlation between them. The simple correlation between royalty rates and franchise fees, after time effects are taken out, is significant at −.103. Since higher-quality firms should charge higher royalties and fixed fees, however, we want to hold quality constant. Thus we turn to the correlation between *changes* in these variables. The simple correlation in changes is −.158 (with time effects taken out again). Thus there is a significant negative correlation between the fees in our data.[6]

We explore this further in figure 3, which shows the mean contem-

[6] To test the significance of these correlation coefficients, we assume that the variables are jointly normally distributed, so that under H_0, $\rho = 0$, $r\sqrt{N-2}/\sqrt{1-r^2} \sim t_{N-2}$.

poraneous change in royalty rates by groups of firms categorized on the basis of how they have changed their franchise fee since the last year. The different lines in the figure represent different samples of firms on the basis of their number of years in franchising. Figure 3 illustrates well the negative correlation between the fees, especially among younger firms (less than 18 years of experience). In that sense, the data suggest that younger firms experiment more with their fees. However, the negative relationship that we observe here and the negative correlations reported above are all due to our definition of franchise fee and the presence, in our data, of 700 observations (from 277 franchisors) that sometimes rely on weekly or monthly fixed payments in lieu of sales-based royalties. Among these firms, the negative correlation between total fixed payments and royalty rates is very strong, at −.43. Whether we eliminate these firms from our sample (i.e., eliminate all 1,043 observations attached to these firms) or eliminate the 700 observations in which they charge ongoing fixed payments, the relationship between the fees becomes positive (in either case, the correlation is .075 in levels and .04 for changes). This suggests that the emphasis on the potential trade-off between those fees in the theoretical literature may be misplaced. We come back to this issue below, in our econometric analyses.

Finally, some models (e.g., Rubin 1978; Gallini and Lutz 1992; Scott 1995) imply that company ownership is a substitute for royalty payments, suggesting that they should also be negatively correlated in the data. The simple correlation between the two (after time effects are taken out) is .046. The same correlation between changes is .003, which is not significant. Similarly, we found no systematic pattern when we explored this relationship graphically or in our regression analyses, so we do not pursue this issue further below.

Overall, the tables and figures above show not only that franchise contract terms change infrequently, but also that when they are modified, the direction of the change is not systematically up or down. This contradicts those theoretical models (Rubin 1978; Mathewson and Winter 1985; Gallini and Lutz 1992) that predict a systematic pattern over time. Finally, there is a trade-off between royalty rates and franchise fees, but the relationship between the two is much weaker than one would expect from theory and is driven by a small minority of firms that sometimes charge ongoing fixed payments in lieu of variable royalties.

IV. Empirical Methodology and Results

In this section, we examine econometrically how contract terms change as the chain becomes mature and larger and the extent to which contract terms are characterized by strong firm-specific effects. The analyses of the raw data suggest that firm-specific effects should play a significant role in our regressions because there is a high variance in contract terms across firms yet, within firms, there is little change in contract terms over time. However, econometric analysis could reveal patterns that are not evident in the simple unconditional nonparametric distributions shown above.

A. *OLS and Fixed-Effects Results*

Consider first a simple parametric model relating royalty rates to franchising experience:

$$R_{it} = \beta X_{it} + u_i + \epsilon_{it}, \tag{1}$$

where R_{it} is the royalty rate; X_{it} is the number of years (at time t) since firm i began franchising; u_i is a firm-specific component that could represent the quality of the firm (such as its technology, the market value of its product concept, the quality of its management, and the quality of other aspects of the contract); and ϵ_{it} is a measurement error or other type of stochastic shock. Control variables included in the estimation of equation (1), including nonlinear terms in X_{it}, are omitted for notational simplicity. Also, we concentrate on royalty rates because the effect of franchising experience on franchise fees, according to theory, should be simply the reverse of the effect for royalty rates. Equation (1) focuses on two key questions: Do R_{it}'s change as firms gain experience, and are they explained by fixed effects?

The treatment of the individual effect u_i depends on the assumptions we make about the relationships between u, e, and X. If, for example, u_i captures differences in franchisor quality and if firms that remain in business and see their experience increase are more likely to be high-quality (high-u_i) firms, then there should be a positive correlation between u and X, and ordinary least squares (OLS) coefficients on X would be biased upward. This source of bias can be eliminated by estimating a fixed-effects model in which all variables are taken as differences from their time-series means. On the other hand, the OLS models currently in the literature are consistent if (1) the firm-specific effects in equation (1) are nonexistent, (2) these firm-specific effects are well captured by sectoral dummy variables included in the OLS regressions, or (3) the firm-specific effects are uncorrelated with the regressors.

Tables 5 and 6 show results obtained from estimating (1) using OLS (cols. 1, 2, and 3) and fixed effects (cols. 4, 5, and 6) for the royalty rate and franchise fee, respectively. The F-tests do support

TABLE 5

OLS and Fixed-Effects Results for the Royalty Rate

Independent Variable	OLS (1)	OLS (2)	OLS (3)	Fixed Effects (4)	Fixed Effects (5)	Fixed Effects (6)
Outlets (100s)	.103***	.103***	.215***	.033	.035*	.056*
	(.016)	(.016)	(.030)	(.020)	(.021)	(.033)
(Outlets)^2 (100s)	−.001***	−.001***	−.003***	−.0006*	−.0006*	−.001
	(.0003)	(.0003)	(.0005)	(.0003)	(.0003)	(.0006)
Years franchising	−.001	−.003	−.016	−.085	−.084	−.178**
	(.009)	(.009)	(.013)	(.060)	(.060)	(.071)
(Years franchising)^2	−.0005***	−.004***	−.0004	.002***	.002***	.001**
	(.0002)	(.0002)	(.0003)	(.0003)	(.0003)	(.0006)
Financing provided		.452***	.355***		.070	−.066
		(.086)	(.123)		(.051)	(.077)
Capital required		.000	−.0001		−.000	.0003
		(.000)	(.0001)		(.000)	(.0002)
Number of states			−.005			.007
			(.005)			(.006)
Canadian franchisor			.891***			
			(.226)			
Canadian × states			−.110***			−.012
			(.023)			(.030)
Training provided			.008**			.007
			(.004)			(.005)
Constant	6.81***	6.63***	6.26***			
	(.161)	(.161)	(.217)			
Sector dummies	yes***	yes***	yes***	na	na	na
Time dummies	yes***	yes***	yes***	yes***	yes***	yes***
Observations	11,947	11,728	5,558	11,947	11,728	5,558
R^2	.072	.074	.105	.022	.023	.028
ρ				.137***	.136***	.150***
				(.009)	(.009)	(.013)

Note.—Heteroskedasticity-consistent standard errors are in parentheses (White 1980).
* α = .10 for two-tail t-tests.
** α = .05 for two-tail t-tests.
*** α = .01 for two-tail t-tests.

TABLE 6

OLS AND FIXED-EFFECTS RESULTS FOR THE NOMINAL FRANCHISE FEE

	OLS			FIXED EFFECTS		
INDEPENDENT VARIABLE	(1)	(2)	(3)	(4)	(5)	(6)
Outlets (100s)	.435***	.338***	.155	−.009	.032	−.512
	(.116)	(.120)	(.176)	(.261)	(.262)	(.362)
$(\text{Outlets})^2$ (100s)	−.007***	−.006***	−.004	−.002	−.003	.005
	(.002)	(.002)	(.003)	(.004)	(.004)	(.006)
Years franchising	.045	.042	.262**	−.292	−.259	1.04
	(.068)	(.067)	(.104)	(.729)	(.733)	(.938)
$(\text{Years franchising})^2$	−.003**	−.003***	−.006***	−.001	−.005	−.008
	(.001)	(.001)	(.002)	(.004)	(.004)	(.007)
Financing provided		2.13**	2.81***		−1.64***	−2.89***
		(.838)	(.924)		(.623)	(.941)
Capital required		.003***	.005***		.0001	.003
		(.001)	(.002)		(.0004)	(.002)
Number of states			−.027			−.034
			(.042)			(.073)
Canadian franchisor			−5.41***			
			(1.74)			
Canadian × states			1.25***			.793**
			(.229)			(.327)
Training provided			.147***			.008
			(.029)			(.055)
Constant	25.86***	24.91***	20.97***			
	(1.31)	(1.33)	(1.44)			
Sector dummies	yes***	yes***	yes***	na	na	na
Time dummies	yes***	yes***	yes***	yes**	yes*	yes**
Observations	11,947	11,728	5,558	11,947	11,728	5,558
R^2	.051	.051	.084	.046	.040	.033
ρ				.192***	.171***	−.104***
				(.009)	(.009)	(.013)

NOTE.—Heteroskedasticity-consistent standard errors are in parentheses (White 1980).
* $\alpha = .10$ for two-tail t-tests.
** $\alpha = .05$ for two-tail t-tests.
*** $\alpha = .01$ for two-tail t-tests.

the introduction of firm-specific fixed effects, relative to OLS with sectoral dummy variables, in these regressions.[7] Furthermore, in the OLS models shown in tables 5 and 6, both the royalty rate and franchise fee rise at a decreasing rate with the number of outlets; in the fixed-effects models, they do not.[8] Apparently, the unobserved fixed effects are positively correlated with outlets, implying that larger chains set higher royalty rates and franchise fees, but there is little increase in these fees with outlet growth within firms. For years franchising, the coefficients also decline markedly in the franchise fee equation. As for royalty rates, a positive coefficient on the quadratic term arises in fixed effects. In fact, under fixed effects, the four experience and outlet effects are jointly significantly different from zero in the royalty rate regression ($F(4, 11{,}930) = 8.6$), but not in the franchise fee regression ($F(4, 11{,}930) = .19$). However, the four experience variables jointly contribute only .003 to the R^2, and the magnitude of the effects in the royalty regression is very small. In particular, despite the significant positive coefficient on squared years franchising, the total effect of years franchising is negative over all the relevant range of our data (up to 43 years). And even at its peak effect (at 21 years), this variable reduces the royalty rate by only 0.9.

Finally, we note that most of the franchising control variables we introduce in our regressions, which include both sectoral and year dummies[9] and several other variables likely to affect contract terms according to theory, account for some of the differences in contract

[7] Compare cols. 1 and 4 of tables 5 and 6. The F-tests are $F(3{,}624, 8{,}307) = 14.39$ and $F(3{,}624, 8{,}307) = 9.81$ for royalty rates and franchise fees, respectively. The fixed-effects results in tables 5 and 6 are all corrected for within-firm serial correlation since the errors were found to be serially correlated. We constrain ρ to be the same across all firms. There is no serial correlation correction in the OLS regressions in tables 5 and 6 because the estimated ρ would approach "one" and approximate fixed-effects estimation.

[8] Similar large reductions in parameters in moving from cross-sectional to within-firm estimation have been found also in the estimation of production functions (see the review by Griliches and Mairesse [1998]). There are two main explanations for this: (1) The errors in the measurement of the independent variable are greatly exaggerated by the fixed-effects transformation, so the noise to signal ratio becomes very large in fixed effects, leading to very imprecise estimated coefficients. Under this explanation, OLS results are closer to the true coefficients. (2) There are significant firm-specific effects in the data that are correlated with other regressors, such that the OLS coefficients are biased. In this case, the within-firm estimates are closer to the truth. The quality of our data, combined with the descriptive evidence in Sec. III on the lack of within-firm experience effects, leads us to favor the second explanation. (See the Appendix, paragraph 4, for details.)

[9] There is a clear time trend in these data: when time is added to col. 1 of tables 5 and 6, respectively, the coefficients are 0.07 and 0.85, with standard errors of 0.01 and 0.09. But we use time dummies in the remainder of the paper since they are more flexible.

terms across firms in columns 2 and 3 (see App. table A1 for detailed variable definitions). But few of these variables play a significant role in fixed-effects regressions (cols. 5 and 6). In light of the hypotheses pertaining to many of these control variables, however, the fixed effects may be overcontrolling.[10]

In sum, the effects of years franchising and outlets are not important in fixed-effects models of contract terms. As these experience variables also explain very little of the variance in the data, we conclude, consistent with our evidence in Section III, that the maturity of the firm—expressed in terms of either the size of the chain or years of franchising experience—is not a major determinant of the change in contract terms within firms over time. This lack of maturity effect again is inconsistent with predictions from theories that rely on signaling arguments, market saturation effects à la Rubin, or franchisor reputation effects à la Mathewson and Winter.

B. The Relationship between Royalty Rates and Franchise Fees

As noted earlier, most models of franchise contracting imply a recursive model for the contract terms in which the royalty rate is chosen first, as a function of incentive and risk issues, and the franchise fee comes second to extract rents left downstream by the royalty rate. Thus the franchise fee is expected to be inversely related to the royalty rate. Alternatively, franchise contracts may be characterized as a set of complementary clauses offered all at once, on a take-it-or-leave-it basis usually, to the franchisee. This implies a simultaneous system, and the regressions presented thus far are all reduced-form equations.

Under either scenario, we need to explore how the two fees are related in the data. Table 7 shows regression coefficients for royalty rates on franchise fees, and vice versa. We also present results obtained when we instrument the "other fee." Unfortunately, when it comes to instrumenting, we do not have good variables to identify separately what causes royalty rates and franchise fees to change. One approach, which we rely on in table 7, is to use own lagged values (along with current and lagged experience and outlets). This approach unfortunately relies on the assumption that the current fee and its lag are not simultaneously determined, a fairly poor as-

[10] The addition of control variables in col. 6 of table 5 produces a reduced sample in which the linear years franchising term has a significant negative effect, but we have verified that this effect is due to the specific odd sample, not to the addition of the control variables.

TABLE 7

RELATIONSHIP BETWEEN ROYALTY RATES AND FRANCHISE FEES

	ROYALTY RATE				FRANCHISE FEE			
	OLS		Fixed Effects		OLS		Fixed Effects	
INDEPENDENT VARIABLE	(1)	(2)	(3)	(4)	(5)	(6)	(7)	(8)
Outlets (100s)	.093***	.101***	.033	.035	.478***	.527***	.066	−.023
	(.015)	(.016)	(.020)	(.021)	(.108)	(.124)	(.256)	(.285)
$(Outlets)^2$ (100s)	−.001***	−.001***	−.001*	−.001*	−.008***	−.008***	−.003	−.002
	(.000)	(.000)	(.000)	(.000)	(.002)	(.002)	(.004)	(.004)
Years franchising	.006	.011	−.086	−.198***	.045	.072	−.474	.301
	(.008)	(.010)	(.060)	(.064)	(.072)	(.102)	(.721)	(.702)
$(Years\ franchising)^2$	−.001***	−.001***	.002***	.002***	−.004***	−.005***	.003	.002
	(.000)	(.000)	(.000)	(.000)	(.001)	(.002)	(.004)	(.005)
Franchise fee	−.010***		−.014***					
	(.001)		(.001)					
Instrumented franchise fee		−.008***		−.007***				
		(.002)		(.001)				
Royalty rate					−1.12***		−2.25***	
					(.132)		(.118)	
Instrumented royalty						−1.12***		−.813***
						(.194)		(.151)
Constant	6.78***	6.81***			33.99***	33.88***		
	(.120)	(.143)			(1.61)	(2.19)		
Observations	11,947	7,714	11,947	7,714	11,947	7,714	11,947	7,714
R^2	.025	.021	.051	.036	.021	.015	.074	.145
ρ			.127***	.120***			.182***	.334***
			(.009)	(.011)			(.009)	(.010)

NOTE.—Heteroskedasticity-consistent standard errors are in parentheses (White 1980). Time dummies are included in all regressions.
* α = .10 for two-tail *t*-tests.
** α = .05 for two-tail *t*-tests.
*** α = .01 for two-tail *t*-tests.

sumption given the strong serial correlation found earlier. An alternative approach is to use as instruments variables measuring expected unit sales (such as the number of employees, sectoral dummies, and contract duration). However, given our limited data on these variables (see the Appendix, paragraph 5) and the fact that they change very rarely within firms, these instruments performed poorly in our fixed-effects regressions.

In tables 5 and 6, the correlation coefficients between the error terms of corresponding regressions of royalty rates and franchise fees are all around −.1. Consistent with this, in all the regressions in table 7, across and within firms and whether we instrument or not, there is a clear negative relationship between the fees. However, it is also true that the coefficients on other explanatory variables are unaffected by the introduction of the other fee, instrumented or not, among the regressors. Thus simultaneity bias is not really an issue in our data.[11]

In addition, in Section III, we showed that the negative correlations between the two contract terms arise entirely from the inclusion, in what we call the franchise fee, of ongoing fixed payments. This is also true for our regressions. When we exclude from our data the 700 observations with ongoing fixed payments (or the firms with such observations), the correlations between the residuals of the franchise fee and royalty rate regressions become positive, though small (around .04). Furthermore, if we separate the instrumented fixed fee in column 4 of table 7 into two parts, namely instrumented up-front and instrumented ongoing fixed payments, we get a positive but insignificant effect for the up-front fee ($\beta = 0.005$, standard error 0.003) and a very significant and large negative effect for ongoing payments ($\beta = -0.009$, standard error 0.001). Finally, among the set of firms that use ongoing fixed payments, a regression of ongoing fixed payments on royalty rates yields a very significant coefficient on royalty rates of −6.75 (standard error 1.12). This implies that, when one starts from these firms' mean royalty rate (3.73) and mean discounted ongoing fixed payments ($53,000), a one-standard-deviation increase in royalty rate, which here amounts to a 100 percent increase, leads to a $50,000, or a nearly 100 percent, decrease in ongoing fixed payments.

Consistent with what we saw in Section III, we conclude that ongoing fixed payments are a very close substitute for royalties; in fact,

[11] This is true with one exception, which is the case in which we introduce the franchise fee in the royalty rate regression. Here, *if* the fee is instrumented, its inclusion affects the relationship between royalty rates and franchising experience (table 7, col. 4). We believe that this result is spurious since it is sensitive to instrumentation.

firms exchange them almost exactly one for one. This is not completely surprising given how franchisors think about such payments: they arise in the data because some franchisors decide to charge their franchisees a fixed monthly or weekly fee *instead of* charging sales-based royalties or advertising fees. However, given that the vast majority of franchisors (92 percent of the firms in our sample) use only up-front franchise fees, what is more surprising is the lack of a negative relationship, *within firms*, between the royalty rate and *up-front* fixed fees.[12]

Why do we find no negative relationship between royalty rates and the type of up-front fixed fees most firms use when the theories all suggest a strong negative link between the two? One possibility would be that other terms of the contract, such as contract duration, exclusive territories, and input purchase requirements, affect the fees and thereby obscure the cross-sectional patterns. But to the extent that these other terms remain fairly constant over time, they cannot explain the zero correlation between changes in royalty rates and changes in up-front fees within firms. More likely, contract terms are simply not set in a way that systematically extracts all downstream rents in all chains.[13] In particular, franchisors may set their up-front franchise fee mostly to cover the costs they incur in setting up a new franchisee, not to recover future rent. We noted in Section II that the up-front fee averages about 8 percent of the expected value of payments by franchisees to franchisors, so it is really quite small. And in his franchisor directory, Bond (1998) notes that "this amount is considered a franchise fee and is a non-recurring expense to reimburse the franchisor for his costs in locating, selecting, qualifying and training new franchisees. . . . Keep in mind that the franchise fee is usually considered a break-even proposition as far as the franchisor is concerned" (p. 21). In this case, the franchise fee would relate to the amount of services rendered by franchisors up front, not to the royalty rate (see also Dnes [1992], Lafontaine [1992*a*], and Sen [1993] on this).

Having established that the weak negative correlation between our notion of franchise fee and royalties arises from those cases of ongoing fixed payments and having found that this weak relationship does not give rise to simultaneity problems in interpreting experi-

[12] Others have found no correlation across firms between the fees even when including ongoing fixed payments in their notion of franchise fees (Dnes 1992; Lafontaine 1992*a*, 1993; Gagné et al. 1998).

[13] See Kaufmann and Lafontaine (1994) for evidence that McDonald's leaves rents with its franchisees. They argue that these rents are a self-enforcement mechanism, similar to efficiency wages. See also Michael and Moore (1995) for evidence from other chains.

ence effects, in the remainder of this paper, we do not drop the 700 observations with ongoing fixed payments, nor change our definition of the franchise fee to exclude ongoing fixed payments, because we consider that our definition best represents the concept of fixed fee that theory relies on.

C. Robustness Issues

The tests for experience effects in tables 5 and 6 impose a quadratic functional form on the experience and outlets variables. Should this functional form be rejected in favor of a more flexible one? We explored this possibility at length and unequivocally rejected it. In the fixed-effects models, we introduced a large number of alternative splines in search of a function that would better fit the data and yet would provide evidence of experience or size effects. We found no such functional form. Moreover, using differences from the firm-specific mean, we used the nonparametric kernel density estimator with alternative bandwidths but still found no evidence of experience effects.

Rather than report these extensive results, we show in figure 4 the mean change in both royalty rates and franchise fees as a function of the years of experience of the franchisor. This figure confirms

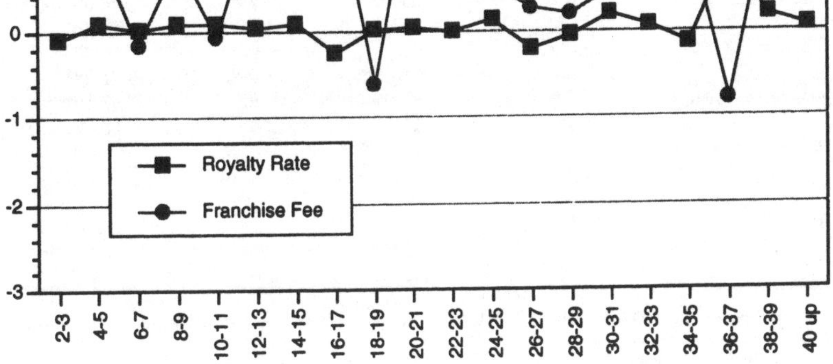

FIG. 4.—Mean changes in contract terms as a function of years in franchising

what we saw earlier in figures 1 and 2, namely, that there is *no systematic age pattern* in the changes in contract terms (though the franchise fee is, on average, adjusted upward to cover inflation).

We also considered the possibility that experience effects on contract terms would be different for important subsamples of the data, namely subsamples based on (1) the type of business the firm is involved in—automotive services, business aids and services, construction, and fast food; (2) the current number of outlets; and (3) the recent growth rate in the number of outlets (negative, zero, or ranges of positive growth). Across all these subsamples, we found no evidence of experience effects.

Two other subsamples are of special interest: franchisors that we observe being successful in franchising over several years and franchisors that will shortly stop franchising. We define the first set as the group of franchised chains for which we have 10 or more years of (not necessarily consecutive) data. This "balanced" subsample is of methodological interest in that it is useful to know how the use of a balanced panel data set might have affected the conclusions reached above. The second subsample, the out-of-business subsample, is the set of firms we know will stop franchising within the next three years (see the Appendix, paragraph 6).

The fixed-effects results from the balanced subsample (in table 8) are not different from those obtained using the whole sample,

TABLE 8

FIXED-EFFECTS SUBSAMPLE RESULTS

Independent Variable	Royalty Rate: Balanced Subsample	Royalty Rate: Out-of-Business Subsample	Franchise Fee: Balanced Subsample	Franchise Fee: Out-of-Business Subsample
Outlets (100s)	.007	−.34*	.29	3.00
	(.03)	(.18)	(.42)	(2.46)
$(\text{Outlets})^2$ (100s)	−.000	.03	−.005	−.35
	(.001)	(.02)	(.006)	(.28)
Years franchising	−.39*	.39**	−.82	−7.12***
	(.23)	(.15)	(2.84)	(2.28)
$(\text{Years franchising})^2$	.002**	.006***	−.005	.020
	(.001)	(.001)	(.008)	(.014)
Observations	2,498	2,785	2,498	2,785
R^2	.15	.04	.23	.10
ρ	.45***	−.15***	.55***	−.43***
	(.02)	(.02)	(.02)	(.02)

NOTE.—Heteroskedasticity-consistent standard errors are in parentheses (White 1980). Time dummies are included in all regressions.

* α = .10 for two-tail t-tests.

** α = .05 for two-tail t-tests.

*** α = .01 for two-tail t-tests.

confirming again the robustness of the results reported above.[14] But results for the firms that will shortly go out of business are different: they *decrease* their franchise fee and *increase* their royalty rate over time.[15] In other words, when they face a high probability of exit, firms reduce the up-front amount that franchisees must pay to get in (by about $7,000 per year) but load up more on the royalties (by 0.4 percent per year of experience). These are sizable changes given mean franchise fees of $23,300 and an average royalty rate of 6.4 percent in our data (see table 1). The reduction in the franchise fee in particular could be an effort to postpone or obviate failure by making the franchise more attractive to potential franchisees who are wealth constrained.[16] However, the sum of the changes can amount to an increase in the average "total" price of the franchise, since 0.4 percent of discounted future sales (estimated at $5,514,000 in 1992 dollars for the average franchise on the basis of Department of Commerce data) is $22,000, which is much greater than the $7,000 reduction in the franchise fee. This net increase in price goes counter to what one would expect a firm facing failure to do and may explain why firms in fact fail in the end.

Finally, our earlier description of the database highlighted a few different reasons why sample selection may be a problem in our data. Of the 3,625 franchisors that appear in our sample, more than 2,700 firms exit the sample before 1992. Of these, 1,674 have stopped franchising, so their departure is a normal part of the evolution of the population of franchisors. The remaining 1,000 or so firms simply are nonrespondents. We need to consider the effect this might have on our results.

We addressed the possibility of selection bias first by estimating OLS and fixed-effects regressions for two subsamples, namely, those firms that drop out of the sample and those that do not. We found no significant differences between these two sets of firms. Second, we used the standard Heckman (1979) selection correction methodology.[17] Though we have reasonable variables to predict selection,

[14] We do not include the instrumented "other fee" in these regressions since the subsamples are already small, and the need for lagged values in the instruments reduces them much further.

[15] Chow tests confirm that the coefficients for the out-of-business sample are significantly different from those of the full sample: $F(17, 2{,}768) = 19.02$ and $F(17, 2{,}768) = 38.12$ for the royalty rate and franchise fee.

[16] One regularly finds ads in the trade press for "low-cost" franchises, meaning those with low franchise fees and initial investment. Apparently, these franchises are desirable to at least some subset of potential franchisees.

[17] More specifically, we add the inverse Mills ratio—obtained from a regression of the sample selection rule on variables we expect affect the likelihood that franchisors respond to the *Entrepreneur* survey—to our fixed-effects regressions in tables 5 and 6. The variables we used to identify the change in the propensity to respond to the

the selection correction modified none of our conclusions. On the basis of these results and the fact that we reached the same conclusion with our overall sample as with our more balanced sample above, we conclude that our results are not sensitive to selection issues, and we do not pursue alternative semiparametric selection correction methods.

D. *The Importance and Stability of Firm-Specific Effects over Time*

In our analyses, we have shown that firm-specific effects play an important role in our data, that they are significant, and that their introduction in regressions changes the coefficients on other right-hand-side variables. In this subsection, we explore further their explanatory power and stability.

1. The Importance of Fixed Effects

The explanatory power of the firm effects in our data is surprisingly large. For the royalty rate regression (table 5, col. 4), we can calculate a pseudo R^2 that allows us to assess how much firm-specific effects add relative to OLS results for the same regression. The R^2 for the OLS only model is .014. When we add fixed effects, the pseudo R^2 is .864! Similarly, for the franchise fee, the R^2 rises from .038 for OLS to .870 following the introduction of fixed effects (table 6, col. 4). And this very sizable explanatory power of the firm-specific effects is not captured well at all by sectoral differences in contract terms: the increases in R^2 arising from sectoral dummies are only .056 for the royalty rate and .059 for the franchise fee.[18]

2. State Dependence or Firm Effects

The explanatory power of the firm effects described above could reflect one of two very different types of behavior on the part of firms, characterized by the distinction between "unobserved hetero-

survey are (1) an indicator of whether the franchise chain is seeking new franchisees—firms recruiting new franchisees should want to participate in the survey—and (2) the firm's ranking in the *Entrepreneur* survey—if a firm is given a low rank in its subsector in a given year, it is less likely to participate in the following year. (See App. table A1 and paragraph 7 for details.)

[18] An analysis of variance confirms the importance of the firm-specific effects. Across firms, the standard deviation of the royalty rate is 3.5 (relative to a mean rate of 6.4), and the standard deviation of the nominal franchise fee is $36,800 (relative to a mean of $23,300). In contrast, the average within-firm standard deviations are 0.74 and $5,600, respectively.

geneity" and "state dependence." The firm effect u_i included in equation (1) models unobserved heterogeneity: if there was only u_i on the right-hand side of (1) as our estimates suggest, then firms choose their contract terms when they begin franchising, and these contract terms remain constant over time. But this firm effect may instead be a proxy for state dependence. More specifically, assume that the *optimal* royalty rate of the firm is not fixed over time, but that the costs of adjusting the actual rate cause the observed rate to be relatively fixed over time. These adjustment costs would cause state dependence: the firm's current royalty rate strongly affects its future rate because it is costly to change R even if the desired R^* changes over time because of changes in X's. Patterns of either heterogeneity or state dependence imply that royalty rates are very persistent over time, but the theoretical source of the persistence varies considerably between the two.

Adjustment costs can hinder the process of changing franchise contract terms for many reasons. For example, many state legislatures require that franchisors file new disclosure documents on making "material changes" in the conditions of sales of their franchise (Kaufmann 1992), and such filings can be costly. Also, frequent changes in royalty rates over time lead to higher administrative costs: at any point in time, the franchisor must keep track of the contracts of each of its franchisees, which is harder when there are many different contracts. In a survey, franchisors have argued that these considerations prevent them from modifying their royalty rates frequently (Lafontaine 1992*b*).

Assume that the costs of adjusting the current royalty rate R_{it} to the desired R^*_{it} can be written as

$$C_{it} = a(R_{it} - R^*_{it})^2 + b(R_{it} - R_{i,t-1})^2. \qquad (2)$$

Costs C reflect both the costs to the franchisor of having the actual rate R diverge from the desired rate R^* (the first term in [2]) and the costs of changing the rate (the second term in [2]).[19] The optimal royalty rate minimizes costs C. Solving for this, we get

$$R_{it} - R_{i,t-1} = (1 - \delta)(R^*_{it} - R_{i,t-1}) + \mu_{it}, \qquad (3)$$

where $1 - \delta = a/(a + b)$, and μ_{it} is an optimization error. If the desired R^* is given by equation (1) above, after substituting and rearranging, we get

$$R_{it} = (1 - \delta)\beta X_{it} + \delta R_{i,t-1} + (1 - \delta)u_i + \eta_{it}, \qquad (4)$$

[19] A more general version of this cost function would include a constant and linear terms. However, this would not affect the econometric model, and so we present the simpler formulation.

where $\eta_{it} = (1 - \delta)\epsilon_{it} + \mu_{it}$. Thus (4) contains a lagged dependent variable whose coefficient is the rate of adjustment of the actual to the desired royalty rate. The relationship between this model and the fixed-effects version is that (4) reduces to the fixed-effects model when the royalty rate is adjusted immediately (when $\delta = 0$).

The fixed-effects regression results with a lagged dependent variable (and the constant term, time dummy variables, and other control variables omitted from eq. [1]) are shown in table 9. Consistent coefficient estimates are obtained here by first-differencing the equation to eliminate the fixed effect and then instrument-

TABLE 9

LAGGED DEPENDENT VARIABLE RESULTS

	Royalty Rate		Franchise Fee	
Independent Variable	(1)	(2)	(3)	(4)
Lagged dependent variable	.633***	.616***	.533***	.433***
	(.078)	(.126)	(.134)	(.094)
Outlets (100s)	.037	.006	−.171	−.521
	(.171)	(.223)	(1.40)	(1.47)
$(\text{Outlets})^2$ (100s)	.000	.001	.001	.006
	(.002)	(.003)	(.019)	(1.021)
$(\text{Years franchising})^2$	.004	−.004	.032	.015
	(.004)	(.006)	(.035)	(.039)
Instrumented franchise fee	−.058	−.047		
	(.064)	(.048)		
Instrumented royalty rate			−.229	−2.58
			(2.69)	(3.07)
Financing provided		.065		−2.66
		(.300)		(2.16)
Capital required		.000		−.001
		(.001)		(.005)
Number of states		−.074		−.064
		(.044)		(.219)
Canadian × states		−.079		3.27
		(.468)		(3.12)
Training provided		.029		.178
		(.021)		(.126)
Time dummies	yes***	yes***	yes***	yes***
Constant	−.073	−.014	−.394	−.184
	(.0956)	(.120)	(1.002)	(1.17)
Observations	5,172	2,387	5,172	2,387
R^2	.020	.009	.020	.003

NOTE.—In this table, we estimate eq. (4) using fixed-effects nonlinear simultaneous equations so that the coefficient on the lagged dependent variable is δ and the coefficients on the other variables are the constrained β. Heteroskedasticity-consistent standard errors are in parentheses (White 1980).

* $\alpha = .10$ for two-tail t-tests.

** $\alpha = .05$ for two-tail t-tests.

*** $\alpha = .01$ for two-tail t-tests.

ing the difference in the lagged dependent variable with a longer lag.[20]

Results imply that, *within firms, the lagged dependent variable has a significant effect* on the current values of royalty rates and franchise fees. The larger the coefficient on the lagged dependent variable, the greater the adjustment costs. The coefficients of about .6 on the lagged royalty rate and .5 on the lagged franchise fee suggest that adjustment costs are relatively high. Looking at the coefficients on the other regressors, we see few significant effects, except that the coefficients on the time dummies (not displayed) are jointly significant.

Finally, given that we found serial correlation in our fixed-effects regressions before a lagged dependent variable was introduced, we test the possibility that the significance of the lagged dependent variable is really reflecting only serial correlation in the residuals. We reject this hypothesis at the 10 percent level.[21] We conclude that while there is serial correlation in the data, the contract terms are also characterized by both heterogeneity and state dependence.

[20] The constructed error term from a regression with both fixed effects and a lagged dependent variable would be correlated with the lagged dependent variable, so that the coefficient on the lagged dependent variable would be biased downward. This bias, which is large when T is small (Hsiao 1986, pp. 74–75), arises because there is a correlation between the difference of the lagged dependent variable from its mean and the difference of the residual from its mean. Thus we instrument the lagged dependent variable with a longer lag. The serial correlation in our data makes our reliance on a longer lag somewhat questionable, but given our data limitations, this remains our best option. Though this is not shown in table 9, results obtained with an instrumented lagged dependent variable are between the OLS and the non-instrumented results, as one would expect given the direction of the biases just described.

[21] The model of serial correlation is $R_{it} = \beta X_{it} + u_i + \epsilon_{it}$, where $\epsilon_{it} = \rho\epsilon_{i,t-1} + e_{it}$. We can rewrite this as

$$R_{it} = \rho R_{i,t-1} + \beta X_{it} - \rho\beta X_{i,t-1} + (1-\rho)u_i + e_{it}$$

or

$$R_{it} = aR_{i,t-1} + bX_{it} - cX_{i,t-1} + (1-\rho)u_i + e_{it}.$$

Thus if $a \cdot b - c = 0$, the lagged effect of R is due to serial correlation, not to state dependence or adjustment costs. As is evident from this last equation, this test depends entirely on having good explanatory variables for R. The intuition is as follows: under state dependence, a change in X has a prolonged effect on R because it changes the optimal R^* in the short run and then alters future R's through the current R. In contrast, under serial correlation, changes in R will appear to be random, not explained by changes in X. If the econometrician does not have good explanatory variables, state dependence must be rejected in favor of serial correlation. We found weak evidence of state dependence, evidence that might be stronger if we had more powerful explanatory variables.

3. The Stability of the Firm Effects over Time

In this subsection, we address some final questions on the stability of firm effects over time. We consider two topics: the possibility of firm-specific growth rates in contract terms and the firm-specific patterns of change.

First, we posit that royalty rates are a function of firm-specific growth rates as well as firm-specific effects, that is,

$$R_{it} = \beta X_{it} + u_i + \gamma_i t + e_{it}, \tag{5}$$

where t is time and the γ_i's are firm-specific growth rates. To estimate (5), we begin by first-differencing the equation to eliminate the firm-specific effect,

$$R_{it} - R_{i,t-1} = \beta(X_{it} - X_{i,t-1}) + \gamma_i + (e_{it} - e_{i,t-1}), \tag{6}$$

and then estimate the regression by taking differences from the firm-specific mean growth to eliminate γ_i. The regression results we obtain show that royalty rates and franchise fees are characterized by firm-specific growth rates (γ_i) as well as fixed effects (u_i). The R^2 for the first-differenced royalty rate regression rises from .003 to .395 when firm-specific growth rates are introduced, and for the first-differenced franchise fee regressions, it goes from .003 to .383. If we limit our sample to those firms that made at least one change in the relevant fee (so we eliminate those with $\gamma_i = 0$), the contribution of the γ_i's to the R^2 is reduced to about half of what it is for the full sample (.15 and .20 for the royalty rate and fee regressions, respectively).

The significance of the firm-specific growth rates is somewhat surprising: such growth rates suggest that changes in a given fee within a firm should be mostly all positive or all negative. Yet the evidence in Section III showed that when firms change their royalty rates several times, the changes are rarely all in the same direction (see the discussion around table 4). To address this puzzle, we add $\phi(R_{i,t-1} - R_{i,t-2})$ to (6). We find that the estimated coefficient, $\hat{\phi}$, is very significantly negative: for the subsample of royalty rate changers, $\hat{\phi} = -.75$ with a standard error of 0.02. Also, again for changers, the R^2 rises from the .15 above to .38 with the addition of this variable. For the franchise fee regressions, the equivalent results are $\hat{\phi} = -.58$ (.02) and an increase in R^2 from .20 to .31. We interpret these results as evidence that there is a "reversion to the mean" in the data: an increase in R_{it} or F_{it} in the past is offset by a decline later on. Note that this result could be caused by measurement error in the dependent variable. To address this, we use differences from sectoral means instead of differences from two-period lags and find very significant reversion to the sectoral means (see Lafontaine and Shaw [1998*b*] for further discussion). Most likely, these "reversion to sectoral means" results reflect the fact that, because of competitive pressures in the franchisee recruiting process, most firms cannot really diverge from industry standards on contract terms for extended periods of time.

V. Conclusion

The primary goal of this research is to provide the first systematic evidence on how franchisors adjust the key monetary terms of their contracts, namely their royalty rates and franchise fees, as they gain franchising experience. In our empirical analyses, we find that they make very few adjustments, so that contract terms are very persistent. In our sample, 58 percent of the firms observed two consecutive years or more never change their royalty rate and 40 percent never change their franchise fee (see table 4). Further, 23 percent of the firms observed 10 years or more in the sample make no changes in their royalty rate over this period. When changes are made, they tend to be fairly large. However, there is no evidence in the data of systematic movement up or down in royalty rates as firms become more mature.

Overall, we find that firm-specific fixed effects explain a very large proportion of the variance in the data. By themselves, fixed effects account for about 85 percent of the variance in royalty rates and franchise fees, and only a small proportion of this firm-level heterogeneity is related to sectoral differences. We expect that these differences reflect unobserved differences in production and monitoring technologies available to the firms or quality differences in the product, the management, or the contract.

We also find evidence that OLS results currently in the literature suffer from omitted variable bias. In OLS, fees increase with the size of the chain. Our fixed-effects results, however, show no such pattern. It appears that more successful firms, or firms with better contracts, have a larger number of outlets and also charge higher fees. Thus, when firm quality is omitted from the OLS models, contract terms erroneously appear to grow with the number of outlets in the chain.

As a whole, our results are unsupportive of signaling models (Gallini and Lutz 1992), of arguments in which firms adjust their fees as they establish their reputation (Mathewson and Winter 1985), and of arguments in which franchisors adjust their fees when their market becomes saturated (Rubin 1978). Instead, our results are more supportive of models in which optimal contract terms remain relatively constant as a chain becomes more mature or grows (such as those of McAfee and Schwartz [1994] and Bhattacharyya and Lafontaine [1995]) or adjustment cost arguments for relatively constant contract terms. Consistent with prior cross-sectional results on this issue, our results also contradict one of the main data patterns suggested by theoretical models of franchising, namely that up-front franchise fees and royalty rates should be inversely related.

In conclusion, our work suggests that once franchisors set the terms of their contract, they change them very little over time. Thus from both empirical and theoretical perspectives, we need to better understand how firms actually set the monetary terms of their contracts when they begin franchising, and what specific factors might prevent them from changing their contract terms over time. Theoretical models that would systematically address the issues that arise when franchisors deal with multiple franchisees, and over long periods of time, might prove especially useful in explaining these data patterns. Similarly, we expect that work that embeds the choice of monetary contract terms in a richer contracting framework, allowing for a more detailed look at how various contract clauses interact with royalty rates and franchise fees, would provide useful guidance for future research in this area.[22]

Appendix

Sources of Data and Variable Definitions

Table A1 presents definitions of the variables used and their sources. Table A2 presents definitions of the sectors.

Other Information about the Data

1. In 1988, the Department of Commerce canceled the publication of *Franchising in the Economy*, the only source of census-type data on franchising in the United States. As a result, data on the extent and growth of franchising in the United States have been unavailable since.

2. When the advertising fee or royalty payments are given as a fixed amount per time period, they are discounted over the average 15 years of franchise contracts and added to the fixed franchise fee. In reality, fixed up-front fees and ongoing fixed payments are different in that liquidity constraints may limit up-front fees in ways that do not affect ongoing payments. In addition, the obligation to make ongoing payments disappears if the outlet goes out of business during the period of the contract. However,

[22] See, e.g., Athey and Stern (1998) for theoretical arguments, and Bercovitz (1997) and Brickley (1997) for some new work on franchise contracts along these lines.

TABLE A1

VARIABLE DEFINITIONS AND SOURCES

Variable	Definition	Source
Royalty rate	Total percentage of sales paid by franchisee to franchisor, including advertising fees. Observations in which this percentage was above 30 percent were excluded from our data set on the assumption that such rates must represent a proportion of profits rather than sales	E
Advertising fee	Usually a percentage of sales paid by franchisees to franchisors, a component of what we call the royalty rate. Sometimes a fixed ongoing payment	E
Franchise fee (nominal)	Fixed up-front payment made by the franchisee to the franchisor at the beginning of the franchise relationship	E
Franchise fee (real)	As above, but deflated using the consumer price index from the *Economic Report of the President*	E
Fixed payments	Ongoing fixed payments sometimes required by the franchisor in lieu of royalties or sales-based advertising fees. We discount these and add them to the up-front franchise fee to get what we call the franchise fee	E
Franchising experience	Number of years since the franchisor started franchising	E
Number of outlets	Total number of units in the chain	E
Percentage company-owned	Proportion of units in the chain that are company-owned and operated	E
Financing provided	A dummy variable set equal to one if the franchisor provides some amount of financing to the franchisee	E
Capital required	Amount of capital franchisors say is needed to open a unit in their chain	E
Canadian franchisor	Dummy variable set equal to one if the franchisor's headquarters' address is in Canada. This variable is also interacted with the number of states variable because the number of states in which a franchisor operates outlets is not an appropriate measure of geographical dispersion for Canadian firms	E
Rank	Rank of the franchisor within its subsector in the survey. Up to the 1988 survey, all firms were ranked by the magazine and listings were organized, within each subsector, on the basis of these rankings. Since 1988, the magazine ranks about half the firms and lists ranked firms first, by rank, within each subsector, followed by unranked firms in the subsector in alphabetical order	E
Seeking USA	Dummy variable equal to one if the franchisor indicates that it is seeking new franchisees in the United States	E
Seeking non-USA	Dummy variable equal to one if the franchisor indicates that it is seeking new franchisees in Canada or anywhere else outside the United States	E
Initial training provided	Number of days of initial training provided to the franchisee by the franchisor	S, F
Number of states with outlets	Number of states in which the franchisor has established outlets	S, F

SOURCE.—E refers to the *Entrepreneur* surveys, various years; S refers to the *Sourcebook of Franchise Opportunities*; and F refers to the *Franchise Opportunities Handbook*. Data found in the latter two sources were obtained from the *Franchise Opportunities Handbook* for the years 1980–87 and 1990 and in the *Source Book of Franchised Opportunities* for 1988, 1989, 1991, and 1992. Unfortunately, the latter sources do not match the samples in the *Entrepreneur* surveys. These sources typically provided data for about half the franchisors included in the *Entrepreneur* survey of the corresponding year.

TABLE A2

SECTOR DEFINITIONS AND NUMBER OF OBSERVATIONS

Department of Commerce Sector	Number of Observations	Number of Franchisors
Automotive products and services	935	270
Business aids and services:		
Accounting, credit, collection agencies, and general business systems	157	44
Employment services	446	122
Printing and copying services	245	44
Tax preparation services	30	12
Real estate	81	34
Miscellaneous business services	717	260
Construction, home improvement, maintenance, and cleaning services	1,192	357
Convenience stores	108	25
Educational products and services	408	140
Restaurants:		
Chicken	206	59
Hamburgers, franks, roast beef, etc.	301	89
Pizza	579	142
Mexican	223	54
Seafood	83	24
Pancakes, waffles	48	12
Steak, full menu	673	204
Sandwich and other	731	229
Hotels, motels, and campgrounds	205	52
Laundry and drycleaning services	79	27
Recreation, entertainment, and travel	219	82
Rental services (auto, truck)	138	36
Rental services (equipment)	124	50
Retailing (nonfood)	1,798	578
Retailing (food other than convenience stores)	998	284
Miscellaneous	1,223	395
Total	11,947	3,625

ongoing fixed payments are very uncommon (arising in only 700 of our 11,947 observations), and outlet failure rates are also low according to Kostecka (1988). Hence, we decided to disregard these differences. We used a discount rate of 3 percent. Given the very small number of cases in which ongoing fixed payments occur, results are not sensitive to the choice of discount rate. Finally, franchise fees of Canadian franchisors were transformed to U.S. dollars using then-current exchange rates.

3. From our original 14,200 observations, we first eliminated 399 observations because the firms levied no royalties, franchise fees, or advertising fees, so they did not fit the definition of business format franchisors. Another 116 observations were lost because of data inconsistencies that we could not resolve even using other sources of data on individual franchisors. Another 54 observations were excluded from our sample because the royalty rate was above our cutoff value of 30 percent. We imposed this upper limit on royalty rates because we gathered that figures above this cutoff

were cases in which royalties were stated as a percentage of profits rather than sales. We chose 30 percent because we know of firms that ask for 30 percent of sales from franchisees. Finally, we lost another 1,684 observations because of missing data on royalty rates, franchise fees, advertising rates, outlets, or franchise fees. In the majority of cases, 1,336 out of 1,684, the missing data pertained to royalty rates or advertising fees. These observations include cases in which the rates were simply not available in the published data, the company responded "varies" (478 cases for royalty rates, 191 for advertising fees, and 303 for both of these fees), or, even less frequent, the fees were a dollar amount per unit of output (105 for royalties, 13 for advertising fee, and 26 for both). Our final sample of 11,947 observations represents 3,625 franchisors.

In some cases, franchisors gave a range of franchise fees or royalty rates. We used the average value in these cases under the assumption that the average fee is close to what the average outlet in the chain pays. Our results were unaffected when we limited ourselves to samples of firms that did not report any range in their fees.

4. Our data on contract terms and on our main explanatory variables are quite accurate. We used the panel nature of the data to check for consistency across years in all variables. Large discrepancies were then investigated using information from other franchisor directories. Furthermore, for the two independent variables we focus on in this paper, namely the years of franchising experience and the number of outlets in the chain, we were able to do even better. The reported datum for years of experience was the year in which the firm started franchising. Thus we had t different observations for this variable for each firm, and we reconciled them using other data sources when discrepancies arose. Similarly, because each survey contains data on outlets (company-owned and franchised) for the current and two previous years, we were able to check the consistency of data on the size of the chain very thoroughly.

5. Robert Bond's *Source Book of Franchised Opportunities* (Irwin, various editions) gives information on the average number of employees per outlet, the length of the franchise contract, whether or not the franchisee must buy some of its inputs from the franchisor, whether or not passive ownership is allowed by the franchisor, and the square footage of the average outlet. We used these data in some of our work to establish the role that these variables might play in the setting of contract terms. We found very little empirical support for including them in our analyses, and as they were not available for all firms or across many years, their use reduced our sample size too much. As a result, we do not really discuss these data in the body of the paper.

6. The information on the year in which the firm exits franchising was obtained by searching the most extensive franchisor directory (Dixon's *Franchise Annual*) for all years in which the firm did not appear in our sample after an initial appearance. If the firm was found in this directory for any given year, it was considered still franchising, and we concluded that it was a nonrespondent. If the firm was not in our sample or in this other directory, it was considered to have stopped franchising or have gone out

of business in the year in which we no longer could find it in either source. Shane (1996) used a similar procedure to track a small subsample of firms. He then contacted the founders of the companies and found that this procedure was a very accurate way to measure exit. Note that the issue of firms merging or being bought by others is not as big a problem in these data as it is in many other longitudinal firm-level data. The reason is that the unit of observation, the franchised chain, most often does not disappear as a result of a merger, because a large part of what buyers of franchised chains purchase is the right to the trade name and franchise contracts. As a result, the franchised chain continues to operate under its own name and contracts. Consequently, it remains a separate potential observation in our data despite having merged with, or being bought out by, another firm.

7. For the selection equation, we use the seeking non-USA dummy variable described in table A1 (seeking USA is almost constant at one). We also use the rank variable, which corresponds to the order in which the firm appears in the survey. The magazine ranks firms using a particular formula (which combines information on firm growth, size, and other characteristics of the franchised chains included in the survey) and, in each subsector, reports data first for the highest-ranking firm, then the second, and so forth. Up to and including the January 1987 survey, all firms were ranked this way. Since then, some subset of firms providing less information are no longer ranked. In each subsector, these firms now appear in alphabetical order below all the ranked firms, giving them all less "standing."

References

Athey, Susan C., and Stern, Scott. "An Empirical Framework for Testing Theories about Complementarity in Organizational Design." Working Paper no. 6600. Cambridge, Mass.: NBER, June 1998.

Berkovitz, J. E. L. "Franchising vs. Company Ownership." Manuscript. Durham, N.C.: Duke Univ., Fuqua School Bus., 1997.

Bhattacharyya, Sugato, and Lafontaine, Francine. "Double-Sided Moral Hazard and the Nature of Share Contracts." *Rand J. Econ.* 26 (Winter 1995): 761–81.

Blair, Roger D., and Kaserman, David L. "Optimal Franchising." *Southern Econ. J.* 49 (October 1982): 494–505.

Bond, Robert E. *Bond's Franchise Guide, 1998.* 11th ed. Oakland, Calif.: Source Book Pubs., 1998.

Brickley, James A. "Incentive Conflicts and Contracting: Evidence from Franchising." Manuscript. Rochester, N.Y.: Univ. Rochester, Simon Grad. School Bus., 1997.

Brickley, James A., and Dark, Frederick H. "The Choice of Organizational Form: The Case of Franchising." *J. Financial Econ.* 18 (June 1987): 401–20.

Caves, Richard E., and Murphy, William F., II. "Franchising: Firms, Markets, and Intangible Assets." *Southern Econ. J.* 42 (April 1976): 572–86.

Cheung, Steven N. S. *The Theory of Share Tenancy, with Special Application to Asian Agriculture and the First Phase of Taiwan Land Reform.* Chicago: Univ. Chicago Press, 1969.

Dant, Rajiv P.; Kaufmann, Patrick J.; and Paswan, Audhesh K. "Ownership Redirection in Franchised Channels." *J. Public Policy and Marketing* 11 (Spring 1992): 33–44.
Dixon, Edward L., ed. *The Franchise Annual.* St. Catharines, Ont.: Info Press, 1986–93.
Dnes, Antony W. *Franchising: A Case-Study Approach.* Aldershot, U.K.: Avebury, 1992.
———. "The Economic Analysis of Franchise Contracts—Survey Article." *J. Inst. and Theoretical Econ.* 152 (June 1996): 297–324.
Gagné, Robert; Sigué, Simon Pierre; and Zaccour, Georges. "Droit d'entree et taux de redevance dans les franchises d'exploitation au Quebec." *L'Actualité Economique* 74 (December 1998): 651–68.
Gallini, Nancy T., and Lutz, Nancy A. "Dual Distribution and Royalty Fees in Franchising." *J. Law, Econ., and Organization* 8 (October 1992): 471–501.
Griliches, Zvi, and Mairesse, Jacques. "Production Functions: The Search for Identification." In *Practicing Econometrics: Essays in Methods and Applications,* by Zvi Griliches. Cheltenham, U.K.: Elgar, 1998.
Hallagan, William S. "Self-Selection by Contractual Choice and the Theory of Sharecropping." *Bell J. Econ.* 9 (Autumn 1978): 344–54.
Heckman, James J. "Sample Selection Bias as a Specification Error." *Econometrica* 47 (January 1979): 153–61.
Hsiao, Cheng. *Analysis of Panel Data.* Cambridge: Cambridge Univ. Press, 1986.
Hunt, Shelby, and Nevin, John. "Tying Agreements in Franchising." *J. Marketing* 39 (1975): 20–26.
Kaufmann, David J. "An Introduction to Franchising and Franchise Law." In *Franchising 1992, Business and Legal Issues.* Commercial Law and Practice Course Handbook series, no. 603. New York: Practising Law Inst., 1992.
Kaufmann, Patrick J., and Lafontaine, Francine. "Costs of Control: The Source of Economic Rents for McDonald's Franchisees." *J. Law and Econ.* 37 (October 1994): 417–53.
Klein, Benjamin, and Saft, Lester F. "The Law and Economics of Franchise Tying Contracts." *J. Law and Econ.* 28 (May 1985): 345–61.
Kostecka, Andrew. *Franchising in the Economy.* Washington: Dept. Commerce, 1988.
Lafontaine, Francine. "Agency Theory and Franchising: Some Empirical Results." *Rand J. Econ.* 23 (Summer 1992): 263–83. (*a*)
———. "How and Why Do Franchisors Do What They Do: A Survey Report." In *Franchising: Passport for Growth and World of Opportunity,* edited by Patrick J. Kaufmann. Sixth annual proceedings of the Society of Franchising. Omaha: Univ. Nebraska, Internat. Center Franchise Studies, 1992. (*b*)
———. "Contractual Arrangements as Signaling Devices: Evidence from Franchising." *J. Law, Econ., and Organization* 9 (October 1993): 256–89.
Lafontaine, Francine, and Shaw, Kathryn L. "Franchising Growth and Franchisor Entry and Exit in the U.S. Market: Myth and Reality." *J. Bus. Venturing* 13 (March 1998): 95–112. (*a*)
———. "Targeting Managerial Control: Evidence from Franchising." Manuscript. Ann Arbor: Univ. Michigan, Bus. School, 1998. (*b*)
Lafontaine, Francine, and Slade, Margaret E. "Retail Contracting: Theory and Practice." *J. Indus. Econ.* 45 (March 1997): 1–25.

———. "Incentive Contracting and the Franchise Decision." In *Advances in Business Applications of Game Theory*, edited by Kalyan Chatterjee and William Samuelson. Dordrecht: Kluwer Academic Press, 1999.

Lal, Rajiv. "Improving Channel Coordination through Franchising." *Marketing Sci.* 9 (Fall 1990): 299–318.

Lyons, Bruce R. "Empirical Relevance of Efficient Contract Theory: Interfirm Contracts." *Oxford Rev. Econ. Policy* 12 (Winter 1996): 27–52.

McAfee, R. Preston, and Schwartz, Marius. "Opportunism in Multilateral Vertical Contracting: Nondiscrimination, Exclusivity, and Uniformity." *A.E.R.* 84 (March 1994): 210–30.

Martin, Robert E. "Franchising and Risk Management." *A.E.R.* 78 (December 1988): 954–68.

Mathewson, G. Frank, and Winter, Ralph A. "The Economics of Franchise Contracts." *J. Law and Econ.* 28 (October 1985): 503–26.

Michael, Steven C., and Moore, Hollie J. "Returns to Franchising." *J. Corporate Finance* 2 (October 1995): 133–55.

Reid, Joseph D., Jr. "The Theory of Share Tenancy Revisited—Again." *J.P.E.* 85 (April 1977): 403–8.

Rubin, Paul H. "The Theory of the Firm and the Structure of the Franchise Contract." *J. Law and Econ.* 21 (April 1978): 223–33.

Scott, Frank A., Jr. "Franchising vs. Company Ownership as a Decision Variable of the Firm." *Rev. Indus. Organization* 10 (February 1995): 69–81.

Sen, Kabir C. "The Use of Initial Fees and Royalties in Business-Format Franchising." *Managerial and Decision Econ.* 14 (March/April 1993): 175–90.

Shane, Scott. "Hybrid Organizational Arrangements and Their Implications for Firm Growth and Survival: A Study of New Franchisors." *Acad. Management J.* 39 (February 1996): 216–34.

Stiglitz, Joseph E. "Incentives and Risk Sharing in Sharecropping." *Rev. Econ. Studies* 41 (April 1974): 219–55.

Udell, Gerald G. "The Franchise Contract." *Cornell Hotel and Restaurant Admin. Q.* 13 (August 1972): 13–21.

White, Halbert J. "A Heteroskedasticity-Consistent Covariance Matrix Estimator and a Direct Test for Heteroskedasticity." *Econometrica* 48 (May 1980): 817–38.

Wimmer, Bradley S., and Garen, John E. "Moral Hazard, Asset Specificity, Implicit Bonding, and Compensation: The Case of Franchising." *Econ. Inquiry* 35 (July 1997): 544–54.

[23]

Journal of Economic Perspectives—Volume 12, Number 4—Fall 1998—Pages 73–94

The Boundaries of the Firm Revisited

Bengt Holmström and John Roberts

Why do firms exist? What is their function, and what determines their scope? These remain the central questions in the economics of organization. They are also central questions for business executives and corporate strategists. The worldwide volume of corporate mergers and acquisitions exceeded $1.6 trillion in 1997. It is hard to imagine that so much time, effort and investment bankers' fees would be spent on adjusting firm boundaries unless there was some underlying economic gain. Indeed, the exceptional levels of merger and acquisition activity over the past two decades are a strong indication that economically significant forces do determine organizational boundaries.

The study of firm boundaries originated with the famous essay by Coase (1937), who raised the question of why we observe so much economic activity inside formal organizations if, as economists commonly argue, markets are such powerful and effective mechanisms for allocating scarce resources. Coase's answer was in terms of the costs of transacting in a world of imperfect information. When the transaction costs of market exchange are high, it may be less costly to coordinate production through a formal organization than through a market.

In large part thanks to the work of Williamson (1975, 1985), recent decades have seen a resurgence of interest in Coase's fundamental insight that firm boundaries can be explained by efficiency considerations. Our understanding of firm boundaries has been sharpened by identifying more precisely the nature and sources of transaction costs in different circumstances. In the process, the focus of

■ *Bengt Holmström is Paul A. Samuelson Professor of Economics, Massachusetts Institute of Technology, Cambridge, Massachusetts. John Roberts is Jonathan B. Lovelace Professor of Economics and Strategic Management, Graduate School of Business, Stanford University, Stanford, California.*

attention has shifted away from the coordination problems originally emphasized by Coase and towards the role of firm boundaries in providing incentives. In particular, the most influential work during the last two decades on why firms exist, and what determines their boundaries, has been centered on what has come to be known as the "hold-up problem."

The classic version of the hold-up story is told by Klein, Crawford and Alchian (1978); its essence is modeled in Grout (1984). One party must make an investment to transact with another. This investment is relation-specific; that is, its value is appreciably lower (perhaps zero) in any use other than supporting the transaction between the two parties.[1] Moreover, it is impossible to draw up a complete contract that covers all the possible issues that might arise in carrying out the transaction and could affect the sharing of the returns from the investment. The classic example, cited by Klein, Crawford and Alchian (1978), involves the dies used to shape steel into the specific forms needed for sections of the body of a particular car model (say, the hood or a quarter panel). These dies are expensive—they can cost tens of millions of dollars. Further, they are next-to-worthless if not used to make the part in question. Suppose the dies are paid for and owned by an outside part supplier. Then the supplier will be vulnerable to hold-up. Because any original contract is incomplete, situations are very likely to arise after the investment has been made that require the two parties to negotiate over the nature and terms of their future interactions. Such ex post bargaining[2] may allow the automobile manufacturer to take advantage of the fact that the dies cannot be used elsewhere to force a price reduction that grabs some of the returns to the investment that the supplier had hoped to enjoy. The supplier may then be unwilling to invest in the specific assets, or it may expend resources to protect itself against the threat of hold-up. In either case, inefficiency results: either the market does not bring about optimal investment, or resources are expended on socially wasteful defensive measures. Having the auto company own the dies solves the problem.

If the supply relationship faces more extensive hold-up problems, the best solution may be vertical integration, with all the parts of the body being procured internally rather than outside. The organization and governance structure of a firm are thus viewed as a mechanism for dealing with hold-up problems.

The next section of the paper will review the two strains of work that have dominated the research on the boundaries of the firm: transaction cost economics and property rights theory. Both theories, while quite different in their empirical implications, focus on the role of ownership in supporting relationship-specific

[1] Thus, once the investment has been sunk, it generates quasi-rents—amounts in excess of the return necessary to keep the invested assets in their current use. There could, but need not, be pure rents—returns in excess of those needed to cause the investment to be made in the first place.

[2] The terms ex ante and ex post–"before the fact" and "after the fact"—are widely used in this literature. In the hold-up story, the investment must be made ex ante, before a binding agreement is reached, while the renegotiation is ex post, after the investment. More generally, the literature refers to negotiations that occur after some irreversible act, including the establishing of the relationship, as ex post bargaining.

investments in a world of incomplete contracting and potential hold-ups. There is much to be learned from this work.

In this essay, however, we argue for taking a much broader view of the firm and the determination of its boundaries. Firms are complex mechanisms for coordinating and motivating individuals' activities. They have to deal with a much richer variety of problems than simply the provision of investment incentives and the resolution of hold-ups. Ownership patterns are not determined solely by the need to provide investment incentives, and incentives for investment are provided by a variety of means, of which ownership is but one. Thus, approaches that focus on one incentive problem that is solved by the use of a single instrument give much too limited a view of the nature of the firm, and one that is potentially misleading.

We support our position first by pointing to situations where relationship-specific investments appear quite high and contracting is incomplete, yet the patterns of ownership are hard to explain either with transaction cost theory or property rights models. The comparison of traditional procurement and subcontracting practices across the U.S. and Japanese automobile industries is the best and most detailed example of this sort that we discuss. Another set of examples illustrates settings in which hold-up problems seem to be small, and therefore boundary choices must be driven by other considerations. Our examples suggest that ownership patterns are responsive to, among other things, agency problems, concerns for common assets, difficulties in transferring knowledge, and the benefits of market monitoring. These suggestions are tentative, and we confess that they are mostly without a good theoretical foundation. They are offered in the hope of inspiring new theoretical research.

We emphasize that this paper is not a survey. We make no claim to having been complete in either our exposition or our citations. Indeed, we are aware of many excellent papers that bear on our arguments or that relate to our examples but that we could not cite because of space considerations. We hope those whose work we have slighted will understand and forgive.

Theoretical Background

Discussions of the hold-up problem and its implications for firm boundaries typically list a standard string of references—including Williamson (1975, 1985), Klein et al. (1978), Grossman and Hart (1986), and Hart and Moore (1990)—as if they were the building blocks in a single coherent theory of ownership. This is not the case. There are certainly points of similarity, particularly that contractual incompleteness necessitates ex post bargaining, causing potential problems for efficiency. But the detailed logic of the stories differs, resulting in quite different empirical predictions.[3] Our brief review of the transaction cost and property rights theories aims at highlighting these distinctions.

[3] Whinston (1997) takes a close look at the empirical distinctions of transaction cost theory and property rights theory.

Modern transaction cost economics originated with Williamson. His views have evolved somewhat over the years. His early work (Williamson, 1975) tended to emphasize ex post inefficiencies that arise in bilateral relationships—for example, when bargaining occurs under asymmetric information—rather than relationship-specific investments and hold-ups, while his later work has paid more attention to initial, specific investments (Williamson, 1979, 1985). But this shift in emphasis has not significantly affected the operational content of his theory, which remains premised on the idea that one can identify key dimensions of individual transactions such that, when described in terms of these dimensions, every transaction can be mapped into a most efficient institutional arrangement.

Williamson (1985) suggests that three transaction characteristics are critical: frequency, uncertainty, and most especially, asset specificity (as measured by the foregone economic benefits of discontinuing a relationship). Each characteristic is claimed to be positively related to the adoption of internal governance. The basic logic is that higher levels of uncertainty and higher degrees of asset specificity, particularly when they occur in combination, result in a more complex contracting environment and a greater need for adjustments to be made after the relationship has begun and commitments have been made. A hierarchical relationship, in which one party has formal control over both sides of the transaction, is presumed to have an easier time resolving potential disputes than does a market relationship. The frequency of a transaction matters because the more often it takes place, the more widely spread are the fixed costs of establishing a non-market governance system.

For the purpose of later comparison, we want to single out a few distinguishing features of Williamson's three-factor paradigm. First, it makes no reference to the direct costs of up-front, ex ante investments. For example, there is no differentiation between a case where a specialized asset costs \$10 million and one in which the asset costs \$100 million, provided that the assets in both cases are worth the same amount more inside the relationship than outside it. There need not even be any up-front expenditures at all: the original, ex ante "investment" could just be an initially costless choice of partner or standard or something similar that limits a party's later options. Williamson (1985) places particular weight on this last case, referring to "The Fundamental Transformation" that occurs when an exchange relationship moves from an ex ante competitive situation, with large numbers of potential trading partners, to an ex post, small-numbers one, once commitments have been made. The theory's indifference to the level of initial investments is consistent with the assumption that the carrying out of such investments is fully contractible (as might well be the case with the investment in automobile dies) and hence poses no incentive problems.

Second, in Williamson's approach the implicit measure of asset specificity is the *aggregate level* of quasi-rents created by the investment. With two parties, say a buyer B and a seller S, asset specificity and aggregate quasi-rents are measured as $V - V_B - V_S$, where V is the capitalized value of the jointly controlled assets in a continued relationship and V_B and V_S are the go-alone values of the individually controlled assets in case B and S separate. In this expression, only the sum $V_B + V_S$

rather than the individual values V_B and V_S matters. On this account, an asymmetric relationship with one party in a dominant position is no different from a symmetric one with the same level of aggregate asset specificity.

Third, taking the transaction as the unit of analysis runs into problems when one starts to consider the costs of bureaucracy and hierarchy more generally, because these costs quite clearly relate not to one single transaction, but to the whole collection of transactions that the hierarchy covers (Milgrom and Roberts, 1992, pp. 32–33).

Finally, Williamson treats market trade as a default that is assumed superior to within-organization trade unless levels of uncertainty, frequency and asset specificity are high enough to pull the transaction out of the market. Because the market is the default, its benefits are not spelled out as clearly as its costs. In transaction cost economics, the functioning market is as much a black box as is the firm in neoclassical microeconomic theory. An assortment of conditions have been adduced by Williamson and others to limit firm size—costs of bureaucracy, the weakening of individual incentives, the hazards of internal politicking, and so on—but none of these costs are easy to measure, and (perhaps for this reason) they have not played much of an empirical role.[4]

A major strength of the modern property rights approach, pioneered by Grossman and Hart (1986),[5] is that it spells out the costs and benefits of integration in a manner that does not rely on the presence of an impersonal market. The theory takes ownership of non-human assets as the defining characteristic of firms: a firm is exactly a set of assets under common ownership. If two different assets have the same owner, then we have a single, integrated firm; if they have different owners, then there are two firms and dealings between them are market transactions. Decisions about asset ownership—and hence firm boundaries—are important because control over assets gives the owner bargaining power when unforeseen or uncovered contingencies force parties to negotiate how their relationship should be continued. The owner of an asset can decide how it should be used and by whom, subject only to the constraints of the law and the obligations implied by specific contracts. Assets become bargaining levers that influence the terms of new agreements and hence the future payoffs from investing in the relationship. In contrast to transaction cost economics, the standard property rights models assume that *all* bargaining, including any that occurs after investments are made, is efficient. Thus, everything turns on how ownership affects initial investments, but unlike Klein et al. (1978), it is essential that these investments are non-contractible.[6]

[4] This is changing. Recently, for example, influence cost ideas (Milgrom and Roberts, 1988, 1990; Meyer, Milgrom and Roberts, 1992) have been used to explain observed inefficiencies in internal capital markets (Scharfstein, 1998; Shin and Stulz, 1998).

[5] Hart and Moore (1990) and many others have developed the property rights approach further. See Hart (1995). Recent additions include DeMeza and Lockwood (1998) and Rajan and Zingales (1998). Holmström (1996) offers a critical commentary.

[6] If the parties can contract on the investments, the assumption of efficient bargaining means that they will be made at the efficient levels, irrespective of ownership patterns.

To illustrate, in Hart and Moore (1990) each agent makes (non-contractible) investments in human capital that are complementary with a set of non-human assets. Each agent necessarily owns his or her own human capital. The ownership of the non-human assets, however, affects the incentives to invest in human capital. Once the investment is made, ex post bargaining determines the allocation of the returns from the investments. This bargaining is assumed to give each party—that is, the buyer B or the seller S—what it could have obtained on its own, V_B or V_S, plus a share of the surplus created by cooperation.

Specifically, payoffs to the parties take the form $P_i = V_i + \frac{1}{2}(V - V_i - V_j)$, $i,j = B,S$, where as before V is the capitalized value of cooperation. Ownership influences the separation payoffs V_B and V_S since the owner of a particular asset gets to deny the other party the use of it if cooperation is not achieved. Ownership does not influence V, since all assets are in use when the parties cooperate. Neither party's investment affects the other's separation payoff, because if they do not cooperate then neither has access to the other's human capital and the investment in it. Individual incentives to invest are driven by the derivatives of the payoff functions P_B and P_S. If $V \equiv V_B + V_S$ for all levels of investment, then individual returns to investments coincide exactly with the social returns, as measured by the derivatives of V. This case corresponds to a competitive market, because no extra value is created by the particular relationship between B and S; both parties would be equally well off if they traded with outsiders. In general, however, the social returns and the individual returns differ, resulting in inefficient investments. In particular, if the payoff functions are supermodular,[7] so that the payoff to incremental investment by one party is increasing in both the volume of non-human assets available to that party and the amount of the other party's investment, then there is under-investment. One can strengthen the incentives of one party by giving that party control over more assets, but only at the expense of weakening the incentives of the other party. There is a trade-off, because ownership shares cannot add up to more than 100 percent. This trade-off determines the efficient allocation of ownership.

Several conclusions follow from this model. For instance, as investment by the buyer B becomes more important (for generating surplus V) relative to investments by the seller S, B should be given more assets. B should be given those assets that make V_B most sensitive to B's investment. If an asset has no influence on B's investment it should be owned by S. For this reason, no outsider should ever own an asset—that would waste bargaining chips that are precious for incentive provision. For the same reason, joint ownership—meaning that both parties have the right to veto the use of the asset—is never optimal. As a consequence, assets that are worthless unless used together should never be separately owned.

[7] Supermodularity of a function means that an increase in one argument increases the incremental return from all the other arguments. With differentiable functions, the cross-partials are all non-negative. In the Hart-Moore model, supermodularity refers both to human capital and to assets, so that having more assets implies a higher marginal return to all investments. See Milgrom and Roberts (1994).

While these implications regarding joint ownership, outside ownership and co-ownership of perfectly complementary assets are often stressed, it is important to keep in mind that they are easy to overturn by slight changes in assumptions. For instance, joint ownership may be desirable when investments improve non-human assets. Third-party control can be desirable if parties would otherwise invest too much in improving their outside opportunities to strengthen their bargaining positions (Holmström and Tirole, 1991; Holmström and Milgrom, 1991, 1994; Rajan and Zingales, 1998). And most conclusions are sensitive to the particular bargaining solution being used (de Meza and Lockwood, 1998). What does survive all variations of the model is the central idea that asset ownership provides levers that influence bargaining outcomes and hence incentives.

In contrast to Williamson's three-factor framework, there is no uncertainty in this model. Frequency plays no role either (although it can be introduced with interesting results, as in Baker, Gibbons and Murphy, 1997, or Halonen, 1994). Most strikingly, the *level* of asset specificity has no influence on the allocation of ownership: the predictions of the model remain unchanged if one increases the total surplus V by adding an arbitrarily large constant to it, because investments are driven by marginal, not total, returns. This is problematic for empirical work, partly because margins are hard to observe when there are no prices and partly because some of the key margins relate to returns from hypothetical investments that in equilibrium are never made. Indeed, as Whinston (1997) has noted, the extensive empirical research geared to testing Williamson's three-factor framework casts no light on the modern property rights models.

As noted earlier, a virtue of the property rights approach is that it simultaneously addresses the benefits *and* the costs of ownership. Markets are identified with the right to bargain and, when necessary, to exit with the assets owned. This greatly clarifies the market's institutional role as well as its value in providing entrepreneurial incentives. On the other hand, firms are poorly defined in property rights models and it is not clear how one actually should interpret the identities of B and S. In an entrepreneurial interpretation, B and S are just single individuals, but this seems of little empirical relevance. If, on the other hand, firms consist of more than one individual, then one has to ask how one should interpret the unobserved investments (in human capital) that cannot be transferred. An even more fundamental question is why firms, as opposed to individuals, should own any assets. At present, the property rights models are so stylized that they cannot answer these questions.[8]

[8] Holmström and Milgrom (1994) and Holmström (1996) argue that the function of firms cannot be properly understood without considering additional incentive instruments that can serve as substitutes for outright ownership. Employees, for instance, typically own no assets, yet they often do work quite effectively. In these theories asset ownership gives access to many incentive instruments and the role of the firm is to coordinate the use of all of them. That may also explain why non-investing parties, including the firm itself, own assets.

Investment Incentives Are Not Provided by Ownership Alone

There is no doubt that hold-up problems are of central concern to business people. In negotiating joint venture agreements, venture capital contracts, or any of a number of other business deals, much time is spent on building in protections against hold-ups. At the same time, such contracts are *prima facie* evidence that hold-up problems do not get resolved solely by integration of buyer and seller into a single party—the firm. Indeed, there seems to be something of a trend today toward disintegration, outsourcing, contracting out, and dealing through the market rather than bringing everything under the umbrella of the organization. This trend has seen the emergence of alternative, often ingenious solutions to hold-up problems.

Japanese Subcontracting

The pattern of relations between Japanese manufacturing firms and their suppliers offers a prominent instance where the make-buy dichotomy and related theorizing have been less than satisfactory. Although the basic patterns apply in a number of industries (including, for example, electronics), the practices in the automobile industry are best documented (Asanuma, 1989, 1992). These patterns have spread from Japan to the auto industry in the United States and elsewhere, and from autos to many other areas of manufacturing. These practices feature long-term, close relations with a limited number of independent suppliers that seem to mix elements of market and hierarchy. Apparently, these long-term relations substitute for ownership in protecting specific assets.

Two points of contrast in the treatment of specific investments between traditional U.S. practice and the Japanese model present particular problems for the received theory. The first concerns investments in designing specialized parts and components. Traditional U.S. practice featured either internal procurement or arm's length, short-term contracting. Design-intensive products were very often procured internally (Monteverde and Teece, 1982).[9] When products were outsourced, the design was typically done by the automaker, with the drawings being provided to the suppliers. This pattern is what hold-up stories would predict, for the investment in design is highly specific and probably cannot be protected fully by contracts; thus, external suppliers will not make such relationship-specific investments, for fear that they will be held up by buyers after their investments are in place. In stark contrast, it is normal practice for Japanese auto firms to rely on their suppliers to do the actual design of the products supplied. The design costs are then to be recovered through the sale price of the part, with the understanding that this price will be adjusted in light of realized volumes.

A second contrast: traditional U.S. practice has been that physical assets specific

[9] However, this pattern did not become standard until decades after the founding of the industry. Earlier, something akin to the practices associated now with the Japanese was the norm. See Helper (1991).

to an automaker's needs are owned by the automaker. This clearly applies in the case of internally procured items, but it also holds in cases where the assets are used by the external supplier in its own factory. For example, the dies used in making a particular car part will belong to the automaker, even though they are used in the supplier's plant on the supplier's presses. Again, this accords well with the transaction cost story of potential hold-up by the automaker.[10] In Japan, in contrast, these specific investments are made by the supplier, who retains ownership of the dies. This would seem to present the automaker with temptations to appropriate the returns on these assets, once the supplier has made the relationship-specific investment. Moreover, because the Japanese auto manufacturers typically have a very small number of suppliers of any part, component or system, the supplier would also seem to be in a position to attempt opportunistic renegotiation by threatening to withhold supply for which there are few good, timely substitutes.

The Japanese pattern is directly at odds with transaction cost theory. Meanwhile, the divergence in ownership of the dies between the two countries presents problems for attempts to explain ownership allocation solely in terms of providing incentives for investment.[11]

In Japanese practice, explicit contracting is not used to overcome the incentive problems involved in outsourced design and ownership of specific assets. In fact, the contracts between the Japanese automakers and their suppliers are short and remarkably imprecise, essentially committing the parties only to work together to resolve difficulties as they emerge. Indeed, they do not even specify prices, which instead are renegotiated on a regular basis. From the hold-up perspective, the prospect of frequent renegotiations over the prices of parts that are not yet even designed would certainly seem problematic.

The key to making this system work is obviously the long-term, repeated nature of the interaction.[12] Although supply contracts are nominally year-by-year, the shared understanding is that the chosen supplier will have the business until the model is redesigned, which lasts typically four or five years. Moreover, the expectation is that the firms will continue to do business together indefinitely. There has been very little turnover of Japanese auto parts suppliers: over a recent eleven-year period, only three firms out of roughly 150 ceased to be members of *kyohokai*, the association of first-level Toyota suppliers (Asanuma, 1989).

The familiar logic of repeated games, that future rewards and punishments motivate current behavior, supports the on-going dealings.[13] An attempted hold-up

[10] An alternative story is more in the line of Williamson's earlier discussions emphasizing inefficiencies in ex post bargaining. The useful life of a die far exceeds the one-year contracting period. If the supplier owned the die, changing suppliers would require negotiating the sale of the die to the new supplier, and this could be costly and inefficient.

[11] Interestingly, Toyota followed U.S. practice in supplying the dies used by at least some of the suppliers to its Kentucky assembly plant (Milgrom and Roberts, 1993).

[12] Taylor and Wiggins (1997) argue that these long-term relations are also the means used in the Japanese system to solve moral hazard problems with respect to quality.

[13] Baker et al. (1997) present a formal analysis of the choice between external and internal procurement,

would presumably bring severe future penalties. As importantly, the amount of future business awarded to a supplier is linked to ratings of supplier performance. The auto companies carefully monitor supplier behavior—including cost reductions, quality levels and improvements, general cooperativeness, and so on—and frequent redesigns allow them to punish and reward performance on an on-going basis. In this sense, supplier relationships in Japan are potentially *less*, not more, locked in than in the traditional U.S. model, where at the corresponding point in the value chain, the supplier is typically an in-house division or department.

Having a small number of suppliers is crucial to the Japanese system. It reduces the costs of monitoring and increases the frequency of transacting, both of which strengthen the force of reputation. Also, the rents that are generated in the production process do not have to be shared too widely, providing the source for significant future rewards. This logic underlies the normal "two-supplier system" used at Toyota. There is more than one supplier to permit comparative performance evaluation, to allow shifting of business as a reward or punishment, to provide insurance against mishaps, and perhaps to limit the hold-up power of each supplier, but the number is not chosen to minimize hold-ups.

The relationship is marked by rich information sharing, including both schedules of production plans necessary for just-in-time inventory management and also details of technology, operations and costs. The automakers also assist the suppliers in improving productivity and lowering costs: technical support engineers are a major part of the automakers' purchasing staff, and they spend significant amounts of time at the suppliers' facilities. All this in turn means that potential information asymmetries are reduced, which presumably facilitates both performance evaluation and the pricing negotiations.[14]

Perhaps the major problem in the system may be that the automakers are inherently too powerful and thus face too great a temptation to misbehave opportunistically. Indeed, many Japanese observers of the system have interpreted it in terms of the automakers' exploitation of their power. One counterbalance to this power asymmetry is the supplier association, which facilitates communication among the suppliers and ensures that if the auto company exploits its power over one, all will know and its reputation will be damaged generally. This raises the cost of misbehavior. In this regard, the fact that Toyota itself organized an association of the leading suppliers for its Kentucky assembly plant is noteworthy (Milgrom and Roberts, 1993).

An alternative solution to this imbalance would be for the automaker to own

taking into account the important fact that long-term relational contracts can be maintained both within a firm as well as across firms.

[14] Strikingly, as automobile electronics have become more sophisticated and a greater part of the cost of a car, Toyota has ceased to rely exclusively on its former sole supplier, Denso, and has developed its own in-house capabilities in this area. Arguably, this was to overcome information asymmetries and their associated costs (Ahmadjian and Lincoln, 1997). In contrast, see the discussion of the effects of Ford's complete reliance on Lear for developing seats for the redesigned 1997 Taurus (Walton, 1997).

the dies, as in the United States. Here a property rights explanation may be useful: under this arrangement, the supplier would not have the same incentives to maintain the dies, since it must be very hard to contract over the amount of wear and tear and its prevention.[15]

Mini-mills, Exclusive Sourcing and Inside Contracting

Another significant shift in the organization of production is illustrated by Nucor, the most successful steel maker in the United States over the past 20 years. Nucor operates mini-mills, which use scrap (mainly car bodies) as raw material for steel production. After an initial technological breakthrough, Nucor started to expand aggressively (Ghemawat, 1995). The strategy required much capital, and to save on capital outlays, Nucor decided to outsource its entire procurement of steel scrap. Traditionally, mini-mills had integrated backwards, partly to secure an adequate supply of raw material and partly because sourcing entails substantial know-how and so was considered "strategically critical." Chaparral Steel, another big mini-mill operator, continues to be integrated backwards, for instance.

In a break with the tradition, Nucor decided to make a single firm, the David J. Joseph Company (DJJ), its sole supplier of scrap. Total dependence on a single supplier would seem to carry significant hold-up risks, but for more than a decade, this relationship has been working smoothly and successfully. Unlike in the Japanese subcontracting system, there are certain contractual supports. Prices are determined by a cost-plus formula to reflect market conditions, and an "evergreen" contract specifies that the parties have to give advance warning (about half a year in advance) if they intend to terminate the relationship. Even so, there is plenty of room for opportunism. Despite transparent cost accounting (essentially, open books), DJJ can misbehave, since realized costs need not be the same as potential costs. Asset specificity remains significant even with the six-month warning period, since a return to traditional sourcing and selling methods would be quite disruptive and expensive for both sides. Indeed, one reason why the partnership has been working so well may be the high degree of mutual dependence: Nucor's share of DJJ's scrap business is estimated to be over 50 percent.

The success of Nucor's organizational model has led other mini-mills to emulate and refine it. In England, Co Steel has gone as far as relying on its sole supplier to make ready-to-use "charges," the final assemblage of materials to go into the steel-making ovens. The production technology for charges is quite complicated: about 20–30 potential ingredients go into each mixture, with the mix depending on the desired properties of the final product, and big cost savings can be had by optimizing the use of the different inputs. This activity entails much know-how and requires extensive information exchange with the steel plant to match inputs with final product demand. The charges must be prepared by the supplier on Co Steel's premises, both for logistical reasons and to facilitate information sharing. In trans-

[15] See Segal and Whinston (1997) for a model in the property rights spirit that is relevant to these issues.

action cost economics, such a cheek-by-jowl situation would be an obvious candidate for integration. Yet, the industry is moving in the direction of disintegration in the belief that specialization will save on costs by eliminating duplicate assets, streamlining the supply chain, and providing better incentives for the supplier through improved accountability.

Related experiments of "inside contracting" include Volkswagen's new car manufacturing plant in Brazil, where the majority of the production workers in the factory are employees, not of Volkswagen, but of subcontractors that provide and install components and systems on the cars as they move along the line. It is too early to tell whether other firms will return to inside contracting, which used to be quite common in the United States up to World War I (Buttrick, 1952), and whether such a move will be successful. But evidently, even potentially large hold-up problems have not deterred recent experimentation.

Airline Alliances

Another illustration of close coordination without ownership is provided by airline alliances, which have proliferated in recent years. Coordinating flight schedules to take advantage of economies of scope requires the parties to resolve an intricate set of issues, particularly ones related to complex "yield management" decisions on how to allocate seats across different price categories and how to shift prices as the flight date approaches. Information and contracting problems abound, and it is hardly surprising that tensions occasionally surface. For instance, KLM and Northwest Airlines recently ran into a dispute that had to be resolved by dismantling their cross-ownership structure. But interestingly, this did not prevent KLM and Northwest from deepening their commitment to their North Atlantic alliance by agreeing to eliminate, over a period of years, all duplicate support operations in the United States and Europe. With the completion of this deal, KLM and Northwest have made themselves extraordinarily interdependent in one of the most profitable segments of their business. A 13-year exclusive contract, with an "evergreen" provision requiring a three-year warning before pull-out, is the main formal protection against various forms of opportunism, but undoubtedly the real safeguard comes from the sizable future rents that can be reaped by continued good behavior.

Why don't the two airlines instead integrate? Regulations limiting foreign ownership and potential government antitrust objections are a factor, as may be tax considerations. However, an explanation we have been given is that airline cultures (and labor unions) are very strong and merging them is extremely difficult. Pilot seniority is a particularly touchy issue.

Contractual Assets and Network Influence

In property rights theory, the boundaries of the firm are identified with the ownership of assets, but in the real world, control over assets is a more subtle matter. "Contractual assets" can often be created rather inexpensively to serve some of the same purposes that the theory normally assigns to ownership: to provide levers that give bargaining power and thereby enhance investment incentives. What we have in mind here are contracts that allocate decision rights much like ownership; for instance, exclusive dealing contracts such as Nucor's, or licensing agreements of various kinds. Such "governance contracts" are powerful vehicles for regulating market relationships. With increased disintegration, governance contracts seem to have become more nuanced and sophisticated. They place firms at the center of a network of relationships, rather than as owners of a clearly defined set of capital assets.

BSkyB, a satellite broadcasting system in Rupert Murdoch's media empire, is an example of a highly successful organization that has created its wealth, not by owning physical assets, but by crafting ingenious contracts that have given it influence over an effective network of media players. Satellite broadcasting requires a variety of highly complementary activities, including acquisition and development of programming, provision of the distribution system (satellites, transmitters and home receivers) and development of encryption devices (to limit reception to those who pay), all of which must be carried out before the service can be offered. Other similarly complex and innovative systems of complements, like electric lighting systems or early computer systems, were largely developed within a single firm. BSkyB instead relies on alliances with other firms. Topsy Tail is even more of a "virtual company." It employs three people, but has sales of personal appearance accessories (combs, hair clips and such) approaching $100 million. Topsy Tail conceives of new products, but essentially everything involved in developing, manufacturing and distributing them is handled through an extensive contractual network. Benetton and Nike, to take some bigger and more conventional firms, also extensively rely on outsourcing and a small asset base. The critical asset in these cases is of course control of the brand name, which gives enormous power to dictate how relationships among the various players are to be organized.

Microsoft and the web of inter-firm relations centered around it provide another illustration. The stock market values Microsoft at around $250 billion, which is more than $10 million per employee. Surely very little of this is attributable to its ownership of physical assets. Instead, by leveraging its control over software standards, using an extensive network of contracts and agreements that are informal as well as formal and that include firms from small start-ups to Intel, Sony and General Electric, Microsoft has gained enormous influence in the computer industry and beyond. We are not experts on Microsoft's huge network of relationships, but it seems clear that the traditional hold-up logic does poorly in explaining how the network has developed and what role it serves. If one were to measure asset specificity simply in terms of separation costs, the estimates for breaking up some of the relationships—say, separating Intel from Microsoft—would likely be large. Yet these potential losses do not seem to cause any moves in the direction of ownership integration.

A similar pattern can be observed in the biotechnology industry (Powell, 1996). As in the computer industry, the activities of the different parties are highly interrelated, with different firms playing specialized roles in the development and marketing of different products. Most firms are engaged in a large number of partnerships; for instance, in 1996 Genentech was reported to have 10 marketing partnerships, 20 licensing arrangements, and more than 15 formal research collaborations (Powell, p. 205). Significant relationship-specific investments are made by many parties, and potential conflicts must surely arise after these investments are in place. Yet the system works, thanks to creative contractual assets—patents and licensing arrangements being the oldest and most ingenious—but also to the force of reputation in a market that is rather transparent, because of the close professional relationships among the researchers.

Firm Boundaries are Responsive to More than Investment Incentives

The examples above make clear that there are many alternatives to integration when one tries to solve hold-up problems. The examples also suggest that ownership may be responsive to problems other than underinvestment in specific assets. Speaking broadly, the problems relate to contractual externalities of various kinds, of which hold-ups are just one.

Resolving Agency Problems

An example of how agency issues can affect the boundaries of an organization is whether a firm employs its sales force directly, or whether it uses outside sales agents. The best-known example here involves electronic parts companies, some of which hire their own sales agents while others sell through separate supply companies (Andersen, 1985; Andersen and Schmittlein, 1984). Originally, Andersen (1985) appears to have expected that the observed variation in this choice would relate to the degree of asset specificity; for example, the extent to which investment by sales people with knowledge about products was specific to a particular company. Instead, measurement costs and agency concerns turned out to be central. An employee sales force is used when individual performance is difficult to measure and when non-selling activities (like giving customer support or gathering information about customers' needs) are important to the firm; otherwise, outside companies are used.

Holmström and Milgrom (1991, 1994) rationalize this pattern with a model of multi-task agency, in which sales people carry out three tasks: making current sales, cultivating long-term customer satisfaction, and gathering and relaying information on customer needs. If the latter two activities are important and if the three activities compete for the agent's time, then the marginal rewards to improved performance on each must be comparable in strength; otherwise, the ill-paid activities will be slighted. Because performance in non-selling activities is arguably hard to measure, it may be best to provide balanced, necessarily lower-powered incentives for all three activities.

Offering weak incentives to an outside sales agent can be problematic, however, because the agent may then divert all effort to selling other firms' products that come with stronger rewards for sales. With an employee, this problem can be handled with a salary and a low commission rate, because the employee's outside activities are more easily constrained and promotion and other broader incentives can be used within the firm to influence the agent's behavior.[16] This logic also explains why outside agents commonly receive higher commission rates than does an inside sales force.

A less familiar illustration of how ownership responds to agency concerns comes from multi-unit retail businesses. Some of these businesses are predominantly organized though traditional franchise arrangements, in which a manufacturer contracts with another party to sell its products in a dedicated facility, as in gasoline retailing. Others, including fast-food restaurants, hotels and pest-control services, are organized in what is called "business concept" franchising. The franchiser provides a brand name and usually other services like advertising, formulae and recipes, managerial training and quality control inspections, collecting a fee from the franchisee in return, but the physical assets and production are owned and managed by the franchisee. Sometimes franchisers (like McDonald's) own and operate a number of outlets themselves. Finally, other businesses are commonly organized with a single company owning all the multiple outlets and hiring the outlet managers as employees. Examples are grocery supermarkets and department stores. What accounts for such differences?

It is hard to see how the specificity of the assets—real estate, cash registers, kitchens and inventories—differs between supermarkets and restaurants in such a way that transactions cost arguments would lead to the observed pattern. Indeed, the assets involved are often not very specific at all. Alternatively, applying the Hart-Moore property rights model here would involve identifying non-contractible investments that are unavailable to the other party if the franchise agreement is terminated or the store manager's employment should end. Noncontractible investments by the center in building the brand might qualify on the one hand, but in many cases it is hard to see what the investments of the operator might be. For example, a fast-food restaurant manager might invest in training the workers and building a clientele, but these investments would presumably still be effective even if the manager were replaced by another. Further, these should also be investments that vary across cases in such a way that it is more important to provide the strong incentives of ownership to the manager of the outlet in one case and to the central party in the other.[17]

An alternative approach based on the need to offer incentives for effort has been proposed by Maness (1996). This approach begins by noting that any elements of the retail outlet's financial costs that are sufficiently difficult to measure must

[16] For a further discussion of the idea that low-powered incentives are a major virtue of firm organization and can help explain firm boundaries, see Holmström (1996).
[17] See Lutz (1995) for a formal model of franchising along these lines.

accrue to the owner of the outlet as residual claimant, because they cannot be passed by contract to another party. Suppose then that all costs are non-contractible in this sense; that is, since the level or appropriateness of various costs cannot be well-monitored from outside, such costs cannot be part of an agreed-upon contract. Then, the only possibility for payments from the owner to the other party is on the basis of revenues. Indeed, actual franchise fees are almost always based on revenues and not on costs (Maness, p. 102) and incentive pay for employee managers is also often based on sales. In such a structure, the employee-manager has no direct incentive to control costs under central ownership, while the franchiser has no incentives for cost-reduction under local ownership. Because the efforts of either party might affect costs, this creates a potential inefficiency. The solution is to lodge ownership with the party to whom it is most important to give incentives for cost control. Maness then argues that cost control in a fast-food operation is more influenced by the local manager's efforts at staffing, training, controlling waste and the like, while costs in supermarkets are most influenced by the inventory and warehousing system, which can be centrally managed. Thus, an explanation emerges for the observed patterns: ownership is assigned to give appropriate incentives for cost control.

A more complex example involves gasoline retailing in the United States and Canada, which has been studied by Shepard (1993) and Slade (1996), respectively. They document a variety of contractual arrangements that are used in each country between the gasoline refining company and the station operator and, in the United States, significant variation in ownership of the station. While the physical assets used in gasoline retailing are quite specific to that use, a station can be switched from one brand to another with a little paint and new signs. Consequently, neither study attempted to explain the variation in contractual and ownership arrangements in terms of specific assets and hold-up.

Both studies find that the observed patterns are consistent with the arrangements being chosen to deal with problems of inducing effort and its allocation among tasks. These arrangements differ over the strengths of the incentives given to sell gasoline and other, ancillary services like repairs, car washes, or convenience store items. In turn, these ancillary services differ in the ease and accuracy of performance measurement. The observed patterns were generally consistent with their being selected to provide appropriately balanced incentives. For example, Shepard's (1993) work notes that in repair services, effort is hard to measure and, more importantly, monitoring the realized costs and revenues by the refiner may be tricky. This should make it less likely that the refinery will own the station and employ the operator and more likely that an arrangement will be adopted where the operator is residual claimant on sales of all sorts, either owning the station outright or leasing it from the refiner on a long-term basis. This is what the data show. In Slade's (1996) data, the presence of repair did not affect the ownership of the station (essentially all the stations were refiner-owned). It did, however, favor leasing arrangements, where the operator is residual claimant on all sales, and diminished the likelihood of commission arrangements, which would offer unbalanced incentives because the operator is residual claimant on non-gasoline business but is paid only a small commission on gasoline sales. The presence of full service rather than just self-serve gasoline sales also favors moving away from the company-owned model, since it matches the returns to relationship-building with the costs, which are borne by the local operator.[18] However, adding a convenience store actually increases the likelihood of using company-owned and -operated stations in the U.S. data, which goes against this logic unless one assumes that monitoring of such sales is relatively easy.

Considering a broad variety of retailing businesses more generally, LaFontaine and Slade (1997) document that the contractual and ownership arrangements that are used are responsive to agency considerations.

Market Monitoring

Ownership also influences agency costs through changes in the incentives for monitoring and the possibilities for performance contracting. A firm that is publicly traded can take advantage of the information contained in the continuous bidding for firm shares. Stock prices may be noisy, but they have a great deal more integrity than accounting-based measures of long-term value. For this reason, stock-related payment schemes tend to be superior incentive instruments. This factor can come to play a decisive role in organizational design as local information becomes more important and firms are forced to delegate more decision authority to sub-units and lower-level employees. Such moves require stronger performance incentives and in many cases the incentives can be offered most effectively by spinning off units and exposing them to market evaluation.

This, at least, is the underlying philosophy of Thermo Electron Corporation and its related companies. Thermo is an "incubator." It finances and supports start-up companies and entrepreneurs within a modern-day variant of the conglomerate. As soon as a unit is thought to be able to stand on its own feet, it is spun off. A minority stake is offered to outside investors, with Thermo and its family of entrepreneurs (particularly the head of the new operation) retaining a substantial ownership share. The principal owners of Thermo, the Hatsapolous brothers, make it very clear that getting to the spin-off stage is the final objective and a key element in their strategy to foster a true entrepreneurial spirit within the company. Besides making managerial incentives dependent on market information, spin-offs limit the

[18] A hold-up story is consistent with the fact that the presence of repair services favors dealer ownership over leasing arrangements in the U.S. data: a lessee who invests in building a clientele for repair work might worry that the refining company will raise the lease payments to appropriate the returns from this investment. This argument, however, does not do much to explain the pattern in the Canadian data, where the refiners own all the stations. One might also attempt to apply this logic to the choice between company-owned and leased stations by arguing that if the company owns the station it cannot motivate the employee-manager to invest in building a clientele because it will appropriate all the returns. However, this argument is not compelling without explaining how firms in other industries succeed in motivating their employees to undertake similar investments.

amount of intervention that Thermo can undertake in the independent units. This, too, will enhance entrepreneurial incentives.[19]

While Thermo has been remarkably successful (at least until recently), few companies have emulated its strategy. One likely reason is that Thermo's approach requires real commitment not to interfere inappropriately in the management of the spun-off units as this would undercut entrepreneurial incentives and would also destroy the integrity of the independent businesses in the eyes of outside investors. While laws protecting minority shareholders help to achieve this commitment to some extent, Thermo's founders have worked for over a decade to establish a reputation for neither intervening excessively nor cross-subsidizing their units. Another reason may be that Thermo has enjoyed all the benefits of a booming stock market since the early 1980s; it is not clear how well Thermo's strategy would work in a flat stock market like the 1970s.

Knowledge Transfers and Common Assets

Information and knowledge are at the heart of organizational design, because they result in contractual and incentive problems that challenge both markets and firms. Indeed, information and knowledge have long been understood to be different from goods and assets commonly traded in markets. In light of this, it is surprising that the leading economic theories of firm boundaries have paid almost no attention to the role of organizational knowledge.[20] The subject certainly deserves more scrutiny.

One of the few economic theory papers to discuss knowledge and firm boundaries is Arrow (1975), who argued that information transmission between upstream and downstream firms may be facilitated by vertical integration. As we saw in the examples of Nucor and the case of Japanese subcontracting, however, this type of information transfer may actually work fairly well even without vertical integration. More significant problems are likely to emerge when a firm comes up with a better product or production technology. Sharing this knowledge with actual or potential competitors would be socially efficient and could in principle enrich both parties, but the dilemma is how to pay for the trade. Until the new ideas have been shown to work, the potential buyer is unlikely to want to pay a lot. Establishing the ideas' value, however, may require giving away most of the relevant information for free. Again, repeated interactions can help here; in fact, even competing firms engage in continuous information exchange on a much larger scale than commonly realized. A common example is the extensive use of benchmarking, in which the costs of particular processes and operations are compared between firms. But when big

[19] See Aghion and Tirole (1997) for a model along these lines. In general, the role of firm boundaries in limiting interventions by more senior managers, thereby improving subordinates' incentives in various ways, has been a basic theme in the influence cost literature (Milgrom and Roberts 1990; Meyer et al., 1992).

[20] In contrast, researchers outside economic theory have made much of the role of knowledge. See, for instance, Teece et al. (1994).

leaps in knowledge occur, or when the nature of the knowledge transfer will involve ongoing investments or engagements, the issues become more complex. A natural option in that case is to integrate. Any claims about the value of knowledge are then backed up by the financial responsibility that comes with pairing cash flow and control rights.[21]

We think that knowledge transfers are a very common driver of mergers and acquisitions and of horizontal expansion of firms generally, particularly at times when new technologies are developing or when learning about new markets, technologies or management systems is taking place. Given the current level of merger and acquisition activity, and the amount of horizontal rather than vertical integration, it seems likely that many industries are experiencing such a period of change. The trend towards globalization of businesses has put a special premium on the acquisition and sharing of knowledge in geographically dispersed firms.

Two organizations that we have studied in which the development and transfer of knowledge are particularly central are ABB, Asea Brown Boveri, the largest electrical equipment manufacturer, and British Petroleum, the fourth-largest integrated oil company. Both firms see the opportunity to learn and share information effectively as key to their competitive advantage, and both operate with extremely lean headquarters that are too small to play a central, direct role in transferring knowledge across units. ABB spends a huge amount of time and effort sharing technical and business information across its more than 1,300 business units around the world through a variety of mechanisms. This would hardly be possible if these businesses were not under the single ABB umbrella. Similarly, BP's 100 business units have been encouraged to share information extensively through "peer assists," which involve business units calling on people from other units to help solve operating problems. BP also has a network of different "federal groups," each of which encourages technologists and managers from units around the world to share knowledge about similar challenges that they face.

The problem with knowledge transfers can be viewed as part of the more general problem of free-riding when independent parties share a common asset. If bargaining is costly, the situation is most easily solved by making a single party responsible for the benefits as well as the costs of using the asset. Brand-names are another example of common assets that typically need to be controlled by a single entity.

Concluding Remarks

It seems to us that the theory of the firm, and especially work on what determines the boundaries of the firm, has become too narrowly focused on the hold-up problem and the role of asset specificity. Think of arraying the set of coordi-

[21] Stuckey (1983), in his extraordinary study of the aluminum industry, reports that knowledge transfer was an important driver of joint ventures.

nation and motivation problems that the firm solves along one dimension of a matrix, and the set of instruments it has available along the other. Put the provision of investment incentives in column one and ownership-defined boundaries in row one. Let an element of the matrix be positive if the corresponding instrument is used to solve the corresponding problem, and zero otherwise. So there is certainly a positive entry in row one, column one: ownership does affect incentives for investment. We have argued, however, that both the first column and the first row have many other positive elements; ownership boundaries serve many purposes and investment incentives are provided in many ways.

Admittedly, most of the evidence we have offered in support of this claim is anecdotal and impressionistic. Our stories are largely based on newspaper reports, case studies, and our own consulting work and they are not the sort of systematic evidence one would ideally want. Nevertheless, we think that of the significant organizational change that seems to be taking place, only a small part can be easily understood in terms of traditional transaction cost theory in which hold-up problems are resolved by integration. Many of the hybrid organizations that are emerging are characterized by high degrees of uncertainty, frequency and asset specificity, yet they do not lead to integration. In fact, high degrees of frequency and mutual dependency seem to support, rather than hinder, ongoing cooperation across firm boundaries. This issue deserves to be explored in future work.[22]

It is also questionable whether it makes sense to consider one transaction at a time when one tries to understand how the new boundaries are drawn. In market networks, interdependencies are more than bilateral, and how one organizes one set of transactions depends on how the other transactions are set up. The game of influence is a complicated one and leads to strategic considerations that transcend simple two-party relationships.

The property rights approach, with its emphasis on incentives driven by ownership, may be a good starting point for investigating these new hybrid structures. These appear to be emerging in response to, among other things, an increase in the value of entrepreneurship and the value of human capital, both of which are features that the property rights approach can in principle model. But this approach also needs to expand its horizon and recognize that power derives from other sources than asset ownership and that other incentive instruments than ownership are available to deal with the joint problems of motivation and coordination. We do not believe that a theory of the firm that ignores contracts and other substitutes for ownership will prove useful for empirical studies. The world is replete with alternative instruments and, as always, the economically interesting action is at the margin of these substitutions.

[22] See Halonen (1994) for a first modeling effort along these lines.

■ *We thank Bradford De Long, Robert Gibbons, Oliver Hart, David Kreps, Timothy Taylor and Michael Whinston for their helpful comments. We are also indebted to the members of the Corporation of the Future initiative at McKinsey & Co., especially Jonathan Day, with whom we have collaborated on the issues discussed here.*

References

Aghion, Philippe, and Jean Tirole, "Formal and Real Authority in Organizations," *Journal of Political Economy*, 1997, *105*, 1–27.

Ahmadjian, Christina, and James Lincoln, "Changing Firm Boundaries in Japanese Auto Parts Supply Networks," draft, Columbia Business School, 1997.

Andersen, Erin, "The Salesperson as Outside Agent or Employee: A Transaction Cost Analysis," *Marketing Science*, 1985, *4*, 234–54.

Andersen, Erin, and David Schmittlein, "Integration of the Sales Force: An Empirical Examination," *Rand Journal of Economics*, 1984, *15*, 385–95.

Arrow, Kenneth, "Vertical Integration and Communication," *Bell Journal of Economics*, 1975, *6*, 173–82.

Asanuma, Banri, "Manufacturer-Supplier Relationships in Japan and the Concept of Relation-Specific Skill," *The Journal of the Japanese and International Economies*, 1989, *3*, 1–30.

Asanuma, Banri, "Japanese Manufacturer-Supplier Relationships in International Perspective." In Paul Sheard, ed., *International Adjustment and the Japanese Economy*. St. Leonards, Australia: Allen & Unwin, 1992.

Baker, George, Robert Gibbons, and Kevin J. Murphy, "Relational Contracts and the Theory of the Firm," draft, Massachusetts Institute of Technology, 1997.

Buttrick, John, "The Inside Contracting System," *Journal of Economic History*, 1952, *12*, 205–21.

Coase, Ronald, "The Nature of the Firm," *Economica*, November 1937, *4*, 386–405.

De Meza, David, and Ben Lockwood, "Does Asset Ownership Always Motivate Managers? Outside Options and the Property Rights Theory of the Firm," *Quarterly Journal of Economics*, 1998, *113*:2, 361–86.

Ghemawat, Pankaj, "Competitive Advantage and Internal Organization: Nucor Revisited," *Journal of Economics and Management Strategy*, 1995, *3*, 685–717.

Grossman, Sanford, and Oliver Hart, "The Costs and Benefits of Ownership: A Theory of Lateral and Vertical Integration," *Journal of Political Economy*, 1986, *94*, 691–719.

Grout, Paul, "Investment and Wages in the Absence of Binding Contracts: A Nash Bargaining Approach," *Econometrica*, 1984, *52*, 449–60.

Halonen, Maija, "Reputation and Allocation of Ownership," STICERD Theoretical Economics Discussion Paper, London School of Economics, 1994.

Hart, Oliver, *Firms, Contracts, and Financial Structure*. Oxford: Clarendon Press, 1995.

Hart, Oliver, and John Moore, "Property Rights and the Nature of the Firm," *Journal of Political Economy*, 1990, *98*, 1119–1158.

Helper, Susan, "Strategy and Irreversibility in Supplier Relations: The Case of the U.S. Automobile Industry," *Business History Review*, 1991, *65*, 781–824.

Holmström, Bengt, "The Firm as a Subeconomy," draft, Department of Economics, Massachusetts Institute of Technology, 1996.

Holmström, Bengt, and Paul Milgrom, "Multitask Principal-Agent Analyses: Incentive Contracts, Asset Ownership, and Job Design," *Journal of Law, Economics, and Organization*, 1991, *7*, 24–51.

Holmström, Bengt, and Paul Milgrom, "The Firm as an Incentive System," *American Economic Review*, 1994, *84*, 972–91.

Holmström, Bengt, and Jean Tirole, "Transfer Pricing and Organizational Form," *Journal of Law, Economics, and Organization*, 1991, *7*:2, 201–28.

Klein, Benjamin, Robert Crawford, and Armen Alchian, "Vertical Integration, Appropriable Rents, and the Competitive Contracting Process," *Journal of Law and Economics*, 1978, *21*, 297–326.

LaFontaine, Francine, and Margaret Slade, "Retail Contracting: Theory and Practice," *Journal of Industrial Economics*, 1997, *45*, 1–25.

Lutz, Nancy, "Ownership Rights and Incentives in Franchising," *Journal of Corporate Finance*, 1995, *2*, 103–31.

Maness, Robert, "Incomplete Contracts and the Choice between Vertical Integration and Franchising," *Journal of Economic Behavior and Organization*, 1996, *32*, 101–15.

Meyer, Margaret, Paul Milgrom, and John Roberts, "Organizational Prospects, Influence Costs and Ownership Changes," *Journal of Economics and Management Strategy*, 1992, *1*:1, 9–35.

Milgrom, Paul, and John Roberts, "An Economic Approach to Influence Activities and Organizational Responses," *American Journal of Sociology*, 1988, *94* (supplement), S154–S179.

Milgrom, Paul, and John Roberts, "Bargaining Costs, Influence Costs and the Organization of Economic Activity." In J. Alt and K. Shepsle, eds., *Perspectives on Positive Political Economy*. Cambridge: Cambridge University Press, 1990, 57–89.

Milgrom, Paul, and John Roberts, *Economics, Organization and Management*. Englewood Cliffs, NJ: Prentice-Hall, 1992.

Milgrom, Paul, and John Roberts, "Johnson Controls, Inc. — Automotive Systems Group:

The Georgetown Kentucky Plant," Stanford Graduate School of Business, Case S-BE-9, 1993.

Milgrom, Paul, and John Roberts, "Comparing Equilibria," *American Economic Review*, 1994, *84*, 441–59.

Monteverde, Kirk, and David Teece, "Supplier Switching Costs and Vertical Integration in the Automobile Industry," *Bell Journal of Economics*, 1982, *13*, 206–13.

Powell, Walter, "Inter-Organizational Collaboration in the Biotechnology Industry," *Journal of Institutional and Theoretical Economics*, 1996, *152*:1, 197–215.

Rajan, Raghuram, and Luigi Zingales, "Power in a Theory of the Firm," *Quarterly Journal of Economics*, 1998, *113*:2, 387–432.

Scharfstein, David, "The Dark Side of Internal Capital Markets II: Evidence from Diversified Conglomerates," NBER Working Paper No. 6352, 1998.

Segal, Ilya, and Michael Whinston, "Exclusive Dealing and Protection of Investments," draft, Department of Economics, University of California, Berkeley, 1997.

Shepard, Andrea, "Contractual Form, Retail Price, and Asset Characteristics," *Rand Journal of Economics*, 1993, *24*, 58–77.

Shin, Hyun-Han, and Rene M. Stulz, "Are Internal Capital Markets Efficient?" *Quarterly Journal of Economics*, 1998, *113*:2, 531–52.

Slade, Margaret, "Multitask Agency and Contract Choice: An Empirical Assessment," *International Economic Review*, 1996, *37*, 465–86.

Stuckey, John, *Vertical Integration and Joint Ventures in the Aluminum Industry*. Cambridge: Harvard University Press, 1983.

Taylor, Curtis, and Steven Wiggins, "Competition or Compensation: Supplier Incentives Under the American and Japanese Subcontracting Systems," *American Economic Review*, 1997, *87*:4, 598–618.

Teece, David, Richard Rumelt, Giovanni Dosi, and Sidney Winter, "Understanding Corporate Coherence, Theory and Evidence," *Journal of Economic Behavior and Organization*, 1994, *23*, 1–30.

Walton, Mary, *Car: A Drama of the American Workplace*. New York: W.W. Norton, 1997.

Whinston, Michael, "On the Transaction Cost Determinants of Vertical Integration," draft, Department of Economics, Northwestern University, 1997.

Williamson, Oliver, *Markets and Hierarchies: Analysis and Antitrust Implications*. New York: The Free Press, 1975.

Williamson, Oliver, "Transaction-Cost Economics: The Governance of Contractual Relations," *Journal of Law and Economics*, 1979, *22*, 233–71.

Williamson, Oliver, *The Economic Institutions of Capitalism*. New York: The Free Press, 1985.

Name Index